D0908232

First Name Reverse Dictionary

SECOND EDITION

First Name Reverse Dictionary

*Given Names
Listed by Meaning*

Second Edition

Yvonne Navarro

McFarland & Company, Inc., Publishers
Jefferson, North Carolina, and London

Library of Congress Cataloguing-in-Publication Data

Navarro, Yvonne, 1957–
    First name reverse dictionary : given names listed by
meaning / Yvonne Navarro. — 2nd ed.
        p.   cm.
    Includes index.

    ISBN-13: 978-0-7864-2934-9
    ISBN-10: 0-7864-2934-8
    (illustrated case binding : 50# alkaline paper) ∞

    1. Names, Personal—Dictionaries.   I. Title.   II. Title:
1st name reverse dictionary.
CS2377.N37   2007
929.4'4—dc22   2006038281

British Library cataloguing data are available

On the cover: details ©2006 PhotoSpin; background ©2006
EclectiCollections

Manufactured in the United States of America

McFarland & Company, Inc., Publishers
  Box 611, Jefferson, North Carolina 28640
    www.mcfarlandpub.com

In memory of
Rochelle Yvonne

Contents

Introduction

You may be using this book for any one of a variety of reasons. Perhaps you are preparing for the birth of a child or know someone who is. Alternatively, this volume may be an important source of information if you are engaged in fiction writing or research. In any case, you will find much unique information about the meanings of names in these pages—though not in the usual fashion of an ordinary "baby name" book. *The First Name Reverse Dictionary* has been prepared in order of *definition* and has been organized like a dictionary.

Using This Dictionary

To General Users:

This expanded edition of *The First Name Reverse Dictionary* has been divided into two sections, one dealing with female names and the other with male names, each arranged in alphabetical order. Previously, if you were a parent-to-be and wanted a name for your daughter which meant "flower," it would have been necessary to search an entire ordinary baby name book to learn which names carry this meaning. Using this book, you can simply turn to the listings under the word "flower" and pick from, in this case, twenty-five names. But the information doesn't stop there. You'll also find sixty-one additional entries that incorporate "flower." For example, "Delfine" is associated with the delphinium or larkspur flower and is Greek in origin; variations of "Delfine" include "Delfina," "Delphine," and "Delphana." Additional variations with even more names which include the word "flower" include "flowering," "flowers" and "flowery." This expanded version of *The First Name Reverse Dictionary* includes hundreds of lovely Hawaiian, Hindi, African, Native American and other names.

Like a dictionary, entries are listed strictly in alphabetical order, regardless of punctuation or word breaks. Subentries, also in alphabetical order, follow immediately and are separated by bullets. The following sample entry illustrates the organization of material in the main entry and the subentries under the definition "powerful" in the female section:

> **powerful** Raina (Old German), Rainah, Rayna, Raynah, Raynata • *ever powerful, ever regal, ever ruler* Erica (Old German), Erika • *powerful battle maiden* Magnilda (Old German) • *powerful, prosperous* Edrea (Old English), Edra • *powerful ruler* Ricarda (Old German) • *strong and powerful* Adira (Hebrew)

As you can see, the language of origin appears in parentheses and immediately follows the main name or names, with derivatives or diminutives (nicknames or the same name as interpreted in other languages) after that. A semicolon within an entry indicates multiple names for the same definition or multiple definitions (different and unrelated).

Definitions with two or more different elements (like "sweetbriar rose; woodbine") will be found in three places (under "rose," "sweetbriar," and "woodbine") or cross-referenced (for "sweetbriar" see "rose").

To Writers:

Finally, an end to the hours spent hunting for that perfect meaning! Fiction writers will find this book to be a valuable and fascinating reference tool for their work, making it possible to appropriately name even the most important character within minutes. As an example, a writer might wish to name a male character after an identifying trait, shown in the following example for "strong." Among the many subentries which include that trait, an author might choose the following:

> • *bow strong* Bogart (Old German)

Everyone remembers the famous actor, Humphrey Bogart. The listing for "strong" supplies seventeen choices, plus thirty more subentries incorporating the word into more detailed definitions. Sometimes the definitions are even more specific:

> **strong-hearted** Dustin *strong-hearted leader* (Old German), Durst, Durstin, Durston

reminiscent of yet another actor, Dustin Hoffman.

Using the Index to Entry Names

Sometimes curiosity gets the best of everyone, and when you just have to know the meaning of your own name or that of your best friend's, turn to the index for help. But remember to use the index as just a starting point, since it will usually direct you only to the *first* key word in a definition. The *f* and *m* in each index entry indicates the female or male section. Thus "**Rilla** *f* brook" in the index will refer you to

> **brook** Rilla *a brook or stream* (German), Rilette

in the female section, and "**Alan** *m* son; cheerful" in the male section will refer you to

> **Alan** Alanson *son of Alan* (Old German), Alansen, Alenson, Allanson

and

> **cheerful...** • *cheerful, handsome, harmonious one* Alan (Irish-Gaelic), Ailin, Alain, Allan, Allen, Allyn

As noted, a listing of more than one word after a name in the index indicates that this particular name has multiple definitions, so be sure to check each one. Also, people are often surprised to discover that the same name has meanings for both female and male, so always check a listing from the index in both sections.

A Matter of Choice

Using the index, in some instances you will see that one name may actually be a derivative or diminutive of others. For instance, **Rita** can mean *motherly* (as a variation of **Jarita**), *girl of the dark* (as a variation of **Maurita**), and *girl of generosity* (as a variation of **Carrita**). It's impossible for this book to include every variation of every name, since additional derivatives and diminutives of any given name are invented nearly every day. Still, it is interesting to note the following:

• Many names have more commonly been used as given names in the past, yet nothing prevents the writer from using these as surnames. This practice is becoming more commonplace.
• Often the same name (though usually the more common ones) may be traced to several different countries of origin.

• At first glance, many of the names in this book may seem archaic or overly formal. Despite this, you can usually find more appropriate or pleasing variations in most listings.

• Different meanings for the same names can sometimes be found within the *same* nationality, while some names have similar definitions in almost every country. Occasionally, a name may be used for either male or female, a practice which is becoming more common. By the same token, many names have, over time, "switched" genders, having started as exclusively a male name and changed to female, or vice versa.

• Many Japanese names consist of several smaller words combined into a specific phrase. In the name **Tanaka**, for instance, "**ta**" means *rice field* and "**naka**" meals *middle*; thus the definition of **Tanaka** is *middle rice field*.

We hope you enjoy the expanded edition of *The First Name Reverse Dictionary* and use it for many years to come!

Meanings Related to Female Names

able Ara *most able maiden* (Old German), Aara

Abraham's Ivria *from Abraham's land* (Hebrew), Ivriah, Ivrit

abstain Ky *carefully; strange; to abstain from, to fear; to sign* (Vietnamese)

abundance Myra (Greek); Zina (Hebrew), Zinah

academic Jignasa *academic curiosity* (Hindi)

accomplished Kane *the doubly accomplished* (Japanese) • *accomplished, perfect one* Perfecta (Spanish)

action Karma (Hindi)

active Malca *active, industrious* (Old German), Malcah • *active one* Kineta (Greek); Radinka (Slavic) • *active sprite* Disa (Old German)

add Josephine *add, increase* (Hebrew), Fifi, Joette, Josefina, Josephina, Josette, Pepita • *she shall add, she shall be fruitful* Pepita (Spanish)

admirable Miranda *admirable, extraordinary* (Latin)

admired Penda *admired or loved* (Swahili) • *admired, praised* Siobhan (Irish-Gaelic)

admonition Monica *admonition, advice* (Latin), Mona

adored Adoree *adored one* (French); Lais (Greek), Laise, Laius; Keiko (Japanese)

adorn Banna *adorn; an ornament, to dress* (Efik/African)

adorned Adaiha *adorned of God* (Hebrew), Ada, Adaha • *adorned one* Adorna, Esmeralda (Latin) • *adorned or beaded* Ena (Efik) • *adorned with jewels* Madai (Hebrew), Ada, Adai, Madi, Madiah

advantage Prapti (Hindi) • *child of advantage or goodness* Tameko (Japanese), Tame

adventuring Fernanda *adventuring, world daring* (Germanic), Ferdinanda, Fernandina

adventurous Ferran (English); Aarini (Hindi)

adversary Atalanta *mighty adversary* (Greek), Atlanta

advice *see* admonition

adviser Moneta (Latin), Monetta

affectionate Fonda *affectionate, tender* (English)

afflicted Jobina *afflicted, persecuted* (Hebrew), Jobi, Jobie, Joby

afraid Alkas *she is afraid* (Native American)

again Renata *born again* (Latin), Renate, Rene, Renee

agate Agate *the agate stone* (Latin); Aggie, Agi (English)

aggressive Alphonsine *an aggressive na-*

ture (Old German), Alphonsa,
Phonsa
agreeable Raziya (African) • *agreeable,
ba lm* Naam (Hebrew), Naaman,
Naamana
ahead Zula *brilliant, ahead* (African)
aid Comfort *strengthening aid and comfort* (French)
aim Laksha (Hindi)
air Alana *light and airy* (Hawaiian),
Alanna, Lana • *of the air, ethereal* Air-
lia (Greek), Airla, Airlee, Airliah,
Airlie • *washed in an air of mystery*
Mystique (French), Mistique
alder La Verne *alder tree grove* (Old
French), Lavergne
alert Nishita (Hindi) • *alert, alert and
awake* Vigilia (Latin) • *quick, alert,
and merry* Zana (Arabic)
alive Vieva (Latin), Viva, Vivi, Vivian,
Viviana, Vivianna, Vivien, Vivienne,
Vivyan • *alive, vivacious* Alvita
(Latin), Alveta, Allveta, Veta,
Vita
all Duka (African) • Altsoba (*all are at
war* (Navajo Indian) • *all honey*
Pamela (Greek), Pamelina • *from all
the gods* Panthea (Greek), Pantheas,
Panthia, Thea, Thia • *loved by all*
Lida, Ludmilla (Slavic), Lidah,
Lidda, Liddie, Lovmilla,
Mila • *ruler of all* Alarice, Elrica, Ulrica (Old German), Alarica, Rica,
Rika, Ulrika • *the all-gifted one* Pandora (Greek) • *the all-loving one* Panphila (Greek)
allegiance Fealty *allegiance, fidelity*
(French)
allures Lena *she who allures* (Latin),
Lina; Liayna (English); Liene (Latvian)
allyssium Alyssa *a flower, flower of the
allyssium* (Old German)
alone Alleen (Dutch); Enola (Native
American) • *alone, standard setter*
Solita (Latin), Lita, Sola, Solitta
aloof Ultima *the most distant, aloof one*
(Latin)
altar Ara (Greek) • *beautiful altar* Arabella (Latin), Arabela, Arabelle,
Bella, Belle
always Aanandi *always happy woman*
(Hindi) • *always laughing* Sasmita
(Hindi) • *always; until the end* Aina

(Scandinavian) • *she was always
selfish* Makadisa (Baduma)
amaryllis Amaryllis *the amaryllis lily*
(Latin)
amazing Vismaya (Hindi)
amber Amber *the amber jewel* (French)
ambitious Meta (Latin), Eta, Mettah
amiable Elma (Greek)
amulet Bua (Vietnamese)
analysis Samiksha (Hindi)
ancestors Den *asked for by her ancestors*
(Japanese)
ancestral Ola *ancestral relic* (Old
Norse)
ancient Kiana (Irish), Kia, Kiandra,
Kiandrea, Kianni; Kianne (English)
• *ancient river goddess* Oba (Yoruban)
• *ancient time* Prasheila (Hindi)
Andros Andria *maiden of Andros*
(Latin)
angel Malaika (African); Malak (Arabic); Anela (Hawaiian) • *an angel*
Tevy (Cambodian); Lavangi (Hindi)
• *angel messenger* Arella (Hebrew),
Arela, Erela; Gelya (Russian) • *angel
of precious stone* Nitika (Native American) • *angel or messenger* Angela
(French), Angelina, Angeline, Angelita; Litsa (Greek) • *bright angel*
Engelberta (Old German)
angelic Angelica *angelic one* (Latin),
Angelique • *spirit angel* Angeni (Native American)
angels Artemas *sound of angels* (Hebrew), Arta, Artamas, Artema, Artima, Artimas, Tema
angry Ireta *angry, enraged one* (Latin),
Iretta, Irette • *angry or fierce* Chandi
(Hindi)
angular (Hindi)
animal Gurit *young animal* (Hebrew),
Gurice
announcement Orela *a divine announcement* (Latin), Orella
announcer Clio (Greek)
answered Eliana *Jehovah has answered
our prayers* (Hebrew); Eliane,
Elianna, Leanna, Liana, Lianne (English)
antelope Gazella *antelope or gazelle*
(Latin) • *a white antelope* Rima (Arabic)
anticipated Raja *the anticipated one;
hoped for* (Arabic)

anything Banna *anything; decay, destruction; this year* (Hausa)

appearance Theophania *appearance of God* (Greek)

apple Elma (Turkish); Tao (Vietnamese) • *apple, fertile* Pomona (Latin)

appointed Sethrida *appointed by the Lord* (Latin)

approval Favor *approval, help; good will conferred* (French)

apricot Anzu (Japanese); Morela (Polish), Morella • *wild apricot* Zerdali (Turkish)

April Averill *born in April* (Old English); Avril, Avrill, Averyl (English) • *born in April, opening* April (Latin)

archer Yvette *a carrier of the bow, archer* (French), Yvonne

ardent Ardccn (Latin), Ignacia, Ignatia, Ignatzia • *ardent one, fiery* Ignatia (Latin) • *burning or ardent one* Seraphina (Hebrew), Serafina, Serafine, Seraphine • *devoted or ardent* Zelia (Greek), Zelina • *little ardent or fiery one* Ena (Irish-Gaelic)

Ark Safina *Noah's Ark* (African)

armed Armida *little armed one* (Latin)

armored Serilda *armored battle maid, girl of war* (Old German), Rilda, Sarilda, Sorilda • *armored warrior maid* Brunhilda, Zerelda (Old German), Serilda, Zarelda

army Mallory *army counselor* (Old German) • *army ruler* Haralda (Old Norse), Hallie, Hally • *place of a famous army* Lorraine (Old German), Loraine • *victorious army* Cosette (French), Cosetta; Colette (French-German), Collette • *victorious army, victorious people* Nicole (Greek), Nichele, Nichelle, Nichola, Nicola, Nicolina, Nicoline, Niki, Nikki

arrived Dinna *the one who has arrived* (Mende)

arrives Dayo *joy arrives* (African)

arrow Yumi (Japanese) • *arrow child* Yumiko (Japanese) • *calm arrow* Tera (Japanese) • *like an arrow* Flo (Native American)

arrows Omusa *to miss with arrows* (Miwok)

art Kala (Hindi)

artichoke Cynara *artichoke or thistle* (Greek)

ash Ashley *from the ash tree meadow* (Old English), Ashleigh • *little one of the ashes* Cinderella (French) • *slim ash tree* Asela (Spanish)

asked Abebe *asked for* (African), Abebi; Shelah (Hebrew), Shaya, Shea, Shela, Sheya • *asked for by her ancestors* Den (Japanese) • *we asked for her and she came to us* Abebi, Abeni (Yoruban)

assistant Sasa (Japanese) • *helper or assistant* Kodi (Irish), Cody, Kodey, Kodie, Kody

aster Astera *the aster flower* (Hebrew), Asta, Asteria, Asteriya

astonishment Tama (Hebrew), Tamah

astray Traviata *one who goes astray* (Italian)

atom Kana (Hindi)

attendant Camille *young ceremonial attendant* (Latin), Camila, Camilla

attract Laka (Hawaiian)

attractive Inu (Hindi) • *graceful, attractive one* Grace (Latin), Engracia, Giorsal, Grazia

august Sebastiane *august, reverenced one* (Latin), Sebastiana

Augustus Austin *belonging to Augustus* (Latine), Augustine

Aunt Tia (Spanish)

aurora Zora *aurora or dawn* (Slavic)

auspicious Prospera *auspicious, favorable* (Latin) • *auspicious speech, good repute* Euphemia (Greek), Eufemia, Euphemie

autumn Aki *born in autumn* (Japanese) • *autumn rain* Jora (Hebrew); Joran (English)

awake Vigilia *alert and awake* (Latin) • *wide awake one* Onawa (Native American)

awakening Jagrati (Hindi)

awareness Jagruti (Hindi)

away Mona *far away, lonely* (Old German)

awe Elmina *awe-inspiring fame* (Old German)

— B —

baby Dola (Mende); Mab (Welsh) • *an Easter baby* Easter (Anglo-Saxon)
background Ermina *noble, of a fine background* (Latin), Erma, Erminna, Mina, Minna
backward Nepa *walking backward* (Arabic)
bakula Bakula *the bakula flower* (Hindi)
ball Mari (Japanese) • *ball child* Mariko (Japanese)
balm *see* agreeable
bamboo Shino *slender bamboo* (Japanese)
baptized Baptista *baptized in God's name* (Greek)
bargain Zora *a bargain* (Hausa), Zorra
bark Ketzia *cinnamonlike bark* (Hebrew), Ketzi, Kezi, Kezia
barren Savanna *the barren one* (Spanish), Savannah
basil Rihana *sweet basil* (Muslin), Rhiana, Rhlanna, Riana, Rianna
basin Pilar *a fountain basin or pillar* (Spanish)
basket Adita (African)
battle Cady (English), Kadee, Kadi, Kadia, Kadie • *armored battle maid, girl of war* Serilda (Old German), Rilda, Sarilda, Sorilda • *battle celebrated or glorious* Hildemar (Old German) • *battle counselor* Hildreth (Old German) • *battle heroine* Valda (Old German) • *battle maid* Bernia (Latin); Heidi (Old German), Heidy, Hidie, Hilda, Hilde, Hildie, Hildy • *battle maid, battle stronghold, battle wand* Hildegarde (Old German) • *battle maiden* Gunda (Old Norse) • *battle of the fortress* Viveca (Scandinavian), Vivica • *brave in battle* Harelda (Old German), Halda, Harilda • *famous battle maid* Clotilda (German), Clothilde • *famous woman warrior, glorious battle maid* Romilda (Old German), Maida, Milda, Romalda, Romelda • *graceful battle maid* Luana (Old German), Lou, Louanna, Luane, Luwanna • *gray battle maiden* Griselda (Old German), Chriselda, Grishilda, Gri-

shilde • *mighty battle maiden* Mathilda (Old German), Maitilde, Matelda, Mathilde, Matilda, Matilde • *powerful battle maiden* Magnilda (Old German) • *shining battle maid* Bertilde (Old English) • *the battle maiden* Armilda (Old German), Armalda, Armelda, Armillda, Milda, Millda • *the maid of battle* Bathilda (Old German), Bathelda, Thilda, Tilda • *victorious battle maid* Solvig (Old English) • *warrior battle maid* Gunhilda (Old Norse)
battles Tracy *one who battles* (Latin), Tracey, Traci, Tracie
bay Daphne *bay or laurel tree* (Greek)
beach Kishi (Japanese)
bead Chuma (Mashona)
beaded *see* adorned
beaming Lewanna *beaming white one, the moon* (Hebrew)
bean Fabia *bean grower* (Latin), Fabiana
bear Nita *a bear* (Choctaw Indian) • *a she-bear* Ursula (Latin), Orsola, Ursola, Ursule, Ursuline • *bear/spear maid* Berengaria (Old English) • *brave as a bear* Bernadette (French), Bernadene, Bernadine, Bernardena, Bernita • *nymph of the sky, she-bear* Ursa (Greek), Ursal, Ursala, Ursas, Ursel, Yursa
bearer Annunciata *bearer of news* (Latin) • *light bearer* Aileen (Anglo-Saxon), Alene, Eileen, Elene, Ileana, Ilene • *rod or staff bearer* Virgilia (Latin) • *shield bearer* Thyra (Greek)
beat Muliya *to beat or hit* (Miwok)
beautiful Jamila (Arabic), Jameela, Jamilah, Jamillah, Jamillia; Belle (French), Bell, Bella, Belva, Belvia; Calla (Greek); Anabela (Hawaiian), Ani; Navit (Hebrew), Nava, Navice; Alpana, Amisha (Hindi); Ilona (Hungarian); Keely (Irish-Gaelic), Kiely, Kiley, Kyley; Olathe, Wyanet (Native American); Hermosa (Spanish); Nizhoni (Navajo Indian) • Zuri (Swahili); Shaina (Yiddish) • *a beautiful life* Kenisha (American) • *beautiful altar* Arabella (Latin), Arabela,

Arabelle, Bella, Belle • *beautiful and clean* Fleta (Anglo-Saxon), Fleda, Flita, Leda, Leta, Lita • *beautiful and fair* Teagan, Tegan (Welsh) • *beautiful blossom* Calantha (Greek), Calantha, Callie • *beautiful, bright* Bertha (Old German) • *beautiful, bright, fair* Alanna (Irish-Gaelic), Alaine, Alayne, Alina, Allene, Lana, Lanna • *beautiful, brilliant* Clarabelle (French); Clarinda (Spanish) • *beautiful Christian* Christabelle (Latin), Cristabel • *beautiful, comely; hyacinth flower* Jacinda (Greek), Jacenta, Jacinta, Jacintha, Jacinthe, Jacynth • *beautiful, compassionate* Ruth (Hebrew) • *beautiful conqueror* Sigrid (Scandinavian) • *beautiful eyes* Maha (African); Shahla (Dari) • *beautiful fairy maiden, elf* Ella (Old English) • *beautiful free diamond* Almaz (Ethiopian) • *beautiful generations* Miyo (Japanese) • *beautiful gift, bountiful gift* Dorinda (Greek), Dorin; Adorabelle (French-Latin) • *beautiful, graceful* Annabelle (Hebrew-Latin), Annabella, Annie, Belle • *beautiful jade* Lin (Chinese) • *beautiful lover* Amabel (Latin), Amabelle • *beautiful maiden* Corabelle (French-German) • *beautiful music, song* Melody (Greek), Melodie • *beautiful nymph of the sea, sea goddess* Thetis (Greek), Heti, Thetes, Thetisa, Thetos • *beautiful one* Mirabel (Spanish), Mirabella, Mirabelle • *beautiful one from heaven* Noelani (Hawaiian) • *beautiful or beautiful jewel* Saphira (English), Sapphire; Sapphira (Hebrew), Phira, Saphra, Sapphera • *beautiful or god-like* Adonia (Greek) • *beautiful or graceful* Kieu (Vietnamese) • *beautiful or lovely* Jafit (Hebrew), Jaffa, Jaffice • *beautiful, pleasant* Farrah (Middle English), Farah, Farand, Fayre • *beautiful, pretty* Belinda (Spanish), Belle, Linda • *beautiful rose* Rosabel (Latin); Rosalinda (Spanish), Rosalind, Rosaline, Rosalynd, Roseline • *eye-catching or beautiful to gaze upon* Rana (Arabic), Raniyah, Ranya • *dawn beautiful* Zerlinda (Hebrew-Spanish) • *great and beautiful one* Maybelle (French-

Latin) • *little beautiful one* Callula (Latin) • *Mary the beautiful* Maribelle (Latin), Marabel, Marabelle, Marybella, Marybelle • *most beautiful* Alika (Nigerian) • *she makes beautiful* Adorna (Latin) • *something beautiful* Isabis (African) • *splendid or beautiful one* Clytie (Greek) • *the beautiful lily* Lilybelle (Latin), Lily, Lilybel

beautifully Alida *beautifully dressed* (Greek), Aleda, Alyda

beauty Uzuri (African); Adara (Greek) • *beauty, loveliness* Venus (Latin), Venita, Vinita • *beauty, sparrow, or trumpet* Zippora (Hebrew) • *child of beauty* Adamma (Nigerian) • *dark as night, dark beauty* Leila (Arabic) • *eternal beauty* Amara (Greek), Amargo, Mara • *girl of beauty* Pulcheria (Latin), Cheri, Cheria, Pulchia • *lady of beauty* Berlinda (Latin), Bellaude, Berlyn • *land of beauty* Madina (Hindi) • *of golden beauty* Oribel (Latin), Orabel, Orabelle, Oribella, Oribelle • *one with a mole or beauty spot* Shaima (Arabic) • *the beauty* Kanani (Hawaiian), Ani, Nani

beaver Beverly *dweller at the beaver meadow* (Old English)

bee Melissa *a bee, honey* (Greek), Lissa, Melicent, Melisse, Melita, Millicent • *the bee* Deborah (Hebrew), Debora, Debra; Devora (Russian) • *the bee's head* Bega (Greek), Begga

beginning Conception (Latin), Concepcion, Conchita • *season's beginning* Kiah (African), Kia

belief Faith *belief in God, fidelity, loyalty* (English), Fay

believer Iman (Arabic) • *believer, thinker* Raissa (Old French)

bell Suzu (Japanese); Zel (Turkish) • *a small bell* Nola (Latin), Nolana

bells Kerani *sacred bells* (Sanskrit), Kera, Keri, Kerie, Kery; Rani (English)

belonging Austin *belonging to Augustus* (Latin), Augustine • *belonging to God* Quanika (American), Nika, Niki, Nikka, Nikki, Quanikka, Quanique • *belonging to Mars* Marcella (Latin), Marcela, Marcelle, Marcellene, Marcellina, Marcie, Marcile, Marcille, Marcy • *belonging to the Lord*

Dominica (Latin), Domenica, Dominga, Domini, Dominique; Dominika (Russian), Mika, Nika • *belonging to the night* Lilith (East Semitic) • *belonging to the stars, glittering* Sidra (Latin)

beloved Habibah, Kalila (Arabic), Kailey, Kylila; Zody (Congo); Amy (French), Aimee, Amata, Amie, Cher, Chere, Cheri, Cherice, Cherise, Cherish, Cherye, Esmee, Sheri; Ema (Hawaiian); Ahava (Hebrew), Davida, Davina, Deedee, Didi, Dodi, Dodie, Dody, Dora, Haviva, Vida; Suki (Japanese); Amice (Latin), Ami, Amoreta, Amorita, Amoritta; Amadika (Rhodesian); Amaliya (Russian); Querida (Spanish); Caryl (Welsh), Carrie, Cary • *admired or loved* Penda (Swahili) • *beloved and pretty* Amelinda (Latin-Spanish), Amilinda • *beloved, dear one* Carita (Latin), Carissa, Karissa, Karisa, Karise, Karisha • *beloved of God* Theophila (Greek), Theophilos • *beloved or concealed* Holda (Old German), Hulda • *dear, beloved one* Cherie (French), Cheri, Chery; Cara (Italian), Carina, Carine, Kara • *gracious or beloved* Hulda (Old German), Haldie • *little beloved one* Luvena (Middle English) • *beloved child; little love* Aiko (Japanese) • *tender beloved* Morna (Celtic), Myrna

below Matsushita *below, pine* (Japanese) • *pool below a fall or waterfall* Lynn (Old English)

benefited Mehitabel *benefited by God* (Hebrew), Mehetabel, Mehitabelle

benevolence Meher (Hindi)

benevolent Charity *benevolent, charitable* (Latin), Charissa, Charita, Cherry

Ben Benquasha, Natene *daughter of Ben* (Native American)

berries Amayeta *big manzanita berries*

best Aretha (Greek)

better Katura *I feel better now* (Babudja)

beyond Tonya *beyond price, inestimable* (Russian), Tonia

big Darrah *big and fine* (Hausa) • *big eyes* Naira (Native American) • *big manzanita berries* Amayeta (Miwok) • *big tree* Adoette (Native American; Ilana (Hebrew)

bird Sakuna (East Indian); Derora, Zipporah (Hebrew), Ceporah, Zippora; Monal (Hindi); Tori (Japanese); Cholena (Native American); Palila (Polynesian) • *a small bird* Jena (Arabic), Jenna • *bird of paradise* Huma (Hindi) • *graceful as a bird* Aletta (Latin), Aleta, Alita, Alitta, Letta, Litta • *large sea bird* Sula (Icelandic) • *motherly bird* Jarita (Hindi), Arita, Gerita, Jari, Jeritah, Rita • *palm bird* Ega (Yoruban) • *yellow bird* Pazi (Native American)

birdlike Ava, Avis (Latin) • *little birdlike one* Birdie (English)

birth Leda (Hebrew), Leda, Lida, Lideah; *of noble birth* Ada (Latin) Adda, Addi, Addie, Adi, Aida • *one of select birth* Asabi (Yoruban)

birthday Natalie (Latin), Natala, Natalia, Nataline, Natasha, Nathalia, Nathalie, Noel, Noelle, Novella

birthstone Amethyst *February birthstone, precious stone* (Greek), Amathist, Amathiste, Amethist

bitter Maryam (Arabic); Malia (Hawaiian); Maire (Irish); Manya (Hebrew), Maralina, Maraline, Marlisa, Mimi, Minnie, Miriam, Mitzi; Masha (Russian); Mara (Slavic); Meryem (Turkish) • *bitter, girl of sadness* Merari (Hebrew), Meraree • *bitter-graceful* Marian (Hebrew), Mariana, Marianna, Marianne, Maryanne • *bitter, myrrh* Muriel (Greek), Merial, Murial • *bitter or bitterness* Mary (Hebrew), Maralyn, Marella, Maretta, Marette, Mari, Maria, Marie, Marietta, Marilla, Marilyn, Marita, Marla, Maura, Maureen, Mayme, Moira, Moya, Muriel; Morena (Spanish); Meli (Zuni) • *bitter princess* Sharma (American), Sharmine

bitterness *see* bitter

black Sierra (Irish) • Kanika *black cloth* (Mwera) • *black cloud* Hana (Arapaho) • *black, dark one* Dee (Welsh) • *black goddess* Kali (Hindi) • *black-haired* Ciara (Irish-Gaelic) • *black or dark* Melanie (Greek), Melany; Melka (Polish); Milena (Slavic) • *black or divine* Devaki (Sanskrit) • *black or sleek* Sable (Middle

English), Sabel, Sabella, Sabelle • *black; time* Kala (Hindi) • *little black one* Kiera (Irish-Gaelic), Keara, Keira, Kieran, Kierra • *girl in black* Chemarin (Hebrew), Chamaran, Chemar • *river of black stones* Guadalupe (Arabic), Lupe, Lupita

blackbird Merle *blackbird, thrush* (Latin), Merl, Merlina, Merline, Merola, Meryl, Myrlene

blessed Benedicta (Latin), Benedetta, Benedikta, Dixie; Anjika (Hindi); Benita (Spanish); Venetia (Welsh) • *blessed by God* Azaria (Hebrew), Azarria, Azeria, Zaria • *blessed, happy one* Beata (Latin) • *blessed joy* Surata (Hindi) • *blessed one* Martiza (Arabic) • *white, blessed one* Gwyneth (Old Welsh)

blessedness Eda *blessedness, prosperity* (Old English)

blessing Nima (Arabic), Nimah, Nimat • *God's blessing* Chinue (African)

blind Kameka (Umbundu) • *blind, dim-sighted one* Cecilia (Latin), Cecile, Celia, Celie; Cicely (American); Cilka (Czech); Kikilia (Hawaiian); Sheila (Irish), Sheela, Sheelah, Sheilah, Shela, Shelia

bliss Ananda (Hindi) • *bliss child, joy* Sachi (Japanese), Sachiko

blissful Elysia *sweetly blissful* (Latin)

blonde Bellanca *blonde one* (Italian), Blanca; Alva (Latin) • *white blonde* Elvira (Latin), Elvera, Elvire; Ela (Polish) • *white or blonde* Albinia (Latin), Albina, Alvina, Aubine

blood Jira *related by blood* (African)

bloom Aiyana, Ayiana *eternal bloom* (Native American) • *to bloom or be successful* Barika (Arabic)

blooming Fullan (Hindi) • *blooming, flourishing, prosperous* Florence (Latin), Fiorenza, Florance, Florencia, Florinda, Florine, Floris • *blooming, flowery* Florida (Latin) • *blooming, luxuriant* Thalia (Greek) • *fresh blooming, green* Viridis (Latin) • *the blooming* Zohra (Arabic)

blossom Kapua (Hawaiian); Hana (Japanese), Hanae, Hanako; Mai (Vietnamese) • *a blossom* Flower (French) • *beautiful blossom* Calantha (Greek), Callantha, Callie • *cherry blossom* Sakura (Japanese) • *from a flower blossom* Evanthe (Greek), Evante, Vanthe; Azalea (Hebrew), Azaleah, Zaelea, Zela, Zelea • *gardenia; fragrant blossom* Kiele (Hawaiian) • *magnolia blossom* Mu-Lan (Chinese) • *of the clover blossom* Clover (Anglo-Saxon), Clovah • *pear blossom* Li-Hua (Chinese) • *plum blossom child* Umeko (Japanese) • *plum blossom, plum tree* Li (Chinese) • *tree peony blossom* Mu-Tan (Chinese) • *violet blossom* Jolan (Greek)

blossoming Pua *a blossoming tree* (Polynesian)

blue Azura *blue sky* (Old French) • *dark blue* Indigo (Greek) • *sapphire blue color or sapphire gem* Sapphira (Greek), Saphira, Sapphire

blueberry Mora *little blueberry* (Spanish)

bluebird Chilalis (Native American) • *bluebird on the mesa* Yoki (Native American)

blushing Lali (Hindi)

bold Ziana (Hindi) • *bold or courageous* Tracy (Latin) • *bold, outspoken* Germaine (Old German) • *bold wise counselor* Conradine (Old German) • *of bold people* Leopoldine (Old German), Dina, Lea, Leopoldeen

boldest Tibelda *boldest of the people* (Old German)

border Kiwa *born on a border* (Japanese)

born Kissa (African); Tawia *born after twins* (Ashanti) • *born again* Renata (Latin), Renate, Rene, Renee • *born at dawn* Cho (Japanese) • *born at Easter time* Easter (Old English) • *born at night* Laila (Arabic), Leila, Layla; Sayo (Japanese) • *born during a journey* Abiona (Yoruban) • *born during a prosperous time* Neema (Swahili) • *born during the rainy season* Nasha (African); Masika (Swahili) • *born in April* Averill (Old English); Avril, Avrill, Averyl (English); *born in April, opening* April (Latin) • *born in autumn* Aki (Japanese) • *born in early spring* Primavera (Latin), Avera, Avaria, Vera • *born in heaven* Divija (Hindi) • *born in January*

Ova (Hausa) • *born in June* June (Latin), Junella • *born in spring* Haru (Japanese), Hayu • *born in spring child* Haruko (Japanese) • *born in summer* Natsu (Japanese) • *born in the evening* Yoi (Japanese) • *born in the morning* Asa (Japanese) • *born in winter* Fuyu (Japanese) • *born on a border* Kiwa (Japanese) • *born on Christmas* Latasha (American), Latacia, Letasha; Natasha (Russian), Tasha • *born on Friday* Afi, Efia, Koffi, Pheba (African), Phibba; Epua (Ghanaian) • *born on Monday* Juba, Kudio (African); Ajua (Ghanaian); Tanisha (Hausa), Tanesha, Tanesha, Tenisha • *born on Saturday* Kwamin, Mimba (African); Ama (Ghanaian) • *born on Sunday* Kwashi, Sisi (African); Adya (East Indian); Esi (Fante); Akosua (Ghanaian); Dominica (Latin), Domenica, Dominga, Dominique • *born on the seventh, seventh* Septima (Latin), Tima • *born on Thursday* Abba, Baba, Kwau (African); Abina (Akan); Aba (Ghanaian); Lakya (Hindi) • *born on Tuesday* Abena, Abla, Beneba, Kwabina (African); Abmaba (Ghanaian) • *born on Wednesday* Cuba, Kwaku (African); Ekua (Ghanaian) • *child born on holy ground* Oni (Yoruban) • *country-born* Kuni (Japanese) • *country-born child* Kuniko (Japanese) • *fifth-born* Quinette (Latin), Quinetta, Quintessa, Quintina • *first-born daughter* Kande (African); Kapuki (Bari); Dede (Ghanaian); Winona (Sioux Indian), Wenona, Winonah • *fourth-born daughter* Pita (Bari) • *ninth born* Tisa (Swahili) • *noble, well-born* Eugenia (Greek), Genie • *nobly born* Nabila (Arabic), Nabeela, Nabiba, Nabilah • *second-born child* Poni (Bari); Kekona (Hawaiian) • *the fourth-born* Rebba (Hebrew), Reba, Rebah; Quartas (Latin), Quartana, Quartis • *the second-born* Secunda (Latin) • *well-born* Owena (Welsh) • *winter-born child* Fuyuko (Japanese)
borrow Becca (Ngombe)
bosom Bronwen *she of the white bosom* (Welsh)

bosomed Rowena *light-haired; white bosomed, white-clad* (Celtic)
boughs Verbena *sacred boughs* (Latin)
bound Rebecca (Hebrew), Reba, Rebeca, Rebeka, Rebekah • *bound to me* Mosera (Hebrew), Mosira, Mosora, Sera
boundary Sabrina *from the boundary line* (Latin)
bountiful Dorene (Greek), Doreen, Dorena, Dorina, Dorine • *beautiful gift, bountiful gift* Dorinda (Greek), Đorin
bow Poloma (Choctaw Indian) • *archer, a carrier of the bow* Yvette (French), Yvonne • *yew-bow* Yvonne (Old French), Yvette
bracelet Tamaki (Japanese) • Armilla *small bracelet* (Latin), Armalla, Armillas, Armillia, Mila, Milla
braid Vanda (Congo); Kumi (Japanese) • *braid child* Kumiko (Japanese)
brainy Jasu (Hindi)
branch Resha *a branch* (Hausa) • *a green branch* Phyllis (Greek), Filide, Phillis; Pilisi (Hawaiian) • *a vine branch* Vidonia (Portuguese) • *leafy branch* Fronde (Latin) • *olive branch or olive tree* Olive (Latin), Livia, Nola, Olga, Olivette, Olivia • *a tree branch* Dalya (Hebrew), Dalia, Dalice, Daliya, Dalit
brave Casey (Irish-Gaelic), Casie, Kacie, Kasey • *brave as a bear* Bernadette (French), Bernadene, Bernadine, Bernardena, Bernita • *brave as a lion* Leontine (Latin), Leonteen, Leontina, Ontina, Ontine • *brave in battle* Harelda (Old German), Halda, Harilda • *child of a brave father* Eudocia (Greek), Docia, Doxia, Eudoca, Eudosia, Eudoxia • *lion-brave* Leonarda (Old German) • *strong and brave* Brice (Celtic), Bryce • *the brave friend* Orva (Anglo-Saxon), Orvah, Orvas • *the brave girl* Devona (Anglo-Saxon), Deva, Devina, Devinna, Devonna, Vona
breath Abelia (Hebrew); Abella (French)
breathe Tho *fiber; poem; to breathe* (Vietnamese)
breeze Rabi (Arabic) • *a gentle summer*

breeze Maili (Polynesian) • *gentle breeze* Aura (Latin), Aurea, Auria
bridge Hashi (Japanese)
bright Ming (Chinese); Urit (Hebrew) • *beautiful, bright* Bertha (Old German) • *beautiful, bright, fair* Alanna (Irish-Gaelic), Alaine, Alayne, Alina, Allene, Lana, Lanna • *bright and fair* Zuleika (Arabic) • *bright and lively* Gay (Old French) • *bright angel* Engelberta (Old German) • *bright as moonlight* Konane (Hawaiian) • *bright, brilliant, illustrious* Clara (Latin), Claire, Clare, Clareta, Clarette, Clarinda, Clarita; Klarissa (German); Klarika (Hungarian) • *bright eyes* Najila (Arabic), Naja, Najah, Najilah; Lochan (Hindi) • *bright, fair, serene one; girl with the tranquil heart* Serena (Latin) • *bright-haired* Calvina (Latin), Calvinna, Vina • *bright leaves; bright spring flower* Akina (Japanese) • *bright, lightness* Leoma (Old English) • *bright one* Aline (Polish) • *bright, polished, splendid* Jala (Arabic) • *bright, shining sword* Egberta (Old English), Egbertina, Egbertine • *bright white* Candida (Latin), Candide • *bright, white light* Farih (Hausa) • *clear or bright* Sorcha (Irish-Gaelic), Sorka • *from the bright meadow* Shirley (Old English), Shirlee, Shirleen, Shirlene • *girl with bright red hair* Rufina (Latin), Fina, Rufena, Ruphina • *light or bright friend* Nellwyn (Greek-Old English) • *the bright child* Zohara (Hebrew), Ohara, Zoha, Zohar
brightly Marya *brightly white or pure* (Arabic)
brightness Mai (Japanese) • *dawn brightness, east* Zara (Hebrew)
brilliance Huette (Old English) • *brilliance of Thor* Thorberta (Old Norse)
brilliant Kalea (Hawaiian); Rajul (Hindi) • *beautiful, brilliant* Clarabelle (French); Clarinda (Spanish) • *bright, brilliant, illustrious* Clara (Latin), Claire, Clare, Clareta, Clarette, Clarinda, Clarita; Klarissa (German); Klarika (Hungarian) • *brilliant, ahead* Zula (African) • *brilliant or shining* Alohi (Hawaiian) •

brilliant heroine Norberta (Old German) • *brilliant little one* Clarice (French), Clarissa, Clarisse • *brilliant mind* Huberta (Old German) • *brilliant, noble* Alberta (Old English), Albertina, Albertine, Elberta • *brilliant one, brilliant star* Electra (Greek), Lectra • *brilliant pledge or hostage, the bright pledge* Gilberta (Old German), Gilbertina, Gilbertine • *brilliant protector* Clarimond (Latin-German) • *light, clear or brilliant* Behira (Hebrew) • *most brilliant one* Claresta (English); Clarissa (Latin) • *noble and brilliant* Alverta (Greek) • *very brilliant one* Philberta (Old English)
brilliantly Bobina *brilliantly famous* (Czech), Berta, Roba
bring Leta (Swahili)
bringer Evangelinc *bringer of good news* (Greek), Eva, Evangelia, Eve • *bringer of light, light* Lucy (Latin), Lucette, Lucia, Luciana, Lucida, Lucie, Lucienne, Lucile, Lucille
broad Brady *broad eye or from a broad islnd* (Old English), Bradi, Bradie, Braedy, Braydee • *broad separation* Eurydice (Greek)
broad-shouldered Platona (Greek)
bronze Kane (Japanese)
brooding Delilah (Hebrew), Dalila, Delila, Lila, Lilah
brook Rilla *a brook or stream* (German), Rilette • *dweller by the brook* Brooke (Old English) • *flowing brook* Derora (Hebrew)
browed Gwendolyn *white-browed* (Old Welsh), Guenna, Gwen, Gwenda
brown Grunella (Old German), Nella • *brown hills* Kiona (Native American)
brownie Nissa *a friendly elf or brownie* (Scandinavian)
brunette Brunetta (Italian)
brushwood Clematis *brushwood or vine* (Greek)
bud Nizana (Hebrew), Nitza, Nitzana, Zana; Kali (Hindi)
budding Yamka *flower budding* (Hopi)
builder Bona (Hebrew)
bull Taura *like a bull* Latin
buoyant Alana *light and buoyant; an offering* (Hawaiian)
burdens Ulla *dearest of all God's burdens* (Hebrew), Ula, Ulah, Ule

burn Brandy *to burn wine* (Old English), Brandee, Brandi, Brandie
burning Seraphina • *burning, flaming* Celosia (Greek) • *burning or ardent one* (Hebrew), Serafina, Serafine, Seraphine
burst Posala *to burst* (Miwok)
bush Sihu *a flower* (Native American)

busy Idona *busy girl* (Old German), Donna, Idonah, Idonna
butterflies Vanessa *a genus of butterflies* (Latin), Vania, Vanna
butterfly Aponi (Hawaiian); Cho (Japanese); Kimama (Shoshone) • *chasing a butterfly* Nova (Hopi)

— C —

cactus Sabra *thorny cactus* (Hebrew), Sabrina
call Nida (Arabic)
caller Nadia (African)
calm Niral (Hindi); Placida (Latin), Cida, Placia, Placidia • *calm arrow* Tera (Japanese) • *calm, merciful, mild* Clementia (Latin), Clemence, Klementine • *calmness of the heavens* Nalani (Hawaiian) • *calm, serene; loving sister* Delphine (Greek), Delphina, Delphinia • *peaceful and calm* Shanti (Sanskrit) • *peaceful, calm* Serenity (Latin)
canal Chanel *dweller near the channel or canal* (Old French), Chanelle, Channelle; Shanel, Shanell, Shanelle (English)
canary Melina *canary yellow colored* (Latin)
candelabrum Menora (Hebrew), Menorah
candle Chandelle *like a candle* (Old French); Chandell, Shandell, Shandelle (English)
capable Kamya (Hindi)
cape Aderes *cape* (Hebrew) Aderet • *cape, headland* Saki (Japanese)
capriciousness Lila *capriciousness of fate* (Hindi)
carefully *see* abstain
caress Milliani *a gentle caress* (Hawaiian)
carrier *see* archer
carry Taborri *voices that carry* (Native American)
Casina Casina *from Casina* (Hausa)
castle Wira *gentlewoman of the castle* (Celtic), Irra, Wera

cat Paka (African); Ula (Hausa)
catlike Faline (Latin)
cedar Sugi (Japanese) • *cedar panels* Ariza (Hebrew), Arza, Arzice, Arzit • *cedar tree* Arna (Hebrew), Arnice, Arnit • *fir or cedar tree* Ornice (Hebrew), Orna, Ornit
celebrated *see* battle celebrated or glorious
celebration Jalsa (Hindi)
celestial Adrika (Hindi)
center Tamaya *in the center* (Native American)
ceremonial *see* attendant
challenger Delaney *descendant of the challenger* (Irish-Gaelic), Delanie
champion Neala (Irish-Gaelic), Nealie, Neela, Neely, Neila, Nelda; Nia (English)
channel *see* canal
chant Inoa *name chant* (Hawaiian)
chaperone Duena (Spanish)
charcoal Ibby *like charcoal* (Bini)
charger Waneta *the charger* (Native American)
charitable Charity *benevolent, charitable* (Latin), Charissa, Charita, Cherry
charity Carita *charity* (Latin), Karita
charm Haiba (African) • *a charm or spell* Jinx (Latin), Jynx • *written charm* Bua (Vietnamese)
charming Nadine (Greek); Lalita, Sarisha (Hindi)
chasing Nova *chasing a butterfly* (Hopi) • *coyote chasing a deer* Kaliska (Miwok)
chaste Kalifa *chaste, holy one* (Somalian) • *chaste or pure* Chastity (Latin) • *the chaste* Sada (Japanese)
chatterer Chiku (African)

chatty Hira (Hausa)
cheer Ailsa *girl of cheer* (Old German), Aillsa, Ilsa
cheerful Damisi (African); Ulani (Hawaiian) • *cheerful expression* Bhavika (Hindi) • *cheerful friend, merry* Hilary (Latin), Hilar, Hilaria, Hillary • *cheerful, full of laughter* Teshi (African) • *cheerful, gay* Allegra (Italian) • *cheerful, good-hearted* Corliss (Old English), Carleas • *cheerful one* Lacey (American), Lacee, Lacie; Lacy (English); Hilaria (Latin) • *cheerful one, joyful* Blythe (Old English), Blithe • *cheerful speaker* Lalage (Greek), Alage, Lallage • *exuberantly cheerful* Allegra (Latin), Allie, Legra • *to be cheerful* Tatum (Middle English), Tate
cherished Sherry (American); Cherie (French)
cherry Cerise (French), Cherise • *cherry blossom* Sakura (Japanese)
chestnut Kuri (Japanese)
chickpea Channa (Hindi)
chief Malvina *polished chief* (Irish-Gaelic), Malva, Melva, Melvina, Melvine • *woman chief* Winema (Modoc Indian)
chieftain Kalani *chieftain from the sky* (Hawaiian), Lani
child Page (Greek), Paget, Pagett, Paige; Keiki (Hawaiian); Bambi (Italian) • *a peaceful child* Peace (Anglo-Saxon) • *arrow child* Yumiko (Japanese) • *ball child* Mariko (Japanese) • *beautiful generations child* Miyoko (Japanese) • *beloved child; little love* Aiko (Japanese) • *bliss child, joy* Sachi (Japanese), Sachiko • *born in spring child* Haruko (Japanese) • *braid child* Kumiko (Japanese) • *child of advantage or goodness* Tameko (Japanese), Tame • *child born on holy ground* Oni (Yoruban) • *child of beauty* Adamma (Nigerian) • *child of a brave father* Eudocia (Greek), Docia, Doxia, Eudoca, Eudosia, Eudoxia • *child of cool, water* Kenda (Modern U.S.) • *child of peace* Evania (Greek), Evannia, Vani, Vania • *child of prosperity* Mieko (Japanese) • *child of the earth* Hermina (Czech); Cassa (Hausa); Herma, Mina (English) •

child of the moon Am (Vietnamese) • *child of the tortoise* Kameko (Japanese) • *child of the wise leader* Mackenzie (Irish-Gaelic), MacKenzie, McKenzie, Kenzie • *child or daughter* Chavi (Gypsy); Chavali (English) • *child to fortune* Zoila (Hebrew), Zoi, Zoilla • *circle child* Mariko (Japanese) • *earth child* Erda (Old German), Erdah, Erdda • *eighth child* Octavia (Latin), Octavie, Ottavia • *fifth child* Penthea (Greek), Pentha, Pentheam, Pentheas • *first child* Kazuko (Japanese); Prima (Latin) • *forest child* Moriko (Japanese) • *forgiveness child* Kaiko (Japanese) • *fortunate child* Machiko (Japanese) • *fourth child* Tessa (Greek) • *generous or magnanimous child* Hiroko (Japanese) • *happy child* Kioko, Tomiko (Japanese) • *heavenly child, heavenly flower* Leilani (Hawaiian) • *humble child* Nariko (Japanese) • *joyous child or child of rapture* Keiko (Japanese) • *lily child* Yuriko (Japanese), Yuri • *middle child* Media (Latin), Madora, Medea, Medora; Dia (Mende) • *next child* Raiko (Japanese), Reiko • *nine, ninth child* Ennea (Greek) • *ninth child* Nona (Latin) • *obedient child* Kazuko (Japanese) • *peak, mountain child* Mineko (Japanese) • *people child* Tamika (Japanese), Tamikee, Tamiko, Tamiyo • *plum blossom child* Umeko (Japanese) • *poem child* Utako (Japanese), Uta • *poetic child* Lee (Irish-Gaelic) • *pretty child* Reiko (Japanese) • *Saturday's child* Ama (Ghanaian), Ami • *second-born child* Poni (Bari); Kekona (Hawaiian) • *shore child* Hamako (Japanese) • *silkcloth child* Kinuko (Japanese), Kinu • *the bright child* Zohara (Hebrew), Ohara, Zoha, Zohar • *the child of a vow* Desma (Greek) • *the third child* Tertia (Latin), Teria, Tertias, Tia • *treasured child* Nyoko (Japanese) • *trembling child* Raama (Hebrew), Rama • *truthful child* Maeko (Japanese) • *twin child* Panya (African) • *valley child* Taniko (Japanese) • *victorious child* Katsu (Japanese) • *water or water child* Nirveli (Todas) • *wave child* Namiko (Japanese), Nami •

winter-born child Fuyuko (Japanese)

children Canice *gentle to children* (Welsh), Canica, Cannice

China China *the country of China* (American), Chyna; Chynna (English)

choir Prochora *choir leader* (Hebrew), Cora, Procora

chosen Moria *chosen by the Lord* (Hebrew), Mori, Moriah, Muriah • *chosen one* Vala (Germanic)

Christian Christine (French), Christiana, Christina, Cristina; Christel (German); Khristina (Russian); Kristin (Scandinavian), Kirsten, Kirstin, Kirsty, Krista, Kristan, Kristin; Krysta (Polish), Tyna • *beautiful Christian* Christabelle (Latin), Cristabel

Christmas *see* born on Christmas

chrysanthemum Chu-Hua (Chinese); Kiku (Japanese) • *chrysanthemum field* Kikuno (Japanese)

chubby Kessie *chubby one* (Ashanti)

cicada Neela (Mende)

cinnamon Kizzy (African)

cinnamonlike *see* bark

circle Mariko *circle child* (Japanese) • *circle of light* Lucerne (Latin), Lucerna

citizen Quirita (Latin)

city Roma *eternal city* (Latin), Romaine, Romelle, Romila, Romilda • *from a city near the sea* Aleria (Greek), Aleras, Alleras, Allerie, Alleris • *from the city of fine vestments* Alida (Greek), Aleda, Alyda, Leda, Lida • *from the city of Ilione or Troy* Ileana (Greek), Ilia • *from the city of Utica* Utica (Old German), Tica, Uticas, Uttica • *from the holy city* Kasi (Hindi) • *laughing girl of the city* Thormora (Hebrew), Omora, Thora, Thorma, Tormoria

clean Nirmala, Vimla (Hindi) • *beautiful and clean* Fleta (Anglo-Saxon), Fleda, Flita, Leda, Leta, Lita • *clean, pure* Rayna (Yiddish)

cleansing Lavelle (Latin), Lavella

clear Shizu (Japanese), Shizue, Shizuko, Shizuyo, Suizuka; Canna (Mende); Ayelen, Aylen (Native American) • *clear as crystal* Crystal (Latin), Chrystal, Krystal • *clear or bright* Sorcha (Irish-Gaelic), Sorka •

clear water Jawole (West African) • *light, clear or brilliant* Behira (Hebrew) • *the clear* Sumi (Japanese), Sumiko

clemency Eir *clemency, peace* (Old German)

clever Haley *clever, ingenious* (Modern U.S.), Hali, Halie, Hallie, Hayley, Haylie

cliff Cleva *dweller at the cliff* (English), Cleve

climbing Liana *a climbing vine* (French), Leana, Leanna, Liane, Lianna, Lianne

cloth Kanika *black cloth* (Mwera) • *silk-cloth child* Kinuko (Japanese), Kinu

clothing Almira *clothing container* (Hindi), Elmira, Mira

cloud Ambuda,Mehal (Hindi) • *a cloud* Nelda (Irish-Gaelic) • *black cloud* Hana (Arapaho) • *cloud, mist or vapor* Nebula (Latin) • *dawn cloud, violet color* Iola (Greek), Iole • *heavenly cloud* Aolani (Hawaiian) • *red cloud coming with sundown* Sanuye (Miwok)

clouds Anan (Arabic)

clove Lavali (Hindi)

clover *see* blossom

collected Samita (Hindi)

collection Nikara (Hindi)

color Iola *dawn cloud, violet color* (Greek), Iole • *sapphire blue color or sapphire gem* Sapphira (Greek), Saphira, Sapphire • *the color of mahogany wood* Mahogany (American)

colored Melina *canary yellow colored* (Latin) • *lilac or violet colored* Mauve (Latin), Malva • *olive colored* Orna (Irish-Gaelic), Ornas • *plum colored* Prunella (Latin), Nella • *scarlet colored* Scarlett (Middle English) • *violet colored flower* Iantha (Greek), Ianthina, Janthina • *violet colored stone* Ione (Greek), Iona

colorful Ayako *colorful, ornamental fabric* (Japanese)

comely Kyla (Irish-Gaelic), Kila, Kilah, Kylah • *beautiful, comely; hyacinth flower* Jacinda (Greek), Jacenta, Jacinta, Jacintha, Jacinthe, Jacynth • *the comely lass* Linette (Celtic), Linetta, Linnette, Lynette, Lynn, Netta

comfort Nahama *comfort from God* (Hebrew), Nahamas • *strengthening aid and comfort* Comfort (French)

comic Nabal *little comic* (Hebrew), Nabala, Nabalas

coming Zara *coming of dawn* (Hebrew), Zarrah • *the coming moon* Magena (Native American), Magen, Magina, Mitena • *war returned with her coming* Manaba (Navajo Indian)

commander Oma (Arabic)

commands Kasmira *commands peace* (Old Slavic)

commit Pham *greedy; to commit* (Vietnamese)

compassion Kripa (Hindi) • *beautiful, compassionate* Ruth (Hebrew) • *compassion, pity* Mercy (Middle English), Mercedes • *compassion, sorrow* Deidre (Celtic)

complete Parinita (Hindi) • *complete wanderer* Deirdre (Irish-Gaelic); Dedra (American) • *complete, whole* Annis (Greek)

complimentary Iditri (Hindi)

concealed Holda *beloved or concealed* (Old German), Hulda • *misunderstood, obscure or concealed* Gabi (Arabic)

concealer Calypso (Greek)

concord Harmony *concord, harmony* (Latin), Harmonia

confederate Farih (Arabic)

confident Renita *confident female* (Latin), Nita, Ranita, Renata, Reneta, Reniti

congratulations Hanna (Arabic)

conquering Vincentia *conquering one* (Latin)

conqueror Sigrid *beautiful conqueror* (Scandinavian) • *fair conqueror* Damalis (Greek), Damal, Damalas, Damali

consciousness Chetana, Sachita (Hindi)

consecrated Elga *consecrated, holy* (Slavic), Olga • *consecrated one* Blessing (Old English) • *consecrated to God* Elizabeth (Hebrew), Elisa, Elisabeth, Elise, Elissa, Eliza, Elyse, Libby, Liesel, Liesl, Lisbeth, Lisette, Liza, Lizabeth, Lizanne; Lusa (Finnish); Isa (German); Zizi (Hungarian); Isabel (Old Spanish); Liseta, Ysabel (Spanish)

consolation Consolata (Italian); Consuela (Spanish), Consuelo, Suela

constancy Constance *constancy, firmness* (Latin), Constanta, Constantina, Constanza; Kani (Hawaiian); Kostya (Russian)

constant Tokiwa *eternally constant* (Japanese)

container *see* clothing container

contemplater Theora *contemplater, watcher* (Greek)

content Prina (Hindi)

contestant Marcella *intelligent contestant* (Old German), Marcelle, Marcelline

continuation Willa (Arabic)

controller Uzzia *masterful controller* (Hebrew), Uzia, Uzial, Uzzial

cool Sheetal (Hindi) • *child of cool, pure water* Kenda (Modern U.S.) • *from a cool land* Daberath (Hebrew), Debarath, Debbra, Deborath, Debra

copper Rez (Hungarian)

coral Penina (Hebrew), Peninah, Peninit • *coral from the sea* Coral (Latin-Greek), Coralie, Coraline, Corel

cord Mio *triple cord* (Japanese)

corn Nahtanha *corn flower* (Native American) • *corn spirit and daughter of the earth* Onatah (Iroquois Indian) • *corn tassel* Takala (Hopi) • *corn tassel flower* Talasi (Hopi) • *rice, wheat, or ears of corn* Gesina (Hausa) • *shelled corn* Humita (Hopi)

corncake Ori (Native American)

cottonwood Alameda *cottonwood grove* (Native American)

cough Kolenya *to cough* (Miwok)

counselor Mallory *army counselor* (Old German) • *battle counselor* Hildreth (Old German) • *bold wise counselor* Conradine (Old German) • *counselor to the elves* Radelle (Old English), Della Delle, Radella • *divine counselor* Alura (Old English) • *elf counselor, good counselor* Alfreda (Old English), Elfreda, Elfrieda, Elva • *elfin counselor* Radella (Old English) • *elfin or good counselor* Elfrida (Old English) • *mild counselor* Mildred (Old English), Mildri • *old, wise counselor* Eldrida (Old English) • *shining counselor* Bertrade (Old English) • *victorious* *counselor* Sigrid (Old Norse) • *wise counselor* Monica (Latin); Monique (French), Mique

country *country-born* Kuni (Japanese) • *country-born child* Kuniko (Japanese) • *from the country estate* Villette (French) • *the country of China* China (American), Chyna; Chynna (English) • *woman of my country* Utina (Native American)

courage Tavishi (Hindi)

courageous Tracy *bold or courageous* (Latin) • *courageous one* Thaddea (Greek)

covered Gilda *covered with gold* (Old English)

coyote Mai (Navajo Indian) • *coyote chasing deer* Kaliska (Miwok)

crag Tara *crag or rocky pinacle* (Irish-Gaelic), Taran, Tarin, Tarina, Taryn

crane Baka (Hindi)

crash Taima *crash of thunder* (Native American)

create Crescent *to create or increase* (Old French), Crescentia

created Rachita (Hindi)

creation Kruti, Rachana, Rachna (Hindi)

creative Aniya, Sarjana, Sarjena (Hindi) • *God's creative power; illusion, fantasy* Maya (Sanskrit), Mayura

creator Raini (Native American), Raine • Nata *speaker or creator* (Native American)

creeper Bela (Hindi) • *golden creeper* Hemlata (Hindi) • *small creeper* Latika (Hindi)

crier Siko (Mashona)

crimson Carmen (Spanish), Carmencita, Karmen

crops Anona *yearly crops* (Latin)

crow Fala (Native American)

crown Taja *a crown* (Hindi), Tajah, Talajara, Tejah, Tejal • *a crown of laurel leaves* Laura (Latin), Laurene, Lauretta, Laurette, Lora, Loren, Lorena, Lorene, Loretta, Lorette, Lorita, Lorna • *a wreath or crown of flowers* Garland (Old French) • *crown* Atara (Hebrew) • *crown, crowned one* Corona (Spanish) • *crown, laurel, victory* Kelilah (Hebrew), Kaile, Kayle, Kelila, Kelula, Kyla • *crown or ornament* Adah (Hebrew) • *honored with a crown* Sade (Yoruban)

crowned Tiara (Latin) • *crown, crowned one* Corona (Spanish) • *crowned in great honor* Garlanda (Old English), Garlinda, Landa • *crowned one* Stephanie (Greek), Stephana, Stephania, Stevana, Stevena; Panya (Russian) • *crowned with laurel* Kaila (Hebrew)

crystal *see* clear as crystal

culture Sanskriti (Hindi)

cultured Lydia *a woman of Lydia, cultured person* (Greek), Lidia, Lydie

cup Lota *portable drinking cup* (Hindi)

curiosity Jignasa *academic curiosity* (Hindi) • *intellectual curiosity* Jigna (Hindi)

curly Crispa *curly-haired* (Hebrew), Crispas

cushion Cody *the cushion* (Old English), Codie

custom Themis *custom, justice, order* (Greek), Tema, Thema

cymbal Zel (Persian)

cypress Tirza *cypress tree* (Hebrew)

Cyprus Cypris *from the island of Cyprus* (Greek), Cipriana; Sipiana (Zuni)

Cyrena Cyrena *from Cyrena* (Greek)

Cythera Cytherea *from the island of Cythera* (Greek)

— **D** —

dainty Aulii (Hawaiian) • *dainty, darling, graceful* Mignon (French), Mignonette • *delicate and dainty* Ling (Chinese)

dance Nartan (Hindi) • *dance lord* Natesa (Hindi) • *to dance* Bina (African), Binah

dancer Binah (African) • *a rope dancer*

Nata (Hindi) • *magic dancer* Satinka (Native American) • *sacred dancer* Kachine (Native American), Kachina

dancing Alima *learned in dancing and music* (Arabic), Alimah

Danish Haldana *half Danish* (Old Norse)

daring *see* adventuring, world daring

dark Ebony *a hard, dark wood* (Greek), Ebonee • *black, dark one* Dee (Welsh) • *black or dark* Melanie (Greek), Melany; Melka (Polish); Milena (Slavic) • *dark as night, dark beauty* Leila (Arabic), Layla, Leilia, Lela, Lila • *dark blue* Indigo (Greek) • *dark flower* Melantha (Greek), Lantha, Melentha • *dark one* Darcie (Irish-Gaelic), Darcey; Adria (Latin), Adrea, Adriana, Adriane, Adrianne, Adrienne • *dark or tawny* Pinga (Hindi) • *girl of dark eyes* Dorcas (Greek), Dorcea, Dorcia • *girl of dark hair* Darcy (Celtic), Darcia, Dercy • *girl of the dark* Maurita (Latin), Aurita, Mauretta, Mauri, Moretta, Morita, Rita • *little dark one* Duana (Irish-Gaelic), Duna, Dwana • *of a dark complexion* Maureen (Old French), Maurine, Moira, Mora, Moreen, Moria • *pitch dark* Neela (Mende)

darkness Ebbie (Bini) • *the darkness before midnight* Lisha (Arabic), Lishe

darling Mignon *dainty, darling, graceful* (French), Mignonette • *darling, little lover* Amorette (Latin), Amarette, Amora, Amoreta, Moretta, Morette

dart Litonya *to dart down* (Miwok)

daughter Hija (African); Natane (Arapaho); Binti (Swahili) • *child or daughter* Chavi (Gypsy); Chavali (English) • *corn spirit and daughter of the earth* Onatah (Iroquois Indian) • *daughter of Ben* Benquasha (Native American) • *daughter of God* Batya (Hebrew) • *daughter of heaven* Efuru (African) • *daughter of our vow* Bathsheba (Hebrew), Bathsheb, Sheba • *daughter of the moon* Cynarra (Greek), Cynara, Cynera, Nara, Narra • *daughter of the ruler* Zoba (Old German), Zoa, Zobe, Zoe •

daughter of the red earth Adamina (Hebrew), Adama • *daughter of the sea, flower of the sea, sea star; warm-hearted* Cordelia (Celtic), Cordalia, Cordeelia, Delia • *daughter of the sun* Drisa (Hindi), Dreesa, Dreesha, Drisana • *daughter of the wind* Canace (Greek) • *first-born daughter* Kande (African); Kapuki (Bari); Dede (Ghanaian); Winona (Sioux Indian), Wenona, Winonah • *fourth-born daughter* Pita (Bari) • *fourth daughter* Pita (African) • *her father's daughter* Adana (Nigerian), Adanna, Adanya • *her mother's daughter* Adanne (African) • *hero's daughter* Ingrid (Old Norse), Inga • *last daughter* Audi (African) • *my daughter* Nituna (Native American)

dawn Oditi (Hindi); Aurore (Latin) • *aurora or dawn* Zora (Slavic) • *born at dawn* Cho (Japanese) • *coming of dawn* Zara (Hebrew), Zarrah • *dawn beautiful* Zerlinda (Hebrew-Spanish) • *dawn brightness, east* Zara (Hebrew) • *dawn cloud, violet color* Iola (Greek), Iole • *golden dawn* Zorina (Slovak), Zora, Zorah, Zorana, Zori, Zorie, Zory • *light of early dawn; sunset glow* Alaula (Hawaiian) • *the dawn of day* Dawn (Old English)

dawning Oriana *the dawning* (Latin) • *the new dawning* Roxanne (Persian), Roxana, Roxene

day Awendela *early day* (Native American • *eye of the day* Daisy (Old English) • *guardian of the sea, mortal day* Meredith (Old Welsh), Meridith • *new day* Dagny (Old Norse) • *the dawn of day* Dawn (Old English)

daybreak Aurora (Latin), Aurore

days Mikka *three days* (Japanese)

dear Carina (Italian), Cara, Rina; Leola (Teutontic) • *beloved, dear one* Carita (Latin), Carissa, Karissa, Karisa, Karise, Karisha • *dear, beloved one* Cheri (French), Cheri, Chery; Cara (Italian), Carina, Carine, Kara • *dear, precious or rare* Azize (Turkish) • *little dear one* Darlene (Old French), Darrelle; Darilynn, Darla (American) • *our dear treasure* Ezara (Hebrew), Ezaria, Ezarra, Ezarras, Zara

dearest Carissa *dearest little schemer* (Latin), Carisa, Chrissa • *dearest of all God's burdens* Ulla (Hebrew), Ula, Ulah, Ule
decay *see* anything
decorated Sajili (Hindi)
dedicated Beta *dedicated to God* (Czech/Slovak) • *she is dedicated to God* Lemmuela (Hebrew), Emmuela, Lemuela, Lemuelah, Uela; Belicia (Spanish)
deep Indrina (Hindi) • *deep snow* Miyuki (Japanese), Yuki • *the deep-* Dooriya (Gypsy); Dooya (English)
deeply Nitara *deeply rooted* (Sanskrit) • *to drink deeply* Dona (Hausa), Donah, Donnah
deer Isi (Choctaw Indian); Harini (Hindi); Shika (Japanese); Dyani, Tacincala (Native American) • *a deer* Hinda (Yiddish) • *a doe deer* Rae (Old English) • *coyote chasing deer* Kaliska (Miwok) • *deer or gazelle* Ayelet (Hebrew) • *female deer* Aphra (Hebrew) • *young deer* Faunia (Latin), Fawn, Fawna, Fawnia
defender Verena *defender, protector* (Old German) • *helper and defender of mankind* Alexandra (Greek), Alejandra, Aleka, Alesandra, Alexa, Alexandrine, Alexis, Lexine, Ritsa, Sandra, Sondra; Leska (Czech); Zandra (English); Alka, Olesia (Polish); Lesya, Sasha, Shura (Russian); Alickina (Scottish), Kina; Xandra (Spanish)
delicate Ling *delicate and dainty* (Chinese) • *delicate one* Tryphena (Latin) • *delicate plant or feather* Fern (Greek), Ferna, Fernas, Ferne
delight Charmaine *delight, joy* (Greek), Charmain, Charmian • *delight or pleasure* (Hebrew), Eden; Delight (Old French) • *she is my delight* Thirza (Hebrew), Hirza, Thirzi, Thirzia, Thissa, Tirza
delightful Krishna (Hindi), Kistna, Kistnah, Krisha, Krisya • *delightful one* Delicia (Latin)
Delos Delia *from the island of Delos* (Greek)
delphinium Delfine *the delphinium or larkspur flower* (Greek), Delfina, Delphina, Delphine

democratic Nadaba (Hebrew), Nadabas, Nadda
deny Canna (Swahili)
descendant Delaney *descendant of the challenger* (Irish-Gaelic), Delanie • *descendant of the protector* Monet (Fresh)
deserted Aud *deserted or empty* (Norwegian)
desirable Tirza (Hebrew); Ishani (Hindi); Ishana (Sanskrit)
desire Aakanksha, Ihita, Ipsita (Hindi) • *desire, expectation, hope* Hope (Old English)
desired Zody (Congo); Oni (Nigerian) • *desired, longed for; so long hoped for* Desiree (French), Desirea, Desireah • *the desired or the wished for* Wilona (Anglo-Saxon), Wilonah • *the desired, the looked-for one* Onida (Native American)
despised Rena *despised, disregarded, or refused* (Hausa)
destiny Karma, Niyati (Hindi) • *destiny, fate* Fortune (Latin), Fortuna • *destiny or fate* Kismet (American); Carma (Sanskrit)
destroyer Aghanashini *destroyer of sins* (Hindi) • *Kali time, the destroyer* Kali (Hindi)
destruction *see* anything
determination Nishtha (Hindi)
determined Wilva (Teutonic) • *determined, positive one* Thetis (Greek) • *direct and determined* Doshi (Hausa)
devoted Zelia *devoted or ardent one* (Greek), Zelina • *devoted to the Lord* Lael (Hebrew), Lail, Lally; Amadis (Latin), Amadas, Ammadas, Ammadis, Madi
devout Oringa (Latin), Oringas
dew Mehika *dew drops* (Hindi); Chumani (Native American) • *the gentle dew from heaven* Talia (Hebrew), Talya • *my father is dew* Abital (Hebrew), Avital
dewy Nadda (Arabic), Nada Naddah
dexterous Dextra *dexterous, skillful* (Latin)
diamond Almas (Hindi); Cara (Vietnamese) • *beautiful free diamond* Almaz (Ethiopian) • *diamond-like* Diamanta (French)
different Nirali (Hindi)

difficult Ciah (Hausa); Kia (English)
dignified Rafiya (African)
diligent Hedva *joy or diligent worker* (Hebrew), Edva, Edveh, Hedvah, Hedve, Hedveh
dim *see* blind
Dionysus Denise *Dionysus, Greek god of wine* (French), Denice, Denisha, Denyse
direct *see* determined
direction Disha (Hindi), Dishi
disagree Eba (Mende)
disciplinarian Imala (Native American)
discussion Jalpa (Hindi)
disgust Liliha (Hawaiian)
dishonest Satha (Hindi)
dispeller Janisha *dispeller of ignorance* (Hindi)
disposition Clementis *of a mild disposition* (Hebrew), Clementas, Clementi, Clementina, Clementine • *of a solemn disposition* Clorinda (Hebrew), Clorinde, Cori, Corin
disregarded *see* despised
distant *see* aloof
distinguished Pallua (Hebrew), Palla, Palnas, Palua; Lakshita (Hindi)
divine Devanshi (Hindi); Deva (Sanskrit) • *a divine annoucement* Orela (Latin), Orella • *black or divine* Devaki (Sanskrit) • *divine counselor* Alura (Old English) • *divine fame* Tecla (Greek), Tekla, Thecia • *divine flower, flower of Zeus* Diantha (Greek), Dianthe, Dianthia • *divine helmet or protection* Aselma (Old German) • *divine name* Theano (Greek) • *divine one, goddess* Diana (Latin), Deana, Deanna, Dianna, Dyan, Dyana, Dyane • *divine power* Astrid (Greek), Astra • *divine queen* Dionne (Greek), Dina, Dynah • *divine strength* Asta (Old Norse) • *divine surprise* Jaala (Hebrew), Jael, Jaela, Jala • *God-like, divine* Devanee (Sanskrit)
divinely Thecla *divinely famous* (Greek), Thekla • *divinely given* Theodosia (Greek), Dosia, Theda
diviner Pythia *a diviner or prophet* (Greek)
doctrine Nori *precept or doctrine* (Japanese), Norie, Noriko

doe Sivia (Hebrew) • *a doe deer* Rae (Old English)
dog Tusa *prairie dog* (Zuni)
doll Doli (African); Putul (Hindi)
donation Donata *donation, gift* (Latin)
door Netta *a door* (Mende), Neata, Neta
double Disa *double or twice* (Greek) • *woven with a double thread* Twyla (Middle English), Twila
doubly *see* accomplished
dove Jemima (Hebrew), Jemena, Jemina, Jeminah, Jemine, Jona, Jonati, Jonina, Mimi, Mina, Yona, Yonah, Yonina, Yonita; Columba (Latin), Coline, Colombe, Columbia; Paloma (Spanish) • *white dove* Chenoa (Native American)
down *see* dart
downward Jardena *to flow downward* (Hebrew)
downy Gillian *downy-haired one, youthful* (Greek), Gilane, Giletta, Gillan, Gilliana, Gilliette, Jill, Julia, Juliana, Juliet, Julietta, Julina, Juline, Julissa; Juliska (Czech); Juliette (French); Julinka (Hungarian); Jula, Julcia (Polish); Iulia (Romanian); Yulinka, Yulka (Russian); Yula (Serbian); Julita (Spanish)
downy-haired Jillian *innocent, downy-haired one* (Latin), Gilli, Gillian, Gillie, Jill, Jilliana, Jillie
draw Dalya *draw water* (Hebrew), Dalia, Dalice, Daliya, Dalit
dream Kanasu, Sapna (Hindi) • *a dream* Imena (Africa) • *dream or vision* Aislinn (Irish-Gaelic), Aisling, Isleen
dress Banna *adorn; an ornament, to dress* (Efik/African) • *beautifully dressed* Alida (Greek), Aleda, Alida, Alyda
drink *see* to drink deeply
drinking *see* cup
drops *see* dew drops
drove Columbine (Latin), Colmbyne
duckweed Ping (Chinese)
dusky Sanvali (Hindi)
dwell Song *to dwell* (Chinese)
dweller Beverly *dweller at the beaver meadow* (Old English) • *dweller at the cliff* Cleva (English), Cleve • *dweller at the gray fortress* Leslie (Irish-

Gaelic), Lesley • *dweller by the brook* Brooke (Old English) • *dweller in a valley or glen* Glenna (Welsh), Glenda, Glenette, Glennette, Glynis • *dweller near the channel or canal* Chanel (Old French), Chanelle, Channelle; Shanel, Shanell, Shanelle (English) • *mountain dweller* Peri (Greek)

dwells Vesta *she who dwells or lingers* (Latin)

dyed Reena *dyed with indigo* (Hausa)

— E —

eagle Erna (Old English), Ernaline • *eagle-like* Aleria (Latin) • *eagle-ruler* Arnalda (Old German) • *eagle valley* Arden (Old English), Ardenia • *fairy eagle* Pari (Persian) • *female eagle* Orlenda (Russian) • *the eagle or heron* Phoenix (Greek)

early Primavera *born in early spring* (Latin), Avera, Avaria, Vera • *early day* Awendela (Native American) • *light of early dawn; sunset glow* Alaula (Hawaiian)

earnest Ernestine *earnest one* (Old English), Erna, Stine

ears *see* corn

earth Dharti, Mahika (Hindi), Dhatri; Tuwa (Hopi); Terra (Latin) • *child of the earth* Hermina (Czech); Cassa (Hausa); Herma, Mina (English) • *corn spirit and daughter of the earth* Onatah (Iroquois Indian) • *daughter of the red earth* Adamina (Hebrew), Adama • *earth child* (Old German), Erdah, Erdda • *of the earth or world* Hermione (Greek), Hermine, Herminia; Hertha (Old English), Erda, Ertha, Herta • *of the red earth* Adaminah (Hebrew), Adama, Adamina • *small earth* Inika (Hindi) • *the earth* Gaea (Greek), Gaia; Eila, Idika (Hindi); Eartha (Old English) • *the good earth* Avani (Sanskrit)

earthen Jarietta *earthen water jug* (Arabic), Jarita

earthly Terrena *of earthly pleasures* (Latin), Terena, Terina, Terrene

ease Yusra (African)

east Zara *dawn brightness, east* (Hebrew) • *from the east* Osten (German); Esta (Italian)

Easter Easter *an Easter baby* (Anglo-Saxon) • *born at Easter time* Easter (Old English) • *from the Easter season* Paschasia (Latin), Pascasia, Pascha, Pascia, Pasia

eastern Sabiya *the eastern wind* (Arabic), Saba, Sabaya, Sabiyah

echo Echo *echo, reflected sound* (Greek) • *echo through the woods* Seda (Armenian), Sedda

Eden Genet (African)

eight Yachi *eight thousand* (Japanese), Yachiko, Yachiyo

eighth *see* child

elder Chi *elder sister; mind; to show* (Vietnamese) • *of the elder tree* Nelda (Old English), Elda, Nell, Nellda • *my elder little sister* Kaya (Hopi)

electricity Vijaya (Hindi)

elegant Araminta *the elegant lady* (Hebrew), Aara, Aramanta, Aramenta

elevated Elata *elevated, lofty, of jolly spirits* (Latin) , Elatia, Ellata, Lati • *from an elevated, magnificent place* Madeline (Greek), Madalaine, Madalena, Madella, Madelle, Madelline, Madelon, Madlen, Magda, Magdalen, Magdalena, Magdalene, Marleen, Marlene

elf Fay *a fairy or elf* (French) • *a friendly elf or brownie* Nissa (Scandinavian) • *beautiful fairy maiden, elf* Ella (Old English) • *elf counselor, good counselor* Alfreda (Old English), Elfreda, Elfrieda, Elva • *famous elf* Ludella (Old English), Loella, Louella, Luella, Luelle • *peaceful elf* Fredella (Old German), Della, Fredela

elfin Elva (Anglo-Saxon), Elvah, Elvia • *an elfin girl* Erlina (Anglo-Saxon), Erleena, Erlinna, Lina • *elfin counselor*

Radella (Old English) • *elfin friend*
Elvina (Old English) • *elfin, good*
Elva (Old German), Elvia • *elfin or good counselor* Elfrida (Old English) • *elfin spear or spike* Ordella (Old German) • *elfin vision* Druella (Old German) • *lucky elfin one* Ruella (Old German), Ruelle

elm Elma *like an elm* (English)

elves Elvina *a friend to elves* (Anglo-Saxon), Elwina • *counselor to the elves* Radelle (Old English), Della, Delle, Radella

embroidered Reena (Hausa)

emerald Mya (Burmese); Masara, Panna (Hindi); Ruri (Japanese); Esmeralda (Spanish)

emotional Bhavi (Hindi), Bhavini

empty *see* deserted or empty

enchantress Naashom (Hebrew), Nashom, Nashoma; Urmila (Hindi)

encircled Jetta *encircled or surrounded* (Congo), Jette

enclosure Gerda *enclosure, protection* (Old Norse)

end *see* always

endearing Caresse *endearing one* (French) • *an endearing woman* Vaclava (Scandinavian), Clava, Vacla

endurance Patience *endurance with fortitude* (French)

enduring Durene *enduring one* (Latin) • *enduring, queenly, womanly* Cornelia (Latin)

enemy Yanaba *she meets the enemy* (Navajo Indian)

energetic Mahira *quick or energetic* (Hebrew), Mehira

energy Shakti (Hindi); Kali (Sanskrit)

engrossed Magana (Hindi)

enjoyment Ranjan (Hindi)

enlightened Jairia *enlightened by God* (Hebrew), Jara, Jari, Jariah

enraged *see* angry, enraged one

ensnare Sidonie *to ensnare* (Hebrew), Sadonia, Sidonia

enthusiasm Ardelle *enthusiasm, warmth* (Latin), Ardeen, Ardelia, Ardella, Ardene, Ardine

enticing Zita (Celtic), Ita, Zitah

equality Samata (Hindi)

Erin Erina *from Erin, Irish lass* (Irish-Gaelic), Erin, Erine, Erinna

essence Quintessa (Latin), Quentessa, Quinta, Quintice

Essex Osyth *saint from Essex* (Anglo-Saxon), Osithe

estate Henrietta *estate or home ruler* (French), Enriqueta, Hariette, Hendrika, Henriette, Henrika; Harriet (Old French); Henka (Polish); Queta (Spanish) • *from the country estate* Villette (French) • *owner of an inherited estate* Ula (Old English) • *ruler of the estate or home* Enrica (Italian)

eternal Nithya, Sanoja (Hindi), Nitya • *eternal beauty* Amara (Greek), Amargo, Mara • *eternal bloom* Aiyana, Ayiana (Native American) • *eternal city* Roma (Latin), Romaine, Romelle, Romila, Romilda • *eternal flame* Keerthi (Hindi) • *my joy is eternal* Gilada (Hebrew), Giladah

eternally *see* constant

ethereal *see* air

ethics Niti, Samskara (Hindi)

evening Tasarla (Gypsy)• *born in the evening* Yoi (Japanese) • *evening or evening star* Hesper (Greek), Hespera, Hespira • *the evening star* Vespera (Latin); Trella (Spanish), Trela, Trellas

everlasting Perpetua (Latin)

ewe Rachel *an ewe* (Hebrew), Rachele, Rachelle, Rae, Rahel, Raquel; Lahela (Hawaiian); Rakel (Swedish)

exalted Raisa (African) • *exalted, fulfillment or truth* Almira (Arabic), Almeria, Almire, Elmira • *exalted of the Lord* Jeremia (Hebrew), Jeri • *exalted or praised* Sami (Arabic) • *lofty, exalted one* Rama (Hebrew) • *noble and exalted* Adara (Hebrew)

excellent Degula (Hebrew) • Jin *super-excellent* (Japanese)

existence Akshi (Hindi) • *the force of present existence* Pemba (Bambara)

expectation *see* desire, expectation, hope

expected Miniya *much is expected of her* (African)

expert Thien *expert; heaven; narrow-minded; to geld* (Vietnamese)

expression *see* cheerful expression

extraordinary *see* admirable, extraordinary

extreme Neva *snow or extreme whiteness* (Spanish)
extremely *see* extremely free
exuberantly *see* cheerful
eye Lochana (Hindi) • *broad eye* Brady (Old English), Bradi, Bradie, Braedy, Braydee • Daisy *eye of the day* (Old English)
eye-catching Rana *eye-catching or beau-* *tiful to gaze upon* (Arabic), Raniyah, Ranya
eyes Najila (Arabic), Naja, Najah, Najilah • *beautiful eyes* Maha (African); Shahla (Dari) • *big eyes* Naira (Native American) • *bright eyes* Lochan (Hindi) • *girl of dark eyes* Dorcas (Greek), Dorcea, Dorcia • *golden eyes* Hemakshi (Hindi)

— **F** —

fabric *see* colorful, ornamental fabric
face Anika *sweetness of face* (Hausa)
fair Enid (English); Gauri (Hindi), Gari, Gouri; Bianca (Italian) • *a soft-spoken woman; fair speech, well-spoken one* Eulalia (Greek), Eula, Eulalie • *beautiful and fair* Teagan, Tegan (Welsh) • *beautiful, bright, fair* Alanna (Irish-Gaelic), Alaine, Alayne, Alina, Allene, Lana, Lanna • *bright and fair* Zuleika (Arabic) • *bright, fair, serene one; girl with the tranquil heart* Serena (Latin) • *fair conqueror* Damalis (Greek), Damal, Damalas, Damali • *fair, harmonious* Alana (Celtic), Alanna, Lana • *fair-shouldered* Nuala (Irish-Gaelic) • *fair, white* Libna (Hebrew), Lebna, Liba, Libnah; Blanche (Old French), Bianca, Blanca, Blinnie; Gwynne (Old Welsh), Gwyn, Wynne • *holy, fair one* Glynnis (Welsh), Glenice, Glenise, Glennice, Glennis, Glenwys, Glenys, Glynis • *just, fair* Adila (African) • *slender-fair* Keelin (Irish-Gaelic), Carolinn • *white, fair-skinned one* Bela (Czech); Balaniki (Hawaii)
fairest Ancelin *fairest handmaid* (Latin), Ancalin, Anceline, Celin, Celine • *fairest, loveliest woman* Vashti (Hebrew), Ashti, Vashtee, Vashtia, Vasti • *fairest of the famous* Euphemia (Greek), Euphemiah, Phemia
fairy Fay *a fairy or elf* (French) • *beautiful fairy maiden, elf* Ella (Old English) • *fairy eagle* Pari (Persian), Parina • *fairy queen* Tiana (Slavic), Tiane, Tianna, Tianne • *little fairy* Fayette (French) • *the fairy queen* Tania (Russian), Tanya • *wood fairy* Sen (Japanese)
faith Aastha, Pratiti (Hindi)
faithful Amineh (Arabic); Emuna (Hebrew); Dilyn (Irish-Gaelic), Dilan, Dilen, Dilinn, Dillan, Dillen, Dillyn • *faithful, loyal one* Leala (Old French), Lealia, Lealie • *faithful woman* Fidelia (Latin), Dela, Fidelas, Fidelity, Fidellia, Idel
facon Taka (Japanese)
fall *see* below
falling Vanda *falling lightly* (Congo) • *rain falling* Huyana (Miwok) • *the falling one* Vega (Arabic)
fame Khyati, Kirti (Hindi) • *awe-inspiring fame* Elmina (Old German) • *divine fame* Tecla (Greek), Tekla, Thecia • *fame, glory* Cleo (Greek) • *of great fame* Orlantha (Old German), Orlanta • *shining with fame* Roberta (Old English), Bobbette, Robina, Robine, Robinia • *the little one of fame* Robinette (Old German), Binetta, Binette, Robin, Robinetta
famed Jasmit (Hindi) • *famed fighter* Aloysia (Old German), Aloisia, Alyose, Lois • *famed one, renowned* Clymene (Greek)
family Lorola *from a great family* (Latin), Lorolla, Lorollas, Ola, Orola • *from a prosperous family* Edina (Anglo-Saxon), Dina, Eddina
famous Bobina (Czech), Berta, Roba; Degula (Hebrew); Nola (Irish-Gaelic), Nolana • *divinely famous* Thecla (Greek), Thekla • *fairest of*

the famous Euphemia (Greek), Euphemiah, Phemia • *famous and pleasant* Mertice (Old English), Merdyce • *famous battle maid* Clotilda (German), Clothilde • *famous elf* Ludella (Old English), Loella, Louella, Luella, Luelle • *famous friend* Rowena (Old English) • *famous, noble one* Elmira (Old English) • *famous one* Kaulana (Hawaiian) • *famous one, shining* Lara (Latin) • *famous protectress* Rosamond (Old German), Rosamund, Rosamunda, Rosamunde, Rozamund • *famous ruler; princess, ruler* Roderica (Old German), Rica • *famous woman warrior, glorious battle maid* Romilda (Old German), Maida, Milda, Romalda, Romelda • *famous warrior maid* Louise (Old German), Alison, Allison, Aloisa, Aloisia, Eloisa, Eloisc, Hcloise, Lisette, Louisa, Louisette, Luisa, Lulu; Iza, Lilka (Polish) • *famous wolf* Rudi (Old German) • *from a famous father* Cleopatra (Greek), Cleopatre • *from a famous place* Cleodel (Greek), Cleodal, Cleodell • *from the famous land* Rolanda (Old German), Orlanda, Rolande • *place of a famous army* Lorraine (Old German), Loraine • *the famous maid of war* Marelda (Old German), Mareld, Marolda

fanciful Caprice (Italian)

fantasy *see* creative

far Mona *far away, lonely* (Old German) • *from the far land* Dacia (Latin), Dachi, Dachia • *from the far valley, from the vale or hollow* Valonia (Latin), Vallonia, Valoniah

farewell Aloha *greetings or farewell* (Hawaiian)

farm Karmel (Hebrew), Carmel, Carmeli, Carmi, Carmia, Carmiel • *girl from the farm* Terza (Greek), Tera, Terzas

farmer Georgia *farmer; watchful one* (Latin), Georgene, Georgette, Georgiana, Georgienne, Georgina, Georgine, Gigi, Giorgia

farming Noma (African)

farseeing Miwako *farseeing child* (Japanese) • *the farseeing* Miwa (Japanese)

fate Karma (Hindi); Destiny (Old French) • *a Viking goddess of fate* Norna (Old Norse) • *capriciousness of fate* Lila (Hindi) • *destiny, fate* Fortune (Latin), Fortuna • *destiny or fate* Carma (Sanskrit)

father Eudocia *child of a brave father* (Greek), Docia, Doxia, Eudoca, Eudosia, Eudoxia • *father of joy* Abigail (Hebrew), Abbey, Gail, Gale • *from a famous father* Cleopatra (Greek), Cleopatre • *my father is dew* Abital (Hebrew), Avital • *the one my father knows* Abida (Hebrew)

father's Adana *her father's daughter* (Nigerian), Adanna, Adanya

faultless Alopa (Hindi)

favor Rida (Arabic)

favorable *see* auspicious, favorable

favorite Kesia (African), Keisha, Keshia, Kessiah, Kissiah, Queisha, Quesha; Prianki (Hindi); Saqui (Native American)

fawn Awenita *a fawn* (Native American); Niabi (Native American) • *a fawn, freshness* Orpah (Hebrew), Oprah, Orpha

fear *see* abstain

fearless Vibhi (Hindi) • *a man's woman, fearless* Andreanna (Greek)

feather Shikoba (Choctaw Indian) • *delicate plant or feather* Fern (Greek), Ferna, Fernas, Ferne

February *see* birthstone

Feel *see* better

female Zaila (African); Cai (Vietnamese) • *confident female* Renita (Latin), Nita, Ranita, Renata, Reneta, Reniti • *female deer* Aphra (Hebrew) • *female eagle* Orlenda (Russian) • *romantic female* Grania (Celtic), Graniah, Grannia, Granniah, Grannias

fertile Arva (Latin) • *apple, fertile* Pomona (Latin) • *fertile field* Yoshino (Japanese) • *from a fertile land, Greek fertility goddess* Demetria (Greek), Demitria • *from the fertile plain* Sharon (Hebrew), Shara

fertility *see* fertile

fervent Ardis *fervent, zealous* (Latin), Arda, Ardelia, Ardella, Ardelle, Ardene

festive Hagia (Hebrew), Hagice,

Hagit • *one who is festive, merry* Habbai (Hebrew)
festivities Utsavi (Hindi)
fiber *see* breathe
fidelity Fealty *allegiance, fidelity* (French) • *belief in God, fidelity, loyalty* Faith (English), Fay
field Kikuno *chrysanthemum field* (Japanese) • *fertile field* Yoshino (Japanese) • *flat, rice field* Hirata (Japanese) • *forest, rice field* Morita (Japanese) • *from a flowering field* Ardath (Hebrew), Arda, Ardeth, Ardith • *from the field* Felda (Old German) • *good field* Yoshino (Japanese) • *pine, rice field* Matsuda (Japanese) • *planted field* Nirel (Hebrew) • *plum tree field* Umeno (Japanese) • *rice field* Arita (Japanese) • *rice field, middle* Tanaka (Japanese) • *rice field, river* Tagawa (Japanese) • *rice field, side* Tanabe (Japanese) • *rice field stork* Tazu (Japanese) • *shore field* Urano (Japanese) • *small field* Ohara (Japanese) • *storehouse field* Kurano (Japanese) • *weaver's field* Orino (Japanese), Ori • *wisteria, rice field* Fujita (Japanese)
fierce *see* angry
fiery Ignatia *ardent one, fiery* (Latin) • *fiery one* Pyrena (Greek) • *fiery woman* Eda (Anglo-Saxon), Edda, Edel • *little ardent or fiery one* Ena (Irish-Gaelic) • *little fiery one* Edana (Irish-Gaelic) • *intense and fiery* Neci (Latin)
fifth Quinette *fifth-born* (Latin), Quinetta, Quintessa, Quintina • *fifth child* Penthea (Greek), Pentha, Pentheam, Pentheas
fight Hedwig *fight, strife; refuge from the storm* (Old German), Heda, Hedvig, Hedvige, Hedy
fighter Dusty *a fighter* (Old German), Dustee, Dusti, Dustin, Dustyn • *famed fighter* Aloysia (Old German), Aloisia, Alyose, Lois • *tiny fighter* Elga (Anglo-Saxon), Ellga
filled Venda (Mende)
final Ultima *final or last* (Latin), Tima
fine Darrah *big and fine* (Hausa) • *fine hair* Kesava (Hindi) • *noble, of a fine background* Ermina (Latin), Erma, Erminna, Mina, Minna

finish Pedzi *to finish* (Rhodesian)
fir *see* cedar
fire Adar (Hebrew); Anala, Banhi (Hindi); Nina (Native American) • *fire of the Lord* Nuria (Hebrew), Nuri, Nuriel • *flames of fire* Agnishikha (Hindi) • *goddess of fire* Analaa (Hindi) • *little fire* Aidlan (Irish-Gaelic) • *the fire* Keahi (Hawaiian)
firebrand Blasia (Old German)
firefly Yola (Hausa)
firmness *see* constancy, firmness
first Primrose *a flower name, little first one* (Latin), Primrosa • *first child* Kazuko (Japanese); Prima (Latin) • *first one* Alpha (Greek), • *first power* Aadhya
first-born Kande *first-born daughter* (African); Kapuki (Bari); Dede (Ghanaian); Winona (Sioux Indian), Wenona, Winonah • *the first-born* Wenonah (Native American), Wanonah, Wenoa, Wenona, Winona
flame Bhanu, Jwala,Shama (Hindi) • *eternal flame* Keerthi (Hindi)
flames *see* flames of fire
flaming Celosia *burning, flaming* (Greek) • *the flaming torch* Kalama (Hawaiian)
flash Levina *a flash, lightning* (Middle English)
flashing Marmara *flashing, glittering, radiating* (Greek)
flat Dessa *flat or unexpressive* (Mende) • *flat, pine* Hiramatsu, Matsuhira (Japanese) • *flat, rice field* Hirata (Japanese)
flatterer Gittle *innocent flatterer* (Hebrew), Gitel, Gittel, Gytle
flattering Ilka *flattering or industrious* (Slavic) • *flattering or industrious one* Amelia (Latin), Amalea, Amalia, Amaline, Amalita, Amilia, Emelina, Emeline, Emilia; Melcia (Polish); Milica (Slavic) • *flattering, winning one* Emily (Latin), Emelda, Emilie, Emlyn, Emlynne
flees Hagar *forsaken, one who flees* (Hebrew), Haggar
fleet Fleta *fleet one, swift* (Old English)
flourishing Virgilia (Latin) • *blooming, flourishing, prosperous* Florence (Latin), Fiorenza, Florance, Floren-

cia, Florinda, Florine, Floris; Flann
(Irish)
flow downward
flower Palesa, Zahara (African); Hua
(Chinese); Fleur (French), Fleurette; Anthea, Malva (Greek), Antheia, Malvia, Malvie; Pua (Hawaiian); Hana (Japanese), Hanae,
Hanako; Flora (Latin), Fiora, Flore,
Floria; Rayen, Xochitl (Native American); Blom (South Africa); Zahra
(Swahili); Hoa (Vietnamese); Blum,
Bluma (Yiddish) • *a flower* Sihu (Native American) • *a flower, flower of the
allyssium* Alyssa (Old German) • *a
flower name, little first one* Primrose
(Latin), Primrosa • *a lilac flower* Lila
(Persian), Lilac • *a lily flower* Lillian
(Latin), Liliane, Lilliana, Lily • *a
poppy flower* Poppy (Latin) • *aster
flower* Astera (Hebrew), Asta, Asteria,
Asteriya • *beautiful, comely; hyacinth
flower* Jacinda (Greek), Jacenta, Jac-
inta, Jacintha, Jacinthe, Jacynth •
bright leaves; bright spring flower Akina
(Japanese) • *corn flower* Nahtanha
(Native American) • *corn tassel flower*
Talasi (Hopi) • *dark flower* Melantha
(Greek), Lantha, Melentha • *daugh-
ter of the sea, flower of the sea, sea star;
warm-hearted* Cordelia (Celtic),
Cordalia, Cordeelia, Delia • *divine
flower, flower of Zeus* Diantha (Greek),
Dianthe, Dianthia • *flower budding*
Yamka (Hopi) • *flower lover* Philan-
tha (Greek) • *flower of forgetfulness,
flower of forgetfulness* Lotus (Egypt-
ian) • *fragile flower* Elodie (Greek),
Elodea, Elodia • *from a flower blossom*
Evanthe (Greek), Evante, Vanthe;
Azalea (Hebrew), Azaleah, Zaelea,
Zela, Zelea • *from a tiny flower, the
mignonette flower* Reseda (Latin),
Raseda, Raseta, Reseta, Seta • *ginger
flower or ginger spice* Ginger (Latin) •
gladiolus flower or small sword Gladys
(Welsh) • *glory flower* Cliantha
(Greek), Cleantha, Cleanthe • *heav-
enly child, heavenly flower* Leilani
(Hawaii) • *heavenly flower* Pualani
(Hawaiian), Puni • *hyacinth flower*
Hyacinth (Greek), Giacinta, Jacinta,
Jacintha • *iris* Ayame (Japanese) •
like the flower marigold Marigolde

(Anglo-Saxon), Mari, Marigold,
Marigolda • *little honey flower* Melita
(Greek), Elita, Malita, Malleta,
Melitta • *little yellow flower* Nurit (He-
brew), Nurice, Nurita • *lotus flower*
Lien-Hua (Chinese) • *lovely flower*
Samantha (Native American), Sama,
Samanthia • *May flower* Valma
(Welsh) • *my golden flower* Meingolda
(Old German), Golda, Meingoldas •
non-sorrow flower Asoka (Hindi) •
plucked flower Mansi (Hopi) • *pluck-
ing flowers* Mausi (Native American)
• *prairie flower* Leotie (Native American) • *pretty flower* Lomasi (Native
American) • *rainbow, the iris flower*
Iris (Greek); Irisa (Russian), Risha •
rose flower Rhodanthe (Greek);
Rozene (Native American); Raizel
(Yiddish), Rayzil, Razil • *saffron
flower* Mamo (Hawaiian) • *spring
flower* Eranthe (Greek) • *the bakula
flower* Bakula (Hindi) • *the delphinium or larkspur flower* Delfine
(Greek), Delfina, Delphina, Delphine • *the fragrant white gardenia
flower* Gardenia (Latin) • *the heather
flower* Brier (French); Erica (Greek),
Erika • *the heather flower or shrub*
Heather (Middle English) • *the jasmine flower* Yasmeen (Arabic); Yasmine (English); Jasmine (Persian),
Jasmin, Jasmina • *the lily flower* Lilia
(Hawaiian) • *the marganit flower* Marganit (Hebrew) • *the marshmallow
plant and flower* Hibiscus (Latin) • *the
tall white flower* Daffodil (Greek),
Dafodil • *the tansy flower* Tansy
(Hopi) • *the tulip flower* Lala (Slavic)
• *thistle flower* Azami (Japanese) • *violet colored flower* Iantha (Greek),
Ianthina, Janthina • *violet flower* Calfuray (Native American); Iolanthe
(Greek), Yolanda; Jolan (Hungarian); Violet (Old French), Viola, Violante, Viole, Violette, Yolande,
Yolanthe • *white flower* Sacnite
(Mayan) • *wind-flower* Anemone
(Greek) • *yellow flower* Caltha (Latin)
flowering Ardath *from a flowering field*
(Hebrew), Arda, Ardeth, Ardith •
rich in flowering, steady Eustacia
(Greek), Eustacie
flowers Kakala *a fragrant garland of*

flowers (Polynesian) • *a wreath or crown of flowers* Garland (Old French) • *goddess of the flowers* Chloris (Greek), Chloras, Chlori, Lori, Loris • *valley of flowers* Algoma (Native American)

flowery *see* blooming, flowery

flowing Sarita (Hindi) • *flowing back of the tide* Ebba (Old English) • *flowing brook* Derora (Hebrew)

flows Cari *flows like water* (Turkish)

fluffy Trilby *a fluffy thing, frivolous, giddy* (Scandinavian), Trilbee, Trillbi, Trilly

flute Bansari, Sanika,Shalika (Hindi) • *flute maiden* Lenmana (Hopi)

fly Suletu *to fly around* (Miwok)

flying Volante *flying one* (Italian)

focus Dishita (Hindi)

foes Artana *vanquisher of all foes* (Hindi)

folded Falda *folded wings* (Icelandic)

follower Tabina *Muhammed's follower* (Arabic)

food Sedna *the goddess of food* (Eskimo)

forbidden Hanna (Hausa)

force Minerva *force, purpose* (Greek), Minette • *the force of present existence* Pemba (Bambara)

forceful Brenna *strong, forceful* (Celtic)

ford Tirtha (Hindi)

forecast Becca *to forecast or predict* (Bobangi)

forehead Tran *forehead; to overflow* (Vietnamese)

forest Lin (Chinese), Ling; Mori (Japanese) • *forest child* Moriko (Japanese) • *forest generation* Moriyo (Japanese) • *forest girl* Kunjana (Hindi) • *forest or wood spirit* Vedis (Old German), Vedi, Veedis • *forest spirit* Asiza (African) • *forest, rice field* Morita (Japanese) • *from the forest* Xylona (Greek)

forgetful Delu *forgetful one* (Mende)

forgetfulness Letha (Greek), Leda, Leitha, Leithia, Leta, Lethia • *flower of forgetfulness, flower of the lotus tree* Lotus (Egyptian)

forgiveness Kai (Japanese) • *forgiveness child* Kaiko (Japanese)

forgiver Sameh (Arabic)

forgotten Kaluwa *the forgotten one* (Umbundu)

forsaken *see* flees

forsight Prudence *foresight, intelligence* (Latin)

forthright Veradis *forthright, genuine* (Latin), Eradis, Vera, Verada, Veradi, Veradia

fortitude *see* endurance with fortitude

fortress Viveca *battle of the fortress* (Scandinavian), Vivica • *dweller at the gray fortress* Leslie (Irish-Gaelic), Lesley • *from the fortress* Darcie (Old French) • *from the royal fortress meadow* Kimberly (Old English)

fortunate Kalyani (Hindi); Halona (Native American) • *fortunate child* Machiko (Japanese) • *fortunate protector* Edmee (Anglo-Saxon), Edme, Edmea, Emee • *most fortunate woman* Audris (Old German), Audras, Audres • *the fortunate one* Kichi (Japanese), Kichiko, Kichiyo

fortune Zoila *child to fortune* (Hebrew), Zoi, Zoilla

fortune-teller Ramila (Swahili) • *a fortune-teller* Dibby (Hausa)

foster Larentia *foster mother* (Latin), Laurena, Laurentia

foundation Fonda (Latin)

fountain Fontainne (French); Endora (Hebrew), Dora, Gali • *a fountain basin or pillar* Pilar (Spanish) • *from a place of fountains* Bethesda (Hebrew), Bathesda, Bathesde, Thesda • *girl of the fountain* Moza (Hebrew), Mosa, Mozza, Oza • *of a fresh fountain* Kelda (Scandinavian), Elda, Kela, Keldah, Kella, Kellda

fourth Pita *fourth-born daughter* (Bari) • *fourth child* Tessa (Greek) • *fourth daughter* Pita (African) • *fourth letter of the Greek alphabet* Delta (Greek) • *the fourth-born* Rebba (Hebrew), Reba, Rebah; Quartas (Latin), Quartana, Quartis

fragile *see* flower

fragrance Moani (Hawaiian) • *the fragrance* Keala (Hawaiian) • *pleasant fragrance* Rufen (Chinese)

fragrant Olinda (Latin), Olida • *a fragrant garland of flowers* Kakala (Polynesian) • *fragrant ointment* Narda

(Latin) • *gardenia; fragrant blossom* Kiele (Hawaiian) • *the fragrant white gardenia flower* Gardenia (Latin) • *to be fragrant* Flair (Latin)

France Francesca *from France* (Italian)

frank Lalita (Greek), Lalitta, Lalittah, Lita

free Fanchon (French); Moksin (Hindi) • *beautiful free diamond* Almaz (Ethiopian) • *extremely free* Parivita (Hindi) • *free and unbounded* Aditi (Hindi) • *free one* Cella (Italian); Fanya (Russian), Fayina • *free woman* Netfa (Ethiopian)

freedom Derora (Hebrew); Willow (Middle English) • *the free one* Kanoa (Polynesian)

fresh Ranana (Hebrew) • Viridis *fresh blooming, green* (Latin) • *fresh, healthy, and pretty* Marini (Swahili) • *fresh, lovely* Blossom (Old English) • *fresh, new* Amaryllis (Greek), Amarillas, Amarillis, Amaryl, Maryl • *of a fresh fountain* Kelda (Scandinavian), Elda, Kela, Keldah, Kella, Kellda

freshness Orpah *a fawn, freshness* (Hebrew), Oprah, Orpha

Friday *see* born on Friday

friend Winna (Congo); Damica (French); Sakhi, Mita (Hindi); Cara (Irish-Gaelic), Carina, Carine, Kara • *a friend* Dakota (Native American) • *a friend to elves* Elvina (Anglo-Saxon), Elwina • *a good friend* Derina (Old English), Derinna, Dorina, Rina • *cheerful friend, merry* Hilary (Latin), Hilar, Hillaria, Hillary • *elfin friend* Elvina (Old English) • *famous friend* Rowena (Old English) • *friend* Amissa (Hebrew) • *friend of our Lord* Photina (Latin), Fhotima, Fina, Fotina, Otina, Tina • *friendly princess, gracious friend* Winola (Old German) • *friend to all* Lakota (Native American) • *light or bright friend* Nellwyn

(Greek-Old English) • *noble friend* Alvina (Old English) • *patient friend* Aleydis (Greek), Aledis, Alidis, Leda • *peaceful friend* Winifred (Old German) • *prosperous friend* Edwina (Old English), Edina • *sea friend* Erwina, Irvette (Old English) • *spear friend* Orva (Old English) • *spiritual friend* Jutta (Latin), Etta, Jueta, Juetta, Juta • *sweet friend, sweet wine* Melvina (Latin), Melva • *the brave friend* Orva (Anglo-Saxon), Orvah, Orvas • *the wise friend* Eldrida (Anglo-Saxon), Dreda, Drida, Eldreda • *trusted friend* Netis (Native American) • *virtuous friend* Areta (Greek), Aretina, Aretta, Arette, Tinaret

friendly Nissa *a friendly elf or brownie* (Scandinavian) • *friendly, friendship* Amity (Latin), Amaty • *friendly princess, gracious friend* Winola (Old German)

friendship Mitali (Hindi) • *friendly, friendship* Amity (Latin), Amaty

frivolous *see* fluffy

fruit Minal (Native American) • *a harvest of fruit* Janna (Arabic), Jana, Janaya • *fruit kernel* Pyrena (Greek)

fruitful Helbona (Hebrew), Elboa, Helbonia, Helbonna, Helbonnah; Pomona (Latin) • *fruitful woman, of the spring* Cerelia (Latin), Cerellia, Cerallua, Cerelly, Erlia • *she shall add, she shall be fruitful* Pepita (Spanish)

fruits Bina (Arapaho)

fulfilled Semira (African)

fulfillment *see* exalted, fulfillment or truth

full Indumati (Hindi)

furrow Sita (Hindi)

future Atida *the future* (Hebrew) • *one who predicts the future* Ramla (African)

•— G —•

gap-toothed Gibby (Hausa)

garden Ganit (Hebrew), Gana, Gan- ice; Karmel (Hebrew), Carmel, Carmeli, Carmi, Carmia • *a gardener,* *of the garden* Hortense (Latin), Hortensia, Ortensia • *garden or God's vineyard* Carmel (Hebrew), Carma, Carmela, Carmelina, Carmelita • *girl of the garden* Garda (Old German), Arda, Gardia

gardener *see* garden

garment Aderes *an outer garment* (Hebrew)

gardenia Kiele *gardenia; fragrant blossom* (Hawaiian) • *the fragrant white gardenia flower* Gardenia (Latin)

garland Fulmala (Hindi) • *a fragrant garland of flowers* Kakala (Polynesian)

gateway Bab *from the gateway* (Arabic), Babette, Barb, Barbara • *gateway, harbor* Portia (Latin)

gay Allegra *cheerful, gay* (Italian) • *gay, lively one* Gail (Old English), Gale, Gayle

gazelle Dorcas (Greek) • *antelope or gazelle* Gazella (Latin) • *deer or gazelle* Ayelet (Hebrew) • *the gazelle, the graceful girl* Tabitha (Aramic) • *young gazelle* Rasha (Arabic)

geld *see* expert; heaven; narrow-minded; to geld

gem Nyoko (Japanese) • *a gem name* Onyx (Greek) • *a gem or precious stone* Gemma (Greek) • *a precious gem or thing* Jewel (Old French) • *a topaz gem* Topaz (Latin) • *sapphire blue color or sapphire gem* Sapphira (Greek), Saphira, Sapphire • *the ruby gem* Ruby (Old French), Rubia, Rubie, Rubina

generation Ede (Greek) • *a generation* Dorit (Hebrew), Dorice • *beautiful generations* Miyo (Japanese) • *beautiful generations child* Miyoko (Japanese) • *forest generation* Moriyo (Japanese)

generosity Carrita *girl of generosity* (Latin), Carita, Rita

generous Karima, Nadda (Arabic), Kareema, Karimah, Nada, Naddah; Eudora (Greek), Dora, Eudore; Winona (Native American) • *generous or magnanimous child* Hiroko (Japanese) • *noble and generous* Nediva (Hebrew)

gentle Lateefah (Arabic); Melina (Greek), Melena; Jin (Japanese); Dalila (Swahili) • *a gentle caress* Mil-

liani (Hawaiian) • *a gentle summer breeze* Maili (Polynesian) • *a gentle woman* Duma (Greek), Dhumma, Dumah • *gentle and polite lady* Urbana (Latin), Urbai, Urbani, Urbanna, Urbannai • *gentle as a lamb* Damara (Greek), Damaris, Damarra, Mara • *gentle breeze* Aura (Latin), Aurea, Auria • *gentle, gracious, kind* Benigna (Latin) • *gentle, humane, kind* Halima (Swahili) • *gentle or languishing* Delilah (Hebrew), Dalila, Delila • *gentle, peaceful one* Placida (Latin) • *gentle, polite* Myrna (Irish-Gaelic), Merna, Mirna, Moina, Morna, Moyna • *gentle to children* Canice (Welsh), Canica, Cannice • *honeylike, sweet or gentle* Melosa (Spanish) • *mild, gentle one* Malinda (Greek), Malena, Malina, Malinde, Melina, Melinda • *soft, gentle* Anana (African) • *the gentle dew from heaven* Talia (Hebrew), Talya

gentlewoman *see* castle

genuine *see* forthright, genuine

genus *see* butterflies

giant Titania (Greek)

giddy *see* fluffy

gift Chipo (African); Nawal (Arabic); Matana (Hebrew); Ahanti (Hindi); Hadiya, Zawadi (Swahili); Gisa (Teutonic) • *a gift, given of God* Nathania (Hebrew), Nathene • *beautiful gift* Adorabelle (French-Latin) • *beautiful gift, bountiful gift* Dorinda (Greek), Dorin • *donation, gift* Donata (Latin) • *gift* Adia (Swahili) • *gift, glory, renown* Adora (Latin) • *gift of God* Noni (African); Dorothy, Theodora (Greek), Dora, Dorothea, Dorthea, Dorthy, Tedora, Theda; Mattea (Hebrew), Mathea, Mathia, Matthea, Matthia, Natania, Natanya, Nathania, Natonya; Godiva (Old English); Dasha, Dosya (Russian) • *gift of Isis* Isadora (Greek) • *gift of the Lord* Matta (Hebrew), Mattah • *gift of the muses* Musidora (Greek) • *gift of the sun* Elidi (Greek) • *gift or present* Makana (Hawaiian) • *gift we prayed for* Matthia (Hebrew), Atthia, Mathi, Mathia, Thia • *God's gift* Lolotea (Zuni) • *God's gracious gift* Ivanna (Hebrew), Ivana, Ivanah, Ivy • *my gift*

Bunme (African), Bunmi • *rich gift* Dita (Czech); Duci (Hungarian); Edith (Old English), Edita, Editha, Edithe, Ediva, Edyth, Edythe • *satisfying gift* Isoke (African); *splendid gift* Eudora (Greek) • *unexpected gift* Halla (African) • *valuable gift* Ekika (Hawaiian); Duci (Hungarian) • *winged gift* Aldora (Greek), Alda, Dora

gifted Eldora *gifted with wisdom* (Latin), Dora • *the all-gifted one* Pandora (Greek)

gilded Eldora *gilded one* (Spanish)

ginger *see* flower

girdle Zona *a girdle* (Latin)

girl Nyako (African); Nenah (American); Alumit (Hebrew); Kani (Hindi); Nina (Spanish), Ninetta, Ninette • *a girl who makes others happy* Beatrice (Latin), Beatrix, Trixie, Trixy • *an elfin girl* Erlina (Anglo-Saxon), Erleena, Erlinna, Lina • *armored battle maid, girl of war* Serilda (Old German), Rilda, Sarilda, Sorilda • *bitter, girl of sadness* Merari (Hebrew), Mera, Meraree • *bright, fair, serene one; girl with the tranquil heart* Serena (Latin) • *busy girl* Idona (Old German), Donna, Idonah, Idonna • *forest girl* Kunjana (Hindi) • *girl from the farm* Terza (Greek), Tera, Terzas • *girl from the sea* Adrienne (Greek), Adria, Adriana, Adriane, Adrianna, Adrianne • *girl in black* Chemarin (Hebrew), Chamaran, Chemar • *girl, maiden* Colleen (Irish-Gaelic), Cailin • *girl of beauty* Pulcheria (Latin), Cheri, Cheria, Pulchia • *girl of cheer* Ailsa (Old German), Aillsa, Ilsa • *girl of dark eyes* Dorcas (Greek), Dorcea, Dorcia • *girl of dark hair* Darcy (Celtic), Darcia, Dercy • *girl of generosity* Carrita (Latin), Carita, Rita • *girl of great talent* Maxentia (Latin), Maxantia, Maxia • *girl of nature, nature lover* Rima (Anglo-Saxon), Ima, Rema, Ria, Rimma • *girl of our hearts* Naarah (Hebrew), Nara, Narah • *girl of peace* Persis (Greek), Persas; Selema (Hebrew), Lema, Selemas, Selima • *girl of purity* Trina (Greek), Trinee, Trinia • *girl of resourcefulness* Fabri-

anne (Latin), Fabria, Fabriane, Fabrianna, Fabrienne • *girl of sadness* Desdemona (Greek), Demona, Desdamona, Desdamonna, Desdee, Mona • *girl of the dark* Maurita (Latin), Aurita, Mauretta, Mauri, Moretta, Morita, Rita • *girl of the fountain* Moza (Hebrew), Mosa, Mozza, Oza • *girl of the garden* Garda (Old German), Arda, Gardia • *girl of the magnolia tree* Magnolia (Anglo-Saxon) • *girl of the sea, sea gull* Larina (Latin), Lareena, Larena, Larianna, Larine, Rina • *girl of the tent* Aholah (Hebrew), Ahola, Aholla, Hollah, Holly • *girl of the valley* Machutte (Old German), Machute • *girl of white skin* Oriana (Celtic), Anna, Oria, Orian, Orianna • *girl or maiden* Betula (Hebrew) • *girl to be trusted* Alethea (Greek), Aleta, Aletha, Alitha, Letha, Litha, Lithea, Thea • *girl who is treasured* Castora (Latin), Casta, Castara, Castera • *girl with bright red hair* Rufina (Latin), Fina, Rufena, Ruphina • *girl with white skin* Yseulte (Celtic), Isolda, Isolde, Yseulta • *golden girl* Hemkanta (Hindi) • *gypsy girl* Zigana (Hungarian) • *holy girl* Diella (Latin), Dielle; Froma (Old German), Fromma • *laughing girl of the city* Thormora (Hebrew), Omora, Thora, Thorma, Tormoria • *little girl* Donella (Latin), Donela, Donell, Nell, Nella; Lassie (Scottish); Ninita (Spanish) • *little girl of purity* Trinette (Greek), Rinee, Trinatte, Trinetta • *rattlesnake girl* Shumana (Hopi), Chuma, Chumana; Shuma (English) • *slim girl* Latangi (Hindi) • *thankful girl* Gratiana (Latin), Atiana, Gratianna, Triana • *the brave girl* Devona (Anglo-Saxon), Deva, Devina, Devinna, Devonna, Vona • *the gazelle, the graceful girl* Tabitha (Aramic) • *the last girl* Maxima (Latin), Maxama, Maxma • *the only girl* Delu (African) • *wholesome young girl* Valeda (Old German), Aleda, Leda, Valeta

girlfriend Kalila (Arabic), Kaleela, Kalilah

give Yetta *giver, to give* (Old English) • *give thanks* Jendayi (African)

given Nathania *a gift, given of God* (Hebrew), Nathene • *divinely given* Theodosia (Greek), Dosia, Theda • *given by God* Bohdana (Slovak); Danya (Russian) • *given to God* Bithia, Helsa (Hebrew), Bitthia, Elsa, Helse, Helsie • *God-given* Theodosia (Greek), Dosia, Feodosia, Teodosia, Theda
giver *see* give
giving Thais *giving joy* (Greek) • *giving praise* Peony (Greek) • *life-giving* Eve (Hebrew), Ebba, Eva, Evaleen, Evalina, Evelyn, Evlyn; Yeva (Russian)
glad Gleda *glad one, glowing* (Old English) • *glad, pleased* Gamada (African)
gladden Gleda *gladden, make happy* (Icelandic)
gladiolus Gladi (Hawaiian) • *gladiolus flower or small sword* Gladys (Welsh)
gladly Simone *hearing gladly, obedient* (Hebrew), Simona, Simonetta • *received gladly, welcome* Welcome (Anglo-Saxon)
gladness Letitia (Latin), Leda, Ledah, Leta, Latisha, Letice, Leticia, Letisha, Lida, Lidah, Tish
glen *see* dweller in a valley or glen
glittering Sidra *belonging to the stars, glittering* (Latin) • *flashing, glittering, radiating* Marmara (Greek) • *glittering, glowing white* Candace (Greek), Candee, Candice, Kandace, Kandee, Kandi, Kandis
glorious Mahima (Hindi); Nilla (Mende), Nola • *battle celebrated or glorious* Hildemar (Old German) • *famous woman warrior, glorious battle maid* Romilda (Old German), Maida, Milda, Romalda, Romelda • *glorious one* Berdine (Old German) • *glorious one, glory* Gloria (Latin), Gloriana, Gloriane • *glorious ruler* Valeska (Old Slavic) • *shining, glorious one* Bertha (Old German), Berta, Berthe; Peke (Hawaiian)
glory Euclea (Greek) • *fame, glory* Cleo (Greek) • *gift, glory, renown* Adora (Latin) • *glorious one, glory* Gloria (Latin), Gloriana, Gloriane • *glory flower* Cliantha (Greek), Cleantha, Cleanthe • *glory to God* Jala (Hausa)

glow Aabha (Hindi) • *light of early dawn; sunset glow* Alaula (Hawaiian) • *red glow* Arunima (Hindi)
glowing Kawena (Hawaiian) • *glad one, glowing* Gleda (Old English) • *glittering, glowing white* Candace (Greek), Candee, Candice, Kandace, Kandee, Kandi, Kandis
goal Meta *a goal, the measurer* (Latin) • *striver toward a goal* Nyssa (Latin)
goat Jael *mountain goat* (Hebrew)
God/god Olisa (Nigerian) • *adorned of God* Adaiha (Hebrew), Adah, Adaha • *a gift, given of God* Nathania (Hebrew), Nathene • *appearance of God* Theophania (Greek) • *belief in God, fidelity, loyalty* Faith (English), Fay • *belonging to God* Quanika (American), Nika, Niki, Nikka, Nikki, Quanikka, Quanique • *beloved of God* Theophila (Greek), Theophilos • *benefited by God* Mehitabel (Hebrew), Mehetabel, Mehitabelle • *blessed by God* Azaria (Hebrew), Azarria, Azeria, Zaria • *comfort from God* Nahama (Hebrew), Nahamas • *consecrated to God* Elizabeth (Hebrew), Elisa, Elisabeth, Elise, Elissa, Eliza, Elyse, Libby, Liesel, Liesl, Lisbeth, Lisette, Liza, Lizabeth, Lizanne; Lusa (Finnish); Isa (German); Zizi (Hungarian); Isabel (Old Spanish); Liseta, Ysabel (Spanish) • *daughter of God* Batya (Hebrew) • *dedicated to God* Beta (Czech/Slovak) • *Dionysus, Greek god of wine* Denise (French), Denice, Denisha, Denyse • *enlightened by God* Jairia (Hebrew), Jara, Jari, Jariah • *gift of God* Noni (African); Dorothy, Theodora (Greek), Dora, Dorothea, Dorthea, Dorthy, Tedora, Theda; Mattea (Hebrew), Mathea, Mathia, Matthea, Matthia, Natania, Natanya, Nathania, Natonya; Godiva (Old English); Dasha, Dosya (Russian) • *given to God* Bithia, Helsa (Hebrew), Bitthia, Elsa, Helse, Helsie • *glory to God* Jala (Hausa) • *God-given* Theodosia (Greek), Dosia, Feodosia, Teodosia, Theda • *God has redeemed* Galya (Hebrew) • *God hath promised good* Amaris (Hebrew), Amaras, Amari, Amary, Mari, Maris • *God is gracious*

Oshana (American), Oshanda, Oshawana; Seana (English), Seanna, Shana, Shanna, Shanice, Shavon, Shavonne, Shawna, Siana; Jane (Hebrew), Geneen, Giovanna, Janae, Janet, Janette, Janice, Janina, Janna, Jayne, Jean, Jeanne, Jeannette, Joan, Joana, Joanne, Juana, Juanita; Kini, Wanita (Hawaiian); Sheena (Irish), Shiona, Sinead; Gianina (Italian), Gianna, Giannetta, Giannina; Zanna (Latvian); Vanya (Russian); Kwanita (Zuni) • *God is my refuge* Adalia (Hebrew), Adal, Adala, Adalee, Adali, Adalie, Adalin, Adall, Adaly, Adalyn, Addal, Addala, Addaly • *God is my strength* Ezrela (Hewbrew), Esraela, Ezraella • *God is my teacher* Moriah (Hebrew), Mariah • *God is with us* Mannuela (Hebrew), Emanuela, Manella, Manuela, Uella • *god-like* Osa (Bini), Ossa • *god, lord* Kyrene (Greek), Kyra • *God loves me* Elom (African) • *god of good luck and wisdom* Ganesa (Hindi) • *God spoke* Mirella (Hebrew), Mireil, Mirela, Mirelle, Miriella, Mirilla • *guarded by God* Samara (Hebrew) • *healed by God* Raphaela (Hebrew), Rafaela • *healer, the god of healing; healing, wholesome* Althea (Greek), Althaia, Thea • *helped by God* Azelia (Hebrew) • *honoring God* Timothea (Greek) • *House of God* Bethel (Hebrew) • *in the image of God* Michaela (Hebrew), Michaele, Michaelina, Michella, Michelle, Mikaela, Miki • *Jehovah is God* Ellice (Greek) • *lioness of God* Ariella (Hebrew), Ariel, Arielle • *loved by God* Tesia (Polish), Taisha, Taysha, Tesha • *loved of God* Amadea (Latin) • *manifestation of God* Tiffany (Greek), Tifanie, Tiffanie • *manuscripts of God* Libni (Hindi) • *miracle of God* Nasya (Hebrew), Nasia • *name of God* Samuela (Hebrew), Ela, Samuella, Uella • *ornament of God* Adiel (Hebrew), Adiella, Ediya, Edia, Ediah, Edya, Edyah • *pray to God* Yobachi (African) • *sent by God to guard, the protectress* Anselma (Old German), Ansela, Ansilma, Sellma, Selma • *she is dedicated to God* Lemmuela (Hebrew), Emmuela,

Lemuela, Lemuelah, Uela; Belicia (Spanish) • *speaker with God* Theola (Greek) • *the god of healing* Peony (Latin) • *the god Siva* Siva (Hindi) • *the sun god* Surya (Hindi) • *the wind god* Anila (Hindi) • *unconquerable, god* Ajay (Hindi); *with God* Binta (African) • *Who is like God* Mia (American); Micah, Misha (Hebrew) • *woman of God* Gabrielle (Hebrew), Gabriela, Gabriella, Gigi • *worship God* Feechi (African)

goddess Thea (Greek); Devi (Sanskrit); Dewi (Malay) • *a little goddess* Devika (Sanskrit) • *ancient river goddess* Oba (Yoruban) • *a Viking goddess of fate* Norna (Old Norse) • *beautiful nymph of the sea, sea goddess* Thetis (Greek), Heti, Thetes, Thetisa, Thetos • *black goddess* Kali (Hindi) • *divine one, goddess* Diana (Latin), Deana, Deanna, Dianna, Dyan, Dyana, Dyane • *from a fertile land, Greek fertility goddess* Demetria (Greek), Demitria • *goddess of fire* Analaa (Hindi) • *goddess of love, lady* Freta (Scandinavian), Freyah • *goddess of spring, youth* Hebe (Greek), Hebbe • *goddess of the flowers* Chloris (Greek), Chloras, Chlori, Lori, Loris • *goddess of the hearth* Hestia (Greek), Hesta • *ivory goddess* Labana (Hebrew), Abana, Labanna, Labannah • *Mars' sister; war goddess* Alala (Greek) • *mother goddess* Nuwa (Chinese); Amma (Hindi), Ellama, Elamma • *spirit or supreme goddess* Isis (Egyptian) • *the goddess Nenet* Nenet (Egyptian) • *the goddess of food* Sedna (Eskimo) • *the goddess of the plague* Pollyam (Hindi) • *the great goddess* Chanda (Sanskrit), Shanda • *warlike or war goddess* Belloma (Latin)

god-like Mikaila (African); Osa (Bini); Adonia (Greek) • *God-like, divine* Devanee (Sanskrit)

godly Theone *godly, God's name* (Greek)

gods Panthea *from all the gods* (Greek), Pantheas, Panthia, Thea, Thia • *mother of the gods* Aditi • *of the mountain of the gods* Olympia (Greek), Olympias, Olympium • *queen of the*

gods Hera (Greek), Herra, Herrah •
sacred to the gods Lehua (Hawaiian)
God's Baptista *baptized in God's name*
(Greek) • *dearest of all God's burdens*
Ulla (Hebrew), Ula, Ulah, Ule • *garden or God's vineyard* Carmel (Hebrew), Carma, Carmela, Carmelina,
Carmelita • Theone *godly, God's name*
(Greek) • *God's creative power; illusion, fantasy* Maya (Sanskrit), Mayura
• *God's blessing* Chinue (African) •
God's gift Lolotea (Zuni) • *God's gra-
cious gift* Ivanna (Hebrew), Ivana,
Ivanah, Ivy • *God's light* Nirel (He-
brew) • *God's promise* Lilybet (Cor-
nish); Elise (Hebrew)
going Anda (Spanish)
gold Nudahr (Arabic); Kanchan
(Hindi); Ora (Latin), Orabel, Ora-
belle • *covered with gold* Gilda (Old
English) • *good as gold* Ah-Kum (Chi-
nese)
golden Oriana (Celtic), Oralia,
Orelda, Orelle, Orlann, Orlene;
Dior (French); Pazia (Hebrew),
Paza, Pazice, Pazit; Haimi (Hindi) •
golden dawn Zorina (Slovak),
Zora,Zorah, Zorana, Zori, Zorie,
Zory • *golden-haired one* Golda
(Old German) • *golden one* Dore
(French); Cressida (Greek), Cresa,
Cresida; Aurelia, Auriel, Oriana
(Latin), Oralia, Orelia, Oriel,
Orielda, Orielle, Oriola, Oriole, Or-
lena; Goldie (Old English); Zarina
(Persian) • *my golden flower* Mein-
golda (Old German), Golda, Mein-
goldas • *of golden beauty* Oribel
(Latin), Orabel, Orabelle, Oribella,
Oribelle
good Bonnie (English); Tobit (He-
brew), Tova, Tovah; Yoshi (Japa-
nese), Yoshie, Yoshiko, Yoshio,
Yoshiyo; Guda (Old English); Lupe
(Old German); Beuna (Spanish);
Hasina (Swahili); Gita (Yiddish) • *a
good friend* Derina (Old English), Derinna, Dorina, Rina • *a good judge of
people* Ethelind (Old German),
Ethel, Ethelinda • *a good jumper*
Pinda (Mende) • *approval, help; good
will conferred* Favor (French) • *at a
good time* Opportuna (Latin), Opportina • *auspicious speech, good repute*

Euphemia (Greek), Eufemia, Euphemie • *bringer of good news* Evangeline (Greek), Eva, Evangelia, Eve •
cheerful, good-hearted Corliss (Old English), Carleas • *elf counselor, good
counselor* Alfreda (Old English), Elfreda, Elfrieda, Elva • *elfin, good* Elva
(Old German), Elvia • *elfin or good
counselor* Elfrida (Old English) • *from
a good home* Bethezel (Hebrew), Betthel, Bettzel • *God hath promised good*
Amaris (Hebrew), Amaras, Amari,
Amary, Mari, Maris • *god of good luck
and wisdom* Ganesa (Hindi) • *golden
creeper* Hemlata (Hindi) • *golden eyes*
Hemakshi (Hindi) • *golden girl*
Hemkanta (Hindi) • *good as gold* Ah-
Kum (Chinese) • *good field* Yoshino
(Japanese) • *good intentions* Benildis
(Latin), Benilda, Benildas • *good,
kind* Agatha (Greek), Agathe • *good
luck and happiness* Ventura (Spanish)
• *good shepherdess* Solange (Latin),
Salangi, Salangia • *good, virtue* Shina
(Japanese), Sheena • *good will* Rid-
haa (African) • *good worker* Millicent
(Old German), Melicent, Mellicent
• *of good repute* Eudocia (Greek),
Docie, Doxie, Doxy, Eudosia, Eu-
doxia • *she who has good news* Nunci-
ata (Latin), Nuncia • *the good earth*
Avani (Sanskrit) • *the Lord is good*
Toby (Hebrew) • *woman of good works*
Fabiola (Latin), Fabiolas, Fabyola
goodness see child
goose Neka *the wild goose* (Native
American)
Goths Gustava *staff of the Goths*
(Swedish)
governor Valda *governor, ruler* (Old
Norse), Velda
grace Charis (Greek), Charie; Annora
(Hebrew), Annorah, Anora, Nora;
Lavani (Hindi) • *grace or mercy* Anya
(Hebrew), Annia, Anyah • *herb of
grace, lenient* Rue (Greek) • *regal
grace* Rexana (Latin), Rexanna, Rex-
anne
graceful Naima, Tabita (African);
Quiana (American), Quianna;
Zarifa (Arabic); Andulka (Czech);
Anais (French); Arete (Greek);
Anabela (Hawaiian) • *beautiful, grace-
ful* Annabelle (Hebrew-Latin),

Annabella, Annie, Belle • *beautiful or graceful* Kieu (Vietnamese) • *bitter-graceful* Marian (Hebrew), Mariana, Marianna, Marianne, Maryanne • *dainty, darling, graceful* Mignon (French), Mignonette *graceful as a bird* Aletta (Latin), Aleta, Alita, Alitta, Letta, Litta • *graceful, attractive one* Grace (Latin), Engracia, Giorsal, Grazia • *graceful battle maid* Luana (Old German), Lou, Louanna, Luane, Luwana • *graceful lily or lily* Shoushan (Armenian); Zuza (Czech); Susan (Hebrew), Sosanna, Susanna, Susannah, Susanne, Susette, Suzanna, Suzanne; Xuxu (Portuguese) • *graceful one* Anne, Hannah (Hebrew), Ana, Anette, Anita, Anna, Anne, Annette, Hana, Nan, Nana, Nanice, Nanci, Nancy; Nusi (Hungarian) • *graceful or lovely* Kaleki (Hawaiian) • *graceful rose* Rosanna (English) • *little graceful one* Nanette (Hebrew), Nanetta • *the gazelle, the graceful girl* Tabitha (Aramic) • *the graceful willow* Lian (Chinese), Liane, Lianne

gracious Hamida (African); Yachne (Hebrew) • *gracious or beloved* Hulda (Old German), Huldie • *friendly princess, gracious friend* Winola (Old German) • *gentle, gracious, kind* Benigna (Latin) • *God is gracious* Oshana (American), Oshanda, Oshawana; Seana (English), Seanna, Shana, Shanna, Shanice, Shavon, Shavonne, Shawna, Siana; Jane (Hebrew), Geneen, Giovanna, Janae, Janet, Janette, Janice, Janina, Janna, Jayne, Jean, Jeanne, Jeannette, Joan, Joana, Joanne, Juana, Juanita; Kini, Wanita (Hawaiian); Sheena (Irish), Shiona, Sinead; Gianina (Italian); Gianna, Giannetta, Giannina; Zanna (Latvian); Vanya (Russian); Kwanita (Zuni) • *God's gracious gift* Ivanna (Hebrew), Ivana, Ivanah, Ivy

grain *a kind of grain* Zea (Latin)

grandmother Nokomis (Chippewa Indian) • *grandmother; poison; residue; three* Ba (Vietnamese)

grass Trava (Czech); Gressa (Norwegian) • *the sacred kusa grass* Kusa (Hindi)

gratitude Thana (Arabic) • *gratitude, propriety* Reiko (Japanese)

gray Leslie *dweller at the gray fortress* (Irish-Gaelic), Lesley • *gray battle maid* Griselda (Old German), Chriselda, Grishilda, Grishilde

great Daron (Irish-Gaelic); Seki (Japanese) • *crowned in great honor* Garlanda (Old English), Garlinda, Landa • *from a great family* Lorola (Latin), Lorolla, Lorollas, Ola, Orola • *girl of great talent* Maxentia (Latin), Maxantia, Maxia • *great and beautiful one* Maybelle (French-Latin) • *great lord* Mahesa (Hindi) • *great, mighty one* Megan (Greek), Meghan • *great one* Moira (Celtic), Moir, Moya, Moyra, Oira; Dai (Japanese); May (Latin), Mae, Maia, Maya • *lady of great wealth* Udele (Anglo-Saxon), Della, Uda, Udela, Udella, Udelle • *of great fame* Orlantha (Old German), Orlanta • *the great goddess* Chanda (Sanskrit), Shanda

greatest Maxine (Latin) • *the greatest* Eyota (Native American)

greatly Bisa *greatly loved* (African)

greedy *see* commit

Greek Denise *Dionysus, Greek god of wine* (French), Denice, Denisha, Denyse • *from a fertile land, Greek fertility goddess* Demetria (Greek), Demitria

green Yarkona (Hebrew); Harita (Hindi); Midori (Japanese); Virida (Spanish) • *a green branch* Phyllis (Greek), Filide, Phillis; Pilisi (Hawaiian) • *fresh blooming, green* Viridis (Latin) • *little green one* Zelenka (Czech) • *the sea green jewel* Beryl (Greek)

greeter Afra *a greeter of people* (Old German), Affra

greetings *see* farewell

grew Shelby *from the village where the willows grew* (Old English), Shelbie, Shellie, Shelly

ground *see* child born on holy ground

grove La Verne *alder tree grove* (Old French), Lavergne • *cottonwood grove* Alameda (Native American) • *from the olive grove* Nolita (Greek), Lita, Nolitta

grower *see* bean grower
growing Papina *a vine growing on an oak tree* (Miwok)
guard *see* God
guarded *see* God
guardian Terentia (Greek), Warda (Old German) • *guardian of the sea, mortal day* Meredith (Old Welsh), Meridith • *guardian or sentinel* Vedette (Italian) • *guardian or watchtower* Atalaya (Spanish) • *prosperous guardian* Nedra (Anglo-Saxon), Neda, Nedrah; Edwardine (Old English)

guide Lodema *guide or pilot* (Old English) • *the guide* Guida (Italian)
guileless Acacia *the guileless one* (Greek), Acaysha, Akaysha, Cacia, Casey, Casia, Casie, Kacey, Kasi, Kassie, Kassya, Kassy
gull Laraine *gull, seabird* (Latin), Larina, Larine
gum Alaqua *sweet gum tree* (Native American)
gypsy Tzigane (Hungarian); Gitana (Spanish) • *gypsy girl* Zigana (Hungarian)

— H —

hair Kesava *fine hair* (Hindi) • *girl of dark hair* Darcy (Celtic), Darcia, Dercy • *girl with bright red hair* Rufina (Latin), Fina, Rufena, Ruphina
haired Calvina *bright-haired* (Latin), Calvinna, Vina • *curly-haired* Crispa (Hebrew), Crispas • *downy-haired one, youthful* Gillian (Greek), Gilane, Giletta, Gillan, Gilliana, Gilliette, Jill, Julia, Juliana, Juliet, Julietta, Julina, Juline, Julissa; Juliska (Czech); Juliette (French); Julinka (Hungarian); Jula, Julcia (Polish); Iulia (Romanian); Yulinka, Yulka (Russian); Yula (Serbian); Julita (Spanish) • *golden-haired one* Golda (Old German) • *lady of the new moon, white-haired* Gwendolyn (Celtic), Gwen, Gwendaline, Gwendoline, Gwendolyn, Gwyn, Gwyneth • *light-haired* Flavia (Latin) • *light-haired; white bosomed, white-clad* Rowena (Celtic) • *red-haired* Flanna (Irish-Gaelic), Flammery • *silver-haired* Tatiana (Latin), Tatia, Tatianas, Tatianna • *snowy or white-haired* Nix (Latin) • *yellow-haired* Flavia (Latin)
half Demi (French) • *half Danish* Haldana (Old Norse) • *half-sister* Beka (Hebrew), Becca, Bekah, Bekka • *of the half moon* Crescentia (Latin), Crescantia

hall Halfrida *peaceful hall or home* (Old English)
hammer Marcella (Latin), Marcelle, Marcelline; Bua (Vietnamese)
hand Yesima *right hand, strength* (Hebrew), Yemina
handmaid *see* fairest handmaid
happiness Hanna, Makenna (African); Hana (Arabic); Felicity (Latin), Felice, Felicia, Felise; Ayelen, Aylen (Native American) • *good luck and happiness* Ventura (Spanish) • *happiness, joy* Fisseha (African)
happy Saida (African); Lidka (Czech); Lydia, Lydie (English); Lydie (French); Lidia (Greek); Lidi (Hungarian); Gada (Hebrew); Samina (Hindi); Aida (Italian); Felice (Latin), Arissa, Felicia, Felicie, Felicity, Felise, Laresa, Larisa, Larissa, Risa, Rissa; Lidka (Russian); Felicidad (Spanish), Feliciana • *a girl who makes others happy* Beatrice (Latin), Beatrix, Trixie, Trixy • *always happy woman* Aanandi (Hindi) • *blessed, happy one* Beata (Latin) • *gladden, make happy* Gleda (Icelandic) • *happy child* Kioko, Tomiko (Japanese) • *happy or prosperous one* Rafa (Arabic) • *happy, prosperous* Ada (Old English), Adda, Aida, Eada, Ida, Idalia, Idalina, Idaline • *happy, victorious one*

Eunice (Greek) • *the happy one*
Aanandita

harbinger Bernice *harbinger of victory*
(German), Berenice, Veronica,
Veronique

harbor *see* gateway, harbor

hard *see* dark

harmonious Alana *fair, harmonious*
(Celtic), Alanna, Lana • *harmonious,*
melodious lady Vevila (Italian-Greek)

harmony Sanjana (Hindi); Concordia
(Latin) • *concord, harmony* Harmony
(Latin), Harmonia • *in harmony*
Unity (Latin) • *harmony, order, the*
world Cosima (Greek) • *harmony,*
peace Miru (Slavic)

harp Koto (Japanese), Kotoko

harvest Arista (Latin) • *a harvest of*
fruit Janna (Arabic), Jana, Janaya •
spring or harvest Rabi (Arabic)

hazelnut Hazel *hazelnut tree* (Old English)

headland *see* cape, headland

healed *see* God

healer *see* God

healing *see* God

healthy Marini *fresh, healthy, and pretty*
(Swahili) • *healthy and large* Vasta
(Latin), Vastah • *healthy and whole*
Sage (Latin) • *strong, healthy one*
Valentina (Latin), Valeda, Valentia,
Valentine, Valida

heap Juji *heap of love* (African)

hearer Simona *hearer, one who hears*
(Hebrew), Simonette

hearing *see* gladly

hears *see* hearer, one who hears

heart Leeba (Hebrew); Hiya, Hridya
(Hindi) • *bright, fair, serene one; girl*
with the tranquil heart Serena (Latin)
• *cheerful, good-hearted* Corliss (Old
English), Carleas • *daughter of the sea,*
flower of the sea, sea star; warm-hearted
Cordelia (Celtic), Cordalia, Cordeelia, Delia • *girl of our hearts*
Naarah (Hebrew), Nara, Narah •
heart of my wife Dara (Hebrew),
Darra • *sun heart* Sadzi (Alaskan)

hearth *see* goddess of the hearth

heather Brier *the heather flower*
(French); Erica (Greek), Erika • *the*
heather flower or shrub Heather (Middle English)

heaven Noelani *beautiful one from*

heaven (Hawaiian) • *born in heaven*
Divija (Hindi) • *daughter of heaven*
Efuru (African) • *expert; heaven;*
narrow-minded; to geld Thien (Vietnamese) • *heavenly, queen of heaven*
Juno (Latin), Jeno, Juna, Juni,
Junna, Junno • *the gentle dew from*
heaven Talia (Hebrew), Talya • *the*
highest point in heaven Lulani (Hawaiian)

heavenly Celeste, Juno, Selena
(Latin), Celene, Celesta, Celestina,
Celia, Celina, Celinda, Sela, Selene,
Selina, Selinda, Tyna; Selinka (Rus-
sian) • *heavenly child, heavenly flower*
Leilani (Hawaiian) • *heavenly cloud*
Aolani (Hawaiian) • *heavenly flower*
Pualani (Hawaiian), Puni • *heavenly,*
queen of heaven Juno (Latin), Jeno,
Juna, Juni, Junna, Junno • *heavenly*
rose Lokelani, Roselani (Hawaiian)

heavens Sema *a sign from the heavens*
(Greenk: • *calmness of the heavens*
Nalani (Hawaiian) • *of the heavens*
Okilani (Hawaiian) • *the height of the*
heavens Semira (Hebrew)

height *see* heavens

helmet Aselma *divine helmet or protec-*
tion (Old German) • *helmut, protector*
Wilhelmina (Old German), Mina,
Valma, Velma, Wilma

help Ophelila (Greek), Ofelia, Ofilia,
Ophelie • *approval, help; good will con-*
ferred Favor (French)

helped *see* God

helper Saada (African); Alesia
(Greek) • *helper and defender of*
mankind Alexandra (Greek), Alejandra, Aleka, Alesandra, Alexa,
Alexandrine, Alexis, Lexine, Ritsa,
Sandra, Sondra; Leska (Czech); Zandra (English); Alka, Olesia (Polish);
Lesya, Sasha, Shura (Russian); Alickina (Scottish), Kina; Xandra (Spanish) • *helper of men* Cassandra
(Greek), Casandra, Kassandra •
helper or assistant Kodi (Irish), Cody,
Kodey, Kodie, Kody

helpful Alma *nourishing, spiritually*
helpful, supportive (Latin)

her Safara *her place* (African)

herb *see* grace

hero Haley (Scandinavian), Haily,
Haleigh, Halie, Hally

heroine Ximena (Greek), Chimene • *battle heroine* Valda (Old German) • *brilliant heroine* Norberta (Old German) • *heroine, strong* Gavrila (Hebrew), Gavriella, Gavrielle • *peaceful heroine* Halfrida (Old German) • *unconquerable heroine* Zelda (Old German), Griselda

heron *see* eagle

hero's *see* daughter

hewn Gazit *hewn stone* (Hebrew), Gisa

hidden Bian (Vietnamese), *hidden or secretive*

high Bly (Native American) • *a jewel, of high value* Esmeralda (Greek), Esmerelda, Esmerolda • *from a high tower* Malina (Hebrew), Lina, Mali, Malin, Mallina • *high mountain* Zaltana (Native American) • *high or lofty* Alta (Latin) • *high-ranking person* Irma (Latin), Erma

highest Maice *highest star* (Latin), Maise, Mayce • *the highest point in heaven* Lulani (Hawaiian)

hill Kirima (Eskimo); Gali, Geva (Hebrew); Oka (Japanese) • *hill, pine* Matsuoka (Japanese)

hills Kiona *brown hills* (Native American) • *from the hills* Obala (Hebrew), Oballa, Obla, Obola; Bryn (Welsh); Brin (English), Brinn, Bryne, Brynn, Brynne

hit *see* to beat or hit

hollow Valonia *from the far valley, from the vale or hollow* (Latin), Vallonia, Valoniah • *from the hollow* Corey (Irish-Gaelic), Corrie, Cory

holly tree Holly (Old English), Holen

holy Kalifa *chaste, holy one* (Somalian) • *child born on holy ground* Oni (Yoruban) • *consecrated, holy* Elga (Slavic), Olga • *from the holy city* Kasi (Hindi) • *holy, fair one* Glynnis (Welsh), Glenice, Glenise, Glennice, Glennis, Glenwys, Glenys, Glynis • *holy girl* Diella (Latin), Dielle; Froma (Old German), Fromma • *holy one* Ariadne (Greek), Ariana, Ariane, Arianna; Olga (Old Norse-Russian), Elga, Olivia, Olva • *holy, pious, religious* Helga (Old German) • *holy reconciliation* Winifred (Welsh), Freda, Wynifred • *very holy or very pleasing* Ariana (Latin)

home Nilaya (Hindi) • *estate or home ruler* Henrietta (French), Enriqueta, Hariette, Hendrika, Henriette, Henrika; Harriet (Old French); Henka (Polish); Queta (Spanish) • *from a good home* Bethezel (Hebrew), Betthel, Bettzel • *peaceful hall or home* Halfrida (Old English) • *ruler of the estate or home* Enrica (Italian)

homeland Utta *from the homeland* (Old German), Uta, Utas, Uttasta

homelover Domella (Latin), Domel, Domela, Mella; Treva (Welsh), Trevah

honest Nishka (Hindi); Masa (Japanese)

honey Dalaja (Hindi) • *a bee, honey* Melissa (Greek), Lissa, Melicent, Melisse, Melita, Millicent • *all honey* Pamela (Greek), Pamelina • *little honey flower* Melita (Greek), Elita, Malita, Malleta, Melitta • *sweet as honey* Devasha (Hebrew), Devash; Melina (Latin)

honeybee Makshi (Hindi)

honeylike *see* gentle

honey-sweet Moema (Native American) • *honey-sweet princess* Sharissa (American), Shari, Sharice, Sharie, Sharine, Sherice, Sherie, Sherissa

honor Anju *an honor or shining* (Hindi) • *a title of honor, safe* Tita (Latin) • *crowned in great honor* Garlanda (Old English), Garlinda, Landa • *honor, honorable one* Honoria (Latin), Nora, Norah • *honor, strength, virtue* Bryna (Irish-Gaelic) • *walks with honor* Fayola (Yoruban)

honorable Taka (Japanese) • *honorable one* Fola (Yoruban), Landa • *honor, honorable one* Honoria (Latin), Nora, Norah

honored Haidee *honored, modest* (Greek) • *honored with a crown* Sade (Yoruban)

honoring *see* God

hope Nadia (Russian), Nadine; Nada (Slavic) • *desire, expectation, hope* Hope (Old English)

hoped Desiree *desired, longed for; so long hoped for* Desiree (French), Desirea, Desireah • *the anticipated one; hoped for* (Arabic)

hopeful Amal (Arabic); Umay (Turkish)

horn Carna (Hebrew), Carniela, Carniella, Carnis, Carnit, Karniela, Karniella, Karnis, Karnit

horse-woman Rechaba (Hebrew), Aba, Rachaba

horses Philippa, Pippa *lover of horses* (Greek), Felipa, Filippa, Pelipa, Philippine, Pippas

hospitable Xenia *hospitable one* (Greek), Xena, Xene, Zenia

hostage Gilberta *brilliant pledge or hostage, the bright pledge* (Old German), Gilbertina, Gilbertine • *hostage or pledge* Giselle (Old German), Gisela, Gisella; Gizi (Hungarian)

hours Horatia *keeper of the hours* (Latin), Horacia

house Aldis *from the largest house* (Old English), Alda, Aldas • *householder* Bo (Old Norse) • *House of God* Bethel (Hebrew) • *house of mercy*

Bethseda (Hebrew) • *house of poverty* Bethany (Aramic), Bethena, Bethina • *lady of the house, mistress* Marta (Aramaic); Maita (Spanish) • *mistress of the house* Yetta (Hebrew), Yeta, Yetah, Yetti • *owner of the new house* Xaviera (Spanish)

hug Sapata *to hug* (Miwok)

humane *see* gentle

humble Vinaya (Hindi) • *humble child* Nariko (Japanese) • *humble; to need* Khiem (Vietnamese)

humorous Jocosa *humorous, joking* (Latin)

hunger Una (Old Irish)

hunt Winda (Swahili) • *a hunt* Evetta (African), Evette

hyacinth Jacinda *beautiful, comely; hyacinth flower* (Greek), Jacenta, Jacinta, Jacintha, Jacinthe, Jacynth • *hyacinth flower* Hyacinth (Greek), Giacinta, Jacinta, Jacintha

hyena Hiti (Eskimo)

— **I** —

idea Diti (Hindi)

idealistic Aadarshini (Hindi)

ignorance Janisha *dispeller of ignorance* (Hindi)

Ilione *see* city

ill Desmona *ill-starred one* (Greek)

illumination Munirah *shedding light or illumination* (Arabic), Muneera, Munira

illusion Shambari (Hindi) • *God's creative power; illusion, fantasy* Maya (Sanskrit), Mayura

illustrious Kalea (Hawaiian) • *bright, brilliant, illustrious* Clara (Latin), Claire, Clare, Clareta, Clarette, Clarinda, Clarita; Klarissa (German); Klarika (Hungarian) • *illustrious, noble* Agave (Greek)

image Imogene *image or likeness* (Latin) • *in the image of God* Michaela (Hebrew), Michaele, Michaelina, Michella, Michelle, Mikaela, Miki

imaginary Kalpita (Hindi)

imagination Kalpana (Hindi)

immortal Ambrosine *she is immortal* (Greek), Amber, Ambrosane, Ambrosia, Brosine

immortality Tansey (Greek)

imperial Imperia *imperial one* (Latin)

incense Ketura, Livona (Hebrew)

inclined Gelasia *inclined to laughter* (Greek)

incomparable Samiya (Hindi)

increase Josephine *add, increase* (Hebrew), Fifi, Joette, Josefina, Josephina, Josette, Pepita • *she shall add, she shall be fruitful* Pepita (Spanish) • *she will increase* Joline (Hebrew) • *to create or increase* Crescent (Old French), Crescentia

independent Fanchon *independent woman* (Old German), Fanchan, Fanchet, Fanchette

indestructible Akshayaa (Hindi)

India Indigo *from India* (Greek)

Indian Zuni *a Zuni Indian* (Zuni)

industrious Malca *active, industrious* (Old German), Malcah • *flattering or industrious* Ilka (Slavic) • *flattering or industrious one* Amelia (Latin), Amalea, Amalia, Amaline, Amalita, Amilia, Emelina, Emeline, Emilia; Melcia (Polish); Milica (Slavic) • *industrious and true* Millicent (Old German), Melisande, Melisenda, Millicent, Milicent • *industrious one* Emily (English), Emelda, Emilie, Emlyn, Emlynne; Ida (Old German) • *very industrious* Almeta (Latin), Alma, Almita, Mita

inestimable *see* beyond price, inestimable

influence Lulu *soothing influence* (Anglo-Saxon)

ingenious *see* clever

inherited *see* estate

initiation Diksha (Hindi)

inner Wakanda *inner magical power* (Sioux)

innermost Batini *innermost thoughts* (Swahili)

innocent Jillian *innocent, downy-haired one* (Latin), Gilli,Gillian, Gillie Jill, Jilliana, Jillie • Gittle *innocent flatterer* (Hebrew), Gitel, Gittel, Gytle

insight Idha (Hindi)

inspired Arnina *inspired; messenger; mountain; shine; singer* (Hebrew)

inspiring Elmina *awe-inspiring fame* (Old German)

instigator Accalia (Latin), Acalia, Calia, Calie

intellect Trayi (Hindi)

intellectual Monisha (Hindi) • *intellectual curiosity* Jigna (Hindi)

intelligence Tomo (Japanese) • *foresight, intelligence* Prudence (Latin) • *intelligence, wisdom* Kyna (Irish-Gaelic) • *understanding or intelligence* Bina (Hebrew)

intelligent Akilah *intelligent or logical* • *intelligent contestant* Marcella (Old German), Marcelle, Marcelline • *intelligent, wise* Frodine (Old German), Frodeen, Frodina, Odeen, Odine • *wise; intelligent* Hui (Chinese)

intense *see* fiery

intentions *see* good intentions

inviolable Sancia *inviolable, sacred* (Latin), Sanchia

Ireland Hibernia (Greek); Ierne (Latin)

iris Ayame (Japanese) • *rainbow, the iris flower* Iris (Greek); Irisa (Russian), Risha

Irish *see* Erin

Iron Tetsu (Japanese)

iron-willed Isa *iron-willed one* (Old German)

Isis *see* gift of Isis

island Shima (Japanese) • *from a broad island* Brady (Old English), Bradi, Bradie, Braedy, Braydee • *from the island* Ila (Old French) • *from the island of Cyprus* Cypris (Greek) • *from the island of Cythera* Cytherea (Greek) • *from the island of Delos* Delia (Greek) • *from the linden tree island* Lindsey (Old English), Lindsay, Lyndsey • *from the ship island* Kelsey (Scandinavian), Kelcie, Kelsy, Kesley, Keslie • *island, pine* Matsushima (Japanese) • *white island* Whitney (Old English)

Italy Italia *from Italy* (Italian)

ivory Galatea (Greek), Alatea, Galatia, Galitea, Latea • *ivory goddess* Labana (Hebrew), Abana, Labanna, Labannah • *ivory-skinned* Fionna (Latin), Fia, Fiona, Phia, Phiona, Phionna

ivy Ivy *ivy vine* (Old English)

— J —

jackal Dilla (Hausa)

jade Yu (Chinese) • *beautiful jade* Lin (Chinese); *jade stone* Jade (Spanish), Ijada

January *see* born in January

jasmine *see* flower

Jehovah Eliana *Jehovah has answered our prayers* (Hebrew); Eliane,

Elianna, Leanna, Liana, Lianne (English) • *Jehovah is God* Ellice (Greek)

jewel Serwa (African); Aabharana (Hindi); Tama (Japanese) • *adorned with jewels* Madai (Hebrew), Ada, Adai, Madaih, Madi • *a jewel* Emerald (Old German) • *a jewel, of high value* Esmeralda (Greek), Esmerelda, Esmerolda • *beautiful or beautiful jewel* Sapphira (Hebrew), Phira, Saphra, Sapphera; Saphira, Sapphire (English) • *jewel or jewel of the sea* Ula (Irish); Cordelia (Welsh), Cordelie, Delia, Della • *precious jewel* Cara (Vietnamese) • *radiant red jewel* Garnet (Old German), Garnette • *sculptured jewel* Cameo (Italian) • *the amber jewel* Amber (French) • *the sea green jewel* Beryl (Greek)

join Levia *to join* (Hebrew)

joined Pega *joined together* (Greek), Pegma

joking *see* humorous, joking

jolly *see* elevated, lofty, of jolly spirits

journey Abiona *born during a journey* (Yoruban) • Odessa *a long journey, The Odyssey* (Greek)

joy Bliss (Anglo-Saxon); Diza (Hebrew), Geela • *blessed joy* Surata (Hindi) • *bliss child, joy* Sachi (Japanese), Sachiko • *delight, joy* Charmaine (Greek), Charmain, Charmian • *father of joy* Abigail (Hebrew), Abbey, Gail, Gale • *giving joy* Thais (Greek) • *happiness, joy* Fisseha (African) • *joy arrives* Dayo (African) • *joy is mine* Ronli (Hebrew), Rona, Roni, Ronia, Ronice • *joy, mirth* Mab (Irish-Gaelic), Mavis, Meave • *joy or diligent worker* Hedva (Hebrew), Edva, Edveh, Hedvah, Hedve, Hedveh • *joy or joyful* Aleeza (Hebrew),

Alisa, Alissa, Alyssa, Leesa, Leeza • *joy, pleasure* Mirth (Anglo-Saxon), Merth • *my joy is eternal* Gilada (Hebrew), Giladah • *one who causes joy all round* Ayoka (Yoruban) • *one who causes joy and rejoicing* Darrah (Efik)

joyful Limber (African); Hagia (Hebrew), Hagice, Hagit • *cheerful one, joyful* Blythe (Old English), Blithe • *joyful, a cause for rejoicing* Fara (Hausa) • *joyful one* Jovita (Latin) • *joyful and young* Leatrice (Latin), Arice, Leatri, Liatrice, Liatris • *joyful song* Ranita (Israeli) • *joy or joyful* Aleeza (Hebrew), Alisa, Alissa, Alyssa, Leesa, Leeza

joyous Mab (Irish-Gaelic), Maeve; Mave, Mavis (English); Leticia (Latin) • *joyous child or child of rapture* Keiko (Japanese)

judge Ethelind *a good judge of people* (Old German), Ethel, Ethelinda • *the Lord will judge* Acima, Joakima (Hebrew), Cima

judged Dinah (Hebrew), Dena, Dina

judges Danette *the Lord judges me* (Greek), Danete

juice Sudha *nectar or juice* (Hindi)

juicy Asisa *juice or ripe* (Hebrew)

jug *see* earthen water jug

jumper *see* a good jumper

June *see* born

jungle Kanan (Hindi)

juniper Geneva *juniper tree* (Old French)

just Adila (African) • *the just one* Jocelyn (Old English), Joceline, Jocelyne, Josceline, Joscelyne, Justine

justice Themis *custom, justice, order* (Greek), Tema, Thema • *the justice of the Lord* Andromeda (Greek), Andra, Andromede, Meda

•— K —•

Kaveri Kaveri *the sacred Kaveri Rover* (Hindi)

keen Jarvia *spear keen* (Old German)

keeper *see* hours

keeps Kay *one who keeps the keys* (Scandinavian), Kaye, Kayla

kernel Eithne (Irish), Enya • *fruit kernel* Pyrena (Greek)

keys *see* keeps

kind Benigna *gentle, gracious, kind* (Latin) • *gentle, humane, kind* Halima (Swahili) • *good, kind* Agatha

(Greek), Agathe • *kind and noble* Adelaide (Teutontic), Adele, Adeline, Della • *kind and shy* Bertilla (Latin), Bertila

kindred Vanda (Old German)

king Naresha *king or lord* (Sanskrit)

kingdom Mercia *from the kingdom of Mercia* (Old English)

kiss Choomia *a kiss* (Gypsy)

kitten Kita (Spanish) • *like a kitten* Sanura (Swahili)

kitty Kisa (Russian)

knife Suri (Todas)

knowing Sage *knowing and wise* (Latin) • *the knowing racoon* Mika (Native American) • *the knowing woman* Kendra (Anglo-Saxon), Kendrah, Kendy

knowledge Minda (Hindi); Tomo (Japanese);Veda (Sanskrit), Vedis • *knowledge, wisdom; the wise maiden* Pallas (Greek), Palla

kola Ibby *the kola nut* (Hausa)

kusa *see* grass

— **L** —

lacking Zella *lacking nothing* (Bobangi), Zela, Zellah

lady Bibi (Arabic); Ladonna (French); Rawnie (Gypsy); Donna (Italian); Domina (Latin); Sita (Swahili) • *a sabine lady* Sabina (Latin), Sabine, Savina • *gentle and polite lady* Urbana (Latin), Urbai, Urbani, Urbanna, Urbannai • *goddess of love, lady* Freta (Scandinavian), Freyah • *harmonious, melodious lady* Vevila (Italian-Greek) • *lady of beauty* Berlinda (Latin), Bellaude, Berlyn • *lady of great wealth* Udele (Anglo-Saxon), Della, Uda, Udela, Udella, Udelle • *lady of the house, mistress* Marta (Aramaic); Maita (Spanish) • *lady of the new moon, white-haired* Gwendolyn (Celtic), Gwen, Gwendaline, Gwendoline, Gwendolyn, Gwyn, Gwyneth • *lady of the river Nile* Nila (Latin), Nilla • *lady of the swans* Swanhilda (Old German) • *lady or mistress* Martha (Aramaic), Martella, Marthena, Martita • *little lady* Kabibe (African) • *little noble lady* Damita (Spanish) • *melodious lady* Bevin (Irish-Gaelic) • *my lady* Mona (Italian) • *noble lady* Freya (Old Norse) • *queen, ruling lady* Hera (Latin) • *ruling lady* Ricadonna (English-Italian) • *the elegant lady* Araminta (Hebrew), Aara, Aramanta, Aramenta • *unwilling lady* Noleta (Latin), Leta, Nola, Noletta, Nolita, Oleta

lamb Una (Old Irish) • *gentle as a lamb* Damara (Greek), Damaris, Damarra, Mara

lame Claudia *lame one* (Latin), Claudette, Claudina, Claudine; Gladys (Welsh), Gleda

land Nuna (Native American) • *from Abraham's land* Ivria (Hebrew), Ivriah, Ivrit • *from a cool land* Daberath (Hebrew), Debarath, Debbra, Deborath, Debra • *from a fertile land, Greek fertility goddess* Demetria (Greek), Demitria • *from the famous land* Rolanda (Old German), Orlanda, Rolande • *from the far land* Dacia (Latin), Dachi, Dachia • *land of beauty* Madina (Hindi)

lane Lanette *from the little lane* (French)

languishing *see* gentle or languishing

large Magna (Latin) • *healthy and large* Vasta (Latin), Vastah • *large sea bird* Sula (Icelandic)

largest *see* house

lark Alauda (Gaelic); Kalli (Greek) • *like a lark* Calandra (Greek), Calendra, Calondra • *singing lark or skylark* Lark (Middle English)

larkspur *see* delphinium

lass Erina *from Erin, Irish lass* (Irish-Gaelic), Erin, Erine, Erinna • *the comely lass* Linette (Celtic), Linetta, Linnette, Lynette, Lynn, Netta

last Ultima *final or last* (Latin), Tima • *last daughter* Audi (African) • *the last* *girl* Maxima (Latin), Maxama, Maxma

laughing Ula (African); Darrah (Hausa) • *always laughing* Sasmita (Hindi) • *laughing girl of the city* Thormora (Hebrew), Omora, Thora, Thorma, Tormoria

laughs Sarina (American) • *one who laughs* Kala (Hawaiian); Sarolta (Hungarian)

laughter Risa (Latin); Hasika (Sanskrit) • *cheerful, full of laughter* Teshi (African) • *inclined to laughter* Gelasia (Greek)

laurel Laura *a crown of laurel leaves* (Latin), Laurene, Lauretta, Laurette, Lora, Loren, Lorena, Lorene, Loretta, Lorette, Lorita, Lorna • *bay or laurel tree* Daphne (Greek) • *crowned with laurel* Kaila (Hebrew) • *crown, laurel, victory* Kelilah (Hebrew), Kelula, Kyla • *of the laurel tree* Dafna (Hebrew), Daphna

law Leya *law, loyalty* (Spanish)

lead Dalma *lead metal or tin* (Hausa)

leader Raidah (Arabic) • *child of the wise leader* Mackenzie (Irish-Gaelic), MacKenzie, McKenzie, Kenzie • *choir leader* Prochora (Latin), Cora, Procora • *sign of the leader* Richmal (Old German), Richma • *woman who leads* Caesaria (Latin), Cesaria

leadership Agrata, Agrima (Hindi)

leaf Patia (Gypsy); Abey (Native American)

leafy *see* branch

leaping Tallulah *leaping water* (Choctaw Indian), Talula

learn Docilla *willing to learn* (Latin), Cilla, Docila, Docile

learned Alma (Arabic); Lopa (Hindi) • *learned in dancing and music* Alima (Arabic), Alimah • *learned one, wise* Ulima (Arabic) • *majestic or learned* Shea (Irish), Shaela, Shaila, Shailyn, Shayana, Shayla, Shaylee, Shayleen, Shaylene, Shaylyn, Sheala

learning Eberta *woman of learning* (Old German), Berta, Ebarta

leaves *see* crown; bright leaves

ledge Shelley *from the ledge or the meadow* (Old English)

lenient *see* grace

leopard Wangari (African)

liberated Mukta (Hindi)

liberation Mukti (Hindi)

liberator Lysandra *liberator of men* (Greek)

life Aisha (African), Asha, Ashia, Asia, Eshe, Maisha; Quanisha (American), Neisha, Nisha, Talisa, Talisha, Talissa • Ayasha, Hayatt (Arabic), Myesha, Myeshia, Myisha; Zoe (Greek), Zoa, Zoie; Janya, Jeevitha, Lekisha (Hindi); Vita (Latin), Veta, Vitia; Eshe (Swahili) • *a beautiful life* Kenisha (American) • *life or living* Chaya (Hebrew), Kaija • *of the quiet life* Wivinia (Latin), Vinia, Wivina, Wivinah

life-giving Eve (Hebrew), Ebba, Eva, Evaleen, Evalina, Evelyn, Evlyn; Yeva (Russian)

light Noura (Arabic); Elaine (French), Elane, Elayne; Ilona (Greek); Leora Hindi); Eileen, Evelyn (Irish-Gaelic); Eli (Norweigian); Eleanore (Old French), Eleanor, Elenora, Elinore, Nora; Galina (Russian), Galya • *an offering; light and buoyant* Alana (Hawaiian) • *a torch, light* Lenka (Czech); Elli, Leena (Estonian); Helen (Greek), Alena, Elaine, Elanore, Elene, Eleni, Elenore, Ellen, Ellette, Ellyn, Helena, Helene, Ileana, Lenora, Lenore, Leonora, Nelly, Nitsa, Nora, Norah; Jelena, Liolya, Olena, Yelena (Russian); Iliana (Spanish) • *bright, lightness* Leoma (Old English) • *bright, white light* Farih (Hausa) • *bringer of light, light* Lucy (Latin), Lucette, Lucia, Luciana, Lucida, Lucie, Lucienne, Lucile, Lucille • *circle of light* Lucerne (Latin), Lucerna • *from the light of the new moon* Neoma (Greek), Neeoma, Neom, Neomah • *God's light* Nirel (Hebrew) • *I have light* Liora (Hebrew), Leora, Leorah • *light and airy* Alana (Hawaiian), Alanna, Lana • *light bearer* Aileen (Anglo-Saxon), Alene, Eileen, Elene, Ileana, Ilene • *light, clear or brilliant* Behira (Hebrew) • *light-haired* Flavia (Latin) • *light-haired; white bosomed, white-clad* Rowena (Celtic) • *light of early dawn; sunset glow* Alaula (Hawaiian) • *light*

or bright friend Nellwyn (Greek-Old English) • *Mary of the light* Lucita, Luz (Spanish) • *shedding light or illumination* Munirah (Arabic), Muneera, Munira • *shining or morning light* Noga (Hebrew) • *the Lord is my light* Eliora (Hebrew), Eleora
lighthearted Jocasta (Italian)
lightly *see* falling lightly
lightning Aashni, Adhira, Ashani (Hindi) • *a flash, lightning* Levina (Middle English)
light-skinned Orinda (Irish)
likeness *see* image or likeness
lilac Lila *a lilac flower* (Persian), Lilac • *lilac or violet colored* Mauve (Latin), Malva
lily Suke (Hawaiian) • *a lily flower* Lillian (Latin), Liliane, Lilliana, Lily • *a water lily* Sida (Greek) • *graceful lily or lily* Shoushan (Armenian); Zuza (Czech); Susan (Hebrew), Sosanna, Susanna, Susannah, Susanne, Susette, Suzanna, Suzanne; Xuxu (Portuguese) • *lily child* Yuriko (Japanese), Yuri • *the amaryllis lily* Amaryllis (Latin) • *the beautiful lily* Lilybelle (Latin), Lily, Lilybel • *the lily flower* Liliana (Hawaiian) • *water lily* Ren (Japanese)
lime tree Linnea (Old Norse)
limitless Aseema (Hindi)
linden *see* island
line *see* boundary
lingers *see* dwells
lion Leola (Latin); Jala (Mende) • *brave as a lion* Leontine (Latin), Leonteen, Leontina, Ontina, Ontine • *lion-brave* Leonarda (Old German) • *lion-like* Leontine (Latin), Leontyne
lioness Tiaret (African); Leonie (French), Leola, Leona, Leonia, Leonice, Liona, Lona, Loni; Liviya (Hebrew), Levia, Leviya, Livia • *lioness-like* Leondra (Greek) • *lioness of God* Ariella (Hebrew), Ariel, Arielle
lisps Blaise *one who lisps or stammers* (Latin), Blaze
listener Samantha *a listener* (Aramaic), Sami • *she who listens* Orella (Latin), Oralla
literature Sahithi, Sahitya (Hindi) •

literature; short; striped tiger; to twist Van (Vietnamese)
lithe Wandis *lithe and slender* (Old German), Wanda
little Primrose *a flower name, little first one* (Latin), Primrosa • *a little goddess* Devika (Sanskrit) • *a little water sprite* Nixie (Old German) • *a little woman* Zoara (Hebrew), Zoa, Zoarah • *a lyric song or little ode* Odelette (French), Odelet • *beloved child; little love* Aiko (Japanese) • *brilliant little one* Clarice (French), Clarissa, Clarisse • *darling, little lover* Amorette (Latin), Amarette, Amora, Amoreta, Moretta, Morette • *dearest little schemer* Carissa (Latin), Carisa, Chrissa • *from the little lane* Lanette (French) • *from the little rock* Rochelle (French), Rochella, Rochette • *little ardent or fiery one* Ena (Irish-Gaelic) • *little armed one* Armida (Latin) • *little beautiful one* Callula (Latin) • *little beloved one* Luvena (Middle English) • *little birdlike one* Birdie (English) • *little black one* Kiera (Irish-Gaelic), Keara, Keira, Kieran, Kierra • *little blueberry* Mora (Spanish) • *little comic* Nabal (Hebrew), Nabala, Nabalas • *little dark one* Duana (Irish-Gaelic), Duna, Dwana • *little dear one* Darlene (Old French), Darrelle • *little fairy* Fayette (French) • *little fiery one* Edana (Irish-Gaelic) • *little fire* Aidlan (Irish-Gaelic) • *little girl* Donella (Latin), Donela, Donell, Nell, Nella; Lassie (Scottish); Ninita (Spanish) • *little girl of purity* Trinette (Greek), Rinee, Trinatte, Trinetta • *little graceful one* Nanette (Hebrew), Nanetta • *little green one* Zelenka (Czech) • *little honey flower* Melita (Greek), Elita, Malita, Malleta, Melitta • *little lady* Kabibe (African) • *little Mary* Maureen (Irish-Gaelic), Maurine, Moira, Mora, Moreen, Moria • *little masterful one, little strong one* Bernadette (Old German) • *little moon* Lunetta (Italian) • *little noble lady* Damita (Spanish) • *little noble one* Edlyn (Old English) • *little one* Tawnie (Gypsy), Tawni, Tawny • Etta, Lorelle (Old German); Chiquita (Spanish) • *little one of the ashes* Cinderella (French) •

little pale one Wannetta (Native American) • *little, pine* Matsuo (Japanese) • *little raven* Brenda (Irish-Gaelic) • *little rock* Paula (Latin), Paulette, Paulina, Pauline, Paulita, Polly; Parnella (Old French), Pernella; Pavla (Russian) • *little rose, pretty rose* Rosaleen (Irish-Gaelic), Rosalie, Rosalind, Roselind, Rosina; Rosa (Spanish) • *little servant of the Lord* Jovita (Latin), Jovi, Jovia, Jovitah, Jovitta, Vita • *little, small* Beti (Gypsy) • *little stammerer* Balbina (Latin-Italian) • *little steadfast one* Pierrette (French) • *little truthful one* Alison (Irish-Gaelic) • *little valley* Glynis (Welsh), Glinys, Glynas • *little vine* Vignette (French) • *little wealthy one* Odelia (Old Anglo-French), Odelinda, Odella, Odetta, Odette, Odilia, Otha, Othilia • *little winged one* Alida (Latin), Aleda, Aleta, Aletta, Alette, Alita, Leda, Lita • *little womanly one* Charlotte (French), Carlene, Carlota, Carlotta, Charlene, Charyl, Cheryl, Sharlene, Sheryl; Sarolta (Hungarian) • Caroline (Latin), Carline, Carol, Carolina, Charline; Carli (Old German), Carla, Carlina, Carlita, Kari, Karla; Karolina (Russian) • *little yellow flower* Nurit (Hebrew), Nurice, Nurita • *majestic little one* Austine (Latin) • *my elder little sister* Kaya (Hopi) • *silent little one* Shysie (Native American) • *the little nymph* Evadne (Greek), Eva, Evadnee, Vadnee • *the little one of fame* Robinette (Old German), Binetta, Binette, Robin, Robinetta

lively Erlinda (Hebrew) • *bright and lively* Gay (Old French) • *gay, lively one* Gail (Old English), Gale, Gayle

living *see* life

lofty Elata *elevated, lofty, of jolly spirits* (Latin), Elatia, Ellata, Lati • *high or lofty* Alta (Latin) • *lofty, exalted one* Rama (Hebrew) • *lofty one* Galiena (Old German), Galiana • *lofty, prominent one* Emina (Latin) • *lofty reputation, renown* Fayme (French)

logical *see* intelligent

lone Lona *lone one, solitary* (Middle English), Loni, Lonna

lonely *see* away

long *see* journey

long-haired Muireann *long-haired one* (Irish-Gaelic); Morrin (English), Moriann, Morianne

long-lasting Hisa (Japanese), Hisae, Hisako, Hisayo

looked *see* desired

Lord/lord Kami (Japanese), Kamiko • *appointed by the Lord* Sethrida (Latin) • *belonging to the Lord* Dominica (Latin), Domenica, Dominga, Dominique; Dominika (Russian), Mika, Nika • *chosen by the Lord* Moria (Hebrew), Mori, Moriah, Muriah • *dance lord* Natesa (Hindi) • *devoted to the Lord* Lael (Hebrew), Lail, Lally; Amadis (Latin), Amadas, Ammadas, Ammadis, Madi • *exalted of the Lord* Jeremia (Hebrew), Jeri • *fire of the Lord* Nuria (Hebrew), Nuri, Nuriel • *friend of our Lord* Photina (Latin), Fhotima, Fina, Fotina, Otina, Tina • *gift of the Lord* Matta (Hebrew), Mattah • *god, lord* Kyrene (Greek), Kyra • *great lord* Mahesa (Hindi) • *king or lord* Naresha (Sanskrit) • *little servant of the Lord* Jovita (Latin), Jovi, Jovia, Jovitah, Jovitta, Vita • *lord* Anisha (Sanskrit) • *mountain lord* Adrisa, Girisa (Hindi) • *ornament of the Lord* Adiel (Hebrew), Addielle, Adiell, Ediya, Edia, Ediah, Edya, Edyah • *praise the Lord* Hosana (Latin); Osanna (English) • *sent from the Lord* Uria (Hebrew), Ria, Uriah, Urial, Urrisa • *strength of the Lord* Ozora (Hebrew) • *the justice of the Lord* Andromeda (Greek), Andra, Andromede, Meda • *the Lord is good* Toby (Hebrew) • *the Lord is mighty* Athalia (Hebrew), Athalla, Athallia • *the lord is my light* Eliora (Hebrew), Eleora • *the Lord is my rock* Gavra (Hebrew), Avra, Gavrah • *the Lord is willing* Joella (Hebrew), Jo Ella, Joelle, Joellen • *the Lord is with you* Muna (African) • *the Lord judges me* Danette (Hebrew), Danete • *the Lord protects me* Daniela (Hebrew), Daniella, Danielle, Niela, Rainelle • *the Lord will judge* Acima, Joakima (Hebrew), Cima

Lordly Cyrilla *Lordly one* (Latin), Cirila

Lorraine Laraine *from Lorraine* (French), Lorain, Loraine, Lorayna, Lorayne, Lorrane

loss Thisbe *romantic loss, the lost lover* (Greek), Thisbee, Tisbe, Tisbee

lost Lorna (Old English), Lora, Loren • *romantic loss, the lost lover* Thisbe (Greek), Thisbee, Tisbe, Tisbee • *the lost* Perdita (Latin)

lotus Padma (Hindi); Ren (Japanese); Kumuda (Sanskrit); Lien (Vietnamese) • *flower of forgetfulness, flower of the lotus tree* Lotus (Egyptian) • *lotus flower* Lien-Hua (Chinese) • *the lotus tree* Sadira (Persian)

loud Kalika (Hindi)

lovable Hita, Priya (Hindi), Priyal, Priyam, Priyanka, Priyata, Pryasha, Pryati; *lovable one* Amabel (Latin), Amabelle • *lovable, pleasant* Elma (Greek)

love Aesha, Lalasa (Hindi); Minna (Old German), Mina, Minda, Mindy, Minetta, Minette; Kama (Sanskrit) • *goddess of love, lady* Freta (Scandinavian), Freyah • *beloved child; little love* Aiko (Japanese) • *I love you* Nayeli (Native American) • *my love* Milada (Czech) • *strong in love* Astrid (Old German) • *worthy of love* Amanda (Latin)

loved Nissa *a remembered loved one* (Hausa) • *greatly loved* Bisa (African) • *heap of love* Juji (African) • *loved by all* Lida, Ludmilla (Slavic), Lidah, Lidda, Liddie, Lodmilla, Lovmilla, Mila • *loved by God* Tesia (Polish), Taisha, Taysha, Tesha • *loved of God* Amadea (Latin) • *loved one* Davina (Hebrew), Daveda, Davena, Daveta, Davida, Davita; Amata, Querida (Spanish), Amanda, Amy, Erida, Queri, Queridas, Rida • *loved one, sweetheart* Kalila (Arabic) • *love me* Femi (Yoruban) • *spear loved* Gertrude (Old German), Gertruda, Gertrudis, Trudy • *the loved one* Kendi (African)

loveliest *see* fairest, loveliest woman

loveliness *see* beauty, loveliness

lovely Arete (Greek) • *beautiful or lovely* Jafit (Hebrew), Jaffa, Jaffice • *fresh, lovely* Blossom (Old English) • *graceful or lovely* Kaleki (Hawaiian) •

lovely flower Samantha (Native American), Sama, Samanthia • *lovely stranger* Barbara (Latin), Babbette, Babete, Babita, Barbette; Johppa (Hebrew), Joappa, Johppah • *lovely temptress* Leda (Hebrew), Eda, Ledah, Ledda • *lovely vision* Idola (Greek), Idolah, Idolla • *lovely white rose* Rosalba (Latin), Alba, Roselba, Salba • *lovely woman* Belda (French), Bellda, Belldame, Belldas, Belle • *most lovely* Calista (Greek), Alisa, Allista, Calise, Calista • *most lovely wife* Ulphia (Latin), Fia, Phia, Ulphi, Ulphiah • *sweet, lovely* Sayen (Native American)

lover Iduna (Old Norse), Idonia; Lubba (Slavic), Luba, Lubbi • *beautiful lover* Amabel (Latin), Amabelle • *darling, little lover* Amorette (Latin), Amarette, Amora, Amoreta, Moretta, Morette • *flower lover* Philantha (Greek) • *girl of nature, nature lover* Rima (Anglo-Saxon), Ima, Rema, Ria, Rimma • *lover of horses* Philippa, Pippa (Greek), Felipa, Filippa, Pelipa, Philippine, Pippas • *lover of song* Philomela (Greek) • *lover of the moon* Philomena (Greek) • *lover of nature* Tivona (Hebrew) • *romantic loss, the lost lover* Thisbe (Greek), Thisbee, Tisbe, Tisbee

loving Charissa, Philana (Greek), Charie, Philene, Philida, Philina; Calida (Latin) • *calm, serene; loving sister* Delphine (Greek), Delphina, Delphinia • *loving memories* Minna (Old German) • *loving woman* Phillida (Greek), Phillada, Vallada • *the all-loving one* Panphila (Greek) • *the peace-loving ruler* Farica (Old German), Arica, Farika, Farrica, Feriga

loyal Misao, Shina (Japanese) • *faithful, loyal one* Leala (Old French), Lealia, Lealie

loyalty Faith *belief in God, fidelity, loyalty* (English), Fay • *law, loyalty* Leya (Spanish)

luck Ganesa *god of good luck and wisdom* (Hindi) • *good luck* Fayola (Yoruban) • *good luck and happiness* Ventura (Spanish)

lucky Gada (Arabic), Zada; Yuki (Japanese), Yukie, Yukiko, Yukiyo;

Fortuna (Latin), Fortunia, Fortunna • *lucky elfin one* Ruella (Old German), Ruelle • *very lucky* Faustina (Latin), Fausta, Faustena, Faustine
luminescent Candra (Latin)
luminous Eta (Hindi)
lunar Am (Vietnamese)
lustrous Aaloka (Hindi)

luxuriant *see* blooming, luxuriant
Lydia *see* cultured
lyre Lyris *music of the lyre* (Greek), Liris
lyric *see* little
lyrical Lirit (Hebrew)
lyrics Shruthi (Hindi)

— M —

magic Tamira (Hindi) • *magic dancer* Satinka • *magic power* Orenda (Iroquois Indian); Oki (Huron Indian)
magical *see* inner magical power
magnanimous *see* generous
magnificent *see* elevated
magnolia Magnolia *girl of the magnolia tree* (Anglo-Saxon) • *magnolia blossom* Mu-Lan (Chinese)
mahogany *see* color
maid Serilda *armored battle maid, girl of war* (Old German), Rilda, Sarilda, Sorilda • *armored warrior maid* Brunhilda, Zerelda (Old German), Serilda, Zarelda • *battle maid* Bernia (Latin); Heidi (Old German), Heidy, Hidie, Hilda, Hilde, Hildie, Hildy • *battle maid, battle stronghold, battle wand* Hildegarde (Old German) • *bear/spear maid* Berengaria (Old English) • *famous battle maid* Clotilda (German), Clothilde • *famous warrior maid* Louise (Old German), Alison, Allison, Aloisa, Aloisia, Eloisa, Eloise, Heloise, Lisette, Louisa, Louisette, Luisa, Lulu; Iza, Lilka (Polish) • *famous woman warrior, glorious battle maid* Romilda (Old German), Maida, Milda, Romalda, Romelda • *graceful battle maid* Luana (Old German), Lou, Louanna, Luane, Luwanna • *gray battle maid* Griselda (Old German), Chriselda, Grishilda, Grishilde • *serpent-maid* Ortrude (Old German) • *shining battle maid* Bertilde (Old English) • *the famous maid of war* Marelda (Old German), Mareld, Marolda • *the maid of battle*

Bathilda (Old German), Bathelda, Thilda, Tilda • *victorious battle maid* Solvig (Old English) • *warrior battle maid* Gunhilda (Old Norse) • *warrior maid* Guida (Italian); Armina (Old German), Armine
maiden Mayda (Anglo-Saxon); Talitha (Aramaic); Corinne (French); Cora, Coren (Greek), Corella, Corette, Corina, Correne, Corrina, Korin; Darika (Hindi); Maida (Old English), Magda, Maidel, Maidie, Mayda, Maydena • *a pure maiden* Atalie (Scandinavian), Attalie, Talie • *battle maiden* Gunda (Old Norse) • *beautiful fairy maiden, elf* Ella (Old English) • *beautiful maiden* Corabelle (French-German) • *flute maiden* Lenmana (Hopi) • *girl, maiden* Colleen (Irish-Gaelic), Cailin • *girl or maiden* Betula (Hebrew) • *knowledge, wisdom; the wise maiden* Pallas (Greek), Palla • *maiden of Andros* Andria (Latin) • *mighty battle maiden* Mathilda (Old German), Maitilde, Matelda, Mathilde, Matilda, Matilde • *most able maiden* Ara (Old German), Aara • *noble maiden* Ilse (Old German), Elsa, Else, Ilsa • *powerful battle maiden* Magnilda (Old German) • *spear maiden* Gari (Old German); Truda (Polish) • *the battle miaden* Armilda (Old German), Armalda, Armelda, Armillda, Milda, Millda • *the snow maiden* Yepa (Native American) • *the vehement maiden* Encratis (Spanish), Engracia, Encratia • *unblossomed maiden* Kali (Hindi) • *warrior maiden* Beda (Old English)

maidenly Parthenia (Greek); Vegenia, Wilikinia (Hawaiian); Virginia (Latin), Ginger; Gina, Ginata, Ginia (Spanish) • *most maidenly one* Corissa (Latin-Greek), Corisa
majestic Austine *majestic little one* (Latin) • *majestic one* Augusta, Majesta (Latin), Auguste • *majestic or learned* Shea (Irish), Shaela, Shaila, Shailyn, Shayana, Shayla, Shaylee, Shayleen, Shaylene, Shaylyn, Sheala
mandara Mandara *the mythical mandara tree* (Hindi)
manifestation *see* God
mankind *see* defender
man's *see* fearless
manuscripts *see* manuscripts of God
manzanita *see* big manzanita berries
marganit *see* flower
marigold *see* flower
marketplace Yarmilla *trader in the marketplace* (Slavic)
married Beulah *married one, she who will marry* (Hebrew), Beula • *married or possessed* Jerusha (Hebrew)
marry *see* married one, she who will marry
Mars *see* belonging to Mars; Mars' sister
Marsh Sawa (Japanese)
marshmallow *see* flower
martial Martina *martial, warlike one* (Latin), Artina, Marta, Martine, Tina
marvelous Shani (African)
Mary Maureen *little Mary* (Irish-Gaelic), Maurine, Moira, Mora, Moreen, Moria • *Mary of the light* Lucita (Spanish), Luz • *Mary the beautiful* Maribelle (Latin), Marabel, Marabelle, Marybella, Marybelle • *the rose of St. Mary* Rosemary (English), Marie, Rose • *the Virgin Mary* Ula (Basque) • *tiny Mary* Marella (Old German), Marela, Marelya, Marla
Mary's Rosemarie *Mary's rose* (Latin), Rosemari, Rosemary
masterful Uzzia *masterful controller* (Hebrew), Uzia, Uzial, Uzzial • *little masterful one, little strong one* Bernadette (Old German)
mature Sharada *mature, ripe* (Sanskrit); Sharda (Hindi)

May Valma *May flower* (Welsh) • *the month of May* Mai (French)
meadow Lee (Anglo-Saxon), Lea • *dweller at the beaver meadow* Beverly (Old English) • *from one's own meadow* Ainsley (Scotch-Gaelic), Ainslee, Ainslie, Ansley • *from the ash tree meadow* Ashley (Old English), Ashleigh, Ashley • *from the bright meadow* Shirley (Old English), Shirlee, Shirleen, Shirlene • *from the ledge or the meadow* Shelley (Old English) • *from the royal fortress meadow* Kimberly (Old English) • *from the west meadow* Wesla (Old English)
measurer *see* goal
meditation Chintanika (Hindi)
melancholy Trista (Latin)
melodious Vevila *harmonious, melodious lady* (Italian-Greek) • *melodious lady* Bevin (Irish-Gaelic) • *melodious song* Mahala (Hebrew), Mahalia, Mahla, Mehala
melody Geeti (Hindi) • *melody, music* Dhwani (Hindi) • *a melody* Aria (Italian) • *melody, song* Odele (Greek), Odelette, Odell • *song or melody* Mangena (Hebrew), Mangina
memories *see* loving memories
memory Una (Hopi Indian)
men Cassandra *helper of men* (Greek), Casandra, Cassandra, Kassandra • *liberator of men* Lysandra (Greek)
Mercia *see* kingdom
merciful Dayanita, Karuna (Hindi) • *calm, merciful, mild* Clementia (Latin), Clemence, Klementine • *the merciful* Mercy (Latin)
mercy Osanna *filled with mercy* (Latin), Osana • *grace or mercy* Anya (Hebrew), Annia, Anyah • *house of mercy* Bethseda (Hebrew)
merit Moira (Greek)
mermaid Sirena *a sweetly singing mermaid siren* (Greek)
merry Hilary *cheerful friend, merry* (Latin), Hilar, Hillaria, Hillary • *merry one* Meave (Celtic); Haggai (Hebrew), Hagai, Haggi, Hagi • *merry, playful* Jocelyn (Latin) • *one who is festive, merry* Habbai (Hebrew) • *quick, alert, and merry* Zana (Arabic)
mesa *see* bluebird

messenger Arnina (Hebrew) • *angel messenger* Arella (Hebrew), Arela, Erela; Gelya (Russian) • *angel or messenger* Angela (French), Angelina, Angeline, Angelita; Litsa (Greek)

metal *see* lead

middle Naka (Japanese); Messina (Latin) • *in the middle of the ocean* Oki (Japanese) • *middle child* Media (Latin), Madora, Medea, Medora • *middle, pine* Matsunaka (Japanese) • *rice field, middle* Tanaka (Japanese)

midnight Lisha *the darkness before midnight* (Arabic), Lishe

mighty Bedelia (Celtic), Delia; Nena, Ninetta, Ninette, Ninnetta, Ninnette (English); Nina (Native American); Rayne (Scandinavian) • *great, mighty one* Megan (Greek), Meghan • *mighty adversary* Atalanta (Greek), Atlanta • *mighty battle maiden* Mathilda (Old German), Maitilde, Matelda, Mathilde, Matilda, Matilde • *mighty or wise protector* Ramona (Spanish), Ramonda • *mighty poet* Kavindra (Hindi) • *mighty power* Ronalda (Old Norse), Rhona, Rona • *mother of a mighty nation; mother of the multitude* Abriana (Hebrew), Abra, Abree, Abrianna, Abrianne, Abrielle, Abrienne, Briana, Brianna • *spear mighty* Geraldine (Old German), Geraldina, Gerhardine, Giralda, Jerri • *the Lord is mighty* Athalia (Hebrew), Athalla, Athallia

mignonette *see* flower

Milan Milana *from Milan* (Italian), Mila, Milan, Milanna

mild Clementia *calm, merciful, mild* (Latin), Clemence, Klementine • *mild counselor* Mildred (Old English), Mildrid • *mild, gentle one* Malinda (Greek), Malena, Malina, Malinde, Melina, Melinda • *mild, smooth, soft* Lenis (Latin), Lena, Leneta, Lenita • *of a mild disposition* Clementis (Hebrew), Clementas, Clementi, Clementina, Clementine

milky Galatea *milky white* (Greek)

mind Huberta *brilliant mind* (Old German) • *elder sister; mind; to show* Chi (Vietnamese) • *expert; heaven; narrow-minded; to geld* Thien (Vietnamese)

minded Alcina *strong-minded* (Greek)

mine Miri (Gypsy); Mia (Italian)

minority Thieu *be missing, be short; the minority* (Vietnamese)

mint Shako (Native American) • *the mint plant* Minta (Greek), Mintha

miracle Keemaya (Hindi) • *a miracle, a wonderful thing* Marvel (Old French), Marvela, Marvella, Marvelle • *miracle of God* Nasya (Hebrew), Nasia

mirror Darpana (Hindi); Kagami (Japanese) • *a mirror* Kyoko (Japanese)

mirth Meara (Irish-Gaelic) • *joy, mirth* Mab (Irish-Gaelic), Mavis, Meave

mirthful Merry *mirthful, pleasant* (Middle English)

miss *see* arrows

missing *see* minority

mist Filma *a mist or veil* (Old English) • *cloud, mist or vapor* Nebula (Latin)

mistress Marta *lady of the house, mistress* (Aramaic); Maita (Spanish) • *lady or mistress* Martha (Aramaic), Martella, Marthena, Martita • *mistress of the house* Yetta (Hebrew), Yeta, Yetah, Yetti • *shrouded in mist* Misty (Old English), Mistie

misty Ninarika (Hindi)

misunderstood *see* concealed

modest Binita, Lajita, Shalini (Hindi) • *honored, modest* Haidee (Greek) • *modest one* Modesty (Latin), Modestia, Modestine • *modest, pious, pure* Casta (Latin) • *modest, shy or violet* Yolanda (Greek), Yolande, Yolante

mole *see* beauty

molecule Kanika (Hindi)

moment Saniya (Hindi)

momentary Nimisha (Hindi)

Monday *see* born on Monday

money Dhanvi (Hindi)

Month *see* May

moon Mahina (Hawaiian); Candra, Indu, Induma, Soma (Hindi); Jaci (Native American) • *beaming white one, the moon* Lewanna (Hebrew) • *daughter of the moon* Cynarra (Greek), Cynara, Cynera, Nara, Narra • *child of the moon* Am (Vietnamese) • *from the light of the new moon* Neoma (Greek), Neeoma, Neom, Neomah • *full moon* Indumati (Hindi) • *lady of* *the new moon, white-haired* Gwendolyn (Celtic), Gwen, Gwendaline, Gwendoline, Gwendolyn, Gwyn, Gwyneth • *little moon* Lunetta (Italian) • *lover of the moon* Philomena (Greek) • *moon, moonlike* Chandra (Sanskrit) • *moon returning* Migina (Native American) • *moon, white* Levana (Hebrew), Levania, Levona, Livana • *new moon* Tainn, Tayen (Native American) • *of the half moon* Crescentia (Latin), Crescantia • *power of the moon* Miakoda (Native American) • *sacred moon* Mitexi (Native American) • *the coming moon* Magena (Native American), Magen, Magina, Mitena • *the moon* Shahar (Arabic); Cynthia, Selena (Greek), Celene, Celina, Celinda, Cynthie, Selene, Selina, Selinda; Salena (Hindi) • *the moon of the third night* Mikazuki (Japanese)

moonbeam Rishima (Hindi)

moonlight Indukala, Iyla (Hindi), Indulala • *bright as moonlight* Konane (Hawaiian) • *of the moonlight* Luna (Latin), Lunna

moonlike Chandra *moon, moonlike* (Sanskrit) • *moonlike* Badria (Afghani); Kamaria (African)

moonshine Suhaila (Hindi)

moral Nita (Hindi)

morning Sabiya (Arabic), Saba, Sabaya, Sabiyah; Tasarla (Gypsy) • *born in the morning* Asa (Japanese) • *shining or morning light* Noga (Hebrew) • *star of the morning* Danica (Slavic), Anica, Dannica, Donica

mortal *see* day

mother Matrika (Hindi); Madra (Latin); Uma (Sanskrit) • *foster mother* Larentia (Latin), Laurena, Laurentia • *mother goddess* Nuwa (Chinese); Amma (Hindi), Ellama, Elamma • *motherly, of the mother* Matronna (Latin), Atronna, Matrona • *mother of multitudes* Abra (Hebrew) • *mother of the gods* Aditi (Hindi) • *mother of the sun* Latonia (Latin), Latia, Latona, Latoniah, Lattonia, Tonia • *mother or nurse* Maia (Greek), Maiah, Maya • *my mother* Ummi (African) • *the mother* Ambika (Hindi)

motherly Jarita *motherly bird* (Hindi), Arita, Gerita, Jari, Jeritah, Rita • *motherly, of the mother* Matronna (Latin), Atronna, Matrona

mother's Adanne *her mother's daughter* (African)

mountain Aadrika (Hindi); Yama (Japanese); Odina (Native American) • *high mountain* Zaltana (Native American) • *inspired; mountain; singer* Arnina (Hebrew) • *mountain dweller* Peri (Greek) • *mountain goat* Jael (Hebrew) • *mountain lord* Adrisa, Girisa (Hindi) • *mountain, pine* Matsuyama (Japanese) • *of the mountain* Orea (Greek) • *of the mountain of the gods* Olympia (Greek), Olympias, Olympium • *peak, mountain child* Mineko (Japanese)

mourner Penthea (Greek)

mouse Panya (Swahili); *a mouse* Musa (Latin), Musetta, Musette

mouth Ria *a river mouth* (Spanish)

movement Sanchali (Hindi)

moving Minowa *moving voice* (Native American)

Muhammed's *see* follower

multitude *see* mother of the multitude

multitudes *see* mother of multitudes

muses *see* gift of the muses

music Aarabi, Sangita (Hindi) • *beautiful music, song* Melody (Greek), Melodie • *learned in dancing and music* Alima (Arabic), Alimah • *melody, music* Dhwani (Hindi) • *music of the lyre* Lyris (Greek), Liris

musical Lirit (Hebrew)

myrrh *see* bitter, myrrh

myrtle Myrtle *the myrtle* (Greek), Mertice, Mertle, Mirtle, Myrtia, Myrtice

mysterious Lisha (African)

mystery Voletta *the veiled woman, woman of mystery* (French), Oletta, Olette, Vola, Voleta; *washed in an air of mystery* Mystique (French), Mistique

mythical *see* mandara

— N —

name Zina (African); Jina (Swahili) • *a flower name, little first one* Primrose (Latin), Primrosa • *divine name* Theano (Greek) • *godly, God's name* Theone (Greek) • *name chant* Inoa (Hawaiian) • *name of God* Samuela (Hebrew), Ela, Samuella, Uella • *to name* Oya (Miwok)

Narmada Reva *the sacred Narmada River* (Hindi)

narrow *see* expert; heaven; narrow-minded; to geld

nation *see* mother of a mighty nation

nature Alphonsine *an aggressive nature* (Old German), Alphonsa, Phonsa • *girl of nature, nature lover* Rima (Anglo-Saxon), Ima, Rema, Ria, Rimma • *lover of nature* Tivona (Hebrew) • *of a noble nature* Auberta (Old German), Aubarta, Auburta • *of a possessive nature* Alysia (Greek), Alisa, Alisia, Alysa

near Chika (Japanese)

nearer Nara *nearer or nearest one* (Old English)

nearest *see* nearer or nearest one

nectar Ami (Hindi), Amidi • *nectar or juice* Sudha (Hindi)

need *see* humble; to need

Nenet *see* goddess

nest Nydia *a nest of refuge* (Latin), Nidia

new Nova (Latin), Novah • *fresh, new* Amaryllis (Greek), Amarillas, Amarillis, Amaryl, Maryl • *from the light of the new moon* Neoma (Greek), Neeoma, Neom, Neomah • *lady of the new moon, white-haired* Gwendolyn (Celtic), Gwen, Gwendaline, Gwendoline, Gwendolyn, Gwyn, Gwyneth • *newcomer* Genesia, Novia (Latin), Genesa, Genisia, Genna, Jenesia • *new day* Dagny (Old Norse) • *new moon* Tainn, Tayen (Native American) • *owner of the new house* Xaviera (Spanish) • *the new dawning* Roxanne (Persian), Roxana, Roxene

news Annunciata *bearer of news* (Latin) • *bringer of good news* Evangeline (Greek), Eva, Evangelia, Eve • *she*

who has good news Nunciata (Latin), Nuncia

next Rai (Japanese) • *next child* Raiko (Japanese), Reiko

night Nyx (Greek); Nakti, Ratri (Hindi); Koko (Native American) • *belonging to the night* Lilith (East Semitic) • *born at night* Laila (Arabic), Leila, Layla; Sayo (Japanese) • *dark as night, dark beauty* Leila (Arabic), Layla, Leilia, Lela, Lila • *night train* Amaya (Japanese) • *the moon of the third night* Mikazuki (Japanese)

nightingale Questa *song of the nightingale* (Latin)

Nile *see* lady of the river Nile

nimble Haya (Japanese)

nine Ennea *nine, ninth child* (Greek)

ninth Ennea *nine, ninth child* (Greek) • *ninth born* Tisa (Swahili) • *ninth child* Nona (Latin)

Noah's Safina *Noah's Ark* (African)

noble Nabila (African); Sharifa (Arabic), Shareefa, Sharifah; Adina (Hebrew), Adena, Adene; Akela (Hawaiian); Elese (Old German); Alida (Spanish) • *brilliant, noble* Alberta (Old English), Albertina, Albertine,Yamya (Hindi), Yamika; Elberta • *famous, noble one* Elmira (Old English) • *illustrious, noble* Agave (Greek) • *kind and noble* Adelaide (Teutontic), Adele, Adeline, Della • *little noble lady* Damita (Spanish) • *little noble one* Edlyn (Old English) • *most noble* Saree (Arabic), Sari • *ornament of God* Adiel (Hebrew), Adiella • *noble and brilliant* Alverta (Greek) • *noble and exalted* Adara (Hebrew) • *noble and generous* Nediva (Hebrew) • *noble and ready* Alfonsine (Old German), Alonza, Alphonsine • *noble friend* Alvina (Old English) • *noble lady* Freya (Old Norse) • *noble maiden* Ilse (Old German), Elsa, Else, Ilsa • *noble, of a fine background* Ermina (Latin), Erma, Erminna, Mina, Minna • *noble one* Adalia, Adelle, Aline (Old German), Ada, Adal, Adala, Adaliah, Adaline,

Adallia, Addy, Adela, Adelina, Adeline, Adelita, Adelka, Akela, Dalia, Dela, Edeline, Lela, Patrice, Patricia, Patrizia, Patti, Pattie, Patsy, Patty, Tisha • *noble protector* Adelma (German) • *noble serpent* Ethelinda (Old English) • *noble strength* Audrey (Old English), Audrie, Audry • *noble, truthful* Alita (Spanish) • *noble, well-born* Eugenia (Greek), Genie • *noble woman* Earlene (Old English), Erlene, Erline • *of a noble nature* Auberta (Old German), Aubarta, Auburta • *of noble birth* Ada (Latin) Adda, Addi, Addie, Adi, Aida *of noble rank* • Adelaide (Old German), Adel, Adela, Della
nobly *see* nobly born
nocturnal Yamini (Hindi)
noisy Rhonda *noisy one* (Welsh), Rhona, Rhonette, Ronda
nomad Numidia *a nomad, one from Numidia* (Latin)
non-sorrow Asoka *non-sorrow flower* (Hindi)
north Kita (Japanese) • *from the north* Nordica (German)

noteworthy Emina *noteworthy one* (Old German), Mina
nothing *see* lacking nothing
nourishing Iku (Japanese) • *nourishing, spiritually helpful, supportive* Alma (Latin)
now Ima (Japanese), Imako
Numidia *see* nomad
nurse Dymphia (Latin), Dimphia, Phia • *mother or nurse* Maia (Greek), Maiah, Maya
nursling Thelma *a nursling* (Greek); Kama (Hawaiian)
nut *see* kola nut
nymph Thetis *beautiful nymph of the sea, sea goddess* (Greek), Heti, Thetes, Thetisa, Thetos • *nymph from the sea; one from the sea, swimmer* Nerine (Greek), Nereen, Neri, Nerice, Nerin, Nerissa • *nymph of the sky, she-bear* Ursa (Greek), Ursal, Ursala, Ursas, Ursel, Yursa • *river or water nymph* Naida (Latin) • *the little nymph* Evadne (Greek), Eva, Evadnee, Vadnee • *wod nymph* Rusalka (Czech)

O

oak Nara (North American Indian-Japanese) • Papina *a vine growing on an oak tree* (Miwok) • *oak tree* Alona (Hebrew) • *the strong, sturdy oak* Ituha (Native American)
oatfield Avena (Latin)
obedient Pulika (African); Jun (Japanese) • *hearing gladly, obedient* Simone (Hebrew), Simona, Simonetta • *obedient child* Kazuko (Japanese) • *obedient woman* Shama (Hebrew), Shamma
obscure *see* concealed
observation Darshana (Hindi)
ocean Derya (Hawaiian); Sagara (Hindi) • *from the ocean* Doris (Greek), Doria, Dorice, Dorise; Kolika (Hawaiian) • *in the middle of the ocean* Oki (Japanese)
ode *see* little

Odyssey *see* journey
offering Desna (Hindi) • *an offering* Portia (Latin) • *light and buoyant; an offering* Alana (Hawaiian)
ointment *see* fragrant ointment
old Alda *old, rich, wise* (Old German) • *old, wise counselor* Eldrida (Old English) • *small, old, wise one* Shannon (Irish-Gaelic), Shani, Shanon, Shannah, Shannan, Shannen, Shauna, Shawna, Shawni
older Aneko *older sister* (Japanese); Minya (Native American)
oleander Oliana (Polynesian)
olive Zayit, Zetta (Hebrew), Zeta, Zetana • *from the olive grove* Nolita (Greek), Lita, Nolitta • *olive colored* Orna (Irish-Gaelic), Ornas • *olive branch or olive tree* Olive (Latin), Livia, Nola, Olga, Olivette, Olivia

omen Senalda *sign, omen* (Spanish), Alda, Enalda, Sena

once Semele *once, a single time; the one and only* Semela (Latin)

one Semele *once, a single time; the one and only* (Latin), Semela • *one, single one* Mona (Greek) • *one, together* Una (Latin) • *the one* Kamea (Hawaiian), Kameo

onions Tiwa (Zuni)

only Semele *once, a single time; the one and only* Semela (Latin) • *the only girl* Delu (African) • *the only one* Unique (Latin)

open Savanna *an open plain* (Spanish) • *secure, open, or protected* Abrial (French), Abeale, Abre, Abreal, Abri, Abriala; Abriale (English)

opening *see* April

opportunity Toki *time of opportunity* (Japanese)

orange Alani *orange; orange tree* (Hawaiian) • *sweetness, like an orange* Cam (Vietnamese)

orator Rheta (Greek)

orchid Ah-Lam *like an orchid* (Chinese)

order Themis *custom, justice, order* (Greek), Tema, Thema • *harmony, order, the world* Cosima (Greek)

origin Matsumoto *origin, pine* (Japanese)

ornament Banna (Efik/African) *adorn; an ornament, to dress* • *crown or ornament* Adah (Hebrew) • *an ornament* Ada (Old English) Adda, Addi, Addie, Adi, Aida • *ornament of God* Adiel (Hebrew), Adiella • *ornament of the Lord* Adiel (Hebrew), Addielle, Adiell

ornamental *see* colorful, ornamental fabric

outer *see* an outer garment

outspoken *see* bold, outspoken

outstanding Fadhila (African)

overflow *see* forehead; to overflow

overtake Sunki (Hopi)

own *see* meadow

owner Ula *owner of an inherited estate* (Old German) • *owner of the new house* Xaviera (Spanish)

ox Ushi (Chinese)

— P —

pacifies Chemosh *she who pacifies* (Hebrew), Chema, Chemash, Chemesh

pageant Tamasha (African)

pain Klesa (Hindi)

pale Wannetta *little pale one* (Native American) • *pale one* Orna (Irish-Gaelic)

Palestine Jordan *from the river in Palestine* (Hebrew), Jardena; Jordanne, Jordyn; Jordane (French); Jordana (Spanish)

palm Palma *a palm* (Latin), Palmira, Palmyra • *a young palm shoot* Hira (Arabic) • *from a palm tree* Phenice (Hebrew), Phenica, Venice • *palm bird* Ega (Yoruban) • *palm tree* Tamara (Hebrew)

panels *see* cedar panels

parade Alameda *parade, promenade; poplar tree* (Spanish)

paradise Huma *bird of paradise* (Hindi)

park Rin (Japanese)

past Priscilla *from past or primitive times* (Latin), Cilla, Prisca; Sila (American)

pastureland Arva *pastureland or seashore* (Latin)

path Hanzila *road, path* (African)

patience Sabra (African); Sabirah (Arabic); Dhriti (Hindi); Jena (Sanskrit)

patient Sabira (Arabic • *patient friend* Aleydis (Greek), Aledis, Alidis, Leda • *the patient wife* Medora (Anglo-Saxon), Dora, Edora, Madora, Medor, Ora

pattern Ona *a pattern* (Bini) • *pattern or precept, rule* Norma (Latin)

peace Irene (Greek), Eirena, Erena,

Irena, Irina, Rena, Rene; Shulamith
(Hebrew); Eirene (Old Norse),
Sula, Sulamith; Aquene (Native
American); Paz (Spanish); Hoa
(Vietnamese) • *child of peace* Evania
(Greek), Evannia, Vani, Vania •
clemency, peace Eir (Old German) •
commands peace Kasmira (Old Slavic)
• *girl of peace* Persis (Greek), Persas;
Selema (Hebrew), Lema, Selemas,
Selima • *harmony, peace* Miru (Slavic)
• *peace, safety or security* An (Viet-
namese) • *the peace-loving ruler* Farica
(Old German), Arica, Farika, Far-
rica, Feriga
peaceful Amina (Arabic); Salome
(Hebrew), Loma, Sally, Salom,
Soloma; Pacifica (Latin), Pacifa,
Pacificia; Frieda (Old German),
Freda, Frida; Chesna (Slavic),
Chessa; Ping (Vietnamese) • *a peaceful child* Peace (Anglo-Saxon) • *gentle, peaceful one* Placida (Latin) •
peaceful and calm Shanti (Sanskrit) •
peaceful and victorious Sigfreda (Old
German) • *peaceful and wise* Elfrida
(Old German), Elfreda • *peaceful,
calm* Serenity (Latin) • *peaceful elf*
Fredella (Old German), Della, Fredela • *peaceful friend* Winifred (Old
German) • *peaceful hall or home* Halfrida (Old English) • *peaceful heroine*
Halfrida (Old German) • *peaceful or
secure* An (Vietnamese) • *peaceful,
quiet one* Tullia (Irish-Gaelic) • *peaceful ruler* Frederica, Fritzi (Old German), Farica, Federica, Frederika,
Frederique • *the peaceful one* Amina
(East African) • *spiritual, serene, and
peaceful* Shanta (Hindi)
peacemaker Shamita (Hindi)
peacock Chandraki (Hindi)
peak Mineko *peak, mountain child*
(Japanese)
pear Li-Hua *pear blossom* (Chinese);
pear tree Le (Chinese)
pearl Gulika, Mukta (Hindi) • *a pearl*
Greta (German), Gretta; Margaret,
Pearl (Latin), Gretal, Gretchen,
Madge, Maisie, Marga, Margareta,
Margarete, Margarita, Margaux,
Margery, Margo, Margory, Margot,
Marjory, Miriam, Pearlina, Pearline,
Peggy; Marjorie (Old French),

Marge, Marje, Marjie; Gita (Slavic),
Perla • *pearl of wisdom* Darda (Hebrew), Dara • *precious pearl* Chau
(Vietnamese)
peerless Kimi (Japanese), Kimie,
Kimiko, Kimiyo
pelican Shada (Native American)
peony *see* blossom
people Dinka (Dinka); Tami (Japanese), Tamiko • *a good judge of people*
Ethelind (Old German), Ethel,
Ethelinda • *a greeter of people* Afra
(Old German), Affra • *boldest of the
people* Tibelda (Old German) • *of
bold people* Leopoldine (Old German), Dina, Lea, Leopoldeen • *people child* Tamika (Japanese), Tamike,
Tamiko, Tamiyo • *the people's ruler*
Derica (German), Dereka, Dericka,
Derika • *victorious army, victorious people* Nicole (Greek), Nichele,
Nichelle, Nichola, Nicola, Nicolina,
Nicoline, Niki, Nikki • *woman of the
people* Leoda (Old German), Leota •
worker for the people Radmilla (Slavic)
perfect Sanemi (Hindi); Dilys
(Welsh), Dalice, Dalicia, Dalisha,
Delicia, Delisha, Dilees, Dylice • Perfecta *accomplished, perfect one* Perfecta
(Spanish) • *the perfect one* Kamilah
(Arabic), Kamila, Kamilla, Kamillah,
Kammile
perfection Kamili (African) • Tammy
perfection (Hebrew)
perfume Kaksi, Shalalu (Hindi)
permanent Akshita (Hindi)
perplexed Farih (Arabic)
persecuted *see* afflicted
person Elita *a special person, select*
(Latin), Ellita, Lita • *a woman of
Lydia, cultured person* Lydia (Greek),
Lidia, Lydie • *high-ranking person*
Irma (Latin), Erma • *young person*
Novia (Latin), Nova
persuasive Casiah (Hausa); Casia,
Cassia (English)
phantom Guinevere *white phantom,
white wave* (Old Welsh), Genevieve,
Guenna, Gwenore, Jenifer, Jeniffer,
Jenni, Jennie, Jennifer, Jenny, Jeny,
Vanora
pheasant Bena (Native American)
photograph Anukriti (Hindi)
piercing Trina (Hindi)

pilgrim Perry *traveler, stranger, or pilgrim* (Latin), Perri, Perriann, Perrie, Perrin
pillar Pilar *a fountain basin or pillar* (Spanish) • *a pointed pillar, rich* Obelia (Greek), Belia, Obel, Obellia, Obiel
pilot *see* guide or pilot
pine Matsu (Japanese) • *below, pine* Matsushita (Japanese) • *flat, pine* Hiramatsu, Matsuhira (Japanese) • *hill, pine* Matsuoka (Japanese) • *island, pine* Matsushima (Japanese) • *little, pine* Matsuo (Japanese) • *middle, pine* Matsunaka (Japanese) • *mountain, pine* Matsuyama (Japanese) • *origin, pine* Matsumoto (Japanese) • *pine, rice field* Matsuda (Japanese) • *pine, river* Matsukawa (Japanese) • *pine tree* Orinda (Hebrew)
pink Hong (Vietnamese)
pinnacle Nadira (Hindi) • *crag or rocky pinnacle* Tara (Irish-Gaelic), Taran, Tarin, Tarina, Taryn
pious Pia (Greek); Joachima (Latin), Joacima, Joacimah, Joshi • *holy, pious, religious* Helga (Old German) • *modest, pious, pure* Casta (Latin)
pipe Piper *a pipe player* (Old English)
pitch *see* dark
pity *see* compassion, pity
place Shantel *from a stony place* (American), Chantal • *her place* Safara (African) • *resting place* Hania (Hebrew), Haniyah; Haniya (English)
plague *see* goddess
plain Wyome (Native American) • *a plain* Sharai (Hebrew) • *an open plain* Savanna (Spanish) • *from the fertile plain* Sharon (Hebrew), Shara
plant Bitski (Turkish) • *delicate plant or feather* Fern (Greek), Ferna, Fernas, Ferne • *plant or shrub* Netia (Hebrew), Neta, Netta • *the marshmallow plant and flower* Hibiscus (Latin) • *the mint plant* Minta (Greek), Mintha • *the sacred Tulasi plant* Tulsi (Hindi)
planted *see* field
player *see* pipe
playful Farih (Arabic) • *merry, playful* Jocelyn (Latin) • *she is playful* Pocahontas (Algonquin Indian)

plays Aleshanee *she plays all the time* (Native American)
pleasant Africa (Celtic), Africah, Afrika, Afrikah; Navit (Hebrew), Nava, Navice • *beautiful, pleasant* Farrah (Middle English), Farah, Farand, Fayre • *famous and pleasant* Mertice (Old English), Merdyce • *lovable, pleasant* Elma (Greek) • *mirthful, pleasant* Merry (Middle English) • *of pleasant times* Halona (Native American), Halonna • *pleasant fragrance* Rufen (Chinese) • *pleasant, sweet* Hedy (Greek) • *the pleasant one* Naomi (Hebrew), Naoma, Noami; Numa (Arabic)
pleasantness Thirza (Hebrew)
pleased Joshitha • *glad, pleased* Gamada (African)
pleases Deka *one who pleases* (Somalian)
pleasing Lalita, Rama (Sanskrit) • *very holy or very pleasing* Ariana (Latin)
pleasure Adna (Hebrew), Adnah • *delight or pleasure* Eden (Hebrew); Delight (Old French) • *joy, pleasure* Mirth (Anglo-Saxon), Merth • *of earthly pleasures* Terrena (Latin), Terena, Terina, Terrene
pledge Arlene *a pledge* (Irish-Gaelic), Arleen, Arlena, Arleta, Arlette, Arline, Arlyne • *brilliant pledge or hostage, the bright pledge* Gilberta (Old German), Gilbertina, Gilbertine • *hostage or pledge* Giselle (Old German), Gisela, Gisella; Gizi (Hungarian)
plentiful Toyo (Japanese)
plow Odera (Hebrew)
plucked *see* flower
plucking *see* flower
plum Lee (Chinese) • *plum blossom child* Umeko (Japanese) • *plum blossom; plum tree* Li (Chinese) • *plum colored* Prunella (Latin), Nella • *plum tree field* Umeno (Japanese)
plums Li (Chinese), Lee
plunging Taki *a plunging waterfall* (Japanese)
poem Kavni *a small poem* (Hindi) • *fiber; poem; to breathe* Tho (Vietnamese) • *poem child* Utako (Japanese), Uta

poet *see* mighty
poetess Kavika (Hindi); Ovida (Latin)
poetic Lirit (Hebrew) • *poetic child* Lee (Irish-Gaelic)
poetry Kavita (Hindi); Eda (Old German); Edda (Old Norse) • *rhyme, poetry* Rima (Spanish)
point Nyssa *starting point* (Greek) • *the highest point in heaven* Lulani (Hawaiian)
pointed Obelia *a pointed pillar, rich* (Greek), Belia, Obel, Obellia, Obiel • Acantha *sharp-pointed, thorned* (Greek)
poison *see* grandmother; poison; residue; three
poke Tiponya *to poke* (Miwok)
polished Jala *bright, polished, splendid* (Arabic) • *polished chief* Malvina (Irish-Gaelic), Malva, Melva, Melvina, Melvine
polite Urbana *gentle and polite lady* (Latin), Urbai, Urbani, Urbanna, Urbannai • *gentle, polite* Myrna (Irish-Gaelic), Merna, Mirna, Moina, Morna, Moyna
politeness Namrata (Hindi)
pomegranate Rimona (Hebrew)
pond Anupa, Simbala (Hindi)
pool *see* below
poppy Rea (Greek) • *a poppy flower* Poppy (Latin)
popular *see* parade, promenade; poplar tree
port Chelsea *ship's port* (Old English), Chelsey
portable *see* cup
positive Thetis *determined, positive one* (Greek) • *the postive* Yoko (Japanese)
possessed *see* married or possessed
possessive *see* nature
poverty *see* house of poverty
power Astrid *divine power* (Greek), Astra • *first power* Aadhya (Hindi) • *God's creative power; illusion, fantasy* Maya (Sanskrit), Mayura • *inner magical power* Wakanda (Sioux) • *magic power* Orenda (Iroquois Indian); Oki (Huron Indian) • *mighty power* Ronalda (Old Norse), Rhona, Rona • *power of the moon* Miakoda (Native American) • *spiritual power* Turya (Hindi) • *supernatural power* Mana

(Hawaiian) • *woman of power* Edra (Hebrew), Eddra, Edrea, Edris
powerful Raina (Old German), Rainah, Rayna, Raynah, Raynata • *ever powerful, ever regal, ever ruler* Erica (Old German), Erika • *powerful battle maiden* Magnilda (Old German) • *powerful, prosperous* Edrea (Old English), Edra • *powerful ruler* Ricarda (Old German) • *strong and powerful* Adira (Hebrew)
prairie Leotie *prairie flower* (Native American) • *prairie dog* Tusa (Zuni)
praise Sansita (Hindi); Eudice (Isreli) • *giving praise* Peony (Greek) • *praise the Lord* Hosana (Latin); Osanna (English) • *worthy of praise* Aenea (Hebrew), Aeniah, Aennela
praised Judith (Hebrew), Jodi, Jody, Judie, Judy • *admired, praised* Siobhan (Irish-Gaelic) • *exalted or praised* Sami (Arabic)
pray *see* pray to God
prayed Matthia *gift we prayed for* (Hebrew), Atthia, Mathi, Mathia, Thia • *prayed for* Oni (African); Amala (Hebrew), Samal
prayer Pranati, Vinati (Hindi) • *a prayer* Atira (Hebrew)
prayers Eliana *Jehovah has answered our prayers* (Hebrew); Eliane, Elianna, Leanna, Liana, Lianne (English)
precept Norma *pattern or precept, rule* (Latin) • *precept or doctrine* Nori (Japanese), Norie, Noriko
precious Ghalyela (African); Nadira (Arabic), Nadirah; Bo (Chinese); Preciosa (Latin); Tahya (Native American); Aziza (Turkish) • *a gem or precious stone* Gemma (Greek) • *angel of precious stone* Nitika (Native American) • *a precious gem or thing* Jewel (Old French) • *a precious stone* Opal (Sanskrit), Opalina, Opaline • *dear, precious or rare* Azize (Turkish) • *February birthstone, precious stone* Amethyst (Greek), Amathist, Amathiste, Amethist • *precious jewel* Cara (Vietnamese) • *precious object* Takara (Japanese) • *precious pearl* Chau (Vietnamese) • *ripe; precious* Alamea (Hawaiian)
predict Ramla *one who predicts the*

future (African) • *to forecast or predict* Becca (Bobangi)

present Makana *gift or present* Makana (Hawaiian) • *the force of present existence* Pemba (Bambara)

pretty Alina (Celtic), Alena, Alinna; Jolie (French); Bonita, Linda (Spanish), Lynda, Nita • *beautiful, pretty* Belinda (Spanish), Belle • *beloved and pretty* Amelinda (Latin-Spanish), Amilinda • *fresh, healthy, and pretty* Marini (Swahili) • *little rose, pretty rose* Rosaleen (Irish-Gaelic), Rosalie, Rosalind, Roselind, Rosina; Rosa (Spanish) • *pretty child* Reiko (Japanese) • *pretty flower* Lomasi (Native American) • *pretty servant* Jolenta (Latin), Jola, Jolanta, Jollanta, Jollenta, Olenta • *pretty smile* Qianru (Chincse) • *the pretty one* Bukeda (South African)

prevented Hanna (Hausa)

price *see* beyond price, inestimable

priceless Amulya (Hindi); Antonia (Latin), Antoinette, Antonetta, Antonietta, Toni, Tonie; Tosia (Polish)

priestess Meda (Native American)

primitive *see* past

princess Gimbya (African); Charron (American), Sarina; Amir (Arabic), Zaira; Zaidee (French); Kala (Hawaiian); Koa, Sarah, Sharai, Sharon (Hebrew), Koah, Sadella, Sally, Sara, Sarene, Sarette, Sari, Sarine, Zara, Zarah, Zaria; Akuti (Hindi); Sarolta (Hungarian); Aldercy (Old English), Aldarcie, Aldarcy, Dercy; Zahira (Spanish), Zaharita • *bitter princess* Sharma (American), Sharmine • *famous ruler; princess, ruler* Roderica (Old German), Rica • *friendly princess, gracious friend* Winola (Old German) • *from a princess* Neala (Celtic), Nealah, Neela, Neila • *honey-sweet princess* Sharissa (American), Shari, Sharice, Sharie, Sharine, Sherice, Sherie, Sherissa

proclaimer Clio *the proclaimer* (Greek)

profound Fonda *profound woman* (Spanish)

project Prakalpa (Hindi)

promenade *see* parade, promenade; poplar tree

prominent Jahia (African) • *lofty, prominent one* Emina (Latin)

promise Amaris *God hath promised good* (Hebrew), Amaras, Amari, Amary, Mari, Maris • *God's promise* Lilybet (Cornish); Elise (Hebrew) • *to promise* Iva (Bini)

promoted Pranita (Hindi)

prophet Pythia *a diviner or prophet* (Greek) • *a prophet* Kaula (Hawaiian)

prophetess Sibyl *a prophetess* (Greek), Cybil, Sibelle, Sibilla, Sibille, Sybil, Sybilla, Sybille • *the wise prophetess* Hulda (Hebrew), Huldah, Ulda

proprietary *see* gratitude, proprietary

prosperity Shaivi (Hindi) • *blessedness, prosperity* Eda (Old English) • *child of prosperity* Mieko (Japanese) • *wealth or worldy prosperity* Arthua (Hindi)

prosperous Zaida (Arabic), Zadam, Zaidah, Zayda; Ede (Old English) • *a prosperous woman* Alodie (Anglo-Saxon), Alodee, Alodi, Lodie • *blooming, flourishing, prosperous* Florence (Latin), Fiorenza, Florance, Florencia, Florinda, Florine, Floris • *born during a prosperous time* Neema (Swahili) • *from a prosperous family* Edina (Anglo-Saxon), Dina, Eddina • *happy or prosperous one* Rafa (Arabic) • *happy, prosperous* Ada (Old English), Adda, Aida, Eada, Ida, Idalia, Idalina, Idaline • *powerful, prosperous* Edrea (Old English), Edra • *prosperous friend* Edwina (Old English), Edina • *properous guardian* Nedra (Anglo-Saxon), Neda, Nedrah; Edwardine (Old English) • *prosperous protector* Edmonda (Anglo-Saxon), Edmanda, Edmunda

protected Aminta (Greek); Gerda (Scandinavian) • *secure, open, or protected* Abrial (French), Abeale, Abre, Abreal, Abri, Abriala; Abriale (English)

protecting Valborga *protecting ruler* (Old German)

protection Helma (Old German) • *divine helmet or protection* Aselma (Old German) • *enclosure, protection* Gerda (Old Norse)

protective Brigid *protective, strong* (Celtic)

protector Brina (Slavic), Brynna • *brilliant protector* Clarimond (Latin-German) • *defender, protector* Verena (Old German) • *descendant of the protector* Monet (French) • *fortunate protector* Edmee (Anglo-Saxon), Edme, Edmea, Emee • *helmut, protector* Wilhelmina (Old German), Mina, Valma, Velma, Wilma • *mighty or wise protector* Ramona (Spanish), Ramonda • *noble protector* Adelma (German) • *prosperous protector* Edmonda (Anglo-Saxon), Edmanda, Edmunda • *resolute protector* Wilhelmina (Old German), Guillelmina, Guillelmine, Guillemette, Helma, Helmine, Minna, Valma, Vihelmina, Wilhelma, Wilhelmine, Willa, Willabelle, Willette, Wilma, Wilmette

protectress Rosamond *famous protectress* (Old German), Rosamund, Rosamunda, Rosamunde, Rozamund • *sent by God to guard, the protectress* Anselma (Old German), Ansela, Ansilma, Sellma, Selma

protects *see* Lord

pure Mariatu, Safiya (African); Anice (American); Nakia (Arabic); Caron (French); Agnes, Catherine, Neysa (Greek), Caitlin, Carina, Catharine, Catriona, Cayla, Ines, Kadee, Kadia, Kadie, Kady, Kara, Karen, Karina, Katelyn, Katherine, Katrina, Katy, Kayla, Neisa, Nessa, Nessi, Nisa, Nysa; Agnella (Greek-Italian), Agnola; Kaitlin, Kaiti, Kaitlan, Kaitleen, Kaitlen, Kaitlyn, Katelyn (Irish); Kalena (Hawaiian); Amishi (Hindi); Pura (Latin); Kassia (Polish); Inessa, Katya, Kiska (Russian); Neza (Slavic); Ynes (Spanish); Kolina (Swedish); Rayna (Yiddish) • *a pure maiden* Atalie (Scandinavian), Attalie, Talie • *brightly white or pure* Marya (Arabic) • *chaste or pure* Chastity (Latin) • *child of cool, pure water* Kenda (Modern U.S.) • *modest, pious, pure* Casta (Latin) • *pure in soul* Enid (Celtic)

purified Laveda *purified one* (Latin), Lavinia, Lavetta, Lavette, Lavina

purity Trina *girl of purity* (Greek), Trinee, Trinia • *little girl of purity* Trinette (Greek), Rinee, Trinatte, Trinetta • *purity, woodlark* Enid (Welsh)

purpose *see* force, purpose

purposeful Canna (Congo)

pussycat Paka (Swahili)

python Dilla (Mende)

• Q •

queen Malika (African); Thema (Akan), Tayma; Regan (American), Reagan, Reaganne, Regin; Takuhi (Armenian), Takoohi • *a queen* Riona (American) Malka (Hebrew); Rani (Hindi), Rania; Regina (Latin), Rane, Reina, Reine, Renia, Reyna; Quenna (Old English) • *divine queen* Dionne (Greek), Dina, Dynah • *fairy queen* Tiana (Slavic), Tiane, Tianna, Tianne • *heavenly, queen of heaven* Juno (Latin), Jeno, Juna, Juni, Junna, Junno • *queen of the gods* Hera (Greek), Herra, Herrah • *queen, ruling lady* Hera (Latin) • *the fairy queen* Tania (Russian), Tanya • *the queen* La Reina (Spanish), Lareina, Larena • *tiny* Halette (Anglo-Saxon), Haletta, Hallette

queenly Daruce (Persian), Darceece, Dari • *enduring, queenly, womanly* Cornelia (Latin) • *queenly, regal* Basilia (Greek) • *queenly, royal* Rana (Hindustani), Ranee, Rani • *queenly, wealthy* Daria (Greek)

quest Anwesha (Hindi)

quick Min (Chinese); Haya (Japanese) • *quick, alert, and merry* Zana (Arabic) • *quick or energetic* Mahira (Hebrew), Mehira

quiet Kafi (African); Shizu (Japanese), Shizue, Shizuko, Shizuyo, Suizuka; Stilla (Latin), Stila, Stillas • *of the quiet life* Wivinia (Latin), Vinia, Wivina, Wivinah • *peaceful, quiet one* Tullia (Irish-Gaelic) • *quiet, silent* Gilly (Mende)

— R —

rabbit Lulu (Native American)
radiant Suchi (Hindi) • *radiant red jewel* Garnet (Old German), Garnette
radiating *see* flashing, glittering, radiating
rain Barkha, Varsha (Hindi), Barsha • *autumn rain* Jora (Hebrew); Joran (English) • *rain falling* Huyana (Miwok)
rainbow Sabrang (Hindi); Amitola (Native American) • *rainbow, the iris flower* Iris (Greek); Irisa (Russian), Risha
rainmaker Ara (Arabic), Aria, Arria
rainwater Eda (Bini), Edda
rainy *see* born during the rainy season
ram Mesha (Hindi)
rambunctious Shandy (Old English), Shandeigh, Shanta
randa Randa *the sweet-smelling randa tree* (Arabic)
rank Adelaide *of noble rank* (Old German), Adel, Adela, Della • *of superior rank* Aldora (Old English), Aleldra
ranking *see* high-ranking person
rapture Kei *rapture or reverence* (Japanese)
rare Nadira (Arabic), Nadirah • *dear, precious or rare* Azize (Turkish)
rattlesnake *see* girl
raven Brenna, Fay (Irish-Gaelic) • *little raven* Brenda (Irish-Gaelic) • *with raven tresses* Brenna (Celtic)
ready *see* noble and ready
reaper Theresa (Greek), Tassos, Teresa, Terese, Teresita, Therese; Resi, Tresa (German); Tereza (Portuguese)
rebellious Meryem (Turkish)
received *see* gladly
reconciliation *see* holy reconciliation
red Arusha (Sanskrit), Arushi; Akako (Japanese) • *daughter of the red earth* Adamina (Hebrew), Adama • Rufina *girl with bright red hair* (Latin), Fina, Rufena, Ruphina • *of the red earth* Adaminah (Hebrew), Adama, Adamina • *radiant red jewel* Garnet (Old German), Garnette • *red cloud*

coming with sundown Sanuye (Miwok) • *red glow* Arunima (Hindi) • *red thunder* Shappa (Native American)
red-haired Flanna (Irish-Gaelic), Flannery; Merah (Malay)
redeemed Galya *God has redeemed* (Hebrew)
redhead La Roux (French)
reed Cattima *slender reed* (Latin), Catima
refined Sumi *the refined* (Japanese), Sumiko
reflected *see* echo, reflected sound
reflection Chhavi (Hindi)
refuge Nydia *a nest of refuge* (Latin), Nidia • *fight, strife; refuge from the storm* Hedwig (Old German), Heda, Hedvig, Hedvige, Hedy • *God is my refuge* Adalia (Hebrew), Adal, Adala, Adalee, Adali, Adalie, Adalin, Adall, Adaly, Adalyn, Addal, Addala, Addaly
refused *see* despised
regain Reva *to regain strength* (Latin)
regal Erica *ever powerful, ever regal, ever ruler* (Old German), Erika • *queenly, regal* Basilia (Greek) • *regal grace* Rexana (Latin), Rexanna, Rexanne • *regal one* Royale (Old French)
rejoice Marni *to rejoice* (Hebrew), Marnie, Marny
rejoicing Yovela (Hebrew); Amadi (Nigerian) • *joyful, a cause for rejoicing* Fara (Hausa) • *one who causes joy and rejoicing* Darrah (Efik)
rejuvenation Edna (Hebrew); Edena (Hawaiian)
related *see* blood
relaxed Winna (Arabic)
reliable Haldis *one who is reliable* (Old German), Halda, Haldas, Haldi
relic *see* ancestral relic
religious *see* holy, pious, religious
remember Una (Hopi)
remembered *see* loved
rendezvous Ina (Efik)
renew Niva (Hindi)
renown Adora *gift, glory, renown* (Latin) • *lofty reputation, renown* Fayme (French)
renowned *see* famed one, renowned

reputation *see* lofty reputation, renown

repute Euphemia *auspicious speech, good repute* (Greek), Eufemia, Euphemie • *of good repute* Eudocia (Greek), Docie, Doxie, Doxy, Eudosia, Eudoxia

request Vinanti (Hindi)

residue *see* grandmother; poison; residue; three

resister Renita (Latin)

resolute Wilhelmina *resolute protector* (Old German), Guillelmina, Guillelmine, Guillemette, Helma, Helmine, Minna, Valma, Vihelmina, Wilhelma, Wilhemine, Willa, Willabelle, Willette, Wilma, Wilmette • *resolute strength, strength* Bridget (Irish-Gaelic), Beret, Berget, Bridgette, Brietta, Brigid, Brigida, Brigitte, Brita

resolution Billie *resolution, willpower* (Old English), Willa

resourcefulness *see* girl of resourcefulness

respectful Yoshi *the respectful* (Japanese), Yoshie, Yoshiko, Yoshio, Yoshiyo

rest Sabba (Hebrew), Sabah • *to rest* Sabra (Hebrew)

resting *see* resting place

restoration Rama (Hausa)

resurrection Anastasia *of the resurrection* (Greek), Anastasie, Anstice, Stacey, Stacy; Nastacia (Russian), Nessa, Tasya

returned *see* coming

returning *see* moon returning

returns Anaba *she returns from war* (Navajo Indian)

reverence *see* rapture

reverenced *see* august, reverenced one

revolution Kranti (Hindi)

reward Lucretia *riches, reward* (Latin), Lucrecia

Rhine Lorelei *siren of the river Rhine* (German)

rhyme *see* poetry

rhythmic Cadence (Latin), Cadena, Candenza

rice Hirata *flat, rice field* (Japanese) • *forest, rice field* Morita (Japanese) • *pine, rice field* Matsuda (Japanese) •

rice field Arita (Japanese) • *rice field, middle* Tanaka (Japanese) • *rice field, river* Tagawa (Japanese) • *rice field, side* Tanabe (Japanese) • *rice field store* Tazu (Japanese) • *rice, wheat, or ears of corn* Gesina (Hausa) • *wisteria, rice field* Fujita (Japanese)

rich Obelia *a pointed pillar, rich* (Greek), Belia, Obel, Obellia, Obiel • *old, rich, wise* Alda (Old German) • *rich gift* Dita (Czech); Duci (Hugarian); Edith (Old English), Edita, Editha, Edithe, Ediva, Edyth, Edythe • *rich in flowering, steady* Eustacia (Greek), Eustacie

riches *see* reward

rider Tasida (Sarcee Indian)

right *see* hand

righteous Rashida (Africa) • *the righteous way* Michiko (Japanese), Michi

ring Alhena (Arabic) *a ring*

ripe Asisa (Hebrew) *juicy or ripe* • *mature, ripe* Sharada (Sanskrit); Sharda (Hindi) • *ripe; precious* Alamea (Hawaiian)

ripened Numa (Hausa); Iva (Swahili)

rising Rohin (Hindi) • *rising star* Citlalic (Aztec) • *rising sun* Levana (Latin)

river India (Sanskrit); Inda, Indee (English) • *ancient river goddess* Oba (Yoruban) • *a river mouth* Ria (Spanish) • *from the river in Palestine* Jordan (Hebrew), Jardena; Jordanne, Jordyn; Jordane (French); Jordana (Spanish) • *lady of the river Nile* Nila (Latin), Nilla • *of the river Tiber* Tiberia (Latin) • *pine, river* Matsukawa (Japanese) • *rice field, river* Tagawa (Japanese) • *river of black stones* Guadalupe (Arabic), Lupe, Lupita • *river or water nymph* Naida (Latin) • *siren of the river Rhine* Lorelei (German) • *the sacred Kaveri River* Kaveri (Hindi) • *the sacred Narmada River* Reva (Hindi)

riverbank Riva *riverbank, shore* (French), Ree, Reeva, Reva

rock Sela (Hebrew), Seleta, Sella; Shila (Hindi); Nelka, Petra (Latin), Nela, Perrine, Petronella, Petronia, Petronila, Pierette, Tona; Sawa (Miwok) • *from the little rock* Rochelle (French), Rochella, Rochette • *little* *rock* Paula (Latin), Paulette, Paulina, Pauline, Paulita, Polly; Parnella (Old French), Pernella; Pavla (Russian) • *the Lord is my rock* Gavra (Hebrew), Avra, Gavrah

rocky *see* crag or rocky pinnacle

road *see* path

rod *see* bearer

roll Mituna *roll up* (Miwok)

Roman Romola *Roman, woman of Rome* (Latin)

romantic Grania *romantic female* (Celtic), Graniah, Grannia, Granniah, Grannias • *romantic loss, the lost lover* Thisbe (Greek), Thisbee, Tisbe, Tisbee

Rome *see* Roman, woman of Rome

rooted *see* deeply rooted

rope Tanika (Hindi) • *a rope dancer* Nata (Hindi)

rose Vardis (Hebrew), Varda, Vardia, Vardice, Vardina • Rose *a rose* (Greek), Raisa, Rasia, Rhoda, Rhodia, Rois, Rosa, Rosalia, Rosalie, Rosella, Roselle, Rosetta, Rosette, Rosina, Rosita, Rozella; Shoshana (Hebrew) • *beautiful rose* Rosabel (Latin); Rosalinda (Spanish), Rosalind, Rosaline, Rosalynd, Roseline • *graceful rose* Rosanna (English) • *heavenly rose* Lokelani, Roselani (Hawaiian) • *little rose, pretty rose* Rosaleen (Irish-Gaelic), Rosalie, Rosalind, Roselind, Rosina, Rosa (Spanish) • *lovely white rose* Rosalba (Latin), Alba, Roselba, Salba • *Mary's rose* Rosemarie (Latin), Rosemari, Rosemary • *rose flower* Rhodanthe (Greek); Rozene (Native American); Raizel (Yiddish), Rayzil, Razil • *sweetbriar rose, woodbine* Eglantine (Old French) • *the rose of St. Mary* Rosemary (English), Marie, Rose • *the wild rose* Ogin (Native American) • *white rose* Semanti, Sevati (Hindi)

rosebud Kalyca (Greek), Kali, Kalica, Kalie, Kalika

round Maru (Japanese)

royal Kimberly *from the royal fortress*

meadow (Old English) • *queenly, royal* Rana (Hindustani), Ranee, Rani

ruby *see* gem

rule *see* pattern or precept, rule

ruler Nagida (Hebrew); Rula (Latin); Walda (Old German), Welda • *army ruler* Haralda (Old Norse), Hallie, Hally • *daughter of the ruler* Zoba (Old German), Zoa, Zobe, Zoe • *eagle-ruler* Arnalda (Old German) • *estate or home ruler* Henrietta (French), Enriqueta, Hariette, Hendrika, Henriette, Henrika; Harriet (Old French); Henka (Polish); Queta (Spanish) • *ever powerful, ever regal, ever ruler* Erica (Old German), Erika • *famous ruler; princess, ruler* Roderica (Old German), Rica • *glorious ruler* Valeska (Old Slavic) • *governor, ruler* Valda (Old Norse), Velda • *peaceful ruler* Frederica, Fritzi (Old German), Farica, Federica, Frederika, Frederique • *powerful ruler* Ricarda (Old German) • *protecting ruler* Valborga (Old German) • *ruler of all* Alarice, Elrica, Ulrica (Old German), Alarica, Rica, Rika, Ulrika • *ruler of the estate or home* Enrica (Italian) • *the peace-loving ruler* Farica (Old German), Arica, Farika, Farrica, Feriga • *the people's ruler* Derica (German), Dereka, Dericka, Derika • *world ruler* Donalda (Irish-Gaelic), Donia; Doni (American); Dony (English)

ruling Media (Greek), Madora, Medea, Medora • *queen, ruling lady* Hera (Latin) • *ruling lady* Ricadonna (English-Italian)

runaway Oprah *a runaway* (Hebrew)

runner Tadita *a runner* (Native American), Tadeta • *swift runner* Atalanta (Greek), Atalani, Atalante, Tala, Talanta

running Saril *the sound of running water* (Turkish)

runs Farih *one who runs well* (Arabic)

rush Kaya *a rush* (Japanese)

• — S — •

Saba Saba *woman of Saba or Sheba* (Greek), Sheba
sabine *see* lady
sacred Edha (Hindi) • *inviolable, sacred* Sancia (Latin), Sanchia • *sacred boughs* Verbena (Latin) • *sacred dancer* Kachine (Native American), Kachina • *sacred moon* Mitexi (Native American) • *sacred to the gods* Lehua (Hawaiian) • *the sacred Kaveri River* Kaveri (Hindi) • *the sacred kusa grass* Kusa (Hindi) • *the sacred Narmada River* Reva (Hindi) • *the sacred Sala tree* Sala (Hindi) • *the sacred tulasi plant* Tulasi (Hindi)
sacrifice Ijaya (Hindi)
sadness Merari *bitter, girl of sadness* (Hebrew), Mera, Meraree • *girl of sadness* Desdemona (Greek), Demona, Desdamona, Desdamonna, Desdee, Mona • *sacred bells* Kerani (Sanskrit), Kera, Keri, Kerie, Kery; Rani (English) • *woman of much sadness* Trista (Latin), Tristas, Tristis
safe *see* honor
safety *see* peace, safety and security
saffron *see* saffron flower
sage Salvia (Latin), Salvina
saint Osyth *saint from Essex* (Anglo-Saxon), Osithe • *the saintly one* Alison (Old German), Alisan, Allisan, Allison
sala *see* the sacred Sala tree
salty Salina *from the salty place* (Latin)
sanctuary Templa (Latin), Tempa, Templas, Templia
sand Sikata (Hindi); Masago (Japanese)
sandalwood Rohana (Hindi)
sane Alyssa *sane one* (Greek), Alysson
sapphire *see* blue color
satisfaction Santosh, Tripti (Hindi)
satisfying Isoke *satisfying gift* (African)
Saturday *see* born on Saturday
Saturday's *see* Saturday's child
saved Moselle *saved from the water* (Egyptian), Mozelle
saw-toothed Sierra (Spanish); Serra (English)

scarlet *see* colored
scented Kasturi (Hindi)
schemer *see* dearest little schemer
scholar Pandita, Pragnya (Hindi); *scholar, student* Medarda (Latin), Meda, Medardas
Scotland Caledonia *from Scotland* (Latin)
sculptured *see* jewel
section Izara *section of a tree* (Hausa)
secure Selma (Arabic) • *peaceful or secure* An (Vietnamese)
sea Kai (Hawaiian) • *a sea urchin* Vana (Polynesian) • *beautiful nymph of the sea, sea goddess* Thetis (Greek), Heti, Thetes, Thetisa, Thetos • *coral from the sea* Coral (Latin-Greek), Coralie, Coraline, Corel • *daughter of the sea, flower of the sea, sea star; warm-hearted* Cordelia (Celtic), Cordalia, Cordeelia, Delia • *from a city near the sea* Aleria (Greek), Aleras, Alleras, Allerie, Alleris • *from the sea* Pasha (Greek); Palasha, Pashka Pelageya (Russian) • *girl from the sea* Adrienne (Greek), Adria, Adriana, Adriane, Adrianna, Adrianne • *girl of the sea, sea gull* Larina (Latin), Lareena, Larena, Larianna, Larine, Rina • *guardian of the sea, mortal day* Meredith (Old Welsh), Meridith • *jewel or jewel of the sea* Cordelia (Welsh), Cordelie, Delia, Della • *large sea bird* Sula (Icelandic) • *nymph from the sea; one from the sea, swimmer* Nerine (Greek), Nereen, Neri, Nerice, Nerin, Nerissa • *of the sea* Maryse (Dutch); Maritza (German); Pelagia (Greek); Dorisa (Hawaiian); Marina (Latin), Marisa, Marisha, Marissa, Marrisa, Merisa, Merissa, Morissa; Dylana (Old Welsh), Dylane; Delma, Marita (Spanish) • *sea friend* Erwina, Irvette (Old English) • *sea or seawater* Kai (Hawaiian) • *sea star* Maris (Latin), Marissa, Marras, Marris • *she lives near the sea* Marola (Latin), Arola, Marala, Maro, Ola • *shore of the sea* Morgana (Old Welsh) • *the sea green jewel* Beryl (Greek) • *thinking of*

the sea Halimeda (Greek), Hallie,
Meda
sea gull *see* girl of the sea, sea gull
seabird *see* gull, seabird
seacoast Ora *seacoast or shore* (Latin-
Old English), Orabel, Orabelle
searches Questa *one who searches*
(French)
seashore Delora *from the seashore*
(Latin), Dellora, Ellora, Lora • *pastureland or seashore* Arva (Latin)
season Nasha *born during the rainy season* (African); Masika (Swahili) •
from the Easter season Paschasia
(Latin), Pascasia, Pascha, Pascia,
Pasia
season's *see* beginning
seawater *see* sea
second *see* born
secret Alumit (Hebrew) • Razilee *my
secret* (Hebrew), Razili • *secret spirit*
Zina (African)
secretive *see* hidden or secretive
secure *see* open
security Amina (Arabic) • *peace, safety
and security* AN (Vietnamese)
seduce Kimatra (Hindi)
seeds Zera (Hebrew)
seek Zita *to seek* (Greek)
seeker Petula *a seeker* (Latin), Petulia
seizer Hara (Hindi)
select Elita *a special person, select*
(Latin), Ellita, Lita • *one of select birth*
Asabi (Yoruban)
selfish Makadisa *she was always selfish*
(Baduma)
sensible Sophronia *sensible one*
(Greek), Sonja, Sonya
sensitive Min (Chinese)
sent *see* Lord
sentence Pankti (Hindi)
sentinel *see* guardian or sentinel
separation *see* broad separation
serene Serena *bright, fair, serene one;
girl with the tranquil heart* (Latin) •
calm, serene; loving sister Delphine
(Greek), Delphina, Delphinia • *spiritual, serene, and peaceful* Shanta
(Hindi)
serpent Ophelia (Greek), Ofelia,
Ofilia, Ophelie • *noble serpent* Ethelinda (Old English) • *serpent-maid*
Ortrude (Old German)
servant Jovita *little servant of the Lord*

(Latin), Jovi, Jovia, Jovitah, Jovitta,
Vita • *pretty servant* Jolenta (Latin),
Jola, Jolanta, Jollanta, Jollenta,
Olenta
seventh *see* born on the seventh, seventh
shade Zillah (Hebrew)
shadow Zilla (Hebrew); Chaaya
(Hindi)
shake Reta *to shake* (African), Reeta,
Rheta, Rhetta
sharp *see* pointed
Sheba *see* Saba
Shedding *see* illumination
shelled *see* corn
shepherdess Solange *good shepherdess*
(Latin), Salangi, Salangia • *sheperdess, wandering one* Wanda (Old
German-Slavic)
shelter Anchal (Hindi)
she-wolf Randi (Old English),
Randie, Randy
shield *see* bearer
shine *see* inspired
shines Zoheret *she shines* (Hebrew)
shining Kunshi (Hindi) • *an honor or
shining* Anju (Hindi) • *bright, shining
sword* Egberta (Old English), Egbertina, Egbertine • *brilliant or shining* Alohi (Hawaiian) • *famous one,
shining* Lara (Latin) • *shining battle
maid* Bertilde (Old English) • *shining counselor* Bertrade (Old English)
• *shining, glorious one* Bertha (Old
German), Berta, Berthe; Peke
(Hawaiian) • *shining or morning light*
Noga (Hebrew) • *shining with fame*
Roberta (Old English), Bobbette,
Robina, Robine, Robinia
Shinto Miya (Japanese)
ship Kelsey *from the ship island* (Scandinavian), Kelcie, Kelsy, Kesley,
Keslie • Chelsea *ship's port* (Old English), Chelsey
shoot *see* palm
shore Kinaari (Hindi); Hama (Japanese) • *riverbank, shore* Riva
(French), Ree, Reeva, Reva • *seacoast
or shore* Ora (Latin-Old English),
Orabel, Orabelle • *shore child* Hamako
(Japanese) • *shore field* Urano (Japanese) • *shore of the sea* Morgana (Old
Welsh) • *the song of the waves on the
shore* Lealiki (Polynesian)

short Thieu *be missing, be short; the minority* (Vietnamese) • *literature; short; striped tiger; to twist* Van (Vietnamese) • *very short* Achla (Hindi)

shouldered Platona *broad-shouldered* (Greek) • *fair-shouldered* Nuala (Irish-Gaelic) • *white-shouldered one* Fenella (Celtic), Nella; Fionnula (Irish-Gaelic), Finella

show *see* elder sister; mind; to show

shrouded *see* mist

shrub Netia *plant or shrub* (Hebrew), Neta, Netta • *the heather flower or shrub* Heather (Middle English)

shy Bertilla *kind and shy* (Latin), Bertila • *modest, shy or violet* Yolanda (Greek), Yolande, Yolante

side *see* field

sight Drishti, Drishya, Dristi, Iksha (Hindi)

sighted *see* dim-sighted one

sign Sema *a sign from the heavens* (Greek) • *carefully; strange; to abstain from, to fear; to sign* Ky (Vietnamese) • *sign of the leader* Richmal (Old German), Richma • *sign, omen* Senalda (Spanish), Alda, Enalda, Sena

signer Signa *a signer* (Latin)

silent Gilly *quiet, silent* (Mende) • *silent little one* Shysie (Native American) • *the silent one* Tacita (Latin), Cita, Tace, Tacey, Tacy

silk *see* silk-cloth child

silken Serica (Latin)

silver Yin (Chinese); Rajata (Hindi) • *like silver* Ariana (Welsh); Ari, Ariane, Adriann, Arianne (English) • *silver-haired* Tatiana (Latin), Tatia, Tatianas, Tatianna

silvery Gina (Japanese) • *silvery one* Argenta (Latin)

sing Yedda *singer, to sing* (Old English) • *sing, singer* Gale (Old Norse), Abigail, Gail • *to sing with trills* Trilby (Italian)

singer Charmaine (Latin), Charmain, Charmian • *a singer* Kokila (Hindi); Signy (Latin); Signe, Signi (Scandinavian) • *a sweetly singing mermaid siren* Sirena (Greek) • *inspired; mountain; singer* Arnina (Hebrew) • *singer, to sing* Yedda (Old English) • *sing, singer* Gale (Old Norse), Abigail, Gail • *singing lark or skylark* Lark

(Middle English) • *sweet singer* Evadne (Greek)

single Gala (Old Norse) • *once, a single time; the one and only* Semele (Latin), Semela • *one, single one* Mona (Greek)

sins *see* destroyer of sins

siren Lurine (German) • *a sweetly singing mermaid siren* Sirena (Greek) • *siren of the river Rhine* Lorelei (German)

sister Delphine *calm, serene; loving sister* (Greek), Delphina, Delphinia • *elder sister; mind; to show* Chi (Vietnamese) • *half-sister* Beka (Hebrew), Becca, Bekah, Bekka • *Mars' sister; war goddess* Alala (Greek) • *my elder little sister* Kaya (Hopi) • *older sister* Aneko (Japanese); Minya (Native American)

sisterly Adelpha (Greek)

sit Magara *to sit or to stay* (Mashona)

Siva *see* the god Siva

skill Metis *skill, wisdom* (Greek)

skilled Praveena (Hindi)

skillful Kaushali (Hindi); Wapeka (Native American) • *dexterous, skillful* Dextra (Latin)

skin Gozy (Swahili)

sky Hana (Arapaho); Lani (Hawaiian); Ambar (Hindi) • *blue sky* Azura (Old French) • *chieftain from the sky* Kulani (Hawaiian), Lani • *nymph of the sky, she-bear* Ursa (Greek), Ursal, Ursala, Ursas, Ursel, Yursa • *space, sky* Antariksha (Hindi)

skylark *see* lark

sleek *see* black

slender Wandis *lithe and slender* (Old German), Wanda • *slender bamboo* Shino (Japanese) • *slender-fair* Keelin (Irish-Gaelic), Caolinn • *slender one* Belisa (Latin) • *slender reed* Cattima (Latin), Catima • *slender, soft* Malva (Greek), Melba, Melva

slenderness Tanima (Hindi)

slim Asela *slim ash tree* (Spanish) • *slim girl* Latangi (Hindi)

slope Saka (Japanese)

small Kiss (Hungarian) • *a small bell* Nola (Latin), Nolana • *a small bird* Jena (Arabic), Jenna • *a small bracelet* Armilla (Latin), Armalla, Armillas, Armillia, Mila, Milla • *a small poem*

Kavni (Hindi) • *a small smile* Koemi (Japanese) • *gladiolus flower or small sword* Gladys (Welsh) • *little, small* Beti (Gypsy) • *small creeper* Latika (Hindi) • *small earth* Inika (Hindi) • *small field* Ohara (Japanese) • *small, old, wise one* Shannon (Irish-Gaelic), Shani, Shanon, Shannah, Shannan, Shannen, Shauna, Shawna, Shawni • *small woman* Kalere (African)

smile Aashi, Misha (Hindi) • Koemi *a small smile* (Japanese) • *pretty smile* Qianru (Chinese) • *smile of truth* Maemi (Japanese)

smiling Basimah (Arabic)

smooth *see* mild, smooth, soft

snow Haima (Hindi); Istas (Native American) • *deep snow* Miyuki (Japanese), Yuki • *snow or extreme whiteness* Neva (Spanish) • *the snow maiden* Yepa (Native American) • *white as snow* Nevada (Spanish)

snowbird Chilali (Native American)

snowflake Nipha (Greek)

snowy Nevada (Latin), Navada, Neva, Neveda • *snowy or white-haired* Nix (Latin)

soft Eulalia *a soft-spoken woman; fair speech, well-spoken one* (Greek), Eula, Eulalia, Eulalie • *mild, smooth, soft* Lenis (Latin), Lena, Leneta, Lenita • *slender, soft* Malva (Greek), Melba, Melva • *soft, gentle* Anana (African)

solemn *see* disposition

solitary Mona (Latin); Casilda (Spanish), Casilde, Cassil, Cassilda, Silda • *lone one, solitary* Lona (Middle English), Loni, Lonna

solution Yukti *trick, solution* (Hindi)

song Chantal (French-Latin), Chandal, Chantalle; Gita (Hindi); Duana (Irish-Gaelic), Dwana; Carmen (Latin), Carmina, Carmine, Carmita, Charmaine • *a lyric song or little ode* Odelette (French), Odelet • *beautiful music, song* Melody (Greek), Melodie • *joyful song* Ranita (Israeli) • *lover of song* Philomela (Greek) • *melodious song* Mahala (Hebrew), Mahalia, Mahla, Mehala • *melody, song* Odele (Greek), Odelette, Odell • *my song* Liron, Shiri (Hebrew), Shira, Shirah • *song of the nightingale* Questa (Latin) • *song or melody* Mangena

(Hebrew), Mangina • *song thrush* Mavis (French) • *the song of the waves on the shore* Lealiki (Polynesian)

songbird Sora *a warbling songbird* (Native American)

soothing Lulu *soothing influence* (Anglo-Saxon)

sorceress Medea (Greek), Edea, Madea, Medeah

sorrow Deidre *compassion, sorrow* (Celtic) • *woman of sorrow* Pelagia (Latin), Pelaga, Pelagi, Pelagias

sorrows Dolores (Spanish), Delora, Delores, Deloris, Delorita

soul Ruhi (Hindi); Duscha (Russian) • *pure in soul* Enid (Celtic) • *soul or spirit* Alma (Spanish)

sound Kani (Hawaiian) • *echo, reflected sound* Echo (Greek) • *the sound of running water* Sarik (Turkish) • *sound of angels* Artemas (Hebrew), Arta, Artamas, Artema, Artima, Artimas, Tema

source Gen (Japanese)

southerner Dacey (Irish-Gaelic), Dacia, Dacie, Dacy

sovereign Kimi (Japanese), Kimie, Kimiko, Kimiyo

space *see* space, sky

spark Fulki (Hindi)

sparrow *see* beauty, sparrow, or trumpet

speak Cheyenne *to speak strangely* (Native American), Cheyanne

speaker Lalage *cheerful speaker* (Greek), Alage, Lallage • *speaker or creator* Nata (Native American) • *speaker with God* Theola (Greek)

speaking Eula *sweet in speaking* (Greek)

spear Ceara (Irish-Gaelic) • *bear/spear maid* Berengaria (Latin) • *elfin spear or spike* Ordella (Old German) • *spear friend* Orva (Old English) • *spear keen* Jarvia (Old German) • *spear loved* Gertrude (Old German), Gertruda, Gertrudis, Trudy • *spear maiden* Gari (Old German); Truda (Polish) • *spear mighty* Geraldine (Old German), Geraldina, Gerhardine, Giralda, Jerri

special Naisha (Hindi) • Elita *a special person, select* (Latin), Ellita, Lita

speech Eulalia *a soft-spoken woman; fair*

speech, well-spoken one (Greek), Eula, Eulalia, Eulalie • *auspicious speech, good repute* Euphemia (Greek), Eufemia, Euphemie • Amira (Hebrew)

spell *see* charm

spent Vana (Congo)

spice Livona (Hebrew) • *ginger flower or ginger spice* Ginger (Latin)

spike *see* elfin spear or spike

spinning Zihna (Hopi)

spiral Helice (Greek)

spirit Kamali (Mashona) • *corn spirit and daughter of the earth* Onatah (Iroquois Indian) • *elevated, lofty, of jolly spirits* Elata (Latin), Elatia, Ellata, Lati • *forest or wood spirit* Vedis (Old German), Vedi, Veedis • *forest spirit* Asiza (African) • *secret spirit* Zina (African) • *soul or spirit* Alma (Spanish) • *spirit angel* Angeni (Native American) • *spirit or supreme goddess* Isis (Egyptian) • *Thor spirit* Thordis (Old Norse), Thordia

spiritual Ruhin (Hindi) • *peaceful friend* Winifred (Old German) • *spiritual power* Turya (Hindi) • *spiritual, serene, and peaceful* Shanta (Hindi)

spiritually *see* helpful

splendid Maja (Arabic), Majidah • *bright, polished, splendid* Jala (Arabic) • *splendid gift* Eudora (Greek) • *splendid one* Indira (Hindi); Indra, Indria • *splendid or beautiful one* Clytie (Greek)

splendor Ojal (Hindi)

spoke Mirella *God spoke* (Hebrew), Mireil, Mirela, Mirelle, Miriella, Mirilla

spoken Eulalia *a soft-spoken woman; fair speech, well-spoken one* (Greek), Eula, Eulalia, Eulalie • *well spoken of* Effie (Greek), Eppie, Euphemia

spot *see* beauty

spread Taipa *to spread wings* (Miwok)

spring Rabia (African); Chun (Chinese); Nana (Hawaiian); Aviva (Hebrew), Avivah, Viva; Gen (Japanese); Kelda (Old Norse), Kelly • *born in early spring* Primavera (Latin), Avera, Avaria, Vera • *born in spring* Haru (Japanese), Hayu • *born in spring child* Haruko (Japanese) • *bright leaves; bright spring flower* Akina (Japanese) • *fruitful woman, of the*

spring Cerelia (Latin), Cerellia, Cerallua, Cerelly, Erlia • *goddess of spring, youth* Hebe (Greek), Hebbe • *of the spring* Cerella (Latin); Cerelia (English) • *spring flower* Eranthe (Greek) • *spring or harvest* Rabi (Arabic)

springlike Verna (Latin), Verda, Verena, Verneta, Vernita, Virina, Virna

springtime Primavera (Spanish) • *the springtime of the year* Spring (Old English)

sprite *active sprite* Disa (Old German) • *a little water sprite* Nixie (Old German)

spy Pranidhi (Hindi)

squashbug Toski *a squashbug* (Hopi)

stable Eustacia *stable, tranquil* (Latin), Stacie, Stacey

staff Virgilia *rod or staff bearer* (Latin) • *staff of the Goths* Gustava (Swedish)

stammerer *see* little stammerer

stammers *see* lisps

standard *see* alone, standard setter

star Estelle (French), Estella, Estrella, Estrellita, Stelle; Hoku (Hawaiian); Esther (Hebrew), Ester, Hester, Hesther, Hetty; Dhruva (Hindi); Hoshi (Japanese); Stella (Latin); Star (Old English); Swetlana (Old German), Svetlana; Esta (Persian) • *brilliant one, brilliant star* Electra (Greek), Lectra • *daughter of the sea, flower of the sea, sea star; warm-hearted* Cordelia (Celtic), Cordalia, Cordeelia, Delia • *evening or evening star* Hesper (Greek), Hespera, Hespira • *highest star* Maice (Latin), Maise, Mayce • *rising star* Citlalic (Aztec) • *sea star* Maris (Latin), Marissa, Marras, Marris • *star-like* Sidra (Latin), Siddra, Sidras • *star of the morning* Danica (Slavic), Anica, Dannica, Donica • *star or star-like* Asta (Greek), Astra • *the evening star* Vespera (Latin); Trella (Spanish), Trela, Trellas

starred *see* ill-starred one

stars *see* belonging to the stars

starting *see* point

stay *see* sit

steadfast *see* little steadfast one

steady *see* flowering

stem Mika (Japanese), Mikie, Mikiyo

stone Ishi (Japanese), Ishie, Ishiko,

Ishiyo • *a gem or precious stone* Gemma (Greek) • *angel of precious stone* Nitika (Native American) • *a precious stone* Opal (Sanskrit), Opalina, Opaline • *February birthstone, precious stone* (Greek), Amathist, Amathiste, Amethist • *hewn stone* Gazit (Hebrew), Gisa • *jade stone* Jade (Spanish), Ijada • *river of black stones* Guadalupe (Arabic), Lupe, Lupita • *violet colored stone* Ione (Greek), Iona • *white stone* Izusa (Native American)

stony *see* from a stony place

storehouse *see* field

stork Koko (Japanese) • *rice field stork* Tazu (Japanese)

storm Storm *a storm or tempest* (Old English) • *fight, strife; refuge from the storm* Hedwig (Old German), Heda, Hedvig, Hedvige, Hedy • *stormy one* Tempest (Old French)

strange Vividha (Hindi) • *carefully; strange; to abstain from, to fear; to sign* Ky (Vietnamese)

strangely *see* speak

stranger Varina (Slavic) • *lovely stranger* Barbara (Latin), Babbette, Babete, Babita, Barbette; Johppa (Hebrew), Joappa, Johppah • Babara (Hawaiian)

stream Rhea (Greek), Rea; Nipa (Todas) • *a brook or stream* Rilla (German), Rillette

strength Birgitta (Norweigian), Gitta, Gitte • *divine strength* Asta (Old Norse) • *God is my strength* Ezrela (Hewbrew), Esraela, Ezraella • *honor, strength, virtue* Bryna (Irish-Gaelic) • *noble strength* Audrey (Old English), Audrie, Audry • *resolute strength, strength* Bridget (Irish-Gaelic), Beret, Berget, Bridgette, Brietta, Brigid, Brigida, Brigitte, Brita • *right hand, strength* Yesima (Hebrew), Yemina • *strength of the Lord* Ozora (Hebrew) • *to regain strength* Reva (Latin) • *traveler, stranger, or pilgrim* Perry (Latin), Perri, Perriann, Perrie, Perrin • *woman of strength* Brianna (Celtic), Briana

strengthening *see* aid

strife Hedda (Old German), Heddi, Heddy • *fight, strife; refuge from the*

storm Hedwig (Old German), Heda, Hedvig, Hedvige, Hedy

string Mala (Hindi)

striped *see* literature; short; striped tiger; to twist

striver *see* goal

strong Abira (Hebrew), Hasina • Meghan (Celtic), Megan; Etana (Hebrew); Kari (Modern U.S.); Lola (Spanish), Lolita • *heroine, strong* Gavrila (Hebrew), Gavriella, Gavrielle • *little masterful one, little strong one* Bernadette (Old German) • *protective, strong* Brigid (Celtic) • *strong and brave* Brice (Celtic), Bryce • *strong and powerful* Adira (Hebrew) • *strong and womanly* Carol (Latin), Caryl, Karol; Kalola (Hawaiian) • *strong, forceful* Brenna (Celtic) • *strong, healthy one* Valentina (Latin), Valeda, Valentia, Valentine, Valida • *strong in love* Astrid (Old German) • *strong-minded* Alcina (Greek) • *strong one* Brianna (Irish-Gaelic) • *strong, womanly* Karla (Modern U.S.), Carla • *the strong one* Drusilla (Latin), Drucie, Drusa, Drusie • *the strong, sturdy oak* Ituha (Native American)

strong-willed Tisha (African)

stronghold *see* battle maid, battle stronghold, battle wand

student *see* scholar, student

sturdy *see* oak

stutterer Ina (Hausa)

succeeds Naila *one who succeeds* (Arabic), Nailah

successful *see* to bloom or be successful

succession Willa *unbroken succession* (Arabic)

sudden Amrusha (Hindi)

sullen Doreen *the sullen one* (Irish-Gaelic), Dorene, Korina

summer Maili *a gentle summer breeze* (Polynesian) • *born in summer* Natsu (Japanese)

sun Drisa *daughter of the sun* (Hindi), Dreesa, DreeshaDrisana • *gift of the sun* Elidi (Greek) • *rising sun* Levana (Latin) • *sun heart* Sadzi • *sun or sunlight* Appoline (Greek) • *sun worshipers* Saura (Hindi) • *the sun* Sula (Icelandic); Nolcha (Native American); Kira (Persian); Kalinda

(Sanskrit), Kaleena, Kalina, Kalindi
• *the sun god* Surya (Hindi)
Sunday *see* born on Sunday
Sunday's *see* child
Sundown *see* cloud
sunlight *see* sun or sunlight
sunny Amshula (Hindi), Anshula
sunrise Usha (Hindi)
sunset *see* sunset glow
sunshine Taniya (Sunshine); Ova
(Bini); Solana (Spanish), Solenne
super-excellent Jin (Japanese)
superior Jigisha (Hindi) • *of superior
rank* Aldora (Old English), Aleldra •
Anevay (Native American)
supernatural *see* power
supplanter Jacoba *the supplanter*
(Hebrew-Latin), Jacobah, Jacobba,
Jacobina, Jakoba, Jaime, Jami, Jamie,
Jayme, Jaymi, Jaymie; Jacqueline
(Old French), Jaclyn, Jacquelyn,
Jacquetta
supportive *see* helpful
supreme *see* goddess
surprise *see* divine surprise
surrender Parbarti (Hindi)
surrendered Vana (Congo); Saranya
(Hindi)
surrounded *see* encircled
swallow Sisika (Native American) •
the swallow Celandine (Greek)
swan Hamsa, Hansa, Marala, Sarasa
(Hindi), Hansini
swans *see* lady of the swans
sweet Nemy (Mende); Mandisa
(Xhosa) • *honeylike, sweet or gentle*
Melosa (Spanish) • *pleasant, sweet*
Hedy (Greek) • *sweet as honey*
Devasha (Hebrew), Devash; Melina
(Latin) • *sweet basil* Rihana (Muslin),
Rhiana, Rhlanna, Riana, Rianna •

sweet friend, sweet wine Melvina
(Latin), Melva • *sweet gum tree*
Alaqua (Native American) • *sweet in
speaking* Eula (Greek) • *sweet, lovely*
Sayen (Native American) • *sweet one*
Dulcie (Latin), Delcine, Dulcea,
Dulciana, Dulcine, Dulcinea; Honey
(Old English); Sakari (Todas) • *sweet
singer* Evadne (Greek) • *sweet-smelling
tree* Chan (Cambodian) • *sweet virgin*
Parthenia (Greek), Parthena,
Parthinia • *sweet-voiced* Islean
(Celtic), Isla, Isleana, Isleen • *the
sweet-smelling randa tree* Randa (Arabic) • *the sweet woman* Vevina (Latin),
Vena, Vevine, Vina
sweet-natured Priya (Hindi), Priyal,
Priyam, Priyanka, Priyata, Pryasha,
Pryati
sweetbriar *see* rose
sweetheart Habika (African); Jiya
(Hindi) • *loved one, sweetheart* Kalila
(Arabic)
sweetly Sirena *a sweetly singing mermaid siren* (Greek) • Elysia *sweetly
blissful* (Latin)
sweetness Anika *sweetness of face*
(Hausa) • *sweetness, like an orange*
Cam (Vietnamese)
swift Rewa, Turanya (Hindi) • *fleet
one, swift* Fleta (Old English) • *swift
runner* Atalanta (Greek), Atalani,
Atalante, Tala, Talanta
swimmer *see* nymph from the sea;
one from the sea, swimmer
sword Zeva (Greek) • *bright, shining
sword* Egberta (Old English), Egbertina, Egbertine • *gladiolus flower
or small sword* Gladys (Welsh)
sympathizes Maurilla *woman who sympathizes* (Latin), Mauralia, Maurilia

—— **T** ——

talent *see* girl of great talent
talents Tabia (Swahili)
talking Vailea *the talking water* (Polynesian)
tall Temira (Hebrew), Timora; Taka
(Japanese) • *the tall white flower*

Daffodil (Greek), Dafodil • *very tall*
Jola (Mende)
tame Laka (Hawaiian)
tansy *see* flower
tassel Takala *corn tassel* (Hopi) • *corn
tassel flower* Talasi (Hopi)

taste Memtba (Miwok)
tasty Ruchira (Hindi)
tawny *see* dark or tawny
teacher Moriah *God is my teacher* (Hebrew), Mariah • *most wise teacher* Fronia (Latin), Fronnia, Fronniah, Onia
tempest *see* storm
tempestuous Tempest *tempestuous one* (French)
temple Miya (Japanese)
temptress *see* lovely temptress
ten Machi *ten thousand* (Japanese) • *ten or tenth* Dixie (French) • *the tenth* Decima (Latin)
tenacious Tansy *tenacious one* (Latin)
tender Komali (Hindi) • *affectionate, tender* Fonda (English) • *tender beloved* Morna (Celtic), Myrna
tenderness Mahala (Hebrew), Mahalah, Mahalia
tent *see* girl of the tent
tenth *see* ten or tenth
test Nissa *to test* (Hebrew), Nisse (Scandinavian)
thankful *see* girl
thanks Jendayi *give thanks* (African)
thin Rama (Hausa)
thinker *see* believer, thinker
thinking Minerva *the thinking one* (Latin), Minette • *thinking of the sea* Halimeda (Greek), Hallie, Meda
third Mikazuki *the moon of the third night* (Japanese) • *the third child* Tertia (Latin), Teria, Tertias, Tia
thirst Trisha (Hindi), Trusha; Ita (Irish-Gaelic)
thistle Cynara *artichoke or thistle* (Greek) • *thistle flower* Azami (Japanese)
Thor Thorberta *brillance of Thor* (Old Norse) • *Thor spirit* Thordis (Old Norse), Thordia
Thorn Meriwa (Eskimo)
thorned *see* pointed
thorny Acacia (Greek) • *thorny cactus* Sabra (Hebrew), Sabrina
thought Vritika, Yochana (Hindi) • *a thought* Pansy (French)
thoughts *see* innermost thoughts
thousand Osen (Japanese) • *eight thousand* Yachi (Japanese), Yachiko, Yachiyo
thread Nima (Hebrew) • *woven with a double thread* Twyla (Middle English), Twila
three Ba *grandmother; poison; residue; three* Ba (Vietnamese) • *three days* Mikka (Japanese)
thrush Sisika (Native American) • *blackbird, thrush* Merle (Latin), Merl, Merlina, Merline, Merola, Meryl, Myrlene • *song thrush* Mavis (French); *thrush* Amaui (Hawaiian)
thunder Bronte (Greek); Thora (Old Norse) • *crash of thunder* Taima (Native American) • *red thunder* Shappa (Native American)
thunderbolt Tama (Native American)
thunderpeal Nari (Japanese), Nariko
Thursday *see* born on Thursday
Tiber *see* river
tide *see* flowing back of the tide
tiger Tora (Japanese) • *literature; short; striped tiger; to twist* Van (Vietnamese)
tigress Namrah (Hindi)
time Bela (Hindi) • *ancient time* Prasheila (Hindi) • *at a good time* Opportuna (Latin), Opportina • *black; time* Kala (Hindi) • *born during a prosperous time* Neema (Swahili) • *once, a single time; the one and only* Semele (Latin), Semela • *time of opportunity* Toki (Japanese) • *time, the destroyer* Kali (Hindi)
times Priscilla *from past or primitive times* (Latin), Cilla, Prisca; Sila (American) • *of pleasant times* Halona (Native American), Halonna
tin *see* lead
tiny Reseda *from a tiny flower, the mignonette flower* (Latin), Raseda, Raseta, Reseta, Seta • *tiny fighter* Elga (Anglo-Saxon), Ellga • *tiny Mary* Marella (Old German), Marela, Marelya, Marla • *tiny queen* Halette (Anglo-Saxon), Haletta, Hallette
title *see* honor
together Syna (Greek) • *joined together* Pega (Greek), Pegma • *one, together* Una (Latin)
topaz *see* gem
torch Beora (Hebrew), Beore • *a torch, light* Lenka (Czech); Elli, Leena (Estonian); Helen (Greek), Alena, Elaine, Elanore, Elene, Eleni, Elenore, Ellen, Ellette, Ellyn,

Helena, Helene, Ileana, Lenora, Lenore, Leonora, Nelly, Nitsa, Nora, Norah; Jelena, Liolya, Olena, Yelena (Russian); Iliana (Spanish) • *the flaming torch* Kalama (Hawaiian)

tortoise Toy (Chinese) • *child of the tortoise* Kameko (Japanese)

touch Helki *to touch* (Miwok)

tower Magdala *a tower* (Greek), Magda • *from a high tower* Malina (Hebrew), Lina, Mali, Malin, Mallina

trader *see* marketplace

tradition Shaili (Hindi)

train *see* night train

tranquil Somila (Hindi); Haruko (Japanese) • *bright, fair, serene one; girl with the tranquil heart* Serena (Latin) • *stable, tranquil* Eustacia (Latin), Stacie, Stacey • *the tranquil* Yasu (Japanese) • *tranquil, untroubled* Evania (Greek), Evannia, Vani, Vania

tranquility Peace (Latin)

transgressor Avera (Hebrew)

traveler Margi (Hindi) • *traveler, stranger, or pilgrim* Perry (Latin), Perri, Perriann, Perrie, Perrin

treasure Seema (Hebrew), Cyma, Seena, Sima, Simah; Takara (Japanese) • *a treasure* Zhen (Chinese) • *girl who is treasured* Castora (Latin), Casta, Castara, Castera • *our dear treasure* Ezara (Hebrew), Ezaria, Ezarra, Ezarras, Zara

treasured *see* child

tree Elmina (Old English) • *a blossoming tree* Pua (Polynesian) • *alder tree grove* La Verne (Old French), Lavergne • *a tree branch* Dalya (Hebrew), Dalia, Dalice, Daliya, Dalit • *a vine growing on an oak tree* Papina (Miwok) • *bay or laurel tree* Daphne (Greek) • *big tree* Adoette (Native American; Ilana (Hebrew) • *cedar tree* Arna (Hebrew), Arnice, Arnit • *cypress tree* Tirza (Hebrew) • *fir or cedar tree* Ornice (Hebrew), Orna, Ornit • *flower of forgetfulness, flower of the lotus tree* Lotus (Egyptian) • *from a palm tree* Phenice (Hebrew), Phenica, Venice • *from the ash tree meadow* Ashley (Old English), Ashleigh, Ashley • *from the linden tree island* Lindsay (Old English), Lindsay,

Lyndsey • *girl of the magnolia tree* Magnolia (Anglo-Saxon) • *hazelnut tree* Hazel (Old English) • *holly tree* Holly (Old English), Holen • *juniper tree* Geneva (Old French) • *lime tree* Linnea (Old Norse) • *oak tree* Alona (Hebrew) • *of the elder tree* Nelda (Old English), Elda, Nell, Nellda • *of the laurel tree* Dafna (Hebrew), Daphna • *olive branch or olive tree* Olive (Latin), Livia, Nola, Olga, Olivette, Olivia • *orange; orange tree* Alani (Hawaiian) • *palm tree* Tamara (Hebrew) • *parade, promenade; poplar tree* Alameda (Spanish) • *pear tree* Le (Chinese) • *pine tree* Orinda (Hebrew) • *plum blossom; plum tree* Li (Chinese) • *plum tree field* Umeno (Japanese) • *section of a tree* Izara (Hausa) • *slim ash tree* Asela (Spanish) • *sweet gum tree* Alaqua (Hawaiian) • *sweet-smelling tree* Chan (Cambodian) • *the lotus tree* Sadira (Persian) • *the mythical mandara tree* Mandara (Hindi) • *tree peony blossom* Mu-Tan (Chinese) • *the sacred Sala tree* Sala (Hindi) • *the sweet-smelling randa tree* Randa (Arabic) • *the willow tree* Willow (Middle English) • *yew tree* Iva (Old French), Ivanna

trembling *see* child

tresses *see* raven

trick *see* trick, solution

trills *see* sing

triple *see* cord

triumphant Sanjaya (Hindi), Sanjita

Troy *see* city

true Vera (Latin), Verena, Verene, Verina, Verine, Verla • *industrious and true* Millicent (Old German), Melisande, Melisenda, Mellicent, Milicent • *true to her word* Willtrude (Old English), Truda, Willa

trumpet *see* beauty, sparrow or trumpet

trusted Alethea *girl to be trusted* (Greek), Aleta, Aletha, Alitha, Letha, Litha, Lithea, Thea • *trusted friend* Netis (Native American)

trustworthy Imani (Hindi); Yori (Japanese), Joriko; Ameena (Swahili), Ameenah, Aminah, Aminae • Menjuiwe *the trustworthy* (West African)

truth Yakini (African); Amissa (Hebrew), Amisa, Amita; Jun (Chinese) • *exalted, fulfillment or truth* Almira (Arabic), Almeria, Almire, Elmira • *the truth* Aletea (Spanish)

truthful Alice (Greek), Alike, Aliz, Alizka, Lici; Alisa (Bulgarian); Alica, Eliska (Czech); Aleta (English), Aletha, Ali, Alicea, Alis, Alisha, Alissa, Alithia, Allie, Ally, Allyce, Allys, Alyce, Alycia, Elisha, Ellie, Elsa, Elsie, Ilisha; Alix (French); Adelicia (German), Alexia, Alexie, Elise, Elschen, Else, Ilse; Alika (Hawaiian); Alise (Latvian); Elza (Slavic); Licha (Spanish) • *little truthful one* Alison (Irish-Gaelic) • *noble, truthful* Alita (Spanish) • *smith of truth* Macmi (Japanese) • *truthful*

child Maeko (Japanese) • *truthful one* Alethea (Greek), Aleta, Aletha, Alitha, Letha, Litha, Lithea, Thea

Tuesday *see* born on Tuesday

tulasi *see* plant

tulip *see* flower

turquoise Phiroza (Hindi)

turtle Awanata (Miwok)

twice *see* double or twice

twilight Sharvari (Hindi)

twin Gemini (Greek), Gemina, Geminine; Mini (English); Nashota (Native American) • *a twin* Thomasa (Greek), Tammy, Thomasina, Thomasine, Tomasina, Tomasine • *twin child* Panya (African)

twins *see* born after twins

twist *see* literature; short; striped tiger; to twist

— U —

unblossomed *see* maiden

unbounded *see* free and unbounded

unbroken *see* succession

unconquerable Ajay (Hindi) • *unconquerable heroine* Zelda (Old German), Griselda

undefeated Aparajita (Hindi)

understanding Eba (Ngala) • *understanding or intelligence* Bina (Hebrew)

unexpected *see* gift

unexpressive *see* flat or unexpressive

union Sanjukta, Yuti (Hindi)

unique Farida (African); Advika, Adwita (Hindi)

unity Ona, Una (Latin)

universal Emma *universal one* (Old German), Ema, Emelina, Emeline, Emelyne, Emmaline

unknown Fatima (Arabic), Fatimah • Cocheta (Native American)

untamed Wilda (Anglo-Saxon) • *wild, untamed* Thera (Greek)

untouched Karida *untouched or virginal* (Arabic)

untroubled *see* tranquil, untroubled

unwilling *see* lady

urchin *see* a sea urchin

useful Ophelia (Greek), Ofelia, Ophelie

— V —

vale *see* far

valley Tani (Japanese); Dena (Native American) • *dweller in a valley or glen* Glenna (Welsh), Glenda, Glenette, Glennette, Glynis • *eagle valley* Arden (Old English), Ardenia • *from the far*

valley, from the vale or hollow Valonia (Latin), Vallonia, Valoniah • *from the valley* Dena (Old English), Deana, Deane, Deena; Dahlia (Old German) • *girl of the valley* Machutte (Old German), Machute • *little valley*

Glynis (Welsh), Glinys, Glynas • *she of the valley* Napea (Latin) • *valley child* Taniko (Japanese) • *valley of flowers* Algoma (Native American)

valuable Anagi (Hindi) • *valuable gift* Ekika (Hawaiian); Duci (Hungarian)

value *see* high

vanquisher *see* vanquisher of all foes

vapor *see* cloud, mist or vapor

vehement *see* maiden

veil *see* mist

veiled *see* mystery

velvety Velvet (Middle English)

veneration Grimonia *woman of veneration* (Latin), Grimona, Mona

verdant Chloe *verdant, young* (Greek)

versatile Dalmar (African)

vestments *see* city

victorious Faiza (African)m Faizah; Jasweer, Jayavanti (Hindi), Jayita; Latoya (Spanish), Toya • *happy, victorious one* Eunice (Greek) • *newly victorious* Signy (Old Norse); Signe, Signi (Scandinavian) • *peaceful and victorious* Sigfreda (Old German) • *to be victorious* Vincentia (Latin), Vincenta • *victorious army* Cosette (French), Cosetta; Colette (Greek-French), Collette • *victorious army, victorious people* Nicole (Greek), Nichele, Nichelle, Nichola, Nicola, Nicolina, Nicoline, Niki, Nikki • *victorious battle maid* Solvig (Old German) • *victorious child* Katsu (Japanese) • *victorious counselor* Sigrid (Old Norse) • *victorious one* Jayne (Sanskrit)

victory Viktoria (Bulgarian); Viktorie, Viktorka (Czech); Victoire (French); Nike (Greek); Jaya, Jayan (Hindi), Jayanti, Jayna; Vitoria (Italian); Victoria (Latin), Vickie, Victorine; Wisia (Polish); Vika, Viki (Serbian); Victoriana, Victorina (Spanish) • *coming before victory* Brona (Greek); Berenice (English) • *crown, laurel, victory* Kelilah (Hebrew), Kaile, Kayle, Kelila, Kelula, Kyla • *harbinger of victory* Bernice (German), Berenice, Veronica, Veronique

Vienna Vienna *from Vienna* (Latin)

vigorous Artemisia (Greek), Artemisa • *a vigorous woman* Sosthenna (He-

brew), Sosthena, Sosthina, Sothena, Thenna

Viking *see* fate

village Mura (Japanese) • *from the village where the willows grew* Shelby (Old English), Shelbie, Shellie, Shelly

vindicated Dena (Native American)

vine Gafna (Hebrew); *a climbing vine* Liana (French), Leana, Leanna, Liane, Lianna, Lianne • *a vine branch* Vidonia (Portuguese) • *a vine growing on an oak tree* Papina (Miwok) • *brushwood or vine* Clematis (Greek) • *ivy vine* Ivy (Old English) • *little vine* Vignette (French) • *of the vine* Vinna (Anglo-Saxon), Vina

vineyard Karmel (Hebrew), Carmel, Carmeli, Carmi, Carmia, Carmiel, • *from the vineyard* Vina (Spanish) • *garden or God's vineyard* Carmel (Hebrew), Carma, Carmela, Carmelina, Carmelita

violet Iola *dawn cloud, violet color* (Greek), Iole • *lilac or violet colored* Mauve (Latin), Malva • *modest, shy or violet* Yolanda (Greek), Yolande, Yolante • *the violet* Fiala (Czech) • *violet blossom* Jolan (Greek) • *violet colored flower* Iantha (Greek), Ianthina, Janthina • *violet colored stone* Ione (Greek), Iona • *violet flower* Calfuray (Native American); Iolanthe (Greek), Yolanda; Jolan (Hungarian); Violet (Old French), Viola, Violante, Viole, Violette, Yolande, Yolanthe

virgin Adara (Arabic), Aludra; Kanya (Hindi), Kania • *sweet virgin* Parthenia (Greek), Parthena, Parthinia • *the Virgin Mary* Ula (Basque)

virginal *see* untouched

virtue Shina *good, virtue* (Japanese), Sheena • *honor, strength, virtue* Bryna (Irish-Gaelic)

virtuous *see* friend

visible Delia (Greek); Ikshita (Hindi)

vision Aislinn *dream or vision* (Irish-Gaelic), Aisling, Isleen • *elfin vision* Druella (Old German) • *lovely vision* Idola (Greek), Idolah, Idolla

vital Quiteria (Latin), Quita, Quiteris, Teria

vitality Uzima (African); Oja (Hindi)

vivacious *see* alive, vivacious

voice *see* moving voice
voiced *see* sweet-voiced
voices *see* voices that carry
voluptuous Adina (Hebrew), Adena, Adine, Dina

vow Bathsheba *daughter of our vow* (Hebrew), Bathsheb, Sheba • *the child of a vow* Desma (Greek)

— W —

walker Andeana (Spanish)
walking *see* walking backward
walks *see* walks with honor
wand *see* battle maid, battle stronghold, battle wand
wanderer Aleta (Greek); Wanda (Old German), Wandis, Wenda, Wendeline, Wendy; Gypsy (unknown origin), Gypsie • *complete wanderer* Deirdre (Irish-Gaelic); Dedra (American) • *sheperdess, wandering one* Wanda (Old German-Slavic) • *the wanderer* Wendelin (Anglo-Saxon), Wendelina, Wendolyn
war Altsoba (Navajo Indian) *all are at war* • *armored battle maid, girl of war* Serilda (Old German), Rilda, Sarilda, Sorilda • *going to war* • Dezba (Navajo Indian) the *famous maid of war* Marelda (Old German), Mareld, Marolda • *Mars' sister; war goddess* Alala (Greek) • *she returns from war* Anaba (Navajo Indian) • *there was no war* Doba (Navajo Indian) • *warlike or war goddess* Belloma (Latin)
warbling *see* songbird
warlike Avice (Old French), Avis; Gytha (Old Norse), Githa • *martial,warlike one* Martina (Latin), Artina, Marta, Martine, Tina • *warlike one* Quirna (Latin) • *warlike or war goddess* Belloma (Latin) • *war returned with her coming* Manaba (Navajo Indian)
warm Wing (Chinese); Calida (Spanish) • *daughter of the sea, flower of the sea, sea star; warm-hearted* Cordelia (Celtic), Cordalia, Cordeelia, Delia
warmth Garima (Hindi) • *enthusiasm, warmth* Ardelle (Latin), Ardeen, Ardelia, Ardella, Ardene, Ardine
warrior Shaka (American); Kelly

(Irish-Gaelic), Keli, Kelia, Kellen, Kelley, Kelli, Kellia, Kellie, Kellina, Kelisa; Gunda (Old Norse); Tyra (Scandinavian) • *armored warrior maid* Brunhilda, Zerelda (Old German), Serilda, Zeralda • *famous warrior maid* Louise (Old German), Alison, Allison, Aloisa, Aloisia, Eloisa, Eloise, Heloise, Lisette, Louisa, Louisette, Luisa, Lulu; Iza, Lilka (Polish) • *famous woman warrior, glorious battle maid* Romilda (Old German), Maida, Milda, Romalda, Romelda • *warrior battle maid* Gunhilda (Old Norse) • *warrior maid* Guida (Italian); Armina (Old German), Armine • *warrior maiden* Beda (Old English)
washed *see* air
washtub Taci (Zuni)
watcher *see* contemplater, watcher
watchful Greer (Latin) • *farmer; watchful one* Georgia (Latin), Georgene, Georgette, Georgiana, Georgienne, Georgina, Georgine, Gigi, Giorgia
watchtower Atalaya *guardian or watchtower* (Spanish) • *of the watchtower* Vedette (French), Detta, Edette, Vedetta
water Ambu, Jeevika, Salila (Hindi) • *a little water sprite* Nixie (Old German) • *a water lily* Sida (Greek) • *child of cool, pure water* Kenda (Modern U.S.) • *clear water* Jawole (West African) • *draw water* Dalya (Hebrew), Dalia, Dalice, Daliya, Dalit • *earthen water jug* Jarietta (Arabic), Jarita • *flows like water* Cari (Turkish) • *from the water* Sadora (Arabic), Dira, Sadirah, Sadiras • *leaping water* Tallulah (Choctaw Indian), Talula •

river or water nymph Naida (Latin) •
saved from the water Moselle (Egyptian), Mozelle • *the sound of running water* Saril (Turkish) • *the talking water* Vailea (Polynesian) • *water lily* Ren (Japanese) • *water or water child* Nirveli (Todas)
waterfall Taki *a plunging waterfall* (Japanese) • *pool below a fall or waterfall* Lynn (Old English)
wave Undine (Latin) • *wave child* Namiko (Japanese), Nami • *white phantom, white wave* Guinevere (Old Welsh), (Old Welsh), Genevieve, Guenna, Gwenore, Jenifer, Jeniffer, Jenni, Jennie, Jennifer, Jenny, Jeny, Vanora • *white wave* Genevieve (Old German); Vanora (Old Welsh)
waves *see* the song of the waves on the shore
wealth Dhanvanti *holding wealth* (Hindi) • *lady of great wealth* Udele (Anglo-Saxon), Della, Uda, Udela, Udella, Udelle • *woman of wealth* Zosima (Greek), Sima, Zima, Zosema, Zosi • *wealth or worldly prosperity* Artha (Hindi)
wealthy Gala (Dutch); Nagida (Hebrew); Ashira (Hindi); Gessica (Italian); Etania (Native American); Ula (Old Norse) • *little wealthy one* Odelia (Old Anglo-French), Odelinda, Odella, Odetta, Odette, Odilia, Otha, Othilia • *queenly, wealthy* Daria (Greek) • *the wealthy* Etenia (Native American) • *wealthy one* Jessica (Hebrew), Jesse, Jessie
weariness Lasca *weary, weariness* (Latin)
weary Leah *weary one* (Hebrew), Le, Lea, Lee • *weariness, weary* Lasca (Latin)
weaver Orino *weaver's field* (Japanese), Ori • *weaver, worker of the web* Penelope (Greek), Penny
web *see* weaver, worker of the web
Wednesday *see* born on Wednesday
weeps Alile (African) *she weeps*
welcome Aspasia (Greek), Aspa, Aspia • *received gladly, welcome* Welcome (Anglo-Saxon)
well Eulalia *a soft-spoken woman; fair speech, well-spoken one* (Greek), Eula, Eulalia, Eulalie • *noble, well-born* Eu-genia (Greek), Genie • *well-born* Owena (Welsh) • *well spoken of* Effie (Greek), Eppie, Euphemia
well-born Zalika *one who's well-born* (Swahili)
west Pratichi (Hindi); Nishi (Japanese) • *from the west meadow* Wesla (Old English)
wet Sikta (Hindi)
wheat *see* corn
white Silver (Anglo-Saxon), Silva, Silvia • *a white antelope* Rima (Arabic) • *beaming white one, the moon* Lewanna (Hebrew) • *bright white* Candida (Latin), Candide • *bright, white light* Farih (Hausa) • *brightly white or pure* Marya (Arabic) • *fair, white* Libna (Hebrew), Lebna, Liba, Libnah; Blanche (Old French), Bianca, Blanca, Blinnie; Gwynne (Old Welsh), Gwyn, Wynne • *girl of white skin* Oriana (Celtic), Anna, Oria, Orian, Orianna • *girl with white skin* Yseulte (Celtic), Isolda, Isolde, Yseulta • *glittering, glowing white* Candace (Greek), Candee, Candice, Kandace, Kandee, Kandi, Kandis • *lady of the new moon, white-haired* Gwendolyn (Celtic), Gwen, Gwendaline, Gwendoline, Gwendolyn, Gwyn, Gwyneth • *light-haired; white bosomed, white-clad* Rowena (Celtic) • *lovely white rose* Rosalba (Latin), Alba, Roselba, Salba • *milky white* Galatea (Greek) • *moon, white* Levana (Hebrew), Levania, Levona, Livana • *she of the white bosom* Bronwen (Welsh) • *snowy or white-haired* Nix (Latin) • *the fragrant white gardenia flower* Gardenia (Latin) • *the tall white flower* Daffodil (Greek), Dafodil • *white as snow* Nevada (Spanish) • *white, blessed one* Gwyneth (Old Welsh) • *white blonde* Elvira (Latin), Elvera, Elvire; Ela (Polish) • *white-browed one* Gwendolyn (Old Welsh), Guenna, Gwen, Gwenda • *white dove* Chenoa (Native American) • *white, fair-skinned one* Bela (Czech); Balaniki (Hawaiian) • *white flower* Sacnite (Mayan) • *white island* Whitney (Old English) • *white or blonde* Albinia (Latin), Albina, Alvina, Aubine • *white phantom, white wave* Guinevere

(Old Welsh), (Old Welsh),
Genevieve, Guenna, Gwenore,
Jenifer, Jeniffer, Jenni, Jennie, Jennifer, Jenny, Jeny, Vanora • *white rose*
Semanti, Sevati (Hindi) • *white-shouldered one* Fenella (Celtic), Nella;
Fionnula (Irish-Gaelic), Finella •
white stone Izusa (Native American) •
white wave Genevieve (Old German);
Vanora (Old Welsh) • *white wood*
Whitley (Middle English)

whiteness *see* extreme

whole Ankal (Hindi) • *complete, whole*
Annis (Greek) • *heathly and whole*
Sage (Latin)

wholesome Althea *healer, the god of
healing; healing, wholesome* (Greek),
Althaia, Thea • *wholesome young girl*
Valeda (Old German), Aleda, Leda,
Valeta

wife Aia, Lillith (Hebrew), Lelith,
Lilith, Lillis • *heart of my wife* Dara
(Hebrew), Darra • *most lovely wife* Ulphia (Latin), Fia, Phia, Ulphi, Ulphiah • *the patient wife* Medora
(Anglo-Saxon), Dora, Edora,
Madora, Medor, Ora

wild Wayra (Native American) • *the
wild goose* Neka (Native American) •
the wild rose Ogin (Native American)
• *wild apricot* Zerdali (Turkish) • *wild
one* Wilda (Old German), Wildee •
wild, untamed Thera (Greek)

will *see* good will

willed *see* iron-willed one

willing Joella *the Lord is willing* (Hebrew), Jo Ella, Joelle, Joellen • *willing to learn* Docilla (Latin), Cilla,
Docila, Docile

willow)Lian *the graceful willow* (Chinese), Liane, Lianne • *the willow tree*
Willow (Middle English)

willows *see* from the village where the
willows grew

willpower *see* resolution, willpower

wind Sarayu (Hindi); Tadewi (Native
American) • *daughter of the wind*
Canace (Greek) • *the eastern wind*
Sabiya (Arabic), Saba, Sabaya,
Sabiyah • *the wind* Makani (Hawaiian) • *the wind god* Anila (Hindi) •
wind-flower Anemone (Greek)

wine Denise *Dionysus, Greek god of wine*
(French), Denice, Denisha, Denyse

• *sweet friend, sweet wine* Melvina
(Latin), Melva • *to burn wine* Brandy
(Old English), Brandee, Brandi,
Brandie

winged Alida *little winged one* (Latin),
Aleda, Aleta, Aletta, Alette, Alita,
Leda, Lita • *winged gift* Aldora
(Greek), Alda, Dora • *winged one*
Alula (Latin)

wings Falda *folded wings* (Icelandic) •
to spread wings Taipa (Miwok)

winner Ajita *a winner* (Hindi)

winning *see* flattering, winning one

winter *see* born

wisdom Athena, Sophie (Greek),
Sofia, Sonja, Sonya, Sophia; Minda
(Hindi); Akili (Tanzanian), Akela,
Akeyla, Akeylah; Zofia (Ukranian) •
gifted with wisdom Eldora (Latin),
Dora • *intelligence, wisdom* Kyna
(Irish-Gaelic) • *knowledge, wisdom; the
wise maiden* Pallas (Greek), Palla •
god of good luck and wisdom Ganesa
(Hindi) • *pearl of wisdom* Darda (Hebrew), Dara • *skill, wisdom* Metis
(Greek)

wise Jada (Hebrew), Ada, Jadda;
Velda (Old German); Maiara (Native American) • *bold wise counselor*
Conradine (Old German) • *child of
the wise leader* Mackenzie (Irish-Gaelic), MacKenzie, McKenzie, Kenzie • *intelligent, wise* Frodine (Old
German), Frodeen, Frodina, Odeen,
Odine • *knowing and wise* Sage
(Latin) • *knowledge, wisdom; the wise
maiden* Pallas (Greek), Palla • *learned
one, wise* Ulima (Arabic) • *mighty or
wise protector* Ramona (Spanish), Ramonda • *most wise teacher* Fronia
(Latin), Fronnia, Fronniah, Onia •
old, rich, wise Alda (Old German) •
old, wise counselor Eldrida (Old English) • *peaceful and wise* Elfrida (Old
German), Elfreda • *small, old, wise
one* Shannon (Irish-Gaelic), Shani,
Shanon, Shannah, Shannan, Shannen, Shauna, Shawna, Shawni • *the
wise* Sabella (Latin), Sabelle • *the
wise friend* Eldrida (Anglo-Saxon),
Dreda, Drida, Eldreda • *the wise one*
Sonia (Greek), Sona, Sonya • *the wise
prophetess* Hulda (Hebrew), Huldah,
Ulda • *wise counselor* Monica (Latin);

Monique (French), Mique • *wise; intelligent* Hui (Chinese)

wish Muna (Arabic); Aarzoo, Akanksha, Kamana, Kamna (Hindi) • *the desired or the wished for* Wilona (Anglo-Saxon), Wilonah

wisteria Fuji (Japanese) • *wisteria, rice field* Fujita (Japanese)

wistful Imelda (Latin), Imalda, Imelida, Melda, Mella

witch Rhiamon *a witch* (Welsh), Rhianon, Rhlanna, Riannon, Rianon

witness Sakshi (Hindi)

wolf Lupe (Spanish); Tala (Native American) • *famous wolf* Rudi (Old German)

woman Quanisha (American), Neisha, Nisha • Aisha (Arabic), Myisha; Pramada (Hindi); Mahala (Native American) • Duma *a gentle woman* (Greek), Dhumma, Dumah • *a little woman* Zoara (Hebrew), Zoa, Zoarah • *a man's woman, fearless* Andreanna (Greek) • *an endearing woman* Vaclava (Scandinavian), Clava, Vacla • *a prosperous woman* Alodie (Anglo-Saxon), Alodee, Alodi, Lodie • *a soft-spoken woman; fair speech, well-spoken one* Eulalia (Greek), Eula, Eulalia, Eulalie • *a vigorous woman* Sosthenna (Hebrew), Sosthena, Sosthina, Sothena, Thenna • *a woman of Lydia, cultured person* Lydia (Greek), Lidia, Lydie • *fairest, loveliest woman* Vashti (Hebrew), Ashti, Vashtee, Vashtia, Vasti • *faithful woman* Fidelia (Latin), Dela, Fidelas, Fidelity, Fidellia, Idel • *famous woman warrior, glorious battle maid* Romilda (Old German), Maida, Milda, Romalda, Romelda • *fiery woman* Eda (Anglo-Saxon), Edda, Edel • *free woman* Netfa (Ethiopian) • *fruitful woman, of the spring* Cerelia (Latin), Cerellia, Cerallua, Cerelly, Erlia • *gentlewoman of the castle* Wira (Celtic), Irra, Wera • *horse-woman* Rechaba (Hebrew), Aba, Rachaba • *independent woman* Fanchon (Old German), Fanchan, Fanchet, Fanchette • *lovely woman* Belda (French), Bellda, Belldame, Belldas, Belle • *loving woman* Phillida (Greek), Phillada, Vallada • *most for-*

tunate woman Audris (Old German), Audras, Audres • *noble woman* Earlene (Old English), Erlene, Erline • *obedient woman* Shama (Hebrew), Shamma • *profound woman* Fonda (Spanish) • *Roman, woman of Rome* Romola (Latin) • *small woman* Kalere (African) • *the happy one* Aanandita (Hindi) • *the knowing woman* Kendra (Anglo-Saxon), Kendrah, Kendy • *the sweet woman* Vevina (Latin), Vena, Vina, Vevine • *the veiled woman, woman of mystery* Voletta (French), Oletta, Olette, Vola, Voleta • *the woman* Alzena (Persian) • *woman* Asha (Arabic) • *woman chief* Winema (Modoc Indian) • *woman of God* Gabrielle (Hebrew), Gabriela, Gabriella, Gigi • *woman of good works* Fabiola (Latin), Fabiolas, Fabyola • *woman of learning* Eberta (Old German), Berta, Ebarta • *woman of much sadness* Trista (Latin), Tristas, Tristis • *woman of my country* Utina (Native American) • *woman of power* Edra (Hebrew), Eddra, Edrea, Edris • *woman of Saba or Sheba* Saba (Greek), Sheba • *woman of sorrow* Pelagia (Latin), Pelaga, Pelagi, Pelagias • *woman of strength* Brianna (Celtic), Briana • *woman of the people* Leoda (Old German), Leota • *woman of veneration* Grimonia (Latin), Grimona, Mona • *woman of wealth* Zosima (Greek), Sima, Zima, Zosema, Zosi • *woman who leads* Caesaria (Latin), Cesaria • *woman who sympathizes* Maurilla (Latin), Mauralia, Maurilia

womanly Andrea (Latin), Andee, Andreana, Andria, Andriana; Zenda (Persian), Zendah • *enduring, queenly, womanly* Cornelia (Latin) • *little womanly one* Charlotte (French), Carlene, Carlota, Carlotta, Charlene, Charyl, Cheryl, Sharlene, Sheryl; Sarolta (Hungarian); Caroline (Latin), Carline, Carol, Carolina, Charline; Carli (Old German), Carla, Carlina, Carlita, Kari, Karla; Karolina (Russian • *strong, womanly* Karla (Modern U.S.), Carla • *strong and womanly* Carol (Latin), Caryl, Karol; Kolala (Hawaiian)

wonderful Saruchi (Hindi) • *a miracle, a wonderful thing* Marvel (Old French), Marvela, Marvella, Marvelle • *wonderful one* Mira (Latin), Mirella, Mirelle, Mirilla, Myra, Myrilla

wood Ebony *a hard, dark wood* (Greek), Ebonee • *forest or wood spirit* Vedis (Old German), Vedi, Veedis • *the color of mahogany wood* Mahogany (American) • *white wood* Whitley (Middle English) • *wood fairy* Sen (Japanese) • *wood nymph* Rusalka (Czech)

woodbine *see* rose

woodlark *see* purity, woodlark

woods *see* echo through the woods

word Sana (Finnish) • *true to her word* Willtrude (Old English), Truda, Willa

worker Millicent *good worker* (Old German), Melicent, Mellicent • *joy or diligent worker* Hedva (Hebrew), Edva, Edveh, Hedvah, Hedve, Hedveh • *the worker* Ayita (Native American) • *weaver, worker of the web* Penelope (Greek), Penny • *worker for the people* Radmilla (Slavic)

works *see* good

world Fernanda *adventuring, world daring* (Germanic), Ferdinanda, Fernandina • *harmony, order, the world* Cosima (Greek) • *of the earth or world* Hermione (Greek), Hermine, Herminia; Hertha (Old English), Erda, Ertha, Herta • *world ruler* Donalda (Irish-Gaelic), Donia; Doni (American); Dony (English)

worldly Jagvi (Hindi) • *wealth or worldly prosperity* Artha (Hindi)

worship Seva (Hindi) • *worship God* Feechi (African)

worshipers *see* sun worshipers

worships Abida (Arabic)

worthy Meras (Hebrew), Meris, Merras • *worthy of love* Amanda (Latin) • *worthy one* Kata (Japanese) • *worthy of praise* Aenea (Hebrew), Aeniah, Aennela

wreath *see* crown

writing Lekha (Hindi)

written *see* charm

wrong Sonesu *what wrong have we done* (South African)

• — Y — •

year Toshi (Japanese) • *anything; decay, destruction; this year* Banna (Hausa) • *the springtime of the year* Spring (Old English) • *yearly crops* Anona (Latin)

yellow Xanthe (Greek); Gauri (Hindi), Gari, Gouri • *canary yellow colored* Melina (Latin) • *little yellow flower* Nurit (Hebrew), Nurice, Nurita • *yellow bird* Pazi (Native American) • *yellow flower* Caltha (Latin) • *yellow-haired* Flavia (Latin)

yellowish Cornelia (Latin), Cornela, Nela; Nelia (Spanish)

yew Kaya *a yew* (Japanese)

yew-bow Yvonne (Old French), Yvette • *yew tree* Iva (Old French), Ivanna

young Wayna (Native American) • *a young palm shoot* Hira (Arabic) • *joyful and young* Leatrice (Latin), Arice, Leatri, Liatrice, Liatris • *verdent,*

young Chloe (Greek) • *very young* Nena (Mende) • *wholesome young girl* Valeda (Old German), Aleda, Leda, Valeta • *young animal* Gurit (Hebrew), Gurice • *young ceremonial attendant* Camille (Latin), Camila, Camilla • *young deer* Faunia (Latin), Fawn, Fawna, Fawnia • *young gazelle* Rasha (Arabic) • *young person* Novia (Latin), Nova

youth *see* goddess of spring, youth

youthful Gillian *downy-haired one, youthful* (Greek), Gilane, Giletta, Gillan, Gilliana, Gilliette, Jill, Julia, Juliana, Juliet, Julietta, Julina, Juline, Julissa; Juliska (Czech); Juliette (French); Julinka (Hungarian); Jula, Julcia (Polish); Iulia (Romanian); Yulinka, Yulka (Russian); Yula (Serbian); Julita (Spanish)

Z

Z Zeta *the letter Z* (Greek)
zealous *see* fervent, zealous
Zeus *see* divine flower, flower of Zeus

Zinnia *see* flower
Zuni *see* Indian

Meanings Related to Male Names

• — A — •

abbey Abbott *abbey father* (Old English), Abott

Abbott Aban *a little abbot* (Irish-Gaelic), Abban • *son of Abbott* Abbottson (Old German), Abbotsen, Abbotson

able Bailey (Old German) • *able, capable* Saksham (Hindi)

abounding Ephraim *abounding in fruitfulness* (Hebrew), Efram, Ephram; Efrain (Spanish) • *abounding in love, beloved* Craddock (Old Welsh)

above Sahale (Native American)

absolute Udom (Thai)

abstain Ky *carefully; strange; to abstain from; to fear; to sign* (Vietnamese)

abundance Zaid *great abundance* (Hindi)

abundant Prachur (Hindi)

accurate Pramesh *master of accurate knowledge* (Hindi)

achievement Manaal *attainment; achievement* (Hindi)

acre Ackerley *dweller at the acre meadow, of the meadow of the oak trees* (Old English) • *owner of a quarter acre* Verge (Anglo-French)

action Udyam (Hindi)

active Chanchal (Hindi) • *active one, energetic* Sproule (Middle English), Sprowle • *little active one* Cavell (Old French)

actor Anoke, Anoki (Native American)

Adam Aiken *little Adam* (Old English), Aikin • *son of Adam* Addis, Addison (Old English), Adis; Adamson (Old German), Adams, Adamsen, Adamsun; MacAdam (Scotch-Gaelic)

add Joseph *he shall add* (Hebrew); Yazid, Yusef, Zaid (Arabic); Yosif (Bulgarian); Joza, Jozef, Jozka (Czech); Joosef (Finnish); Josephe (French); Josef (German); Iosif (Greek); Joska, Joszef, Jozsi (Hungarian); Ioseph (Irish); Giuseppe (Italian); Jo (Japanese); Jazeps (Latvian); Jozio, Juzef, Juziu (Polish); José (Portuguese); Osip, Osya, Yeska, Yesya, Yusif, Yuzef (Russian); Josep, Josip, Joze, Jozef, Jozhe, Jozhef (Servian); Josecito, Joseito, Joselito (Spanish); Yusuf (Swahili); Osip (Ukrainian); Yousef (Yiddish)

addition Garibald *a welcome addition* (Old English), Aribold, Garibold, Ribal

adherent Ansel *adherent of a nobleman* (Old French), Ansell • *adherent of Nicholas* Coleman (Old English), Colman • *adherent or attendant* Lance (Old French) • *faithful one's adherent* Truman (Old English)

administrator Proctor (Latin), Proctor • *administrator, foreman, magistrate, overseer, sheriff* Schultz (German) • *God's chief administrator* Mukasa (African)

admired Sanjiro (Japanese), Sanji; Hieu (Vietnamese)

adoration Bhajan, Vandan (Hindi)

advancer Wade *the advancer* (Old English)

advancer's Weddell *dweller at the advancer's hill* (Old English) • *from the advancer's estate, from Wade's castle* Wadsworth (Old English), Wade, Wadesworth • *the advancer's meadow* Wadley (Old English)

advancing Wolfgang *advancing wolf, path of a wolf* (Old German)

adventuring Ferdinand *life adventuring, world daring* (Old German), Ferdinando, Ferdnando, Fernando, Hernando

adventurous Gan (Chinese)

adviser Redmond *adviser, protector* (Old German) • *adviser, so wise* Eldwin (Anglo-Saxon), Eldwen • *the adviser* Aldred (Anglo-Saxon), Alded

afar Paxton *a traveler, from afar* (Old German), Packston, Packton, Paxon

affection Mamraj *lord of affection* (Hindi)

affectionate Sanurag, Sujal, Vatsal (Hindi) • *affectionate one, kind one* Oliver (Old Norse), Oliverio, Olivier • *lovable or affectionate* Prem (Sanskrit)

aflame Brendan *aflame, inspirational* (Scandinavian), Brandon, Brannon, Brendon, Brennan

against Pariket *against desire* (Hindi)

aggressive Cavill *aggressive warrior* (Old German), Cavil

agreeable Naamann (Hebrew), Naaman, Naman

agriculture Lono *god of peace and agriculture* (Hawaiian)

ahead Nigan (Native American)

aided Mansur *divinely aided* (Arabic)

aim Lakshan (Hindi) • *aim, target* Laksh (Hindi)

air Bavol (Gypsy); Vyan (Hindi) • *child of the air or wind* Anil (Hindi)

Aku Shadrach *command of Aku* (Babylonian), Shad

Alan Alanson *son of Alan* (Old German), Alansen, Alenson, Allanson

alder Worcester *alder forest army camp* (Old English) • *at the alder tree* Alder (Old English) • *dweller by the alder river* Garnock (Old Welsh) • *dweller near the alder tree* Fernald (Old German) • *from the alder grove* Varney (Celtic); Verney (Old French) • *grove of alders* Delano (Latin), Delanos

alert Suchet (Hindi) • *alert, watchful one* Wake (Old English) • *little alert one* Howell (Old Welsh)

Alexander Callister (Irish-Gaelic); *son of Alexander* Sanders (Middle English), Sanderson, Saunders, Saunderson

alien Frayne (Old English)

alike Simen (Gypsy)

alive Alair *alive, cheerful* (Celtic), Allare • *alive, live, living* Vito (Latin)

all Tutto (Latin) • *all given to him* Wemilat (Native American) • *all pervasive* Ehimay (Hindi) • *all speak to him* Wemilo (Native American) • *all wise* Alvis, Elvis (Old Norse) • *borrowed all* Rance (African), Rancell, Ransell • *famous or royally peaceful, the ruler of all* Vladimir (Slavic), Vlad, Vladamar, Vladi, Vladimar • *friend of all* Alvin (Old German), Alvan, Alwin, Alwyn; Albin (Russian) • *lord of all* Varindra (Hindi) • *lord of all lords* Devadeva (Hindi) • *my father is still alive* Nnamdi (Nigerian) • *noble ruler, ruler of all* Alaric (Old German), Alric, Alrick • *vigorous and alive* Ziven (Slavic); Zivon (English)

alligator Polo (African)

almond Mandel (German)

alone Alein (Yiddish)

aloof Nazarius *the aloof* (Latin)

always Prosper *always blessed* (Latin), Prospero, Prosperus • *always careful* Ware (Anglo-Saxon), Wier

ambition Zhiyuan (Chinese); Tanish (Hindi)

ambitious Brice *ambitious, awake* (Celtic), Bryce

ambush Akando (Native American); Zared (Hebrew)

amiable Camlo (Gypsy); *an amiable friend* Haymo (Latin), Aimo

amulet Shen *sacred amulet* (Egyptian)
ancestor Olin *reminder of his ancestor* (Old Norse), Olen
ancestral Olaf *ancestral relic* (Old Norse), Olav; Cawley (Scotch-Norse)
ancient Kedem (Hebrew); Chirantan (Hindi); Cian, Kian (Irish-Gaelic); Kean, Keane, Keene (English) • *an ancient king* Trishanku (Hindi) • *an ancient philosopher* Naagarjun (Hindi) • *an ancient physician* Charak (Hindi) • *an ancient sage* Naarad, Shameek (Hindi) • *crossing the old ford or river, of the ancient ford* Alford (Old English), Alvord • *dweller at the ancient oak tree* Orrick (Old English) • *from the ancient cow barn* Byram (Old English) • *little ancient one* Kccnan (Irish-Gaelic), Kenan, Kienan • *old and ancient man* Kumush (Hindi)
angel Malak (Hindi); Tuyen (Vietnamese) • *angel brilliant* Inglebert (Old German), Engelbert, Englebert • *angel of Jehovah* Malachi (Hebrew), Malchus • *angel of the Lord* Azriel (Hebrew), Azrae • *angel messenger* DeAngelo (American) • *angel or messenger* Angelo (Latin), Angel
angry Gaal *angry son* (Hebrew)
animal Derwin *animal lover* (Old German), Dorwin, Durwin
animal's Bodua *an animal's tail* (Akan)
Ann's Ainsworth *from Ann's estate* (Old English)
anointed Krister *anointed one, believer in Christ* (Swedish); Christian (Greek), Christiano, Kristian • *the anointed one* Cristo (Greek); Criston, Cristos
anvil Anyon (Celtic-Welsh)
anything Cata *a calabash; anything; a salty cake; gourd; in daylight* (Hasua/African)
appearance Pradarsh *appearance, order* (Hindi)
apple Pomeroy *from the apple orchard* (Old French)
appointed Seth (Hebrew) • *appointed of Jehovah, exalted by God* Jeremy (Hebrew), Jereme, Jeremiah, Jeremias; Yerik (Russian)
appreciates Enlai *one who appreciates* (Chinese)

apprentice Prentice *an apprentice or learner* (Middle English)
April Averell *born in the month of April* (Middle English), Averil, Averill
archer Sarngin (Hindi); Ivon (Teutonic) • *archer, bowman* Archer (Old English) • *renowned archer* Bevus (Old German), Bevis
ardent Arden *ardent, fiery; eager, fervent, sincere* (Latin), Ardin • *ardent, fiery one* Egan (Irish-Gaelic) • *ardent one* Reece (Old Welsh), Reese • *son of the ardent one* Price (Old Welsh)
arising Rajas *arising from passion* (Hindi)
aristocrat Gibrian *aristocrat; from a high place; stern* (Latin)
arm Armstrong *with a strong arm* (Old English)
armed Searle *armed one, armor* (Old German), Serle • *armed, protective* Armand (Latin-Old German), Arman, Armando, Armin, Armond, Ormond
armor *see* armed one, armor
army Sena (Hindi) • *alder forest army camp* Worcester (Old English) • *army brilliant, glorious warrior* Herbert (Old German) • *army guard, guardian army* Garner (Old French) • *army man* Harry (Old English); Armand (Old German), Armin; Mandek (Polish) • *army man; soldier* Armino (Italian) • *army man, warrior* Herman (Old German), Armand, Armando, Hamlin, Harman, Harmon • *army of gods* Devsena (Hindi) • *army of the Varini, defending warrior or army* Werner (Old German) • *army or people's friend* Arvin (Old German) • *army ruler* Hale (Hawaiian); Herrick (Old German); Harold (Old Norse), Araldo, Aralt, Hal; Enric (Romanian) • *army ruler; mason, wall builder* Waller (Old English); Herrick (Old German); Harold (Old Norse), Araldo, Aralt, Hal • *army ruler, powerful warrior* Walter (Old German), Gauthier, Walther • *army warrior* Harvey (Old German) • *a son's army* Inger (Old Norse), Ingar, Ingvar • *battle army* Gunther (Old Norse), Gunter • *bold army* Balder (Old English), Baldur, Baudier • *defending army or warrior*

Warner (Old German), Werner • *dweller at the fortified army camp* Chester (Old English), Chet; Cheslav (Russian) • *from the army land* Harlan (Old English) • *mighty army* Ragnar, Raynor (Old Norse), Ragnor, Rainer, Rainier, Rayner, Raynor • *national army* Thayer (Old Frankish) • *powerful army* Mather, Ricker (Old English) • *victorious army* Colin (French-Greek) • *victorious army, victorious people* Klaus (German); Nicholas (Greek), Cole, Nichol, Nicol, Nicolas, Nikki; Kolya (Russian); Nicanor (Spanish) • *victory over army* Senajit (Hindi) • *yew bow army* Ivar (Old Norse), Ivor

arrival Aagam *coming, arrival* (Hindi)

arrow Belen (Greek); Vishikh (Hindi) • *an arrow* Shalya (Hindi) • *arrow maker* Fletcher (Middle English) • Flo *like an arrow* (Native American) • *new arrow* Motega (Native American) • *the arrow* Ouray (Native American)

arrows Nibaal (Hindi)

Artemis Artemas *gift of the goddess Artemis* (Greek), Art, Artemus, Artimas, Artimis, Tamus, Taymus

ascending Rohan (Hindi)

ascetic Zahid (Arabic)

ash Ashburn *ash tree brook* (Old English) • *ash tree farm* Ashby (Old English) • *dweller at the ash tree farm* Ashton (Old English) • *dweller at the ash tree meadow, from the ash tree ford* Ashford (Old English) • *dweller at the ash tree pool* Ashlin (Old English)

asked Saul *asked for* (Hebrew)

aspen Waverly *quaking aspen tree meadow* (Old English)

aspiration Maraam (Hindi)

assistant Bello *helper, assistant* (African)

astrologer Ganak *an astrologer* (Hindi)

athlete Carvey *athlete, game player* (Irish-Gaelic)

attainment *see* attainment

attendant Lance *adherent or attendant* (Old French) • *attendant, officer* Sargent (Old French), Sergeant, Sergent • *attendant or lad* Ladd (Middle English) • *follower or warrior attendant* Thane (Old English), Thaine, Thayne • *herdsman, knight's attendant* Swain (Middle English), Swayne • *knight's attendant, shield bearer* Squire (Middle English) • *servant to the royal court, youthful attendant* Page (French), Pagas, Pegasus • *the attendant* Serge (Latin) • *young attendant* Padgett (French), Padget

attentive Suchet *attentive* (Hindi)

attractive Mohul (Hindi); Mohan (Sanskrit) • *attractive, charming servant* Mohandas (Sanskrit)

august Sebastian *august one, reverenced one* (Latin), Sebastiano, Sebastien

Augustus Augustine *belonging to Augustus* (Latin), Austen, Austin

auspicious Faust *auspicious, lucky* (Latin)

austere Sterne *austere one* (Middle English), Stearn, Stearne • *austere, strong man* Hartman (Old German)

autumn Sarad *born in autumn* (Hindi); Thu (Vietnamese)

avenges Alastair *one who avenges* (Greek), Alaster, Allaster, Alister, Allister, Alastar

awake *see* ambitious, awake

awakened Jagrav (Hindi)

aware Subhan (Hindi)

away Nicabar *to take away* (Gypsy)

awe Oglesby *awe-inspiring* (Old English) • *awe-inspiring guardian, noble guardian* Aylward (Old English) • *awe-inspiring one's farmland* Aylworth (Old English) • *dweller in the valley of the awe-inspiring one* Anscom (Old English), Anscomb • *from the awe-inspiring one's pasture meadow* Ansley (Old English) • *the awe-inspiring one's meadow* Ainsley (Old English) • *the awe-inspiring one's son* Anson (Old English)

axe Bardrick *axe-ruler* (Old English) • *axe-wolf* Bardolf (Old English), Bardolph, Bardou, Bardoul

B

Baal Hannibal *grace of Baal* (Phoenician)

baby Shishul (Hindi)

badger Brock (Celtic) • *a badger* Shafan (Hebrew), Shaphan; Shayfan (English) • *from the badger meadow* Brockley (Old English)

bailiff Woodruff *bailiff or forest warden* (Old English) • *bailiff or steward* Reeve (Old English), Reave, Steward, Stewart, Stuart; Bailey (Old French), Bailie, Baily, Bayley

baker Ferran (Arabic)

balanced Pratul *a balanced person* (Hindi)

bald Calvin *bald one* (Latin), Calvino, Kalvin

ballad Baird *ballad singer, minstrel* (Irish-Gaelic), Bard • *folk song or ballad* Cadao (Vietnamese)

bamboo Takeshi (Japanese) • *large bamboo* Luong (Vietnamese) • *strong as bamboo* Takeo (Japanese)

bank Windsor *at the river's bend, boundary bank* (Old English) • *dweller at the bank or slope* Bink (North English) • *from the bank or ridge* Link (Old English)

banner Patakin *holder of a banner* (Hindi)

barber Holic (Czech)

barberry Arlo (Spanish)

bard Riordan *bard or royal poet* (Irish-Gaelic)

bare Barlow *dweller at the bare hill, he lives on the boar's hill* (Old English), Borlow • *little and bare* Loman (Irish-Gaelic)

barley Barton *barley estate or farmstead* (Old English) • *from the barley fields* Berwick (Old German) • *from the barley ford* Beresford (Old English)

barn *see* ancient

barrel Cade (Middle English), Kade • *barrel maker* Kiefer (German), Keefe; Cooper (Old English)

Bart's Bartley *Bart's meadow* (Old English)

base Honda *base, rice field* (Japanese)

basin Pilar *a fountain basin or pillar* (Spanish)

basket Almiron *clothes basket* (Hindi), Miron

bat Adan *a large bat* (Yoruban)

battle Narong (Thai) • *battle army* Gunther (Old Norse), Gunter • *battle brave* Hilliard (Old German), Hilier • *battle chief* Kincaid (Celtic) • *battle chieftain* Cedric (Old English); Kedrick (American) • *battle counselor* Eldred (Old German), Eldrid • *battle follower* Coyle (Irish-Gaelic) • *battle keenness* Caddock (Old Welsh) • *battle man* Cadman (Old Anglo-Welsh) • *battle spirit* Cadell (Old Welsh) • *battle stone* Wystand (Anglo-Saxon) • *comrade in battle* Gereron (French), Gere • *dear friend in battle* Hadwin (Old German), Hadwyn, Wynn • *eager for battle* Alfonso (Old German), Alonso, Alonzo, Alphonso; Fonzi (Spanish) • *famous in battle* Wymer (Old English) • *from the battle place* Keith (Irish-Gaelic) • *helmeted, ready for battle* Coryell (Greek) • *hero of the battle* Ranveer (Hindi) • *lively in battle* Valdis (Old German), Valdas, Valdes • *valorous in battle* Duer (Celtic) • *wise in battle* Balthasar (Persian), Balthazar

battlefield Ronsher *lion of the battlefield* (Hindi)

battler Tracy (Latin); Boris (Slavic)

bay Kang *one from a river or bay* (Korean)

beach Sanborn *dweller at the sandy brook, of the sandy beach* (Old English), Sanborne, Sanburn

beacon Brandon *from the beacon hill* (Old English)

bead Chuma (Zimbabwean)

bean Fabian *bean grower* (Latin), Faber, Fabio, Fabiano, Fabien • *from the bean field* Bancroft (Old English)

bear Arthur (Celtic); Artis (Czech); Arto (Finnish); Anthanasios (Greek), Thanos; Shaurav (Hindi); Artur (Irish); Arturo, Urso (Italian); Kuma (Japanese); Honon (Miwok); Kuruk, Yana (Native American); Bern (Old German), Baer, Berne; Artek (Polish); Artair (Scottish);

Dov (Yiddish) • *bear growling* Liwanu (Miwok) • *bear with lots of hair* Huslu (Miwok) • *brave as a bear* Bernard (Old German), Barnard, Barney, Bernardo, Bernhard, Burnard; Bjorn (Scandinavian) • *divine bear* Osborn (Old Norse) • *holy bear* Esbern (Danish), Esburn; Esben (Old Norse) • *little bear* Orson (Old French) • *mighty bear* Barret (Old German), Barrett • *noble bear* Adelbern (Teutonic) • *Thor's bear* Thorburn (English); Thorbjörn (Scandinavian) • *war bear* Wyborn (Old Norse)

beard Lombard *a long beard* (Old German), Lombardo, Lombardy • *man with a mustache or beard* Algernon (Old French) • *man with an unusual beard* Brody (German); Brodie (English)

bearded Julius *downy-bearded one, youthful* (Latin), Jule, Jules, Julio; Giles (Old French), Gil

bearer Amasa *burden bearer* (Hebrew) • *Christ bearer* Stoffel (German); Christopher (Greek), Kristo, Kristopher; Kriss (Latvian); Christobal (Spanish), Tobal • *cup bearer* Burl (Old English) • *knight's attendant, shield bearer* Squire (Middle English) • *rod or staff bearer* Virgil (Latin), Virge, Virgilio • *sceptre bearer* Macy (Old English) • *the bearer of good news* Ewald (Latin), Ewold, Wald

bearing Palmer *palm bearing pilgrim* (Old English)

beautiful Hasani (Arabic); Navrang, Rupang, Sohil (Hindi) • *beautiful child* Sheehan (Hindi) • *beautiful dawn* Akemi (Japanese) • *beautiful friend* Bellamy (Latin) • *beautiful man* Apollo (Greek) • *beautiful sea* Mervin (Scotch-Gaelic), Merwin, Merwyn • *dweller in the beautiful glen* Belden (Old English), Beldon • *from a beautiful valley* Belden (Old German) • *from the beautiful mountain* Beaumont (Old French) • *of the beautiful fortress* Beaufort (French), Beau, Beaufert • *radiant, beautiful* Ruchir (Hindi)

beauty Noy (Hebrew) • *embodied beauty* Rupin (Hindi) • *little beauty* Husain (Arabic), Husain, Hussain,

Hussein • *lord of beauty* Rupesh (Hindi) • *man of great beauty* Philemon (Greek)

beaver Adriel (Native American); Bobar (Czech); Castor (Greek) • *the beaver* Ahmik (Native American)

bee Miland (Hindi)

beggar Hahnee *a beggar* (Native American) • *long-haired beggar* Kesin (Hindi)

beguiling Wylie *beguiling, charming* (Anglo-Saxon)

behold Reuben *behold a son* (Hebrew), Ruben

believer Krister *anointed one, believer in Christ* (Swedish); Christian (Greek), Christiano, Kristian • *true believer* Hanif (Arabic), Haneef

belligerent Callahan *small, belligerent one* (Irish-Gaelic), Callaghan

belonging Augustine *belonging to Augustus* (Latin), Austen, Austin • *belonging to Demeter, Greek fertility goddess* Demetrius (Greek), Demetre, Demetrio; Dimitri (Russian) • *belonging to Ireland* Argyle (Celtic), Argile • *belonging to Julius* Halian (Zuni) • *belonging to the castle* Castel (Latin) • *belonging to the god Olorun* Olorun (African) • *belonging to the Lord; born on Sunday, the Lord's day* Dominic (Latin), Domenico, Domingo, Dominick, Dominico, Dominique, Nick

belongs Elkan *he belongs to God* (Hebrew)

beloved Azizi (African); Dathan (American), Dathin, Dathon; Habib (Arabic); Wilbur (Anglo-Saxon), Wilber; Aziz (Arabic); Esme (French); Erastus (Greek); David (Hebrew), Dave, Lal, Sajan (Hindi); Cam (Gypsy); Leif (Old Norse); Dewey (Old Welsh); Daudi (Swahili); Sevilen (Turkish) • *abounding in love, beloved* Craddock (Old Welsh) • *beloved descendant* Judd (Hebrew), Jedd, Judus • *beloved friend* Derwin, Durwin (Old English) • *beloved of God* Amadeo (Spanish), Amadis, Amado, Amando • *beloved of God, beloved stranger* Elidad (Hebrew) • *beloved of the Lord* Jedidiah (Hebrew), Jed, Jediah • *beloved one* Daudi (Swahili) • *beloved or dear one*

Anwell (Celtic-Welsh), Anwyl, Anwyll • *from a beloved place* Livingston (Old English) • *from the beloved one's farmstead* Truesdale (Old English) • *little beloved one* Lovell (Old English), Lowell • *little beloved or dear one* Darrell (Old French), Darold, Darryl, Daryl • *powerful and beloved* Aziz (Arabic) • *son of the beloved one* Davis (Old English) • *Thor's beloved* Thorleif (Scandinavian)

below Matsushita *below, pine* (Japanese)

bend *see* bank

benediction Ashesh (Hindi)

benefactor's Maddox *the benefactor's son* (Old Anglo-Welsh)

beneficent Maddock *beneficent and good* (Old Welsh), Madock

benevolent Naeem (African); Shanyu (Hindi)

Benjamin Benson *son of Benjamin* (Hebrew-English)

bent Benton *from the bent grass farm* (Old English)

best Uttam (Hindi) • *best of kings* Rajdeep (Hindi) • *the best* Rishit (Hindi)

bewitch Dukker *to bewitch* (Gypsy); Duke (English)

bewitching Mohan (Sanskrit)

beyond Yul *beyond the horizon* (Mongolian)

big Naag *a big serpent* (Hindi) • *from the big meadow* Grantham (Old English), Grantland, Grantley

birch Birch *at the birch tree* (Old English), Birk • *birch tree* Burch (Middle English) • *dweller at the birch headland* Birkett (Middle English) • *dweller at the birch tree meadow* Barclay (Old English), Berkeley • *from the birch tree island* Birkey (North English)

bird Gozal (Hebrew); Pakhi, Pakshi (Hindi); Chim (Vietnamese) • *a bird* Kaling, Titir (Hindi) • *bird of prey* Hawk (American); Hawke, Hawkeye (English) • *the night bird* Kibbe (Native American) • *yellow bird* Mamo (Hawaiian)

birdlike Byrd (Old English)

bird's Tas *bird's nest* (Gypsy)

birth Kesse *fat at birth* (Ashanti) • *of noble birth* Payton (Irish-Gaelic), Paton, Peyton

bishop Bishop *the bishop* (Old English)

bitter Marion (Hebrew), Mario, Marius • *bitter, of the terebinth tree* Elah (Hebrew)

black Aswad (Arabic); Ham (Hebrew); Kala (Hindi); Li (Korean); Wattan (Native American); Blake (Old English); Taman (Serbo-Croatian) • *black, dark blue* Shyamal (Hindi) • *black, rice field* Kuroda (Japanese) • *dark blue, black* Shyam (Hindi) • *dark or black man* Dunham (Celtic), Dunam • *from the black ford* Hamford (Old German) • *from the black fort* Cardew (Celtic) • *from the black meadow* Blakeley (Old English) • *from the black or dark settlement* Colby (Old Anglo-Norse), Kolby • *from the black or dark water* Douglas (Scotch-Gaelic), Douglass, Dugald • *healthy black man* Delano (Irish-Gaelic) • *little black one* Ciaran (Irish-Gaelic) • *little jet black one* Kerwin (Irish-Gaelic), Kerwen, Kirwin • *the black god* Mayon (Hindi) • *the black raven* Branduff (Irish-Gaelic), Brandubh • *the black stranger* Dougal (Irish-Gaelic)

blackbird Merle (French) • *blackbirdlike* Kass (German)

black-eyed Sullivan *black-eyed one* (Irish-Gaelic)

black-haired Dolan, Dow (Irish-Gaelic); Colley (Old English), Collis

blacksmith Smith *blacksmith, worker with a hammer* (Old French) • Fabron *little blacksmith* (French), Fabrioni

blemish Niramay *without blemish* (Hindi)

blessed Prosper *always blessed* (Latin), Prospero, Prosperus • *blessed coming* Kaloosh (Armenian) • *blessed, happy* Seeley (Old English), Sealey; Selig (Old German) • *blessed one* Karsten (Greek), Kersten, Kirsten, Kirt; Benedict (Latin), Bendix, Benedetto, Benedicto, Benito, Bennet, Benoit • *God has blessed me* Olushola (Nigerian) • *little blessed one* Bennett (French-Latin)

blessing Sampada (Hindi) • *God's blessing* Adom (Ghanaian) • *the god Chi's own blessing* Chinua (Nigerian)

blind Cecil *blind or dim-sighted* (Latin)

bliss Anando (African); Prahalad (Hindi)

blond Boyd *blond one* (Irish-Gaelic); Alva (Latin), Alba; DeWitt (Old Flemish); Alpin (Scotch) • *blond or tawny* Flavio (Latin) • *blond ruler, elf ruler, spirit ruler* Aubrey (Old French) • *blond, white* Blanco (Spanish) • *fair, blond one* Aubin (Old French); Gwynn (Old Welsh), Guin • *little blond one* Banning (Irish-Gaelic) • *white or blond one* Dwight (Old Dutch)

blood Barron *of noble blood* (Old English), Baron, Barr

bloodhound Talbott *the bloodhound* (Anglo-Saxon), Talbot, Tallbot, Tallbott

blooming Praful (Hindi)

blowing Nirvan *a blowing out* (Sanskrit)

blue Neel, Vinil (Hindi); Hinto (Native American) • *black, dark blue* Shymal (Hindi) • *blue-eyed* Sullivan (Celtic) • *blue jay* Jay (Old French) • *blue sky* Neelambar (Hindi) • *dark blue, black* Shyam (Hindi) • *little blue-eyed one* Gorman (Irish-Gaelic) • Neel *sapphire blue* (Hindi)

bluebird Yahto (Native American)

bluff Dohosan *a small bluff* (Native American)

boar York *boar estate* (Old English) • *brave or strong as a boar* Everard (Old English), Eberhard, Evered, Everett, Everhart • *first son of the wild boar* Haro (Japanese), Haroko, Haroku • *from the boar valley* Borden (Old English) • *pugilist; the wild boar* Evers (Anglo-Saxon) • *wild-boar brave* Eberhard (Old German)

boar's Barlow *dweller at the bare hill, he lives on the boar's hill* (Old English), Borlow • *he lives near the boar's den* Barden (Old English), Borden

boat Nauka (Hindi) • *boat, sun* Tarani (Hindi)

body Wong *wide body of water* (Chinese)

bodyguard Ekanga (Hindi)

boisterous Shandy *little boisterous one* (Old English)

bold Diallo (African); Kyne (Anglo-Saxon); Tristram (Celtic); Caleb (Hebrew), Cale, Kaleb; Cort (Old German) • *a bold son* Grimbald (French), Grimbal • *bold and daring* Hardy (Old German), Hardey • *bold and royal, chief warrior* Kimball (Old Welsh), Kimble • *bold army* Balder (Old English), Baldur, Baudier • *bold counselor* Conrad (Old German), Conrade, Contrado, Cort, Curt, Konni, Konrad, Kurt • *bold, courageous one* Tracy (Latin) • *bold for the people* Leopold (Old German), Leopoldo • *bold friend or protector* Baldwin (Old German), Balduin, Baudoin • *bold guardian or royal guardian* Kenward (Old English) • *bold man* Frick (Old English) • *bold, noble and sacred* Archibald (Anglo-Saxon/German), Archibaldo • *bold or princely and famous* Baldemar (Old German) • *bold or princely ruler* Baldric (Old German), Baudric • *bold, outspoken* Germain (Old German), Germaun, Germin • *bold raven* Brainard (Old English) • *bold, sharp one* Keane (Middle English), Kean, Keene • *bold spear* Gerbold (Old German) • *bold, strong* Kennard, Trumble (Old English); Ballard (Old German) • *bold warrior* Gunter (French); Guenter, Guenther, Gunther (German); Guntero (Italian); Gunnar (Norwegian); Gunnar (Teutonic) • *bold warrior or royal warrior* Kenway (Old English)

boldest Theobald *boldest of the people* (Old German), Tibold, Tybalt

born Daegal *a son born at daylight* (Scandinavian), Dagall, Dygal, Dygall • *belonging to the Lord; born on Sunday, the Lord's day* Dominic (Latin), Domenico, Domingo, Dominick, Dominico, Dominique, Nick • *born after twins* Kizza (Ugandan) • *born at Christmas* Noel (French), Natal, Nowell; Yule (Old English) • *born at Easter* Pascal (Italian) • *born at night* Okon (African); Daren (Hausa) • *born during a journey* Uzoma (Nigerian) • *born during a rain* Brishen (Gypsy) • *born during the month of March* Mart (Turkish) • *born during the pilgrimage* Haji

(Egyptian) • *born during war* Abiodun (Nigerian) • *born free* Azad (Turkish) • *born in autumn* Sarad (Hindi); Thu (Vietnamese) • *born in honor* Abiola (African) • *born in January* Janus (Latin); Jarek (Polish) • *born in May* Geminian (Latin), Geminius • *born in the month of April* Averell (Middle English), Averil, Averill • *born in the month of Ramadan* Ramadan (Swahili) • *born in the ninth month* Sivan (Hebrew) • *born in the wintertime* Winter (Old English) • *born in winter* Wen (Gypsy); Huyu (Japanese); Abejide (Nigerian) • *born of clay* Clayborne (Old German), Clayborn • *born of fire* Vasuman (Hindi) • *born of the spear* Waitimu (African) • *born on Friday* Cuffee, Jimoh, Juma (African), Cuffy; Jumah (Swahili) • *born on Monday* Cudjo (African) • *born on Saturday* Kwame, Kwamin, Quami (African); Atu, Kwam (Ghanaian) • *born on Sunday* Danladi, Kwasi, Kwesi, Quashee (African); Danladi (Hausa) • *born on the hill* Gibeon (Hebrew), Gibbon, Gibe • *born on the willow farm* Saville (Latin), Saval, Savil, Savill • *born on Thursday* Quao (African); Hamisi (Swahili) • *born on Tuesday* Cubbenah (African); Akua (Ghanaian) • *born on Wednesday* Kwaco, Kwaku, Quaco (African); Abeeku (Ghanaian) • *born while traveling* Chenzira (Zimbabwean) • *born with long hair, leader* Caesar (Latin), Cesar, Cesare; Kesar (Russian) • *born with teeth* Danior (Gypsy) • *bright; second-born son* Kenji (Japanese) • *eighth-born child* Octavius (Latin), Octavio; Tam (Vietnamese) • *fifteenth-born child* Odinan (African) • *fifth-born child* Anum (Ghanaian); Quenton, Quintin (Latin), Quent, Quentin, Quenton, Quint; Quito (Spanish); *first born* Pehlaj (Hindi); Kazuo (Japanese); Mosi (Swahili) • *first-born male* Taro (Japanese) • *first-born male twin* Ulan (Sudan) • *first-born son* Chaska (Sioux) • *first child born to a family* Primo (Italian) • *fourth-born, fourth son* Annan (African); Quartus (Latin) • *fourth-born*

son Shiro (Japanese) • *he is born of God* Jabin (Hebrew), Jaban, Jabon • *newly born* Navaj (Hindi) • *ninth-born son* Akron (African), Akan • *noble, well-born* Eugene (Greek), Eugenio, Gene, Gino • *second-born boy* Lado (Sudan) • *second-born son* Manu (Ghanaian); Eiji, Zinan (Japanese); Pili (Swahili) • *seventh-born child* Bay (Vietnamese) • *seventh-born son* Ashon (African) • *sixth-born son* Essien (African) • *sun born* Ramses (African) • *third-born* Trey (Middle English) • *third-born male* Saburo (Japanese) • *third-born son* Taizo (Japanese) • *thirteenth-born child* Adusa (Ghanaian) • *thirteenth-born son* Odissan (African) • *town born* Urien (Welsh) • *twelfth-born son* Adeben (Akan) • *well-born* Ewan (Celtic), Ewen • *well-born one, young warrior* Evan (Irish-Gaelic), Ewan, Ewen; Owen (Old Welsh)

borrowed *see* all

boss Russom *boss, head* (African)

bound Tye *bound or tied* (Old English) • *homeward bound* Kerey (Gypsy); Keir English)

boundary Severn (Old English) • *at the river's bend, boundary bank* Windsor (Old English)

boundless Anirudh (Hindi)

bow Chang *a bow* (Chinese) • *bow strong* Bogart (Old German) • *little yew bow* Iven (Old French) • *son of yew bow* Ives (Old English), Yves • *yew bow army* Ivar (Old Norse), Ivor

bowman Archer *archer, bowman* (Old English) • *the bowman or hunter* Arley (Old English)

boy Chal (Gypsy); Batuk (Hindi); Swaine (Old German), Swain, Swane; Lathan (Old Norse) • *a young boy* Kishor (Hindi) • *boy of the tribe, follower* Sabu (Indian) • *bright boy* Akio (Japanese) • *second-born boy* Lado (Sudan) • *snow boy* Yukio (Japanese), Yuki, Yukiko • *tiger boy* Torao (Japanese) • *we have a boy* Akinlabi (Nigerian) • *year boy* Toshio (Japanese), Toshi • *young boy* Kumar, Tuka (Hindi)

bramblebush Bramwell *from the bram-*

blebush spring, of Bram's well (Old English), Bram

Bram's *see* bramblebush

brass Phineas *mouth of brass* (Greek)

brave Pravir, Randhir, Sahas, Vir (Hindi); Ubald (Latin), Ube; Mato (Native American); Akinlana (Nigerian); Akin (Yoruban), Ahkeen • *battle brave* Hilliard (Old German), Hilier • *brave and noble* Adlar (Old German), Adlare • *brave and resolute* Willard (Old English) • *brave and sacred* Allard (Old English), Alard • *brave as a bear* Bernard (Old German), Barnard, Barney, Bernardo, Bernhard, Burnard; Bjorn (Scandinavian) • *brave, dark man* Donnelly (Celtic), Donely, Donnel, Donnell • *brave friend* Hardwin (Old English); Darwin (Old German), Darwen • *brave man* Dreng (Norwegian) • *brave lord* Virendra, Viresh (Hindi) • brave *one* Jabari (Swahili) • *brave one's son* Harding (Old English) • *brave or strong as a boar* Everard (Old English), Eberhard, Evered, Everett, Everhart • *brave, powerful* Maynard (Old German), Menard • *brave sailor* Cadmar (Celtic), Cadmarr • *brave, valorous, watchful* Casey (Irish-Gaelic) • *brave warrior* Cadman (Celtic), Cadmann; Kenelm (Old English) • *firm spear, spear brave* Garrett (Old English), Garrard, Garret, Garritt • *gift brave* Gifford (Old English), Gifferd • *lion brave* Leonard (Old German), Leonardo • *lord of the brave* Viranath (Hindi) • *mighty brave* Reynard (Old German), Raynard, Reinhard, Renard, Renaud • *nobly brave* Adalard (Old German), Adallard • *nobly brave, warrior* Ellard (Old German), Ellerd, Ellord • *powerful brave* Richard (Old German), Ricard, Ricardo, Riccardo, Richerd, Rickert • *resolute, brave* Sudhir (Hindi) • *royally brave* Kensell (Old German) • *spear brave, spear strong* Gerard (Old English), Gerardo, Geraud, Gerrard, Jerard • *the brave charioteer* Cormac (Irish-Gaelic) • *the brave defender* Tracey (Anglo-Saxon), Tracay, Tracy • *the brave soldier* Kenway, Sherard (Anglo-Saxon), Kenay,

Kenweigh • *wild-boar brave* Eberhard (Old German)

bravery Shaurya, Virata (Hindi)

breath Avel (Greek); Hevel (Hebrew); Ettan, Shwas (Hindi) • *breath, evanescence* Abel (Hebrew) • *breath of life* Pranjivan (Hindi) • *breath of the gods* Spiro (Greek)

breathe Tho *fiber; poem; to breathe; workman* (Vietnamese)

breeze Rabi (Arabic), Rabbi

brewer Brewster (Old English), Brewer, Bruce

brick Ziegler *brick and tile maker* (German)

bridge Hashi (Japanese) • *a dweller by the bridge* Brigham (Anglo-Saxon) • *bridge builder; dweller at the bridge* Bridger (Old English) • *bridge over white water* Bainbridge (Old English)

bridges Pierrepont *stone bridges* (French), Pierpont

brigadier Zaim *brigadier general* (Arabic)

bright Javier (Arabic); Ming (Chinese); Sudip, Sudir, Tejal, Vivash (Hindi); Acar (Turkish) • *a diamond, bright protector* Diamond (Old English) • *bright boy* Akio (Japanese) • *bright, clear* Sinclair (English-Scottish) • *bright, clear water* Kenn (Old Welsh), Cain • *bright Finn, the bright man* Davin (Scandinavian), Daven, Davon • *bright forest* Sherwood (Old English) • *bright gem* Halbert (Old German) • *bright moonlight* Konane (Hawaiian) • *bright one* Quon (Chinese) • *bright or shining with fame* Robert (Old English), Bert, Roberto, Robertson, Robin, Rupert • *bright pupil* Teillo (Latin), Teilo • *bright raven, he shall be famous* Bertram (Old German), Bartram • *bright; second-born son* Kenji (Japanese) • *bright, shining sword* Egbert (Old English) • *bright, shining white* Galvin (Irish-Gaelic), Galvan, Galven • *bright star* Gelasius (Latin), Gelasias • *bright, the shining son* Fulbert (Old German), Philbert • *bright, victory* Seiberth (German) • *bright, white* Kent (Old Welsh) • *day bright* Delbert (Old English) • *from a bright field* Campbell (French), Campball •

from a bright hope Guibert (Old German) • *from the bright valley or clear river valley* Kendall (Old English), Kendal, Kendell • *little bright one* Galen (Irish-Gaelic); Jalen (American) • *the bright one's forest* Dagwood (Old English)

brightest Anwar (African)

brightly Yu *shining brightly* (Chinese)

brightness Prajval (Hindi) • *brightness of the north, brilliant hero* Norbert (Old German) • *brightness, radiance* Ronak (Hindi)

brilliance Thorbert *brilliance of Thor or thunder glorious, thunder* (Old Norse) • *man of brilliance* Hebert (Old German)

brilliant Rajul (Hindi) • *a famous and brilliant man* Cuthbert (Anglo-Saxon), Cuthburt • *angel brilliant* Inglebert (Old German), Engelbert, Englebert • *army brilliant, glorious warrior* Herbert (Old German) • *brightness of the north, brilliant hero* Norbert (Old German) • *brilliant among the people* Tab (Old German) • *brilliant and graceful* Hulbert (Old German), Hulbard, Hulburt • *brilliant and noble or illustrious* Berty (Czech); Albert (Old English), Adelbert, Ailbert, Alberto, Aubert, Berto, Elbert • *brilliant counselor* Radbert (Old English) • *brilliant hero* Halbert (Old English) • *brilliant hostage or pledge* Gilbert (Old English), Gilberto, Guilbert • *brilliant, light* Deepak (Sanskrit) • *brilliant mind* Hobart (Old German) • *brilliant mind or spirit* Hubert (Old German), Bert, Huberto, Hugh; Berdy (Russian) • *brilliant one's estate* Berton (Old English) • *brilliant, prosperous* Edbert (Old English) • *brilliant; quick friend* Egwin (Anglo-Saxon), Egin, Winn • *brilliant raven* Bertram (Old English), Bertrand • *brilliant ruler* Berthold (Old German), Bertold, Bertoldi, Bertoud • *brilliant seafarer* Colbert (Old English), Colvert, Culbert • *brilliant son* Sanson (Hebrew), Sansen • *brilliant, splendor* Mayukh (Hindi) • *divinely brilliant* Osbert (Old English) • *from the firm fortress, resolute brilliant one*

Wilbur (Old German) • *his country's light, land brilliant* Lambert (Old German), Landbert, Landberto • *mighty brilliant* Rambert (Old German) • *proud, brilliant one* Dalbert (Old English), Delbert • *very brilliant one* Filbert (Old English), Filberte, Filberto, Philbert • *wealthy, brilliant one* Obert (Old German)

bringer Abayomi *bringer of happiness* (Nigerian) • *bringer of knowledge or light, light* Luke (Latin), Luca, Lucan, Lucas, Lucian, Lucius

brings Olukayode *my Lord brings happiness* (Nigerian) • *the one who brings hope* Navashen (Hindi)

Briton Brett (Celtic), Bret

broad Prithu, Vishaal (Hindi) • *broad brook* Bradburn (Old English) • *broad field, forest* Bradshaw (English) • *broad one, broad-shouldered* Plato (Greek) • *broad, wide place* Brad (Old English) • *from the broad island* Brady (Old English) • *from the broad meadow* Bradley (Old English) • *from the broad ridge* Broderick (Middle English) • *from the broad river crossing* Bradford (Old English) • *from the broad spring* Bradwell (Old English), Brad

broad-shouldered Platon (Spanish) • *broad one, broad-shouldered* Plato (Greek)

bronze Ardon (Hebrew)

brook Yuval (Hindi) • *a brook* Beck (Middle English); Burne, Calder (Old English), Bourne, Byrne • *ash tree brook* Ashburn (Old English) • *broad brook* Bradburn (Old English) • *dweller at the brook in the hollow* Holbrook (Old English) • *dweller at the brooks* Brooks (Middle English) • *dweller at the flooding brook* Washburn (Old English) • *dweller at the sandy brook, of the sandy beach* Sanborn (Old English), Sanborne, Sanburn • *dweller at the spring brook* Welborne (Old English) • *dweller on the brook island* Birney (Old English), Burney • *from a brook by the sea* Seabrooke (Old English) • *from the brook* Bourne (Old English) • *from the clay brook* Clayborne (Old English), Claiborn, Clay, Claybourne • *from the clear brook*

Sherborne (Old English), Sherbourn, Sherbourne • *from the deer
brook* Dearborn (Old English) • *from
the roe deer brook, of the flower fields*
Rayburn (Old English), Raybin, Raybourne • *from the west brook* Westbrook (Old English) • *from the wildcat brook* Chadburn (Old English) •
he lives by the red brook Rad burn (Old
English), Radbourne

broom Bromley *a dweller in the
meadow, dweller at the broom meadow*
(Old English), Bromleigh

Brosna Brosnan *dweller near the Brosna
River* (Irish-Gaelic)

brother Adelpho (Greek); Pal
(Gypsy); Ekodar (Hindi) • *elder
brother* Abi (Hebrew) • *the brother* Sibley (Anglo-Saxon), Siblee

brown Dunstan *brown fortress, brown
stone* (Old English) • *brown warrior*
Donahue (Irish-Gaelic); Duncan
(Scotch-Gaelic) • *reddish-brown complexion* Burrell (Old French) •
reddish-brown hair Sorrell (Old
French) • *son of the brown one* Bronson (Old English)

brown-complected Burnett *little
brown-complected one* (Middle English)

brown-haired Bruno *brown-haired one*
(Italian) • *dark or brown-haired* Bruns
(German) • *little brown-haired one*
Burnell (Old French) • *small brown-
haired one* Donnan (Irish-Gaelic)

brushwood Riston *from the brushwood
estate or town* (Old English) • *from the
brushwood meadow* Risley (Old English) • *from the home in the brushwood*
Ruston (Old English), Rusten,
Rustin

bubbly Gilboa (Hebrew)

buck Buck *buck deer* (Old English) •
dweller at the buck deer meadow Buckley
(Old English) • *roe buck deer estate*
Renton (Old English)

bud Mukul (Hindi)

Buddhist Liko *Buddhist nun* (Chinese)

builder Waller *army ruler; mason, wall
builder* (Old English) • *bridge builder;
dweller at the bridge* Bridger (Old English)

building Newbold *of the new building*
(Old English)

bull Fairleigh *from thebull meadow* (Old
English), Farlay, Farlee, Farley

burden Amos *a burden* (Hebrew) •
burden bearer Amasa (Hebrew)

Burleigh Burl *from the town of Burleigh*
(Anglo-Saxon), Beryl, Burley

burned Brandeis *dweller on a burned
clearing* (Czech); Brand, Brandt,
Brant (English)

burning Jomo *burning spear* (East
African) • *burning torch* Quidel (Native American)

busy Emlyn *son of a busy father* (Old
German), Emelin, Emlen

butcher Metzger (German)

— C —

cabinet Schreiner *cabinet maker* (German)

cake *see* anything

calabash *see* anything

calm Yen *calm, serene* (Vietnamese) •
calm, tranquil one Sereno (Latin) •
calm, unflappable Gedraitis (Lithuanian) • *tranquil and calm* Placido
(Latin); Placedo, Placijo, Plasido,
Plasio (Spanish) • *very calm* Prashant
(Hindi)

camel Gamal (Arabic), Gamali, Jamal,

Jammal • *a camel hump* Gilad (Arabic); Giladi, Gilead (English)

camp Worcester *alder forest army camp*
(Old English) • *camp by the road*
Cilombo (African) • *chosen camp, legion camp* Lester (Latin) • *dweller at
the fortified army camp* Chester (Old
English), Chet; Cheslav (Russian) •
from the camp Tabor (Hungarian)

canal Nehru (Sanskrit)

candid Guyapi (Native American)

candle Deepak *light, candle* (Hindi)

candler Chandler *candle maker* (Middle English). Shandler

canon Channing *canon, church dignitary* (Old French)

capable Inas, Layak (Hindi) • *able, capable* Saksham (Hindi) • *skillful, capable* Pravin (Hindi)

cape Saki *cape, headland* (Japanese)

capricious Varian *capricious, clever* (Latin), Varien, Varion

captain Rais (Arabic) • Kerry *ship captain* (English)

captive Tillo (Latin), Tillio

careful Ware *always careful* (Anglo-Saxon), Wier • *careful traveler* Trevor (Celtic), Trevar • *careful, wary guard* Gardell (Old German), Gardal, Gardel

carefully *see* abstain

caretaker Crandall *caretaker of the valley; from the valley of cranes* (Old English), Crandale, Crandell

caribou Ahdik (Native American)

Carl's Carlton *from Carl's farm* (Old English), Carleton

carpenter Zimmerman (German), Zimmermann; Wright (Old English); Sayer (Welsh), Sayers, Sayre

Carr Carson *son of Carr* (Welsh)

carried Amos (Hebrew)

cart Carter *cart driver* (Old English) • *the cart maker* Carter (Anglo-Saxon), Cart

carter Jagger *carter, teamster* (North English)

carve Cata *cut or cut down, to carve* (Swahili/African)

carver Carver *the meat carver* (Anglo-Saxon)

cask Cade (Middle English)

castle Armon (Hebrew), Armani, Armoni • *belonging to the castle* Castel (Latin) • *castle dweller* Borg (Norse) • *castle, fortress, stronghold* Burke (Old German) • *castle tower* Carlisle (Old English) • *dweller at the castle ford* Burford (Old English) • *dweller at the castle meadow* Burley (Old English), Burleigh • *dweller at the castles* Carey (Old Welsh), Cary • *dweller on the castle hill* Burdon (Old English) • *dweller on the castle hill slope* Burbank (Old English) • *from the advancer's estate, from Wade's castle* Wadsworth (Old English), Wade, Wadesworth • *from the castle of the king* Rexford (Latin), Rexferd; Hallvard (Scandinavian) • *from the enduring castle town* Warburton (Old English) • *from the wealthy one's hill or hill castle* Montgomery (Old French) • *governor of a castle* Castellan (Spanish) • *strong as a castle* Burchard (Old English), Burgard, Burgaud, Burkhart

catfish Cata *a connecting wall; catfish; nut; to confine* (Mende/African)

cattle Bosworth *at the cattle enclosure* (Old English) • *cattle shed on the meadow* Birley (Old English) • *from the cattle ford* Rutherford (Old English), Rutherfurd • *keeper of the cattle, little cow* Vachel (French), Vachell, Vachil, Vachill • *of the valley of cattle* Orford (Old English), Ford, Orford

cautious Waring *the cautious soul* (Anglo-Saxon), Warrin, Warring

cave Covell *dweller at the cave slope* (Old English)

celebrated Kirtin (Hindi); Kayin (Yoruban)

celebration Parvesh *lord of celebration* (Hindi)

celestial Mandar *a celestial tree* (Hindi)• *divine, celestial* Saurav (Hindi)

challenger Delaney *descendant of the challenger* (Irish-Gaelic), Delan, Delane, Delainey

chamberlain Camerero *chamberlain, monastery worker* (Spanish) • *son of the chamberlain or overseer* Chalmers (Old Scotch)

champion Carroll, Neal (Irish-Gaelic), Neale, Neall, Neil, Nial, Niall, Niels; Nels, Nils (Scandinavian) • *champion or hero* Curran (Irish-Gaelic), Currey, Curry • *champion's son* Nelson (English), Nealson, Nilson • *champion, warrior* Kemp (Middle English) • *little champion* Carlin, Carollan (Irish-Gaelic), Carling • *the people's champion* Sayer (Old German), Sayre

chancellor Chauncey *chancellor church official* (Middle English)

changeable Geary *changeable one* (Middle English), Gery

chanting Japa (Hindi)
chapel Chapell *a man of the chapel, pious* (Anglo-Saxon)
chaplain Chapin *chaplain, man of God* (French), Chapen, Chapland
character Taksheel *strong character* (Hindi)
charcoal Colman *charcoal maker* (Icelandic) • *charcoal merchant, miner* Collier (Old English), Colier, Colis, Collyer, Colyer
charioteer Cormick (Irish-Gaelic), Cormack • *the brave charioteer* Cormac (Irish-Gaelic)
charitable Danvir (Hindi) • *charitable, good* Khairiya (Hindi)
charming Rushil (Hindi) • *attractive, charming servant* Mohandas (Sanskrit) • *beguiling, charming* Wylie (Anglo-Saxon)
cheeked Julian *downy-cheeked one, youthful* (Latin), Julius
cheerful Vidor (Hungarian); Tate (Middle English), Taite • *alive, cheerful* Alair (Celtic), Allare • *cheerful, handsome, harmonious one* Alan (Irish-Gaelic), Ailin, Alain, Allan, Allen, Allyn • *cheerful, kind friend* Gladwin (Old English) • *pleasant, cheerful* Prafulla (Hindi)
cherry Kersen (Indonesian)
chess Nard *the game of chess* (Persian)
Chi Chioke *gift of the god Chi* Chioke (Nigerian) • *power of the god Chi* Chike (Nigerian) • *the god Chi is our defender* Chileogu (Nigerian) • *the god Chi is our protector* Chileogu (Nigerian) • *the god Chi is protecting* Cinese (Nigerian) • *the god Chi's own blessing* Chinua (Nigerian) • *thought of the god Chi* Chinelo (Nigerian)
chick Cicero *chick-pea or vetch* (Latin); Ciceron (Spanish)
chief Ohin (Ghanaian); Meer, Vea (Hindi); Lenox, Torin (Irish-Gaelic); Minco, Tyee (Native American), Minko • *a chief* Rosh (Hebrew) • *a little chief* Okemos (Native American) • *battle chief* Kincaid (Celtic) • *bold and royal, chief warrior* Kimball (Old Welsh), Kimble • *chief guardian* Howard (Old English) • *chief, nobleman* Earl (Old English), Earle, Erl, Errol; Jarl (Scandinavian) • *chief,*

ruler Kim (Old English) • *commander in chief* Tartan (Hebrew), Tarton, Tarttan • *fierce chief* Griffith (Old Welsh) • *God's chief administrator* Mukasa (African) • *great chief* Melvern (Native American) • *polished chief* Malvin, Melvin (Irish-Gaelic) • *son of a chief* Yuma (Native American) • *swarthy chief* Duncan (Celtic) • *the chief* Kelii (Hawaiian)
chieftain *see* battle chieftain
child Moses (Egyptian); Koji (Japanese); Eudo (Old Norse) • *beautiful child* Sheehan (Hindi) • *child, cub* Colin (Irish-Gaelic) • *child from the south* Nam (Vietnamese) • *child of Passover* Pascal (Hebrew), Pasco • *child of the air or wind* Anil (Hindi) • *child of the hunting dog keeper* Connery (Irish-Gaelic), Conaire, Conary, Conray; Conrey, Conroy, Conry • *child of the valley* Slade (English) • *eighth-born child* Octavius (Latin), Octavio; Tam (Vietnamese) • *excellent male child* Hideo (Japanese) • *fifteenth-born child* Odinan (African) • *fifth-born child* Anum (Ghanaian); Quenton, Quintin (Latin), Quent, Quentin, Quenton, Quint; Quito (Spanish) • *fifth child* Quinton (Latin) • *first child born to a family* Primo (Italian) • *male child* Godana (African) • *ninth child* Ennis (Greek) • *only child* Kontar (Ghanaian) • *seventh-born child* Bay (Vietnamese) • *small child* Chiumbo (Kenyan) • *thirteenth-born child* Adusa (Ghanaian) • *wonderful child* Gyasi (Ghanaian); Jahsee, Jaysee (English)
choice Ennis *one choice, only choice* (Irish-Gaelic) • *one choice, unique strength* Angus (Scotch-Gaelic) • *strong man, very choice one* Fergus (Irish-Gaelic)
chosen Mustafa (Arabic); Seth (Hebrew) • *chosen camp, legion camp* Lester (Latin) • *man chosen by Jehovah* Moriah (Hebrew)
Christ Krister *annointed one, believer in Christ* (Swedish); Christian (Greek), Christiano, Kristian • *Christ bearer* Stoffel (German); Christopher (Greek), Kristo, Kristophyer; Kriss (Latvian); Cristobal (Spanish),

Tobal • *servant of Christ* Gilchrist (Irish-Gaelic)
Christmas *see* born at Christmas
chronicler Kaga (Native American)
church Channing *canon, church dignitary* (Old French) • *chancellor church official* Chauncey (Middle English) • *church legal officer, summoner* Sumner (Middle English) • *church meadow* Kirkley (Old North English) • *church official or sacristan* Sexton (Middle English) • *dweller at the church* Kirk (Old Norse) • *dweller at the church hill* Churchill (Old English) • *from the church area* Parrish (Middle English) • *from the church forest* Kirkwood (Old North English) • *from the church village* Kirby (Old Norse), Kerby
citizen Burgess *citizen of a fortified town* (Middle English) • *citizen of Rome* Romulus (Latin)
city Chapman *a man of the city, urbane* (Anglo-Saxon) • *from a walled city* Carlisle (Latin), Carl, Carlyle, Lisle, Lyle • *friend of city* Purumitra (Hindi) • *from the city* Orban (Hungarian); Urban (Latin), Urbaine, Urbano • *from the city of Milan* Milan (Latin) • *from the city of Tarrsus* Tarsus (Hebrew), Tarrsus • *from the city of Tyre* Tyrus (Latin), Ty • *from the dark estate or farm; of a dark city* Colton (Old English), Coltin, Coltson, Coltun • *from the earthquake city* Bela (Hebrew) • *of a foreign city* Ernald (Old German), Ernaldus • *of the fortified city* Walton (Old English) • *of the new city* Napier (Spanish), Neper
civilized Sabhya (Hindi)
clad Digvastra *sky clad* (Hindi)
Clair Sinclair *from St. Clair* (French)
claw Yutu *to claw* (Miwok)
clay Clayborne *born of clay* (Old German), Clayborn • *from the clay brook* Clayborne (Old English), Claiborn, Clay, Claybourne • *from the clay estate or town* Clayton (Old English) • *from the place of clay* Clay (Old English)
clean Amal (Hindi)
cleaner Walker *cleaner of cloth* (Middle English)
cleanliness Joben *one who enjoys cleanliness* (Japanese)

clear Sinclair *bright, clear* (English-Scottish) • *bright, clear water* Kenn (Old Welsh), Cain • *from the bright valley or clear river valley* Kendall (Old English), Kendal, Kendell • *from the clear brook* Sherborne (Old English), Sherbourn, Sherbourne • *luminous and clear* Minh (Vietnamese) • *pure, clear* Nirmal (Hindi) • *the clear one* Adisa (Nigerian)
clearing Brandeis *dweller on a burned clearing* (Czech); Brand, Brandt, Brant (English) • *from the clearing in the forest* Royd (Scandinavian), Roid • *from the high clearing* Henley (Old English), Henleigh
cleft Erskine *from the height of the cleft* (Scotch-Gaelic)
clever Chapal, Kaushal, Sumedh (Hindi), Chatur, Chatura • *capricious, clever* Varian (Latin), Varien, Varion • *clever, ingenious one; curly-haired one* Cassidy (Irish-Gaelic)
cliff Cleavant (Old English), Cleavon • *dweller at the red cliff* Radcliff (Old English) • *from the cliff* Clive (Old English), Cleve, Clyve • *from the cliff estate or town* Clifton (Old English) • *from the cliff ford* Clifford (Old English); Telem (Hebrew) • *from the cliff land* Cleveland (Old English) • *from the head of the cliff* Kinnell (Irish-Gaelic) • *from the heath cliff* Heathcliff (Middle English) • *from the rocky cliff* Stancliff (Old English) • *from the south cliff* Sutcliff (Old English) • *from the steep cliff or rock* Cliff (Old English) • *from the white cliff* Wycliff (Old English)
cloak Lennon *little cloak* (Irish-Gaelic)
close Sameep (Hindi)
cloth Walker *cleaner of cloth* (Middle English) • *cloth thickener* Fuller (Middle English) • *warm cloth* Nishar (Hindi)
clothes *see* basket
cloud Abhin, Badal, Barid, Megh, Mehal, Payod, Vanad, Varid (Hindi)
clouds Jaldhar, Neerad (Hindi) • *god of clouds and rain* Hinun (Native American) • *king of clouds* Meghraj (Hindi)
clump Saravana *clump of reeds* (Hindi)

coatmaker Manning *coatmaker, son of a good man* (Old German)

cobra Takshak *a cobra* (Hindi) • *one who wears cobra* Naagdhar (Hindi)

coincidence Sanjog (Hindi)

cold Caldwell *cold spring* (Old English)

collected Sanchit (Hindi)

collection Sanchay (Hindi)

collector Asaph (Hebrew) • *a toll collector* Tolman (Old English), Tollman, Tollmann, Tolmann

colony Lincoln *from the colony by the pool* (Old English)

color Moswen *light in color* (African) • *of a dark color* Morrell (Latin), Morel, Morril

colored Cornell *horn colored hair* (Old French), Cornall, Cornel • *horn colored, hornlike* Cornelius (Latin), Cornelio • *the color red* Gulal (Hindi)

colt Colter *colt herder* (Old English)

Columbia Malcolm *disciple of St. Columbia* (Scotch-Gaelic)

combatant's Patton *from the combatant's estate* (Old English)

comfort Nehemiah *a comfort from God* (Hebrew) • *comfort, rest* Noah (Hebrew)

comforter Jabir (Arabic); Menachem (Yiddish), Mendeley; *the compassionate or comforter* Nahum (Hebrew)

coming Kaloosh *blessed coming* (Armenian) • *he is coming* Payat (Native American); Pay, Payatt (English)

command Aadesh (Hindi) • *command of Aku* Shadrach (Babylonian), Shad

commander Penn (Old German) • *commander in chief* Tartan (Hebrew), Tarton, Tarttan • *famous commander* Penrod (Old German) • *helpful commander* Raoul (Old German) • *noble commander* Adelric (Old German)

commanding Bodil (Scandinavian)

commands Casimir *commands peace* (Old Slavic), Casimiro, Kasimir

coming *see* arrival

commit Pham *greedy; to commit* (Vietnamese)

companion Kadin (Arabic); Abhisar (Hindi) • *entertaining companion* Samir (Arabic) • *gallant companion* Sancho (Spanish) • *little companion* Keller (Irish-Gaelic)

comparison Nirupam *without comparison* (Hindi)

compassionate Rahim (Arabic), Rahman; Kripal (Hindi); Rabmet (Turkish) • *the compassionate or comforter* Nahum (Hebrew)

complete Pooran, Puran (Hindi) • *complete knowledge* Sambodh (Hindi)

completed Hoang (Vietnamese)

compulsion Garnett *spear compulsion* (Old English), Garnet

comrade Mikul (Hindi) • *comrade in battle* Gereron (French), Gere • *stable comrade* Stacy (Latin), Stacey

consciousness Chaitan, Pramit, Sambit, Sanhata (Hindi), Chaitanya

condor Antiman *condor of the sun* (Native American) • *wild condor* Aucaman (Native American)

conferring Ravi (Hindi)

confine *see* catfish

congratulate Ho *to congratulate* (Chinese)

congregation Adriel *from God's congregation* (Hebrew)

connected Sashang (Hindi)

connecting *see* catfish

connoisseur Kashif (Hindi)

conquering Vincent *conquering one* (Latin), Vince, Vincente, Vincenz; Wicent (Polish)

conqueror Jayin, Tarusa (Hindi); Victor (Latin), Vitorio; Fenyang (Botswanan) • *conqueror of the mind* Manjeet (Hindi) • *conqueror of truth* Rutajit (Hindi) • *heroic conqueror* Herrod (Hebrew), Herod

consecrated Enoch *consecrated, dedicated* (Hebrew) • *consecrated to God* Lemuel (Hebrew)

conservative Hosyi (Japanese)

consolation Faraji (African) • *patience, consolation* Dheeraj (Hindi) • *son of consolation or exhortation* Barnabas (Greek), Barnaby, Barney; Bane (Hawaiian)

constant Constantine *constant, firm one* (Latin), Constantin, Constantino, Costantin, Costantino, Dinos; Costa, Konstandinos, Konstantinos, Kostas, Kostis, Kostos (Greek); Stancio (Spanish) • *constant one, tamer* Damon (Greek), Damian, Damien

constantly Chang (Korean)

consul Sergius (Latin), Serge, Sergei, Sergias, Sergu; Sergio (Italian)

contend Jareb *he will contend* (Hebrew), Jarib

content Samvar (Hindi) • *content, satisfied* Prineet (Hindi)

contest Havelock *sea contest* (Old Norse)

continuity Ji (Chinese)

continuous Anram (Hindi), Aviral, Avirat

control Jarlath *man of control* (Latin), Jari, Jarlathus

cook Cocinero (Spanish)

copper Kuper (Yiddish) • *copper; to move* Doug (Vietnamese) • *red, made of copper, Mars* Lohit (Hindi)

coppersmith Saffar (Hindi)

corn Dagan (Hebrew), Dagen, Dagon, Daygon

corner Walston *corner stone* (Anglo-Saxon) • *from the corner property* Wray (Old Norse) • *from the slope or corner of land* Yale (Old English) • *from the wether-sheep corner* Wetherell (Old English)

cornstalk Hokolesqua (Shawnee Indian)

Cornwall Denzel *from a place in Cornwall* (Cornish)

correct Uchit (Hindi) • *correct message* Udant (Hindi) • *correct or true* Chan (Vietnamese)

cosmic Shesh *cosmic serpent* (Hindi)

cottage Ascot *dweller at the east cottage* (Old English), Ascott • *dweller at the wall enclosed cottage* Walcott (Old English) • *dweller at west cottage* Wescott (Old German), Wes • *dweller in the old cottage* Alcott (Old English); Olcott (Old German) • *from a stone cottage* Alcott (Celtic), Alcot, Allcot • *from a vined cottage* Haines (Old German), Haynes • *from the cottage on the winding path* Chetwin (Old English) • *from the cottage or country estate* Byron (Old French) • *from the west cottage* Westcott (Old English) • *he dwells at Wolfe's cottage* Wolcott (Old English), Woolcott

cougar Tohon (Native American)

council Rashid *one of good council* (Swahili), Rasheed

counsel Redman *counsel man, horse-*

man (Old English) • *counsel mighty* Redwald (Old English) • *counsel protector* Redmond (Old English), Radmund, Redmund • *counsel wolf, swift wolf* Radolf, Ralph (Old English), Raoul, Raul, Rolph • *peaceful counsel* Sanfred (Old German) • *son of the little counsel wolf* Rawlins (Old Anglo-French); Rawson (Old English) • *wolf counsel* Rolf (Old German); Rolfe, Rolph (Scandinavian)

counselor Daly (Irish-Gaelic); Rad (Old English) • *a wise counselor* Mordecai (Hebrew) • *battle counselor* Eldred (Old German), Eldrid • *bold counselor* Conrad (Old German), Conrade, Contrado, Cort, Curt, Konni, Konrad, Kurt • *brilliant counselor* Radbert (Old English) • *divine counselor* Osred (Old English) • *elfin or good counselor* Alfred (Old English), Alfredo

count Conde (Spanish)

country Bourey (Cambodian); Tem (Gypsy); Deshad (Hindi), Deshal, Deshan • *from the cottage or country estate* Byron (Old French) • *from the country* Rusticus (Latin), Rustice • *of the country of taxes* Toland (Anglo-Saxon), Tolland, Towland • *one from the country, villager* Payne (Latin)

country's *see* brilliant

couple Jugal (Hindi)

courage Himmat (Hindi) • *helmet courage* Helmut (Old German)

courageous Ojayit (Hindi); Adal (Old German), Adall, Adel • *bold, courageous one* Tracy (Latin) • *courageous, stout hearted* Thaddeus (Greek), Taddeo, Tadeo • *ever courageous* Sadavir (Hindi) • *highly courageous* Ardal (Irish-Gaelic), Artegal, Arthgallo

court Courtland *dweller at the court land or farmstead* (Old English), Court • *dweller at the court or farmstead* Courtney (Old French) • *from the enclosed court* Courtland (French) • *servant to the royal court, youthful attendant* Page (French), Pagas, Pegasus • *the fortified court* Harcourt (French)

courteous Shalina (Hindi); Bonar (Old French) • *courteous, ingenious, majestic, scientific one* Shea (Irish-Gaelic) • *courteous one, courtly,* *elegant, well-bred* Curtis (Old French), Curt, Kurt, Kurtis

courtly *see* courteous one, courtly, elegant, well-bred

cover Oni *shelter, cover* (Hindi)

cow Byram *from the ancient cow barn* (Old English) • *keeper of the cattle, little cow* Vachel (French), Vachell, Vachil, Vachill • *white cow* Boyne (Irish-Gaelic)

cowherd Gorakh (Hindi), Govind

crag Craig *dweller at the crag;* Kraig (Scotch-Gaelic)

crane Cranston *from the crane estate or town* (Old English) • *from the crane meadow* Cranley (Old English)

cranes *see* caretaker of the valley; from the valley of cranes

created Nirmit (Hindi) • *God has created him* Asiel (Hebrew)

creates Marnin *one who creates joy* (Hebrew)

creation Srijan (Hindi) • *lord of creation* Kartar (Hindi)

creative Kaliq (Arabic) • *creative one* Adwin (Ghanaian)

Creator Brahma *creator of the universe* (Hindi) • *the Creator* Raini (Native American)

creek Creighton *dweller at the creek estate or town* (Middle English)

creeper Parnik (Hindi)

crest Dinh *mountain summit; crest* Vietnamese)

crested Corydon *crested or helmeted one* (Greek), Korudon

cried for Arvell (Celtic)

crier Scully *town crier or herald* (Irish-Gaelic)

crooked Cromwell *dweller at the crooked or winding spring* (Old English) • *from the crooked field* Sheffield (Old English) • *from the crooked or winding valley* Camden (Anglo-Gaelic) • *wry or crooked mouth* Campbell (Scotch-Gaelic) • *wry or crooked nose* Cameron (Scotch-Gaelic)

cross Quade *cross, ill-tempered one* (German); Quaid (English) • *the shrine of the Cross* Crosby (Old Norse) • *from the cross meadow* Crosley (Old English)

crossing Sanford *by the sandy crossing, dweller at the sandy ford* (Old English), Sanferd, Sanfo, Sanfourd • *crossing the old ford or river, of the ancient ford* Alford (Old English), Alvord • *dweller at the mill ford, from the crossing by the mill* Milford (Old English), Millford • *dweller at the river crossing* Wade (Old English) • *dweller by the river crossing* Byford (Old English) • *from the broad river crossing* Bradford (Old English) • *from the spring by the crossing, from the spring ford* Welford (Old English) • *gray-haired one's river crossing* Blanford (Old English) • *one who lives near a shallow stream crossing* Brodny (Slavic) • *river crossing* Ford (Old English)

crossroads Travers *from the crossroads* (Old French), Travis

crown Taji (African); Pollux (Greek), Pol; Mukut, Sartaj (Hindi) • *the crown needs honor* Adesola (Nigerian), Adejola • *wearing a crown* Kiritan (Hindi)

crowned Taj (Hindi) • *crowned in great honor* Garland (Old English), Garlan • *crowned one* Stephen (Greek), Estefan, Estevan, Etienne, Stefan, Stefano, Stephan, Stephenson, Steven, Stevenson; Esteban (Spanish) • *laurel crowned one* Lenci, Lorant (Hungarian); Lorcan (Jewish); Lawrence (Latin), Lars, Laurenz, Lawry, Lorenz, Lorenzo; Brencis (Latvian); Ralis (Lithuanian); Lorens (Scandinavian); Lorne (Scottish), Lorn

crow's Crawford *of the crow's ford* (Old English)

crucifix Rhodes *dweller at the crucifixes* (Middle English) • *dweller at the crucifix spring* Rodwell (Old English)

crusader Palmer (English)

cry Jaron *to cry out* (Hebrew)

cub Quillan (Irish-Gaelic) • *child, cub* Colin (Irish-Gaelic) • *lion cub* Gur (Hebrew) • *little wolf cub* Channing (Irish-Gaelic); Chane, Channe, Channon (English) • *my lion cub* Guri (Hebrew)

cuckoo Piki (Hindi)

cup *see* bearer

Cupid Atanu (Hindi)

cultivator Harith (African)

curious Chiman (Hindi)

curiosity Jignesh *intellectual curiosity* (Hindi)

curly Troy *at the place of the curly-haired people* (Old French) • *clever, ingenious one; curly-haired one* Cassidy (Irish-Gaelic) • *curly-haired* Krispin (Czech); Crepin, Frazier (French), Fraser, Frasier, Frazer; Crespino (Italian); Crispin (Latin), Crispino, Crispus; Crispo (Spanish)

curving Romney *curving river* (Old Welsh) • *curving river, famous power* Rolt (Old German)

cushion Cody *a pillow or cushion* (Old English), Kody

cut *see* carve

cutter Telek *iron cutter* (Polish) • *iron cutter or hewer* Telford (Old French), Telfor, Telfour • *wool cutter* Sherman (Old English)

cutting Dulani (African)

Cyprus Cyprian *a man of Cyprus* (Greek), Ciprian, Cyprio

Cyrene Cyrano *from Cyrene* (Greek)

— D —

Daegal's Dalston *from Daegal's place* (Anglo-Saxon)

dance Nartana *makes others dance* (Hindi)

dancer Namid *star dancer* (Native American) • *the supreme dancer* Natraj (Hindi)

Dane Denby *a loyal Dane, from the Danish settlement* (Scandinavian), Danby • *from the Dane's settlement* Danby (Old Norse) • *half Dane* Halden (Old Norse), Haldan

Danish *see* Dane

daring Ferdinand *life adventuring, world daring* (Old German), Ferdinando, Ferdnando, Fernando, Hernando • *bold and daring* Hardy (Old German), Hardey

dark Taman (Serbo-Croatian) • *a friend from the dark* Colwin (Anglo-Saxon), Colvin, Colwen • *black, dark blue* Shyamal (Hindi) • *brave, dark man* Donnelly (Celtic), Donely, Donnel, Donnell • *dark blue, black* Shyam (Hindi) • *dark complexioned one* Duff, Dugan (Irish-Gaelic), Duffy; Maurice (Latin), Mauricio, Maury, Moritz, Morrell, Morris; Black (Old English); Dunn (Old English); Moore (Old French) • *dark hero* Dooley (Irish-Gaelic) • *dark one* Kerwin (Celtic), Corwin, Kerwon; Kerr (Irish-Gaelic); Adrian, Nigel (Latin), Adriano, Adrien; Blake (Old En-

glish); Hadrian (Swedish) • *dark or black man* Dunham (Celtic), Dunam • *dark or brown-haired* Bruns (German) • *dark or gray* Tynan (Irish-Gaelic) • *dark warrior* Donovan (Celtic) • *from the black or dark settlement* Colby (Old Anglo-Norse), Kolby • *from the black or dark water* Douglas (Scotch-Gaelic), Douglass, Dugald • *from the dark estate or farm; of a dark city* Colton (Old English), Coltin, Coltson, Coltun • *from the dark farm* Colby (Old English) • *from the dark valley* Blagden (Old English) • *little dark complexioned one* Kieran (Irish-Gaelic); Moreno (Italian-Spanish) • *little dark one* Duane, Dwayne, Kern (Irish-Gaelic) • *newcomer, the dark stranger* Doyle (Celtic) • *of a dark color* Morrell (Latin), Morel, Morril • *son of the dark complexioned one* Morse (Old English) • *son of the dark man* Collis (Old English) • *son of the dark one* Kerry (Irish-Gaelic) • *son of the dark stranger* MacDougal (Scotch-Gaelic)

dark-haired Duff (Irish-Gaelic)

darkness Tamas (Hindi) • *god of darkness* Tamish (Hindi)

dark-skinned Keir (Celtic); Mauli (Hawaiian); Cole (Old English); Merrick (Welsh), Merick, Merik, Merrik

darling Drury *darling, sweetheart* (Old French)

dawn Nishant, Vibhat (Hindi); Roshan (Persian) • Akemi *beautiful dawn* (Japanese) • *sun, dawn* Sahar (Hindi)

day Dack (Old Norse); *belonging to the Lord; born on Sunday, the Lord's day* Dominic (Latin), Domenico, Domingo, Dominick, Dominico, Dominique, Nick • *day bright* Delbert (Old English) • *day lord* Dinesh (Sanskrit) • *sunny day* Helaku (Native American)

daylight Cata *a calabash; anything; a salty cake; gourd; in daylight* (Hasua/African) • *a son born at daylight* Daegal (Scandinavian), Dagall, Dygal, Dygall

dead Jolon *valley of the dead oaks* (Native American)

dear Dyre (Norse) • *beloved or dear one* Anwell (Celtic-Welsh), Anwyl, Anwyll • *dear friend in battle* Hadwin (Old German), Hadwyn, Wynn • *little beloved or dear one* Darrell (Old French), Darold, Darryl, Daryl

death Merripen (Gypsy)

decisive Hasim *decisive one* (Arabic); Haseem (English)

decorated Rajit (Hindi)

dedicated *see* consecrated, dedicated

dedicating Samarpan (Hindi)

decoration Rushabh (Hindi)

deeds Jaskaran *good deeds* (Hindi)

deep Holcomb *deep valley* (Old English) • *of the deep forest* Lockwood (Old English)

deeply Shen *deeply spiritual* (Chinese)

deer Isi (Choctaw Indian); Jelinek (Czech); Hart (English); Cerf (French); Hersh (German), Hirsch; Hershel (Hebrew), Hersch, Herschel; Harshul, Sharang (Hindi); Sarna (Polish); Reno (Spanish) • *a fawn or little deer* Ossian (Irish-Gaelic), Oisin; Ossin (English) • *buck deer* Buck (Old English) • *deer guardian or warden* Derward (Old English) • *deer park or estate, from the deer farm* Darton (Old English) • *dweller at the buck deer meadow* Buckley (Old English) • *from the deer brook* Dearborn (Old English) • *from the deer estate* Darby (Irish-Gaelic), Derby • *from the deer hill* Rawdon (Old Ger-

man), Rawdan, Rawden, Rawdin • *from the deer meadow* Raleigh (Old English), Ralaigh, Ralleigh • *from the roe deer brook, of the flower fields* Rayburn (Old English), Raybin, Raybourne • *from the roe deer forest* Roscoe (Old Norse) • *from the roe deer spring* Rowell (Old English) • *roe buck deer estate* Renton (Old English) • *small deer field* Ogano (Japanese) • *spotted deer* Sarang (Hindi)

deer's Hartwell *deer's spring* (English)

defender Naasir (African); Asim (Arabic), Azim, Azeem; Patr (Hindi) • *army of the Varini, defending warrior or army* Werner (Old German) • *defender of men* Alastair (Scotch-Gaelic), Alaster, Alister, Allister • *defender, true man or watchman* Warren (Old German) • *defending army or warrior* Warner (Old German), Werner • *fortress of the defender's family* Warwick (Old English), Warrick • *helper and defender of mankind* Alexander (Greek), Alec, Alexandre, Alexandro, Alexio, Alexis, Alister, Sander, Saunders; Elek (Hungarian); Oles (Polish) • *the brave defender* Tracey (Anglo-Saxon), Tracay, Tracy • *the god Chi is our defender* Chileogu (Nigerian)

delegate Leggett *delegate or envoy* (Old French), Leggitt, Liggett

delicate Loman (Serbo-Croatian) • *delicate or good* Tayib (Indian) • *tender, delicate* Mridul (Hindi)

delight Pramod, Pratosh (Hindi) • *merriment, delight* Rahas (Hindi)

delightful Krishna, Madin (Hindi), Krisha, Krishnah; Harshal, Mohan, Pramad (Sanskrit), Harshad, Harshil, Harshul

delighting Ranjan (Hindi)

dell Dalton *from the farm in the dell, from the valley estate or town* (Old English) • *lion of the woodland dell* Napoleon (Greek) • *of the dell* Ardell (Old English), Ardel • *of the dell of eagles* Arundell (Old English), Arondel, Arondell, Arundel • *of the open dell* Lydell (Old English)

Demeter *see* belonging to Demeter, Greek fertility goddess

den *see* boar's

Denis Sidney *from St. Denis* (Old English), Sydney
Demark Dana *one from Denmark* (Old English)
Dennis Tennyson *son of Dennis* (Middle English); Dennison (Old English)
departer Nestor *departer or traveler; wisdom* (Greek)
descendant Judd *beloved descendant* (Hebrew), Jedd, Judus • *descendant of Lucius* Lucian (Latin), Luciano, Lucien • *descendant of the challenger* Delaney (Irish-Gaelic), Delan, Delaine, Delainey • *descendant, the inheritor* Jared (Hebrew), Jarred; Jerrod (American) • *the descendants of John* Jennings (Anglo-Saxon)
descending Jordon (Hebrew), Giordano
desert Marudeva *lord of the desert* (Hindi)
designer Mandell *a designer* (Old German), Mandel
desire Ichaa, Manorath (Hindi) • *against desire* Pariket (Hindi) • *of high desire* Connor (Irish-Gaelic), Conner • *wish, desire* Muna (Hindi)
desired Hau *longed for; desired* (Vietnamese) • *the desired one* Desi (Latin); Desito (Spanish)
destined Deston (Latin), Dustin
destroyer Nandin (Hindi) • *destroyer, hewer* Gideon (Hebrew); Hedeon (Russian) • *destroyer of enemies* Areehah (Hindi), Arihant, Arindam • *destroyer of evil* Hashim (Arabic), Hasheem • *destroyer of ignorance* Tamonash (Hindi)
determination Sankalp *will, determination* (Hindi)
determined Liam (Irish-Gaelic) • *determined, firm, resolute* Will (Old English) • *determined peacemaker, resolute peaceful one* Wilfred (Old German)
development Vikas (Hindi)
devoted Sofian (Arabic) • *devoted, pious* Cuyler (Irish-Gaelic), Cyler • *devoted to God* Amyas (Latin), Amias • *devoted to Sunday worship* Maloney (Irish-Gaelic) • *devoted to the will of God; peaceful, quiet one; people mighty* Tully (Irish-Gaelic)
devotee Bhagat (Hindi)

devout Arshad (Sanskrit); Darweshi (Swahili)
dew Tal (Hebrew) • *dew of the morning* Talor (Hebrew) • *father of dew* Avital (Hebrew) • Camlo *sweet dew* (Vietnamese)
dexterous Dexter *dexterous one* (Latin)
diamond *see* bright
Dick's Dickson *Dick's son, of Dick's land* (Old English), Dixon
different Abhin, Vipreet (Hindi)
dignified Jahi (Hindi)
dignitary Channing *canon, church dignitary* (Old French) • *exalted, majestic dignitary* August (Latin), Auguste, Augustin, Augusto, Augustus
dignity Ekbal (Hindi); Jahi (Swahili)
dike Thorndyke *from the thorny dike or embankment* (Old English), Thorndike
dim-sighted *see* blind or dim-sighted
directs Jahdal *the man God directs* (Hebrew), Jahdai, Jahdiel, Jahdol
dirt Marar (Rhodesian); Marana (African)
discerning Basir *discerning and intelligent* (Turkish) • *discerning truth from falsehood* Faruq (Arabic), Farouk
disciple *see* Columbia
discreet Trevor *discreet, prudent, wise* (Irish-Gaelic)
dispenser of provisions Spencer (Middle English)
distaff Quigley (Irish-Gaelic)
distinguished Bertin *distinguished friend* (Spanish)
ditch Brodie *a ditch* (Irish-Gaelic), Brody
divided Kasim (Arabic); Kaseem (English)
divine Devak (Hindi) • *divine bear* Osborn (Old Norse) • *divine, celestial* Saurav (Hindi) • *divine counselor* Osred (Old English) • *divine, famous ruler* Amory (Old German), Amery • *divine friend* Orwin (Anglo-Saxon); Godwin (Old English), Goodwin • *divine helmet* Anselm (Old German), Ansel, Anselme, Anselmo • *divine, immortal one* Ambrose (Greek), Ambrogio, Ambros, Ambrosi, Ambrosio • *divine jewel* Devmani (Hindi) • *divine protection* Wingate (Old English) • *divine protector* Osmond (Old

English), Osmund; Amund (Scandinavian) • *divine reward* (Scandinavian), Axell • *divine ruler* Osric (Old German), Osrick, Osrock, Rick • *divine spear, divine spearman* Oscar (Old Norse) • *divine warrior* Osborn (Old English) • *god-like, divine* Deval (Sanskrit)

divinely Mansur *divinely aided* (Arabic) • *divinely brilliant* Osbert (Old English) • *divinely glorious* Osmar (Old English) • *divinely good* Osgood (Old English) • *divinely peaceful* Jeffrey (Old French), Geoffrey, Jefferey; Godfrey (Old German), Gottfried • *divinely powerful* Oswald (Old English), Oswell

doctor Hakim (Ethiopian); Kaviraj (Hindi); Tabib (Turkish)

document Lekh (Hindi)

dog Kalb (Arabic), Kaleb, Kilah • *child of the hunting dog keeper* Connery (Irish-Gaelic), Conaire, Conary, Conray; Conrey, Conroy, Conry

doer Baruch *doer of good* (Greek); Boniface (Latin) • *well-doer* Evander (Greek)

door Tariq *one who knocks on the door* (Arabic); Tareek, Tarick, Tarik (English) • *open door* Tenskwatawa (Shawnee Indian)

Doria Dorian *from Doria, from the sea* (Greek)

double Twyford *from the double river ford* (Old English)

dove Jonah (Hebrew); Yamha (Hindi); Yunus (Turkish) • *dove, peace* Jonas (Hebrew) • *like a dove* Holleb (Teutonic), Holley, Holluh, Holuh • *little dove* Coleman (Irish-Gaelic), Colman • *the dove, peace loving* Culver (Old English), Colver

down Doane *from the down or hill* (Old English) • *one who smites down* Sihonn (Hebrew), Sihon, Sihun, Sihunn

downy Julius *downy-bearded one, youthful* (Latin), Jule, Jules, Julio; Giles (Old French), Gil • *downy-cheeked one, youthful* Julian (Latin), Julius

dragon Tatsu (Japanese) • *sign of the dragon* Drake (Middle English)

drawer Winchell *drawer of water* (Anglo-Saxon)

dream Swapan (Hindi)

dreams Swapnesh *kind of dreams* (Hindi)

driver Carter *cart driver* (Old English)

drummer Tabber *the wee drummer* (Arabic), Taber

dry Senwe *a dry stalk of grain* (African) • *from the dry valley* Dryden (Old English)

duke Duque (Spanish)

duty Karmendra *duty performer* (Hindi)

dwell Song *to dwell* (Chinese)

dweller Brigham *a dweller by the bridge* (Anglo-Saxon) • *a dweller in the meadow, dweller at the broom meadow* Bromley (Old English), Bromleigh • *bridge builder; dweller at the bridge* Bridger (Old English) • *by the sandy crossing, dweller at the sandy ford* Sanford (Old English), Sanferd, Sanfo, Sanfourd • *castle dweller* Borg (Norse) • *dweller at a forest* Forrest (Old French), Forest • *dweller at a grove of trees* Shaw (Old English) • *dweller at a marsh* Carr (Old Norse) • *dweller at ship island* Delsey (Old Norse) • *dweller at Simon's estate* Symington (Old English) • *dweller at the acre meadow, of the meadow of the oak trees* Ackerley (Old English) • *dweller at the advancer's hill* Weddell (Old English) • *dweller at the ancient oak tree* Orrick (Old English) • *dweller at the ash tree farm* Ashton (Old English) • *dweller at the ash tree meadow, from the ash tree ford* Ashford (Old English) • *dweller at the ash tree pool* Ashlin (Old English) • *dweller at the bank or slope* Bink (North English) • *dweller at the bare hill, he lives on the boar's hill* Barlow (Old English), Borlow • *dweller at the birch headland* Birkett (Middle English) • *dweller at the birch tree meadow* Barclay (Old English), Berkeley • *dweller at the brook in the hollow* Holbrook (Old English) • *dweller at the brooks* Brooks (Middle English) • *dweller at the buck deer meadow* Buckley (Old English) • *dweller at the castle ford* Burford (Old English) • *dweller at the castle meadow* Burley (Old English), Burleigh • *dweller at the castles* Carey (Old

Welsh), Cary • *dweller at the cave slope*
Covell (Old English) • *dweller at the
church* Kirk (Old Norse) • *dweller at
the church hill* Churchill (Old English) • *dweller at the court land or
farmstead* Courtland (Old English),
Court • *dweller at the court or farmstead*
Courtney (Old French) • *dweller at
the crag* Craig (Scotch-Gaelic); Kraig
• *dweller at the creek estate or town*
Creighton (Middle English) • *dweller
at the crooked or winding spring*
Cromwell (Old English) • *dweller at
the crucifixes* Rhodes (Middle English) • *dweller at the crucifix spring*
Rodwell (Old English) • *dweller at the
east cottage* Ascot (Old English), Ascott • *dweller at the elder tree* Elder
(Old English) • *dweller at the elm tree
moor* Elmore (Old English) • *dweller
at the enclosed land or park* Park (Old
English), Parke • *dweller at the field*
Fielding (Old English) • *dweller at
the fifth son's estate* Quincy (Old
French) • *dweller at the fighter's estate*
Payton (Old English) • *dweller at the
flooding brook* Washburn (Old English) • *dweller at the forest* Hurst
(Middle English) • *dweller at the
fortified army camp* Chester (Old English), Chet; Cheslav (Russian) •
dweller at the fortified town Burton
(Old English) • *dweller at the fortress*
Burke (Old French), Berk, Berke,
Bourke, Burk • *dweller at the fowl enclosure* Fulton (Old English) • *dweller
at the friend's estate* Winthrop (Old
English) • *dweller at the gates* Yates
(Middle English) • *dweller at the gray
forest* Leslie (Scotch-Gaelic), Lesley •
dweller at the hare or rabbit lake
Arledge (Old English) • *dweller at the
hedge by the forest* Woodrow (Old English) • *dweller at the hedged enclosure*
Haig (Old English) • *dweller at the island* Nye (Middle English) • *dweller
at the king's ford* Rexford (Old English) • *dweller at the king's spring*
Kingswell (Old English) • *dweller at
the ledge meadow* Shelley (Old English) • *dweller at the linden tree valley*
Lindell (Old English) • *dweller at the
little oak tree* Quennel (Old French) •
dweller at the long ford Langford (Old

English) • *dweller at the long hill*
Langdon (Old English), Landon •
dweller at the marshy valley Marsden
(Old English), Marsdon • *dweller at
the meadow* Atley (Old English) •
*dweller at the mill ford, from the crossing
by the mill* Milford (Old English),
Millford • *dweller at the mill town* Milton (Old English) • *dweller at the new
pool* Newlin (Old Welsh), Newlyn •
dweller at the noble one's island Adney
(Old English) • *dweller at the oak forest* Cheney (Old French), Cheyney •
dweller at the oak tree meadow Ackley
(Old English) • *dweller at the oat field*
Avenall (Old French), Avenel,
Avenell • *dweller at the old estate or
town, from the old manor* Alton (Old
English), Elton • *dweller at the pointed
hill* Montague (French), Monte,
Monty • *dweller at the priest's meadow*
Presley (Old English) • *dweller at the
priest's place* Preston (Old English) •
*dweller at the prince's hill, of the low
lands* Ludlow (Old English), Ludlew,
Ludly • *dweller at the red cliff* Radcliff
(Old English) • *dweller at the red
meadow* Redley (Old English) •
dweller at the river crossing Wade (Old
English) • *dweller at the rocky forest*
Stanwood (Old English) • *dweller at
the rocky meadow* Stanley (Old English), Stanleigh • *dweller at the rocky
village* Stanwick (Old English) •
dweller at the rough meadow Rowley
(Old English) • *dweller at the ryeland*
Rylan (Old English), Ryland •
*dweller at the sandy brook, of the sandy
beach* Sanborn (Old English), Sanborne, Sanburn • *dweller at the sheep
estate* Shipton (Old English) • *dweller
at the sheep meadow* Shipley (Old English) • *dweller at the shrine of the Cross*
Crosby (Old Norse) • *dweller at the
slopes* Hallam (Old English) • *dweller
at the spring* Atwell (Old English) •
dweller at the spring brook Welborne
(Old English) • *dweller at the spring
estate or town* Welton (Old English) •
dweller at the spring farm Atherton
(Old English) • *dweller at the sword
grass place* Sedgwick (Old English) •
dweller at the thicket Bruce (Old
French) • *dweller at the triangular

farmstead Garton (Old English) • *dweller at the valley edge, green valley* Denver (Old English) • *dweller at the vegetable enclosure* Worton (Old English) • *dweller at the village in the thicket* Busby (Scotch-Norse) • *dweller at the wall enclosed cottage* Walcott (Old English) • *dweller at the water* Atwater (Old English) • *dweller at the watercress spring* Carswell (Old English) • *dweller at the wet field* Wakefield (Old English) • *dweller at the wether-sheep meadow* Wetherly (Old English) • *dweller at the white field* Whittaker (Old English) • *dweller at the willow ford* Wilford (Old English) • *dweller at the woman's estate* Quimby (Old Norse), Quinby • *dweller at west cottage* Wescott (Old German), Wes • *dweller by a hollow or by a seething pool* Corey (Irish-Gaelic), Cory • *dweller by a holy spring* Halliwell (Old English) • *dweller by a thorn tree* Thorne (Old English) • *dweller by a willow tree* Wythe (Middle English) • *dweller by the alder river* Garnock (Old Welsh) • *dweller by the enclosure or stronghold* Locke (Old English) • *dweller by the river crossing* Byford (Old English) • *dweller by the spring* Wells (Old English) • *dweller by the stiles* Styles (Old English) • *dweller by the water* Kelwin (Celtic), Kelley, Kelwen; Lach (Old English) • *dweller in a glen or valley* Glenn (Irish-Gaelic-Old Welsh), Glen, Glyn, Glynn • *dweller in a hut* Booth (Middle English), Boothe • *dweller in the beautiful glen* Belden (Old English), Beldon • *dweller in the house at the rock* Tremayne (Old Cornish) • *dweller in the old cottage* Alcott (Old English); Olcott (Old German) • *dweller in the valley* Dale, Dean, Slade (Old English) • *dweller in the valley meadow* Denley (Old English) • *dweller in the valley of the awe-inspiring one* Anscom (Old English), Anscomb • *dweller in the woodlands* Boyce (French) • *dweller near the alder tree* Fernald (Old German) • *dweller near the Brosna River* Brosnan (Irish-Gaelic • *dweller on a burned clearing* Brandeis (Czech); Brand, Brandt, Brant (English) • *dweller on reclaimed land* Newland (Old English) • *dweller on the brook island* Birney (Old English), Burney • *dweller on the castle hill* Burdon (Old English) • *dweller on the castle hill slope* Burbank (Old English) • *dweller on the mountain* Bergen (Old German) • *dweller on the pointed hill* Kill (Old English) • *forest dweller* Silvanus (Latin), Silvano, Sylvanus • *hillside estate dweller* Houghton (Old German) • *sea dweller* Morgan (Welsh) • *son of the dweller at a marsh* Carson (Middle English) • *valley dweller* Vail (Middle English), Vale

dwelling Zebulon *dwelling place* (Hebrew) • *from the home or dwelling place* Case (Latin), Cayce, Cayse • *from the priest's dwelling* Prescott (Old English)

dwells Wolcott *he dwells at Wolfe's cottage* (Old English), Woolcott • *he dwells by the stream* Brooks (Old English) • *keeper of the dyke* Van Dyke (Dutch)

— E —

eager Arden *ardent, fiery; eager, fervent, sincere* (Latin), Ardin • *eager for battle* Alfonso (Old German), Alonso, Alonzo, Alphonso; Fonzi (Spanish) • *eager helper or foreign helper* Gallagher (Irish-Gaelic)

eagle Ajax (Greek); Washi (Japanese); Aleron (Middle Latin); Dyami (Native American); Aren (Norse); Adler, Ahren (Old German), Ahrens • *an eagle* Dyami (Native American) • *eagle gracious* Arnall (Old German), Arnell • *eagle hunter* Makya (Native American) • *eagle of the sun* Antinanco (Native American) • *eagle ruler* Arnold (Old

German), Arnaldo, Arnaud, Arnoldo • *eagle wolf* Arno (Old German), Arnon, Arnoux • *little eagle* Arnett (Old English-Old French), Arnatt; Arnot (Old French-Old German) • *noble eagle* Erland (Old German), Erlond; Adelar (Teutonic) • *of the eagle forest* Arvid (Scandinavian) • *power of an eagle* Arne (Old German) • *the flying eagle* Altair (Arabic)

eagles *see* dell

earned Arjit (Hindi) • *Ogun has earned honor* Ogunkeye (Nigerian)

earnest Ernest *earnest one* (Old English), Ernesto, Ernestus, Ernst; Neto (Spanish)

earth Chik, Pov (Gypsy); Prithvi (Hindi) • *king of the earth* Ilisa, Prithviraj (Hindi) • *king of the ocean* Iravan, Ratnakar (Hindi) • *lord of earth* Ilesh, Talish (Hindi) • *man of the earth* Damek (Slavik), Adamek, Adamik, Adham, Damick, Damicke • *man of the red earth* Damek (Czech); Adam (Hebrew); Keddy (Scottish), Keady, Keddie • Adan (Spanish) • *master of the earth* Avaneesh (Hindi) • *of the earth, mortal* Clay (Old German) • *peace on earth* Aiyetoro (Nigerian) • *prince of earth* Parthiv (Hindi) • *red earth* Addison (Old English) • *the earth* Dagan (East Semitic), Dagon; Mahin, Prithvee (Hindi)

earthquake *see* city

east Kedem (Hebrew); *dweller at the east cottage* Ascot (Old English), Ascott • *from the east* Este (Italian), Estes • *man from the east* Anatole, Cadmus (Greek), Anarolio, Anatol • *the east* Poorv (Hindi) • *the east wind* (Native American)

Easter *see* born at Easter

easy Sahaj (Hindi)

ecstasy Pulak *ecstacy, rapture* (Hindi)

edge *see* dweller at the valley edge

Edward Edison *son of Edward* (Old English), Edson

Egyptian Keb *the Egyptian god Keb* (Egyptian)

eighth-born *see* eighth-born child

elder Elder *dweller at the elder tree* (Old English) • *elder brother* Abi (Hebrew)

• *from the elder tree island* Ellery (Middle English), Ellerey • *elder twin* Zesiro (Ugandan)

eldest Baakir (African)

elegance Jamal (African)

elegant *see* courteous one, courtly, elegant, well-bred

elephant Hastin (Hindi); Sele (West African)

elf Aubrey *blond ruler, elf ruler, spirit ruler* (Old French) • *elf ruler* Avery (Old English) • *elf valley* Elden (Old English)

elfin Alf (Old Norse) • *elfin friend* Elwin (Old English), Elvin • *elfin or good counselor* Alfred (Old English), Alfredo • *elfin warrior* Elvy (Old English)

Ellis Ellison *son of Ellis* (Old English)

elm Elmore *dweller at the elm tree moor* (Old English) • *from the place of the elm trees* Lennox (Scottish-Gaelic) • *like an elm tree* Elman (German), Elmen, Elmon • *the elm tree* Du (Vietnamese)

eloquent Dibri *eloquent and forthright* (Hebrew), Dibbrun, Dibrin, Dibru

embankment *see* dike

embodied *see* embodied beauty

embrace Ashlesh *to embrace* (Hindi)

emerald Neelam, Panna, Pannalal (Hindi)

eminent Howell (Welsh) • *high, eminent one* Howe (Old German)

Emory Emerson *son of Emory* (Old English), Emersen

emperor Ekaraj, Shalang (Hindi) • *an emperor* Huang (Chinese)

enchanter Nahson *great enchanter* (Hebrew), Nahshu, Nahshun, Nahshunn

enchanting Nikunja (Hindi)

encircle Dur (Hebrew)

enclosed Park *dweller at the enclosed land or park* (Old English), Parke • *dweller at the wall enclosed cottage* Walcott (Old English) • *enclosed pasture meadow* Penley (Old English) • *from the enclosed court* Courtland (French) • *from the enclosed farm* Crofton (Old English) • *from the enclosed meadow* Yardley (Old English) • *high or enclosed wood* Heywood (English)

enclosure • *at the cattle enclosure*

Bosworth (Old English) • *dweller at the fowl enclosure* Fulton (Old English) • *dweller at the hedged enclosure* Haig (Old English) • *dweller at the vegetable enclosure* Worton (Old English) • *dweller by the enclosure or stronghold* Locke (Old English) • *from the enclosure with the winding path* Wyndham (Old English) • *from the flax enclosure* Linton (Old English) • *from the long enclosure* Langworth (Old English) • *from the red enclosure* Rudyard (Old English) • *from the riverbank enclosure* Oram (Old English) • *from the rye enclosure* Ryton (Old English) • *from the village enclosure or meadow* Wickham (Old English) • *hedged enclosure keeper* Hayward (Old English) • *sandy enclosure or town* Santon (Old English)

encounter Akanni *profitable encounter* (Nigerian)

end Ahir *end or last* (Turkish) • Townsend *from the end of town* (Old English)

enduring Warburton *from the enduring castle town* (Old English) • *the enduring one* Durant (Latin)

enemies Areehah *destroyer of enemies* (Hindi), Arihant, Arindam • *killer of enemies* Ripudaman (Hindi) • *killing enemies* Arihan (Hindi) • *my enemies are many* Ilomerika (Nigerian), Ilom • *protector against enemies* Zareb (Sudanese)

enemy Ripu (Hindi)

energetic *see* active one, energetic

Englishman Yancy (Native American)

engrossed Magan (Hindi)

enjoyment Modal (Hindi)

enjoys *see* one who enjoys cleanliness

enlightened Tanveer (Hindi) • *a man whom God has enlightened* Jair (Hebrew)

enough Samyak (Hindi)

enterprising Fachan *enterprising, skilled* (Latin), Fachanan

entertaining Samir *entertaining companion* (Arabic)

enthusiasm Oojam (Hindi)

entire Akhill, Nikhil (Hindi)

envious Diarmit *not envious* (Irish-Gaelic), Darby, Dermot, Dermott

envoy *see* delegate or envoy

equal Simen (Gypsy); Adeela, Sarish (Hindi)

equality Samesh *lord of equality* (Hindi)

ermine Fitch *European ermine or marten* (Middle English)

essence Jawhar (Arabic); Asav (Hindi) • *supreme essence* Pillan (Native American); Pilan (English)

establish Yakim *God will establish* (Hebrew); Akim (Russian)

estate Barton *barley estate or farmstead* (Old English) • *boar estate* York (Old English) • *brilliant one's estate* Berton (Old English) • *deer park or estate, from the deer farm* Darton (Old English) • *dweller at Simon's estate* Symington (Old English) • *dweller at the creek estate or town* Creighton (Middle English) • *dweller at the fifth son's estate* Quincy (Old French) • *dweller at the fighter's estate* Payton (Old English) • *dweller at the friend's estate* Winthrop (Old English) • *dweller at the old estate or town, from the old manor* Alton (Old English), Elton • *dweller at the sheep estate* Shipton (Old English) • *dweller at the spring estate or town* Welton (Old English) • *dweller at the woman's estate* Quimby (Old Norse), Quinby • *from a farm in Kent, from the royal estate* Kenton (Old English) • *from an estate by a pool* Pelton (Old English) • *from Ann's estate* Ainsworth (Old English) • *from the advancer's estate, from Wade's castle* Wadsworth (Old English), Wade, Wadesworth • *from the brushwood estate or town* Riston (Old English) • *from the clay estate or town* Clayton (Old English) • *from the cliff estate or town* Clifton (Old English) • *from the combatant's estate* Patton (Old English) • *from the cottage or country estate* Byron (Old French) • *from the crane estate or town* Cranston (Old English) • *from the dark estate or farm; of a dark city* Colton (Old English), Coltin, Coltson, Coltun • *from the deer estate* Darby (Irish-Gaelic), Derby • *from the estate of the keen one's family* Washington (Old English) • *from the estate on the projecting ridge* Hutton (Old English) • *from the estate* or town on the ledge Skelton (Old English) • *from the farm in the dell, from the valley estate or town* Dalton (Old English) • *from the field estate or town* Felton (Old English) • *from the friend's estate* Winton (Old English) • *from the friend's estate or town* Winston (Old English) • *from the golden estate or town* Orville (Old French) • *from the good, liberal one's estate* Tilton (Old English) • *from the gray estate* Horton (Old English) • *from the great estate* Manville (Old French) • *from the great estate or town* Granville (Old French) • *from the great hill* Brynmor (Welsh) • *from the headland estate or town* Clinton (Old English) • *from the hero's estate* Manton (Old English) • *from the hill slope estate* Halton (Old English) • *from the industrious one's estate* Melville (Old French) • *from the iron one's estate* Isham (Old English) • *from the moor estate or town* Morton (Old English) • *from the new estate* Neville (Old French), Nevil, Nevile • *from the new estate or town* Newton (Old English) • *from the north estate* Norville (Old Anglo-French), Norvel, Norvil • *from the north estate or north town* Norton (Old English) • *from the old estate or town* Elton (Old English) • *from the quiet river estate or town* Tanton (Old English) • *from the raven family estate* Remington (Old English) • *from the riverside estate* Eaton (Old English) • *from the rook estate* Rugby (Old English) • *from the Scotchman's estate* Scoville (Old French) • *from the sheep estate* Skipton (Old English) • *from the south estate* Sutton (Old English) • *from the stony estate* Stanton (Old English), Staunton • *from the summer estate* Somerton (Old English); Somerville (Old French-German) • *from the thorny estate* Thornton (Old English) • *from the tree stump estate or town* Stockton (Old English) • *from the wealthy estate* Wellington (Anglo-Saxon) • *from the west estate* Weston (Old English) • *from the wise man's estate* Witton (Old English) • *hillside estate dweller* Houghton (Old German) • *hillside estate or town* Litton (Old

English) • *home lover's estate* Hamilton (Old English) • *home or private property, ruler of an estate* Henry (Old German), Enrique, Heinrich, Hendrick, Henri; Quico (Spanish) • *hunting estate* Huntington (Old English) • *marsh estate or farm* Fenton (Old English) • *marshy estate, spearman's estate* Carvell (Old French), Carvel • *noble one's estate* Alston, Elsworth (Old English) • *noble one's estate or town, noble stone* Elston (Old English) • *of the estate of Ralph* Ralston (Old English), Ralfston, Rolfston • *owner of a rented estate* Galton (Old English) • *pledge or hostage's estate* Gilby (Old Norse) • *roe buck deer estate* Renton (Old English) • *tall man's estate or town* Langston (Old English) • *thunder ruler's estate* Tarleton (Old English) • *upper estate or town* Upton (Old English) • *warrior's estate* Burnaby (Old Norse) • *warrior's estate or town* Chadwick (Old English) • *wheat estate or town* Wheaton (Old English) • *white one's estate* Wentworth (Old English) • *willow estate* Saville (North French) • *yew tree estate* York (Old English)

Estes Estes *of the house of Estes* (Latin), Estas, Estis

eternal Sadiva, Sashwat, Suchir (Hindi) • *eternal flame* Ajanta (Hindi) • *the eternal king's son* Arkin (Norwegian)

European *see* ermine

Evan Bevan *the son of Evan* (Celtic), Bevin

evanescence *see* breath, evanescence

evening Saanjh (Hindi)

everywhere Chou, Chow (Chinese)

evil *see* destroyer of evil

evolved Ednit (Hindi)

ewe Ewert *ewe herder* (Old English)

exalted Alvah, Sion (Hebrew); Austin (Latin), Austen, Auston • *appointed of Jehovah, exalted by God* Jeremy (Hebrew), Jereme, Jeremiah, Jeremias; Yerik (Russian) • *exalted, majestic dignitary* August (Latin), Auguste, Augustin, Augusto, Augustus • *exalted, noble* Kareen (Arabic), Karim • *exalted or lofty* Haroun (Arabic); Aaron (Hebrew), Aharon, Aron • *of the*

exalted or high race Hakon (Old Norse), Hako
exalting Rafi (Arabic), Raffin
excellence Ubora (African) • *greatest in excellence* Maximillian (Latin), Maxim, Maximo; Maksim (Russian)
excellent Liang (Chinese); Benzi (Hebrew); Ghalib (Hindi) • *an excellent warrior, king* Praveer (Hindi) • *excellent male child* Hideo (Japanese) • *excellent one* Variya (Hindi) • *most excellent* Pravar (Hindi)
excitement Urav (Hindi)
exhortation *see* consolation

exile Gershom *exile or stranger* (Hebrew), Gersham
exists Chidi *God exists* (African)
experienced Maalik (African)
expert Mahir (Hebrew) • *expert; heaven; narrow-minded; to geld* Thien (Vietnamese) • *expert, skilled* Praveen, Pravin (Hindi)
exquisite Apoorva (Hindi)
extensive Vipul (Hindi)
eye Lokanetra *eye of the world* (Hindi) • *the eye* Vilochan (Hindi)
eyes Nayan (Hindi)

— F —

fair Kyle *fair and handsome* (Celtic), Kile • *fair, blond one* Aubin (Old French); Gwynn (Old Welsh), Guin • *fair-complexioned* Dhaval, Kapil (Hindi) • *fair-complexioned one* Alben (Latin), Alban, Albin, Aubin • *fair-haired and complexioned* Finn (Irish-Gaelic) • *fair-minded* Adley (Hebrew), Adalai, Adlai, Adlay, Adlei • *fair or white* Albion, Alver, Remus (Latin), Alvar, Aubyn • *fair or white-haired, with short hair* Sherlock (Old English), Sherlocke • *fair view* Bevis (Old French), Beauvais • *fair, white one* Wynn (Old Welsh), Winn • *little and fair* Finan (Irish-Gaelic), Fionan; Finn, Finnin, Fintan, Finton (English) • *little fair-complexioned one* Gannon (Irish-Gaelic) • *little fair-haired one* Blakey (Old English) • *little fair-haired valorous one* Finley (Irish-Gaelic), Findlay, Findley, Finlay • *son of the fair head* Gaynor (Irish-Gaelic), Gainer, Gainor, Gayner
fairest Japheth *fairest son* (Hebrew), Japeth
faith Iman (African); Vishvas (Hindi)
faithful Amin (Arabic), Ameen, Amitan, Amnon; Hamon (Greek); Dillon (Irish-Gaelic) • *faithful and true* Pin (Vietnamese) • *faithful, loyal* Leal (Latin) • *faithful, loyal, true one* True (Old English) • *faithful one's ad-*

herent Truman (Old English) • *faithful servant* Tadashi (Japanese) • *faithful, sincere, true* Fidel (Latin), Fidele, Fidelio, Fidelis
falcon Sahen (Hindi) • *falcon flying* Elsu (Miwok) • *falcon or hawk* Merlin (Middle English) • *little falcon or hawk* Marlon (Old French), Marlin
falsehood *see* discerning truth from falsehood
fame Kirti, Yash, Yashas (Hindi) • *bright or shining with fame* Robert (Old English), Bert, Roberto, Robertson, Robin, Rupert • *famous ruler, rich in fame* Roderick (Old German), Broderick, Roderich, Rodrick, Rodriego, Rodrigo, Rurik • *from the fountain of fame* Engedi (Hebrew) • *lord of fame* Yashodev (Hindi) • *of holy fame* Alisen (Old German)
famed Karnam, Yashmit (Hindi)
family Primo *first child born to a family* (Italian) • *fortress of the defender's family* Warwick (Old English), Warrick • *from a good family* Benon (Irish-Gaelic) • *from a venerated family* Gatian (Hebrew), Gati, Gatias • *from a wandering family* Gurias (Hebrew) • *from the estate of the keen one's family* Washington (Old English) • *from the raven family estate* Remington (Old English)

famous Rowan (Celtic); Cleon (Greek), Kleon; Parag (Hindi); Clarence (Latin) • *a famous and brilliant man* Cuthbert (Anglo-Saxon), Cuthburt • *a famous warrior* Lashi (Gypsy), Lash, Lasho • *bold or princely and famous* Baldemar (Old German) • *bright raven, he shall be famous* Bertram (Old German), Bartram • *curving river, famous power* Rolt (Old German) • *divine, famous ruler* Amory (Old German), Amery • *famous commander* Penrod (Old German) • *famous friend* Marvin, Mervin (Old English), Merwyn • *famous hero or man* Rodman (Old German) • *famous hostage* Gilmer (Old English) • *famous, illustrious one* Clair (English) • *famous in battle* Wymer (Old English) • *famous noble* Hilmar (Old Norse) • *famous, noble* Nolan (Irish-Gaelic); Almo (Old English), Aylmer, Edelmar, Elmer • *famous one's island* Rodney (Old English) • *famous or royally peaceful, the ruler of all* Vladimir (Slavic), Vlad, Vladamar, Vladi, Vladimar • *famous protector* Rodmond (Old German), Rodmund • *famous ruler* Roarke (Irish-Gaelic), Rourke, Ruark; Roald, Valdemar (Old German), Waldemar • *famous ruler, rich in fame* Roderick (Old German), Broderick, Roderich, Rodrick, Rodriego, Rodrigo, Rurik • *famous son* Ingemar (Old Norse) • *famous spearman* Roger (Old German), Rodger, Rogerio, Rutger • *famous, strong* Waldemar (Old English) • *famous warrior* Aloysius, Lothar, Louis, Luther (Old German), Aloisus, Clovis, Lewis, Lotario, Ludvig, Ludwig, Luigi, Luis, Lutero, Luthais; Humberto (Teutonic); Umberto (Spanish) • *famous wolf* Rule (Old French); Rudolph (Old German), Rodolf, Rodolfo, Rodolph, Rudolf; Ulmer (Old Norse), Ulmar; Rolon (Spanish) • *from the famous land* Roland (Old German), Orlando, Roldan, Rolland, Rollin, Rollins, Rowland; Ordando (Spanish) • *land famous* Lamar (Old German) • *little famous one* Merritt (Old English); Merrill

(Old French) • *resolute, famous one* Wilmer (Old German) • *son of famous in war* Loring (Old German) • *very famous one* Filmer (Old English), Fillmore, Filmore

farm Karmel (Hebrew) • *ash tree farm* Ashby (Old English) • *a small farm* Toft (Old English) • *born on the willow farm* Saville (Latin), Saval, Savil, Savill • *deer park or estate, from the deer farm* Darton (Old English) • *dweller at the ash tree farm* Ashton (Old English) • *dweller at the spring farm* Atherton (Old English) • *farm worker* Hoffman (German) • *from a farm* Bolton (Old English), Bolten; Kelby (Old German), Kilby • *from a farm in Kent, from the royal estate* Kenton (Old English) • *from Carl's farm* Carlton (Old English), Carleton • *from the bent grass farm* Benton (Old English) • *from the dark farm* Colby (Old English) • *from the dark estate or farm; of a dark city* Colton (Old English), Coltin, Coltson, Coltun • *from the enclosed farm* Crofton (Old English) • *from the farm by the spring* Wilton (English); Kilby (Old German); Welby (Scandinavian) • *from the farm in the dell, from the valley estate or town* Dalton (Old English) • *from the farm in the valley* Denton (Old English) • *from the farm near the ledge* Shelby (Anglo-Saxon) • *from the ledge farm or town* Shelton (Old English) • *from the manor house farm* Selby (Old English) • *from the meadow farm* Leighton (Old English) • *from the north farm* Northrop (Old English) • *from the rush farm* Leverton (Old English) • *from the spring farm* Chilton, Wilton (Old English) • *from the Welshman's farm* Walworth (Old English) • *from the wether-sheep farm* Wetherby (Old English) • *from the willow farm* Willoughby (Old English) • *from the winding farm* Crompton (Old English) • *marsh estate or farm* Fenton (Old English) • *of the farm by the water* Marston (Old English) • *of the farm in the forest* Silsby (Old English) • *of the farm over the hill* Dunton (Old English), Dunston, Duntson • *wolf guardian's farm* Wordsworth (Old English)

farmer Granger, Stedmann (Old English), Stedman; Karl, Mayer (Old German), Meyer, Myer; Parlan (Scottish) • *a farmer, son of the furrows* Bartholomew (Hebrew), Bartel, Barthel, Bartholomaus; Bartkus (Lithuanian) • *farmer, land worker* Jorn (Danish); Juri (Estonian); Joji (Japanese); George (Latin), Georg, Giorgio, Jorge; Goran (Scandinavian); Yuri (Russian) • *farmer, steward* Meyer (German)

farmer's Carleton *farmer's settlement* (Old English), Carlton

farmland *see* awe-inspiring one's farmland

farmstead Worth (Old English) • *at the farmstead* Atworth (Old English) • *barley estate or farmstead* Barton (Old English) • *dweller at the court land or farmstead* Courtland (Old English), Court • *dweller at the court or farmstead* Courtney (Old French) • *dweller at the triangular farmstead* Garton (Old English) • *farmstead owner* Stedman (Old English) • *from the beloved one's farmstead* Truesdale (Old English) • *from the farmstead* Worth (Old English) • *from the white farmstead* Whitby (Old English) • *peasant's farmstead or town* Charlton (Old English)

fascinating Mohin (Hindi)

fast Hector *holds fast, steadfast* (Greek)

fat *see* fat at birth

fate Karm (Hindi); Deston (Latin), Dustin

father Abu (African); Avi (Hebrew); Tadd (Old Welsh); Fadey (Ukranian) • *abbey father* Abbott (Old English), Abott • *Father, Lord* Uba (African) • *father of a generation* Avidor (Hebrew) • *father of dew* Avital (Hebrew) • *father of gods and men* Zeus (Greek) • *father of justice* Avidan (Hebrew) • *father of light* Abner (Hebrew), Avner • *father of peace* Absalom (Hebrew), Absa; Axel (Old German) • *father of the multitude* Bram (Dutch); Abraham (Hebrew), Ibrahim • *God is my father* Aviel (Hebrew) • *like his father* Antipas (Hebrew); Atalik (Hungarian) • *my father is my rock; my father is my strength*

Avniel (Hebrew) • *my father is still alive* Nnamdi (Nigerian) • *son of a busy father* Emlyn (Old German), Emelin, Emlen • *the Lord is my father* Abijah (Hebrew), Abisha, Abisia, Abixah

fatherhood Zaci *god of fatherhood* (African)

favor Rida (Arabic)

fawn *see* a fawn or little deer

fear *see* abstain

fearless Nirbhay (Hindi), Nirbhik

feather Shikoba (Choctaw Indian)

feeling Rasik *full of feeling, passion* (Hindi)

feet Charan (Hindi)

fence Han *a fence* (Chinese)

fern Farnham *from the fern field* (Old English) • *from the fern meadow* Farnley (Old English) • *from the fern slope* Farnell (Old English), Farnall, Fernald

fertile Kasib (Arabic); Kaseem (English) • *a tiller of fertile soil* Tilford (Old English), Tillford, Tillfourd

fertility Demetrius *belonging to Demeter, Greek fertility goddess* (Greek), Demetre, Demetrio; Dimitri (Russian) • *the Syrian god of fertility* Hadad (Arabic), Adad, Haddad

fervent *see* ardent, fiery; eager, fervent, sincere

festival Tiet (Vietnamese)

fiber *see* breathe

field shoda *a level field* (Japanese) • *a resident of Stanfield, from the rocky field* Stanfield (Old English) • *base, rice field* Honda (Japanese) • *black, rice field* Kuroda (Japanese) • *broad field, forest* Bradshaw (English) • *dweller at the field* Fielding (Old English) • *dweller at the oat field* Avenall (Old French), Avenel, Avenell • *dweller at the wet field* Wakefield (Old English) • *dweller at the white field* Whittaker (Old English) • *flat, rice field* Hirata (Japanese) • *forest, rice field* Morita (Japanese) • *from a bright field* Campbell (French), Campball • *from the bean field* Bancroft (Old English) • *from the crooked field* Sheffield (Old English) • *from the fern field* Farnham (Old English) • *from the field by the small river* Mansfield (Old English) •

from the field estate or town Felton (Old English) • *from the field or plain* Blair (Irish-Gaelic) • *from the flax field* Linley (Old English) • *from the friend's field* Winfield (Old English) • *from the hawk field* Gavin (Old Welsh), Gavan, Gaven • *from the little field* Dalziel (Scotch-Gaelic) • *from the ravine field or waterfall field* Dallas (Scotch-Gaelic) • *from the red field, red pasture meadow* Radley (Old English) • *from the red meadow, he lives by the red field* Ridley (Old English) • *from the rye field* Rycroft (Old English) • *from the smooth field* Riddock (Irish-Gaelic) • *from the south field* Suffield (Old English) • *from the warrior's field* Mayfield (Old English) • *from the white field* Whitfield (Old English) • *good fortune, rice field* Fukuda (Japanese) • *middle, rice field* Tanaka (Japanese) • *of the field near the sea* Seadon (Old English), Seaden • *old, rice field* Furuta (Japanese) • *pine, rice field* Matsuda (Japanese) • *rice field, river* Tagawa (Japanese) • *rice field, rock* Iwata (Japanese) • *rice field, side* Tanabe (Japanese) • *rice field, wisteria* Fujita (Japanese) • *small deer field* Ogano (Japanese) • *small field* Ohara (Japanese) • *triangular field* Garfield (Old English)

fields Berwick *from the barley fields* (Old German) • *from the roe deer brook, of the flower fields* Rayburn (Old English), Raybin, Raybourne • *man of prosperity, owner of fields* Forbes (Irish-Gaelic)

fierce Griffith *fierce chief* (Old Welsh) • *fierce raven* Brainard (Old German), Braynard • *fierce, strong* Praval (Hindi); Lon, Lunn (Irish-Gaelic) • *fierce valor* Devlin (Irish-Gaelic)

fiery Hakan (Native American); Adar (Hebrew) • *ardent, fiery; eager, fervent, sincere* Arden (Latin), Ardin • *ardent, fiery one* Egan (Irish-Gaelic) • *fiery one* Ignacio (Latin); Ignace, Ignatius, Ignatz (English); Ignatius (Dutch); Ignaz (German); Ignazio (Italian); Hignacio, Ignasio, Ygnocio (Spanish • *little fiery one* Aidan, Fagan, Keegan (Irish-Gaelic), Aden, Fagin, Aiden • *of the fiery hair, redhead*

Bayard (French), Baird, Beard • *son of the fiery one* Key, Magee (Irish-Gaelic)

fifteenth *see* fifteenth born child

fifth Quincy *dweller at the fifth son's estate* (Old French) • *fifth child* Quinton (Latin)

fighter Goar (Latin), Goer, Gore; Palladin (Native American), Pallaton • *dweller at the fighter's estate* Payton (Old English) • *fifth-born child* Anum (Ghanaian); Quenton, Quintin (Latin), Quent, Quentin, Quenton, Quint; Quito (Spanish) • *fighter, stranger* Boris (Slavic) • *guerrilla fighter* Magaidi (East African) • *the spear fighter* Ordway (Anglo-Saxon)

filled Gyan *filled with knowledge* (Sanskrit)

Finn Davin *bright Finn, the bright man* (Scandinavian), Daven, Davon • *thunder Finn* Torpin (Old Norse)

fir Garwood *from the fir forest* (Old English)

fire Edan (Celtic); Adar, Nuri (Hebrew), Nuriel, Nuris; Basdev, Jugnu, Krishanu, Pavak, Shami, Vanhi (Hindi) • *born of fire* Vasuman (Hindi) • *son of fire, son of light* Orion (Greek)

firebrand Brand, Brant (Old English) • *firebrand, sword* Brander (Old Norse)

firm Allard (Old German), Alard • *constant, firm one* Constantine (Latin), Constantin, Constantino, Costantin, Costantino, Dinos; Costa, Konstandinos, Konstantinos, Kostas, Kostis, Kostos (Greek); Stancio (Spanish) • *determined, firm, resolute* Will (Old English) • *firm, constant one* Constantine (Latin), Constantin, Constantino, Costantin, Costantino • *firm spear, spear brave* Garrett (Old English), Garrard, Garret, Garritt • *firm, strong one* Firmin (Old French) • *from the firm fortress, resolute brilliant one* Wilbur (Old German) • *god of fire* Agni, Varad (Hindi) • *nobly firm* Adelhart (Teutonic) • *of a firm nature* Goddard (Old German), Godderd, Godred • *solid, firm or rugged* Berk (Turkish) • *the fire* Keahi (Hawaiian)

firmness Ethan *firmness, strength* (Hebrew)

first Shaka (African) • *first born* Pehlaj (Hindi); Kazuo (Japanese) • *first child born to a family* Primo (Italian) • *first light* Ujas (Hindi) • *first of twins* Odion (Nigerian) • *first son of the wild boar* Haro (Japanese), Haroko, Haroku • *the first one* Thien (Vietnamese)

first-born Mosi (Swahili) • *first-born male* Taro (Japanese) • *first-born male twin* Ulan (Sudan) • *first-born son* Chaska (Sioux)

fish Fiske (Middle English); Pat (Native American) • *large fish* Timin (Hindi) • *little fish* Dagan (East Semitic), Dagon

fisherman Siddon (Hebrew), Sidon, Sidonius • *the fisherman* Fisk (Scandinavian), Fiske

flame Prajvala (Hindi) • *flame of God* Uriel (Hebrew), Uri, Ury • *flame of Jehovah, my light is Jehovah* Uriah (Hebrew) • *silver flame* Shiamak, Siamak (Hindi)

flaming Pierro *with flaming hair* (Greek)

flank Hong *flank, side; red, rosy* (Vietnamese)

flat Hiramatsu, Matsuhira *flat, pine* (Japanese) • *flat, rice field* Hirata (Japanese) • *from the flat land* Platt (Old French) • *from the flat meadow* Smedley (Old English)

flatnosed Harim (Hebrew)

flattering Millard *flattering, strong and winning* (Old French) • *flattering, winning one; industrious one* Emil (Old German), Emilio

flattery Du (Vietnamese)

flax Linton *from the flax enclosure* (Old English) • *from the flax field* Linley (Old English)

flaxen-haired Linus (Hebrew), Linis, Lynus

flight Nissan (Hebrew)

flint Lonato (Native American)

flint-like Shamir (Hebrew)

flocks Gothard *from God's flocks* (Old German), Gothar

flooding *see* brook

flowing Akar (Turkish) • *free-flowing* Deror (Hebrew), Derori

flower Zahur (Swahili) • *from the roe deer brook, of the flower fields* Rayburn

(Old English), Raybin, Raybourne

flowered Royden *from the flowered valley* (Old English)

flute Len (Hopi); Banshi, Bansi, Murli, Tanav (Hindi) • *a flute* Murali, Tunava (Hindi) • *the flute* Muralee (Hindi)

flying Elsu *falcon flying* (Miwok) • *the flying eagle* Altair (Arabic)

foes Jitamitra *vanquisher of foes* (Hindi)

fog Nihaar (Hindi)

folk *see* ballad

follower Coyle *battle follower* (Irish-Gaelic) • *boy of the tribe, follower* Sabu (Indian) • *follower or warrior attendant* Thane (Old English), Thaine, Thayne

follows Rashad *one who follows the right path* (Arabic), Rasheed, Rashid

food Purvis *to provide food* (English-French)

force Uziel *a mighty force* (Hebrew), Uzziel • *soul, life force* Janu (Hindi)

ford Sanford *by the sandy crossing, dweller at the sandy ford* (Old English), Sanferd, Sanfo, Sanfourd • *crossing the old ford or river, of the ancient ford* Alford (Old English), Alvord • *dweller at the ash tree meadow, from the ash tree ford* Ashford (Old English) • *dweller at the castle ford* Burford (Old English) • *dweller at the king's ford* Rexford (Old English) • *dweller at the long ford* Langford (Old English) • *dweller at the mill ford, from the crossing by the mill* Milford (Old English), Millford • *dweller at the willow ford* Wilford (Old English) • *ford of the national spearman* Tuxford (Old Norse-English) • *from Gil's ford* Gilford (Old English) • *from the barley ford* Beresford (Old English) • *from the black ford* Hamford (Old German) • *from the cattle ford* Rutherford (Old English), Rutherfurd • *from the cliff ford* Clifford (Old English); Telem (Hebrew) • *from the double river ford* Twyford (Old English) • *from the ford at the hill* Lawford (Old English) • *from the ford at the peak* Pickford (Old English) • *from the iron ford* Telford (Old English), Telfore,

Tellford • *from the linden tree ford* Linford (Old English) • *from the oak tree ford* Adair (Scotch-Gaelic) • *from the oxen ford* Oxford (Old English) • *from the raven's ford* Ransford (Old English) • *from the red ford* Radford, Redford (Old English), Ruford • *from the rocky ford* Stanford (Old English) • *from the rough ford* Rufford (Old English) • *from the rush ford* Rushford (Old English) • *from the spring by the crossing, from the spring ford* Welford (Old English) • *from the stony ford* Stamford (Old English) • *from the tall ford* Hanford (Old German) • *from the white ford* Whitford (Old English) • *from the wide ford* Rumford (Old English) • *from the willow ford* Safford (Old English) • *Hugh's ford* Huxford (Old English) • *of the crow's ford* Crawford (Old English) • *of the ford by the wall* Warford (Old English), Warfourd • *of the landing ford* Stafford (Old English), Staford • *river ford on the street* Stratford (Old English)

forehead Tran *forehead; to overflow* (Vietnamese)

foreign Gallagher *eager helper or foreign helper* (Irish-Gaelic) • *of a foreign city* Ernald (Old German), Ernaldus

foreigner Gall (Irish-Gaelic) • *foreigner, stranger* Frayne (Middle English), Fraine, Freyne

foreman *see* administrator, foreman, magistrate, overseer

forest Lin (Chinese), Ling; Nahele (Hawaiian); Kaanan (Hindi) • *a forest* Malaya (Hindi); *alder forest army camp* Worcester (Old English) • *a roe, from the forest* Dorcas (Hebrew), Dorcus • *at the forest* Atwood (Old English) • *bailiff or forest warden* Woodruff (Old English) • *bright forest* Sherwood (Old English) • *broad field, forest* Bradshaw (English) • *dweller at a forest* Forrest (Old French), Forest • *dweller at the forest* Hurst (Middle English) • *dweller at the gray forest* Leslie (Scotch-Gaelic), Lesley • *dweller at the hedge by the forest* Woodrow (Old English) • *dweller at the oak forest* Cheney (Old French), Cheyney • *dweller at the rocky forest*

Stanwood (Old English) • *forest dweller* Silvanus (Latin), Silvano, Sylvanus • *forester, forest warden* Woodward (Old English) • *forest grove* Vipin (Hindi) • *forest guardian* Forrester (Middle English), Forester, Foster • *forest guide* Guido (Italian) • *forest keeper* Ranger (Old French), Rainger • *forest, rice field* Morita (Japanese) • *forest town* Boswell (Old French) • *friend guardian, friend's forest* Winward (Old English) • *from the church forest* Kirkwood (Old North English) • *from the clearing in the forest* Royd (Scandinavian), Roid • *from the fir forest* Garwood (Old English) • *from the forest* Xylon (Greek); Wesh (Gypsy); Silvester, Sylvan (Latin), Silvain, Silvan, Silvestro, Sylvester; Holt (Old English); Boyce (Old French) • *from the forest of nut trees* Delano (Old French) • *from the forest of oak trees* Cheney (French), Chenay • *from the forest valley* Walden (Old English) • *from the gray forest* Griswold (Old German) • *from the hedged forest* Haywood (Old English), Heywood • *from the lake forest* Marwood (Old English) • *from the narrow forest* Calhoun (Irish-Gaelic) • *from the north forest* Norwood (Old English) • *from the old forest* Elwood (Old English), Ellwood • *from the raven forest* Renshaw (Old English) • *from the roe deer forest* Roscoe (Old Norse) • *from the upper forest* Upwood (Old English) • *gamekeeper, warden of a forest* Forest (English) • *lord of the forest* Vanadev, Vanajit (Hindi) • *of the deep forest* Lockwood (Old English) • *of the eagle forest* Arvid (Scandinavian) • *of the farm in the forest* Silsby (Old English) • *the bright one's forest* Dagwood (Old English)

forested Odell *from the forested hill* (Middle English)

forester *see* forest

forever Junius *forever young* (Latin)

forgiving Fordel (Gypsy)

formless Amoorta (Hindi)

forsaken Almon (Hebrew)

fort Carson (Welsh) • *from the black fort* Cardew (Celtic) • *of the winning fort* Seaver (Anglo-Saxon), Seavir

forth Siloam *he is sent forth* (Hebrew), Siloa, Siloum

forthright Dibri *eloquent and forthright* (Hebrew), Dibbrun, Dibrin, Dibru • *forthright, noble* Elbert (Old German), Bart, Elbart, Elburt

fortified Burgess *citizen of a fortified town* (Middle English) • *dweller at the fortified army camp* Chester (Old English), Chet; Cheslav (Russian) • *dweller at the fortified town* Burton (Old English) • *of the fortified city* Walton (Old English) • *the fortified court* Harcourt (French)

fortress Dunstan *brown fortress, brown stone* (Old English) • *castle, fortress, stronghold* Burke (Old German) • *dweller at the fortress* Burke (Old French), Berk, Berke, Bourke, Burk • *fortress of the defender's family* Warwick (Old English), Warrick • *fortress of the moon* London (Middle English) • *fortress resident* Brougher (Old English) • *from the firm fortress, resolute brilliant one* Wilbur (Old German) • *from the fortress* Darcy (Old French), Darsey • *from the fortress town* Broughton (Old English) • *from the glen fortress* Glendon (Scottish-Gaelic), Glenden, Glenn • *from the stone fortress* Stanbury (Old English) • *from this fortress* Carew (Celtic), Carr, Carrew • *great hill fortress* Dunmore (Scotch-Gaelic) • *of the beautiful fortress* Beaufort (French), Beau, Beaufert • *rocky fortress or sky fortress* Rochester (Old English)

fortunate Masud (Arabic); Asher (Hebrew); Subhag (Hindi); Sachio (Japanese) • *fortunate, lucky one* Felix (Latin); Feliks (Russian) • *the fortunate* Gadmann (Hebrew), Gadmon

fortune Mestipen (Gypsy) • Cappi *good fortune* (Gypsy); Chance (Middle English) • *good fortune, rice field* Fukuda (Japanese) • *my fortune* Gadi (Arabic); Gadiel (Israeli)

fortune-teller Durriken (Gypsy)

founder Shaka (African) • *the founder* Sawandi (South African)

fountain Pilar *a fountain basin or pillar* (Spanish) • *fountain; water source* Fontaine (French); Fontayne (English); Fontana (Italian); *from the*

fountain of fame Engedi (Hebrew) • *from the fountain of youth* Endor (Hebrew), Dorr, Ender, Nandor

fourth *see* born

fowl *see* dweller at the fowl enclosure

fox Liska *a fox* (Czech); Voss (Dutch); Todd (North English)

fragrant Quanah (Comanche Indian); Myron (Greek)

free Nirish (Hindi) • *born free* Azad (Turkish) • *free holder of land* Franklin (Middle English), Frank, Franklyn • *free man* Palani (Hawaiian); Darby, Dermot, Kermit (Irish-Gaelic), Derby, Dermott; Francis (Latin), Francesco, Franchot, Francisco, Francois, Frans, Franz; Bundy, Freeman (Old English); Frank (Old French); Chico, Pancho (Spanish) • *free, noble friend* Frewin (Old English), Frewen • *free or noble protector* Fremont (Old German) • *smooth, free, and unhindered* Chang (Chinese)

freedom Deror *freedom, free-flowing* (Hebrew), Derori

free-flowing *see* freedom

fresh Tan *fresh and new* (Vietnamese)

Friday *see* born on Friday

friend Rafiki (African); Kadin, Khalil (Arabic); Bandhu, Bheru, Mitali, Mitul, Sachiv, Vayya (Hindi); Dakota (Native American); Akiiki (Ugandan) • *a friend* Mitra (Hindi) • *a friend from the dark* Colwin (Anglo-Saxon), Colvin, Colwen • *a friend of a soldier* Chatwin (Anglo-Saxon) • *a friend of nature* Stanwin (Old English), Stonwin • *a good friend* Subandhu (Hindi) • *an amiable friend* Haymo (Latin), Aimo • *army or people's friend* Arvin (Old German) • *beautiful friend* Bellamy (Latin) • *beloved friend* Derwin, Durwin (Old English) • *bold friend or protector* Baldwin (Old German), Balduin, Baudoin • *brave friend* Hardwin (Old English); Darwin (Old German), Darwen • *brilliant; quick friend* Egwin (Anglo-Saxon), Egin, Winn • *cheerful, kind friend* Gladwin (Old English) • *dear friend in battle* Hadwin (Old German), Hadwyn, Wynn • *distinguished friend* Bertin (Spanish) • *divine friend* Orwin (Anglo-Saxon);

Godwin (Old English), Goodwin • *elfin friend* Elwin (Old English), Elvin • *famous friend* Marvin, Mervin (Old English), Merwyn • *free, noble friend* Frewin (Old English), Frewen • *friend from the north* Norvin (Old English), Norwin, Norwyn • *friend guardian, friend's forest* Winward (Old English) • *friend of all* Alvin (Old German), Alvan, Alwin, Alwyn; Albin (Russian) • *friend of city* Purumitra (Hindi) • *friend of gold* Goldwin (Anglo-Saxon) • *friend of St. Michael, from Michael's stronghold* Carmichael (Scotch-Gaelic) • *friend of the harvest* Berwin (Middle English) • *friend of the sea* Merwyn (Celtic), Mervin, Merwin • *friend or old, wise protector* Alden (Old English), Aldin, Aldwin, Aldwyn, Elden, Eldin • *friend to all* Lakota (Native American), Takoda • *God's friend* Oswin (Old English) • *golden friend* Aurelius (Latin), Arelus • *good friend* Kalil (Arabic), Kahaleel, Kahlil; Bellamy (French); Saumitr (Hindi); Nitis (Native American) • *handsome friend* Bellamy (Old French) • *heart friend* Corwin (Old French-English) • *intimate friend* Halil (Turkish) • *law friend* Ewing (Old English) • *manor house friend* Selwyn (Old English), Selwin • *noble friend, wealthy friend* Audwin (Old German) • *not a friend* Unwin (Old English) • *old friend or protector* Aldwin (Anglo-Saxon), Aldwon • *peaceful friend* Jakarious (Hindi); Winfred (Old English) • *powerful friend* Medwin (Old English) • *prosperous friend* Edwin (Old English) • *protector or spear friend* Aswin (Old English) • *proud friend* Delwyn (Old English),

Delwin • *sea friend* Erwin, Irving (Old English), Irvin, Irvine, Irwin; Marvin (Old Welsh) • *spear friend* Garvin, Orvin (Old English), Garwin • *sword friend* Melvin (Old English) • *the raven's friend* Corwin (Anglo-Saxon), Corvin, Korwin • *valued friend* Levin (Anglo-Saxon) • *Welsh friend* Walwyn (Old English)

friendly Maitreya, Mitrajit, Sumant (Hindi); Elan (Native American) • *friendly, lovable* Elmo (Latin-Greek) • *friendly, loving* Philo (Greek)

friend's Winthrop *dweller at the friend's estate* (Old English) • *friend guardian, friend's forest* Winward (Old English) • *from the friend's estate* Winton (Old English) • *from the friend's estate or town* Winston (Old English) • *from the friend's field* Winfield (Old English) • *from the friend's hill* Winslow (Old English)

friendship Salokh (Hindi) • *love, friendship* Pranya (Hindi)

from Van (Dutch) • *from me* Mander (Gypsy)

frost Tushaar (Hindi)

fruit Samar *fruit of paradise* (Hindi)

fruitful Helbon *from the fruitful valley* (Hebrew)

fruitfulness see abounding in fruitfulness

full Rip *full grown* (Dutch), Ripp • *full moon* Badrani (African); Badar (Arabic) • *full of feeling, passion* Rasik (Hindi) • *full of grace* Elu (Native American) • *full of life* Jeeval, Sajiva (Hindi) • *full of love* Premal (Hindi)

fun Pias (Gypsy)

furrows see farmer

future Huang-Fu *wealthy future* (Chinese)

— **G** —

Gabriel Gable *little Gabriel* (Old French)
gain Labh (Hindi)
gallant see companion
game Carvey *athlete, game player* (Irish-

Gaelic) • *the game of chess* Nard (Persian)
gamekeeper see forest
Gar Garson *son of Gar* (Old English), Gershon

garden Munda (African); Udyan (Hindi); Mundan (Rhodesian) • *a garden* Ginton (Hebrew), Ginson • *from the garden* Garth (Old Norse)

gardener Arber (Latin); Gardner (Middle English), Gardiner

garland Vencel *wreath or garland* (Hungarian) • *garland or wreath of glory* Wenceslaus (Old Slavic)

Garret Garrison *son of Garret (Old English)*

Gary· Garron *son of Gary, a spearman* (Old English)

Gascony Gaston *from Gascony* (Old German)

gate Stiggur (Gypsy) • *dweller at the gates* Yates (Middle English) • *from the high gate* Hyatt (Old English) • *guardian of the gate* Yemon (Japanese) • *the guard at the northern gate* Norward (Old German), Norwood, Norword

gatekeeper Porter (French); Durward (Old English) • *gatekeeper, royal messenger* Portero (Spanish)

gateway Barr *a gateway* (Old English)

gave Olujimi *God gave me this* (Nigerian)

gay Festus *gay, jubilant* (Latin), Festatus • *gay, lively one* Gale (Old English), Gaile, Gayle

gaze Vilokan (Hindi)

gazelle Maha (Hindi)

geld *see* expert; heaven; narrow-minded; to geld

gem *see* bright gem

general Zaim *brigadier general* (Arabic) • *lieutenant general* Fariq (Arabic)

generation *see* father

generosity Hisham (Arabic); Samaah (Hindi)

generous Fadil, Kareem (Arabic), Fadeel, Fahdeel; Hiroshi (Japanese) • *a generous soul* Edbert (Anglo-Saxon)

gentle Latif (African); Adiv (Hebrew); Syon (Hindi); Daman (Irish); Lindo (Old German); Gareth (Welsh), Garth • *gentle and patient* Halim (Arabic) • *gentle, good, kind* Bonar (Old French) • *gentle, handsome, lovable, noble* Keefe (Irish-Gaelic) • *gentle, kind one, merciful* Kelemen (Hungar-

ian); Clement (Latin), Clemence, Clemens, Clemente, Clementius; Kliment (Russian) • *gentle, lovable* Kevin (Irish-Gaelic), Kevan, Keven • *gentle peace* Linfred (Old German) • *quiet, gentle* Shamindra (Hindi)

Gerald Fitzgerald *a son of Gerald* (Old German), Fitz, Fitzger

German Almund (Old German) • *son of the Teuton or German* Tyson (Old German) • *the German* Jermaine (Latin); Jamaine, Jermain, Jermane (English); Jarman (Old German), Jerman

giant Viraat (Hindi); Orion (Latin)

giants Titus *of the giants* (Greek), Tito

gift Suday (Hindi) • *a gift* Doran (Greek), Dorein, Doren, Dorin, Dorren, Dorrin, Dorran; Tesher (Hebrew); Donato (Latin) • *a gift, given of God* Nathan (Hebrew), Nate • *gift brave* Gifford (Old English), Gifferd • *gift from God* Enam (Ghanaian) • *gift of God* Theodore (Greek), Teodoro, Theodorus; Coniah, Nathaniel (Hebrew), Conah, Conias, Jecoa; Fedor (Russian) • *gift of Jehovah* Johanan, Matthew (Hebrew), Mateo, Mathew, Mathias, Matteo, Matthaeus, Mattias; Mayhew (Old French) • *gift of our Lord* Osgood (Old German) • *gift of the god Chi* Chioke (Nigerian) • *gift of the goddess Artemis* Artemas (Greek), Art, Artemus, Artimas, Artimis, Tamus, Taymus • *gift of the Lord* Jeconiah, Zebadiah (Hebrew), Econah, Jecon, Zebe, Zebedee; Tudor (Welsh) • *God's gift* Yohance (African); Todor (Hungarian); Dorek (Polish) • *Jehovah's gift* Jonathan (Hebrew) • *Jupiter's gift* Zenas (Greek), Zenos

Gilbert Gibson *son of Gilbert* (Old English)

Gil's *see* ford

give Jivan *to give life* (Hindi); Jeeven, Jeven, Jiven, Jivin (English)

given Nathan *a gift, given of God* (Hebrew), Nate • *all given to him* Wemilat (Native American) • *given by water* Nirad (Hindi) • *given by Zeus* Senon (Spanish)

gives Del *he gives* (Gypsy) • *Ogun gives help* Ogunsanwo (Nigerian)

giving Sanjeev *giving life, reanimating* (Hindi)

glacier Brede (Scandinavian)

glad Faine *glad, joyful* (Middle English); Fane (Old English)

glade Nemo *from the glade or glen* (Greek)

glen Glenn *dweller in a glen or valley* (Irish-Gaelic/Old Welsh), Glen, Glyn, Glynn • *dweller in the beautiful glen* Belden (Old English), Beldon • *from the glade or glen* Nemo (Greek) • *from the glen fortress* Glendon (Scottish-Gaelic), Glenden, Glenn

glorified Rajab (Arabic); Raj (English)

glorious Ala, Majid (Arabic), Magid, Jajdi, Majeed; Dyumna, Mahasvin (Hindi); Huy (Vietnamese) • *army brilliant, glorious warrior* Herbert (Old German) • *brilliance of Thor or thunder glorious, thunder* Thorbert (Old Norse) • *divinely glorious* Osmar (Old English) • *glorious peace* Siegfried (Old German), Siegfrid, Sigfrid, Sigvard • *glorious position, stand of glory* Stane (Serbian); Stanislaus (Slavic), Stanislas, Stanislav • *glorious raven* Bartram (Old English), Barthram • *glorious ruler, royal glory* Vladislav (Old Slavic) • *little glorious warrior* Harbin (Old French-German) • *sea glorious* Seabert (Old English), Sebert • *shining, glorious one* Bert (Old English)

glory Wing (Chinese); Shaan (Hindi) • *garland or wreath of glory* Wenceslaus (Old Slavic) • *glorious position, stand of glory* Stane (Serbian); Stanislaus (Slavic), Stanislas, Stanislav • *glorious ruler, royal glory* Vladislav (Old Slavic) • *glory of God* Jochebed (Hebrew), Jochbed • *glory of spring* Jaroslav (Slavic) • *glory, prosperity* Blade (Old English) • *glory, vigor* Pratap (Hindi)

goat Jael *mountain goat* (Hebrew)

God/god Thakur (Hindi); Chi (Nigerian) • *a comfort from God* Nehemiah (Hebrew) • *a gift, given of God* Nathan (Hebrew), Nate • *a man whom God has enlightened* Jair (Hebrew) • *appointed of Jehovah, exalted by God* Jeremy (Hebrew), Jereme, Jere-

miah, Jeremias; Yerik (Russian) • *belonging to the god Olorun* Olorun (African) • *beloved of God* Amadeo (Spanish), Amadis, Amado, Amando • *beloved of God, beloved stranger* Elidad (Hebrew) • *chaplain, man of God* Chapin (French), Chapen, Chapland • *consecrated to God* Lemuel (Hebrew) • *devoted to God* Amyas (Latin), Amias • *devoted to the will of God; peaceful, quiet one; people mighty* Tully (Irish-Gaelic) • *flame of God* Uriel (Hebrew), Uri, Ury • *gift from God* Enam (Ghanaian) • *gift of God* Theodore (Greek), Teodoro, Theodorus; Coniah, Nathaniel (Hebrew), Conah, Conias, Jecoa; Fedor (Russian) • *gift of the god Chi* Chioke (Nigerian) • *glory of God* Jochebed (Hebrew), Jochbed • *God exists* Chidi (African) • *God gave me this* Olujimi (Nigerian) • *God has blessed me* Olushola (Nigerian) • *God hears* Ismael (Arabic), Ismail, Ismeil; Ishmael (English); Ismael (Hebrew); Esmael, Isamel, Ysmael (Spanish) • *God is gracious* Deshawn (American), Deshane, Deshawne; Sean (Celtic), Shane, Shawn; Jean (French); Hans (German); Yannis (Greek); Hanan, John (Hebrew), Giovanni, Ivan, Johann, Jon, Juan, Sean, Shane; Ansis (Latvian); Janis, Jonas (Lithuanian), Janulis; Kwam (Native American); Zane (Old English); Jens (Scandinavian), Yens; Ian (Scotch-Gaelic); Jovan (Slavic); Evan, Jone (Welsh) • *God has created him* Asiel (Hebrew) • *God is good* Wunand (Native American) • *God is my judge* Daniel (Hebrew), Dane • *God is my lion* Guriel (Hebrew) • *God is salvation* Jesus (Hebrew); Jesu, Jesuso, Jezus (Spanish) • *God is the victor* Olushegun (Nigerian) • *God is with us* Emmanuel (Hebrew), Emanuel, Emanuele, Immanuel, Manuel • *God loves me* Olufemi (Nigerian) • *God, my rock or stone* Zuriel (Hebrew) • *God, my salvation, the Lord is salvation* Elisha (Hebrew), Eliseo • *god of clouds and rain* Hinun (Native American) • *god of darkness* Tamish (Hindi) • *god of fatherhood* Yaci

(African) • *god of fire* Agni, Varad
(Hindi) • *god of love* Madan (Hindi);
Amadis (Latin), Amadus • *god of love
and passions* Kamadev (Hindi) • *god
of mind* Manish (Hindi) • *god of
mountain* Girish (Hindi) • *god of
peace and agriculture* Lono (Hawaiian) • *God of salvation* Joshua (Hebrew) • *god of serpents* Naagesh
(Hindi) • *god of the midday sun* Orun-
jan (African) • *god of the multitude*
Ganesh (Sanskrit) • *God of the river*
Alpheus (Greek), Alfeus • *god of the
stars* Taresh (Hindi) • *god of the world*
Jagdeo (Hindi) • *god of war* Ogun
(Nigerian) • *god of waters* Varun
(Hindi) • *god of wine* Dennis
(Greek), Denis, Dion, Dionsio,
Dionysus • *God is just* Avidan (He-
brew) • *God is my father* Aviel (He-
brew) • *God is perfect* Jotham (He-
brew) • *God rules* Elrad (Hebrew) •
God the highest Omari, Omarr
(Swahili) • *God, the Lord* Elihu (He-
brew) • *God will establish* Yakim (He-
brew); Akim (Russian) • *God will help*
Lazarus (Hebrew), Lazario, Lazaro •
God will increase Jo (Japanese) • *God
will judge* Joachim, Yadim (Hebrew);
Yadon (Israeli); Ioakim (Russian),
Jov; Joaquin (Spanish) • *healed by
God* Raphael (Hebrew), Rafael,
Rafaelle, Rafaello, Rafe • *he belongs to
God* Elkan (Hebrew) • *he is born of
God* Jabin (Hebrew), Jaban, Jabon •
he is protected by God Osmond (Old
German), Osman, Osmen, Osmo,
Osmund, Ozmo • *help from God*
Adom (Akan) • *hidden by the god*
Zephaniah (Hebrew) • *his name is
God* Samuel (Hebrew), Samuele •
honoring God Timothy (Greek), Tim-
oteo, Timotheus • *Jehovah is my God*
Elliot (French-Hebrew), Elliott; Ilias
(Greek); Elijah (Hebrew), Elia,
Elias, Ellis • *Kamdev, god of love*
Darpak (Hindi) • *lion of God* Arel
(Hebrew), Areli • *loved by God* Joash
(Hebrew), Hoashis, Joashus; Priyesh
• *man of God* Gabriel, Obadiah (He-
brew), Obed, Obeded • *power of God*
Chike (African) • *power of the god Chi*
Chike (Nigerian) • *ruling through
God* Godric (Anglo-Saxon) • *seeker of*

god Sutapa (Hindi) • *servant of God*
Abdalla (Swahili) • *song of God* Ronel
(Hebrew) • *strength of God* Ezekiel
(Hebrew), Ezechiel, Ezechiele, Ezequiel, Zeke • *sun god* Dinesh (Sanskrit) • *thanking God* Hamid (Arabic)
• *the black god* Mayon (Hindi) • *the
Egyptian god Keb* Keb (Eyptian) • *the
god Chi is our defender* Chileogu
(Nigerian) • *the god Chi is our protector* Chileogu (Nigerian) • *the god Chi
is protecting* Cinese (Nigerian) • *the
god Chi's own blessing* Chinua (Nigerian) • *the god Kalkin* Kalkin (Hindi)
• *the god Odin* Odin (Old Norse) •
the god Ogun Oko (African) • *the god
Vishnu* Narain (Hindi) • *the Lord is
God* Joel (Hebrew) • *the man God di-
rects* Jahdal (Hebrew), Jahdai,
Jahdiel, Jahdol • *the Syrian god of fer-
tility* Hadad (Arabic), Adad, Haddad
• *thought of the god Chi* Chinelo
(Nigerian) • *thunder god* Raiden
(Japanese) • *to whom God is a help*
Eleazar (Hebrew), Eleazaro • *who is
like God* Mihail (Bulgarian); Minka,
Misko (Czech); Mihkel (Estonian);
Mikko (Finnish); Dumichel, Michau
(French); Makis, Michail, Mikhail,
Mikhalis, Mikhos (Greek); Michael
(Hebrew), Micah, Michel, Miguel,
Mikael, Mischa; Miska (Hungarian);
Mikelis, Mikus (Latvian); Mitchell
(Middle English); Mikkel (Norwe-
gian); Machas, Michak, Michael,
Michalek, Mietek (Polish); Miguel
(Portuguese); Mihas (Romanian);
Mikhalka (Russian); Micheil (Scot-
tish); Mickel, Mihalje (Swedish); Mi-
haio (Ukranian); Mihangel (Welsh)
• *village god* Muni (Hindi) • *wrestling
with God* Israel (Hebrew)
goddess Demetrius *belonging to
Demeter, Greek fertility goddess*
(Greek), Demetre, Demetrio;
Dimitri (Russian) • *gift of the goddess
Artemis* Artemas (Greek), Art, Artemus, Artimas, Artimis, Tamus,
Taymus
god-like Deven (Sanskrit) • *god-like,
divine* Deval (Sanskrit)
godly Theon (Greek); Devank, Vinesh
(Hindi)
gods Devsena *army of gods* (Hindi) •

breath of the gods Spiro (Greek) •
father of gods and men Zeus (Greek)
God's Adriel *from God's congregation*
(Hebrew) • *from God's flocks* Gothard
(Old German), Gothar • *God's bless-*
ing Adom (Ghanaian) • *God's chief*
administrator Mukasa (African) •
God's friend Oswin (Old English) •
God's gift Yohance (African); Todor
(Hungarian); Dorek (Polish) • *God's*
hero Gavril (Russian) • *God's light*
Madison (English) • *God's mountain*
Harel (Hebrew) • *God's planter*
Jezreel (Hebrew) • *placed in God's*
hands Foluke (Nigerian) • *ruler of the*
Gods Devraj (Hindi)
goes Tuan *goes smoothly* (Vietnamese)
• *he goes* Jal (Gypsy)
gold Jin (Chinese); Rukm (Hindi);
Kim (Korean); Zeheb (Turkish) •
friend of gold Goldwin (Anglo-Saxon)
golden Kin (Japanese) • *from the*
golden estate or town Orville (Old
French) • *golden friend* Aurelius
(Latin), Arelus • *golden-haired* Aurel
(Czech); Aurek (Finnish); Aurele,
Dory (French); Aurelio (Italian);
Aurelius (Latin); Aureli (Polish);
Aurelian (Romanian); Avrel, Avreliy
(Russian) • *golden one* Sovann (Cambodian); Oro (Spanish) • *golden yel-*
low hair Flavius (Latin) • *son of the*
golden one Golding (Old English) •
the golden-haired Xanthus (Latin)
good Husni, Salih (Arabic); Tavi (Aramaic); Liang (Chinese); Tobit (Hebrew), Tova, Tovah; Dobry (Polish) •
a good friend Subandhu (Hindi) • *a*
good judge Faisal (Arabic), Faisel,
Faizal, Faysal, Faysul, Fayzal, Fayzel •
beneficient and good Maddock (Old
Welsh), Madock • *charitable, good*
Khairiya (Hindi) • *coatmaker, son of a*
good man Manning (Old German) •
delicate or good Tayib (Indian) • *di-*
vinely good Osgood (Old English) •
doer of good Baruch (Greek); Boniface (Latin) • *elfin or good counselor*
Alfred (Old English), Alfredo • *from*
a good family Benon (Irish-Gaelic) •
from the good, liberal one's estate Tilton
(Old English) • *from the good, liberal*
one's valley Tilden (Old English) •
gentle, good, kind Bonar (Old French)

• *God is good* Wunand (Native Ameri-
can) • *good deeds* Jaskaran (Hindi) •
good fortune Saad (African); Cappi
(Gypsy); Chance (Middle English) •
good fortune, rice field Fukuda (Japa-
nese) • *good friend* Kalil (Arabic), Ka-
haleel, Kahlil; Bellamy (French);
Saumitr (Hindi); Nitis (Native
American) • *good luck* Cheung (Chi-
nese) • *good man* Goodman (Old
German) • *good one* Boone (Old
French) • *good seafarer* Godrich (Old
German), Goodrich • *my good* Tovi
(Hebrew) • *one of good council* Rashid
(Swahili), Rasheed • *son of a good*
man Odoric (Latin), Odericus,
Odrick • *the bearer of good news* Ewald
(Latin), Ewold, Wald • *the good* Ho
(Chinese) • *the Lord is good* Tobias
(Hebrew), Tobia
good-hearted Suhruda (Hindi)
good-looking Zuri (African)
good-natured Hien *good-naturedand*
sweet (Vietnamese)
goodness Joed *witness our Lord's good-*
ness (Hebrew)
gooseberry Durril *the gooseberry*
(Gypsy)
gopher Suskov (Russian)
gore Gordon *from the triangular or gore*
shaped hill (Old English), Gordan,
Gorden
Goths Gustavo *staff of the Goths* (Italian); Gustave (Swedish), Gustaf,
Gustaff, Gustav
gourd *see* anything
government Sigwald *government or vic-*
torious ruler (Old German)
governor *see* castle
grace Hannibal *grace of Baal* (Phoenician) • *full of grace* Elu (Native American)
graceful Sulalit (Hindi) • *brilliant and*
graceful Hulbert (Old German), Hulbard, Hulburt
gracious Arnall *eagle gracious* (Old
German), Arnell • *God is gracious*
God is gracious Deshawn (American),
Deshane, Deshawne; Sean (Celtic),
Shane, Shawn; Jean (French); Hans
(German); Yannis (Greek); Hanan,
John (Hebrew), Giovanni, Ivan, Johann, Jon, Juan, Sean, Shane; Ansis
(Latvian); Janis, Jonas (Lithuanian),

Janulis; Kwam (Native American); Zane (Old English); Jens (Scandinavian), Yens; Ian (Scotch-Gaelic); Jovan (Slavic); Evan, Jone (Welsh) • *gracious protector* Esmond (Old English) • *gracious son* Ethbin (Latin), Ethban, Ethben

grain Dagan (Hebrew), Dagen, Dagon, Daygon • *a dry stalk of grain* Senwe (African)

grand Manvell *from the grand house* (Latin), Manvel, Manvil

grandfather Babu (African)

grasp Chin *to grasp* (Korean) • *to grasp or hold* Cata (Bangi/African)

grass Kakar (Indian); Pezi (Sioux) • *dweller at the sword grass place* Sedgwick (Old English) • *from the bent grass farm* Benton (Old English)

grassy hill Hamilton (English), Hambleton • *owner of a grassy plain* Lander (Middle English), Landers, Landor

grateful Haamid (African)

gray Tynan *dark or gray* (Irish-Gaelic) • *dweller at the gray forest* Leslie (Scotch-Gaelic), Lesley • *from the gray estate* Horton (Old English) • *from the gray forest* Griswold (Old German) • *from the gray home or gray land* Graham (Old English) • *from the gray meadow* Greeley (Old English) • *gray-haired one* Lloyd (Old Welsh), Floyd • *gray-haired one's river crossing* Blanford (Old English) • *gray wolf* Mingan (Native American) • *iron gray hair* Ferrand (Old French), Farrand, Farrant, Ferrand

grazing Winfield *place for grazing* (Old German)

great Chen (Chinese); Magnus (Latin); Grant (Middle English) • *a man of the great plains* Conway (Celtic) • *crowned in great honor* Garland (Old English), Garlan • *from the great estate* Manville (Old French) • *from the great estate or town* Granville (Old French) • *from the great hill* Brynmor (Welsh) • *great abundance* Zaid (Hindi) • *great chief* Melvern (Native American) • *great enchanter* Nahson (Hebrew), Nahshu, Nahshun, Nahshunn • *great hero* Anlon (Irish-Gaelic), Anluan • *great*

hill fortress Dunmore (Scotch-Gaelic) • *great judge* Ramiro (Spanish), Ramirez • *great lord* Ainmire (Irish-Gaelic); Mahesh (Sanskrit) • *great talker* Kuzih, Tate (Native American) • *great warrior* Cathmor (Irish-Gaelic) • *little great one* Darren (Irish-Gaelic), Daren • *man of great beauty* Philemon (Greek) • *man of great wealth* Orton (Old German), Orten • *of great joy* Tait (Scandinavian), Taite • *of great worth* Aylsworth (Old German), Alsworth, Ellsworth • *the great leaper* Gosheven (Native American) • *thinker with a great purpose* Aristotle (Greek)

greater Major, Mayer (Latin)

greatest Ali (Arabic) • *greatest in excellence* Maximillian (Latin), Maxim, Maximo; Maksim (Russian) • *greatest star* Urian (Greek), Urion

greatly Hillell *greatly praised* (Hebrew), Hilel, Hillel

Greece Javan *one from Greece* (Hebrew), Javin, Javon

greedy *see* commit

Greek *see* belonging to Demeter, Greek fertility goddess

green Kadir (Arabic); Harit (Hindi) • *dweller at the valley edge, green valley* Denver (Old English) • *from the green hill* Varden (Celtic), Vardon • *of the green lawn* Landers (Old English)

gritty Chesmu (Native American)

grocer Samman (Arabic), Sammon

ground Galt *high ground* (Old Norse)

grove Shaw *dweller at a grove of trees* (Old English) • *forest grove* Vipin (Hindi) • *from the alder grove* Varney (Celtic); Verney (Old French) • *from the grove* Lunt (Old Norse) • *from the grove of trees* Grover (Old English) • *from the hare grove* Hargrove (Old English), Hargrave • *from the holly tree grove* Hollis (Old English) • *grove of alders* Delano (Latin), Delanos • *grove of trees* Nahele (Hawaiian) • *island grove* Lundy (French)

grower *see* bean grower

growing Crescen (Latin), Crescin, Crescint, Cris, Crist

growling Liwanu *bear growling* (Miwok)

grown Rip *full grown* (Dutch), Ripp

guard Garner *army guard, guardian army* (Old French) • *careful, wary guard* Gardell (Old German), Gardal, Gardel • *from the guarded palace* Salisbury (Old English) • *guard, watchman* Waite (Middle English) • *the guard at the northern gate* Norward (Old German), Norwood, Norword • *unfailing guard* Durward (Old German)

guardian Hafiz *a guardian* (Arabic) • *army guard, guardian army* Garner (Old French) • *awe-inspiring guardian, noble guardian* Aylward (Old English) • *bold guardian or royal guardian* Kenward (Old English) • *chief guardian* Howard (Old English) • *deer guardian or warden* Derward (Old English) • *forest guardian* Forrester (Middle English), Forester, Foster • *friend guardian, friend's forest* Winward (Old English) • *from the guardian's meadow* Wardley (Old English) • *guardian at the gate* Yemon (Japanese) • *guardian from the sea* Meredith (Old Welsh) • *guardian, watchman* Ward (Old English), Warde, Warden • *hall guardian or warden* Allward (Old English) • *park guardian or keeper* Parker (Middle English) • *powerful guardian* Rickward (Old English), Rickwood • *prosperous guardian* Edward (Old English), Edouard, Eduard, Eduardo, Edvard • *sea guardian* Seward (Old English) • *victorious guardian* Sigurd (Old Norse) • *watchful guardian* Argus (Greek) • *wealthy guardian* Edik (Russian) • *wolf guardian's farm* Wordsworth (Old English)

guerrilla *see* fighter

guest Atithi (Hindi) • *guest or stranger* Xenos (Greek)

guide Sahil (Hindi) • *a guide or leader* Hadi (Arabic) • *forest guide* Guido (Italian) • *guide to righteousness* Haadiya (Hindi)

guided Rashid *rightly guided* (Arabic), Rasheed

⟶ H ⟶

hacker Hackett *little hacker* (Old French-German)

hair Huslu *bear with lots of hair* (Miwok) • *born with long hair, leader* Caesar (Latin), Cesar, Cesare; Kesar (Russian) • *fair or white-haired, with short hair* Sherlock (Old English), Sherlocke • *golden yellow hair* Flavius (Latin) • *horn colored hair* Cornell (Old French), Cornall, Cornel • *iron gray hair* Ferrand (Old French), Farrand, Farrant, Ferrant • *long hair, noted for his hair* Esau (Hebrew) • *of the fiery hair, redhead* Bayard (French), Baird, Beard • *reddish-brown hair* Sorrell (Old French) • *renowned for his hair* Faxon (Old German), Faxan, Faxen • *with flaming hair* Pierro (Greek)

haired Troy *at the place of the curly-haired people* (Old French) • *black-haired* Dolan, Dow (Irish-Gaelic); Colley (Old English), Collis • *brown-haired one* Bruno (Italian) • *clever, ingenious one; curly-haired one* Cassidy (Irish-Gaelic) • *curly-haired curly-haired* Krispin (Czech); Crepin, Frazier (French), Fraser, Frasier, Frazer; Crespino (Italian); Crispin (Latin), Crispino, Crispus; Crispo (Spanish) • *dark-haired* Duff (Irish-Gaelic) • *dark or brown-haired* Buns (German) • *fair-haired and complexioned* Finn (Irish-Gaelic) • *fair or white-haired, with short hair* Sherlock (Old English), Sherlocke • *flaxen-haired* Linus (Hebrew), Linis, Lynus • *from the white-haired one's island* Whitney (Old English) • *golden-haired* Aurel (Czech); Aurek (Finnish); Aurele, Dory (French); Aurelio (Italian); Aurelius (Latin); Aureli (Polish); Aurelian (Romanian); Avrel, Avreliy (Russian) • *gray-haired one* Lloyd

(Old Welsh), Floyd • *gray-haired one's river crossing* Blanford (Old English) • *light-haired* Fairfax (English) • *little brown-haired one* Burnell (Old French) • *little red-haired one* Ruskin (French-German); Roslin (Old French) • *long-haired beggar* Kesin (Hindi) • *red-haired* Ruff, Rush (French), Ruffe, Rufus; Flann, Rogan, Rowan (Irish-Gaelic), Rowe, Rowen; Rust (Latin), Rufe, Rusty; Reid (Old English), Read, Reed; Russell (Old French); Roth (Scottish-Gaelic) • *reddish-brown haired* Arun (Sanskrit) • *red-haired youth* Alroy (Irish-Gaelic) • *sandy-haired* Sandy (Middle English) • *servant of the red-haired youth* Gilroy (Irish-Gaelic) • *small brown-haired one* Donnan (Irish-Gaelic) • *son of the red-haired man* Flynn (Irish-Gaelic), Flinn • *the golden-haired* Xanthus (Latin) • *white-haired* Finbar (Irish), Finbur • *white-haired man* Whitman (Old English) • *yellow-haired* Bowie (Irish-Gaelic); Flavian (Latin)

hairy Issay (African)

half Halden *half Dane* (Old Norse), Haldan • *half-speaker, mumbler* Lawler (Irish-Gaelic)

hall Edsel *a prosperous man's manor hall or house* (Old English) • *from the manor hall* Halford (Old English) • *hall guardian or warden* Allward (Old English) • *the hall* LaSalle (French)

halo Bimb (Hindi)

Hal's Halsey *from Hal's island* (Old English)

hammer Smith *blacksmith, worker with a hammer* (Old French) • *little hammer* Marcel (Latin), Marcello, Marcellus, Marcelo

hand Dumaka *help me with hands* (Nigerian) • *left hand* Nawat (Native American) • *son of the right hand* Benjamin (Hebrew), Beathan • *the hand* Jed (Arabic); Jedd (English)

hands Fabron *he works with his hands, the mechanic* (Latin), Fabrin • *placed in God's hands* Foluke (Nigerian)

handsome Runako (African); Cemal, Hassan, Husni, Jamil, Shakil, Shaquille (Arabic), Jamill; Beauregard (French), Beau; Adonis (Greek);

Manjul, Nehal, Prakrit, Saumya (Hindi); Cavan, Cullen, Keeley, Kenneth (Irish-Gaelic), Cullan, Cullin, Kavan, Kealy, Keely • *cheerful, handsome, harmonious one* Alan (Irish-Gaelic), Ailin, Alain, Allan, Allen, Allyn • *fair and handsome* Kyle (Celtic), Kile • *gentle, handsome, lovable, noble* Keefe (Irish-Gaelic) • *handsome friend* Bellamy (Old French) • *handsome, kind* Hasim (Arabic), Hassim • *handsome or keen* Keene (Celtic), Kean, Keane

Hans Hansen *son of Hans* (Scandinavian), Hansan, Hanson

happiness Santosh (Hindi); Ayo (Nigerian); Dakarai (Zimbabwean) • Abayomi *bringer of happiness* (Nigerian) • *my Lord brings happiness* Olukayode (Nigerian)

happy Said (African); Asher (Hebrew); Kantu, Nishok, Prasanna, Samen, Sunar (Hindi); Farhani (Swahili) • *blessed, happy* Seeley (Old English), Sealey; Selig (Old German) • *he was happy* Adebayo (Nigerian)

hard Hart (Anglo-Saxon) • *hard, strong minded* Hurd (Anglo-Saxon) • *hard worker* Cham (Vietnamese)

hardy Hardy *from a hardy stock* (Old German), Harday

hare Krolik (Czech-Polish), Zajicka; Haas (Dutch-German); Cooney (English); Zajac (Polish-Ukranian); Kune (Yugoslavian) • *dweller at the hare or rabbit lake* Arledge (Old English) • *from the hare grove* Hargrove (Old English), Hargrave • *from the hare pasture* Harley (Old English), Arley

harmonious *see* cheerful, handsome, harmonious one

harmony Cosmo *harmony, order, the universe* (Greek), Cosimo, Cosme

harp player Harper (Old English)

Harris Harrison *son of Harris* (Old English), Harry

Harry Harris *son of Harry* (Old English); Barris (Old Welsh) • *Harry's son* Parry (Welsh)

hater Ulysses (Greek), Ulises

harvest Hasad (Turkish) • *friend of the harvest* Berwin (Middle English)

hawk Horus (African); Taka (Japanese); • *falcon or hawk* Merlin (Middle English) • *from the hawk field* Gavin (Old Welsh), Gavan, Gaven • *little falcon or hawk* Marlon (Old French), Marlin • *sparrow hawk* Kele (Hopi); Kelle (English) • *white hawk* Gavin (Irish-Gaelic)

hawks Keaton *place of the hawks* (English)

he Delsin *he is so* (Native American)

head Russom *boss, head* (African) • Kinnell *from the head of the cliff* (Irish-Gaelic) • *head man* Colman (Icelandic) • *head of the monastery* Pryor (Latin); Prior (English) • *helmeted head* Kennedy (Irish-Gaelic) • *son of the fair head* Gaynor (Irish-Gaelic), Gainer, Gainor, Gayner • *to shake the head* Luyu (Miwok)

headland Pembroke (Welsh) • *cape, headland* Saki (Japanese) • *dweller at the birch headland* Birkett (Middle English) • *from the headland estate or town* Clinton (Old English) • *rocky headland* Carrick (Irish-Gaelic)

healed Raphael *healed by God* (Hebrew), Rafael, Rafaelle, Rafaello, Rafe • *he is healed by the Lord* Josiah (Hebrew)

healer Daktari (African); Jason (Greek), Jayson • *healer; tranquil* Gaylen (Greek), Galen, Gailen, Galen; Jalen (American) • *physician, healer* Asa (Hebrew)

healthy Sage *healthy and whole* (Latin) • *healthy black man* Delano (Irish-Gaelic) • *healthy, powerful, strong* Valerian (Late Latin) • *healthy, strong, valorous* Valentine (Latin), Valentino

hear Sam *to hear* (Hebrew)

hearing Simon *hearing, one who hears* (Hebrew), Simeon, Simone

hears Ismael *God hears* Ismail, Ismeil (Arabic); Ishmael (English); Ismael (Hebrew); Esmael, Isamel, Ysmael (Spanish) • Simon *hearing, one who hears* (Hebrew), Simeon, Simone

heart Thaddeus *courageous, stout hearted* (Greek), Taddeo, Tadeo • *heart friend* Corwin (Old French-English) • *of man's heart* Hartmann (Old German), Hartman • *strong-hearted leader* Dustin (Old German), Durst, Durstin, Durston

hearty Khang *robust, hearty one* (Vietnamese)

heat Grishm (Hindi)

heath Heathcliff *from the heath cliff* (Middle English) • *from the heath meadow* Hadley (Old English) • *heath or wasteland* Heath (Middle English)

heaven Phalak, Sumanyu, Tavish, Tridiva (Hindi); Yakez (North American Indian) • *expert; heaven; narrow-minded; to geld* Thien (Vietnamese) • *host of heaven* Sabian (Hebrew) • *raft, heaven* Taran (Hindi) • *sky, heaven* Gagan (Hindi) • *the highest point in heaven* Lulani (Hawaiian) • *towards heaven* Swarit (Hindi)

heavy Amasa (Hebrew)

hedge *see* dweller at the hedge by the forest

hedged Haig *dweller at the hedged enclosure* (Old English) • *from the hedged forest* Haywood (Old English), Heywood • *from the hedged meadow* Hawley (Old English) • *from the hedged pasture* Hagley (Old English) • *from the hedged valley* Hayden (Old English), Haydon • *hedged enclosure keeper* Hayward (Old English)

height *see* cleft

heights Givon *hill or heights* (Hebrew)

heir Arve (Scandinavian) • *son of the heir* MacNair (Irish-Gaelic)

helmet *divine helmet* Anselm (Old German), Ansel, Anselme, Anselmo • *helmet courage* Helmut (Old German) • *helmet, protected* Elmo (Italian) • *one with a helmet* Caffar (Irish-Gaelic)

helmeted Corydon *crested or helmeted one* (Greek), Korudon • *helmeted head* Kennedy (Irish-Gaelic) • *helmeted, ready for battle* Coryell (Greek)

help Betserai (Zimbabwean) • *God will help* Lazarus (Hebrew), Lazario, Lazaro • *help from God* Adom (Akan) • *help, helper* Ezra (Hebrew), Esra • *help out* Dumaka (Nigerian) • *help me with hands* Dumaka (Nigerian) • *my help* Ezri (Hebrew) • *Ogun gives help* Ogunsanwo (Nigerian) • *stone or rock of the help* Ebenezer (Hebrew), Eben • *to whom God is a help* Eleazar (Hebrew), Eleazaro

helper Alexis (Greek) • *eager helper or foreign helper* Gallagher (Irish-Gaelic) • *helper, assistant* Bello (African) • *helper and defender of mankind* Alexander (Greek), Alec, Alexandre, Alexandro, Alexio, Alexis, Alister, Sander, Saunders; Elek (Hungarian); Oles (Polish) • *help, helper* Ezra (Hebrew), Esra

helpful Sarin (Hindi) • *helpful commander* Raoul (Old German)

helps Sandor *he helps people* (Slavic), Alexander, Sander, Sanders • *one who helps people* Janardan (Hindi)

Henry Harris *son of Henry* (Old English), Henderson • *son of Henry, royal ruler* Kendrick (Irish-Gaelic)

Henry's Haland *of Henry's land* (Old English), Halland

herald Boyden (Celtic); Booth (Old Norse), Boothe • *herald, messenger* Boden (Old French) • *herald or messenger* Budd (Old English), Bud • *herald wolf* Botolf (Old English) • *town crier or herald* Scully (Irish-Gaelic)

herb Yarb (Gypsy); Edi (Hindi)

herder Colter *colt herder* (Old English) • *ewe herder* Ewert (Old English)

herdsman Calvert (Old English) • *herdsman, knight's attendant* Swain (Middle English), Swayne

heritage Gildas *of wise heritage* (Latin), Gildus, Gilus

hermit Sola (Greek); Saire (Old German), Sair, Sayre

hero Pravit, Sinha (Hindi); Conlan (Irish-Gaelic), Conley, Conlin, Conlon; Hale (Old English); Igor (Scandinavian-Slavic), Ingmar • *brightness of the north, brilliant hero* Norbert (Old German) • *brilliant hero* Halbert (Old English) • *champion or hero* Curran (Irish-Gaelic), Currey, Curry • *dark hero* Dooley (Irish-Gaelic) • *famous hero or man* Rodman (Old German) • *God's hero* Gavril (Russian) • *great hero* Anlon (Irish-Gaelic), Anluan • *hero of the battle* Ranveer (Hindi) • *little hero* Sweeney (Irish-Gaelic) • *noble hero, noble wolf* Adolph (Old German), Adolf, Adolfo, Adolphe, Adolphus • *old hero* Shanley (Irish-Gaelic) •

peaceful hero, peaceful man Manfred (Old English) • *son of the hero* Manning (Old English)

heroic Akin (Yoruban), Ahkeen • *heroic conqueror* Herrod (Hebrew), Herod

hero's Manton *from the hero's estate* (Old English) • *from the hero's or man's meadow* Manley (Old English)

hewer Gideon *destroyer, hewer* (Hebrew); Hedeon (Russian) • Telford *iron cutter or hewer* (Old French), Telfor, Telfour

hid Garridan *you hid* (Gypsy)

hidden Darnell *from the hidden nook* (Old English) • *hidden by the god* Zephaniah (Hebrew) • *the hidden* Ammon (Egyptian)

hide Schuyler *scholar, teacher; shield or to hide* (Dutch)

high Gibrian *aristocrat; from a high place; stern* (Latin) • *from the high clearing* Henley (Old English), Henleigh • *from the high gate* Hyatt (Old English) • *from the high hill* Kinnard (Irish-Gaelic); Brent (Old English) • *from the high pasture, high meadow* Hanley (English) • *from the high peak* Ogilvie (Pictish-Scotch) • *high, eminent one* Howe (Old German) • *high ground* Galt (Old Norse) • *high hill* Talvrin (Old Welsh); Talfryn (English) • *high, lofty* Tungar (Hindi) • *high or enclosed wood* Heywood (English) • *high quality* Utkarsh (Hindi) *high, tall* Pransu (Hindi) • *of high desire* Connor (Irish-Gaelic), Conner • *of the exalted or high race* Hakon (Old Norse), Hako

highest Omari, Omarr *God the highest* (Swahili) • *highest success* Paramjeet (Hindi) • *highest truth* Paramartha (Hindi) • *highest truth, salvation* Parmaarth (Hindi) • *Jehovah, the highest* Eli (Hebrew) • *the highest point in heaven* Lulani (Hawaiian)

highly Ardal *highly courageous* (Irish-Gaelic), Artegal, Arthgallo • *most highly praised* Ahmad (Arabic) • *highly respected* Manit (Hindi) • *highly spirited* Keegan (Celtic), Kegan, MacEgan

hill Chew (Chinese); Oka (Japanese); Howe (Middle English) • *born on the* *hill* Gibeon (Hebrew), Gibbon, Gibe • *dweller at the advancer's hill* Weddell (Old English) • *dweller at the bare hill, he lives on the boar's hill* Barlow (Old English), Borlow • *dweller at the church hill* Churchill (Old English) • *dweller at the long hill* Langdon (Old English), Landon • *dweller at the pointed hill* Montague (French), Monte, Monty • *dweller at the prince's hill, of the low lands* Ludlow (Old English), Ludlew, Ludly • *dweller on the castle hill* Burdon (Old English) • *dweller on the castle hill slope* Burbank (Old English) • *dweller on the pointed hill* Kipp (Old English) • *from a hill near the well* Weldon (Old German) • *from the beacon hill* Brandon (Old English) • *from the deer hill* Rawdon (Old German), Rawdan, Rawden, Rawdin • *from the down or hill* Doane (Old English) • *from the ford at the hill* Lawford (Old English) • *from the forest hill* Odell (Middle English) • *from the friend's hill* Winslow (Old English) • *from the green hill* Varden (Celtic), Vardon • *from the high hill* Kinnard (Irish-Gaelic); Brent (Old English) • *from the hill* Bryn (Welsh), Brin, Brinn • *from the hill meadow* Dunley, Lawley (Old English) • *from the hill slope estate* Halton (Old English) • *from the holy hill* Eldon (Old English) • *from the house on the hill* Hilton (Old English), Hiltan, Hilten • *from the king's hill* Kingdon (Old English) • *from the ledge hill* Sheldon (Old English), Shelley • *from the rye hill* Ryle (Old English) • *from the sandy hill* Sandon (Old English) • *from the snowy hill* Snowden (Old English) • *from the spring hill* Weldon (Old English) • *from the steep hill* Brenton (Old English), Brent • *from the triangular or gore shaped hill* Gordon (Old English), Gordan, Gorden • *from the watch hill* Wardell (Old English) • *from the wealthy one's hill or hill castle* Montgomery (Old French) • *from the white hill* Whitelaw (Old English) • *from the wooded hill* Waldon (Old English) • *from Thor's hill, of Thor's mountain* Thurlow (Old English), Thorlow, Torrlow • *grassy hill*

Hamilton (English), Hambleton • *great hill fortress* Dunmore (Scotch-Gaelic) • *high hill* Talvrin (Old Welsh); Talfryn (English) • *hill or heights* Givon (Hebrew) • *hill, pine* Matsuoka (Japanese) • *hunter's hill* Huntingdon (Old English) • *linden tree hill* Lindberg (Old German) • *noble one's hill* Elsdon (Old English) • *of the farm over the hill* Dunton (Old English), Dunston, Duntson • *of the hill by the water* Marlow (Old English) • *of the mill on the hill* Meldon (Old English) • *of the rough hill* Harlow (Old English) • *of the town on the top of the hill* Egerton (Old English), Egarton

hills Howland, Knox *of the hills* (Old English), Howlend, Howlond, Howlyn

hills Tirumala *seven hills* (Hindi)

hillside Wildon *from the woody hillside* (Old English) • *hillside estate dweller* Houghton (Old German) • *hillside estate or town* Litton (Old English) • *hillside hollow* Cowan (Irish-Gaelic)

hillslope Brawley *from the hillslope meadow* (Old English)

hilltop Drummond *he lives on the hilltop* (Celtic)

historian Skelly *historian, storyteller* (Irish-Gaelic)

hold see grasp

holder Franklin *free holder of land* (Middle English), Frank, Franklyn • *holder of a banner* Patakin (Hindi)

holds see fast

hole Kong (Korean)

hollow Holbrook *dweller at the brook in the hollow* (Old English) • *dweller by a hollow or by a seething pool* Corey (Irish-Gaelic), Cory • *from the hollow in the valley* Holden (Old English) • *from the kettle shaped hollow* Bing (Old German) • *from the rocky hollow* Stanhope (Old English) • *hillside hollow* Cowan (Irish-Gaelic) • *little hollow* Logan (Scotch-Gaelic)

holly see grove

holy Punit, Tahir (Hindi) • *dweller by a holy spring* Halliwell (Old English) • *from the holy hill* Eldon (Old English) • *holy bear* Esbern (Danish), Esburn; Esben (Old Norse) • *holy, little saint*

Nevan (Irish-Gaelic), Nevin, Nevins, Niven • *holy man* Shaman (Native American) • *holy name* Jerome (Latin) • *holy river* Varana (Hindi) • *holy, sacred, saintly* Santo (Italian) • *holy star* Sutara (Hindi) • *of holy fame* Alisen (Old German) • *the holy sandalwood tree* Chandan (Sanskrit)

home Dor (Hebrew) • *from a shepherd's home* Norvall (Irish-Gaelic), Norval, Norvil • *from the gray home or gray land* Graham (Old English) • *from the home in the brushwood* Ruston (Old English), Rusten, Rustin • *from the home lover's meadow* Ardley (Old English) • *from the home or dwelling place* Case (Latin), Cayce, Cayse • *home lover* Aidan (Celtic) • *home lover's estate* Hamilton (Old English) • *home loving wolf* Ardolph (Old English) • *home or private property, ruler of an estate* Henry (Old German), Enrique, Heinrich, Hendrick, Henri; Quico (Spanish) • *little home* Hamlet (Old French-German), Hamet, Hamlin, Hamlyn, Hammet • *little home lover* Hamlin (Old French-German) • *lover of his home* Hume (Old German) • *nobleman's home* Barnum (Old English) • *protector of the home* Hammond (Middle English) • *ruler of the home* Hendrik (Dutch), Hendrick, Henri; Rico (Italian-Spanish), Enrico, Heinrich, Henry

homeless Aniket (Hindi)

homeward *see* homeward bound

honest Sharif (Arabic); Sujan (Hindi) • *honest one* Liem (Vietnamese) • *sincere and honest* Makoto (Japanese) • *simple, honest* Rujul (Hindi) • *straight, honest* Pragun (Hindi)

honor Ekram (Hindi) • *born in honor* Abiola (African) • *crowned in great honor* Garland (Old English), Garlan • *honor, reward, value* Timon (Greek) • • *in honor of St. Kabir* Kabir (Hindi) • *Ogun has earned honor* Ogunkeye (Nigerian) • *the crown needs honor* Adesola (Nigerian), Adejola

honorable Ehren, Gervase *honorable one* (Old German), Garvey, Gervais, Jarvey

honorably Ogunsheye *Ogun has performed honorably* (Nigerian)

honored Mahit (Hindi) • *honored son, loved* Erastus (Greek), Erasatus, Erastes, Estus

honoring *see* God

hooded Hudson *son of the hooded one* (Old English)

hope Tesfay (Ethiopian); Hy (Vietnamese) • *from a bright hope* Guibert (Old German) • *the one who brings hope* Navashen (Hindi)

horizon Digant, Kshitij, Shitiz (Hindi) • *beyond the horizon* Yul (Mongolian)

horn Nelek (Polish) • *horn colored hair* Cornell (Old French), Cornall, Cornel • *horn colored, hornlike* Cornelius (Latin), Cornelio

hornlike *see* colored

horse Arvan, Pramath (Hindi) • *horse keeper* Stoddard (Old English) • *horse keeper, steward* Marshall (Middle English) • *horse mighty* Roswald (Old German), Roswell • *horse rider* Revanth (Hindi) • *little horse* Eachan (Irish-Gaelic)

horseman Susi (Greek), Sussi • *counsel man, horseman* Redman (Old English) • *horseman or knight* Rider (Old English), Ryder

horses Ahern *horse lord, owner of many horses* (Celtic), Ahearn, Aherin, Aherne, Hearn, Hearne • *lover of horses* Philip (Greek), Felipe, Filippo, Philipp, Phillip; Lorimer (Latin), Larimer, Larimor

host *see* heaven

hostage Cole *a fellow hostage* (Old Irish) • *brilliant hostage or pledge* Gilbert (Old English), Gilberto, Guilbert • *famous hostage* Gilmer (Old English) • *pledge or hostage's estate* Gilby (Old Norse)

hound Conway *hound of the plain* (Irish-Gaelic)

hours Horace *keeper of the hours, light of the sun* (Latin), Horatio

house Edsel *a prosperous man's manor hall or house* (Old English) • *a soldier's son, of the warrior's house* Etam (Latin) • *dweller in the house at the rock* Tremayne (Old Cornish) • *from the grand house* Manvell (Latin), Manvel, Manvil • *from the house on the hill* Hilton (Old English), Hiltan, Hilten • *from the manor house farm* Selby

(Old English) • *from the manor house place* Halstead (Old English), Halsted • *from the master's house* Hall (Old English) • *from the old house* Aldis (Old English), Aldous, Aldus • *from the yellow house* Sterling (Old Welsh) • *house, mansion* Niket (Hindi), Niketan (Hindi) • *manor house friend* Selwyn (Old English), Selwin • *of the house of Estes* Estes (Latin), Estas, Estis • *owner of the new house* Xavier (Spanish), Javier

householder Bo (Old Norse); Bosse (Swedish)

huge Vishal (Hindi) • *a huge serpent* Kaaliya (Hindi)

Hugh Hewitt *little Hugh* (Old French); Hewett, Hewlett, Hewson (English) • *the son of little Hugh* Hutchinson (Middle English), Hutchens, Hutchins, Hutchison

Hugh's Huxford *Hugh's ford* (Old English) • *Hugh's meadow* Huxley (Old English) • *Hugh's town* Houston (Scottish)

humble Donkor (African); Subinay, Vinamar (Hindi) • *humble; to need* Khiem (Vietnamese)

hump *see* a camel hump

Hun Humphrey *peaceful Hun* (Old German)

hundreds Satish *ruler of hundreds* (Hindi)

hunt Hunt *a hunt* (Old English) • *he who likes to hunt* Oringo (African)

hunter Kenaz (Hebrew); Kiraat (Hindi); Chase (Old French) • *eagle hunter* Makya (Native American) • *from the hunter's meadow* Huntley (Old English) • *from the woods, the hunter* Hayes (Old English) • *hunter's hill* Huntingdon (Old English) • *the bowman or hunter* Arley (Old English) • *the hunter* Theron (Greek), Therron; Hunter (Old English)

hunting Connery *child of the hunting dog keeper* (Irish-Gaelic), Conaire, Conary, Conray, Conrey, Conroy, Conry • *hunting estate* Huntington (Old English)

huntsman Montero (Spanish) • *a huntsman* Jaeger (German)

husband Isman *a loyal husband* (Hebrew), Isma

husky Nagy *husky, large* (Hungarian)

hut *see* dweller in a hut

hyacinth Jacinto (Spanish)

I

idea Yukta (Hindi)

ideal Adarsh (Hindi)

ideas Nadabb *man of liberal ideas* (Hebrew), Nadab, Nadabus

idol Moorti *an idol* (Hindi)

ignorance *see* destroyer of ignorance

ill-tempered *see* cross

illuminate Pradvot *to illuminate* (Hindi)

illuminated Nirajit (Hindi)

illumination Nuren, Ronshan (Arabic); Sakash (Hindi)

illustrious Majid (Arabic), Magid, Majdi, Majeed; Sujash (Hindi) • *brilliant and noble or illustrious* Albert (Czech), Berty; (Old English), Adelbert, Ailbert, Alberto, Aubert, Berto,

Elbert • *famous, illustrious one* Clair (English) • *illustrious, noble* Grady (Irish-Gaelic)

immortal Akshay, Chiranjiv, Kaustubh (Hindi); Tanek (Polish), Atanazy, Atek; Arius (German); Afon, Afonya, Fonya, Opanas, Panas, Tanas (Russian) • *divine, immortal one* Ambrose (Greek), Ambrogio, Ambros, Ambrosi, Ambrosio

immovable Atal (Hindi)

inaccessible Amil (Hindi)

incarnation Avatar (Hindi)

inconceivable Achintya (Hindi)

increase Chin (Chinese) • Jo *God will increase* (Japanese)

independent Maverick *independent nonconformist* (American)

indestructible Achyuthan (Hindi), Avinash, Avinashi
indirect Balbo *the indirect speaker* (Latin), Bailby
industrious Mahir (Hebrew) • *flattering, winning one; industrious one* Emil (Old German), Emilio • *from the industrious one's estate* Melville (Old French) • *industrious ruler* Emery (Old German), Amerigo, Emeri, Emerson, Emory • *industrious, strong* Emmett (Old German), Emmet, Emmott
inestimable Anthony *inestimable, priceless one* Antony (English); Anton (Bulgarian); Antonin, Tonda, Tonik (Czech); Antoine (French); Andonios, Andonis (Greek); Akoni (Hawaiian); Tonese (Hungarian); Tonio (Italian); Antaine (Irish); (Latin), Antonio; Antons (Latvian); Antavas, Tavas (Lithuanian); Antek, Antoni, Antos, Tolek, Tonek (Polish); Antinko, Tosya, Tusya (Russian)
inexperienced Cahil *young, inexperienced, and naïve* (Turkish)
infinite Anant (Hindi)
ingenious Cassidy *clever, ingenious one; curly-haired one* (Irish-Gaelic) • *courteous, ingenious, majestic, scientific one* Shea (Irish-Gaelic) • *ingenious, scientific* Haley (Irish-Gaelic)
ingenuity Hamar (Old Norse)
Ing's Ingram *Ing's raven* (Old German), Ingraham
inheritor Jared *descendant, the inheritor* (Hebrew), Jerred; Jerrod (American) • *inheritor of property* Arve (Scandinavian)
injure Talman *to injure* (Aramaic); Talmon (English)
injuring Sarana (Hindi)
innocent Riju, Rijul (Hindi) • *innocent one* Ince (Latin) • *most innocent* Kilian (Celtic), Kilan
inspirational *see* aflame, inspirational
inspiring Oglesby *awe-inspiring* (Old English) • *awe-inspiring guardian, noble guardian* Aylward (Old English) • *awe-inspiring one's farmland* Aylworth (Old English) • *dweller in the valley of the awe-inspiring one* Anscom (Old English), Anscomb • *from the*

awe-inspiring one's pasture meadow Ansley (Old English) • *the awe-inspiring one's meadow* Ainsley (Old English) • *the awe-inspiring one's son* Anson (Old English)
instrument Karan (Hindi)
intellectual *see* intellectual curiosity
intelligence Praket (Hindi) • *discerning and intelligent* Basir (Turkish) • *intelligence, spirit* Hugh (Old English), Hugo • *intelligence, wisdom* Conan (Celtic)
intelligent Elewa (African); Akil (Arabic), Ahkeel, Zaki; Dheeman, Pradhi, Vijval (Hindi); Zeki (Turkish) • *discerning and intelligent* Basir (Turkish) • *intelligent and learned* Fahim (Arabic), Faheem • *intelligent; smart* Akira (Japanese) • *intelligent, wise* Quinn (Irish-Gaelic) • *son of the intelligent one* Fitzhugh (Old English) • *wise and intelligent* Arif (Turkish); Areef (English) • *wise; intelligent* Hui (Chinese); Dheemant (Hindi)
interesting Romir (Hindi); Eddy (Scandinavian)
interpreter Latimer (Middle English)
intimate *see* friend
invention Rachit (Hindi)
investigation Anvesh (Hindi)
invincible Avijit, Durja (Hindi) • *he is invincible* Lachish (Hebrew), Lach, Lachus • *invincible, mighty oak* Elon (Hebrew), Ellon
Ireland Argyle *belonging to Ireland* (Celtic), Argile
iron Telek *iron cutter* (Polishy) • *from the iron ford* Telford (Old English), Telfore, Tellford • *from the iron one's estate* Isham (Old English) • *iron gray hair* Ferrand (Old French), Farrand, Farrant, Ferrant • *iron hewer or cutter* Telford (Old French), Telfor, Telfour • *super iron, super strength* Trahern (Old Welsh)
is *see* he is so
island Shima (Japanese) • *dweller at ship island* Delsey (Old Norse) • *dweller at the island* Nye (Middle English) • *dweller at the noble one's island* Adney (Old English) • *dweller on the brook island* Birney (Old English), Burney • *famous one's island* Rodney (Old English) • *from Hal's island*

Halsey (Old English) • *from the birch tree island* Birkey (North English) • *from the broad island* Brady (Old English) • *from the elder tree island* Ellery (Middle English), Ellerey • *from the river island* Innis (Irish-Gaelic), Innes, Inness; Holmes (Middle English); Holmann (Old German), Holman, Holmen • *from the rocky island* Skerry (Old Norse) • *from the*

white-haired one's island Whitney (Old English) • *island grove* Lundy (French) • *island, pine* Matsushima, Shimatsu (Japanese) • *persevering one's island* Pitney (Old English) • *ram's island; raven's island* Ramsey (Old English)

isle Lyle *from the isle* (Old French), Lyell • *from the linden tree isle* Lindsey (Anglo-Saxon), Lindsay, Lynd

— J —

Jack Jackson *son of Jack* (Old English)
jaguar Nahuel (Native American)
James Santiago *St. James* (Spanish), Antiago, Sandiago, Sandiego, Saniago •
January *see* born in January
jasper Jasper *jasper stone* (Old French)
jay *see* blue jay
jealous Ehioze *not jealous* (Nigerian)
Jeffrey Jefferson *son of Jeffrey* (Old English)
Jehovah Ali (Arabic) • *angel of Jehovah* Malachi (Hebrew), Malchus • *appointed of Jehovah, exalted by God* Jeremy (Hebrew), Jereme, Jeremiah, Jeremias; Yerik (Russian) • *flame of Jehovah, my light is Jehovah* Uriah (Hebrew) • *gift of Jehovah* Johanan, Matthew (Hebrew), Mateo, Mathew, Mathias, Matteo, Matthaeus, Mattias; Mayhew (Old French) • *his life is Jehovah's* Jehiah (Hebrew), Jehias, Jehius, Johiah • *Jehovah hath remembered* Zachary (Hebrew), Zacaria, Zacarias, Zacharias • *Jehovah is my God* Elliot (French-Hebrew), Elliott; Ilias (Greek); Elijah (Hebrew), Elia, Elias, Ellis • *Jehovah is my splendor* Hodiah (Hebrew), Hodia, Hodiya • *Jehovah's gift* Jonathan (Hebrew) • *Jehovah, the highest* Eli (Hebrew) • *loyal servant of Jehovah* Jehosah (Hebrew) • *man chosen by Jehovah* Moriah (Hebrew) • *the son of Jehovah* Jehiel (Hebrew), Jehial
jet *see* black

jewel Jawhar (Arabic); Johar, Lalam (Hindi); Kito (Swahili) • *divine jewel* Devmani (Hindi)
jewels Navratan *nine jewels* (Hindi)
John Jennings *the descendants of John* (Anglo-Saxon) • *the son of John* Johnston (Irish-Gaelic), Johnsten; Jones (Welsh) • *Thor's stone or jewel* Thurstan (English), Thurston
joined Levi *joined, united* (Hebrew), Levy
journey Fulumirani (African) • *born during a journey* Uzoma (Nigerian)
joy Kautik, Sammad, Shahalad (Hindi); Radman (Slavic) • *joy of life* Pransukh (Hindi) • *my joy* Roni (Hebrew) • *of great joy* Tait (Scandinavian), Taite • *one who creates joy* Marnin (Hebrew) • *shouts of joy* Kallol (Hindi) • *with joy* Saharsh (Hindi)
joyful Sachit (Hindi); Lear (Old German) • *glad, joyful* Faine (Middle English); Fane (Old English)
joyous Pulakesh (Hindi); Pramod (Sanskrit) • *to be joyous* Ranon (Hebrew); Ranen (Israeli)
jubilant *see* gay, jubilant
Judd Judson *the son of Judd* (Old German), Judsen
judge Hatim (Arabic); Hateem, Hatem (English) • *a good judge* Faisal (Arabic), Faisel, Faizal, Faysal, Faysul, Fayzal, Fayzel • *a judge, wise* Dempster (Old English), Dempsey, Dempstor • *God is my judge* Daniel

(Hebrew), Dane • *God will judge*
Joachim, Yadin (Hebrew); Yadon (Israeli); Ioakim (Russian), Jov;
Joaquin (Spanish) • *great judge*
Ramiro (Spanish), Ramirez • *Lord and judge* Dusan (Slavic) • *son of the judge* Deems (Old English)
judge's Grayson *a judge's son* (Old English), Gray, Grey, Greyson
Julius Halian *belonging to Julius* (Zuni)

Jupiter's *see* gift
just Adli (Turkish) • *God is just* Avidan (Hebrew) • *just, righteous one* Zadok (Hebrew), Zakoc • *just one, upright* Justin (Old French) • *lawful and just* Seiji (Japanese)
justice Masato (Japanese); Justis (Old French), Justus • *father of justice* Avidan (Hebrew) • *justice of the Lord* Zedekiah (Hebrew)

⎯ K ⎯

Kabir *see* in honor of St. Kabir
Kalkin *see* the god Kalkin
Kamdev *see* god of love
Keb *see* Egyptian
keen Washington *from the estate of the keen one's family* (Old English) • *handsome or keen* Keene (Celtic), Kean, Keane • *spear keen* Jarvis (Old German), Jervis
keenness *see* battle keenness
keeper Connery *child of the hunting dog keeper* (Irish-Gaelic), Conaire, Conary, Conray, Conrey, Conroy, Conry • *forest keeper* Rnager (Old French), Rainger • *hedged enclosure keeper* Hayward (Old English) • *horse keeper* Stoddard (Old English) • *horse keeper, steward* Marshall (Middle English) • *keeper of the cattle, little cow* Vachel (French), Vachell, Vachil, Vachill • *keeper of the dyke* Van Dyke (Dutch) • *keeper of the hours, light of the sun* Horace (Latin), Horatio • *keeper of the keys* Clavero (Spanish) • *keeper of the mountain* Van Ness (Dutch) • *park guardian or keeper* Parker (Middle English)
Kent *see* estate
kettle *see* hollow
keys *see* keeper of the keys
killer *see* killer of enemies
killing *see* killing enemies
kind Prajin, Prajit, Sudhit (Hindi) • *affectionate one, kind one* Oliver (Old Norse), Oliverio, Olivier • *cheerful, kind friend* Gladwin (Old English) • *gentle, good, kind* Bonar (Old French)

• *gentle, kind one, merciful* Kelemen (Hungarian); Clement (Latin), Clemence, Clemens, Clemente, Clementius; Kliment (Russian) • *handsome, kind* Hasim (Arabic), Hassim • *kind soul* Gentilis (Latin) • *kind to the poor* Dindayal (Hindi) • *noble and kind* Kerem (Turkish)
kindling Bodhan (Hindi)
kindly Erasmus (Greek)
kindness Jaidayal *victory of kindness* (Hindi)
king Eze, Mansa, Reth (African); Roy (French), Roi; Kini, Loe (Hawaiian); Adheesh, Adhip, Adhiraj, Natesh, Nrip, Raajaa, Rajan, Rajesh, Ranak (Hindi); Rex (Latin); Sakima (Native American); Tor (Nigerian); Elroy, Leroy (Old French); Aldrich (Old German), Aldredge, Aldridge, Eldridge; Manco (Peruvian); Soma (South African); Alroy, Rey (Spanish), Reyes; Kiral (Turkish) • *an ancient king* Trishanku (Hindi) • *an excellent warrior, king* Praveer (Hindi) • *from the castle of the king* Rexford (Latin), Rexferd; Hallvard (Scandinavian) • *king of clouds* Meghraj (Hindi) • *kind of dreams* Swapnesh (Hindi) • *king of kings* Nripendra, Nripesh (Hindi) • *king of mountains* Shattesh (Hindi) • *king of seasons* Rutesh (Hindi) • *king of serpents* Naagpati (Hindi) • *king of stars* Naksatraraja (Hindi) • *king of the earth* Ilisa, Prithviraj (Hindi) • *king of the serpents* Naagendra (Hindi) • *king*

of the world Jagdish (Hindi) • *king or lord* Naresh (Sanskrit) • *little king* Regan, Ryan (Irish-Gaelic), Reagan, Reagen, Regen • *may the Lord protect the king* Balthasar (Greek), Baltasar, Balthazar; Zarek (Polish) • *red king* Rory (Irish-Gaelic), Rurik • *son of the king* Royce (French), Roi, Roice, Roy • *the king* Kiros (African)

kingdom Mithil (Hindi) • *from the Lord's kingdom* Adriel (Hebrew), Adrell, Adrial, Adriell

kingly Royal (French) • *kingly, magnificent* Basil (Latin), Basile, Basilio, Basilius

king's/kings Rajdeep *best of kings* (Hindi) • *dweller at the king's ford* Rexford (Old English) • *dweller at the king's spring* Kingswell (Old English) • *from the king's hill* Kingdon (Old English) • *from the king's residence* Kingston (Old English) • *king of kings* Nripendra, Nripesh (Hindi) • *king's secretary* Chancellor (Middle English), Chaunce • *of the king's meadow* Kenley, Kingsley (Old English), Kenlay, Kenleigh, Kinsley • *royalty, kingdom* Raj (Hindi) • *the eternal king's son* Arkin (Norwegian)

kinship Chibale (African)

knife Cutler *the knife maker* (Old English), Cutlor, Cuttler

knight Faris (Arabic); Aleron, Chevalier (French); Ritter (North German); Chevy (Old French) • *born at night* Daren (Hausa); Okon (African) • *horseman or knight* Rider (Old English), Ryder

knightly Vasilis *knightly, magnificent* (Greek)

knight's Squire *knight's attendant, shield bearer* (Middle English) • *herdsman, knight's attendant* Swain (Middle English), Swayne

knocks *see* one who knocks on the door

knolls Torrance *from the knolls* (Anglo-Irish), Torey, Torrey, Torry

knot Knute (Danish); Canute (English); Knut (Old Norse)

knowing Channing *a regent, knowing* (Anglo-Saxon) • Sage *wise and knowing* (Latin)

knowledge Anuva, Gyan, Nibodh (Hindi) • *bringer of knowledge or light, light* Luke (Latin), Luca, Lucan, Lucas, Lucian, Lucius • *complete knowledge* Sambodh (Hindi) • *filled with knowledge* Gyan (Sanskrit) • *knowledge, wisdom* Mendel (East Semitic) • *master of accurate knowledge* Pramesh (Hindi)

knows Nian *one who knows* (Cambodian)

•— L —•

labor Tristram *sorrowful labor* (Latin-Welsh)

lad Chal (Gypsy) • *attendant or lad* Ladd (Middle English)

lake Sarasi (Hindi) • *dweller at the hare or rabbit lake* Arledge (Old English) • *from the lake forest* Marwood (Old English) • *from the lake land* Marland (Old English) • *from the lake meadow* Marley (Old English) • *from the rocky lake* Stanmore (Old English) • *lake of paradise* Kausar (Hindi)

lamb Hamal (Arabic); Owain (Old Welsh)

lame Claude *the lame one* (Latin), Claudio, Claudius

lamp Pradeep (Hindi)

land Dickson *Dick's son, of Dick's land* (Old English), Dixon • *dweller at the court land or farmstead* Courtland (Old English), Court • *dweller at the enclosed land or park* Park (Old English), Parke • *dweller on reclaimed land* Newland (Old English) • *farmer, land worker* Jorn (Danish); Juri (Estonian); Joji (Japanese); George (Latin), Georg, Giorgio, Jorge; Goran (Scandinavian); Yuri (Russian) • *free holder of land* Franklin (Middle English), Frank, Franklyn • *from a noble land* Uland (Old German), Ulland, Ullund • *from the army* *land* Harlan (Old English) • *from the cliff land* Cleveland (Old English) • *from the famous land* Roland (Old German), Orlando, Roldan, Rolland, Rollin, Rollins, Rowland • *from the flat land* Platt (Old French) • *from the gray home or gray land* Graham (Old English) • *from the lake land* Marland (Old English) • *from the pathway land or property* Wayland (Old English) • *from the pointed land* Orlan (Old English), Orland • *from the root or stump land* Rutland (Old Norse) • *from the slope or corner of land* Yale (Old English) • *from the southern land* Sutherland (Old Norse) • *his country's light, land brilliant* Lambert Old German), Landbert, Landberto • *land between the streams* Cartland (English-Scotch) • *land famous* Lamar (Old German) • *nobleman's land* Erland (Old English) • *of Henry's land* Haland (Old English), Halland • *of the land* Amiel (Hebrew) • *soldier's land* Chatham (Old English)

landing *see* ford

landowner Swithbert *the respected landowner* (Old German), Swithbart

lands *see* dweller at the prince's hill, of the low lands

large Aiken (Anglo-Saxon) • *husky, large* Nagy (Hungarian) • *large bamboo* Luong (Vietnamese) • *large fish* Timin (Hindi) • *large stork* Ozuru (Japanese) • *large, very tall* Rustam (Hindi)

Lars Larson *son of Lars* (Scandinavian)

last Antim (Hindi) • Ahir *end or last* (Turkish)

lasting Dante (Latin) • *lasting power* Reynold (Old German), Rennold

lathe Turner *worker with the lathe* (Latin)

laugh Ochi (African)

laughing Hasin (Indian), Hasen, Hassin; Ryan (Latin)

laughs Isaac *he laughs* (Hebrew), Ike; Ahanu (Native American)

laughter Hasan, Suhas (Hindi)

laurel Lenci, Lorant *laurel crowned one* (Hungarian); Lorcan (Jewish); Lawrence (Latin), Lars, Laurenz, Lawry, Lorenz, Lorenzo; Brencis (Latvian); Ralis (Lithuanian); Lorens (Scandinavian); Lorne (Scottish), Lorn • *laurel, victory* Lorant (Hungarian); Lars (Scandinavian)

law Dotan (Hebrew), Dothan • *law friend* Ewing (Old English) • *law powerful* Ewald (Old English) • *lord of law* Niteesh (Hindi) *right in the law* Jude (Latin)

lawful Seiji *lawful and just* (Japanese)

lawn *see* green

Lawrence Lawson *son of Lawrence* (Old English)

lawyer Wakil (Arabic) • Lamont *a lawyer* (Scandinavian), Lamond

leader Pranet, Savir, Thakur (Hindi); Duke, Proctor (Latin), Procterl Pomo (Native American) • *a guide or leader* Hadi (Arabic) • *a powerful leader* Gazo (Hebrew), Gazzo • *born with long hair, leader* Caesar (Latin), Cesar, Cesare; Kesar (Russian) • *leader, nobleman* Barnett (Old English) • *leader of men* Naruna (Hindi) • *learned or skillful leader* MacKinley (Irish-Gaelic) • *powerful leader* Trahern (Celtic), Trahurn; Edrei (Hebrew), Edroi • *strong-hearted leader* Dustin (Old German), Durst, Durstin, Durston • *strong leader* Farley (Irish-Gaelic) • *warrior leader* Einar (Old Norse)

leaf Pattin *a leaf* (Gypsy) • *leaf trail* Patrin (Gypsy) • *red leaf* Wapasha (Dakota Indian) • *weaving leaf* Chane (Swahili)

leafy Parnal (Hindu)

lean Kawacatoose *lean man* (Cree Indian) • *lean or thin* Blaine (Celtic); Blayne (English); Blane (Irish-Gaelic)

leaper *see* the great leaper

learned Fahim (African); Alim (Arabic), Aleem; Budhil, Sarasvat (Hindi) • *intelligent and learned* Fahim (Arabic), Faheem • *learned or skillful leader* MacKinley (Irish-Gaelic) • *most learned man* Hachmann (Hebrew), Hachman, Hachmin

learner *see* apprentice

leather Tanner *leather maker* (Old English)

leaves Pallab *new leaves* (Hindi)

ledge Shelley *dweller at the ledge meadow* (Old English) • *from the estate or town on the ledge* Skelton (Old English) • *from the farm near the ledge* Shelby (Anglo-Saxon) • *from the ledge farm or town* Shelton (Old English) • *from the ledge hill* Sheldon (Old English), Shelley

left *see* left hand

legal *see* church legal officer, summoner

legendary Anka *the legendary phoenix* (Turkish)

legion *see* camp

leopard Namir (Hebrew)

level Shoda *a level field* (Japanese)

liberal Tilton *from the good, liberal one's estate* (Old English) • *from the good, liberal one's valley* Tilden (Old English) • *man of liberal ideas* Nadabb (Hebrew), Nadab, Nadabus

liberated Muktananda (Hindi)

liberation Nirvan (Hindi)

lieutenant *see* general

life Jibben,Merripen (Gypsy); Chaim (Hebrew), Hyam, Leben; Jeevan (Hindi); Chaimek, Haim (Polish); Khaim (Russian); Guy (Old German) • *breath of life* Pranjivan (Hindi) • *full of life* Jeeval, Sajiva (Hindi) • *giving life, reanimating* Sanjeev (Hindi) • *his life is Jehovah's* Jehiah (Hebrew), Jehias, Jehius, Johiah • *joy of life* Pransukh (Hindi) • *life adventuring, world daring* Ferdinand (Old German), Ferdinando, Ferdnando, Fernando, Hernando • *lord of life* Pranesh (Hindi) • *soul, life force* Janu (Hindi)

life-giving Jaival (Hindi)

light Nuren (Arabic); Prakash, Ullas (Hindi); Roshan (Persian); Luz (Spanish) • Kiran *a light ray* (Sanskrit) • *brilliant, light* Deepak (Sanskrit) • *bringer of knowledge or light, light* Luke (Latin), Luca, Lucan, Lucas, Lucian, Lucius • *father of light* Abner (Hebrew), Avner • *first light* Ujas (Hindi) • *flame of Jehovah, my light is Jehovah* Uriah (Hebrew) • *God's light* Madison (English) • *his country's light, land brilliant* Lambert (Old German), Landbert, Land-

berto • *keeper of the hours, light of the sun* Horace (Latin), Horatio • *light, candle* Deepak (Hindi) • *light-haired* Fairfax (English) • *light in color* Moswen (African) • *light of the mind* Mandeep (Hindi) • *lord of light* Urmiya (Hindi) • *new light* Navtej (Hindi) • *ray of light* Mareechi (Hindi) • *son of fire, son of light* Orion (Greek) Jivan • *to give life* (Hindi); Jeeven, Jeven, Jiven, Jivin (English) • *victory to the light* Jaideep (Hindi)

lighted Deepit (Hindi)

lighting Deepan *lighting up* (Hindi)

lightning Bijal, Chapal, Tarit (Hindi); Llewellyn (Welsh)

lights *see* lord of lights

lime Lyndon *from the lime wood* (Old English)

limitless Avkash *limitless space* (Hindi)

linden Lindell *dweller at the linden tree valley* (Old English) • *from the linden tree ford* Linford (Old English) • *from the linden tree isle* Lindsey (Anglo-Saxon), Lindsay, Lynd • *linden tree hill* Lindberg (Old German) • *of the linden meadow* Lindley (Old English), Lindly, Lindy

lion Kosey, Lencho, Tau (African), Kosse; Haidar, Asad (Arabic), Aleser; Lais (East Indian); Leibel (English), Leib; Lio (Hawaiian); Ari (Hebrew), Lavi; Parindra (Hindi); Leo (Latin); Arslan (Turkish) • *a lion* Gurion (Hebrew) • *God is my lion* Guriel (Hebrew) • *lion brave* Leonard (Old German), Leonardo • *lion cub* Gur (Hebrew) • *lion like* Leon (French); Lev (Czech/Russian) • *lion man* Leander (Greek), Leandre, Leandro • *lion of God* Arel (Hebrew), Areli • *lion of the battlefield* Ronsher (Hindi) • *lion of the woodland dell* Napoleon (Greek) • *my lion cub* Guri (Hebrew) • *the lion* Mrigendra (Hindi), Mrigesh • *young lion* Lionel (Old French)

lionlike Llewellyn (Old Welsh)

liquid Taral (Hindi)

lisps Blaisot *one who lisps or stammers* (French); Blasi, Blasius (German); Balas, Ballas, Balasz (Hungarian); Biagio (Italian); Blaise (Latin), Blaze; Blazek (Polish); Braz (Portuguese); Vlas (Russian)

listener Luister *a listener* (Afrikaans)
literature Van *literature; short; striped tiger; to twist* (Vietnamese)
little Vaughn (Celtic), Vaughan; Paul (Latin), Pablo, Paolo • *a fawn or little deer* Ossian (Irish-Gaelic), Oisin; Ossin (English) • *a little chief* Okemos (Native American) • *a little stream* Jafar (Arabic) • *dweller at the little oak tree* Quennel (Old French) • *from the little field* Dalziel (Scotch-Gaelic) • *from the little stronghold* Burkett (Old French) • *holy, little saint* Nevan (Irish-Gaelic), Nevin, Nevins, Niven • *keeper of the cattle, little cow* Vachel (French), Vachell, Vachil, Vachill • *little active one* Cavell (Old French) • *little Adam* Aiken (Old English), Aikin • *little alert one* Howell (Old Welsh) • *little ancient one* Keenan (Irish-Gaelic), Kenan, Kienan • *little and bare* Loman (Irish-Gaelic) • *little and fair* Finan (Irish-Gaelic), Fionan; Finn, Finnin, Fintan, Finton (English) • *little bear* Orson (Old French) • *little beauty* Husain (Arabic), Husain, Hussain, Hussein • *little beloved one* Lovell (Old English), Lowell • *little beloved or dear one* Darrell (Old French), Darold, Darryl, Daryl • *little black one* Ciaran (Irish-Gaelic) • *little blacksmith* Fabron (French), Fabrioni • *little blessed one* Bennett (French-Latin) • *little blond one* Banning (Irish-Gaelic) • *little blue-eyed one* Gorman (Irish-Gaelic) • *little boisterous one* Shandy (Old English) • *little bright one* Galen (Irish-Gaelic); Jalen (American) • *little brown-complected one* Burnett (Middle English) • *little brown-haired one* Burnell (Old French) • *little champion* Carlin, Carollan (Irish-Gaelic), Carling • *little cloak* Lennon (Irish-Gaelic) • *little companion* Keller (Irish-Gaelic) • *little dark complexioned one* Kieran (Irish-Gaelic); Moreno (Italian-Spanish) • *little dark one* Duane, Dwayne, Kern (Irish-Gaelic) • *little dove* Coleman (Irish-Gaelic), Colman • *little eagle* Arnett (Old English-Old French), Arnatt; Arnot (Old French-Old German), Arnott • *little*

fair-complexioned one Gannon (Irish-Gaelic) • *little fair-haired one* Blakey (Old English) • *little fair-haired valorous one* Finley (Irish-Gaelic), Findlay, Findley, Finlay • *little falcon or hawk* Marlon (Old French), Marlin • *little famous one* Merritt (Old English); Merrill (Old French) • *little fiery one* Aidan, Fagan, Keegan (Irish-Gaelic), Aden, Aiden, Fagin • *little fish* Dagan (East Semitic), Dagon • *little Gabriel* Gable (Old French) • *little glorious warrior* Harbin (Old French-German) • *little great one* Darren (Irish-Gaelic), Daren • *little hacker* Hackett (Old French-German) • *little hammer* Marcel (Latin), Marcello, Marcellus, Marcelo • *little hero* Sweeney (Irish-Gaelic) • *little hollow* Logan (Scotch-Gaelic) • *little home* Hamlet (Old French-German), Hamet, Hamlin, Hamlyn, Hammet • *little home lover* Hamlin (Old French-German) • *little horse* Eachan (Irish-Gaelic) • *little Hugh* Hewitt (Old French); Hewett, Hewlett, Hewson (English) • *little jet black one* Kerwin (Irish-Gaelic), Kerwen, Kirwin • *little king* Regan, Ryan (Irish-Gaelic), Reagan, Reagen, Regen • *little, mighty and powerful* Renny (Irish-Gaelic) • *little old wise one* Shannon (Irish-Gaelic) • *little one* Koji (Japanese) • *little Paul* Pollock (Old English) • *little peaceful one* Sheehan (Irish-Gaelic) • *little Peter* Parkin, Perkin (Old English); Parle, Parnell, Perrin (Old French) • *little, pine* Matsuo (Japanese) • *little raven* Brendan (Irish-Gaelic) • *little red-haired one* Ruskin (French-German); Roslin (Old French) • *little rope maker* Cordell (Old French), Kordell • *little rough one* Girvin (Irish-Gaelic), Garvan, Garvey, Girvan, Girven • *little scandal or snarer* Scanlon (Irish-Gaelic), Scanlan • *little seal* Ronan (Irish-Gaelic) • *little shield* Rankin (Old English); Burdett (Old French) • *little, short* Klein (German), Cline, Kline • *little slender one* Keelan (Irish-Gaelic), Kealan, Kelan • *little smart one* Hewitt (English) • *little son* Sonny (Middle English) •

little spear Bercan, Corrigan (Irish-Gaelic), Bearchan, Korigan, Korrigan • *little Thomas* Maslin (Old French) • *little Tom* Tomkin (Old English), Tomlin • *little victorious one* Bowen (Irish-Gaelic) • *little warlike one* Killian (Irish-Gaelic) • *little war mighty one* Malin (Old English) • *little warrior* Wyatt (Old French) • *little wealthy one* Odell (Old Anglo-French) • *little wolf* Phelan (Irish-Gaelic) • *little wolf cub* Channing (Irish-Gaelic); Chane, Channe, Channon (English) • *little yew bow* Iven (Old French) • *little young one* Hagen (Irish-Gaelic), Hagan • *small stone, the little one* Elstan (Anglo-Saxon), Elston • *son of the little counsel wolf* Rawlins (Old Anglo-French); Rawson (Old English) • *the little man* Malik (Slavic) • *the son of little Hugh* Hutchinson (Middle English), Hutchens, Hutchins, Hutchison

live *see* alive, live, living

lively Sajiv (Hindi) • *gay, lively one* Gale (Old English), Gaile, Gayle • *lively in battle* Valdis (Old German), Valdas, Valdes • *lively one* Gaylord (Old French), Gallard, Gayler, Gaylor • *lively son* Jareb (Hebrew) • *of the lively town* Harden (Old English), Hardan

lives Jivvel *he lives* (Gypsy) • *one who lives by the pond* Putnam (Old English) • *one who lives in a parish* Parish (Middle English), Parrish

living Zeno (French); Zenas (Greek), Zenon, Zeus; Ziv (Old Slavic); Zewek (Polish); Zinon (Russian); Cenon, Senon (Spanish) • *alive, live, living* Vito (Latin)

lizard Cata (Ngombe/African)

local Landry *the local ruler* (Anglo-Saxon), Landre, Landri

lofty Haroun *exalted or lofty* (Arabic); Aaron (Hebrew), Aharon, Aron • *high, lofty* Tungar (Hindi) • *the lofty one* Abram (Hebrew)

lonely Bedad (Hebrew)

lonesome Iggi (African); Ehud *lonesome, only son* (Hebrew)

long Lombard *a long beard* (Old German), Lombardo, Lombardy • *born with long hair, leader* Caesar (Latin),

Cesar, Cesare; Kesar (Russian) • *dweller at the long ford* Langford (Old English) • *dweller at the long hill* Langdon (Old English), Landon • *from the long enclosure* Langworth (Old English) • *from the long meadow* Langley (Old English) • *long hair, noted for his hair* Esau (Hebrew) • *long or tall man* Lang (Old Norse)

longevity Umar (African)

long-haired *see* long-haired beggar

long-lived Ayush (Hindi)

look Onani (African)

looks Akule *he looks up* (Native American)

Lord/lord Tyrone (Greek), Tye; Vasin (Hindi); Frey (Old English); Adon (Phoenician), Adonis • *angel of the Lord* Azriel (Hebrew), Azrae • *belonging to the Lord; born on Sunday, the Lord's day* Dominic (Latin), Domenico, Domingo, Dominick, Dominico, Dominique, Nick • *beloved of the Lord* Jedidiah (Hebrew), Jed, Jediah • *brave lord* Virendra, Viresh (Hindi) • *day lord* Dinesh (Sanskrit) • *gift of our Lord* Osgood (Old German) • *gift of the Lord* Jeconiah, Zebadiah (Hebrew), Econah, Jecon, Zebe, Zebedee; Tudor (Welsh) • *God, my salvation, the Lord is salvation* Elisha (Hebrew), Eliseo • *God, the Lord* Elihu (Hebrew) • *great lord* Ainmire (Irish-Gaelic); Mahesh (Sanskrit) • *he is healed by the Lord* Josiah (Hebrew) • *horse lord, owner of many horses* Ahern (Celtic), Ahearn, Aherin, Aherne, Hearn, Hearne • *in the Lord is strength* Boaz (Hebrew), Boas, Boase • *justice of the Lord* Zedekiah (Hebrew) • *king or lord* Naresh (Sanskrit) • *Lord and judge* Dusan (Slavic) • *Lord, Father* Uba (African) • *lord, nobleman* Hidalgo (Spanish) • *lord of affection* Mamraj (Hindi) • *lord of all* Varindra (Hindi) • *lord of all lords* Devadeva (Hindi) • *lord of beauty* Rupesh (Hindi) • *lord of celebration* Parvesh (Hindi) • *lord of creation* Kartar (Hindi) • *lord of earth* Ilesh, Talish (Hindi) • *lord of equality* Samesh (Hindi) • *lord of fame* Yashodev (Hindi) • *lord of law* Niteesh (Hindi) • *lord of life* Pranesh

(Hindi) • *lord of light* Urmiya
(Hindi) • *lord of lights* Deependra
(Hindi) • *lord of love* Pritish, Renesh
(Hindi) • *lord of mercy* Karunesh
(Hindi) • *lord of men* Janesh (Hindi)
• *lord of mind* Monish (Hindi) • *lord
of my people* Amiel (Hebrew) • *lord of
peace* Shantidev, Shantinath (Hindi)
• *lord of pearls* Shringesh (Hindi) •
lord of perfection Kalpesh (Hindi) •
lord of piousness Suchendra (Hindi) •
lord of prosperity Shivadev (Hindi) •
lord of sound Hakesh (Hindi) • *lord of
stars* Udupati, Uduraj (Hindi) • *lord
of strength* Urjani (Hindi) • *lord of the
brave* Viranath (Hindi) • *lord of the
desert* Marudeva (Hindi) • *lord of the
forest* Vanadev, Vanajit (Hindi) • *lord
of the manor* Orville (French), Orvil •
lord of the night Raakesh, Rakesh
(Hindi) • *lord of the pious* Poonish
(Hindi) • *lord of the ridge* Selfridge
(Old German) • *lord of the sea* Barun,
Paranjay (Hindi) • *lord of the snow*
Himesh (Hindi) • *lord of the soul*
Chitesh (Hindi), Chittesh • *lord of
the universe* Jagesh (Hindi), Jagish •
lord of the world Bhavesh, Loknaath,
Vishvesh (Hindi) • *lord of three worlds*
Lohendra (Hindi) • *lord of treasure*
Nidhish (Hindi) • *lord of truth* Ritesh
(Hindi) • *lord of virtue* Shubendra
(Hindi) • *lord of water* Jalesh, Toyesh,
Varunesh (Hindi) • *lord of wealth*
Vittesh (Hindi) *lord of wisdom* Prad-
nesh (Hindi) • *lord or master* Tiernan
(Irish-Gaelic) • *may the Lord protect
the king* Balthasar (Greek), Baltasar,
Balthasar; Zarek (Polish) • *my Lord
brings happiness* Olukayode (Niger-
ian) • *noble son of the Lord* Nodab
(Hebrew), Odab • *praise the Lord*
Joab, Ramiah (Hebrew), Joub,
Ramah • *protected by the Lord* Pedaiah
(Hebrew), Pedaias • *salvation of the
Lord* Isaiah (Hebrew), Isak • *the Lord*
Adon (Hebrew); Sahib (Hindi) • *the
Lord be praised* Jehu (Hebrew), Jeu •
the Lord is God Joel (Hebrew) • *the
Lord is good* Tobias (Hebrew), Tobia
• *the Lord is my father* Abijah (He-
brew), Abisha, Abisia, Abixah • *the
Lord loves him* Joses (Hebrew) • *the
lord Vishnu* Harish (Sanskrit),

Haresh • *the praise of the Lord* Yehudi
(Hebrew) • *this in praise of the Lord*
Jedthus (Hebrew) • *visited by the Lord*
Eliathan (Hebrew), Eli, Eliath,
Eliathas
lordly Kiril *lordly one* (Bulgarian);
Cyril (Greek), Cirill, Cirilo, Cyrille,
Cyrillus; Tierney (Irish-Gaelic)
lords/Lord's Dominic *belonging to the
Lord; born on Sunday, the Lord's day*
(Latin), Domenico, Domingo, Dominick, Dominico, Dominique, Nick
• *from the Lord's kingdom* Adriel (Hebrew), Adrell, Adrial, Adriell • *lord of
all lords* Devadeva (Hindi) • *witness
our Lord's goodness* Joed (Hebrew)
lotus Kamal, Mrinal (Hindi)
lotuslike Sarojin (Hindi)
loud Harod *the loud terror* (Hebrew),
Harrod
lovable Mungo (Irish-Gaelic) •
friendly, lovable Elmo (Latin-Greek) •
gentle, handsome, lovable, noble Keefe
(Irish-Gaelic) • *gentle, lovable* Kevin
(Irish-Gaelic), Kevan, Keven • *lovable
or affectionate* Prem (Sanskrit) • *lovable, worthy of love* Erasmus (Greek),
Erasme, Erasmo, Rasmus
love Rudo (African); Moh, Prem
(Hindi) • *abounding in love, beloved*
Craddock (Old Welsh) • *full of love*
Premal (Hindi) • *god of love* Madan
(Hindi); Amadis (Latin), Amadus •
god of love and passions Kamadev
(Hindi) • *Kamdev, god of love* Darpak
(Hindi) • *lord of love* Pritish, Renesh
(Hindi) • *lovable, worthy of love* Erasmus (Greek), Erasme, Erasmo, Rasmus • *love, friendship* Pranay (Hindi)
• *love, respect* Prashray (Hindi) • *tears
of love* Laramie (French) • *witness our
love* Jegar (Hebrew), Jeggar, Jegger
loved Erastus *honored son, loved*
(Greek), Erasatus, Erastes, Estus •
loved by God Joash (Hebrew),
Hoashis, Joashus; Priyesh (Hindi)
lovely Camlo (Gypsy)
lover Preetam (Hindi) • *animal lover*
Derwin (Old German) • Dorwin,
Durwin • *home lover* Aidan (Celtic) •
little home lover Hamlin (Old French-
German) • *lover, loving* Amory
(Latin), Amery • *lover of his home*
Hume (Old German) • *lover of horses*

Philip (Greek), Felipe, Filippo, Philipp, Phillip; Lorimer (Latin), Larimer, Larimor • *lover of nature* Tivon (Hebrew) • *lover of peace* Radomil (Slavic) • *lover of wealth* Srikant (Hindi) • *of the sea, lover of water* Pontius (Latin), Pontias, Pontus

lover's Ardley *from the home lover's meadow* (Old English) • *home lover's estate* Hamilton (Old English)

loves Olufemi *God loves me* (Nigerian) • *he loves the sea, shipmaker* Omar (Arabic), Omarr, Omer, Omor • *man who loves mankind* Philander (Greek), Fillander, Fillender, Philan, Philender • *the Lord loves him* Joses (Hebrew)

loving Iddo (Hebrew); Kama, Kami (Hindi) • *friendly, loving* Philo (Greek) • *home loving wolf* Ardolph (Old English) • *lover, loving* Amory (Latin), Amery • *self-loving* Narcissus (Greek) • *the dove, peace loving* Culver (Old English), Colver

low Ludlow *dweller at the prince's hill, of the low lands* (Old English), Ludlew, Ludly • *from the low valley* Loudon (Teutonic);Lowden (English)

loyal Denby *a loyal Dane, from the Danish settlement* (Scandinavian), Danby • *a loyal husband* Isman (Hebrew), Isma • *a loyal swallow* Howin (Chinese) • *faithful, loyal* Leal (Latin) • *faithful, loyal, true one* True (Old English) • *loyal servant of Jehovah* Jehosah (Hebrew) • *loyal son, reliable* Barabbas (Hebrew), Barabas

Lucius *see* descendant of Lucius

luck Mestipen (Gypsy); Sudi (Swahili) • *good luck* Cheung (Chinese)

lucky Maimun (Arabic); Wapi (Native American); Fortune (Old French), Fortunio; Madox (Welsh), Madoc • *auspicious, lucky* Faust (Latin) • *fortunate, lucky one* Felix (Latin); Feliks (Russian)

luminous Anshumat, Etash, Idhant, Kashi (Hindi) • *luminous and clear* Minh (Vietnamese)

luster Ojas, Sutej (Hindi)

lustrous Kantilal (Hindi), Kantimoy

— M —

magician Jamnes *wisest magician* (Hebrew), Jamnis

magistrate *see* administrator, foreman, magistrate, overseer

magnificent Basil *kingly, magnificent* (Latin), Basile, Basilio, Basilius • *knightly, magnificent* Vasilis (Greek)

majestic Adir (Hebrew) • *courteous, ingenious, majestic, scientific one* Shea (Irish-Gaelic) • *exalted, majestic dignitary* August (Latin), Auguste, Augustin, Augusto, Augustus

maker Fletcher *arrow maker* (Middle English) • *a sail maker* Naylor (Old English), Nalor • *barrel maker* Kiefer (German), Keefe; Cooper (Old English) • *brick and tile maker* Ziegler (German) • *cabinet maker* Schreiner (German) • *candle maker* Chandler (Middle English), Shandler • *charcoal maker* Colman (Icelandic) • *leather maker* Tanner (Old English) • *little rope maker* Cordell (Old French), Kordell • *maker of the peace* Renfred (Old German), Renferd • *roofer and tile maker* Tyler (Middle English) • *rope maker* Roper (Old English) • *shoe maker* Schuman (German) • *the cart maker* Carter (Anglo-Saxon), Cart • *the knife maker* Cutler (Old English), Cutlor, Cuttler • *wagon maker* Dewayne (American); Wagner (German); Wainwright, Wayne (Old English) • *wheel maker* Wheeler (Old English)

male Taro *first-born male* (Japanese) • *first-born male twin* Ulan (Sudan) • *excellent male child* Hideo (Japanese) • *male child* Godana (African) • *the second male* Jiro (Japanese) • *third-born male* Saburo (Japanese)

man Manav (Hindi); Lenno, Patwin

(Native American), Leno • *a famous and brilliant man* Cuthbert (Anglo-Saxon), Cuthburt • *a man of Cyprus* Cyprian (Greek), Ciprian, Cyprio • *a man of strength* Ozen (Hebrew), Ozan • *a man of the chapel, pious* Chapell (Anglo-Saxon) • *a man of the city, urbane* Chapman (Anglo-Saxon) • *a man of the great plains* Conway (Celtic) • *a man of the sea, sailor* Ithaman (Latin) • *a man of understanding* Favian (Latin), Favianus, Favient, Favin • *a man of wisdom* Jeuz (Hebrew) • *a man whom God has enlightened* Jair (Hebrew) • *an upright man* Jesher (Hebrew), Jesh • *army man* Harry (Old English); Armand (Old German), Armin; Mandek (Polish) • *army man; soldier* Armino (Italian) • *army man, warrior* Herman (Old German), Armand, Armando, Hamlin, Harman, Harmon • *a together man* Kamal (Arabic) • *austere, strong man* Hartman (Old German) • *battle man* Cadman (Old Anglo-Welsh) • *beautiful man* Apollo (Greek) • *bold man* Frick (Old English) • *brave man* Dreng (Norwegian) • *brave, dark man* Donnelly (Celtic), Donely, Donnel, Donnell • *bright Finn, the bright man* Davin (Scandinavian), Daven, Davon • *chaplain, man of God* Chapin (French), Chapen, Chapland • *coatmaker, son of a good man* Manning (Old German) • *counsel man, horseman* Redman (Old English) • *defender, true man or watchman* Warren (Old German) • *famous hero or man* Rodman (Old German) • *free man* Palani (Hawaiian); Darby, Dermot, Kermit (Irish-Gaelic), Derby, Dermott; Francis (Latin), Francesco, Franchot, Francisco, Francois, Frans, Franz; Bundy, Freeman (Old English); Frank (Old French); Chico, Pancho (Spanish) • *good man* Goodman (Old German) • *head man* Colman (Icelandic) • *healthy black man* Delano (Irish-Gaelic) • *holy man* Shaman (Native American) • *lean man* Kawacatoose (Cree Indian) • *lion man* Leander (Greek), Leandre, Leandro • *long or tall man* Lang (Old

Norse) • *man chosen by Jehovah* Moriah (Hebrew) • *man from the muddy place* Brody (Scottish); Brodie (English) • *man from south Munster* Desmond (Irish-Gaelic) • *man from the east* Anatole, Cadmus (Greek), Anarolio, Anatol • *man from Wales, Welshman* Wallace (Old English), Wallache, Walsh • *man of brilliance* Hebert (Old German) • *man of control* Jarlath (Latin), Jari, Jarlathus • *man of God* Gabriel, Obadiah (Hebrew), Obed, Obeded • *man of great beauty* Philemon (Greek) • *man of great wealth* Orton (Old German), Orten • *man of liberal ideas* Nadabb (Hebrew), Nadab, Nadabus • *man of many possessions* Darius (Persian), Darian, Derian, Dorian • *man of peace* Axel (Hebrew); Pacian (Latin), Pace, Pacien • *man of poetry* Teague (Celtic), Teage • *man of prosperity, owner of fields* Forbes (Irish-Gaelic) • *man of refinement* Lawton (Old English), Latton, Laughton • *man of the earth* Damek (Slavik), Adamek, Adamik, Adham, Damick, Damicke • *man of the mill* Millman (Old English), Milman • *man of the moors* Moreland (Old English) • *man of the people* Publius (Latin), Publias • *man of the plains* Lyman (Old English), Liman, Limann, Lymann • *man of the red earth* Damek (Czech); Adam (Hebrew); Keddy (Scottish), Keady, Keddie; Adan (Spanish) • *man of the sword* Saber (Old German), Sabir • *man of the woods* Sawyer (Celtic), Sawyor • *man of wisdom* Jadda (Hebrew), Jaddan, Jaddo • *man of zeal* Phelgon (Latin), Phelgen • *man who loves mankind* Philander (Greek), Filander, Fillender, Philan, Philender • *man with a mustache or beard* Algernon (Old French) • *man with an unusual beard* Brody (German); Brodie (English) • *man with strength of ten thousand* Michio (Japanese) • *most learned man* Hachmann (Hebrew), Hachman, Hachmin • *medicine man* Jabilo (African) • *mountain man* Orestes (Greek), Oreste • *noble man* Ola (West African) • *old, wise man* Altman (Old German) • *peaceful hero, peaceful man* Manfred (Old English) • *poor man* Kawacatoose (Cree Indian) • *powerful man* Richman (Old English) • *prosperous man* Othman (Old German) • *quiet man* Stillman (Old English) • *son of a good man* Odoric (Latin), Odericus, Odrick • *son of the dark man* Collis (Old English) • *son of the red-haired man* Flynn (Irish-Gaelic), Flinn • *son of the wise man* Druce (Old Anglo-Welsh) • *son's man or splendid son* Sampson (Hebrew), Samson, Sanson, Sansone • *strong man, very choice one* Fergus (Irish-Gaelic) • *the little man* Malik (Slavic) • *the man God directs* Jahdal (Hebrew), Jahdai, Jahdiel, Jahdol • *the man who is unafraid* Pollard (Old German), Polard, Pollerd • *the prosperous man* Idden (Anglo-Saxon), Iden • *the refuge of man* Naaraayan (Hindi) • *white-haired man* Whitman (Old English) • *wild man or satyr* Sheridan (Irish-Gaelic) • *wisdom, wise man* Solon (Greek) • *wise man* Morathi (African); Witt (Old English) • *young man* Kerel (Afrikaans)

mankind Alexander *helper and defender of mankind* (Greek), Alec, Alexandre, Alexandro, Alexio, Alexis, Alister, Sander, Saunders; Elek (Hungarian); Oles (Polish) • *man who loves mankind* Philander (Greek), Fillander, Fillender, Philan, Philender • *teacher of mankind* Plato (Latin), Platto, Platus

manly Drew (English); Veryl (Old German), Verald, Verrill; Naren (Sanskrit) • *manly, strong* Keandre (American); Kalman (German); Andrew (Greek-Hebrew), Anders, Andre, Andrej, Andres; Kale (Hawaiian); Charles (Old German), Carl, Carlo, Carlos, Chaz, Karl; Jedrek (Polish); Kalle (Scandinavian); Kendrew (Scottish)

manor Edsel *a prosperous man's manor hall or house* (Old English) • *dweller at the old estate or town, from the old manor* Alton (Old English), Elton • *from the manor hall* Halford (Old English) • *from the manor house farm* Selby (Old English) • *from the manor*

house place Halstead (Old English), Halsted • *lord of the manor* Orville (French), Orvil • *manor house friend* Selwyn (Old English), Selwin • *servant in a manor* Berry (Old English)

man's Manley *from the man's or hero's meadow* (Old English) • *from the wise man's estate* Witton (Old English) • *of man's heart* Hartmann (Old German), Hartmann • *tall man's estate or town* Langston (Old English)

mansion *see* house

many Thai (Vietnamese)

March *see* born during the month of March

mariner Morven (Scottish-Gaelic) • *mariner, sea warrior* Murray (Scotch-Gaelic) • *son of the mariner* MacMurray (Irish-Gaelic)

marquis Marques (Spanish)

Mars Marcus *offspring of Mars* (Latin), Marc • *red, made of copper, Mars* Lohit (Hindi)

marsh Delmore *at a marsh* (Anglo-Saxon) • *dweller at a marsh* Carr (Old Norse) • *marsh estate or farm* Fenton (Old English) • *son of the dweller at a marsh* Carson (Middle English) • *wood by a marsh* Morley (English)

marshy *dweller at the marshy valley* Marsden (Old English), Marsdon • *from the marshy place* Marsh (Old English) • *marshy estate, spearman's estate* Carvell (Old French), Carvel

marten *see* ermine

martial Mario *martial one* (Latin); DeMarco (American)

Mary Gilmore *servant of the Virgin Mary* (Celtic)

masculine Arsenio *masculine and virile* (Greek), Arsanio, Arsemio; Eresenio (Spanish)

mason *see* army ruler; mason, wall builder

master Wirt (German) • *lord or master* Tiernan (Irish-Gaelic) • *master of accurate knowledge* Pramesh (Hindi) • *master of the earth* Avaneesh (Hindi) • *master of the right path* Nitin (Hindi) • *ship master* Skipper (Middle English) • *treasure master* Caspar (Persian), Casper, Gaspar, Gasper, Jasper, Kasper

master's Hall *from the master's house* (Old English)

matchless Atul (Hindi)
Maur Seymour *from St. Maur* (Old French)
Maurice Morrison *son of Maurice* (Old English)
May *see* born in May
me *see* from me
meadow Bentley (Old English), Bently • *a dweller in the meadow, dweller at the broom meadow* Bromley (Old English), Bromleigh • *Bart's meadow* Bartley (Old English) • *cattle shed on the meadow* Birley (Old English) • *church meadow* Kirkley (Old North English) • *dweller at the acre meadow, of the meadow of the oak trees* Ackerley (Old English) • *dweller at the ash tree meadow, from the ash tree ford* Ashford (Old English) • *dweller at the birch tree meadow* Barclay (Old English), Berkeley • *dweller at the buck deer meadow* Buckley (Old English) • *dweller at the castle meadow* Burley (Old English), Burleigh • *dweller at the ledge meadow* Shelley (Old English) • *dweller at the meadow* Atley (Old English) • *dweller at the oak tree meadow* Ackley (Old English) • *dweller at the priest's meadow* Presley (Old English) • *dweller at the red meadow* Redley (Old English) • *dweller at the rocky meadow* Stanley (Old English), Stanleigh • *dweller at the rough meadow* Rowley (Old English) • *dweller at the sheep meadow* Shipley (Old English) • *dweller at the wether-sheep meadow* Wetherly (Old English) • *dweller in the valley meadow* Denley (Old English) • *enclosed pasture meadow* Penley (Old English) • *from the awe-inspiring one's pasture meadow* Ansley (Old English) • *from the badger meadow* Brockley (Old English) • *from the big meadow* Grantham (Old English), Grantland, Grantley • *from the black meadow* Blakeley (Old English) • *from the broad meadow* Bradley (Old English) • *from the brushwood meadow* Risley (Old English) • *from the bull meadow* Fairleigh (Old English), Farlay, Farlee, Farley • *from the crane meadow* Cranley (Old English) • *from the cross meadow* Crosley (Old English) • *from*

the deer meadow Raleigh (Old English), Ralaigh, Ralleigh • *from the enclosed meadow* Yardley (Old English) • *from the fern meadow* Farnley (Old English) • *from the flat meadow* Smedley (Old English) • *from the gray meadow* Greeley (Old English) • *from the guardian's meadow* Wardley (Old English) • *from the heath meadow* Hadley (Old English) • *from the hedged meadow* Hawley (Old English) • *from the hero's or man's meadow* Manley (Old English) • *from the high pasture, high meadow* Hanley (English) • *from the hill meadow* Dunley, Lawley (Old English) • *from the hillslope meadow* Brawley (Old English) • *from the home lover's meadow* Ardley (Old English) • *from the hunter's meadow* Huntley (Old English) • *from the lake meadow* Marley (Old English) • *from the long meadow* Langley (Old English) • *from the meadow* Balfore, Cluny (Irish-Gaelic), Balfour; Mead, Sully (Old English) • *from the meadow farm* Leighton (Old English) • *from the moor meadow* Morley (Old English) • *from the oak meadow* Oakley (Old English) • *from the pasture meadow* Lee (Old English), Leigh • *from the people's meadow* Dudley (Old English) • *from the rabbit meadow* Arley (Old English), Harley • *from the raven's meadow* Ransley (Old English) • *from the red field, red pasture meadow* Radley (Old English) • *from the red meadow, he lives by the red field* Ridley (Old English) • *from the rocky meadow* Rockley (Old English) • *from the root or stump meadow* Rutley (Old English) • *from the sheep meadow* Shepley (Anglo-Saxon), Shep, Sheply • *from the south meadow* Sully (Old English) • *from the split meadow* Spalding (Old English), Spaulding • *from the thorny meadow* Thornley (Old English) • *from the town meadow* Townley (Old English) • *from the tree stump meadow* Stockley (Old English) • *from the village enclosure or meadow* Wickham (Old English) • *from the village meadow* Wickley (Old English) • *from the weaver's meadow* Webley (Old English) • *from the west meadow*

Wesley (Old English), Westleigh • *from the wet meadow* Wakeley (Old English) • *from the white meadow* Whitley (Old English) • *Hugh's meadow* Huxley (Old English) • *of a near meadow* Ainsley (Old English), Ainslie • *of the king's meadow* Kenley, Kingsley (Old English), Kenlay, Kenleigh, Kinsley • *of the linden meadow* Lindley (Old English), Lindly, Lindy • *of the meadowlands* Leland, Leighland (Anglo-Saxon) • *quaking aspen tree meadow* Waverly (Old English) • *the advancer's meadow* Wadley (Old English) • *the awe-inspiring one's meadow* Ainsley (Old English) • *Thor's meadow* Thorley (Old English), Totley • *wheat meadow* Wheatley (Old English)

meat *see* carver

mechanic *see* hands

meddlesome Connor (Irish-Gaelic), Conner, Connors, Conor

medicinal Kamuzu (African)

medicine Jabilo *medicine man* (African)

meditation Chintan (Hindi)

meditative Dhyanesh (Hindi)

meek Sudama (Hindi)

melodious Madhur (Hindi)

men Alastair *defender of men* (Scotch-Gaelic), Alaster, Alister, Allister • *father of gods and men* Zeus (Greek) • *leader of men* Naruna (Hindi) • *lord of men* Janesh (Hindi) • *peace among men* Manfred (Old German)

merchant Mercer (Latin), Merce, Merceer; Chapman (Old English) • *charcoal merchant, miner* Collier (Old English), Colier, Colis, Collyer, Colyer • *merchant, peddler, tradesman* Kauffman (German)

merciful Rahim (Arabic), Rahman; Dayaram, Karuna (Hindi); Rabmet (Turkish) • *gentle, kind one, merciful* Kelemen (Hungarian); Clement (Latin), Clemence, Clemens, Clemente, Clementius; Kliment (Russian)

mercy Daya, Hanan (Hindi) • *lord of mercy* Karunesh (Hindi) • *ocean of mercy* Kripasagar (Hindi)

meritorious Isas *meritorious one* (Japanese)

merriment *see* delight

message Sandesh (Hindi) • *correct message* Udant (Hindi)

messenger Rasul (African); Nuncio (Latin); Nunzio (Spanish) • *angel messenger* DeAngelo (American) • *angel or messenger* Angelo (Latin), Angel • *gatekeeper, royal messenger* Portero (Spanish) • *herald, messenger* Boden (Old French) • *herald or messenger* Budd (Old English), Bud

Michael *see* friend of St. Michael, from Michael's stronghold

Michael's *see* friend of St. Michael, from Michael's stronghold

midday Orunjan *god of the midday sun* (African)

middle Naka (Japanese) • *middle, pine* Matsunaka (Japanese) • *middle, rice field* Tanaka (Japanese)

mighty Jelani (African); Conall (Celtic), Connell, Congal; Sahasya, Saubal, Udbal (Hindi); Walden, Waldo (Old German) • *a mighty force* Uziel (Hebrew), Uzziel • *a mighty warrior* Kellen (Irish-Gaelic), Kalin, Kelin, Kellan, Kelle, Kellin • *counsel mighty* Redwald (Old English) • *devoted to the will of God; peaceful, quiet one; people mighty* Tully (Irish-Gaelic) • *horse mighty* Roswald (Old German), Roswell • *invincible, mighty oak* Elon (Hebrew), Ellon • *little, mighty and powerful* Renny (Irish-Gaelic) • *little war mighty one* Malin (Old English) • *mighty and peaceful* Renfred (Old English) • *mighty and powerful* Reginald (Old English), Reinald, Reinhold, Reinold, Renato, Renault, Reynold, Ronald • *mighty army* Ragnar, Raynor (Old Norse), Ragnor, Rainer, Rainier, Rayner, Raynor • *mighty bear* Barret (Old German), Barrett • *mighty brave* Reynard (Old German), Raynard, Reinhard, Renard, Renaud • *mighty brilliant* Rambert (Old German) • *mighty or ruling protector* Walmond (Old German) • *mighty or wise protector* Raymond (Old German), Ramon; Ramiro (Spanish), Ramirez • *mighty power* Ronald (Old Norse), Renaldo • *mighty soldier* Balin (Hindi), Bali, Valin • *mighty traveler* Farold (Old English) • *mighty* *warrior* Tredway (Old English) • *son of mighty power* Ronson (Old English) • *son of spear mighty* Fitzgerald (Old English) • *son of war mighty* Madison (Old English) • *son of world mighty* MacDonald (Scotch-Gaelic) • *spear mighty* Orval (Old French); Gerald (Old German), Geraldo, Geraud, Gerault, Gerold, Giraldo, Giraud; Gerhard (Scandinavian) • *very strong, mighty* Prabal (Hindi) • *world mighty, world ruler* Donald (Scotch-Gaelic); Tauno (Finnish)

Milan *see* city

military Cadal *of the military* (Celtic), Cadel

milk Piyush (Hindi)

mill Milford *dweller at the mill ford, from the crossing by the mill* (Old English), Millford • *dweller at the mill town* Milton (Old English) • *from the mill stream* Melbourne (Old English), Melburn, Milburn • *man of the mill* Millman (Old English), Milman • *of the mill on the hill* Meldon (Old English) • *of the stream by the mill* Milburn (Old English), Milburt, Millburn

miller Milo *a miller* (Latin); Millard (Old English), Miller, Millman, Milman

mind Chitt, Manas (Hindi) • *brilliant mind* Hobart (Old German) • *brilliant mind or spirit* Hubert (Old German), Bert, Huberto, Hugh; Berdy (Russian) • *conqueror of the mind* Manjeet (Hindi) • *expert; heaven; narrow-minded; to geld* Thien (Vietnamese) • *god of mind* Manish (Hindi) • *light of the mind* Mandeep (Hindi) • *lord of mind* Monish (Hindi) • *mind; to show* Chi (Vietnamese) • *resolute spirit or mind* Wilmot (Old German)

minded *see* hard, strong minded

mine Ronli *song is mine* (Hebrew)

miner *see* charcoal merchant, miner

minister Wazir (Arabic) • Khatib *religious minister* (Arabic)

minority Thieu *be missing, be short; the minority* (Vietnamese)

minstrel *see* ballad singer, minstrel

miracle Nissim (Hebrew)

mirror Darpan (Hindi)

misfortune Tavor (Aramaic); Tabor (Israeli)

missing *see* minority

mist Duman (Turkish)

mock Kaseko *to mock, or to ridicule* (Rhodesian)

modest Unni (Hebrew); Pranit, Shalin (Hindi)

modesty Vinay (Hindi)

moist Sajal (Hindi)

monastery Camerero *chamberlain, monastery worker* (Spanish) • *head of the monastery* Pryor (Latin); Prior (English)

Monday *see* born on Monday

month Mart *born during the month of March* (Turkish) • *born in the month of Ramadan* Ramadan (Swahili)

moon Chander, Kalanath, Kumudesh, Mayank, Mehtab, Mrigank, Naakesh, Nishesh, Rajnish, Saras, Subhendu, Yamir (Hindi), Chandra, Kalan • *born at full moon* Badru (African) • *fortress of the moon* London (Middle English) • *full moon* Badrani (African); Badar (Arabic) • *moon in the water* Jalendu (Hindi) • *new moon* Nabhendu, Nabhendu *new moon* (Hindi) • *son of the moon* Mrigaj (Hindi) • *the moon* Chandak, Savan (Hindi); Jacy (Native American), Jaycee; Chand (Sanskrit) • *the new moon* Hilel (Arabic) • *victory of the moon* Jaichand (Hindi) • *white moon* Muraco (Native American) • *young moon* Balachandar (Hindi), Balendu

moonlight Chandran (Sanskrit) • *bright moonlight* Konane (Hawaiian)

moonshine Mudil (Hindi)

moonstone Sushim (Hindi)

moor Elmore *dweller at the elm tree moor* (Old English) • *from the moor estate or town* Morton (Old English) • *from the moor meadow* Morley (Old English) • *from the moor or wasteland* Muir (Scotch-Gaelic) • *from the white moor* Whitmore (Old English)

moors Moreland *man of the moors* (Old English) • *of the moors* Hadden (Old English), Haden

moral Duc (Vietnamese), Duy

morality Rishabh (Hindi)

morally Deshi *morally upright* (Chinese)

morning Addae (Ghanaian) • *dew of the morning* Talor (Hebrew)
mortal *see* earth
motion Riti (Hindi)
mound Teng (Chinese)
mountain Parvat, Shail (Hindu) • *a mountain* Chang (Chinese); Yama (Japanese); Montel (Latin), Monteil, Montell • *dweller on the mountain* Bergen (Old German) • *from the beautiful mountain* Beaumont (Old French) • *from the mountain* Berg (German) • *from Thor's hill, of Thor's mountain* Thurlow (Old English), Thorlow, Torrlow • *god of mountain* Girish (Hindi) • *God's mountain* Harel (Hebrew) • *keeper of the mountain* Van Ness (Dutch) • *mountain goat* Jael (Hebrew) • *mountain man* Orestes (Greek), Oreste • *mountain peak* Kruin (Afrikaans) • *mountain, pine* Matsuyama (Japanese) • *mountain stream* Bergren (Scandinavian), Berg • *mountain summit* Kiri (Cambodian) • *mountain summit; crest* Dinh (Vietnamese) • *snow mountain*

Himaadri (Hindi) • *son of mountain* Girilal (Hindi)
mountaineer Haruni (African); Orestes (Greek); Slevin (Irish-Gaelic), Slaven, Slavin, Sleven
mountainous Montana *from a mountainous region* (Latin)
mountains *see* king of mountains
mouth Phineas *mouth of brass* (Greek) • *wry or crooked mouth* Campbell (Scotch-Gaelic)
move *see* copper; to move
muddy *see* man from the muddy place
mule Moulton *of the mule stable* (Old English), Molton, Mouldon, Muldon
multiple Thai (Vietnamese)
multitude Bram *father of the multitude* (Dutch); Abraham (Hebrew), Ibrahim • *god of the multitude* Ganesh (Sanskrit)
mumbler *see* half-speaker, mumbler
Munster *see* man from south Munster
musical Sargam *musical notes* (Hindi)
mustache *see* beard
mustard Kardal *mustard seed* (Arabic)

• — N — •

naïve *see* inexperienced
name Nav (Hungarian); Shem (Yiddish)
narrow Thien *expert; heaven; narrow-minded; to geld* (Vietnamese) • *from the narrow forest* Calhoun (Irish-Gaelic) • *from the narrow river* Kelvin (Irish-Gaelic), Kelvan, Kelven • *from the narrow road* Lane (Middle English)
nation Deshad (Hindi), Deshal, Deshan • Baram *son of a nation* (Israeli)
national Tuxford *ford of the national spearman* (Old Norse-English) • *most popular, national or people's spirit* Volney (Old German) • *national army* Thayer (Old Frankish) • *national protector* Tedmond (Old English)
native Landis (Old German)
nature Teva (Hebrew); Prakrit (Hindi) • *a friend of nature* Stanwin

(Old English), Stonwin • *lover of nature* Tivon (Hebrew) • *religion, nature* Dharma (Hindi)
near Stanway *from near the stony road* (Old English) • *he lives near the bear's den* Barden (Old English), Borden • *he lives near the spring* Maxwell (Anglo-Saxon) • *of a near meadow* Ainsley (Old English), Ainslie • *to be near* Gan (Vietnamese)
nearby Lathan *he lives nearby* (Old German)
need *see* humble; to need
Nen Nen *the spirit of Nen* (Egyptian)
nephew Nevin (Irish-Gaelic), Niven
nest Tas *bird's nest* (Gypsy) • *from where the ravens nest* Renwick (Old German)
net Pasha *net, snare* (Hindi)
new Naveen, Navin (Hindi) • *dweller at the new pool* Newlin (Old Welsh),

Newlyn • *fresh and new* Tan (Vietnamese) • *from the new estate* Neville (Old French), Nevil, Nevile • *from the new estate or town* Newton (Old English) • *from the new spring* Newlin (Celtic) • *from the new valley* Seldon (Old English), Seldan, Selden • *new arrow* Motega (Native American) • *new leaves* Pallab (Hindi) • *new light* Navtej (Hindi) • *new moon* Nabendu, Nabhendu (Hindi) • *new, surprise* Nawal (Hindi) • *new town* Newton (English-Scottish); Neville (French) • *of the new building* Newbold (Old English) • *of the new city* Napier (Spanish), Neper • *owner of the new house* Xavier (Spanish), Javier • *the new moon* Hilel (Arabic)

newcomer Newman (Old English) • *newcomer, the dark stranger* Doyle (Celtic)

newly *see* newly born

news *see* bearer

nice Birju *nice singer* (Hindi)

Nicholas Coleman *adherent of Nicholas* (Old English), Colman • *son of Nicholas* Nixon (Old English)

night Nishil, Rajani (Hindi) • *lord of the night* Raakesh, Rakesh (Hindi) • *the night bird* Kibbe (Native American)

nightmare Musenda (African)

nimble *see* quick-moving, nimble

nine *see* nine jewels

ninth Akron *ninth-born son* (African), Akan • *ninth child* Ennis (Greek)

noble Coman, Nabil (Arabic); Adir (Hebrew); Adel (Teutonic) • *awe-inspiring guardian, noble guardian* Aylward (Old English) • *bold, noble and sacred* Archibald (Anglo-Saxon/German), Archibaldo • *brave and noble* Adlar (Old German), Adlare • *brilliant and noble or illustrious* Berty (Czech); Albert (Old English), Adelbert, Ailbert, Alberto, Aubert, Berto, Elbert • *dweller at the noble one's island* Adney (Old English) • *exalted, noble* Kareen (Arabic), Karim • *famous noble* Hilmar (Old Norse) • *famous, noble* Nolan (Irish-Gaelic); Almo (Old English), Aylmer, Edelmar, Elmer • *forthright, noble* Elbert (Old German), Bart, Elbart, Elburt • *free,*

noble friend Frewin (Old English), Frewen • *free or noble protector* Fremont (Old German) • *from a noble land* Uland (Old German), Ulland, Ullund • *gentle, handsome, lovable, noble* Keefe (Irish-Gaelic) • *illustrious, noble* Grady (Irish-Gaelic) • *most noble one* Hiram (Hebrew) • *noble and kind* Kerem (Turkish) • *noble and ready* Alphonso (Old German), Alfonso, Alphonse, Lanzo • *noble bear* Adelbern (Teutonic) • *noble commander* Adelric (Old German) • *noble eagle* Erland (Old German), Erlond; Adelar (Teutonic) • *noble friend, wealthy friend* Audwin (Old German) • *noble hero, noble wolf* Adolph (Old German), Adolf, Adolfo, Adolphe, Adolphus • *noble man* Ola (West African) • *noble one* Padraig (Irish); Patrick (Latin), Patrice, Patrizio; Edel (Old German); Adel (Tuetonic), Adal; Arthur (Welsh), Artair, Arturo, Artus • *noble one's estate* Alston, Elsworth (Old English) • *noble one's estate or town, noble stone* Elston (Old English) • *noble one's hill* Elsdon (Old English) • *noble one's son* Alison (Old English) • *noble ruler* Audric (Old German) • *noble ruler, ruler of all* Alaric (Old German), Alric, Alrick • *noble son of the Lord* Nodab (Hebrew), Odab • *noble spearman* Alger (Old German), Algar • *noble warrior* Albern (Old English) • *noble, well-born* Eugene (Greek), Eugenio, Gene, Gino • *of noble birth* Payton (Irish-Gaelic), Paton, Peyton • *of noble blood* Barron (Old English), Baron, Barr

nobleman Marquis (Old French); *adherent of a nobleman* Ansel (Old French), Ansell • *chief, nobleman* Earl (Old English), Earle, Erl, Errol; Jarl (Scandinavian) • *leader, nobleman* Barnett (Old English) • *lord, nobleman* Hidalgo (Spanish) • *nobleman's son* Erling (Old English) • *nobleman, warrior* Baron (Old English), Barron

nobleman's Barnum *nobleman's home* (Old English) • *nobleman's land* Erland (Old English)

nobly Adalard *nobly brave* (Old German), Adallard • *nobly brave, warrior*

Ellard (Old German), Ellerd, Ellord • *nobly firm* Adelhart (Teutonic) • *nobly resolute* Abelard (Old German); Adelard (Teutonic)

noisy Tristan *noisy one* (Old Welsh)

nonconformist *see* independent

nook *see* hidden

north Norbert *brightness of the north, brilliant hero* (Old German) • *friend from the north* Norvin (Old English), Norwin, Norwyn • *from the north estate* Norville (Old Anglo-French), Norvel, Norvil • *from the north estate or north town* Norton (Old English) • *from the north farm* Northrop (Old English) • *from the north forest* Nor-wood (Old English) • *from the north spring* Norwell (Old English) • *man from the north* Norris, Norvin (Old German), Norvan, Norven

northern *see* gate

northman Norman *a northman* (Old French)

nose *see* crooked

noted *see* hair

notes *see* musical notes

nun *see* Buddhist

nurturing Jatan (Hindi)

nut Cata *a connecting wall; catfish; nut; to confine* (Mende/African) • *from the forest of nut trees* Delano (Old French)

O

oak Ackerley *dweller at the acre meadow, of the meadow of the oak trees* (Old English) • *dweller at the ancient oak tree* Orrick (Old English) • *dweller at the little oak tree* Quennel (Old French) • *dweller at the oak forest* Cheney (Old French), Cheyney • *dweller at the oak tree meadow* Ackley (Old English) • *from the forest of oak trees* Cheney (French), Chenay • *from the oak meadow* Oakley (Old English) • *from the oak tree ford* Adair (Scotch-Gaelic) • *from the oak valley* Ogden (Old English) • *invincible, mighty oak* Elon (Hebrew), Ellon • *oak tree* Alon (Hebrew), Allon • *oak wood* Chaney (Old French); Cheney (English) • *the oak tree* Oakes (Old English)

oaks Jolon *valley of the dead oaks* (Native American)

oarsman Remy (Latin)

oat *see* dweller at the oat field

oath Kenneth *royal oath* (Irish-Gaelic)

obedient Jun (Chinese); Praney (Hindi)

ocean Barindra, Nadeen, Nadish, Saagar, Shankhi (Hindi); Han (Vietnamese), Hai • *king of the ocean* Iravan (Hindi) • *ocean of mercy* Kripasagar (Hindi) • *sea, ocean* Sagar (Hindi) • *the ocean* Jatasya (Hindi)

Odin Odin *the god Odin* (Old Norse)

officer Sargent *attendant, officer* (Old French), Sergeant, Sergent • *church legal officer, summoner* Sumner (Middle English)

official Chauncey *chancellor church official* (Middle English) • *church official or sacristan* Sexton (Middle English)

offspring *see* offspring of Mars

often Dichali *he speaks often* (Native American)

Ogun Ogunsanwo *Ogun gives help* • *Ogun has earned honor* Ogunkeye (Nigerian) • *Ogun has performed honorably* Ogunsheye (Nigerian) • *the god Ogun* Oko (African)

old Chan (Chinese); Kedem (Hebrew); Sani (Navajo Indian); Geraint (Welsh) • *crossing the old ford or river, of the ancient ford* Alford (Old English), Alvord • *dweller at the old estate or town, from the old manor* Alton (Old English), Elton • *dweller in the old cottage* Alcott (Old English); Olcott (Old German) • *friend or old, wise protector* Alden (Old English), Aldin, Aldwin, Aldwyn, Elden, Eldin • *from the old estate or town* Elton (Old English) • *from the old forest* Elwood (Old English), Ellwood • *from the old* *house* Aldis (Old English), Aldous, Aldus • *from the old spring* Elwell (Old English) • *little old wise one* Shannon (Irish-Gaelic) • *old and wise* Aldo (Old German) • *old friend or protector* Aldwin (Anglo-Saxon), Aldwon • *old hero* Shanley (Irish-Gaelic) • *old, rice field* Furuta (Japanese) • *old, wise man* Altman (Old German) • *old, wise one* Sennett (French) • *old, wise ruler* Aldrich (Old English), Aldric, Audric, Eldric

Olney Olney *from the town of Olney* (Old English), Olnay, Olnton

Olorun Olorun *belong to the god Olorun* (African)

one Ekani (Hindi) • *little one* Koji (Japanese) • *one choice, only choice* Ennis (Irish-Gaelic) • *one choice, unique strength* Angus (Scotch-Gaelic) • *one year* Bersh (Gypsy) • *the first one* Tien (Vietnamese)

only Keval (Hindi), Kewal • *lonesome, only son* Ehud (Hebrew) • *one choice, only choice* Ennis (Irish-Gaelic) • *only child* Kontar (Ghanaian) • *only son* Iggi (African)

open Chang (Chinese) • *of the open dell* Lydell (Old English) • *open door* Tenskwatawa (Shawnee Indian)

opponent Faustus *strong opponent* (Latin), Faust

opposite Prateep (Hindi)

opposition Virudh (Hindi)

oppress Talman *to oppress* (Aramaic); Talmon (English)

oracle Phineas (Hebrew), Pincas, Pinchas

orange Alani *orange; orange tree* (Hawaiian)

orchard *see* apple

order Pradarsh *appearance, order* (Hindi) • *harmony, order, the universe* Cosmo (Greek), Cosimo, Cosme

organized Shrenik (Hindi)

origin Bron (African) • Matsumoto *origin, pine* (Japanese)

ornament Adin *an ornament* (Hebrew) • *my ornament, my witness* Adlai (Hebrew)

out *see* a blowing out

outspoken *see* bold, outspoken

overflow *see* forehead; to overflow

overseer *administrator, foreman, magistrate, overseer, sheriff* Schultz (German) • *son of the chamberlain or overseer* Chalmers (Old Scotch)

Owen Bowen *son of Owen* (Celtic)

owl Sowa (Slavic)

owner Stedman *farmstead owner* (Old English) • *horse lord, owner of many horses* Ahern (Celtic), Ahearn, Aherin, Aherne, Hearn, Hearne • *man of prosperity, owner of fields* Forbes (Irish-Gaelic) • *owner of a grassy plain* Lander (Middle English), Landers, Landor • *owner of a quarter acre* Verge (Anglo-French) • *owner of a rented estate* Galton (Old English) • *owner of the new house* Xavier (Spanish), Javier • *ship owner* Skipp (Old Norse)

ox Eleph *strong as an ox* (Hebrew)

oxen *see* ford

oyster Trai (Vietnamese)

— P —

pack Paco *to pack* (Italian)

pain Brirar *without pain* (Hindi)

painless Vishalya (Hindi)

palace *see* guarded

pale Oran *pale complexioned one* (Irish-Gaelic), Oren, Orin, Orrin

Palestine Jordan *from the river in Palestine* (Hebrew); Jori (American), Jory

palm Palmer *palm bearing pilgrim* (Old English) • *palm tree* Dekel (Arabic)

panther Numair (Arabic); Koi (Native American)

paradise Samar *fruit of paradise* (Hindi) • Kausar *lake of paradise* (Hindi)

parents Lendar *from his parents* (Gypsy) • Lensar *with his parents* (Gypsy)

parish Parish *one who lives in a parish* (English), Parrish

park Darton *deer park or estate, from the deer farm* (Old English) • *dweller at the enclosed land or park* Park (Old English), Parke • *park guardian or keeper* Parker (Middle English)

partner Sathi (Hindi)

passage Lane *at the passage* (Old English)

passion Rajas *arising from passion* (Hindi) • *full of feeling, passion* Rasik (Hindi)

passions *see* god of love and passions

passover *see* child of Passover

past Ateet (Hindi)

pasture Penley *enclosed pasture meadow* (Old English) • *from the awe-inspiring one's pasture meadow* Ansley (Old English) • *from the hare pasture* Harley (Old English), Arley • *from the hedged pasture* Hagley (Old English) • *from the high pasture, high meadow* Hanley (English) • *from the pasture meadow* Lee (Old English), Leigh • *from the red field, red pasture meadow* Radley (Old English)

path Wolfgang *advancing wolf, path of a wolf* (Old German) • *from the cottage on the winding path* Chetwin (Old English) • *from the enclosure with the winding path* Wyndham (Old English) • *master of the right path* Nitin (Hindi) • *one who follows the right path* Rashad (Arabic), Rasheed, Rashid • *on the upward path* Rohin (Hindi)

pathway *see* land

patience Dhairya (Hindi), Dhiraj • *patience, consolation* Dheeraj (Hindi)

patient Kshantu (Hindi) • *gentle and patient* Halim (Arabic)

Patrick Fitzpatrick *a son of Patrick* (Old German), Fitz, Patrick

Paul *see* little Paul

pea *see* chick-pea or vetch

peace Salim (African); Sholom (Hebrew), Shalom, Sholem; Prasham (Hindi); Bem (Nigerian); Paz (Spanish); An (Vietnamese) • *commands peace* Casimir (Old Slavic), Casimiro, Kasimir • *dove, peace* Jonas (Hebrew) • *father of peace* Absalom (Hebrew), Absa; Axel (Old German) • *gentle peace* Linfred (Old German)

• *glorious peace* Siegfried (Old German), Siegfrid, Sigfrid, Sigvard • *god of peace and agriculture* Lono (Hawaiian) • *he wishes peace* Zelimir (Slavic) • *lord of peace* Shantidev, Shantinath (Hindi) • *lover of peace* Radomil (Slavic) • *maker of the peace* Renfred (Old German), Renferd • *makes peace* Shamak (Hindi) • *man of peace* Axel (Hebrew); Pacian (Latin), Pace, Pacien • *peace among men* Manfred (Old German) • *peace on earth* Aiyetoro (Nigerian) • *peace, safe* Salim (Arabic), Saleem • *rough peace or rough one* Garvey (Irish-Gaelic) • *the dove, peace loving* Culver (Old English), Colver • *wolf peace* Ulfred (Old English)

peaceful Salim (African); Solomon (Hebrew), Saloman, Salomon; Rusham, Samik, Shantimay, Vitola (Hindi); Salaman (Hungarian); Langundo (Native American); Saleem (Swahili) • *determined peacemaker, resolute peaceful one* Wilfred Old German) • *devoted to the will of God; peaceful, quiet one; people mighty* Tully (Irish-Gaelic) • *divinely peaceful* Jeffrey (Old French), Geoffroy, Jefferey; Godfrey (Old German), Gottfried • *famous or royally peaceful, the ruler of all* Vladimir (Slavic), Vlad, Vladamar, Vladi, Vladimar • *little peaceful one* Sheehan (Irish-Gaelic) • *mighty and peaceful* Renfred (Old English) • *peaceful counsel* Sanfred (Old German) • *peaceful friend* Jakarious (Hindi); Winfred (Old English) • *peaceful hero, peaceful man* Manfred (Old English) • *peaceful Hun* Humphrey (Old German) • *peaceful or secure* Shanon (Hebrew); Shanan (English) • *peaceful ruler* Bedrich (Czech); Riki (Estonian); Frederick, Walfred (Old German), Frederic, Frederik, Fredric, Fredrich, Fredrick, Friedrich • *peaceful, victorious* Siegfried (Old German), Sigfrid, Sigvard • *peaceful wolf* Fridolf (Old English)

peacemaker \Shamita (Hindi) • *determined peacemaker, resolute peaceful one* Wilfred (Old German)

peach Salaam (African)

peacock Mayur, Vrishin (Hindi)
peak Aadit, Shekhar, Shikhar (Hindi)
• *from the ford at the peak* Pickford
(Old English) • *from the high peak*
Ogilvie (Pictish-Scotch) • *mountain
peak* Kruin (Afrikaans)
pear Le *pear tree* (Chinese) • *from the
pear tree* Perry (Middle English)
pearl Tautik (Hindi); Trai (Vietnamese)
pearls Shringesh *lord of pearls* (Hindi)
peasant's *see* farmstead
peddler *see* merchant, peddler,
tradesman
peninsula Ross *from the peninsula*
(Scotch-Gaelic)
Penrose Penrose *from the town of Penrose* (Old English)
peony Botan (Japanese)
people Troy *at the place of the curly-
haired people* (Old French) • *bold for
the people* Leopold (Old German),
Leopoldo • *boldest of the people*
Theobald (Old German), Tibold,
Tybalt • *brilliant among the people* Tab
(Old German) • *devoted to the will of
God; peaceful, quiet one; people mighty*
Tully (Irish-Gaelic) • *he helps people*
Sandor (Slavic), Alexander, Sander,
Sanders • *Lord of my people* Amiel
(Hebrew) • *man of the people* Publius
(Latin), Publias • *of the people* Folki
(Danish); Folk (English); Folke
(Old Norse) • *one who helps people* Ja-
nardan (Hindi) • *pride's people* Dallin
(Old English), Dalan, Dalen, Dalin,
Dallan, Dallen, Dallon, Dalon, Day-
lan, Daylen • *ruler of the people*
Dedric, Derrick, Theodoric (Old
German), Dedrick, Derek, Dietrich,
Dirk • *the people* Demos (Greek);
Tomi (Nigerian) • *victorious army,
victorious people* Klaus (German);
Nicholas (Greek), Cole, Nichol,
Nicol, Nicolas, Nikki; Kolya (Rus-
sian); Nicanor (Spanish)
people's Arvin *army or people's friend*
(Old German) • *from the people's
meadow* Dudley (Old English) • *most
popular, national or people's spirit* Volney (Old German) • *the people's champion* Sayer (Old German), Sayre
perceptive Darshan *perceptive one*
(Sanskrit)

perfect Kamil, Khushal (Arabic),
Kameel
perfection *see* lord of perfection
performed *see* honorably
performer *see* duty performer
permanent Sanaatan (Hindi)
persevering *see* island
persistent Conroy (Celtic)
person Pratul *a balanced person*
(Hindi) • *a respectable person* Shreeman (Hindi)
pervasive Ehimay *all pervasive* (Hindi)
pet Cullen (Celtic)
Peter Parkin, Perkin *little Peter* (Old
English); Parle, Parnell, Perrin (Old
French) • *son of Peter* Pierson
(Greek), Pearson, Peirsen, Pierce
petitioner Pepin (Old German)
phantom Drew *phantom, vision* (Old
Welsh)
philosopher *see* an ancient philosopher
phoenix *see* legendary
physician Tabib (Turkish) • *an ancient
physician* Charak (Hindi) • *physician,
healer* Asa (Hebrew)
piercer Percival *valley piercer* (Old
French), Percy
pilgrim Dewar (Irish-Gaelic) • *palm
bearing pilgrim* Palmer (Old English)
• *pilgrim to Rome* Romeo (Latin),
Romeon • *traveler, stranger, or pilgrim*
Perry (Latin)
pilgrimage Haji *born during the pilgrimage* (Egyptian)
pillager Talbot (Old French)
pillar Ande (African) • Pilar *a fountain basin or pillar* (Spanish)
pillow *see* cushion
pine Matsu (Japanese) • *below, pine*
Matsushita (Japanese) • *flat, pine* Hiramatsu, Matsuhira (Japanese) •
hill, pine Matsuoka (Japanese) • *island, pine* Matsushima, Shimatsu
(Japanese) • *little, pine* Matsuo
(Japanese) • *middle, pine* Matsunaka
(Japanese) • *mountain, pine* Matsuyama (Japanese) • *origin, pine* Matsumoto (Japanese) • *pine, rice field*
Matsuda (Japanese) • *pine, river* Matsukawa (Japanese)
pious Saatvik (Hindi); Arshad (Sanskrit) • Chapell *a man of the chapel,
pious* (Anglo-Saxon) • *devoted, pious*

Cuyler (Irish-Gaelic), Cyler • *lord of the pious* Poonish (Hindi)

piousness *see* lord of piousness

piper Whistler *piper or whistler* (Old English); Peverell (Old French), Peverel, Peveril

place Eng *a place* (Chinese) • *from a place in Cornwall* Denzel (Cornish) • *from the home or dwelling place* Case (Latin), Cayce, Cayse • *man from the muddy place* Brody (Scottish); Brodie (English) • *place of rest* Paulo (African) • *place of the hawks* Keaton (English)

placed *see* placed in God's hands

placid Shvant, Suval (Hindi)

plain Blair *from the field or plain* (Irish-Gaelic) • *hound of the plain* Conway (Irish-Gaelic) • *owner of a grassy plain* Lander (Middle English), Landers, Landor

plains Conway *a man of the great plains* (Celtic) • *man of the plains* Lyman (Old English), Liman, Limann, Lymann • *of the plains* Maitland (Old English), Mailand, Matland

planet Mangal (Hindi)

planner Yojit (Hindi)

plant Chane (African) • *small plant* Taru (Hindi)

planter *see* God's planter

player Carvey *athlete, game player* (Irish-Gaelic) • *harp player* Harper (Old English)

playful Du (Vietnamese)

pleasant Adiv (Hebrew); Shushil (Hindi); Adunbi (Nigerian) • *pleasant, cheerful* Prafulla (Hindi) • *pleasant sound* Suran (Hindi)

pleased Mudit, Prina (Hindi)

pleasing Bandhul, Modak, Nandak, Raman, Vinod (Hindi)

pledge Arlen (Celtic); Gage (Old French) • *a pledge* Cole (Old Irish) • *brilliant hostage or pledge* Gilbert (Old English), Gilberto, Guilbert • *pledge or hostage's estate* Gilby (Old Norse) • *pledge, security* Homer (Greek)

plentiful Toyo (Japanese)

plenty Otadan (Native American); Tadan (English)

plowman Harith (Arabic), Harithah

plums Lee (Chinese), Li

poem *see* breathe

poet Kirin (Hindi); Ovid (Latin) • *a poet* Kavi (Sanskrit) • *bard or royal poet* Riordan (Irish-Gaelic) • *poet and singer* Bard (Irish-Gaelic), Baird, Barde • *poet, saint* Narsi (Hindi) • *poet, savant* Devin (Irish-Gaelic) • *poet, wise man* Strahan (Irish-Gaelic) • *royal poet* Riorden (Irish-Gaelic)

poetic Lee (Irish-Gaelic), Leigh

poetry *see* man of poetry

point *see* heaven

pointed Montague *dweller at the pointed hill* (French), Monte, Monty • *dweller on the pointed hill* Kipp (Old English) • *from the pointed land* Orlan (Old English), Orland • *spearlike or pointed* Barry (Irish-Gaelic)

poison Ba *poison; residue; three* (Vietnamese)

policeman Rendor (Hungarian)

polished Malvin, Melvin *polished chief* (Irish-Gaelic) • *smooth, polished one* Terence (Latin), Terencio

polite Baneet (Hindi)

pomegranate Rimon (Hebrew)

pond *see* one who lives by the pond

pool Ashlin *dweller at the ash tree pool* (Old English) • *dweller at the new pool* Newlin (Old Welsh), Newlyn • *dweller by a hollow or by a seething pool* Corey (Irish-Gaelic), Cory • *from an estate by a pool* Pelton (Old English) • *from the colony by the pool* Lincoln (Old English) • *from the red pool* Rutledge (Old English) • *from the valley of the pool* Marden (Old English)

poor Dindayal *kind to the poor* (Hindi) • *poor man* Kawacatoose (Cree Indian)

popular Volney *most popular, national or people's spirit* (Old German) • *popular one* Demas (Greek)

porter Porter (French)

portion Ansh (Hindi)

position *see* glorious position, stand of glory

possessed Cain *possessed or possession* (Hebrew); Kabil (Turkish)

possession *see* possessed or possession

possessions *see* man of many possessions

power Shakuni (Hindi); Naldo (Old German) • *curving river, famous power*

Rolt (Old German) • *lasting power* Reynold (Old German), Rennold • *mighty power* Ronald (Old Norse), Renaldo • *power of God* Chike (African) • *power of the god Chi* Chike (Nigerian) • *power of the sea* Zale (Greek) • *son of mighty power* Ronson (Old English) • *wise power* Renaud (Hindi)

powerful Kedar (Arabic), Kadar; Oorjit, Vibhu, Vikrant (Hindi); Maska (Native American) • *a powerful leader* Gazo (Hebrew), Gazzo • *army ruler, powerful warrior* Walter (Old German), Gauthier, Walther • *brave, powerful* Maynard (Old German), Menard • *divinely powerful* Oswald (Old English), Oswell • *ever powerful, ever ruler* Eric (Old Norse), Erich, Erik • *healthy, powerful, strong* Valerian (Late Latin) • *law powerful* Ewald (Old English) • *little, mighty and powerful* Renny (Irish-Gaelic) • *mighty and powerful* Reginald (Old English), Reinald, Reinhold, Reinold, Renato, Renault, Reynold, Ronald • *powerful and beloved* Aziz (Arabic) • *powerful and royal* Cynric (Old English) • *powerful army* Mather, Ricker (Old English) • *powerful brave* Richard (Old German), Ricard, Ricardo, Riccardo, Richerd, Rickert • *powerful friend* Medwin (Old English) • *powerful guardian* Rickward (Old English), Rickwood • *powerful leader* Trahern (Celtic), Trahurn; Edrei (Hebrew), Edroi • *powerful man* Richman (Old English) • *powerful protector* Richmond (Old German) • *powerful ruler* Richard (Old German), Ricard, Ricardo, Riccardo, Richart, Rickert • *powerful, sacred* Archard (Anglo-Saxon/ German), Archerd • *powerful, strength* Haile (Ethiopian) • *power of an eagle* Arne (Old German) • *sea powerful* Sewell (Old English), Sewald, Sewall • *strong or powerful* Hamza (Arabic)

praise Judah (Hebrew), Judas, Jude; Ohas, Prashansa, Shansa (Hindi) • *praise the Lord* Joab, Ramiah (Hebrew), Joub, Ramah • *the praise of the Lord* Yehudi (Hebrew) • *the praised one, worthy of praise* Aeneas (Greek), Eneas • *this in praise of the Lord* Jedthus (Hebrew)

praised Judd (Hebrew); Sanjiro (Japanese), Sanji • *greatly praised* Hillell (Hebrew), Hilel, Hillel • *highly praised* Ahmad (Arabic) • *most highly praised* Ahmed (Arabic) • *the Lord be praised* Jehu (Hebrew), Jeu • *the praised one* Muhammad (Arabic), Ahmad, Ahmed, Amad, Amed, Hamid, Hammad, Hammed, Humayd, Mahmud, Mahmoud, Mehemet, Mehmet, Mohamad, Mohamet, Muhammed; Mehmet (Turkish) • *the praised one, worthy of praise* Aeneas (Greek), Eneas

praiser Thaddeus (Latin), Taddeo, Tadeo

prayed Rambert *for whom we prayed* (Latin), Ramburt, Rombert

precious Jhulier, Maulik (Hindi); Dyre (Norse) • *precious one* Azizi (African) • *precious second son* Tanjiro (Japanese) • *precious stone* Ratan (Hindi)

preeminence Jethro (Hebrew)

prelate Taggart *son of the prelate* (Irish-Gaelic)

prepared Jephum *he is prepared* (Hebrew), Jepum

prey *see* bird of prey

priceless *see* inestimable, priceless one

pride Garv (Hindi)

pride's *see* pride's people

priest Khoury (Arabic); Ritvik (Hindi)

priest's Presley *dweller at the priest's meadow* (Old English) • *dweller at the priest's place* Preston (Old English) • *from the priest's dwelling* Prescott (Old English)

prince Amiri (African); Amir (Arabic), Ameer; Mylor (Celtic), Melar, Milore; Wang (Chinese); Mehtar (East Indian); Panav, Rajkumar (Hindi); Adar (Syrian) • *a prince* Yuvraj (Hindi) • *prince of earth* Parthiv (Hindi) • *royal prince, ruler* Xerxes (Persian)

princely Baldemar *bold or princely and famous* (Old German) • *bold or princely ruler* Baldric (Old German), Baudric

prince's *see* dweller at the prince's hill, of the low lands
private *see* estate
prize Tanak (Hindi)
profit Saad (African); Cappi (Gypsy)
profitable *see* profitable encounter
projecting *see* estate
promotion Sarwar (Hindi)
property Wray *from the corner property* (Old Norse) • *from the pathway land or property* Wayland (Old English) • *home or private property, ruler of an estate* Henry (Old German), Enrique, Heinrich, Hendrick, Henri; Quico (Spanish) • *inheritor of property* Arve (Scandinavian)
proprietor Laird (Celtic)
prospering Audley (Anglo-Saxon), Audly
prosperity Raju (Hindi) • *glory, prosperity* Blade (Old English) • *man of prosperity, owner of fields* Forbes (Irish-Gaelic) • *prosperity, success* Speed (Old English)
prosperous Sashreek (Hindi); Odell (Old German); Onan (Turkish) • *a prosperous man's manor hall or house* Edsel (Old English) • *brilliant, prosperous* Edbert (Old English) • *from the prosperous village* Edlun (Anglo-Saxon) • *lord of prosperity* Shivadev (Hindi) • *prosperous and rich* Rafferty (Irish-Gaelic) • *prosperous friend* Edwin (Old English) • *prosperous from the sea* Murdock (Scotch-Gaelic) • *prosperous guardian* Edward (Old English), Edouard, Eduard, Eduardo, Edvard • *prosperous man* Othman (Old German) • *prosperous protector* Odon (Hungarian); Edmund (Old English), Eamon, Edmond, Edmundo • *prosperous ruler* Edric, Edwald (Old English) • *prosperous spearman* Edgar (Old English), Edgard, Edgardo; Gerik (Polish) • *prosperous, stable* Stacey (Middle Latin) • *prosperous, wealthy one* Otto (Old German) • *prosperous wolf* Edolf, Udolf (Old English) • *the prosperous man* Idden (Anglo-Saxon), Iden
protect Kivi (Hebrew), Akiba, Akiva, Kiva • *may the Lord protect the king* Balthasar (Greek), Baltasar, Balthasar; Zarek (Polish)

protected Osmond *he is protected by God* (Old German), Osman, Osmen, Osmo, Osmund, Ozmo • *of the protected town* Arlo (Old English) • *protected by the Lord* Pedaiah (Hebrew), Pedaias
protecting Palin (HindI) • *the god Chi is protecting* Cinese (Nigerian)
protection Fremont (Anglo-Saxon); Gopan (Hindi) • *divine protection* Wingate (Old English) • *protection, wolf* Raoul (French), Ralph, Randolph • *under Thor's protection* Thormond (Old English), Thormund, Thurmond; Thurman (Scandinavian), Thorman, Thurmann
protective *see* armed, protective
protector Asim (Arabic); Chadwick (Celtic), Chad; Dinanath, Tarak (Hindi); Tedman (Old German), Teddman, Tedmann, Tedmund; Chionesu (Zimbabwean) • *a diamond, bright protector* Diamond (Old English) • *adviser, protector* Redmond (Old German) • *bold friend or protector* Baldwin (Old German), Balduin, Baudoin • *counsel protector* Redmond (Old English), Radmund, Redmund • *divine protector* Osmond (Old English), Osmund; Amund (Scandinavian) • *famous protector* Rodmond (Old German), Rodmund • *free or noble protector* Fremont (Old German) • *friend or old, wise protector* Alden (Old English), Aldin, Aldwin, Aldwyn, Elden, Eldin • *gracious protector* Esmond (Old English) • *helmet, protected* Elmo (Italian) • *mighty or ruling protector* Walmond (Old German) • *mighty or wise protector* Raymond (Old German), Ramon; Ramiro (Spanish), Ramirez • *national protector* Tedmond (Old English) • *old friend or protector* Aldwin (Anglo-Saxon), Aldwone • *powerful protector* Richmond (Old German) • *prosperous protector* Odon (Hungarian); Edmund (Old English), Eamon, Edmond, Edmundo • *protector against enemies* Zareb (Sudanese) • *protector or spear friend* Aswin (Old English) • *protector of the home* Hammond (Middle English) • *resolute protector* Viljo (Finnish); William (Old

German), Wilhelm, Wilkes, Williamson, Willis, Wilson; Guillermo (Spanish) • *spear protector* Garmond, Ormond (Old English), Garmund • *the god Chi is our protector* Chileogu (Nigerian) • *true protector* Warmond (Old English) • *unwavering protector* Vassily (Slavic-German), Vasilek, Vasya, Vasyuta • *victorious protector* Sigmund (Old German), Sigismond, Sigismund • *wealthy protector* Eamon (Irish-Gaelic)

protestor Eskill *a protestor* (Scandinavian), Eskil

proud Chimalsi (African); Shandar (Hindi) • *proud, brilliant one* Dalbert (Old English), Delbert • *proud friend*

Delwyn (Old English), Delwin • *proud one* Avan (Hebrew), Evan; Bryant (Old English)

provide *see* food

provisions *see* dispenser of provisions

prudent Trevor *discreet, prudent, wise* (Irish-Gaelic) • *prudent warrior* Rainer (Old German)

pugilist *see* boar

pupil *see* bright pupil

pure Hanbal, Tahir, Nirmay, Taha (Arabic); Bimal, Pavitra, Vimal (Hindi); Jing, Manchu (Chinese); Amal (Hindi) • *pure, clear* Nirmal (Hindi) • *pure one* Gower (Old Welsh)

purpose *see* great

quaking *see* aspen
quality Utkarsh *high quality* (Hindi)
quarter *see* acre
quick Brice (Celtic); Javas (Sanskrit) • *brilliant; quick friend* Egwin (Anglo-Saxon), Egin, Winn • *the quick one* Sprague (Old English), Sprage
quick-moving Aiolos *quick-moving, nimble* (Greek)
quick-witted Zeki (Turkish)
quiet Sushant (Hindi); Kiyoshi (Japanese), Yoshi • *devoted to the will of*

God; peaceful, quiet one; people mighty Tully (Irish-Gaelic) • *from the quiet river estate or town* Tanton (Old English) • *from the quiet spring* Stilwell (Anglo-Saxon) • *quiet, gentle* Shamindra (Hindi) • *quiet man* Stillman (Old English) • *quiet, silent* Neerav (Hindi)
quietly Dovev *to whisper or speak quietly* (Hebrew), Dov • *walks quietly* Kijika (Native American)

R

rabbit Arledge *dweller at the hare or rabbit lake* (Old English) • *from the rabbit meadow* Arley (Old English), Harley • *young rabbit* Leverett (Old French)
radiance Ronak *brightness, radiance* (Hindi)
radiant Anshul, Pradyun (Hindi) • *a radiant soul* Philbert (Old German), Bert, Filbert • *radiant as sunlight* Huy

(Vietnamese) • *radiant, beautiful* Ruchir (Hindi)
raft *see* raft, heaven
raging Patamon (Native American)
rain Tal (Hebrew); Barsaat (Hindi) • *born during a rain* Brishen (Gypsy) • *god of clouds and rain* Hinun (Native American)
raindrop Dalfon (Hebrew)
rainmaker Gowon (Nigerian)

rainy Nehal (Hindi)
raiser Tupper *ram raiser* (Old English)
Ralph *see* estate
ram Aries *a ram* (Latin) • *ram raiser* Tupper (Old English)
Ramadan Ramadan *born during the month of Ramadan* (Swahili)
rambler Rover *rambler, wanderer* (Middle English)
ram's Ramsey *ram's island; raven's island* (Old English) • *ram's valley* Ramsden (Old English)
rapid Trent *rapid stream, torrent; swift* (Latin)
rapture *see* ecstacy, rapture
rare Nadir (Arabic); Viral (Hindi)
rational Sachetan (Hindi)
raven Corbin (Latin), Korban, Korben, Korbin; Bran (Old Celtic), Bram; Corbett (Old French), Corbet, Corby; Kangi (Sioux); Kangee, Kanjee (English) • *bold raven* Brainard (Old English) • *bright raven, he shall be famous* Bertram (Old German), Bartram • *brilliant raven* Bertram (Old English), Bertrand • *fierce raven* Brainard (Old German), Braynard • *from the raven family estate* Remington (Old English) • *from the raven forest* Renshaw (Old English) • *glorious raven* Bartram (Old English), Barthram • *Ing's raven* Ingram (Old German), Ingraham • *little raven* Brendan (Irish-Gaelic) • *ruling raven* Waldron (Old German) • *the black raven* Branduff (Irish-Gaelic), Brandubh
ravens *see* nest
raven's Ransford *from the raven's ford* (Old English) • *from the raven's meadow* Ransley (Old English) • *ram's island; raven's island* Ramsey (Old English) • *the raven's friend* Corwin (Anglo-Saxon), Corvin, Korwin
ravine *see* field
ray Kiran *a light ray* (Sanskrit) • *ray of light* Mareechi (Hindi)
rays *see* sun rays
ready helmeted, ready for battle Coryell (Greek) • *noble and ready* Alphonso (Old German), Alfonso, Alphonse, Lanzo
reanimating *see* giving life, reanimating

reason Akil *one who uses reason* (Arabic), Ahkeel
rebellious Marid (Arabic)
reborn Rene (Latin) • *one who is reborn* Anastatius (Greek)
reckless Ohanko (Native American)
reclaimed *see* dweller on reclaimed land
red Rohit (Hindi) • *at the red shore* Radnor (Old English) • *dweller at the red cliff* Radcliff (Old English) • *dweller at the red meadow* Redley (Old English) • *flank, side; red, rosy* Hong (Vietnamese) • *from the red enclosure* Rudyard (Old English) • *from the red field, red pasture meadow* Radley (Old English) • *from the red ford* Radford, Redford (Old English), Ruford • *from the red meadow, he lives by the red field* Ridley (Old English) • *from the red pool* Rutledge (Old English) • *from the red spring* Rothwell (Old Norse) • *from the red stream* Radborne (Old English) • *from the red swamp* Monroe (Irish-Gaelic) • *he lives by the red brook* Radburn (Old English), Radbourne • *he lives by the red valley* Radford (Old English), Radley • *little red-haired one* Ruskin (French-German); Roslin (Old French) • *man of the red earth* Damek (Czech); Adam (Hebrew); Keddy (Scottish), Keady, Keddie; Adan (Spanish) • *red earth* Addison (Old English) • *red-haired* Ruff, Rush (French), Ruffe, Rufus; Flann, Rogan, Rowan (Irish-Gaelic), Rowe, Rowen; Rust (Latin), Rufe, Rusty; Reid (Old English), Read, Reed; Russell (Old French); Roth (Scottish-Gaelic) • *red-haired youth* Alroy (Irish-Gaelic) • *red king* Rory (Irish-Gaelic), Rurik • *red leaf* Wapasha (Dakota Indian) • *red, made of copper, Mars* Lohit (Hindi) • *red one* Derry, Rooney, Rory (Irish-Gaelic) • *servant of the red-haired youth* Gilroy (Irish-Gaelic) • *son of the red-haired man* Flynn (Irish-Gaelic), Flinn • *son of the red warrior* Clancy (Irish-Gaelic); Clancey (English) • *the color red* Gulal (Hindi)
reddish Corcoran *of reddish complexion* (Irish-Gaelic) • *reddish-brown complexion* Burrell (Old French) • *reddish-*

brown hair Sorrell (Old French) •
reddish-brown haired Arun (Sanskrit)

redeemer Goel *the redeemer* (Hebrew)

redhead Rodman (Old German),
Rodmann, Rodmun, Rodmur • *of the
fiery hair, redhead* Bayard (French),
Baird, Beard

reed Roden *from the reed valley* (Old
English) • *stalk or reed* Kaniel (Hebrew)

reeds *see* clump of reeds

refined Odo *the refined son* (Latin),
Odilo, Odlo

refinement *see* man of refinement

refuge Van Wyck *from the refuge*
(Dutch) • *the refuge of man*
Naaraayan (Hindi)

regal Regis (Latin) • *regal one* Royal
(Old French)

regent *see* knowing

region Montana *from a mountainous region* (Latin) • *of a rocky region* Gilead
(Hebrew), Gillead, Gilleod

reindeer Ahdik (Native American)

rejoicer Gaius (Welsh)

reliable *see* loyal son, reliable

relic *see* ancestral relic

religion Dharma *religion, nature*
(Hindi) • *sword of religion* Seif (Arabic)

religious Khatib *religious minister* (Arabic) • *religious town or temple* Templeton (Old English)

remainder Avashesh (Hindi)

remembered Simrit, Smrita (Hindi) •
Jehovah hath remembered Zachary (Hebrew), Zacaria, Zacarias, Zacharias

remembrance Smaran (Hindi)

reminder *see* ancestor

remover Hara *the remover of sins*
(Hindi)

renowned Torbert *as renowned as Thor*
(Old English), Torbart • *renowed
archer* Bevus (Old German), Bevis •
renowned for his hair Faxon (Old German), Faxan, Faxen • *renowned warrior* Ludwig (Old German)

rented *see* estate

repairman Schuster *shoe repairman*
(German)

reputed Pingal *a reputed sage* (Hindi)

request Funsan (African)

reserved Hisoka (Japanese)

residence *see* king's

resident Stanfield *a resident of
Stanfield, from the rocky field* (Old En-
glish) • *a resident of Walford* Walford
(Old English), Ford • *a resident of
Warfield* Warfield (Old English),
Warfeld, Warfold • *fortress resident*
Brougher (Old English) • *valley resi-
dent* Denman (Old English)

residue *see* poison; residue; three

resists Steele *he resists* (Sanskrit)

resolute Willard *brave and resolute*
(Old English) • *determined, firm, res-
olute* Will (Old English) • *determined
peacemaker, resolute peaceful one* Wil-
fred (Old German) • *from the firm
fortress, resolute brilliant one* Wilbur
(Old German) • *nobly resolute*
Abelard (Old German); Adelard
(Teutonic) • *resolute, brave* Sudhir
(Hindi) • *resolute, famous one* Wilmer
(Old German) • *resolute protector*
Viljo (Finnish); William (Old Ger-
man), Wilhelm, Wilkes, Williamson,
Willis, Wilson; Guillermo (Spanish)
• *resolute spirit or mind* Wilmot (Old
German)

respect *see* love, respect

respectable *see* a respectable person

respected Manit *highly respected*
(Hindi) • *respected or admired* Hieu
(Vietnamese) • *Swithbert the respected
landowner* (Old German), Swithbart

respectful Sadar (Hindi)

rest Rowe (Anglo-Saxon); Vishram
(Hindi) • *comfort, rest* Noah (Hebrew) • *place of rest* Paulo (African)

restless Chapal (Hindi)

restraint Ankush (Hindi)

result Nishkarsh (Hindi)

resurrected Anstice *resurrected one*
(Greek)

retainer Yeoman (Middle English)

return Shevi (Hebrew)

reverenced *see* august one, reverenced one

revive Soo (Chinese)

revolt Mered (Hebrew)

revolution Kraanti, Viplav (Hindi)

reward Timon *honor, reward, value*
(Greek) • *divine reward* Axel (Scandinavian), Axell

rice Honda *base, rice field* (Japanese) •
black, rice field Kuroda (Japanese) •
flat, rice field Hirata (Japanese) •

forest, rice field Morita (Japanese) • *good fortune, rice field* Fukuda (Japanese) • *middle, rice field* Tanaka (Japanese) • *old, rice field* Furuta (Japanese) • *pine, rice field* Matsuda (Japanese) • *rice field, river* Tagawa (Japanese) • *rice field, rock* Iwata (Japanese) • *rice field, side* Tanabe (Japanese) • *rice field, wisteria* Fujita (Japanese)

rich Tomi (Japanese); Powa (Native American) • *famous ruler, rich in fame* Roderick (Old German), Broderick, Roderich, Rodrick, Rodriego, Rodrigo, Rurik • *prosperous and rich* Rafferty (Irish-Gaelic) • *rich ruler* Edric (Anglo-Saxon) • *the rich* Hashum (Hebrew), Heshum

Richard Ryker *son of Richard* (Middle English); Dixon (Old English)

Rider Tasida (Sarcee Indian) • *a rider* Kistur (Gypsy) • *horse rider* Revanth (Hindi)

ridicule *see* mock

ridge Link *from the bank or ridge* (Old English) • *from the broad ridge* Broderick (Middle English) • *from the estate on the projecting ridge* Hutton (Old English) • *from the ridge* Ridge, Rigg (Old English) • *from the ridge road* Ridgeway (Old English) • *he lives by the ridge* Ridgley (Old English), Ridglea, Ridglee • *lord of the ridge* Selfridge (Old German)

right Salih (Arabic) • *master of the right path* Nitin (Hindi) • *one who follows the right path* Rashad (Arabic), Rasheed, Rashid • *right in the law* Jude (Latin) • *right side* Teman (Hebrew) • *son of the right hand* Benjamin (Hebrew), Beathan

righteous Rashad (African); Adio (Nigerian) • *just, righteous one* Zadok (Hebrew), Zakoc

righteousness *see* guide to righteousness

righthanded Jamin (Hebrew), Jammin

rightly Rashid *rightly guided* (Arabic), Rasheed

ripe Rip (Dutch), Ripp

rippling Misu *rippling water* (Miwok)

rising Rohak (Hindi)

river Orrin (English); Sarit (Hindi) • *a river* Sutoya (Hindi) • *at the river's bend, boundary bank* Windsor (Old English) • *crossing the old ford or river, of the ancient ford* Alford (Old English), Alvord • *curving river* Romney (Old Welsh) • *curving river, famous power* Rolt (Old German) • *dweller at the river crossing* Wade (Old English) • *dweller by the alder river* Garnock (Old Welsh) • *dweller by the river crossing* Byford (Old English) • *dweller near the Brosna River* Brosnan (Irish-Gaelic) • *from the bright valley or clear river valley* Kendall (Old English), Kendal, Kendell • *from the broad river crossing* Bradford (Old English) • *from the double river ford* Twyford (Old English) • *from the field by the small river* Mansfield (Old English) • *from the narrow river* Kelvin (Irish-Gaelic), Kelvan, Kelven • *from the quiet river estate or town* Tanton (Old English) • *from the river in Palestine* Jordan (Hebrew); Jori (American), Jory • *from the river island* Innis (Irish-Gaelic), Innes, Inness; Holmes (Middle English); Holmann (Old German), Holman, Holmen • *from the river of stones* Calder (Celtic) • *from the wide river* Leith (Celtic) • *God of the river* Alpheus (Greek), Alfeus • *gray-haired one's river crossing* Blanford (Old English) • *holy river* Varana (Hindi) • *of the Severn river* Severin (Old English), Severen • *one from a river or bay* Kang (Korean) • *pine, river* Matsukawa (Japanese) • *rice field, river* Tagawa (Japanese) • *river crossing* Ford (Old English) • *river ford on the street* Stratford (Old English) • *small river* Jaafar (African) • *the river Tano* Tano (Ghanaian), Tanno

riverbank Deverell *from the riverbank* (English-Old Welsh); Rye (Old French) • *from the riverbank enclosure* Oram (Old English)

rivers Hiawatha *he makes rivers* (Native American)

riverside Worthington *from the riverside* (Anglo-Saxon) • *from the riverside estate* Eaton (Old English)

road Tobbar (Gypsy) • *camp by the road* Cilombo (African) • *from near the stony road* Stanway (Old English) •

Lane *from the narrow road* (Middle English) • *from the ridge road* Ridgeway (Old English)

robust *see* hearty

rock Bour (African); Ferris (Celtic); Adri (Hindi) • *dweller in the house at the rock* Tremayne (Old Cornish) • *from the steep cliff or rock* Cliff (Old English) • *God, my rock or stone* Zuriel (Hebrew) • *like a rock* Rock (Modern), Rocky • *my father is my rock; my father is my strength* Avniel (Hebrew) • *rice field, rock* Iwata (Japanese) • *rock or stone* Takis (Greek); Peter (Latin), Pedro, Pero, Piero, Pierre, Pieter, Pietro; Pierce (Old Anglo-French) • *stone or rock of the help* Ebenezer (Hebrew), Eben

rocky Stanfield *a resident of Stanfield, from the rocky field* (Old English) • *dweller at the rocky forest* Stanwood (Old English) • *dweller at the rocky meadow* Stanley (Old English), Stanleigh • *dweller at the rocky village* Stanwick (Old English) • *from the rocky cliff* Stancliff (Old English) • *from the rocky ford* Stanford (Old English) • *from the rocky hollow* Stanhope (Old English) • *from the rocky island* Skerry (Old Norse) • *from the rocky lake* Stanmore (Old English) • *from the rocky meadow* Rockley (Old English) • *from the rocky spring* Rockwell (Old English) • *of a rocky region* Gilead (Hebrew), Gillead, Gilleod • *of the rocky valley* Standish (Old English), Standice • *rocky fortress or sky fortress* Rochester (Old English) • *rocky headland* Carrick (Irish-Gaelic)

rod *see* bearer

roe Dorcas *a roe, from the forest* (Hebrew), Dorcus • *from the roe deer brook, of the flower fields* Rayburn (Old English), Raybin, Raybourne • *from the roe deer forest* Roscoe (Old Norse) • *from the roe deer spring* Rowell (Old English) • *roe buck deer estate* Renton (Old English)

Rome Romulus *citizen of Rome* (Latin) • *of Rome* Roman (Latin), Romain • *pilgrim to Rome* Romeo (Latin), Romeon

roof thatcher Thatcher (Middle English)

roofer *see* maker

rook *see* estate

root Rutland *from the root or stump land* (Old Norse) • *from the root or stump meadow* Rutley (Old English)

rope Cordell *little rope maker* (Old French), Kordell • *rope maker* Roper (Old English)

rose Vartan (Armenian) • *a rose* Vered (Hebrew)

roses Rhodes *place of the roses* (Greek)

rosy *see* flank, side; red, rosy

rough Rowley *dweller at the rough meadow* (Old English) • *from the rough ford* Rufford (Old English) • *little rough one* Girvin (Irish-Gaelic), Garvan, Garvey, Girvan, Girven • *of the rough hill* Harlow (Old English) • *rough peace or rough one* Garvey (Irish-Gaelic)

royal Alroy (Latin), Elroy; Kyne (Old English) • *bard or royal poet* Riordan (Irish-Gaelic) • *bold and royal, chief warrior* Kimball (Old Welsh), Kimble • *bold guardian or royal guardian* Kenward (Old English) • *bold warrior or royal warrior* Kenway (Old English) • *from a farm in Kent, from the royal estate* Kenton (Old English) • *gatekeeper, royal messenger* Portero (Spanish) • *glorious ruler, royal glory* Vladislav (Old Slavic) • *powerful and royal* Cynric (Old English) • *royal oath* Kenneth (Irish-Gaelic) • *royal poet* Riordan (Irish-Gaelic) • *royal prince, ruler* Xerxes (Persian) • *royal ruler* Kenrick (Old English) • *royal, victorious one* Kinsey (Old English) • *servant to the royal court, youthful attendant* Page (French), Pagas, Pegasus • *son of Henry* Harris (Old English), Henderson • *son of Henry, royal ruler* Kendrick (Irish-Gaelic)

royally Vladimir *famous or royally peaceful, the ruler of all* (Slavic), Vlad, Vladamar, Vladi, Vladimar • *royally brave* Kensell (Old German)

royalty *see* royalty, kingdom

ruby Manik (Hindi) • *a ruby* Rubin (Latin)

rugged *see* firm

ruins Tremain *of the ruins* (Anglo-Saxon), Tremayne

rule Aren (Norse)

ruler Hakem (Arabic); Nagid (Hebrew); Vasin (Hindi); Walden (Old German); Sultan (Swahili); Adar (Syrian); Nyagwa (West African) • *army ruler* Hale (Hawaiian); Herrick (Old German); Harold (Old Norse), Araldo, Aralt, Hal; Enric (Romanian) • *army ruler; mason, wall builder* Waller (Old English) • *army ruler, powerful warrior* Walter (Old German), Gauthier, Walther • *a ruler* Rozen (Hebrew); Rosen (English) • *axe-ruler* Bardrick (Old English) • *blond ruler, elf ruler, spirit ruler* Aubrey (Old French) • *bold or princely ruler* Baldric (Old German), Baudric • *brilliant ruler* Berthold (Old German), Bertold, Bertoldi, Bertoud • *chief, ruler* Kim (Old English) • *divine, famous ruler* Amory (Old German), Amery • *divine ruler* Osric (Old German), Osrick, Osrock, Rick • *eagle ruler* Arnold (Old German), Arnaldo, Arnaud, Arnoldo • *elf ruler* Avery (Old English) • *ever powerful, ever ruler* Eric (Old Norse), Erich, Erik • *famous or royally peaceful, the ruler of all* Vladimir (Slavic), Vlad, Vladamar, Vladi, Vladimar • *famous ruler* Roarke (Irish-Gaelic), Rourke, Ruark; Roald, Valdemar (Old German), Waldemar • *famous ruler, rich in fame* Roderick (Old German), Broderick, Roderich, Rodrick, Rodriego, Rodrigo, Rurik • *glorious ruler, royal glory* Vladislav (Old Slavic) • *government or victorious ruler* Sigwald (Old German) • *home or private property, ruler of an estate* Henry (Old German), Enrique, Heinrich, Hendrick, Henri; Quico (Spanish) • *industrious ruler* Emery (Old German), Amerigo, Emeri, Emerson, Emory • *like a ruler* Llewellyn (Old Welsh) • *noble ruler* Audric (Old German) • *noble ruler, ruler of all* Alaric (Old German), Alric, Alrick • *old, wise ruler* Aldrich (Old English), Aldric, Audric, Eldric • *peaceful ruler* Bedrich (Czech); Riki (Estonian); Frederick, Walfred (Old German), Frederic, Frederik, Fredric, Fredrich, Fredrick, Friedrich • *powerful ruler* Richard (Old German), Ricard, Ricardo, Riccardo, Richart, Rickert • *prosperous ruler* Edric, Edwald (Old English) • *rich ruler* Edric (Anglo-Saxon) • *royal prince, ruler* Xerxes (Persian) • *royal ruler* Kenrick (Old English) • *ruler of all* Alrik, Olery (Old German) • *ruler of hundreds* Satish (Hindi) • *ruler of the gods* Devraj (Hindi) • *ruler of the home* Hendrik (Dutch), Hendrick, Henri; Rico (Italian-Spanish), Enrico, Heinrich, Henry • *ruler of the people* Dedric, Derrick, Theodoric (Old German), Dedrick, Derek, Dietrich, Dirk • *ruler, thunder* Terrell (Old English), Terrill • *sacred ruler* Aric (Old English) • *son of Henry, royal ruler* Kendrick (Irish-Gaelic) • *spear ruler* Garrick (Old English) • *the local ruler* Landry (Anglo-Saxon), Landre, Landri • *the wise ruler* Alberic (Old German), Albric • *Thor ruler, thunder ruler* Thorald (Old Norse), Terrell, Tyrell; Thorvald (Scandinavian) • *wolf ruler* Ulric (Old German) • *world mighty, world ruler* Donald (Scotch-Gaelic); Tauno (Finnish) • *world ruler* Bohdan (Ukranian); Bogdan, Bogdashka, Danya (Russian)

ruler's Rigby *ruler's valley* (Old English) • *thunder ruler's estate* Tarleton (Old English)

rules Elrad *God rules* (Hebrew) • *one who rules* Sasta (Hindi)

ruling Walmond *mighty or ruling protector* (Old German) • *ruling raven* Waldron (Old German) • *ruling through God* Godric (Anglo-Saxon)

runner Angell (Greek), Angel, Angelo • *swift runner* Sherwin (Middle English)

running Akar (Turkish)

rush Leverton *from the rush farm* (Old English) • *from the rush ford* Rushford (Old English)

rushing Arnon *rushing stream* (Hebrew)

rye Ryton *from the rye enclosure* (Old English) • *from the rye field* Rycroft (Old English) • *from the rye hill* Ryle (Old English) • *rye seller* Ryman (Old English)

ryeland *see* dweller at the ryeland

• S •

sacred Sadoc (Hebrew) • *bold, noble and sacred* Archibald (Anglo-Saxon/German), Archibaldo • *brave and sacred* Allard (Old English), Alard • *holy, sacred, saintly* Santo (Italian) • *powerful, sacred* Archard (Anglo-Saxon/German), Archerd • *sacred amulet* Shen (Egyptian) • *sacred ruler* Aric (Old English) • *sacred symbol* Setu (Hindi) • *sacred urn* Kalash (Hindi)
sacrifice Yagya (Hindi)
sacrifices Fasto *one who makes sacrifices* (Latin), Fasta
sacristan *see* church official or sacristan
safe Nanji (African) • *peace, safe* Salim (Arabic), Saleem
safety Haven *place of safety* (Old English)
sagacious Shanahan *sagacious, wise one* (Irish-Gaelic)
sage Naarad, Shameek *an ancient sage* (Hindi) • *a reputed sage* Pingal (Hindi) • *a sage* Lomash, Pusan, Sarat, Shalik, Yaj (Hindi) • *a saint, sage* Rishi (Hindi)
sail *see* maker
sailor Nevlin (Celtic) • *a man of the sea, sailor* Ithaman (Latin) • *a summer sailor* Sorley (Irish-Gaelic); Somhairle (Irish) • *brave sailor* Cadmar (Celtic), Cadmarr • *the strong sailor* Ithnan (Hebrew)
saint Mudgal, Rithwik (Hindi); Meletius (Latin) • *a saint, sage* Rishi (Hindi) • *holy, little saint* Nevan (Irish-Gaelic), Nevin, Nevins, Niven • *poet, saint* Narsi (Hindi) • *worshiper of the saint* Nevin (Irish-Gaelic), Niven
St. James *see* James
saintly Ultann (Welsh), Ultan • *holy sacred, saintly* Santo (Italian)
salesman Dalal *vendor or salesman* (Hindi)
salty Slane (Czech); *a calabash; anything; a salty cake; gourd; in daylight* Cata (Hasua/African)
salvation Jesus *God is salvation* (Hebrew); Jesu, Jesuso, Jezus (Spanish)

• *God, my salvation, the Lord is salvation* Elisha (Hebrew), Eliseo • *God of salvation* Joshua (Hebrew) • *highest truth, salvation* Parmaarth (Hindi) • *salvation of the Lord* Isaiah (Hebrew), Isak
sanctified Sancho *sanctified, sincere, truthful* (Spanish)
sandalwood Rohan (Hindi) • Chandan *the holy sandalwood tree* (Sanskrit)
sandy Sanford *by the sandy crossing, dweller at the sandy ford* (Old English), Sanferd, Sanfo, Sanfourd • *dweller at the sandy brook, of the sandy beach* Sanborn (Old English), Sanborne, Sanburn • *from the sandy hill* Sandon (Old English) • *sandy enclosure or town* Santon (Old English) • *sandy-haired* Sandy (Middle English)
sapphire *see* blue
satisfaction Josha (East Indian); Paritosh, Toshan (Hindi)
satisfied *see* content, satisfied
Saturday *see* born on Saturday
satyr *see* man
savant *see* poet, savant
savior Naagpal, Nagpal *savior of serpents* (Hindi) • *the savior* Salvador (Spanish), Salvatore, Xavier
Saxon Saxon *from a Saxon town* (Old German), Saxen
scandal *see* little scandal or snarer
sceptre *see* bearer
scholar Pandita, Pramsu, Vidvan (Hindi); Cleary (Irish-Gaelic); Clark (Old French) • *scholar, teacher; shield or to hide* Schuyler (Dutch)
schoolmaster Skyler (Dutch); Skylar, Skylor (English)
scientific Shea *courteous, ingenious, majestic, scientific one* (Irish-Gaelic) • *ingenious, scientific* Haley (Irish-Gaelic)
Scotchman's Scoville *from the Scotchman's estate* (Old French)
Scotland Scott *from Scotland* (Old English)
scribe Escriba (Spanish)
sculptor Kritiman
sea Kai (Hawaiian); Samudra (Hindi); Deniz (Turkish) • *a man of the sea, sailor* Ithaman (Latin) •

beautiful sea Mervin (Scotch-Gaelic), Merwin, Merwyn • *friend of the sea* Merwyn (Celtic), Mervin, Merwin • *from a brook by the sea* Seabrooke (Old English) • *from Doria, from the sea* Dorian (Greek) • *from the place by the sea* Merton (Anglo-Saxon) • *from the sea* Morven (Celtic), Morvin; Bainbridge (Irish-Gaelic); Delmar (Latin); Delmer (Old French); Dylan (Old Welsh) • *from the town by the sea* Seaton (Old English), Seton • *guardian from the sea* Meredith (Old Welsh) • *he loves the sea, shipmaker* Omar (Arabic), Omarr, Omer, Omor • *lord of the sea* Barun, Paranjay (Hindi) • *mariner, sea warrior* Murray (Scotch-Gaelic) • *of the field near the sea* Seadon (Old English), Seaden • *of the sea, lover of water* Pontius (Latin), Pontias, Pontus • *of the well by the sea* Sidwell (Anglo-Saxon), Sidwel, Sidwohl • *power of the sea* Zale (Greek • *prosperous from the sea* Murdock (Scotch-Gaelic) • *sea contest* Havelock (Old Norse) • *sea dweller* Morgan (Welsh) • *sea friend* Erwin, Irving (Old English), Irvin, Irvine, Irwin; Marvin (Old Welsh) • *sea glorious* Seabert (Old English), Sebert • *sea guardian* Seward (Old English) • *sea, ocean* Sagar (Hindi) • *sea serpent* Timin (Arabic) • *sea powerful* Sewell (Old English), Sewald, Sewall • *sea spear, sea warrior* Seger (Old English), Seager, Segar • *sea tide* Hurley (Irish-Gaelic) • *sea warrior* Murphy (Irish-Gaelic) • *victorious on the sea* Sewell (Old German), Sewole, Sewoll • *white sea* Morgan (Old Welsh), Morgen
seafarer Colbert *brilliant seafarer* (Old English), Colvert, Culbert • *good seafarer* Godrich (Old German), Goodrich
seal *see* little seal
seaman Bahari (African); Zeeman (Dutch)
season Basant *season of spring* (Hindi) • Tiet (Vietnamese)
seasons *see* king of seasons
secluded Yale *from a secluded place* (English)
second Tanjiro *precious second son*

(Japanese) • *second of twins* Odongo (African) • *the second male* Jiro (Japanese)
second-born Kenji *bright; second-born son* (Japanese) • *second-born boy* Lado (Sudan) • *second-born son* Manu (Ghanaian); Eiji, Zinan (Japanese); Pili (Swahili) • *the second male* Jiro (Japanese)
secret Razi *my secret* (Aramaic); Raziel (Israeli)
secretary *see* king's secretary
secretive Hisoka (Japanese)
secure *see* peaceful
security An (Vietnamese) • *pledge, security* Homer (Greek)
see Vilok *to see* (Hindi)
seed *see* mustard seed
seeker Talib (Arabic) • *seeker of god* Sutapa (Hindi)
seething *see* dweller by a hollow or by a seething pool
self Atman *the self* (Hindi)
self-denying Zahid (Arabic)
self-disciplined Samin (Hindi)
self-loving Narcissus (Greek)
seller *see* rye seller
sent *see* he is sent forth
separation Nivrutti *separation from the world* (Hindi)
serene Yen *calm, serene* (Vietnamese)
serious Taarank (Hindi) • *a serious soul; stern, severe one* Tearle (Old English), Terle, Tierell
serpent Naag *a big serpent* (Hindi) • *a huge serpent* Kaaliya (Hindi) • *cosmic serpent* Shesh (Hindi) • *sea serpent* Timin (Arabic)
serpents Naagesh *god of serpents* (Hindi) • Naaghpati *kind of serpents* (Hindi) • Naagendra *king of the serpents* (Hindi) • *savior of serpents* Naagpal, Nagpal (Hindi)
servant Umi (African); Sweyn (Anglo-Saxon); Sevak (Hindi); Gill (Irish-Gaelic), Gialla; Gilley (English) • *attractive, charming servant* Mohandas (Sanskrit) • *faithful servant* Tadashi (Japanese) • *loyal servant of Jehovah* Jehosah (Hebrew) • *servant in a manor* Berry (Old English) • *servant of Christ* Gilchrist (Irish-Gaelic) • *servant of God* Abdalla (Swahili) • *servant of the red-haired youth* Gilroy

(Irish-Gaelic) • *servant of the Virgin Mary* Gilmore (Celtic) • *servant to the royal court, youthful attendant* Page (French), Pagas, Pegasus

serves Lance *he who serves* (Latin)

settle Adnan *to settle* (Arabic)

settled Garai *to be settled* (Rhodesian)

settlement Denby *a loyal Dane, from the Danish settlement* (Scandinavian), Danby • *farmer's settlement* Carleton (Old English), Carlton • *from the black or dark settlement* Colby (Old Anglo-Norse), Kolby • *from the Dane's settlement* Danby (Old Norse) • *from the white settlement* Whitby (Scandinavian) • *warrior's settlement* Cadby (Old Norse-English)

settlers Somerset *from the place of the summer settlers* (Old English)

seven *see* seven hills

seventh Bay *seventh-born child* (Vietnamese) • *seventh-born son* Ashon (African) • *seventh son* Septimus (Latin)

severe Tearle *a serious soul; stern, severe one* (Old English), Terle, Tierell • *son of the severe, violent one* Hastings (Old English)

Severn *see* of the Severn river

shady Glendon *from the shady valley* (Celtic)

shake *see* to shake the head

shallow *see* crossing

shame Inteus *he has no shame* (Native American)

shape Aakaar (Hindi) • *shape, summit* Prakhar (Hindi)

shaped Quinlan *well shaped one* (Irish-Gaelic)

sharp *see* bold, sharp one

shed *see* cattle shed on the meadow

sheep Shipton *dweller at the sheep estate* (Old English) • *dweller at the sheep meadow* Shipley (Old English) • *dweller at the wether-sheep meadow* Wetherly (Old English) • *from the sheep estate* Skipton (Old English) • *from the sheep meadow* Shepley (Anglo-Saxon), Shep, Sheply • *from the wether-sheep corner* Wetherell (Old English) • *from the wether-sheep farm* Wetherby (Old English)

shell Shankh *a shell* (Hindi)

shelter Ashray, Sharan (Hindi) • *shelter, cover* Oni (Hindi)

shepherd Berger (French); Schaffer (German) • *from a shepherd's home* Norvall (Irish-Gaelic), Norval, Norvil

sheriff *see* administrator, foreman, magistrate, overseer, sheriff

shield Squire *knight's attendant, shield bearer* (Middle English) • *little shield* Rankin (Old English); Burdett (Old French) • *scholar, teacher; shield or to hide* Schuyler (Dutch) • *shield wolf* Randolph (Old English), Randall, Randell, Randolf • *son of shield* Ransom (Old English)

shine Viraaj *to shine* (Hindi)

shining Zahir (African); Sambha, Surush (Hindi) • *bright or shining with fame* Robert (Old English), Bert, Roberto, Robertson, Robin, Rupert • *bright, shining sword* Egbert (Old English) • *bright, shining white* Galvin (Irish-Gaelic), Galvan, Galven • *bright, the shining son* Fulbert (Old German), Philbert • *shining brightly* Yu (Chinese) • *shining, glorious one* Bert (Old English) • *very shining one* Delling (Old Norse)

ship Delsey *dweller at ship island* (Old Norse) • *ship captain* Kerry (English) • *ship master* Skipper (Middle English) • *ship owner* Skipp (Old Norse) • *victory ship* Kelsey (Old English); Kelsy (English)

shipmaker *see* loves

shipman Orman (Old English)

shoe Schuman *shoe maker* (German) • *shoe repairman* Schuster (German)

shopkeeper Kramer (German), Cramer; Hackman (Old German)

shore *see* red

short Waman (Hindi); Cort (Old Norse) • *be missing, be short; the minority* Thieu (Vietnamese) • *fair or white-haired, with short hair* Sherlock (Old English), Sherlocke • *literature; short; striped tiger; to twist* Van (Vietnamese) • *little, short* Klein (German), Cline, Kline

shouldered Platon (Spanish) • *broad one, broad-shouldered* Plato (Greek)

shouts *see* shouts of joy

show *see* mind; to show

shrine *see* Cross

shut Kwan *to shut* (Chinese)

side Hong *flank, side; red, rosy* (Vietnamese) • *rice field, side* Tanabe (Japanese) • *right side* Telman (Hebrew)

sight Ikshan (Hindi)

sighted *see* blind or dim-sighted

sign Missim (Hebrew); Rupak (Hindi) • *carefully; strange; to abstain from; to fear; to sign* Ky (Vietnamese) • *sign of the dragon* Drake (Middle English)

signal Sanket (Hindi)

silent Neerav *quiet, silent* (Hindi)

silk Resham (Hindi)

silver Yin (Chinese); Rajat (Hindi) • *silver flame* Shiamak, Siamak (Hindi)

Simon Simpson *son of Simon* (Old English), Simson

Simon's *see* dweller at Simon's estate

simple Rujul *simple, honest* (Hindi) • *simple, straightforward* Pranjal, Saral (Hindi)

sincere Arden *ardent, fiery; eager, fervent, sincere* (Latin), Ardin • *faithful, sincere, true* Fidel (Latin), Fidele, Fidelio, Fidelis • *sanctified, sincere, truthful* Sancho (Spanish) • *sincere and honest* Makoto (Japanese)

sing Jaron, Ranon *to sing* (Hebrew); Ranen (Israeli)

singer Baird *ballad singer, minstrel* (Irish-Gaelic), Bard • *nice singer* Birju (Hindi) • *poet and singer* Bard (Irish-Gaelic), Baird, Barde

singing Gayan *singing, the sky* (Hindi)

sinless Anagh (Hindi)

sins *see* the remover of sins

sixth Essien *sixth-born son* (African) • *sixth son* Sextus (Latin)

skilled Kritanu (Hindi) • *enterprising, skilled* Fachan (Latin), Fachanan • *expert, skilled* Praveen, Pravin (Hindi) • *learned or skillful leader* MacKinley (Irish-Gaelic)

skillful Vidur (Hindi) • *skillful, capable* Pravin (Hindi)

sky Lani (Hawaiian); Akash, Vyom (Hindi); Yakecan (Native American) • *blue sky* Neelambar (Hindi) • *rocky fortress or sky fortress* Rochester (Old English) • *singing, the sky* Gayan (Hindi) • *sky clad* Digvastra (Hindi) • *sky, heaven* Gagan (Hindi) • *sky on song* Yakecen (North American Indian)

slender Keelan *little slender one* (Irish-Gaelic), Kealan, Kelan • *slender, thin* Caley (Irish), Cale, Calen, Calin

slim Yasti (Hindi)

slope Saka (Japanese) • *dweller at the bank or slope* Bink (North English) • *dweller at the cave slope* Covell (Old English) • *dweller on the castle hill slope* Burbank (Old English) • *from the fern slope* Farnell (Old English), Farnall, Fernald • *from the hill slope estate* Halton (Old English) • *from the slope or corner of land* Yale (Old English)

slopes *see* dweller at the slopes

slumber Lutherum (Gypsy)

small Tawno (Gypsy); Kiss (Hungarian); Vaughn (Old Welsh); Pavel (Slavic), Paul • *a small bluff* Dohosan (Native American) • *a small farm* Toft (Old English) • *from the field by the small river* Mansfield (Old English) • *small, belligerent one* Callahan (Irish-Gaelic), Callaghan • *small brown-haired one* Donnan (Irish-Gaelic) • *small child* Chiumbo (Kenyan) • *small deer field* Ogano (Japanese) • *small field* Ohara (Japanese) • *small plant* Taru (Hindi) • *small river* Jaafar (African) • *small stone, the little one* Elstan (Anglo-Saxon), Elston • *small thing* Cheche (African) • *very small one* Kea (Kongo/African); Marmion (Old French)

smart Akira *intelligent; smart* (Japanese) • *little smart one* Hewitt (English)

smiling Baasima (Hindi) • *ever smiling* Sasmit (Hindi)

smites *see* down

smith Haddad (Arabic); Kovar (Czech)

smoke Duman (Turkish)

smooth Riddock *from the smooth field* (Irish-Gaelic) • *smooth, free, and unhindered* Chang (Chinese) • *smooth, polished one* Terence (Latin), Terencio

smoothly Tuan *goes smoothly* (Vietnamese)

snail Baul (Gypsy)

snake Phani (Hindi)

snare *see* net

snarer *see* little scandal or snarer
snow Tuhin (Hindi) • *lord of the snow* Himesh (Hindi) • *snow boy* Yukio (Japanese), Yuki, Yukiko • *snow mountain* Himaadri (Hindi) • *white as snow* Tuhinsurra (Hindi)
snowy *see* hill
soaring Wuyi *turkey vulture soaring* (Miwok)
soft-spoken Subhash (Hindi)
softness Mardav (Hindi)
soil Tilford *a tiller of fertile soil* (Old English), Tillford, Tillfourd • *tiller of the soil* Bond (Old English), Bonde, Bondon, Bonds
sojourner Farmann *a sojourner* (Anglo-Saxon), Farman
soldier Gerlac (Dutch); Knight (Middle English) • *a friend of a soldier* Chatwin (Anglo-Saxon) • *army man; soldier* Armino (Italian) • *mighty soldier* Balin (Hindi), Bali, Valin • *strong soldier, warrior* Bornani (African) • *soldier, warrior* Miles (Latin), Myles • *the brave soldier* Kenway, Sherard (Anglo-Saxon), Kenay, Kenweigh • *valiant soldier* Carney (Celtic), Carnay; Roque (Latin), Rochus, Rock, Rocky
soldier's Etam *a soldier's son, of the warrior's house* (Latin) • *soldier's land* Chatham (Old English)
solid *see* firm
solitary Ekaant (Hindi)
somebody Awan (Native American)
son Yaro (African); Chal (Gypsy); Ben (Hebrew), Benn; Nandan, Tanay, Vatsa (Hindi); Fitz (Old French) • *a bold son* Grimbald (French), Grimbal • *a farmer, son of the furrows* Bartholomew (Hebrew), Bartel, Barthel, Bartholomaus; Bartkus (Lithuanian) • *a judge's son* Grayson (Old English), Gray, Grey, Greyson • *angry son* Gaal (Hebrew) • *a soldier's son, of the warrior's house* Etam (Latin) • *a son* Kumar (Sanskrit) • *a son born at daylight* Daegal (Scandinavian), Dagall, Dygal, Dygall • *a son of Gerald* Fitzgerald (Old German), Fitz, Fitzger • *a son of Patrick* Fitzpatrick (Old German), Fitz, Patrick • *a son's army* Inger (Old Norse), Ingar, Ingvar • *behold a son* Reuben (Hebrew),

Ruben • *brave one's son* Harding (Old English) • *bright; second-born son* Kenji (Japanese) • *bright, the shining son* Fulbert (Old German), Philbert • *brilliant son* Sanson (Hebrew), Sansen • *champion's son* Nelson (English), Nealson, Nilson • *coatmaker, son of a good man* Manning (Old German) • *Dick's son, of Dick's land* Dickson (Old English), Dixon • *dweller at the fifth son's estate* Quincy (Old French) • *excellent son* Benzi (Hebrew) • *fairest son* Japheth (Hebrew), Japeth • *famous son* Ingemar (Old Norse) • *first-born son* Chaska (Sioux) • *first son of the wild boar* Haro (Japanese), Haroko, Haroku • *fourth-born, fourth son* Annan (African); Quartus (Latin) • *fourth-born son* Shiro (Japanese) • *gracious son* Ethbin (Latin), Ethban, Ethben • *Harry's son* Parry (Welsh) • *honored son, loved* Erastus (Greek), Erasatus, Erastes, Estus • *little son* Sonny (Middle English) • *lively son* Jareb (Hebrew) • *lonesome, only son* Ehud (Hebrew), Ehudd • *loyal son, reliable* Barabbas (Hebrew), Barabas • *ninth-born son* Akron (African), Akan • *nobleman's son* Erling (Old English) • *noble one's son* Alison (Old English) • *noble son of the Lord* Nodab (Hebrew), Odab • *precious second son* Tanjiro (Japanese) • *second-born boy* Lado (Sudan) • *second-born son* Manu (Ghanaian); Eiji, Zinan (Japanese); Pili (Swahili) • *seventh-born son* Ashon (African) • *seventh son* Septimus (Latin) • *sixth-born son* Essien (African) • *sixth son* Sextus (Latin) • *son of* Mac (Celtic) • *son of* Abdul (Arabic), Abdel • *son of Abbott* Abbottson (Old German), Abbotsen, Abbotson • *son of a busy father* Emlyn (Old German), Emelin, Emlen • *son of a chief* Yuma (Native American) • *son of Adam* Addis, Addison (Old English), Adis; Adamson (Old German), Adams, Adamsen, Adamsun; MacAdam (Scotch-Gaelic) • *son of a good man* Odoric (Latin), Odericus, Odrick • *son of Alan* Alanson (Old German), Alansen, Alenson, Allanson • *son of Alexander* Callister (Irish-

Gaelic); Sanders (Middle English), Sanderson, Saunders, Saunderson • *son of a nation* Baram (Israeli) • *son of Benjamin* Benson (Hebrew-English) • *son of Carr* Carson (Welsh) • *son of consolation or exhortation* Barnabas (Greek), Barnaby, Barney; Bane (Hawaiian) • *son of Dennis* Tennyson (Middle English); Dennison (Old English) • *son of Edward* Edison (Old English), Edson • *son of Ellis* Ellison (Old English) • *son of Emory* Emerson (Old English), Emersen • *son of famous in war* Loring (Old German) • *son of fire, son of light* Orion (Greek) • *son of Gar* Garson (Old English), Gershon • *son of Garret* Garrison (Old English) • *son of Gary, a spearman* Garron (Old English) • *son of Gilbert* Gibson (Old English) • *son of Hans* Hansen (Scandinavian), Hansan, Hanson • *son of Harris* Harrison (Old English), Harry • *son of Harry* Harris (Old English); Barris (Old Welsh) • *son of Henry* Harris (Old English) • *son of Henry, royal ruler* Kendrick (Irish-Gaelic) • *son of Jack* Jackson (Old English) • *son of Jeffrey* Jefferson (Old English) • *son of Lars* Larson (Scandinavian) • *son of Lawrence* Lawson (Old English) • *son of Maurice* Morrison (Old English) • *son of mighty power* Ronson (Old English) • *son of mountain* Girilal (Hindi) • *son of my sorrow* Benoni (Hebrew) • *son of Nicholas* Nixon (Old English) • *son of Owen* Bowen (Celtic) • *son of Peter* Pierson (Greek), Pearson, Peirsen, Pierce • *son of Richard* Ryker (Middle English); Dixon (Old English) • *son of shield* Ransom (Old English) • *son of Simon* Simpson (Old English), Simson • *son of spear mighty* Fitzgerald (Old English) • *son of stone* Stinson (Old English) • *son of Terrence* Terris (Anglo-Saxon), Territus • *son of the ardent one* Price (Old Welsh) • *son of the beloved one* Davis (Old English) • *son of the brown one* Bronson (Old English) • *son of the chamberlain or overseer* Chalmers (Old Scotch) • *son of the dark complexioned one* Morse (Old English) • *son of the dark man*

Collis (Old English) • *son of the dark one* Kerry (Irish-Gaelic) • *son of the dark stranger* MacDougal (Scotch-Gaelic) • *son of the dweller at a marsh* Carson (Middle English) • *son of the fair head* Gaynor (Irish-Gaelic), Gainer, Gainor, Gayner • *son of the fiery one* Key, Magee (Irish-Gaelic) • *son of the golden one* Golding (Old English) • *son of the heir* MacNair (Irish-Gaelic) • *son of the hero* Manning (Old English) • *son of the hooded one* Hudson (Old English) • *son of the intelligent one* Fitzhugh (Old English) • *son of the judge* Deems (Old English) • *son of the king* Royce (French), Roi, Roice, Roy • *son of the little counsel wolf* Rawlins (Old Anglo-French); Rawson (Old English) • *son of the mariner* MacMurray (Irish-Gaelic) • *son of the moon* Mrigaj (Hindi) • *son of the prelate* Taggart (Irish-Gaelic) • *son of the red-haired man* Flynn (Irish-Gaelic), Flinn • *son of the red warrior* Clancy (Irish-Gaelic); Clancey (English) • *son of the right hand* Benjamin (Hebrew), Beathan • *son of the severe, violent one* Hastings (Old English) • *son of the Teuton or German* Tyson (Old German) • *son of the wave* Dylan (Welsh) • *son of the wise man* Druce (Old Anglo-Welsh) • *son of the wolf* Weylin (Celtic) • *son of Vincent* Vinson (Old English) • *son of Walter* Quade (Irish-Gaelic); Quaid (English); Watkins, Watson (Old English) • *son of war mighty* Madison (Old English) • *son of William* Willis (Old English); Wilson (Old German) • *son of world mighty* MacDonald (Scotch-Gaelic) • *son of yew bow* Ives (Old English), Yves • *son's man or splendid son* Sampson (Hebrew), Samson, Sanson, Sansone • *spearman's son* Orson (Old English) • *ten thousand-fold strong third son* Manzo (Japanese) • *the awe-inspiring one's son* Anson (Old English) • *the benefactor's son* Maddox (Old Anglo-Welsh) • *the eternal king's son* Arkin (Norwegian) • *the refined son* Odo (Latin), Odilo, Odlo • *the son of Evan* Bevan (Celtic), Bevin • *the son of Jehovah* Jehiel (Hebrew), Jehial • *the son of John* Johnston (Irish-Gaelic), John-sten; Jones (Welsh) • *the son of Judd* Judson (Old German), Judsen • *the son of little Hugh* Hutchinson (Middle English), Hutchens, Hutchins, Hutchison • *the son of Vandyke; the son of Van Ness* Vance (Dutch), Van • *third-born son* Taizo (Japanese) • *third son* Teritus (Latin) • *thirteenth-born son* Odissan (African) • *thoughtful son* Tullus (Latin), Tullius, Tullusus, Tully • *twelfth-born son* Adeben (Akan)

song Gillie *a song* (Gypsy); Zamir (Hebrew); Geet (Hindi); Carvel (Manx); Yakecan (Native American) • Cadao *folk song or ballad* (Vietnamese) • *my song* Leron (Hebrew), Lerone, Liron, Lirone • *sky on song* Yakecen (North American Indian) • *song is mine* Ronli (Hebrew) • *song of God* Ronel (Hebrew)

sophisticated Desmond *sophisticated, worldly* (French)

sorrow Brone (Irish-Gaelic) • *son of my sorrow* Benoni (Hebrew) • *without sorrow* Ashok (Hindi)

sorrowful *see* labor

soul Atma (Hindi) • *a generous soul* Edbert (Anglo-Saxon) • *a radiant soul* Philbert (Old German), Bert, Filbert • *a serious soul; stern, severe one* Tearle (Old English), Terle, Tierell • *kind soul* Gentilis (Latin) • *lord of the soul* Chitesh (Hindi), Chittesh • *soul, life force* Janu (Hindi) • *spirit or soul* Hoyt (Old Norse) • *the cautious soul* Waring (Anglo-Saxon), Warrin, Warring • *the soul, the spirit* Dusan (Czech) • *the universal soul* Hansin (Hindi) • *universal soul* Vishvatma (Hindi)

sound Ninad (Hindi) • *lord of sound* Hakesh (Hindi) • *pleasant sound* Suran (Hindi) • *without sound* Nirav (Hindi)

south Nam *child from the south* (Vietnamese) • *from the south cliff* Sutcliff (Old English) • *from the south estate* Sutton (Old English) • *from the south field* Suffield (Old English) • *from the south meadow* Sully (Old English) • *from the south spring* Southwell (Old English) • *man from south Munster* Desmond (Irish-Gaelic)

southern *see* land

southerner Dacey (Irish-Gaelic), Dacy

sovereign Tynan (Irish-Gaelic)

sovereignty Rajata (Hindi)

space Antariksh (Hindi) • *limitless space* Avkash (Hindi)

sparrow *see* hawk

speak Wemilo *all speak to him* (Native American) • Dovev *to whisper or speak quietly* (Hebrew), Dov

speaker Vadin (Hindi) • *half-speaker, mumbler* Lawler (Irish-Gaelic) • *the indirect speaker* Balbo (Latin), Bailby

speaks *see* he speaks often

spear Kerr (Irish-Gaelic) • *bold spear* Gerbold (Old German) • *burning spear* Jomo (East African) • *divine spear, divine spearman* Oscar (Old Norse) • *firm spear, spear brave* Garrett (Old English), Garrard, Garret, Garritt • *little spear* Bercan, Corrigan (Irish-Gaelic), Bearchan, Korigan, Korrigan • *protector or spear friend* Aswin (Old English) • *sea spear, sea warrior* Seger (Old English), Seager, Segar • *son of spear mighty* Fitzgerald (Old English) • *spear brave, spear strong* Gerard (Old English), Gerardo, Geraud, Gerrard, Jerard • *spear compulsion* Garnett (Old English), Garnet • *spear friend* Garvin, Orvin (Old English), Garwin • *spear keen* Jarvis (Old German), Jervis • *spear mighty* Orval (Old French); Gerald (Old German), Geraldo, Geraud, Gerault, Gerold, Giraldo, Giraud; Gerhard (Scandinavian) • *spear protector* Garmond, Ormond (Old English), Garmund • *spear ruler* Garrick (Old English) • *spear, spearman* Gary (Old English), Garey, Gari, Garry • *spear warrior* Garroway (Old English) • *the spear fighter* Ordway (Anglo-Saxon) • *wolf spear* Ulger (Old English)

spearlike *see* pointed

spearman Garman, Orman (Old English) • *divine spear, divine spearman* Oscar (Old Norse) • *famous spearman* Roger (Old German), Rodger, Rogerio, Rutger • *ford of the national spearman* Tuxford (Old Norse-English) • *marshy estate, spearman's estate* Carvell (Old French), Carvel •

noble spearman Alger (Old German), Algar • *prosperous spearman* Edgar (Old English), Edgard, Edgardo; Gerik (Polish) • *son of Gary, a spearman* Garron (Old English) • *spear, spearman* Gary (Old English), Garey, Gari, Garry

spearman's *see* son

special Vishesh (Hindi)

speech Rasna, Rutva (Hindi)

spellbound Mohit (Hindi)

spirit Prana (Hindi); Kamali (Mashona) • *battle spirit* Cadell (Old Welsh) • *blond ruler, elf ruler, spirit ruler* Aubrey (Old French) • *brilliant mind or spirit* Hubert (Old German), Bert, Huberto, Hugh; Berdy (Russian) • *brought by a spirit* Aniweta (Nigerian) • *intelligence, spirit* Hugh (Old English), Hugo • *most popular, national or people's spirit* Volney (Old German) • *resolute spirit or mind* Wilmot (Old German) • *spirit or soul* Hoyt (Old Norse) • *the soul, the spirit* Dusan (Czech) • *the spirit of Nen* Nen (Egyptian) • *Thor or thunder spirit* Tormey (Irish-Gaelic)

spirited Keegan *highly spirited* (Celtic), Kegan, MacEgan • Brady *spirited one* (Irish-Gaelic)

spiritual Devrat, Ruhan (Hindi) • *deeply spiritual* Shen (Chinese)

splendid Hod (Hebrew) • *son's man or splendid son* Sampson (Hebrew), Samson, Sanson, Sansone

splendor Mayukh, Ramra (Hindi) • *Jehovah is my splendor* Hodiah (Hebrew), Hodia, Hodiya

split *see* meadow

spokesman Nantan (Native American)

sport Ullock *wolf sport* (Old English)

spotted *see* spotted deer

spring Lennor (Gypsy); Aviv (Hebrew); Vasant (Hindi) • *cold spring* Caldwell (Old English) • *deer's spring* Hartwell (English) • *dweller at the crooked or winding spring* Cromwell (Old English) • *dweller at the crucifix spring* Rodwell (Old English) • *dweller at the king's spring* Kingswell (Old English) • *dweller at the spring* Atwell (Old English) • *dweller at the spring brook* Welborne (Old English)

• *dweller at the spring estate or town* Welton (Old English) • *dweller at the spring farm* Atherton (Old English) • *dweller at the watercress spring* Carswell (Old English) • *dweller by a holy spring* Halliwell (Old English) • *dweller by the spring* Wells (Old English) • *from the bramblebush spring, of Bram's well* Bramwell (Old English), Bram • *from the broad spring* Bradwell (Old English), Brad • *from the farm by the spring* Wilton (English); Kilby (Old German); Welby (Scandinavian) • *from the new spring* Newlin (Celtic) • *from the north spring* Norwell (Old English) • *from the old spring* Elwell (Old English) • *from the quiet spring* Stilwell (Anglo-Saxon) • *from the red spring* Rothwell (Old Norse) • *from the rocky spring* Rockwell (Old English) • *from the roe deer spring* Rowell (Old English) • *from the south spring* Southwell (Old English) • *from the spring* Kell (Old Norse) • *from the spring by the crossing, from the spring ford* Welford Old English) • *from the spring farm* Chilton, Wilton (Old English) • *from the spring hill* Weldon (Old English) • *from the tree stump spring* Stockwell (Old English) • *glory of spring* Jaroslav (Slavic) • *he lives near the spring* Maxwell (Anglo-Saxon) • *season of spring* Basant (Hindi)

springlike Verne, Vernon *springlike, youthful* (Latin)

stable Moulton *of the mule stable* (Old English), Molton, Mouldon, Muldon • *prosperous, stable* Stacey (Middle Latin) • *stable comrade* Stacy (Latin), Stacey • *stable, tranquil* Eustace (Latin), Eustasius, Eustazio

staff Virgil *rod or staff bearer* (Latin), Virge, Virgilio • *staff of the Goths* Gustavo (Italian); Gustave (Swedish), Gustaf, Gustaff, Gustav

stalk Senwe *a dry stalk of grain* (African) • *stalk or reed* Kaniel (Hebrew)

stallion Stallone *a stallion* (Middle English)

stammers *see* lisps

stand Stane *glorious position, stand of glory* (Serbian); Stanislaus (Slavic),

Stanislas, Stanislav • *I stand up* Nibaw (Native American)

Stanfield *see* field

star Hoku (Hawaiian); Nakshatra, Tarachand (Hindi); Hoshi (Japanese); Hute (Native American); Zorya (Ukranian) • *a star* Bahula (Hindi) • *bright star* Gelasius (Latin), Gelasias • *greatest star* Urian (Greek), Urion • *holy star* Sutara (Hindi) • *king of stars* Naksatraraja (Hindi) • *star dancer* Namid (Native American)

stars Taresh *god of the stars* (Hindi) • *lord of the stars* Udupati, Uduraj (Hindi)

start Samay (Hindi)

stately Timur *tall or stately* (Hebrew)

steadfast Gerius (Latin) • *holds fast, steadfast* Hector (Greek)

steady Heman (Hebrew) • *steady and strong* Maynard (Old German)

steal Nicabar *to steal* (Gypsy)

steel Chisulo (African)

steep Cliff *from the steep cliff or rock* (Old English) • *from the steep hill* Brenton (Old English), Brent

stern Neron (Bulgarian); Nerone (Italian); Nero (Latin); Abasi (Swahili) • *aristocrat; from a high place; stern* Gibrian (Latin) • *a serious soul; stern, severe one* Tearle (Old English), Terle, Tierell • *strict or stern* Soren (Latin), Soran, Sorin, Sorran, Sorren, Sorrin

steward Reeve, Stewart *bailiff or steward* (Old English), Reave, Steward, Stuart; Bailey (Old French), Bailie, Baily, Bayley • *farmer, steward* Meyer (German) • *horse keeper, steward* Marshall (Middle English)

stiles *see* dweller by the stiles

still Mortimer *from the still water* (Old French) • *my father is still alive* Nnamdi (Nigerian)

stock Hardy *from a hardy stock* (Old German), Harday • *from sturdy stock* Hale (Old English), Hal

stone Stein (German) • *battle stone* Wystand (Anglo-Saxon) • *brown fortress, brown stone* Dunstan (Old English) • *corner stone* Walston (Anglo-Saxon) • *from a stone cottage* Alcott (Celtic), Alcot, Allcot • *from the stone fortress* Stanbury (Old English) •

God, my rock or stone Zuriel (Hebrew) • *jasper stone* Jasper (Old French) • *noble one's estate or town, noble stone* Elston (Old English) • *precious stone* Ratan (Hindi) • *rock or stone* Takis (Greek); Peter (Latin), Pedro, Pero, Piero, Pierre, Pieter, Pietro; Pierce (Old Anglo-French) • *small stone, the little one* Elstan (Anglo-Saxon), Elston • *son of stone* Stinson (Old English) • *stone bridges* Pierrepont (French), Pierpont • *stone or rock of the help* Ebenezer (Hebrew), Eben • *stone worker* Mason (Old French) • *sword wielder's stone* Axton (Old English) • *Thor's stone or jewel* Thurstan (Old English), Thurston

stones *see* river

stony Stanway *from near the stony road* (Old English) • *from the stony estate* Stanton (Old English), Staunton • *from the stony ford* Stamford (Old English) • *from the stony vale* Stanhope (Old English) • *from the stony woods* Stanwood (Old English)

stork Ozuru *large stork* (Japanese)

storm Asifa (Arabic); Tufan (Hindi)

storyteller *see* historian, storyteller

stout *see* courageous, stout hearted

straight Bankim *not straight* (Hindi) • *straight, honest* Pragun (Hindi)

straightforward *see* simple, straightforward

strange Dorran (Celtic), Doran, Dorein, Doren, Dorin, Dorren, Dorrin • *carefully; strange; to abstain from; to fear; to sign* Ky (Vietnamese)

stranger Newcomb (Anglo-Saxon); Doran (Celtic) • *beloved of God, beloved stranger* Elidad (Hebrew) • *exile or stranger* Gershom (Hebrew), Gersham • *fighter, stranger* Boris (Slavic) • *foreigner, stranger* Frayne (Middle English), Fraine, Freyne • *guest or stranger* Xenos (Greek) • *newcomer, the dark stranger* Doyle (Celtic) • *son of the dark stranger* MacDougal (Scotch-Gaelic) • *the black stranger* Dougal (Irish-Gaelic) • *traveler, stranger, or pilgrim* Perry (Latin)

stream Rithik (Hindi); Flint (Old English) • *a little stream* Jafar (Arabic) • *from the mill stream* Melbourne (Old English), Melburn, Milburn • *from* *the red stream* Radborne (Old English) • *from the stream* Annan (Celtic); Struthers (Irish-Gaelic) • *he dwells by the stream* Brooks (Old English) • *land between the streams* Cartland (English-Scotch) • *mountain stream* Bergren (Scandinavian), Berg • *of the stream by the mill* Milburn (Old English), Milburt, Millburn • *one who lives near a shallow stream crossing* Brodny (Slavic) • *rapid stream, torrent; swift* Trent (Latin)

street Stratford *river ford on the street* (Old English)

strength Zeeshan (Hindi); Drew (Old German) • *a man of strength* Ozen (Hebrew), Ozan • *firmness, strength* Ethan (Hebrew) • *honor, strength, virtue* Brian (Celtic), Briant, Brien, Bryan, Bryant, Bryon • *in the Lord is strength* Boaz (Hebrew), Boas, Boase • *lord of strength* Urjani (Hindi) • *man with strength of ten thousand* Michio (Japanese) • *my father is my rock; my father is my strength* Avniel (Hebrew) • *one choice, unique strength* Angus (Scotch-Gaelic) • *powerful, strength* Haile (Ethiopian) • *rushing stream* Arnon (Hebrew) • *strength of God* Ezekiel (Hebrew), Ezechiel, Ezechiele, Ezequiel, Zeke • *super iron, super strength* Trahern (Old Welsh) • *with strength* Sabal (Hindi)

strict Soren *strict or stern* (Latin), Soran, Sorin, Sorran, Sorren, Sorrin

striped *see* literature; short; striped tiger; to twist

strong Chacha, Ekon (African); Neron (Bulgarian); Bryant (Celtic); Gibor (Hebrew); Balaraj, Balbir, Baldev, Sahat, Subali, Tanvir, Vibhut (Hindi); Nerone (Italian); Nero, Val (Latin); Honovi, Songan (Native American) • *austere, strong man* Hartman (Old German) • *bold, strong* Kennard, Trumble (Old English); Ballard (Old German) • *bow strong* Bogart (Old German) • *brave or strong as a boar* Everard (Old English), Eberhard, Evered, Everett, Everhart • *famous, strong* Waldemar (Old English) • *fierce, strong* Praval (Hindi) • Lon, Lunn (Irish-Gaelic) •

firm, strong one Firmin (Old French) • *flattering, strong and winning* Millard (Old French) • *hard, strong minded* Hurd (Anglo-Saxon) • *healthy, powerful, strong* Valerian (Late Latin) • *healthy, strong, valorous* Valentine (Latin), Valentino • *industrious, strong* Emmett (Old German), Emmet, Emmott • *manly, strong* Keandre (American); Kalman (German); Andrew (Greek-Hebrew), Anders, Andre, Andrej, Andres; Kale (Hawaiian); Charles (Old German), Carl, Carlo, Carlos, Chaz, Karl; Jedrek (Polish); Kalle (Scandinavian); Kendrew (Scottish) • *spear brave, spear strong* Gerard (Old English), Gerardo, Geraud, Gerrard, Jerard • *steady and strong* Maynard (Old German) • *strong as a castle* Burchard (Old English), Burgard, Burgaud, Burkhart • *strong as an ox* Eleph (Hebrew) • *strong as a sword* Rapier (Middle French) • *strong as bamboo* Takeo (Japanese) • *strong character* Taksheel (Hindi) • *strong leader* Farley (Irish-Gaelic) • *strong man, very choice one* Fergus (Irish-Gaelic) • *strong one* Quilin (Irish-Gaelic), Quinley; Quinn (English) • *strong opponent* Faustus (Latin), Faust • *strong or powerful* Hamza (Arabic) • *strong soldier, warrior* Bornani (African) • Hhhhhjjhjhkhjk *swift and strong* Boaz (Hebrew) • *ten thousand-fold strong third son* Manzo (Japanese) • *the strong sailor* Ithnan (Hebrew) • *very strong, mighty* Prabal (Hindi) • *with a strong arm* Armstrong (Old English)

strong-hearted Dustin *strong-hearted leader* (Old German), Durst, Durstin, Durston

strong-willed Connor (Irish-Gaelic), Conner, Connors, Conor

stronghold Varick (Old English), Vareck • *castle, fortress, stronghold* Burke (Old German) • *dweller by the enclosure or stronghold* Locke (Old English) • *friend of St. Michael, from Michael's stronghold* Carmichael (Scotch-Gaelic) • *from the little stronghold* Burkett (Old French) • *from the white stronghold* Whitlock (Old English)

strongly Connor *strongly wise* (Irish-Gaelic), Conner, Connors, Conor
struggle Ajani *he who wins the struggle* (African)
studious Hoc *studious one* (Vietnamese)
stump Rutland *from the root or stump land* (Old Norse) • *from the root or stump meadow* Rutley (Old English) • *from the tree stump estate or town* Stockton (Old English) • *from the tree stump meadow* Stockley (Old English) • *from the tree stump spring* Stockwell (Old English)
sturdy *see* stock
sturgeon Nahma *the sturgeon* (Native American)
sublime Yucel (Turkish)
succeed Safal (Hindi)
success Kamran (Hindi) • *highest success* Paramjeet (Hindi) • *prosperity, success* Speed (Old English)
sugar Istu *sugarpine sugar* (Miwok)
sugarcane Ikshu (Hindi)
sugarpine *see* sugar
suitor Alvis *a suitor* (Scandinavian), Elvis
summer Lennor (Gypsy) • *a summer sailor* Sorley (Irish-Gaelic); Somhairle (Irish) • *from the place of the summer settlers* Somerset (Old English) • *from the summer estate* Somerton (Old English); Somerville (Old French-German)
summit Kiri *mountain summit* (Cambodian) • *mountain summit; crest* Dinh (Vietnamese) • *shape, summit* Prakhar (Hindi)
summoner *see* church legal officer, summoner
sun Arun (Cambodian); Kem (Gypsy); Patag, Pratyush, Sulek, Tamila, Viraj (Hindi); Sol (Latin) • *boat, sun* Tarani (Hindi) • *condor of the sun* Antiman (Native American) • *eagle of the sun* Antinanco (Native American) • *from the wide valley, of the village of the sun* Braden, Siddell (Old English), Brad • *god of the midday sun* Orunjan (African) • *keeper of the hours, light of the sun* Horace (Latin), Horatio • *morning sun* Addae (Ghanaian) • *related to the sun* Amon (Hebrew) • *sun born* Ramses

(African) • *sun, dawn* Sahar (Hindi) • *sun god* Dinesh (Sanskrit) • *sun rays* Rashmi (Hindi) • *the sun* Mihir, Rave, Ravi, Suvan, Virochan (Hindi), Raviv; Sol (Latin); Etu (Native American); Cyrus (Old Persian), Ciro, Cy
Sunday Dominic *belonging to the Lord; born on Sunday, the Lord's day* (Latin), Domenico, Domingo, Dominick, Dominico, Dominique, Nick • *born on Sunday* Danladi, Kwasi, Kwesi, Quashee (African); Danladi (Hausa) • *devoted to Sunday worship* Maloney (Irish-Gaelic)
sunlight *see* radiant
sunny Arpiar (Armenian) • *sunny day* Helaku (Native American)
sunrise Uday (Hindi)
super *see* iron
superior Ishat, Nirek, Rishab, Shreyas (Hindi)
supplant Kivi (Hebrew), Akiba, Akiva, Kiva
supplanter Jacob *the supplanter* (Hebrew), Jake, Jayme; Ikov (Bulgarian); Hakub, Kokubas (Czech); Shamus (English), Shaymus; Jacques (French); Jakob (German); Seamus (Irish), Seumas; Giacomo (Italian), Giamo; Jeks (Latvian); James (Old Spanish); Diego, Jaime (Spanish)
supreme Virat *supreme being* (Hindi) • *supreme essence* Pillan (Native American); Pilan (English) • *the supreme dancer* Natraj (Hindi)
surprise Atuanya (African); Ashcharya, Vismay (Hindi) • *new, surprise* Nawal (Hindi)
survives Anstice *one who survives* (Greek), Anstus
survivors Sarid *one of the survivors* (Hebrew), Sarad
swallow Yen *a swallow* (Vietnamese)
swamp *see* red
swarthy Colley (Old English), Collis • *swarthy chief* Duncan (Celtic)
sweet Hien *good-natured and sweet* (Vietnamese) • *sweet dew* Camlo (Vietnamese)
sweetheart *see* darling, sweetheart
swift Achilles (Greek); Skeet (Middle English), Skeat, Skeeter; Reece (Old German); Javas (Sanskrit) • *counsel*

wolf, swift wolf Radolf, Ralph (Old English), Raoul, Raul, Rolph • *rapid stream, torrent; swift* Trent (Latin) • *swift and strong* Boaz (Hebrew) • *swift runner* Sherwin (Middle English)

sword Husam (Arabic); Kaditula (Hindi) • *bright, shining sword* Egbert (Old English) • *dweller at the sword grass place* Sedgwick (Old English) • *firebrand, sword* Brander (Old Norse)

• *man of the sword* Saber (Old German), Sabir • *strong as a sword* Rapier (Middle French) • *sword friend* Melvin (Old English) • *sword of religion* Seif (Arabic) • *sword wielder's stone* Axton (Old English) • *war sword* Hildebrand (Old German)

symbol Pratik (Hindi) • *sacred symbol* Setu (Hindi)

Syrian *see* fertility

— **T** —

tail Bodua *an animal's tail* (Akan)

tailor Schneider *a tailor* (German); Taylor (Middle English), Snyder, Tailor

take *see* to take away

taken Moses *taken out of the water* (Hebrew), Moshe

takes Lel *he takes* (Gypsy)

talented Chinelo, Chuioke (Nigerian) • *talented one* Tai (Vietnamese)

talker *see* great talker

talks Demothi *talks walking* (Native American)

tall Hanford *from the tall ford* (Old German) • *high, tall* Pransu (Hindi) • *large, very tall* Rustam (Hindi) • *long or tall man* Lang (Old Norse) • *tall man's estate or town* Langston (Old English) • *tall or stately* Timur (Hebrew) • *very tall* Jola (Menda/African)

taloned Salmalin (Hindi)

tamer *see* constant one, tamer

Tano Tano *the river Tano* (Ghanaian), Tanno

target Lakshya (Hindi) • Laksh *aim, target* (Hindi)

Tarsus *see* city

tasty Rochak (Hindi)

tawny Hari (Hindi)

taxes *see* country

teacher Dabir (Arabic); Baruti (Botswanan); Fu (Chinese); Socrates (Greek) • *scholar, teacher; shield or to hide* Schuyler (Dutch) • *teacher of mankind* Plato (Latin), Platto, Platus

teamster *see* carter, teamster

tears *see* tears of love

teeth *see* born with teeth

temple *see* religious town or temple

ten Michio *man with strength of ten thousand* (Japanese) • *ten thousand-fold strong third son* Manzo (Japanese)

tender Sukumar (Hindi) • *tender, delicate* Mridul (Hindi)

terebinth *see* bitter, of the terebinth tree

Terrence *see* son of Terrence

terror *see* loud

Teuton *see* German

thank Zikomo *thank you* (African)

thanking *see* God

thatcher *see* roof thatcher

thickener *see* cloth thickener

thicket Bruce *dweller at the thicket* (Old French) • *dweller at the village in the thicket* Busby (Scotch-Norse) • *from the thicket* Stroud (Old English)

thin Blaine *lean or thin* (Celtic); Blayne (English); Blane (Irish-Gaelic) • *slender, thin* Caley (Irish), Cale, Calen, Calin • *thin one* Ottah (African)

thing *see* small thing

thinker Rashidi (African); Chintak (Hindi) • *thinker with a great purpose* Aristotle (Greek)

thinking Manan (Hindi)

third Manzo *strong third son* (Japanese) • *ten thousand-fold* • *third son* Teritus (Latin)

third-born Trey (Middle English) • *third-born male* Saburo (Japanese) • *third-born son* Taizo (Japanese)

thirteenth-born *see* son

Thomas *see* little Thomas

Thor Torbert *as renowned as Thor* (Old English), Torbart • *brilliance of Thor or thunder glorious, thunder* Thorbert (Old Norse) • *Thor or thunder spirit* Tormey (Irish-Gaelic) • *Thor ruler, thunder ruler* Thorald (Old Norse), Terrell, Tyrell; Thorvald (Scandinavian)

thorn *see* dweller by a thorn tree

thorny Thorndyke *from the thorny dike or embankment* (Old English), Thorndike • *from the thorny estate* Thornton (Old English) • *from the thorny meadow* Thornley (Old English)

thorough Gomer *the thorough one* (Anglo-Saxon), Gomar

Thor's Thorbjörn *Thor's bear* Thorburn (English); (Scandinavian) • *Thor's beloved* Thorleif (Scandinavian) • *Thor's stone or jewel* Thurstan (English), Thurston • *from Thor's hill, of Thor's mountain* Thurlow (Old English), Thorlow, Torrlow • *Thor's meadow* Thorley (Old English), Totley • *Thor's stone* Thurstan (Old English) • *under Thor's protection* Thormond (Old English), Thormund, Thurmond; Thurman (Scandinavian), Thorman, Thurmann

thought Mannan (Hindi) • *a thought* Turag (Hindi) • *thought of the god Chi* Chinelo (Nigerian)

thoughtful Akil (Arabic), Ahkeel • *son of the intelligent one* Fitzhugh (Old English)

thousand *see* man with strength of ten thousand

thousand-fold *see* ten thousand-fold strong third son

three Lohendra *lord of three worlds* (Hindi) • *poison; residue; three* Ba (Vietnamese)

thunder Garjan, Meghnad (Hindi); Tarrant (Old Welsh) • *brilliance of Thor or thunder glorious, thunder* Thorbert (Old Norse) • *Thor or thunder spirit* Tormey (Irish-Gaelic) • *Thor ruler, thunder ruler* Thorald (Old Norse), Terrell, Tyrell; Thorvald (Scandinavian) • *thunder Finn* Tor-

pin (Old Norse) • *thunder god* Raiden (Japanese) • *thunder ruler's estate* Tarleton (Old English)

thunderous Thorr *the thunderous one* (Scandinavian), Thor, Torr

Thursday *see* born on Thursday

thyself Kanko (Hausa)

tide *see* sea tide

tied *see* bound or tied

tiger Hu (Chinese); Shaardul, Shardul (Hindi) • *literature; short; striped tiger; to twist* Van (Vietnamese) • *tiger boy* Torao (Japanese)

tile Ziegler *brick and tile maker* (German) • *roofer and tile maker* Tyler (Middle English)

tiller Tilford *a tiller of fertile soil* (Old English), Tillford, Tillfourd • *tiller of the soil* Bond (Old English), Bonde, Bondon, Bonds

time Kala (Hindi) • *time of trouble* Iniko (Nigerian)

tin Kangi (Japanese); Kangee, Kanjee (English)

tinker Spengler *tinker, tinsmith* (German)

tinsmith *see* tinker, tinsmith

tiny Tawno (Gypsy); Alpesh (Hindi) • *tiny one* Joktan (Hebrew); Beacan (Irish-Gaelic), Beagan; Becan (English)

together *see* man

tolerant Dheer (Hindi)

toll *see* collector

Tom *see* little Tom

top *see* hill

topaz Pukhraj (Hindi)

torch *see* burning

torrent *see* rapid stream, torrent; swift

tortoise Toy (Chinese)

touch Sparsh (Hindi) • *to touch* Helki (Miwok) • *touchstone* Paras (Hindi)

towards *see* towards heaven

tower Carlisle *castle tower* (Old English) • *from the tower* Torr (Old English) • *he lives by the tower* Torrey (Celtic), Torray, Towrey, Towroy

town Burgess *citizen of a fortified town* (Middle English) • *dweller at the creek estate or town* Creighton (Middle English) • *dweller at the fortified town* Burton (Old English) • *dweller at the mill town* Milton (Old English) • *dweller at the old estate or town, from the* *old manor* Alton (Old English), Elton • *dweller at the spring estate or town* Welton (Old English) • *forest town* Boswell (Old French) • *from a Saxon town* Saxon (Old German), Saxen • *from the brushwood estate or town* Riston (Old English) • *from the clay estate or town* Clayton (Old English) • *from the cliff estate or town* Clifton (Old English) • *from the crane estate or town* Cranston (Old English) • *from the end of town* Townsend (Old English) • *from the enduring castle town* Warburton (Old English) • *from the estate or town on the ledge* Skelton (Old English) • *from the farm in the dell, from the valley estate or town* Dalton (Old English) • *from the field estate or town* Felton (Old English) • *from the fortress town* Broughton (Old English) • *from the friend's estate or town* Winston (Old English) • *from the golden estate or town* Orville (Old French) • *from the great estate or town* Granville (Old French) • *from the headland estate or town* Clinton (Old English) • *from the ledge farm or town* Shelton (Old English) • *from the moor estate or town* Morton (Old English) • *from the new estate or town* Newton (Old English) • *from the north estate or north town* Norton (Old English) • *from the old estate or town* Elton (Old English) • *from the quiet river estate or town* Tanton (Old English) • *from the town by the sea* Seaton (Old English), Seton • *from the town by the wall* Warton (Old English) • *from the town meadow* Townley (Old English) • *from the town of Burleigh* Burl (Anglo-Saxon), Beryl, Burley • *from the town of Olney* Olney (Old English), Olnay, Olnton • *from the town of Penrose* Penrose (Old English) • *from the tree stump estate or town* Stockton (Old English) • *hillside estate or town* Litton (Old English) • *Hugh's town* Houston (Scottish) • *new town* Newton (English-Scottish); Neville (French) • *noble one's estate or town, noble stone* Elston (Old English) • *of the lively town* Harden (Old English), Hardan • *of the protected town* Arlo (Old English) • *of the town on the top of the hill*

Egerton (Old English), Egarton • *peasant's farmstead or town* Charlton (Old English) • *religious town or temple* Templeton (Old English) • *sandy enclosure or town* Santon (Old English) • *tall man's estate or town* Langston (Old English) • *town born* Urien (Welsh) • *town crier or herald* Scully (Irish-Gaelic) • *upper estate or town* Upton (Old English) • *warrior's estate or town* Chadwick (Old English) • *wheat estate or town* Wheaton (Old English)

tradesman *see* merchant, peddler, tradesman

trail *see* leaf

tranquil Sereno *calm, tranquil one* (Latin) • *healer; tranquil* Gaylen (Greek), Galen, Gailen, Galen; Jalen (American) • *stable, tranquil* Eustace (Latin), Eustasius, Eustazio • *tranquil and calm* Placido (Latin); Placedo, Placijo, Plasido, Plasio (Spanish)

traveler Pathik, Pathin, Raahi (Hindi); Farr, Tripp (Old English) • *a traveler, from afar* Paxton (Old German), Packston, Packton, Paxon • *careful traveler* Trevor (Celtic), Trevar • *departer or traveler; wisdom* Nestor (Greek) • *mighty traveler* Farold (Old English) • *traveler, stranger, or pilgrim* Perry (Latin)

traveling Saju (Hindi) • *born while traveling* Chenzira (Zimbabwean)

treasure Ezar, Segel (Hebrew); Nigam (Hindi) • *lord of treasure* Nidhish (Hindi) • *treasure master* Caspar (Persian), Casper, Gaspar, Gasper, Jasper, Kasper

tree Chin (Chinese); Palash (Hindi); Miki (Japanese) • *a celestial tree* Mandar (Hindi) • *ash tree brook* Ashburn (Old English) • *ash tree farm* Ashby (Old English) • *a tree* Nishat, Pival, Piyali, Santan (Hindi) • *at the alder tree* Alder (Old English) • *at the birch tree* Birch (Old English), Birk • *birch tree* Burch (Middle English) • *bitter, of the terebinth tree* Elah (Hebrew) • *dweller at a grove of trees* Shaw (Old English) • *dweller at the ancient oak tree* Orrick (Old English) • *dweller at the acre meadow, of the meadow of the*

oak trees Ackerley (Old English) •
dweller at the ash tree farm Ashton
(Old English) • *dweller at the ash tree
meadow, from the ash tree ford* Ashford
(Old English) • *dweller at the ash tree
pool* Ashlin (Old English) • *dweller at
the birch tree meadow* Barclay (Old English), Berkeley • *dweller at the elder
tree* Elder (Old English) • *dweller at
the elm tree moor* Elmore (Old English) • *dweller at the linden tree valley*
Lindell (Old English) • *dweller at the
little oak tree* Quennel (Old French) •
dweller at the oak tree meadow Ackley
(Old English) • *dweller by a thorn tree*
Thorne (Old English) • *dweller by a
willow tree* Wythe (Middle English) •
dweller near the alder tree Fernald (Old
German) • *from the birch tree island*
Birkey (North English) • *from the
elder tree island* Ellery (Middle English), Ellerey • *from the forest of oak
trees* Cheney (French), Chenay • *from
the grove of trees* Grover (Old English)
• *from the holly tree grove* Hollis (Old
English) • *from the linden tree ford* Linford (Old English) • *from the linden
tree isle* Lindsey (Anglo-Saxon), Lindsay, Lynd • *from the oak tree ford* Adair
(Scotch-Gaelic) • *from the pear tree*
Perry (Middle English) • *from the tree
stump estate or town* Stockton (Old
English) • *from the tree stump meadow*
Stockley (Old English) • *from the tree
stump spring* Stockwell (Old English)
• *from the willow tree valley* Selden
(Old English) • *from the yew tree valley*
Udell (Old English), Udale, Udall •
like an elm tree Elman (German),
Elmen, Elmon • *linden tree hill* Lind-
berg (Old German) • *oak tree* Alon
(Hebrew), Allon • *orange; orange tree*
Alani (Hawaiian) • *palm tree* Dekel
(Arabic) • *pear tree* Le (Chinese) •
quaking aspen tree meadow Waverly
(Old English) • *the elm tree* Du (Viet-
namese) • *the holy sandalwood tree*
Chandan (Sanskrit) • *the oak tree*
Oakes (Old English) • *yew tree estate*
York (Old English)
trees Shaw *dweller at a grove of trees*
(Old English) • *dweller at the acre
meadow, of the meadow of the oak trees*
Ackerley (Old English) • *from the for-*

est of nut trees Delano (Old French) •
from the forest of oak trees Cheney
(French), Chenay • *from the grove of
trees* Grover (Old English) • *from the
place of the elm trees* Lennox (Scottish-
Gaelic) • *grove of trees* Nahele
(Hawaiian)
triangular Garton *dweller at the triangular farmstead* (Old English) • *from the
triangular or gore shaped hill* Gordon
(Old English), Gordan, Gorden • *triangular field* Garfield (Old English)
tribe *see* boy of the tribe, follower
tribute Kane (Irish-Gaelic), Kain,
Kaine, Kayne
tricky Harsho (Hebrew)
triumphant Jishnu (Hindi)
trouble *see* time of trouble
true Chan *correct or true* (Vietnamese)
• *defender, true man or watchman* Warren (Old German) • *faithful and true*
Pin (Vietnamese) • *faithful, loyal,
true one* True (Old English) • *faithful,
sincere, true* Fidel (Latin), Fidele, Fidelio, Fidelis • *true believer* Hanif
(Arabic), Haneef • *true one* Verrill
(Old French), Verrall, Verrell • *true
protector* Warmond (Old English) •
true, trusty one Trigg (Old Norse)
trumpeter Dudas (Lithuanian)
trustworthy Aman (African)
trusty *see* true, trusty one
truth Jun (Chinese) • *conqueror of truth*
Rutajit (Hindi) • *discerning truth from
falsehood* Faruq (Arabic), Farouk •
highest truth Paramartha (Hindi) •
highest truth, salvation Parmaarth
(Hindi) • *lord of truth* Ritesh
(Hindi)
truthful Sancho *sanctified, sincere,
truthful* (Spanish) • *truthful one*
Delsin (Native American)
Tuesday *see* born on Tuesday
turkey Wuyi *turkey vulture soaring*
(Miwok)
turtledove Howi (Miwok)
twelfth-born *see* born
twilight Pradosh (Hindi)
twin Thomas *a twin* (Greek), Tomaso;
Tamas (Hungarian); Cowan (Irish-
Gaelic); Tavis (Scotch-Gaelic),
Tavish, Tevis; Tomas (Slavic) • *elder
twin* Zesiro (Ugandan) • *first-born
male twin* Ulan (Sudan)

twins Kizza *born after twins* (Ugandan) • *first of twins* Odion (Nigerian) • *second of twins* Odongo (African)

twist *see* literature; short; striped tiger; to twist
Tyre *see* city

U

ultimate Shekhar (Hindi)
unafraid *see* man
unassuming Vineet (Hindi)
unattached Nirmohi (Hindi)
unbending Takeshi *unbending one* (Japanese)
unborn Aja (Hindi), Ajaat
unbounded Nissim (Hindi)
uncle Ahab (Hebrew)
unconquerable Ajay (Hindi), Ajit
understand Yarin (Hebrew); Javin (English)
understanding Haskel (Hebrew), Haskell • *a man of understanding* Favian (Latin), Favianus, Favient, Favin
undying Anirvan (Hindi)
unencumbered Digambar
unending Amogh (Hindi)
unequaled Atulya (Hindi)
unexpected Atwan (Nigerian)
unfailing *see* guard
unflappable *see* calm, unflappable
unforgettable Smirtiman (Hindi)
unhindered *see* free
unifying Harmon (Greek)
union Mithun (Hindi)
unique Farid (Arabic), Fareed • *one choice, unique strength* Angus (Scotch-Gaelic)
united *see* joined, united

unity Ace (Latin)
universal Yu (Chinese); Vishvam (Hindi) • *the universal soul* Hansin (Hindi) • *universal soul* Vishvatma (Hindi)
universe Brahma *creator of the universe* (Hindi) • Cosmo *harmony, order, the universe* (Greek), Cosimo, Cosme • *lord of the universe* Jagesh (Hindi), Jagish
unmoveable Nishchal *unmoveable, unshakeable* (Hindi)
unreachable Durga (Hindi)
unshakeable *see* unmoveable
unusual *see* man with an unusual beard
unwavering *see* protector
up *see* I stand up
upper Upwood *from the upper forest* (Old English) • *upper estate or town* Upton (Old English)
upright Jesher *an upright man* (Hebrew), Jesh • *just one, upright* Justin (Old French) • *morally upright* Deshi (Chinese)
upward Rohin *on the upward path* (Hindi)
urbane *see* city
urn *see* sacred urn
usurper Waldo (Old English), Waldos

V

vain Cash, Cassius *vain one* (Latin), Cass, Caz
vale *see* stony
valiant Carney *valiant soldier* (Celtic), Carnay; Roque (Latin), Rochus, Rock, Rocky • *valiant, warlike one* Riley (Latin), Reilly, Ryley

valley Tani (Japanese) • *caretaker of the valley; from the valley of cranes* Crandall (Old English), Crandale, Crandell • *child of the valley* Slade (English) • *deep valley* Holcomb (Old English) • *dweller at the linden tree valley* Lindell (Old English) • *dweller at* *the marshy valley* Marsden (Old English), Marsdon • *dweller at the valley edge, green valley* Denver (Old English) • *dweller in a glen or valley* Glenn (Irish-Gaelic/Old Welsh), Glen, Glyn, Glynn • *dweller in the valley* Dale, Dean, Slade (Old English) • *dweller in the valley meadow* Denley (Old English) • *dweller in the valley of the awe-inspiring one* Anscom (Old English), Anscomb • *elf valley* Elden (Old English) • *from a beautiful valley* Belden (Old German) • *from the boar valley* Borden (Old English) • *from the bright valley or clear river valley* Kendall (Old English), Kendal, Kendell • *from the crooked or winding valley* Camden (Anglo-Gaelic) • *from the dark valley* Blagden (Old English) • *from the dry valley* Dryden (Old English) • *from the farm in the dell, from the valley estate or town* Dalton (Old English) • *from the farm in the valley* Denton (Old English) • *from the flowered valley* Royden (Old English) • *from the forest valley* Walden (Old English) • *from the fruitful valley* Helbon (Hebrew) • *from the good, liberal one's valley* Tilden (Old English) • *from the hedged valley* Hayden (Old English), Haydon • *from the hollow in the valley* Holden (Old English) • *from the low valley* Loudon (eutonic); Lowden (English) • *from the new valley* Seldon (Old English), Seldan, Selden • *from the oak valley* Ogden (Old English) • *from the reed valley* Roden (Old English) • *from the shady valley* Glendon (Celtic) • *from the valley of the pool* Marden (Old English) • *from the wide valley, of the village of the sun* Braden, Siddell (Old English), Brad • *from the willow tree valley* Selden (Old English) • *from the yew tree valley* Udell (Old English), Udale, Udall • *he lives by the red valley* Radford (Old English), Radley • *he lives in the valley* Ripley (Old English), Ripleigh • *of the rocky valley* Standish (Old English), Standice • *of the valley of cattle* Orford (Old English), Ford, Orferd • *ram's valley* Ramsden (Old English) • *ruler's valley* Rigby (Old English) • *valley dweller* Vail (Middle English),

Vale • *valley of the dead oaks* Jolon (Native American) • *valley piercer* Percival (Old French), Percy • *valley resident* Denman (Old English)

valor Vikram (Hindi) • *fierce valor* Devlin (Irish-Gaelic)

valorous Casey (Celtic) • *brave, valorous, watchful* Casey (Irish-Gaelic) • *healthy, strong, valorous* Valentine (Latin), Valentino • *little fair-haired valorous one* Finley (Irish-Gaelic), Findlay, Findley, Finlay • *most valorous one* Farrell (Irish-Gaelic), Farrel, Ferrell • *valorous in battle* Duer (Celtic)

valuable Moulik (Hindi)

value *see* honor, reward, value

valued *see* friend

Vandyke *see* son

Van Ness *see* son

vanquisher *see* vanquisher of foes

variable Varian (Latin)

Varini *see* army of the Varini, defending warrior or army

vassal Vasallo (Spanish)

vegetable *see* dweller at the vegetable enclosure

veiled Lot (Hebrew)

vendor *see* salesman

venerable Austin *venerable one* (Latin), Austen

venerated *see* family

vetch *see* chick-pea or vetch

victor Harjit, Ranjit (Hindi) • *God is the victor* Olushegun (Nigerian)

victorious Nasser (Arabic); Shing (Chinese); Harjeet, Jaiman, Prajeet, Ranajay, Ranajit, Ranjiv, Sanjay, Satvik, Sikander, Ujjay, Vijendra, Vijeta (Hindi); Carney (Irish-Gaelic), Carny; Nassor (Swahili) • *government or victorious ruler* Sigwald (Old German) • *little victorious one* Bowen (Irish-Gaelic) • *peaceful, victorious* Siegfried (Old German), Sigfrid, Sigvard • *royal, victorious one* Kinsey (Old English) • *victorious army* Colin (French-Greek) • *victorious army, victorious people* Klaus (German); Nicholas (Greek), Cole, Nichol, Nicol, Nicolas, Nikki, Kolya (Russian); Nicanor (Spanish) • *victorious guardian* Sigurd (Old Norse) • *victorious on the sea* Sewell (Old German),

Sewole, Sewoll • *victorious protector* Sigmund (Old German), Sigismond, Sigismund • *victorious wolf* Woolsey (Old English)

victory Fath (Arabic); Sheng (Chinese); Nico (Greek); Sujit (Hindi) • *bright, victory* Seiberth (German) • *from the village of victory* Sedgewick (Old English) • *laurel, victory* Lorant (Hungarian); Lars (Scandinavian) • *victory of kindness* Jaidayal (Hindi) • *victory of the moon* Jaichand (Hindi) • *victory over army* Senajit (Hindi) • *victory ship* Kelsey (Old English); Kelsy (English) • *victory to the light* Jaideep (Hindi)

view *see* fair view

vigilant Gregor (Greek), Gregorio, Gregory, Grigor

vigor Vigor (Celtic) • *glory, vigor* Pratap (Hindi)

village Mura (Japanese), Stoke (Middle English) • *dweller at the rocky village* Stanwick (Old English) • *dweller at the village in the thicket* Busby (Scotch-Norse) • *from the church village* Kirby (Old Norse), Kerby • *from the prosperous village* Edlun (Anglo-Saxon) • *from the village enclosure or meadow* Wickham (Old English) • *from the village meadow* Wickley (Old English) • *from the village of victory* Sedgewick (Old English) • *from the wide valley, of the village of the sun*

Braden, Siddell (Old English), Brad • *of the village* Lathrop (Anglo-Saxon); Thorpe (Old English); Vick (Old French) • *village god* Muni (Hindi)

villager *see* country

vigorous Hod (Hebrew) • *vigorous and alive* Ziven (Slavic); Zivon (English)

Vincent *see* son of Vincent

vined *see* cottage

violent *see* severe

virgin *see* Mary

virile Arsenio *masculine and virile* (Greek), Arsanio, Arsemio; Eresenio (Spanish) • *virile and young* Colin (Celtic), Cole

virtue Brian *honor, strength, virtue* (Celtic), Briant, Brien, Bryan, Bryant, Bryon • *lord of virtue* Shubendra (Hindi)

virtuous Shilang (Hindi); Duc (Vietnamese)

Vishnu Harish (Sanskrit), Haresh • *the god Vishnu* Narain (Hindi)

vision Darshan *one with vision* (Sanskrit) • *phantom, vision* Drew (Old Welsh)

visited *see* Lord

vital Sanjiv (Hindi)

voice Liu (African)

vulture Nasr (Arabic), Nusair; Geier (Slavic), Geyer • *turkey vulture soaring* Wuyi (Miwok)

W

Wade's *see* advancer's

wagon *see* maker

Wales *see* man from Wales, Welshman

Walford *see* resident

walking Demothi *talks walking* (Native American) • *walking wonder* Manipi (Native American

walks *see* walks quietly

wall Cata *a connecting wall; catfish; nut; to confine* (Mende/African) • *army ruler; mason, wall builder* Waller (Old English) • *dweller at the wall enclosed cottage* Walcott (Old English) • *from*

the town by the wall Warton (Old English) • *of the ford by the wall* Warford (Old English), Warfourd

walled *see* city

Walter *see* son of Walter

wanderer Arvad (Hebrew), Arpad; Wendell (Old German) • *a wanderer* Igasho (Native American) • *rambler, wanderer* Rover (Middle English) • *the wanderer* Ishmael (Hebrew), Ishmul

wandering Errol (Latin) • *from a wandering family* Gurias (Hebrew)

wanted Oni *the wanted one* (Nigerian)
war Harb (Arabic) • *born during war*
Abiodun (Nigerian) • *god of war*
Ogun (Nigerian) • *little war mighty
one* Malin (Old English) • *son of famous in war* Loring (Old German) •
son of war mighty Madison (Old English) • *war bear* Wyborn (Old
Norse) • *war sword* Hildebrand (Old
German)
warden Woodruff *bailiff or forest warden*
(Old English) • *deer guardian or war-
den* Derward (Old English) • *forester,
forest warden* Woodward (Old En-
glish) • *gamekeeper, warden of a forest*
Forest (English) • *hall guardian or
warden* Allward (Old English)
Warfield *see* resident
warlike Killian *little warlike one* (Irish-
Gaelic) • *valiant, warlike one* Riley
(Latin), Reilly, Ryley • *warlike one* De-
Marco (American); Ashur (East Se-
mitic); Mark, Martin (Latin), Marc,
Marco, Marcos, Marcus, Marten,
Martino, Marton, Marty; Chad (Old
English); Lachlan (Scotch-Gaelic);
Arrio (Spanish), Ario
warm Wing (Chinese); Clyde (Welsh)
• *warm cloth* Nishar (Hindi)
warrior Gamba, Hondo (African);
Hanley, Kelly, Sloan (Irish-Gaelic),
Kelley, Sloane; Adofo (Nigerian);
Wyman (Old English); Guy (Old
German); Bowen (Welsh) • *a famous
warrior* Lashi (Gypsy), Lash, Lasho •
aggressive warrior Cavill (Old German), Cavil • *a mighty warrior* Kellen
(Irish-Gaelic), Kalin, Kelin, Kellan,
Kelle, Kellin • *an excellent warrior,
king* Praveer (Hindi) • *army ruler,
powerful warrior* Walter (Old German), Gauthier, Walther • *army warrior* Harvey (Old German) • *army
brilliant, glorious warrior* Herbert
(Old German) • *army man, warrior*
Herman (Old German), Armand,
Armando, Hamlin, Harman, Harmon • *army of the Varini, defending
warrior or army* Werner (Old German) • *a soldier's son, of the warrior's
house* Etam (Latin) • *bold and royal,
chief warrior* Kimball (Old Welsh),
Kimble • *bold warrior* Gunter
(French); Guenter, Guenther, Gun-

ther (German); Guntero (Italian);
Gunnar (Norwegian); Gunnar (Teu-
tonic) • *bold warrior or royal warrior*
Kenway (Old English) • *brave warrior*
Cadman (Celtic), Cadmann;
Kenelm (Old English) • *brown war-
rior* Donahue (Irish-Gaelic); Duncan
(Scotch-Gaelic) • *champion, warrior*
Kemp (Middle English) • *dark warrior* Donovan (Celtic) • *defending
army or warrior* Warner (Old German), Werner • *divine warrior* Os-
born (Old English) • *elfin warrior*
Elvy (Old English) • *famous warrior*
Aloysius, Lothar, Louis, Luther (Old
German), Aloisus, Clovis, Lewis,
Lotario, Ludvig, Ludwig, Luigi, Luis,
Lutero, Luthais; Humberto (Teu-
tonic); Umberto (Spanish) • *follower
or warrior attendant* Thane (Old English), Thaine, Thayne • *from the warrior's field* Mayfield (Old English) •
great warrior Cathmor (Irish-Gaelic)
• *little glorious warrior* Harbin (Old
French-German) • *little warrior* Wyatt
(Old French) • *mariner, sea warrior*
Murray (Scotch-Gaelic) • *mighty warrior* Tredway (Old English) • *nobleman, warrior* Baron (Old English),
Barron • *noble warrior* Albern (Old
English) • *nobly brave, warrior* Ellard
(Old German), Ellerd, Ellord • *prudent warrior* Rainer (Old German) •
renowned warrior Ludwig (Old German) • *sea spear, sea warrior* Seger
(Old English), Seager, Segar • *sea
warrior* Murphy (Irish-Gaelic) • *soldier, warrior* Miles (Latin), Myles •
son of the red warrior Clancy (Irish-
Gaelic); Clancey (English) • *spear
warrior* Garroway (Old English) •
warrior leader Einar (Old Norse) •
strong soldier, warrior Bornani
(African) • *warrior's estate* Burnaby
(Old Norse) • *warrior's estate or town*
Chadwick (Old English) • *warrior's
settlement* Cadby (Old Norse-English)
• *well-born one, young warrior* Evan
(Irish-Gaelic), Ewan, Ewen; Owen
(Old Welsh) • *wise warrior* Witter
(Old English)
wary *see* careful, wary guard
wasteland Muir *from the moor or wasteland* (Scotch-Gaelic) • *from the*

wasteland Moore (Middle English) • *heath or wasteland* Heath (Middle English)
watch *see* hill
watchful Eran (Hebrew) • *alert, watchful one* Wake (Old English) • *brave, valorous, watchful* Casey (Irish-Gaelic) • *watchful guardian* Argus (Greek) • *watchful one* Ira (Hebrew) • *watchful one, watchman* Gregory (Latin), Gregor
watchman Wakeman (Old English) • *defender, true man or watchman* Warren (Old German) • *guardian, watchman* Ward (Old English), Warde, Warden • *guard, watchman* Waite (Middle English) • *watchful one, watchman* Gregory (Latin), Gregor
water Payas, Salil, Toya,Udu (Hindi) • *bridge over white water* Bainbridge (Old English) • *bright, clear water* Kenn (Old Welsh), Cain • *dweller at the water* Atwater (Old English) • *dweller by the water* Kelwin (Celtic), Kelley, Kelwen; Lach (Old English) • *drawer of water* Winchell (Anglo-Saxon) • *fountain; water source* Fontaine (French); Fontayne (English); Fontana (Italian) • *from the black or dark water* Douglas (Scotch-Gaelic), Douglass, Dugald • *from the still water* Mortimer (Old French) • *from the water* Lachlan (Scotch-Gaelic) • *given by water* Nirad (Hindi) • *lord of water* Jalesh, Toyesh, Varunesh (Hindi) • *moon in the water* Jalendu (Hindi) • *of the farm by the water* Marston (Old English) • *of the hill by the water* Marlow (Old English) • *of the sea, lover of water* Pontius (Latin), Pontias, Pontus • *rippling water* Misu (Miwok) • *taken out of the water* Moses (Hebrew), Moshe • *wide body of water* Wong (Chinese)
watercress *see* dweller at the watercress spring
waterfall Emlyn (Welsh) • *from the ravine field or waterfall field* Dallas (Scotch-Gaelic)
waters *see* god of waters
wave Lahar, Tarang (Hindi) • Dylan *son of the wave* (Welsh)
wealth Yasar (Arabic), Yaser, Yasir, Yasser; Jesse (Hebrew), Jess, Jessie;

Shriyans (Hindi) • *lord of wealth* Vittesh (Hindi) • *lover of wealth* Srikant (Hindi) • *man of great wealth* Orton (Old German), Orten
wealthy Huang (Chinese) • Wellington *from the wealthy estate* (Anglo-Saxon) • *from the wealthy one's hill or hill castle* Montgomery (Old French) • *little wealthy one* Odell (Old Anglo-French) • *noble friend, wealthy friend* Audwin (Old German) • *prosperous, wealthy one* Otto (Old German) • *wealthy, brilliant one* Obert (Old German) • *wealthy future* Huang-Fu (Chinese) • *wealthy guardian* Edik (Russian) • *wealthy one* Darius (Greek); Otis (Old German) • *wealthy protector* Eamon (Irish-Gaelic) • *wealthy wolf* Odolf (Old German)
wearing *see* wearing a crown
wears *see* one who wears cobra
weaver Weber (German); Webb, Webster (Old English)
weaver's *see* meadow
weaving *see* weaving leaf
Wednesday *see* born on Wednesday
wee *see* drummer
welcome Garibald *a welcome addition* (Old English), Aribold, Garibold, Ribal • *welcome rain* Barsaat (Hindi)
welfare Kalyan (Hindi)
well Weldon *from a hill near the well* (Old German) • *from the bramblebush spring, of Bram's well* Bramwell (Old English), Bram • *I do well* Faro (Latin), Farro, Farron • *of the well by the sea* Sidwell (Anglo-Saxon), Sidwel, Sidwohl • *to do well* Wuliton (Native American) • *well shaped one* Quinlan (Irish-Gaelic) • *well wisher* Iqbal (Arabic)
well-born Benon (Irish-Gaelic); Sachio (Japanese) • *noble, well-born* Eugene (Greek), Eugenio, Gene, Gino • *well-born* Ewan (Celtic), Ewen • *well-born one, young warrior* Evan (Irish-Gaelic), Ewan, Ewen; Owen (Old Welsh)
well-bred Curtis *courteous one, courtly, elegant, well-bred* (Old French), Curt, Kurt, Kurtis
well-doer Evander (Greek)
Welsh *see* friend

Welshman *see* man from Wales, Welshman

Welshman's *see* farm

wept over Arval (Latin), Arvel

west Wescott *dweller at west cottage* (Old German), Wes • *from the west brook* Westbrook (Old English) • *from the west cottage* Westcott (Old English) • *from the west estate* Weston (Old English) • *from the west meadow* Wesley (Old English), Westleigh

wet Wakefield *dweller at the wet field* (Old English) • *from the wet meadow* Wakeley (Old English)

wether Wetherly *dweller at the wether-sheep meadow* (Old English) • *from the wether-sheep corner* Wetherell (Old English) • *from the wether-sheep farm* Wetherby (Old English)

what Ho (Chinese)

wheat Wheaton *wheat estate or town* (Old English) • *wheat meadow* Wheatley (Old English)

wheel *see* maker

whisper *see* to whisper or speak quietly

whistler *piper or whistler* Whistler (Old English); Peverell (Old French), Peverel, Peveril • *the whistler* Hototo (Native American)

white DeWitt (Dutch); Laban (Hebrew); Banan (Irish) • *blond, white* Blanco (Spanish) • *bridge over white water* Bainbridge (Old English) • *bright, shining white* Galvin (Irish-Gaelic), Galvan, Galven • *bright, white* Kent (Old Welsh) • *dweller at the white field* Whittaker (Old English) • *fair or white* Albion, Alver, Remus (Latin), Alvar, Aubyn • *fair or white-haired, with short hair* Sherlock (Old English), Sherlocke • *fair, white one* Wynn (Old Welsh), Winn • *from the white cliff* Wycliff (Old English) • *from the white farmstead* Whitby (Old English) • *from the white field* Whitfield (Old English) • *from the white ford* Whitford (Old English) • *from the white-haired one's island* Whitney (Old English) • *from the white hill* Whitelaw (Old English) • *from the white meadow* Whitley (Old English) • *from the white moor* Whitmore (Old English) • *from the white settlement*

Whitby (Scandinavian) • *from the white stronghold* Whitlock (Old English) • *not white* Asit (Hindi) • *white as snow* Tuhinsurra (Hindi) • *white cow* Boyne (Irish-Gaelic) • *white-haired* Finbar (Irish), Finbur • *white-haired man* Whitman (Old English) • *white hawk* Gavin (Irish-Gaelic) • *white headed* Kenyon (Irish-Gaelic) • *white moon* Muraco (Native American) • *white one's estate* Wentworth (Old English) • *white or blond one* Dwight (Old Dutch) • *white sea* Morgan (Old Welsh), Morgen

whole Ankal, Ekansh, Sarvak, Shantanu (Hindi) • *healthy and whole* Sage (Latin)

wide Brad *broad, wide place* (Old English) • *from the wide ford* Rumford (Old English) • *from the wide river* Leith (Celtic) • *from the wide valley, of the village of the sun* Braden, Siddell (Old English), Brad • *wide body of water* Wong (Chinese) • *wide valley* Braden, Siddell (Old English)

widower Almon (Hebrew)

wielder's *see* stone

wild Haro *first son of the wild boar* (Japanese), Haroko, Haroku • *pugilist; the wild boar* Evers (Anglo-Saxon) • *wild-boar brave* Eberhard (Old German) • *wild condor* Aucaman (Native American) • *wild man or satyr* Sheridan (Irish-Gaelic)

wildcat Zbik (Polish) • *from the wildcat brook* Chadburn (Old English)

will Tully *devoted to the will of God; peaceful, quiet one; people mighty* (Irish-Gaelic) • *will, determination* Sankalp (Hindi)

William *see* son of William

willing Wichado, Wingi (Native American)

willow Saville *born on the willow farm* (Latin), Saval, Savil, Savill • *dweller at the willow ford* Wilford (Old English) • *dweller by a willow tree* Wythe (Middle English) • *from the willow farm* Willoughby (Old English) • *from the willow ford* Safford (Old English) • *from the willow tree valley* Selden (Old English) • *one from the willow place* Lazauskas (Lithuanian) • *willow estate* Saville (North French)

wind Bavol (Gypsy); Anil, Marut, Pavan, Samir, Sarayu, Suka (Hindi); Tadi (Native American) • *child of the air or wind* Anil (Hindi) • *like the wind* Beval (Gypsy) • *the east wind* Waban (Native American) • *the wind* Nodin (Native American), Noton

winding Cromwell *dweller at the crooked or winding spring* (Old English) • *from the cottage on the winding path* Chetwin (Old English) • *from the crooked or winding valley* Camden (Anglo-Gaelic) • *from the enclosure with the winding path* Wyndham (Old English) • *from the winding farm* Crompton (Old English)

windy Tate (Native American) • *from the windy place* Guthrie (Irish-Gaelic)

wine *see* God of wine

winegrower Tychonn (Celtic), Tichon, Tichonn, Ticon, Tychon

winner Ghalib (African); Budd (Celtic), Bud, Buddy

winning Millard *flattering, strong and winning* (Old French) • *flattering, winning one; industrious one* Emil (Old German), Emilio • *of the winning fort* Seaver (Anglo-Saxon), Seavir

wins *see* he who wins the struggle

winter Tushar (Hindi) • *born in winter* Wen (Gypsy)

wintertime *see* born in the wintertime

wisdom Parmeet (Hindi) • *a man of wisdom* Jeuz (Hebrew) • *departer or traveler; wisdom* Nestor (Greek) • *intelligence, wisdom* Conan (Celtic) • *knowledge, wisdom* Mendel (East Semitic) • *lord of wisdom* Pradnesh (Hindi) • *man of wisdom* Jadda (Hebrew), Jaddan, Jaddo • Solon *wisdom, wise man* (Greek)

wise Alim (Arabic), Aleem, Hakeem, Hakim; Dheemanth, Kovidh, Sambuddha, Shaunak, Sukrit, Sumay, Sumed (Hindi), Dhir • *adviser, so wise* Eldwin (Anglo-Saxon), Eldwen • *a judge, wise* Dempster (Old English), Dempsey, Dempstor • *all wise* Alvis, Elvis (Old Norse) • *a wise counselor* Mordecai (Hebrew) • *discreet, prudent, wise* Trevor (Irish-Gaelic) • *friend or old, wise protector* Alden (Old English), Aldin, Aldwin, Aldwyn, Elden, Eldin • *from the wise man's estate* Witton (Old English) • *intelligent, wise* Quinn (Irish-Gaelic) • *little old wise one* Shannon (Irish-Gaelic) • *mighty or wise protector* Raymond (Old German), Ramon; Ramiro (Spanish), Ramirez • *of wise heritage* Gildas (Latin), Gildus, Gilus • *old and wise* Aldo (Old German) • *old, wise man* Altman (Old German) • *old, wise one* Sennett (French) • *old, wise ruler* Aldrich (Old English), Aldric, Audric, Eldric • *poet, wise man* Strahan (Irish-Gaelic) • *sagacious, wise one* Shanahan (Irish-Gaelic) • *son of the wise man* Druce (Old Anglo-Welsh) • *strongly wise* Connor (Irish-Gaelic), Conner, Connors, Conor • *the wise ruler* Alberic (Old German), Albric • *wise and intelligent* Arif (Turkish); Areef (English) • *wise and knowing* Sage (Latin) • *wise in battle* Balthasar (Persian), Balthazar • *wise; intelligent* Hui (Chinese); Dheemant (Hindi) • *wise man* Morathi (African); Witt (Old English) • *wise one* Hakeen (Arabic), Hakim; Conroy (Irish-Gaelic); Catto (Latin), Cato, Caton, Catton; Drew (Old Welsh) • *wise power* Renaud (Hindi) • *wise warrior* Witter (Old English)

wisest *see* magician

wish Murad, Sidak, Umed (Hindi); Hy (Vietnamese) • *wish, desire* Munda (Hindi)

wisher *see* well wisher

wishes *see* he wishes peace

wisteria *see* field

without Niramay *without blemish* (Hindi) • *without comparison* Nirupam (Hindi) • *without sound* Nirav (Hindi)

witness Paki (African); *my ornament, my witness* Adlai (Hebrew) • *witness our Lord's goodness* Joed (Hebrew) • *witness our love* Jegar (Hebrew), Jegar, Jegger

wolf Welk (Czech); Farkas (Hungarian); Wolfe (Old English), Wulff; Volkow (Polish); Volkov (Russian); Gonzalo (Spanish), Gonsalve, Gonzales; Vovcenko (Ukranian) • *advancing wolf, path of a wolf* Wolfgang (Old German) • *axe-wolf* Bardolf

(Old English), Bardolph, Bardou, Bardoul • *counsel wolf, swift wolf* Radolf, Ralph (Old English), Raoul, Raul, Rolph • *eagle wolf* Arno (Old German), Arnon, Arnoux • *famous wolf* Rule (Old French); Rudolph (Old German), Rodolf, Rodolfo, Rodolph, Rudolf; Ulmer (Old Norse), Ulmar; Rolon (Spanish) • *gray wolf* Mingan (Native American) • *herald wolf* Botolf (Old English) • *home loving wolf* Ardolph (Old English) • *little wolf* Phelan (Irish-Gaelic) • *little wolf cub* Channing (Irish-Gaelic); Chane, Channe, Channon (English) • *noble hero, noble wolf* Adolph (Old German), Adolf, Adolfo, Adolphe, Adolphus • *peaceful wolf* Fridolf (Old English) • *prosperous wolf* Edolf, Udolf (Old English) • *protection, wolf* Raoul (French), Ralph, Randolph • *shield wolf* Randolph (Old English), Randall, Randell, Randolf • *son of the little counsel wolf* Rawlins (Old Anglo-French); Rawson (Old English) • *son of the wolf* Weylin (Celtic) • *victorious wolf* Woolsey (Old English) • *wealthy wolf* Odolf (Old German) • Rolf (Old German); Rolfe, Rolph (Scandinavian) • *wolf guardian's farm* Wordsworth (Old English) • *wolf peace* Ulfred (Old English) • *wolf ruler* Ulric (Old German) • *wolf spear* Ulger (Old English) • *wolf sport* Ullock (Old English)

Wolfe's *see* cottage

woman Quimby *dweller at the woman's estate* (Old Norse), Quinby • *of the womb of woman* Quinby (Scandinavian)

womb *see* woman

wonder Naval (Hindi) • Manipi *walking wonder* (Native American)

wonderful *see* child

wood Lyndon *from the lime wood* (Old English) • *high or enclosed wood* Heywood (English) • *oak wood* Chaney (Old French); Cheney (English) • *wood by a marsh* Morley (English)

woodcutter Hackman (Old English); *woodcutter, woodsman* Woodman (Old English)

wooded Waldon *from the wooded hill* (Old English)

woodland Culley *at the woodland* (Irish-Gaelic), Cully • *dweller in the woodlands* Boyce (French) • *lion of the woodland dell* Napoleon (Greek)

woods Wesh (Gypsy) • *from the stony woods* Stanwood (Old English) • *from the woods, the hunter* Hayes (Old English) • *man of the woods* Sawyer (Celtic), Sawyor

woodsman *see* woodcutter, woodsman

woody *see* hillside

wool *see* cutter

word Sana (Finnish)

worker Smith *blacksmith, worker with a hammer* (Old French) • *chamberlain, monastery worker* Camerero (Spanish) • *farmer, land worker* Jorn (Danish); Juri (Estonian); Joji (Japanese); George (Latin), Georg, Giorgio, Jorge; Goran (Scandinavian); Yuri (Russian) • *farm worker* Hoffman (German) • *hard worker* Cham (Vietnamese) • *stone worker* Mason (Old French) • *worker with the lathe* Turner (Latin)

workman *see* breathe

works *see* hands

world Alem (African); Jagat (Hindi) • *eye of the world* Lokenetra (Hindi) • *god of the world* Jagdeo (Hindi) • *king of the world* Jagdish (Hindi) • *life adventuring, world daring* Ferdinand (Old German), Ferdinando, Ferdnando, Fernando, Hernando • *lord of the world* Bhavesh, Loknaath, Vishvesh (Hindi) • *separation from the world* Nivrutti (Hindi) • *son of world mighty* MacDonald (Scotch-Gaelic) • *the world* Mahi (Hindi); Jahan (Sanskrit) • *world mighty, world ruler* Donald (Scotch-Gaelic); Tauno (Finnish) • *world ruler* Bohdan (Ukranian); Bogdan, Bogdashka, Danya (Russian)

worldly *see* sophisticated, worldly

worlds *see* lord of three worlds

worship *see* devoted to Sunday worship

worshiper Abedi (African) • *worshiper of the saint* Nevin (Irish-Gaelic), Niven

worth *see* great

worthy Erasmus *lovable, worthy of love* (Greek), Erasme, Erasmo, Rasmus •

the praised one, worthy of praise Aeneas (Greek), Eneas • *worthy one* Wirt (Old English)

wreath Vencel *wreath or garland* (Hungarian) • *garland or wreath of glory* Wenceslaus (Old Slavic)

wrestler Nayati *the wrestler* (Native American)

wrestling *see* wrestling with God

writer Kateb (Arabic); Kaga (Native American)

wry Campbell *wry or crooked mouth* (Scotch-Gaelic) • *wry or crooked nose* Cameron (Scotch-Gaelic)

Y

yardkeeper Garth (Anglo-Saxon)

year Nien *a year* (Vietnamese) • *one year* Bersh (Gypsy) • *year boy* Toshio (Japanese), Toshi

yellow Wang (Chinese); Hwang, Ko (Korean) • *from the yellow house* Sterling (Old Welsh) • *golden yellow hair* Flavius (Latin) • *yellow bird* Mamo (Hawaiian) • *yellow-haired* Bowie (Irish-Gaelic); Flavian (Latin)

yesterday Sef (Egyptian)

yew Udell *from the yew tree valley* (Old English), Udale, Udall • *little yew bow* Iven (Old French) • *son of yew bow* Ives (Old English), Yves • *yew bow army* Ivar (Old Norse), Ivor • *yew tree estate* York (Old English)

young Tarun (Hindi); Owain (Irish-Gaelic) • *a young boy* Kishor (Hindi) • *forever young* Junius (Latin) • *little young one* Hagen (Irish-Gaelic), Hagan • *virile and young* Colin (Celtic), Cole • *well-born one, young warrior* Evan (Irish-Gaelic), Ewan, Ewen; Owen (Old Welsh) • *young at-*

tendant Padgett (French), Padget • *young boy* Kumar, Tuka (Hindi) • *young, inexperienced, and naïve* Cahil (Turkish) • *young lion* Lionel (Old French) • *young man* Kerel (Afrikaans) • *young moon* Balachandar (Hindi), Balendu • *young rabbit* Leverett (Old French)

youth Svend (Danish); Hogan (Irish-Gaelic); Azi (Nigerian); Burr (Old Norse); Sven (Scandinavian) • *from the fountain of youth* Endor (Hebrew), Dorr, Ender, Nandor • *red-haired youth* Alroy (Irish-Gaelic) • *servant of the red-haired youth* Gilroy (Irish-Gaelic)

youthful Halian (Native American) • *servant to the royal court, youthful attendant* Page (French), Pagas, Pegasus • *springlike, youthful* Verne, Vernon (Latin) • *downy-bearded one, youthful* Julius (Latin), Jule, Jules, Julio; Giles (Old French), Gil • *downy-cheeked one, youthful* Julian (Latin), Julius • *youthful one* Tarun (Sanskrit)

Z

zeal *see* man of zeal

zealous Zelotes *zealous one* (Greek)

Zeus Senon *given by Zeus* (Spanish)

Index to Names

These brief references are to every name in the dictionary, with an indication of f for the female names section and m for the male, followed by the definition heading (or headings if separated by a semicolon). These headings do not necessarily constitute a definition; one should read the entry to obtain a full understanding.

Aabha *f* glow
Aabharana *f* jewel
Aadarshini *f* idealistic
Aadesh *m* command
Aadhya *f* first; power
Aadit *m* peak
Aadrika *f* mountain
Aagam *m* arrival
Aakaar *m* shape
Aakanksha *f* desire
Aaloka *f* lustrous
Aanandi *f* always; happy
Aanandita *f* happy;
  woman
Aara *f* able; elegant; lady;
  maiden
Aarabi *f* music
Aarini *f* adventurous
Aaron *m* exalted; lofty
Aarzoo *f* wish
Aashi *f* smile
Aashni *f* lightning
Aastha *f* faith
Aba *f* born; horse-woman;
  woman
Aban *m* Abbott
Abana *f* goddess; ivory
Abasi *m* stern
Abayomi *m* bringer; happi-
  ness
Abba *f* born
Abban *m* Abbott
Abbey *f* father; joy
Abbotsen *m* Abbott; son
Abbotson *m* Abbott; son
Abbott *m* abbey; father

Abbottson *m* Abbott;
  son
Abdalla *m* God/god;
  servant
Abdel *m* son
Abdul *m* son
Abeale *f* open; protected
Abebe *f* asked
Abebi *f* asked
Abedi *m* worshiper
Abeeku *m* born
Abejide *m* born
Abel *m* breath
Abelard *m* nobly; reso-
  lute
Abelia *f* breath
Abella *f* breath
Abena *f* born
Abeni *f* asked
Abey *f* leaf
Abhin *m* cloud; differ-
  ent
Abhisar *m* companion
Abi *m* brother; elder
Abida *f* father; worships
Abigail *f* father; joy; sing;
  singer
Abijah *m* father; Lord/
  lord
Abina *f* born
Abiodun *m* born; war
Abiola *m* born; honor
Abiona *f* born; journey
Abira *f* strong
Abisha *m* father; Lord/
  lord

Abisia *m* father; Lord/lord
Abital *f* dew; father
Abixah *m* father; Lord/
  lord
Abla *f* born
Abmaba *f* born
Abner *m* father; light
Abott *m* abbey; father
Abra *f* mighty; mother
Abraham *m* father; multi-
  tude
Abram *m* lofty
Abre *f* open; protected
Abreal *f* open; protected
Abree *f* mighty
Abri *f* open; protected
Abrial *f* open; protected
Abriala *f* open; protected
Abriale *f* open; protected
Abriana *f* mighty
Abrianna *f* mighty
Abrianne *f* mighty
Abrielle *f* mighty
Abrienne *f* mighty
Absa *m* father; peace
Absalom *m* father;
  peace
Abu *m* father
Acacia *f* guileless;
  thorny
Acalia *f* instigator
Acantha *f* pointed
Acar *m* bright
Acaysha *f* guileless
Accalia *f* instigator
Ace *m* unity

Achilles *m* swift
Achintya *m* inconceivable
Achla *f* short
Achyuthan *m* indestructible
Acima *f* judge; Lord/lord
Ackerley *m* acre; dweller; meadow; oak; tree; trees
Ackley *m* dweller; meadow; oak; tree
Ada *f* adorned; birth; happy; jewel; noble; ornament; prosperous; wise
Adad *m* fertility; God/god
Adah *f* crown; God/god; ornament
Adaha *f* adorned; God/god
Adai *f* adorned; jewel
Adaiha *f* adorned; God/god
Adair *m* ford; oak; tree
Adal *f* God/god; noble; refuge
Adal *m* courageous; noble
Adala *f* God/god; noble; refuge
Adalai *m* fair
Adalard *m* brave; nobly
Adalee *f* God/god; refuge
Adali *f* God/god; refuge
Adalia *f* God/god; noble; refuge
Adaliah *f* noble
Adalie *f* God/god; refuge
Adalin *f* God/god; refuge
Adaline *f* noble
Adall *f* God/god; refuge
Adall *m* courageous
Adallard *m* brave; nobly
Adallia *f* noble
Adaly *f* God/god; refuge
Adalyn *f* God/god; refuge
Adam *m* earth; man; red
Adama *f* daughter; earth; red
Adamek *m* earth; man
Adamik *m* earth; man
Adamina *f* daughter; earth; red
Adaminah *f* earth; red
Adamma *f* beauty; child
Adams *m* Adam; son
Adamsen *m* Adam; son
Adamson *m* Adam; son
Adamsun *m* Adam; son
Adan *m* bat; earth; man; red
Adana *f* daughter; father's
Adanna *f* daughter; father's

Adanne *f* daughter; mother's
Adanya *f* daughter; father's
Adar *f* fire
Adar *m* fiery; fire; prince; ruler
Adara *f* beauty; exalted; noble; virgin
Adarsh *m* ideal
Adda *f* birth; happy; noble; ornament; prosperous
Addae *m* morning; sun
Addal *f* God/god; refuge
Addala *f* God/god; refuge
Addaly *f* God/god; refuge
Addi *f* birth; noble; ornament
Addie *f* birth; noble; ornament
Addielle *f* Lord/lord; ornament
Addis *m* Adam; son
Addison *m* Adam; earth; red; son
Addy *f* noble
Adebayo *m* happy
Adeben *m* born; son
Adeela *m* equal
Adejola *m* crown; honor
Adel *f* noble; rank
Adel *m* courageous; noble
Adela *f* noble; rank
Adelaide *f* kind; noble; rank
Adelar *m* eagle; noble
Adelard *m* nobly; resolute
Adelbern *m* bear; noble
Adelbert *m* brilliant; illustrious; noble
Adele *f* kind; noble
Adelhart *m* firm; nobly
Adelicia *f* truthful
Adelina *f* noble
Adeline *f* kind; noble
Adelita *f* noble
Adelka *f* noble
Adelle *f* noble
Adelma *f* noble; protector
Adelpha *f* sisterly
Adelpho *m* brother
Adelric *m* commander; noble
Aden *m* fiery; little
Adena *f* noble; voluptuous
Adene *f* noble
Aderes *f* cape; garment
Aderet *f* cape
Adesola *m* crown; honor
Adham *m* earth; man

Adheesh *m* king
Adhip *m* king
Adhira *f* lightning
Adhiraj *m* king
Adi *f* birth; noble; ornament
Adia *f* gift
Adiel *f* God/god; Lord/lord; noble; ornament
Adiell *f* Lord/lord; ornament
Adiella *f* God/god; noble; ornament
Adila *f* fair; just
Adin *m* ornament
Adina *f* noble; voluptuous
Adine *f* voluptuous
Adio *m* righteous
Adir *m* majestic; noble
Adira *f* powerful; strong
Adis *m* Adam; son
Adisa *m* clear
Adita *f* basket
Aditi *f* free; gods; mother
Adiv *m* gentle; pleasant
Adlai *m* fair; ornament; witness
Adlar *m* brave; noble
Adlare *m* brave; noble
Adlay *m* fair
Adlei *m* fair
Adler *m* eagle
Adley *m* fair
Adli *m* just
Adna *f* pleasure
Adnah *f* pleasure
Adnan *m* settle
Adney *m* dweller; island; noble
Adoette *f* big; tree
Adofo *m* warrior
Adolf *m* hero; noble; wolf
Adolfo *m* hero; noble; wolf
Adolph *m* hero; noble; wolf
Adolphe *m* hero; noble; wolf
Adolphus *m* hero; noble; wolf
Adom *m* blessing; God's; God/god; help
Adon *m* Lord/lord
Adonia *f* beautiful; godlike
Adonis *m* handsome; Lord/lord
Adora *f* gift; glory; renown
Adorabelle *f* beautiful; gift
Adoree *f* adored
Adorna *f* adorned; beautiful

Alair *m* alive; cheerful
Alala *f* goddess; sister; war
Alamea *f* precious; ripe
Alameda *f* cottonwood; grove; parade; tree
Alan *m* cheerful; handsome
Alana *f* air; buoyant; fair; harmonious; light; offering
Alani *f* orange; tree
Alani *m* orange; tree
Alanna *f* air; beautiful; bright; fair; harmonious; light
Alansen *m* Alan; son
Alanson *m* Alan; son
Alaqua *f* gum; sweet; tree
Alard *m* brave; firm; sacred
Alaric *m* all; noble; ruler
Alarica *f* all; ruler
Alarice *f* all; ruler
Alastair *m* avenges; defender; men
Alastar *m* avenges
Alaster *m* avenges; defender; men
Alatea *f* ivory
Alauda *f* lark
Alaula *f* dawn; glow; light
Alayne *f* beautiful; bright; fair
Alba *f* lovely; rose; white
Alba *m* blond
Alban *m* fair
Alben *m* fair
Alberic *m* ruler; wise
Albern *m* noble; warrior
Albert *m* brilliant; illustrious; noble
Alberta *f* brilliant; noble
Albertina *f* brilliant; noble
Albertine *f* brilliant; noble
Alberto *m* brilliant; illustrious; noble
Albin *m* all; fair; friend
Albina *f* blonde; white
Albinia *f* blonde; white
Albion *m* fair; white
Albric *m* ruler; wise
Alcina *f* minded; strong
Alcot *m* cottage; stone
Alcott *m* cottage; dweller; old; stone
Alda *f* gift; house; old; omen; rich; sign; winged; wise
Aldarcie *f* princess
Aldarcy *f* princess
Aldas *f* house

Alded *m* adviser
Alden *m* friend; old; protector; wise
Alder *m* alder; tree
Aldercy *f* princess
Aldin *m* friend; old; protector; wise
Aldis *f* house
Aldis *m* house; old
Aldo *m* old; wise
Aldora *f* gift; rank; superior; winged
Aldous *m* house; old
Aldred *m* adviser
Aldredge *m* king
Aldric *m* old; ruler; wise
Aldrich *m* king; old; ruler; wise
Aldridge *m* king
Aldus *m* house; old
Aldwin *m* friend; old; protector; wise
Aldwon *m* friend; old
Aldwone *m* protector
Aldwyn *m* friend; old; protector; wise
Alec *m* defender; helper; mankind
Aleda *f* beautifully; city; dress; girl; little; wholesome; winged; young
Aledis *f* friend; patient
Aleem *m* learned; wise
Aleeza *f* joy; joyful
Alein *m* alone
Alejandra *f* defender; helper
Aleka *f* defender; helper
Aleldra *f* rank; superior
Alem *m* world
Alena *f* Lenka; light; pretty
Alene *f* bearer; light
Alenson *m* Alan; son
Aleras *f* city; sea
Aleria *f* city; eagle; sea
Aleron *m* eagle; knight
Alesandra *f* defender; helper
Aleser *m* lion
Aleshanee *f* plays
Alesia *f* helper
Aleta *f* bird; girl; graceful; little; trusted; truthful; wanderer; winged
Aletea *f* truth
Aletha *f* girl; trusted; truthful
Alethea *f* girl; trusted; truthful
Aletta *f* bird; graceful; little; winged

Alette *f* little; winged
Alexa *f* defender; helper
Alexander *m* defender; helper; helps; mankind; people
Alexandra *f* defender; helper
Alexandre *m* defender; helper; mankind
Alexandrine *f* defender; helper
Alexandro *m* defender; helper; mankind
Alexia *f* truthful
Alexie *f* truthful
Alexio *m* defender; helper; mankind
Alexis *f* defender; helper
Alexis *m* defender; helper; mankind
Aleydis *f* friend
Alf *m* elfin
Alfeus *m* God/god; river
Alfonsine *f* noble
Alfonso *m* battle; eager; noble; ready
Alford *m* ancient; crossing; ford; old; river
Alfred *m* counselor; elfin; good
Alfreda *f* counselor; elf; good
Alfredo *m* counselor; elfin; good
Algar *m* noble; spearman
Alger *m* noble; spearman
Algernon *m* beard; man
Algoma *f* flowers; valley
Alhena *f* ring
Ali *f* truthful
Ali *m* greatest; Jehovah
Alica *f* truthful
Alice *f* truthful
Alicea *f* truthful
Alickina *f* defender; helper
Alida *f* beautifully; city; dress; little; noble; winged
Alidis *f* friend; patient
Alika *f* beautiful; truthful
Alike *f* truthful
Alile *f* weeps
Alim *m* learned; wise
Alima *f* dancing; learned; music
Alimah *f* dancing; learned; music
Alina *f* beautiful; bright; fair; pretty
Aline *f* bright; noble

Alinna *f* pretty
Alis *f* truthful
Alisa *f* joy; joyful; lovely; nature; truthful
Alisan *f* saint
Alise *f* truthful
Alisen *m* fame; holy
Alisha *f* truthful
Alisia *f* nature
Alison *f* famous; little; maid; saint; truthful; warrior
Alison *m* noble; son
Alissa *f* joy; joyful; truthful
Alister *m* avenges; defender; helper; mankind; men
Alita *f* bird; graceful; little; noble; truthful; winged
Alitha *f* girl; trusted; truthful
Alithia *f* truthful
Alitta *f* bird; graceful
Alix *f* truthful
Aliz *f* truthful
Alizka *f* truthful
Alka *f* defender; helper
Alkas *f* afraid
Allan *m* cheerful; handsome
Allanson *m* Alan; son
Allard *m* brave; firm; sacred
Allare *m* alive; cheerful
Allaster *m* avenges
Allcot *m* cottage; stone
Alleen *f* alone
Allegra *f* cheerful; gay
Allen *m* cheerful; handsome
Allene *f* beautiful; bright; fair
Alleras *f* city; sea
Allerie *f* city; sea
Alleris *f* city; sea
Allie *f* cheerful; truthful
Allisan *f* saint
Allison *f* famous; maid; saint; warrior
Allista *f* lovely
Allister *m* avenges; defender; men
Allon *m* oak; tree
Allveta *f* alive
Allward *m* guardian; hall; warden
Ally *f* truthful
Allyce *f* truthful
Allyn *m* cheerful; handsome
Allys *f* truthful

Alma *f* helpful; industrious; learned; nourishing; soul; spirit
Almas *f* diamond
Almaz *f* beautiful; diamond; free
Almeria *f* exalted; truth
Almeta *f* industrious
Almira *f* clothing; exalted; truth
Almire *f* exalted; truth
Almiron *m* basket
Almita *f* industrious
Almo *m* famous; noble
Almon *m* forsaken; widower
Almund *m* German
Alodee *f* prosperous; woman
Alodi *f* prosperous; woman
Alodie *f* prosperous; woman
Aloha *f* farewell
Alohi *f* brilliant; shining
Aloisa *f* famous; maid; warrior
Aloisia *f* famed; famous; fighter; maid; warrior
Aloisus *m* famous; warrior
Alon *m* oak; tree
Alona *f* oak; tree
Alonso *m* battle; eager
Alonza *f* noble
Alonzo *m* battle; eager
Alopa *f* faultless
Aloysia *f* famed; fighter
Aloysius *m* famous; warrior
Alpana *f* beautiful
Alpesh *m* tiny
Alpha *f* first
Alpheus *m* God/god; river
Alphonsa *f* aggressive Alphonsine; nature
Alphonse *m* noble; ready
Alphonsine *f* nature; noble
Alphonso *m* battle; eager; noble; ready
Alpin *m* blond
Alric *m* all; noble; ruler
Alrick *m* all; noble; ruler
Alrik *m* ruler
Alroy *m* haired; king; red; royal; youth
Alston *m* estate; noble
Alsworth *m* great
Alta *f* high; lofty
Altair *m* eagle; flying
Althaia *f* God/god; wholesome

Althea *f* God/god; wholesome
Altman *m* man; old; wise
Alton *m* dweller; estate; manor; old; town
Altsoba *f* all; war
Aludra *f* virgin
Alula *f* winged
Alumit *f* girl; secret
Alura *f* counselor; divine
Alva *f* blonde
Alva *m* blond
Alvah *m* exalted
Alvan *m* all; friend
Alvar *m* fair; white
Alver *m* fair; white
Alverta *f* brilliant; noble
Alveta *f* alive
Alvin *m* all; friend
Alvina *f* blonde; friend; noble; white
Alvis *m* all; suitor; wise
Alvita *f* alive
Alvord *m* ancient; crossing; ford; old; river
Alwin *m* all; friend
Alwyn *m* all; friend
Alyce *f* truthful
Alycia *f* truthful
Alyda *f* beautifully; city; dress
Alyose *f* famed; fighter
Alysa *f* nature
Alysia *f* nature
Alyssa *f* allyssium; flower; joy; joyful; sane
Alysson *f* sane
Alzena *f* woman
Am *f* child; lunar; moon
Ama *f* born; child
Amabel *f* beautiful; lovable; lover
Amabelle *f* beautiful; lovable; lover
Amad *m* praised
Amadas *f* devoted; Lord/lord
Amadea *f* God/god; loved
Amadeo *m* beloved; God/god
Amadi *f* rejoicing
Amadika *f* beloved
Amadis *f* devoted; Lord/lord
Amadis *m* beloved; God/god; love
Amado *m* beloved; God/god
Amadus *m* God/god; love
Amal *f* hopeful
Amal *m* clean; pure

Amala *f* prayed
Amalea *f* flattering; industrious
Amalia *f* flattering; industrious
Amaline *f* flattering; industrious
Amalita *f* flattering; industrious
Amaliya *f* beloved
Aman *m* trustworthy
Amanda *f* love; loved; worthy
Amando *m* beloved; God/god
Amara *f* beauty; eternal
Amaras *f* God/god; good; promise
Amarette *f* darling; little; lover
Amargo *f* beauty; eternal
Amari *f* God/god; good; promise
Amarillas *f* fresh; new
Amarillis *f* fresh; new
Amaris *f* God/god; good; promise
Amary *f* God/god; good; promise
Amaryl *f* fresh; new
Amaryllis *f* amaryllis; fresh; lily; new
Amasa *m* bearer; burden; heavy
Amata *f* beloved; loved
Amathist *f* birthstone; precious; stone
Amathiste *f* birthstone; precious; stone
Amaty *f* friendly; friendship
Amaui *f* thrush
Amaya *f* night
Amayeta *f* berries; big
Ambar *f* sky
Amber *f* amber; immortal; jewel
Ambika *f* mother
Ambrogio *m* divine; immortal
Ambros *m* divine; immortal
Ambrosane *f* immortal
Ambrose *m* divine; immortal
Ambrosi *m* divine; immortal
Ambrosia *f* immortal
Ambrosine *f* immortal
Ambrosio *m* divine; immortal

Ambu *f* water
Ambud *f* cloud
Amed *m* praised
Ameen *m* faithful
Ameena *f* trustworthy
Ameenah *f* trustworthy
Ameer *m* prince
Amelia *f* flattering; industrious
Amelinda *f* beloved; pretty
Amerigo *m* industrious; ruler
Amery *m* divine; famous; lover; loving; ruler
Amethist *f* birthstone; precious; stone
Amethyst *f* birthstone; precious
Ami *f* beloved; child; nectar
Amias *m* devoted; God/god
Amice *f* beloved
Amidi *f* nectar
Amie *f* beloved
Amiel *m* land; Lord/lord; people
Amil *m* inaccessible
Amilia *f* flattering; industrious
Amilinda *f* beloved; pretty
Amin *m* faithful
Amina *f* peaceful; security
Aminah *f* trustworthy
Amineh *f* faithful; trustworthy
Aminta *f* protected
Amir *f* princess
Amir *m* prince
Amira *f* speech
Amiri *m* prince
Amisa *f* truth
Amisha *f* beautiful
Amishi *f* pure
Amissa *f* friend; truth
Amita *f* truth
Amitan *m* faithful
Amitola *f* rainbow
Amity *f* friendly; friendship
Amma *f* goddess; mother
Ammadas *f* devoted; Lord/lord
Ammadis *f* devoted; Lord/lord
Ammon *m* hidden
Amnon *m* faithful
Amogh *m* unending
Amon *m* sun
Amoorta *m* formless
Amora *f* darling; little; lover

Amoreta *f* beloved; darling; little; lover
Amorette *f* darling; little; lover
Amorita *f* beloved
Amoritta *f* beloved
Amory *m* divine; famous; lover; loving; ruler
Amos *m* burden; carried
Amrusha *f* sudden
Amshula *f* sunny
Amulya *f* priceless
Amund *m* divine; protector
Amy *f* beloved; loved
Amyas *m* devoted; God/god
An *f* peace; peaceful; secure; security
An *m* peace; security
Ana *f* graceful
Anaba *f* returns; war
Anabela *f* beautiful; graceful
Anagh *m* sinless
Anagi *f* valuable
Anais *f* graceful
Anala *f* fire
Analaa *f* fire; goddess
Anan *f* clouds
Anana *f* gentle; soft
Ananda *f* bliss
Anando *m* bliss
Anant *m* infinite
Anarolio *m* east; man
Anastasia *f* resurrection
Anastasie *f* resurrection
Anastatius *m* reborn
Anatol *m* east; man
Anatole *m* east; man
Ancalin *f* fairest
Ancelin *f* fairest
Anceline *f* fairest
Anchal *f* shelter
Anda *f* going
Ande *m* pillar
Andeana *f* walker
Andee *f* womanly
Anders *m* manly; strong
Andonios *m* inestimable
Andonis *m* inestimable
Andra *f* justice; Lord/lord
Andre *m* manly; strong
Andrea *f* womanly
Andreana *f* womanly
Andreanna *f* fearless; woman
Andrej *m* manly; strong
Andres *m* manly; strong
Andrew *m* manly; strong
Andria *f* Andros; maiden; womanly

Andriana *f* womanly
Andromeda *f* justice; Lord/lord
Andromede *f* justice; Lord/lord
Andulka *f* graceful
Aneko *f* older; sister
Anela *f* angel
Anemone *f* flower; wind
Anette *f* graceful
Anevay *f* superior
Angel *m* angel; messenger; runner
Angela *f* angel; messenger
Angelica *f* angelic
Angelina *f* angel; messenger
Angeline *f* angel; messenger
Angelique *f* angelic
Angelita *f* angel; messenger
Angell *m* runner
Angelo *m* angel; messenger; runner
Angeni *f* angelic; spirit
Angus *m* choice; one; strength; unique
Ani *f* beautiful; beauty
Anica *f* morning; star
Anice *f* pure
Anika *f* face; sweetness
Aniket *m* homeless
Anil *m* air; child; wind
Anila *f* God/god; wind
Anirudh *m* boundless
Anirvan *m* undying
Anisha *f* Lord/lord
Anita *f* graceful
Aniweta *m* spirit
Aniya *f* creative
Anjika *f* blessed
Anju *f* honor; shining
Anka *m* legendary
Ankal *f* whole
Ankal *m* whole
Ankush *m* restraint
Anlon *m* great; hero
Anluan *m* great; hero
Anna *f* girl; graceful; white
Annabella *f* beautiful; graceful
Annabelle *f* beautiful; graceful
Annan *m* born; son; stream
Anne *f* graceful
Annette *f* graceful
Annia *f* grace; mercy
Annie *f* beautiful; graceful
Annis *f* complete; whole

Annora *f* grace
Annorah *f* grace
Annunciata *f* bearer; news
Anoke *m* actor
Anoki *m* actor
Anona *f* crops; year
Anora *f* grace
Anram *m* continuous
Anscom *m* awe; dweller; inspiring; valley
Anscomb *m* awe; dweller; inspiring; valley
Ansel *m* adherent; divine; helmet; nobleman
Ansela *f* God/god; protectress
Ansell *m* adherent; nobleman
Anselm *m* divine; helmet
Anselma *f* God/god; protectress
Anselme *m* divine; helmet
Anselmo *m* divine; helmet
Ansh *m* portion
Anshul *m* radiant
Anshula *f* sunny
Anshumat *m* luminous
Ansilma *f* God/god; protectress
Ansis *m* God/god; gracious
Ansley *f* meadow
Ansley *m* awe; inspiring; meadow; pasture
Anson *m* awe; inspiring; son
Anstice *f* resurrection
Anstice *m* resurrected; survives
Anstus *m* survives
Antaine *m* inestimable
Antariksh *m* space
Antariksha *f* sky
Antavas *m* inestimable
Antek *m* inestimable
Anthanasios *m* bear
Anthea *f* flower
Antheia *f* flower
Anthony *m* inestimable
Antiago *m* James
Antim *m* last
Antiman *m* condor; sun
Antinanco *m* eagle; sun
Antinko *m* inestimable
Antipas *m* father
Antoine *m* inestimable
Antoinette *f* priceless
Anton *m* inestimable
Antonetta *f* priceless
Antoni *m* inestimable
Antonia *f* priceless

Antonietta *f* priceless
Antonin *m* inestimable
Antonio *m* inestimable
Antons *m* inestimable
Antony *m* inestimable
Antos *m* inestimable
Anukriti *f* photograph
Anum *m* born; child; fighter
Anupa *f* pond
Anuva *m* knowledge
Anvesh *m* investigation
Anwar *m* brightest
Anwell *m* beloved; dear
Anwesha *f* quest
Anwyl *m* beloved; dear
Anwyll *m* beloved; dear
Anya *f* grace; mercy
Anyah *f* grace; mercy
Anyon *m* anvil
Anzu *f* apricot
Aolani *f* cloud; heavenly
Aparajita *f* undefeated
Aphra *f* deer; female
Apollo *m* beautiful; man
Aponi *f* butterfly
Apoorva *m* exquisite
Appoline *f* sun
April *f* April; born
Aquene *f* peace
Ara *f* able; altar; maiden; rainmaker
Arabela *f* altar; beautiful
Arabella *f* altar; beautiful
Arabelle *f* altar; beautiful
Araldo *m* army; ruler
Aralt *m* army; ruler
Aramanta *f* elegant; lady
Aramenta *f* elegant; lady
Araminta *f* elegant; lady
Arber *m* gardener
Archard *m* powerful; sacred
Archer *m* archer; bowman
Archerd *m* powerful; sacred
Archibald *m* bold; noble; sacred
Archibaldo *m* bold; noble; sacred
Arda *f* fervent; field; flowering; garden; girl
Ardal *m* courageous; highly
Ardath *f* field; flowering
Ardeen *f* ardent; enthusiasm; warmth
Ardel *m* dell
Ardelia *f* enthusiasm; fervent; warmth
Ardell *m* dell

Ardella *f* enthusiasm; fervent; warmth
Ardelle *f* enthusiasm; fervent; warmth
Arden *f* eagle; valley
Arden *m* ardent; eager; fiery; sincere
Ardene *f* enthusiasm; fervent; warmth
Ardenia *f* eagle; valley
Ardeth *f* field; flowering
Ardin *m* ardent; eager; fiery; sincere
Ardine *f* enthusiasm; warmth
Ardis *f* fervent
Ardith *f* field; flowering
Ardley *m* home; lover's; meadow
Ardolph *m* home; loving; wolf
Ardon *m* bronze
Areef *m* intelligent; wise
Areehah *m* destroyer; enemies
Arel *m* God/god; lion
Arela *f* angel; messenger
Areli *m* God/god; lion
Arella *f* angel; messenger
Arelus *m* friend; golden
Aren *m* eagle; rule
Areta *f* friend
Arete *f* graceful; lovely
Aretha *f* best
Aretina *f* friend
Aretta *f* friend
Arette *f* friend
Argenta *f* silvery
Argile *m* belonging; Ireland
Argus *m* guardian; watchful
Argyle *m* belonging; Ireland
Ari *f* silver
Ari *m* lion
Aria *f* melody; rainmaker
Ariadne *f* holy
Ariana *f* holy; pleasing; silver
Ariane *f* holy; silver
Arianna *f* holy
Arianne *f* silver
Aribold *m* addition; welcome
Aric *m* ruler; sacred
Arica *f* loving; peace; ruler
Arice *f* joyful; young
Ariel *f* God/god; lioness
Ariella *f* God/god; lioness
Arielle *f* God/god; lioness

Aries *m* ram
Arif *m* intelligent; wise
Arihan *m* enemies
Arihant *m* destroyer; enemies
Arindam *m* destroyer; enemies
Ario *m* warlike
Arissa *f* happy
Arista *f* harvest
Aristotle *m* great; thinker
Arita *f* bird; field; motherly; rice
Arius *m* immortal
Ariza *f* cedar
Arjit *m* earned
Arkin *m* eternal; king's/ kings; son
Arledge *m* dweller; hare; lake; rabbit
Arleen *f* pledge
Arlen *m* pledge
Arlena *f* pledge
Arlene *f* pledge
Arleta *f* pledge
Arlette *f* pledge
Arley *m* bowman; hare; hunter; meadow; pasture; rabbit
Arline *f* pledge
Arlo *m* barberry; protected; town
Arlyne *f* pledge
Armalda *f* battle; maiden
Armalla *f* bracelet; small
Arman *m* armed
Armand *m* armed; army; man; warrior
Armando *m* armed; army; man; warrior
Armani *m* castle
Armelda *f* battle; maiden
Armida *f* armed; little
Armilda *f* battle; maiden
Armilla *f* bracelet; small
Armillas *f* bracelet; small
Armillda *f* battle; maiden
Armillia *f* bracelet; small
Armin *m* armed; army; man
Armina *f* maid; warrior
Armine *f* maid; warrior
Armino *m* army; man; soldier
Armon *m* castle
Armond *m* armed
Armoni *m* castle
Armstrong *m* arm; strong
Arna *f* cedar; tree
Arnalda *f* eagle; ruler
Arnaldo *m* eagle; ruler

Arnall *m* eagle; gracious
Arnatt *m* eagle; little
Arnaud *m* eagle; ruler
Arne *m* eagle; powerful
Arnell *m* eagle; gracious
Arnett *m* eagle; little
Arnice *f* cedar; tree
Arnina *f* inspired; messenger; mountain; singer
Arnit *f* cedar; tree
Arno *m* eagle; wolf
Arnold *m* eagle; ruler
Arnoldo *m* eagle; ruler
Arnon *m* eagle; rushing; strength; wolf
Arnot *m* eagle; little
Arnott *m* little
Arnoux *m* eagle; wolf
Arola *f* sea
Aron *m* exalted; lofty
Arondel *m* dell
Arondell *m* dell
Arpad *m* wanderer
Arpiar *m* sunny
Arria *f* rainmaker
Arrio *m* warlike
Arsanio *m* masculine; virile
Arsemio *m* masculine; virile
Arsenio *m* masculine; virile
Arshad *m* devout; pious
Arslan *m* lion
Art *m* Artemis; gift; goddess
Arta *f* angels; sound
Artair *m* bear; noble
Artamas *f* angels; sound
Artana *f* foes
Artegal *m* courageous; highly
Artek *m* bear
Artema *f* angels; sound
Artemas *f* angels; sound
Artemas *m* Artemis; gift; goddess
Artemisa *f* vigorous
Artemisia *f* vigorous
Artemus *m* Artemis; gift; goddess
Artha *f* wealth; worldly
Arthgallo *m* courageous; highly
Arthua *f* prosperity
Arthur *m* bear; noble
Artima *f* angels; sound
Artimas *f* angels; sound
Artimas *m* Artemis; gift; goddess
Artimis *m* Artemis; gift; goddess

Aurelia *f* golden
Aurelian *m* golden; haired
Aurelio *m* golden; haired
Aurelius *m* friend; golden; haired
Auria *f* breeze; gentle
Auriel *f* golden
Aurita *f* dark; girl
Aurora *f* daybreak
Aurore *f* dawn; daybreak
Austen *m* Augustus; belonging; exalted; venerable
Austin *f* Augustus; belonging
Austin *m* Augustus; belonging; exalted; venerable
Austine *f* little; majestic
Auston *m* exalted
Ava *f* birdlike
Avan *m* proud
Avaneesh *m* earth; master
Avani *f* earth; good
Avaria *f* born; early; spring
Avashesh *m* remainder
Avatar *m* incarnation
Avel *m* breath
Avena *f* oatfield
Avenall *m* dweller; field
Avenel *m* dweller; field
Avenell *m* dweller; field
Avera *f* born; early; spring; transgressor
Averell *m* April; born
Averil *m* April; born
Averill *f* April; born
Averill *m* April; born
Avery *m* elf; ruler
Averyl *f* April; born
Avi *m* father
Avice *f* warlike
Avidan *m* father; God/god; just; justice
Avidor *m* father
Aviel *m* father; God/god
Avijit *m* invincible
Avinash *m* indestructible
Avinashi *m* indestructible
Aviral *m* continuous
Avirat *m* continuous
Avis *f* birdlike; warlike
Avital *f* dew; father
Avital *m* dew; father
Aviv *m* spring
Aviva *f* spring
Avivah *f* spring
Avkash *m* limitless; space
Avner *m* father; light
Avniel *m* father; rock; strength

Avra *f* Lord/lord; rock
Avrel *m* golden; haired
Avreliy *m* golden; haired
Avril *f* April; born
Avrill *f* April; born
Awan *m* somebody
Awanata *f* turtle
Awendela *f* day; early
Awenita *f* fawn
Axel *m* father; man; peace; reward
Axell *m* divine; reward
Axton *m* stone; sword
Ayako *f* colorful
Ayame *f* flower; iris
Ayasha *f* life
Ayelen *f* clear; happiness
Ayelet *f* deer; gazelle
Ayiana *f* bloom; eternal
Ayita *f* worker
Aylen *f* clear; happiness
Aylmer *m* famous; noble
Aylsworth *m* great
Aylward *m* awe; guardian; inspiring; noble
Aylworth *m* awe; inspiring
Ayo *m* happiness
Ayoka *f* joy
Ayush *m* long-lived
Azad *m* born; free
Azalea *f* blossom; flower
Azaleah *f* blossom; flower
Azami *f* flower; thistle
Azaria *f* blessed; God/god
Azarria *f* blessed; God/god
Azeem *m* defender
Azelia *f* God/god
Azeria *f* blessed; God/god
Azi *m* youth
Azim *m* defender
Aziz *m* beloved; powerful
Aziza *f* precious
Azize *f* dear; precious; rare
Azizi *m* beloved; precious
Azrae *m* angel; Lord/lord
Azriel *m* angel; Lord/lord
Azura *f* blue; sky

Ba *f* grandmother; three
Ba *m* poison; three
Baakir *m* eldest
Baasima *m* smiling
Bab *f* gateway
Baba *f* born
Babara *f* stranger
Babbette *f* lovely; stranger
Babete *f* lovely; stranger
Babette *f* gateway
Babita *f* lovely; stranger

Babu *m* grandfather
Badal *m* cloud
Badar *m* full; moon
Badrani *m* full; moon
Badria *f* moonlike
Badru *m* moon
Baer *m* bear
Bahari *m* seaman
Bahula *m* star
Bailby *m* indirect; speaker
Bailey *m* able; bailiff; steward
Bailie *m* bailiff; steward
Baily *m* bailiff; steward
Bainbridge *m* bridge; sea; water; white
Baird *m* ballad; fiery; hair; poet; redhead; singer
Baka *f* crane
Bakula *f* bakula; flower
Balachandar *m* moon; young
Balaniki *f* fair; white
Balaraj *m* strong
Balas *m* lisps
Balasz *m* lisps
Balbina *f* little
Balbir *m* strong
Balbo *m* indirect; speaker
Baldemar *m* bold; famous; princely
Balder *m* army; bold
Baldev *m* strong
Baldric *m* bold; princely; ruler
Balduin *m* bold; friend; protector
Baldur *m* army; bold
Baldwin *m* bold; friend; protector
Balendu *m* moon; young
Balfore *m* meadow
Balfour *m* meadow
Bali *m* mighty; soldier
Balin *m* mighty; soldier
Ballard *m* bold; strong
Ballas *m* lisps
Baltasar *m* king; Lord/lord; protect
Balthasar *m* battle; king; Lord/lord; protect; wise
Balthazar *m* battle; king; wise
Bambi *f* child
Banan *m* white
Bancroft *m* bean; field
Bandhu *m* friend
Bandhul *m* pleasing
Bane *m* consolation; son
Baneet *m* polite
Banhi *f* fire

Bankim *m* straight
Banna *f* adorn; anything; dress; ornament; year
Banning *m* blond; little
Bansari *f* flute
Banshi *m* flute
Bansi *m* flute
Baptista *f* baptized; God's
Barabas *m* loyal; son
Barabbas *m* loyal; son
Baram *m* nation; son
Barb *f* gateway
Barbara *f* gateway; lovely; stranger
Barbette *f* lovely; stranger
Barclay *m* birch; dweller; meadow; tree
Bard *m* ballad; poet; singer
Barde *m* poet; singer
Barden *m* boar's; near
Bardolf *m* axe; wolf
Bardolph *m* axe; wolf
Bardou *m* axe; wolf
Bardoul *m* axe; wolf
Bardrick *m* axe; ruler
Barid *m* cloud
Barika *f* bloom
Barindra *m* ocean
Barkha *f* rain
Barlow *m* bare; boar's; dweller; hill
Barnabas *m* consolation; son
Barnaby *m* consolation; son
Barnard *m* bear; brave
Barnett *m* leader; nobleman
Barney *m* bear; brave; consolation; son
Barnum *m* home; nobleman's
Baron *m* blood; noble; nobleman; warrior
Barr *m* blood; gateway; noble
Barret *m* bear; mighty
Barrett *m* bear; mighty
Barris *m* Harry; son
Barron *m* blood; noble; nobleman; warrior
Barry *m* pointed
Barsaat *m* rain; welcome
Barsha *f* rain
Bart *m* forthright; noble
Bartel *m* farmer; son
Barthel *m* farmer; son
Bartholomaus *m* farmer; son
Bartholomew *m* farmer; son

Barthram *m* glorious; raven
Bartkus *m* farmer; son
Bartley *m* Bart's; meadow
Barton *m* barley; estate; farmstead
Bartram *m* bright; famous; glorious; raven
Baruch *m* doer; good
Barun *m* Lord/lord; sea
Baruti *m* teacher
Basant *m* season; spring
Basdev *m* fire
Basil *m* kingly; magnificent
Basile *m* kingly; magnificent
Basilia *f* queenly; regal
Basilio *m* kingly; magnificent
Basilius *m* kingly; magnificent
Basimah *f* smiling
Basir *m* discerning; intelligence; intelligent
Bathelda *f* battle; maid
Bathesda *f* fountain
Bathesde *f* fountain
Bathilda *f* battle; maid
Bathsheb *f* daughter; vow
Bathsheba *f* daughter; vow
Batini *f* innermost
Batuk *m* boy
Batya *f* daughter; God/god
Baudier *m* army; bold
Baudoin *m* bold; friend; protector
Baudric *m* bold; princely; ruler
Baul *m* snail
Bavol *m* air; wind
Bay *m* born; child; seventh
Bayard *m* fiery; hair; redhead
Bayley *m* bailiff; steward
Beacan *m* tiny
Beagan *m* tiny
Bearchan *m* little; spear
Beard *m* fiery; hair; redhead
Beata *f* blessed; happy
Beathan *m* hand; right; son
Beatrice *f* girl; happy
Beatrix *f* girl; happy
Beau *m* beautiful; fortress; handsome
Beaufert *m* beautiful; fortress
Beaufort *m* beautiful; fortress

Beaumont *m* beautiful; mountain
Beauregard *m* handsome
Beauvais *m* fair
Becan *m* tiny
Becca *f* borrow; forecast; half; predict; sister
Beck *m* brook
Beda *f* maiden; warrior
Bedad *m* lonely
Bedelia *f* mighty
Bedrich *m* peaceful; ruler
Bega *f* bee
Begga *f* bee
Behira *f* brilliant; clear; light
Beka *f* half; sister
Bekah *f* half; sister
Bekka *f* half; sister
Bela *f* creeper; fair; time; white
Bela *m* city
Belda *f* lovely; woman
Belden *m* beautiful; dweller; glen; valley
Beldon *m* beautiful; dweller; glen
Belen *m* arrow
Belia *f* pillar; pointed; rich
Belicia *f* dedicated; God/god
Belinda *f* beautiful; pretty
Belisa *f* slender
Bell *f* beautiful
Bella *f* altar; beautiful
Bellamy *m* beautiful; friend; good; handsome
Bellanca *f* blonde
Bellaude *f* beauty; lady
Bellda *f* lovely; woman
Belldame *f* lovely; woman
Belldas *f* lovely; woman
Belle *f* altar; beautiful; graceful; lovely; pretty; woman
Bello *m* assistant; helper
Belloma *f* goddess; war; warlike
Belva *f* beautiful
Belvia *f* beautiful
Bem *m* peace
Ben *m* son
Bena *f* pheasant
Bendix *m* blessed
Beneba *f* born
Benedetta *f* blessed
Benedetto *m* blessed
Benedict *m* blessed
Benedicta *f* blessed
Benedicto *m* blessed
Benedikta *f* blessed

Benigna *f* gentle; gracious; kind
Benilda *f* good
Benildas *f* good
Benildis *f* good
Benita *f* blessed
Benito *m* blessed
Benjamin *m* hand; right; son
Benn *m* son
Bennet *m* blessed
Bennett *m* blessed; little
Benoit *m* blessed
Benon *m* family; good; well-born
Benoni *m* son; sorrow
Benquasha *f* Ben; daughter
Benson *m* Benjamin; son
Bentley *m* meadow
Bently *m* meadow
Benton *m* bent; farm; grass
Benzi *m* excellent; son
Beora *f* torch
Beore *f* torch
Bercan *m* little; spear
Berdine *f* glorious
Berdy *m* brilliant; mind; spirit
Berengaria *f* bear; maid; spear
Berenice *f* harbinger; victory
Beresford *m* barley; ford
Beret *f* resolute; strength
Berg *m* mountain; stream
Bergen *m* dweller; mountain
Berger *m* shepherd
Berget *f* resolute; strength
Bergren *m* mountain; stream
Berk *m* dweller; firm; fortress
Berke *m* dweller; fortress
Berkeley *m* birch; dweller; meadow; tree
Berlinda *f* beauty; lady
Berlyn *f* beauty; lady
Bern *m* bear
Bernadene *f* bear; brave
Bernadette *f* bear; brave; little; masterful; strong
Bernadine *f* bear; brave
Bernard *m* bear; brave
Bernardena *f* bear; brave
Bernardo *m* bear; brave
Berne *m* bear
Bernhard *m* bear; brave
Bernia *f* battle; maid
Bernice *f* harbinger; victory

Bernita *f* bear; brave
Berry *m* manor; servant
Bersh *m* one; year
Bert *m* bright; brilliant; fame; glorious; mind; radiant; shining; soul; spirit
Berta *f* brilliantly; famous; glorious; learning; shining; woman
Bertha *f* beautiful; bright; glorious; shining
Berthe *f* glorious; shining
Berthold *m* brilliant; ruler
Bertila *f* kind; shy
Bertilde *f* battle; maid; shining
Bertilla *f* kind; shy
Bertin *m* distinguished; friend
Berto *m* brilliant; illustrious; noble
Bertold *m* brilliant; ruler
Bertoldi *m* brilliant; ruler
Berton *m* brilliant; estate
Bertoud *m* brilliant; ruler
Bertrade *f* counselor; shining
Bertram *m* bright; brilliant; famous; raven
Bertrand *m* brilliant; raven
Berty *m* brilliant; illustrious; noble
Berwick *m* barley; fields
Berwin *m* friend; harvest
Beryl *f* green; jewel; sea
Beryl *m* Burleigh; town
Beta *f* dedicated; God/god
Bethany *f* house
Bethel *f* God/god; house
Bethena *f* house
Bethesda *f* fountain
Bethezel *f* good; home
Bethina *f* house
Bethseda *f* house; mercy
Beti *f* little; small
Betserai *m* help
Betthel *f* good; home
Bettzel *f* good; home
Betula *f* girl; maiden
Beula *f* married
Beulah *f* married
Beuna *f* good
Beval *m* wind
Bevan *m* Evan; son
Beverly *f* beaver; dweller; meadow
Bevin *f* lady; melodious
Bevin *m* Evan; son
Bevis *m* archer; fair; renowned
Bevus *m* archer; renowned

Bhagat *m* devotee
Bhajan *m* adoration
Bhanu *f* flame
Bhavesh *m* Lord/lord; world
Bhavi *f* emotional
Bhavika *f* cheerful
Bhavini *f* emotional
Bheru *m* friend
Biagio *m* lisps
Bian *f* hidden
Bianca *f* fair; white
Bibi *f* lady
Bijal *m* lightning
Billie *f* resolution
Bimal *m* pure
Bimb *m* halo
Bina *f* dance; fruits; intelligence; understanding
Binah *f* dance; dancer
Binetta *f* fame; little
Binette *f* fame; little
Bing *m* hollow
Binita *f* modest
Bink *m* bank; dweller; slope
Binta *f* God/god
Binti *f* daughter
Birch *m* birch; tree
Birdie *f* birdlike; little
Birgitta *f* strength
Birju *m* nice; singer
Birk *m* birch; tree
Birkett *m* birch; dweller; headland
Birkey *m* birch; island; tree
Birley *m* cattle; meadow
Birney *m* brook; dweller; island
Bisa *f* greatly; loved
Bishop *m* bishop
Bithia *f* given; God/god
Bitski *f* plant
Bitthia *f* given; God/god
Bjorn *m* bear; brave
Black *m* dark
Blade *m* glory; prosperity
Blagden *m* dark; valley
Blaine *m* lean; thin
Blair *m* field; plain
Blaise *f* lisps
Blaise *m* lisps
Blaisot *m* lisps
Blake *m* black; dark
Blakeley *m* black; meadow
Blakey *m* fair; little
Blanca *f* blonde; fair; white
Blanche *f* fair; white
Blanco *m* blond; white
Blane *m* lean; thin

Blanford *m* crossing; gray; haired; river
Blasi *m* lisps
Blasia *f* firebrand
Blasius *m* lisps
Blayne *m* lean; thin
Blaze *f* lisps
Blaze *m* lisps
Blazek *m* lisps
Blessing *f* consecrated
Blinnie *f* fair; white
Bliss *f* joy
Blithe *f* cheerful; joyful
Blom *f* flower
Blossom *f* fresh; lovely
Blum *f* flower
Bluma *f* flower
Bly *f* high
Blythe *f* cheerful; joyful
Bo *f* house; precious
Bo *m* householder
Boas *m* Lord/lord; strength
Boase *m* Lord/lord; strength
Boaz *m* Lord/lord; strength; strong; swift
Bobar *m* beaver
Bobbette *f* fame; shining
Bobina *f* brilliantly; famous
Boden *m* herald; messenger
Bodhan *m* kindling
Bodil *m* commanding
Bodua *m* animal's; tail
Bogart *m* bow; strong
Bogdan *m* ruler; world
Bogdashka *m* ruler; world
Bohdan *m* ruler; world
Bohdana *f* given
Bolten *m* farm
Bolton *m* farm
Bona *f* builder
Bonar *m* courteous; gentle; good; kind
Bond *m* soil; tiller
Bonde *m* soil; tiller
Bondon *m* soil; tiller
Bonds *m* soil; tiller
Boniface *m* doer; good
Bonita *f* pretty
Bonnie *f* good
Boone *m* good
Booth *m* dweller; herald
Boothe *m* dweller; herald
Borden *m* boar; boar's; near; valley
Borg *m* castle; dweller
Boris *m* battler; fighter; stranger

Borlow *m* bare; boar's; dweller; hill
Bornani *m* soldier; strong; warrior
Bosse *m* householder
Boswell *m* forest; town
Bosworth *m* cattle; enclosure
Botan *m* peony
Botolf *m* herald; wolf
Bour *m* rock
Bourey *m* country
Bourke *m* dweller; fortress
Bourne *m* brook
Bowen *m* little; Owen; son; victorious; warrior
Bowie *m* haired; yellow
Boyce *m* dweller; forest; woodland
Boyd *m* blond
Boyden *m* herald
Boyne *m* cow; white
Brad *m* broad; spring; sun; valley; village; wide
Bradburn *m* broad; brook
Braden *m* sun; valley; village; wide
Bradford *m* broad; crossing; river
Bradi *f* broad; eye; island
Bradie *f* broad; eye; island
Bradley *m* broad; meadow
Bradshaw *m* broad; field; forest
Bradwell *m* broad; spring
Brady *f* broad; eye; island
Brady *m* broad; island; spirited
Braedy *f* broad; eye; island
Brahma *m* Creator; universe
Brainard *m* bold; fierce; raven
Bram *m* bramblebush; father; multitude; raven; spring; well
Bramwell *m* bramblebush; spring; well
Bran *m* raven
Brand *m* burned; clearing; dweller; firebrand
Brandee *f* burn; wine
Brandeis *m* burned; clearing
Brander *m* firebrand; sword
Brandi *f* burn; wine
Brandie *f* burn; wine
Brandon *m* aflame; beacon; hill
Brandt *m* burned; clearing; dweller

Brandubh *m* black; raven
Branduff *m* black; raven
Brandy *f* burn; wine
Brannon *m* aflame
Brant *m* burned; clearing; dweller; firebrand
Brawley *m* hillslope; meadow
Braydee *f* broad; eye; island
Braynard *m* fierce; raven
Braz *m* lisps
Brede *m* glacier
Brencis *m* crowned; laurel
Brenda *f* little; raven
Brendan *m* aflame; little; raven
Brendon *m* aflame
Brenna *f* forceful; raven; strong
Brennan *m* aflame
Brent *m* high; hill; steep
Brenton *m* hill; steep
Bret *m* Briton
Brett *m* Briton
Brewer *m* brewer
Brewster *m* brewer
Brian *m* strength; virtue
Briana *f* mighty; strength; woman
Brianna *f* mighty; strength; strong; woman
Briant *m* strength; virtue
Brice *f* brave; strong
Brice *m* ambitious; quick
Bridger *m* bridge; builder; dweller
Bridget *f* resolute; strength
Bridgette *f* resolute; strength
Brien *m* strength; virtue
Brier *f* flower; heather
Brietta *f* resolute; strength
Brigham *m* bridge; dweller
Brigid *f* protective; resolute; strength; strong
Brigida *f* resolute; strength
Brigitte *f* resolute; strength
Brin *f* hills
Brin *m* hill
Brina *f* protector
Brinn *f* hills
Brinn *m* hill
Brirar *m* pain
Brishen *m* born; rain
Brita *f* resolute; strength
Brock *m* badger
Brockley *m* badger; meadow

Broderick *m* broad; fame; famous; rich; ridge; ruler
Brodie *m* beard; ditch; man; place
Brodny *m* crossing; stream
Brody *m* beard; ditch; man; place
Bromleigh *m* broom; dweller; meadow
Bromley *m* broom; dweller; meadow
Bron *m* origin
Brona *f* victory
Brone *m* sorrow
Bronson *m* brown; son
Bronte *f* thunder
Bronwen *f* bosom; white
Brooke *f* brook; dweller
Brooks *m* brook; dweller; dwells; stream
Brosine *f* immortal
Brosnan *m* Brosna; dweller; river
Brougher *m* fortress; resident
Broughton *m* fortress; town
Bruce *m* brewer; dweller; thicket
Brunetta *f* brunette
Brunhilda *f* armored; maid; warrior
Bruno *m* brown-haired; haired
Bruns *m* brown-haired; dark
Bryan *m* strength; virtue
Bryant *m* proud; strength; strong; virtue
Bryce *f* brave; strong
Bryce *m* ambitious
Bryn *f* hills
Bryn *m* hill
Bryna *f* honor; strength; virtue
Bryne *f* hills
Brynmor *m* estate; great
Brynn *f* hills
Brynna *f* protector
Brynne *f* hills
Bryon *m* strength; virtue
Bua *f* amulet; charm; hammer
Buck *m* buck; deer
Buckley *m* buck; deer; dweller; meadow
Bud *m* herald; messenger; winner
Budd *m* herald; messenger; winner
Buddy *m* winner

Budhil *m* learned
Bukeda *f* pretty
Bundy *m* free; man
Bunme *f* gift
Bunmi *f* gift
Buns *m* haired
Burbank *m* castle; dweller; hill; slope
Burch *m* birch; tree
Burchard *m* castle; strong
Burdett *m* little; shield
Burdon *m* castle; dweller; hill
Burford *m* castle; dweller; ford
Burgard *m* castle; strong
Burgaud *m* castle; strong
Burgess *m* citizen; fortified; town
Burk *m* dweller; fortress
Burke *m* castle; dweller; fortress; stronghold
Burkett *m* little; stronghold
Burkhart *m* castle; strong
Burl *m* bearer; Burleigh; town
Burleigh *m* castle; dweller; meadow
Burley *m* Burleigh; castle; dweller; meadow; town
Burnaby *m* estate; warrior
Burnard *m* bear; brave
Burne *m* brook
Burnell *m* brown-haired; haired; little
Burnett *m* brown-complected; little
Burney *m* brook; dweller; island
Burr *m* youth
Burrell *m* brown; reddish
Burton *m* dweller; fortified; town
Busby *m* dweller; thicket; village
Byford *m* crossing; dweller; river
Byram *m* ancient; cow
Byrd *m* birdlike
Byrne *m* brook
Byron *m* cottage; country; estate

Cacia *f* guileless
Cadal *m* military
Cadao *m* ballad; song
Cadby *m* settlement; warrior
Caddock *m* battle

Cade *m* barrel; cask
Cadel *m* military
Cadell *m* battle; spirit
Cadena *f* rhythmic
Cadence *f* rhythmic
Cadman *m* battle; brave; man; warrior
Cadmann *m* brave; warrior
Cadmar *m* brave; sailor
Cadmarr *m* brave; sailor
Cadmus *m* east; man
Cady *f* battle
Caesar *m* born; hair; leader; long
Caesaria *f* leader; woman
Caffar *m* helmet
Cahil *m* inexperienced; young
Cai *f* female
Cailin *f* girl; maiden
Cain *m* bright; clear; possessed; water
Caitlin *f* pure
Calandra *f* lark
Calantha *f* beautiful; blossom
Calder *m* brook; river
Caldwell *m* cold; spring
Cale *m* bold; slender; thin
Caleb *m* bold
Caledonia *f* Scotland
Calen *m* slender; thin
Calendra *f* lark
Caley *m* slender; thin
Calfuray *f* flower; violet
Calhoun *m* forest; narrow
Calia *f* instigator
Calida *f* loving; warm
Calie *f* instigator
Calin *m* slender; thin
Calise *f* lovely
Calista *f* lovely
Calla *f* beautiful
Callaghan *m* belligerent; small
Callahan *m* belligerent; small
Callantha *f* beautiful; blossom
Callie *f* beautiful; blossom
Callister *m* Alexander; son
Callula *f* beautiful; little
Calondra *f* lark
Caltha *f* flower; yellow
Calvert *m* herdsman
Calvin *m* bald
Calvina *f* bright; haired
Calvinna *f* bright; haired
Calvino *m* bald
Calypso *f* concealer
Cam *f* orange; sweetness

Cam *m* beloved
Camden *m* crooked; valley; winding
Cameo *f* jewel
Camerero *m* chamberlain; monastery; worker
Cameron *m* crooked; wry
Camila *f* attendant; young
Camilla *f* attendant; young
Camille *f* attendant; young
Camlo *m* amiable; dew; lovely; sweet
Campball *m* bright; field
Campbell *m* bright; crooked; field; mouth; wry
Canace *f* daughter; wind
Candace *f* glittering; glowing; white
Candee *f* glittering; glowing; white
Candenza *f* rhythmic
Candice *f* glittering; glowing; white
Candida *f* bright; white
Candide *f* bright; white
Candra *f* luminescent; moon
Canica *f* children; gentle
Canice *f* children; gentle
Canna *f* clear; deny; purposeful
Cannice *f* children; gentle
Canute *m* knot
Caolinn *f* slender
Cappi *m* fortune; good; profit
Caprice *f* fanciful
Cara *f* beloved; dear; diamond; friend; jewel; precious
Cardew *m* black; fort
Caresse *f* endearing
Carew *m* fortress
Carey *m* castle; dweller
Cari *f* flows; water
Carina *f* beloved; dear; friend; pure
Carine *f* beloved; dear; friend
Carisa *f* dearest; little
Carissa *f* beloved; dear; dearest; little
Carita *f* beloved; charity; dear; generosity; girl
Carl *m* city; manly; strong
Carla *f* little; strong; womanly
Carleas *f* cheerful; good; heart
Carlene *f* little; womanly

Carleton *m* Carl's; farm; farmer's; settlement
Carli *f* little; womanly
Carlin *m* champion; little
Carlina *f* little; womanly
Carline *f* little; womanly
Carling *m* champion; little
Carlisle *m* castle; city; tower
Carlita *f* little; womanly
Carlo *m* manly; strong
Carlos *m* manly; strong
Carlota *f* little; womanly
Carlotta *f* little; womanly
Carlton *m* Carl's; farm; farmer's; settlement
Carlyle *m* city
Carma *f* destiny; fate; garden; God's; vineyard
Carmel *f* farm; garden; God's; vineyard
Carmela *f* garden; God's; vineyard
Carmeli *f* farm; garden; vineyard
Carmelina *f* garden; God's; vineyard
Carmelita *f* garden; God's; vineyard
Carmen *f* crimson; song
Carmencita *f* crimson
Carmi *f* farm; garden; vineyard
Carmia *f* farm; garden; vineyard
Carmichael *m* friend; stronghold
Carmiel *f* farm; vineyard
Carmina *f* song
Carmine *f* song
Carmita *f* song
Carna *f* horn
Carnay *m* soldier; valiant
Carney *m* soldier; valiant; victorious
Carniela *f* horn
Carniella *f* horn
Carnis *f* horn
Carnit *f* horn
Carny *m* victorious
Carol *f* little; strong; womanly
Carolina *f* little; womanly
Caroline *f* little; womanly
Carolinn *f* fair
Carollan *m* champion; little
Caron *f* pure
Carr *m* dweller; fortress; marsh
Carrew *m* fortress

Carrick *m* headland; rocky
Carrie *f* beloved
Carrita *f* generosity; girl
Carroll *m* champion
Carson *m* Carr; dweller; fort; marsh; son
Carswell *m* dweller; spring
Cart *m* cart; maker
Carter *m* cart; driver; maker
Cartland *m* land; stream
Carvel *m* estate; marshy; song; spearman
Carvell *m* estate; marshy; spearman
Carver *m* carver
Carvey *m* athlete; game; player
Cary *f* beloved
Cary *m* castle; dweller
Caryl *f* beloved; strong; womanly
Casandra *f* helper; men
Case *m* dwelling; home; place
Casey *f* brave; guileless
Casey *m* brave; valorous; watchful
Cash *m* vain
Casia *f* guileless; persuasive
Casiah *f* persuasive
Casie *f* brave; guileless
Casilda *f* solitary
Casilde *f* solitary
Casimir *m* commands; peace
Casimiro *m* commands; peace
Casina *f* Casina
Caspar *m* master; treasure
Casper *m* master; treasure
Cass *m* vain
Cassa *f* child; earth
Cassandra *f* helper; men
Cassia *f* persuasive
Cassidy *m* clever; curly; haired; ingenious
Cassil *f* solitary
Cassilda *f* solitary
Cassius *m* vain
Casta *f* girl; modest; pious; pure; treasure
Castara *f* girl; treasure
Castel *m* belonging; castle
Castellan *m* castle
Castera *f* girl; treasure
Castor *m* beaver
Castora *f* girl; treasure
Cata *m* anything; carve; catfish; daylight; grasp; lizard; nut; salty

Catharine *f* pure
Catherine *f* pure
Cathmor *m* great; warrior
Catima *f* reed; slender
Cato *m* wise
Caton *m* wise
Catriona *f* pure
Cattima *f* reed; slender
Catto *m* wise
Catton *m* wise
Cavan *m* handsome
Cavell *m* active; little
Cavil *m* aggressive; warrior
Cavill *m* aggressive; warrior
Cawley *m* ancestral
Cayce *m* dwelling; home; place
Cayla *f* pure
Cayse *m* dwelling; home; place
Caz *m* vain
Ceara *f* spear
Cecil *m* blind
Cecile *f* blind
Cecilia *f* blind
Cedric *m* battle
Celandine *f* swallow
Celene *f* heavenly; moon
Celesta *f* heavenly
Celeste *f* heavenly
Celestina *f* heavenly
Celia *f* blind; heavenly
Celie *f* blind
Celin *f* fairest
Celina *f* heavenly; moon
Celinda *f* heavenly; moon
Celine *f* fairest
Cella *f* free
Celosia *f* burning; flaming
Cemal *m* handsome
Cenon *m* living
Ceporah *f* bird
Cerallua *f* fruitful; spring; woman
Cerelia *f* fruitful; spring; woman
Cerella *f* spring
Cerellia *f* fruitful; spring; woman
Cerelly *f* fruitful; spring; woman
Cerf *m* deer
Cerise *f* cherry
Cesar *m* born; hair; leader; long
Cesare *m* born; hair; leader; long
Cesaria *f* leader; woman
Chaaya *f* shadow
Chacha *m* strong

Chad *m* protector; warlike
Chadburn *m* brook; wildcat
Chadwick *m* estate; protector; town; warrior
Chaim *m* life
Chaimek *m* life
Chaitan *m* consciousness
Chaitanya *m* consciousness
Chal *m* boy; lad; son
Chalmers *m* chamberlain; overseer; son
Cham *m* hard; worker
Chamaran *f* black; girl
Chan *f* sweet; tree
Chan *m* correct; old; true
Chance *m* fortune; good
Chancellor *m* king's/kings
Chanchal *m* active
Chand *m* moon
Chanda *f* goddess; great
Chandak *m* moon
Chandal *f* song
Chandan *m* holy; sandalwood; tree
Chandell *f* candle
Chandelle *f* candle
Chander *m* moon
Chandi *f* angry
Chandler *m* candler; maker
Chandra *f* moon; moonlike
Chandra *m* moon
Chandraki *f* peacock
Chandran *m* moonlight
Chane *m* cub; leaf; little; plant; wolf
Chanel *f* canal; dweller
Chanelle *f* canal; dweller
Chaney *m* oak; wood
Chang *m* bow; constantly; free; mountain; open; smooth
Channa *f* chickpea
Channe *m* cub; little; wolf
Channelle *f* canal; dweller
Channing *m* canon; church; cub; dignitary; knowing; little; wolf
Channon *m* cub; little; wolf
Chantal *f* place; song
Chantalle *f* song
Chapal *m* clever; lightning; restless
Chapell *m* chapel; man; pious
Chapen *m* chaplain; God/god; man
Chapin *m* chaplain; God/god; man

Chapland *m* chaplain; God/god; man
Chapman *m* city; man; merchant
Charak *m* ancient; physician
Charan *m* feet
Charie *f* grace; loving
Charis *f* grace
Charissa *f* benevolent; charitable; loving
Charita *f* benevolent; charitable
Charity *f* benevolent; charitable
Charlene *f* little; womanly
Charles *m* manly; strong
Charline *f* little; womanly
Charlotte *f* little; womanly
Charlton *m* farmstead; town
Charmain *f* delight; joy; singer
Charmaine *f* delight; joy; singer; song
Charmian *f* delight; joy; singer
Charron *f* princess
Charyl *f* little; womanly
Chase *m* hunter
Chaska *m* born; first-born; son
Chastity *f* chaste; pure
Chatham *m* land; soldier's
Chatur *m* clever
Chatura *m* clever
Chatwin *m* friend; soldier
Chau *f* pearl; precious
Chaunce *m* king's/kings
Chauncey *m* chancellor; church; official
Chavali *f* child; daughter
Chavi *f* child; daughter
Chaya *f* life
Chaz *m* manly; strong
Cheche *m* small
Chelsea *f* port; ship
Chelsey *f* port; ship
Chema *f* pacifies
Chemar *f* black; girl
Chemarin *f* black; girl
Chemash *f* pacifies
Chemesh *f* pacifies
Chemosh *f* pacifies
Chen *m* great
Chenay *m* forest; oak; tree; trees
Cheney *m* dweller; forest; oak; tree; trees; wood
Chenoa *f* dove; white
Chenzira *m* born; traveling

Cher *f* beloved
Chere *f* beloved
Cheri *f* beauty; beloved; dear; girl
Cheria *f* beauty; girl
Cherice *f* beloved
Cherie *f* beloved; cherished
Cherise *f* beloved; cherry
Cherish *f* beloved
Cherry *f* benevolent; charitable
Chery *f* beloved; dear
Cherye *f* beloved
Cheryl *f* little; womanly
Cheslav *m* army; camp; dweller; fortified
Chesmu *m* gritty
Chesna *f* peaceful
Chessa *f* peaceful
Chester *m* army; camp; dweller; fortified
Chet *m* army; camp; dweller; fortified
Chetana *f* consciousness
Chetwin *m* cottage; path; winding
Cheung *m* good; luck
Chevalier *m* knight
Chevy *m* knight
Chew *m* hill
Cheyanne *f* speak
Cheyenne *f* speak
Cheyney *m* dweller; forest; oak
Chhavi *f* reflection
Chi *f* elder; mind; sister
Chi *m* God/god; mind
Chibale *m* kinship
Chico *m* free; man
Chidi *m* exists; God/god
Chik *m* earth
Chika *f* near
Chike *m* Chi; God/god; power
Chiku *f* chatterer
Chilali *f* snowbird
Chilalis *f* bluebird
Chileogu *m* Chi; defender; God/god; protector
Chilton *m* farm; spring
Chim *m* bird
Chimalsi *m* proud
Chiman *m* curious
Chimene *f* heroine
Chin *m* grasp; increase; tree
China *f* China; country
Chinelo *m* Chi; God/god; talented; thought
Chintak *m* thinker

Chintan *m* meditation
Chintanika *f* meditation
Chinua *m* blessing; Chi; God/god
Chinue *f* blessing; God's
Chioke *m* Chi; gift; God/god
Chionesu *m* protector
Chipo *f* gift
Chiquita *f* little
Chiranjiv *m* immortal
Chirantan *m* ancient
Chisulo *m* steel
Chitesh *m* Lord/lord; soul
Chitt *m* mind
Chittesh *m* Lord/lord; soul
Chiumbo *m* child; small
Chloe *f* verdant; young
Chloras *f* flowers; goddess
Chlori *f* flowers; goddess
Chloris *f* flowers; goddess
Cho *f* born; butterfly; dawn
Cholena *f* bird
Choomia *f* kiss
Chou *m* everywhere
Chow *m* everywhere
Chriselda *f* battle; gray; maid
Chrissa *f* dearest; little
Christabelle *f* beautiful; Christian
Christel *f* Christian
Christian *m* anointed; believer; Christ
Christiana *f* Christian
Christiano *m* anointed; believer; Christ
Christina *f* Christian
Christine *f* Christian
Christobal *m* bearer
Christopher *m* bearer; Christ
Chrystal *f* clear
Chu-Hua *f* chrysanthemum
Chuioke *m* talented
Chuma *f* bead; girl
Chuma *m* bead
Chumana *f* girl
Chumani *f* dew
Chun *f* spring
Churchill *m* church; dweller; hill
Chyna *f* China; country
Chynna *f* China; country
Ciah *f* difficult
Cian *m* ancient
Ciara *f* black
Ciaran *m* black; little

Cicely *f* blind
Cicero *m* chick
Ciceron *m* chick
Cida *f* calm
Cilka *f* blind
Cilla *f* learn; past; times; willing
Cilombo *m* camp; road
Cima *f* judge; Lord/lord
Cinderella *f* ash; little
Cinese *m* Chi; God/god; protecting
Ciprian *m* Cyprus; man
Cipriana *f* Cyprus
Cirila *f* Lordly
Cirill *m* lordly
Cirilo *m* lordly
Ciro *m* sun
Cita *f* silent
Citlalic *f* rising; star
Claiborn *m* brook; clay
Clair *m* famous; illustrious
Claire *f* bright; brilliant; illustrious
Clancey *m* red; son; warrior
Clancy *m* red; son; warrior
Clara *f* bright; brilliant; illustrious
Clarabelle *f* beautiful; brilliant
Clare *f* bright; brilliant; illustrious
Clarence *m* famous
Claresta *f* brilliant
Clareta *f* bright; brilliant; illustrious
Clarette *f* bright; brilliant; illustrious
Clarice *f* brilliant; little
Clarimond *f* brilliant; protector
Clarinda *f* beautiful; bright; brilliant; illustrious
Clarissa *f* brilliant; little
Clarisse *f* brilliant; little
Clarita *f* bright; brilliant; illustrious
Clark *m* scholar
Claude *m* lame
Claudette *f* lame
Claudia *f* lame
Claudina *f* lame
Claudine *f* lame
Claudio *m* lame
Claudius *m* lame
Clava *f* endearing; woman
Clavero *m* keeper
Clay *m* brook; clay; earth
Clayborn *m* born; clay

Clayborne *m* born; brook; clay
Claybourne *m* brook; clay
Clayton *m* clay; estate; town
Cleantha *f* flower; glory
Cleanthe *f* flower; glory
Cleary *m* scholar
Cleavant *m* cliff
Cleavon *m* cliff
Clematis *f* brushwood; vine
Clemence *f* calm; merciful; mild
Clemence *m* gentle; kind; merciful
Clemens *m* gentle; kind; merciful
Clement *m* gentle; kind; merciful
Clementas *f* disposition; mild
Clemente *m* gentle; kind; merciful
Clementi *f* disposition; mild
Clementia *f* calm; merciful; mild
Clementina *f* disposition; mild
Clementine *f* disposition; mild
Clementis *f* disposition; mild
Clementius *m* gentle; kind; merciful
Cleo *f* fame; glory
Cleodal *f* famous
Cleodel *f* famous
Cleodell *f* famous
Cleon *m* famous
Cleopatra *f* famous; father
Cleopatre *f* famous; father
Cleva *f* cliff; dweller
Cleve *f* cliff; dweller
Cleve *m* cliff
Cleveland *m* cliff; land
Cliantha *f* flower; glory
Cliff *m* cliff; rock; steep
Clifford *m* cliff; ford
Clifton *m* cliff; estate; town
Cline *m* little; short
Clinton *m* estate; headland; town
Clio *f* announcer; proclaimer
Clive *m* cliff
Clorinda *f* disposition
Clorinde *f* disposition
Clothilde *f* battle; famous; maid

Clotilda *f* battle; famous; maid
Clovah *f* blossom
Clover *f* blossom
Clovis *m* famous; warrior
Cluny *m* meadow
Clyde *m* warm
Clymene *f* famed
Clytie *f* beautiful; splendid
Clyve *m* cliff
Cocheta *f* unknown
Cocinero *m* cook
Codie *f* cushion
Cody *f* assistant; cushion; helper
Cody *m* cushion
Colbert *m* brilliant; seafarer
Colby *m* black; dark; farm; settlement
Cole *m* army; dark-skinned; hostage; people; pledge; victorious; virile; young
Coleman *m* adherent; dove; little; Nicholas
Colette *f* army; victorious
Colier *m* charcoal; merchant
Colin *m* army; child; cub; victorious; virile; young
Coline *f* dove
Colis *m* charcoal; merchant
Colleen *f* girl; maiden
Collette *f* army; victorious
Colley *m* black-haired; haired; swarthy
Collier *m* charcoal; merchant
Collis *m* black-haired; dark; haired; man; son; swarthy
Collyer *m* charcoal; merchant
Colman *m* adherent; charcoal; dove; head; little; maker; man; Nicholas
Colmbyne *f* drove
Colombe *f* dove
Colter *m* colt; herder
Coltin *m* city; dark; estate; farm
Colton *m* city; dark; estate; farm
Coltson *m* city; dark; estate; farm
Coltun *m* city; dark; estate; farm
Columba *f* dove
Columbia *f* dove

Columbine *f* drove
Colver *m* dove; loving; peace
Colvert *m* brilliant; seafarer
Colvin *m* dark; friend
Colwen *m* dark; friend
Colwin *m* dark; friend
Colyer *m* charcoal; merchant
Coman *m* noble
Comfort *f* aid; comfort
Conah *m* gift; God/god
Conaire *m* child; dog; hunting; keeper
Conall *m* mighty
Conan *m* intelligence; wisdom
Conary *m* child; dog; hunting; keeper
Concepcion *f* beginning
Conception *f* beginning
Conchita *f* beginning
Concordia *f* harmony
Conde *m* count
Congal *m* mighty
Coniah *m* gift; God/god
Conias *m* gift; God/god
Conlan *m* hero
Conley *m* hero
Conlin *m* hero
Conlon *m* hero
Connell *m* mighty
Conner *m* desire; high; meddlesome; strong-willed; strongly; wise
Connery *m* child; dog; hunting; keeper
Connor *m* desire; high; meddlesome; strong-willed; strongly; wise
Connors *m* meddlesome; strong-willed; strongly; wise
Conor *m* meddlesome; strong-willed; strongly; wise
Conrad *m* bold; counselor
Conrade *m* bold; counselor
Conradine *f* bold; counselor; wise
Conray *m* child; dog; hunting; keeper
Conrey *m* child; dog; hunting; keeper
Conroy *m* child; dog; hunting; keeper; persistent; wise
Conry *m* child; dog; hunting; keeper

Consolata *f* consolation
Constance *f* constancy
Constanta *f* constancy
Constantin *m* constant; firm
Constantina *f* constancy
Constantine *m* constant; firm
Constantino *m* constant; firm
Constanza *f* constancy
Consuela *f* consolation
Consuelo *f* consolation
Contrado *m* bold; counselor
Conway *m* great; hound; man; plain; plains
Cooney *m* hare
Cooper *m* barrel; maker
Cora *f* choir; leader; maiden
Corabelle *f* beautiful; maiden
Coral *f* coral; sea
Coralie *f* coral; sea
Coraline *f* coral; sea
Corbet *m* raven
Corbett *m* raven
Corbin *m* raven
Corby *m* raven
Corcoran *m* reddish
Cordalia *f* daughter; flower; heart; sea; star; warm
Cordeelia *f* daughter; flower; heart; sea; star; warm
Cordelia *f* daughter; flower; heart; jewel; sea; star; warm
Cordelie *f* jewel; sea
Cordell *m* little; maker; rope
Corel *f* coral; sea
Corella *f* maiden
Coren *f* maiden
Corette *f* maiden
Corey *f* hollow
Corey *m* dweller; hollow; pool
Cori *f* disposition
Corin *f* disposition
Corina *f* maiden
Corinne *f* maiden
Corisa *f* maidenly
Corissa *f* maidenly
Corliss *f* cheerful; good; heart
Cormac *m* brave; charioteer
Cormack *m* charioteer

Cormick *m* charioteer
Cornall *m* colored; hair; horn
Cornel *m* colored; hair; horn
Cornela *f* yellowish
Cornelia *f* enduring; queenly; womanly; yellowish
Cornelio *m* colored; horn
Cornelius *m* colored; horn
Cornell *m* colored; hair; horn
Corona *f* crown; crowned
Correne *f* maiden
Corrie *f* hollow
Corrigan *m* little; spear
Corrina *f* maiden
Cort *m* bold; counselor; short
Corvin *m* friend; raven's
Corwin *m* dark; friend; heart; raven's
Cory *f* hollow
Cory *m* dweller; hollow; pool
Corydon *m* crested; helmeted
Coryell *m* battle; helmeted; ready
Cosetta *f* army; victorious
Cosette *f* army; victorious
Cosima *f* harmony; order; world
Cosimo *m* harmony; order; universe
Cosme *m* harmony; order; universe
Cosmo *m* harmony; order; universe
Costa *m* constant; firm
Costantin *m* constant; firm
Costantino *m* constant; firm
Court *m* court; dweller; farmstead; land
Courtland *m* court; dweller; enclosed; farmstead; land
Courtney *m* court; dweller; farmstead
Covell *m* cave; dweller; slope
Cowan *m* hillside; hollow; twin
Coyle *m* battle; follower
Craddock *m* abounding; beloved; love
Craig *m* crag; dweller
Cramer *m* shopkeeper

Crandale *m* caretaker; valley
Crandall *m* caretaker; valley
Crandell *m* caretaker; valley
Cranley *m* crane; meadow
Cranston *m* crane; estate; town
Crawford *m* crow's; ford
Creighton *m* creek; dweller; estate; town
Crepin *m* curly; haired
Cresa *f* golden
Crescantia *f* half; moon
Crescen *m* growing
Crescent *f* create; increase
Crescentia *f* create; half; increase; moon
Crescin *m* growing
Crescint *m* growing
Cresida *f* golden
Crespino *m* curly; haired
Cressida *f* golden
Cris *m* growing
Crispa *f* curly; haired
Crispas *f* curly; haired
Crispin *m* curly; haired
Crispino *m* curly; haired
Crispo *m* curly; haired
Crispus *m* curly; haired
Crist *m* growing
Cristabel *f* beautiful; Christian
Cristina *f* Christian
Cristo *m* anointed
Cristobal *m* Christ
Criston *m* anointed
Cristos *m* anointed
Crofton *m* enclosed; farm
Crompton *m* farm; winding
Cromwell *m* crooked; dweller; spring; winding
Crosby *m* cross; dweller
Crosley *m* cross; meadow
Crystal *f* clear
Cuba *f* born
Cubbenah *m* born
Cudjo *m* born
Cuffee *m* born
Cuffy *m* born
Culbert *m* brilliant; seafarer
Cullan *m* handsome
Cullen *m* handsome; pet
Culley *m* woodland
Cullin *m* handsome
Cully *m* woodland
Culver *m* dove; loving; peace

Curran *m* champion; hero
Currey *m* champion; hero
Curry *m* champion; hero
Curt *m* bold; counselor; courteous; well-bred
Curtis *m* courteous; well-bred
Cuthbert *m* brilliant; famous; man
Cuthburt *m* brilliant; famous; man
Cutler *m* knife; maker
Cutlor *m* knife; maker
Cuttler *m* knife; maker
Cuyler *m* devoted; pious
Cy *m* sun
Cybil *f* prophetess
Cyler *m* devoted; pious
Cyma *f* treasure
Cynara *f* artichoke; daughter; moon; thistle
Cynarra *f* daughter; moon
Cynera *f* daughter; moon
Cynric *m* powerful; royal
Cynthia *f* moon
Cynthie *f* moon
Cyprian *m* Cyprus; man
Cyprio *m* Cyprus; man
Cypris *f* Cyprus; island
Cyrano *m* Cyrene
Cyrena *f* Cyrena
Cyril *m* lordly
Cyrilla *f* Lordly
Cyrille *m* lordly
Cyrillus *m* lordly
Cyrus *m* sun
Cytherea *f* Cythera; island

Daberath *f* cool; land
Dabir *m* teacher
Dacey *f* southerner
Dacey *m* southerner
Dachi *f* far; land
Dachia *f* far; land
Dacia *f* far; land; southerner
Dacie *f* southerner
Dack *m* day
Dacy *f* southerner
Dacy *m* southerner
Daegal *m* born; daylight; son
Daffodil *f* flower; tall; white
Dafna *f* laurel; tree
Dafodil *f* flower; tall; white
Dagall *m* born; daylight; son
Dagan *m* corn; earth; fish; grain; little

Dagen *m* corn; grain
Dagny *f* day; new
Dagon *m* corn; earth; fish; grain; little
Dagwood *m* bright; forest
Dahlia *f* valley
Dai *f* great
Daisy *f* eye
Dakarai *m* happiness
Dakota *f* friend
Dakota *m* friend
Daktari *m* healer
Dalaja *f* honey
Dalal *m* salesman
Dalan *m* people
Dalbert *m* brilliant; proud
Dale *m* dweller; valley
Dalen *m* people
Dalfon *m* raindrop
Dalia *f* branch; draw Dalya; noble; tree; water
Dalice *f* branch; draw Dalya; perfect; tree; water
Dalicia *f* perfect
Dalila *f* brooding; gentle
Dalin *m* people
Dalisha *f* perfect
Dalit *f* branch; draw Dalya; tree; water
Daliya *f* branch; draw Dalya; tree; water
Dallan *m* people
Dallas *m* field; waterfall
Dallen *m* people
Dallin *m* people
Dallon *m* people
Dalma *f* lead
Dalmar *f* versatile
Dalon *m* people
Dalston *m* Daegal's
Dalton *m* dell; estate; farm; town; valley
Daly *m* counselor
Dalya *f* branch; tree; water
Dalziel *m* field; little
Damal *f* conqueror; fair
Damalas *f* conqueror; fair
Damali *f* conqueror; fair
Damalis *f* conqueror; fair
Daman *m* gentle
Damara *f* gentle; lamb
Damaris *f* gentle; lamb
Damarra *f* gentle; lamb
Damek *m* earth; man; red
Damian *m* constant
Damica *f* friend
Damick *m* earth; man
Damicke *m* earth; man
Damien *m* constant
Damisi *f* cheerful
Damita *f* lady; little; noble

Damon *m* constant
Dana *m* Demark
Danby *m* Dane; loyal; settlement
Dane *m* God/god; judge
Danete *f* judges; Lord/lord
Danette *f* judges; Lord/lord
Danica *f* morning; star
Daniel *m* God/god; judge
Daniela *f* Lord/lord
Daniella *f* Lord/lord
Danielle *f* Lord/lord
Danior *m* born
Danladi *m* born; Sunday
Dannica *f* morning; star
Dante *m* lasting
Danvir *m* charitable
Danya *f* given
Danya *m* ruler; world
Daphna *f* laurel; tree
Daphne *f* bay; laurel; tree
Dara *f* heart; pearl; wife; wisdom
Darby *m* deer; envious; estate; free; man
Darceece *f* queenly
Darcey *f* dark
Darcia *f* dark; girl; hair
Darcie *f* dark; fortress
Darcy *f* dark; girl; hair
Darcy *m* fortress
Darda *f* pearl; wisdom
Daren *m* born; great; knight; little
Dari *f* queenly
Daria *f* queenly; wealthy
Darian *m* man
Darika *f* maiden
Darilynn *f* dear
Darius *m* man; wealthy
Darla *f* dear
Darlene *f* dear; little
Darnell *m* hidden
Darold *m* beloved; dear; little
Daron *f* great
Darpak *m* God/god; love
Darpan *m* mirror
Darpana *f* mirror
Darra *f* heart; wife
Darrah *f* big; fine; joy; laughing; rejoicing
Darrell *m* beloved; dear; little
Darrelle *f* dear; little
Darren *m* great; little
Darryl *m* beloved; dear; little
Darsey *m* fortress

Darshan *m* perceptive; vision
Darshana *f* observation
Darton *m* deer; estate; farm; park
Daruce *f* queenly
Darwen *m* brave; friend
Darweshi *m* devout
Darwin *m* brave; friend
Daryl *m* beloved; dear; little
Dasha *f* gift; God/god
Dathan *m* beloved
Dathin *m* beloved
Dathon *m* beloved
Daudi *m* beloved
Dave *m* beloved
Daveda *f* loved
Daven *m* bright; Finn; man
Davena *f* loved
Daveta *f* loved
David *m* beloved
Davida *f* beloved; loved
Davin *m* bright; Finn; man
Davina *f* beloved; loved
Davis *m* beloved; son
Davita *f* loved
Davon *m* bright; Finn; man
Dawn *f* dawn; day
Daya *m* mercy
Dayanita *f* merciful
Dayaram *m* merciful
Daygon *m* corn; grain
Daylan *m* people
Daylen *m* people
Dayo *f* arrives; joy
Dean *m* dweller; valley
Deana *f* divine; goddess; valley
Deane *f* valley
DeAngelo *m* angel; messenger
Deanna *f* divine; goddess
Dearborn *m* brook; deer
Debarath *f* cool; land
Debbra *f* cool; land
Debora *f* bee
Deborah *f* bee
Deborath *f* cool; land
Debra *f* bee; cool; land
Decima *f* ten
Dede *f* born; daughter; first-born
Dedra *f* complete; wanderer
Dedric *m* people; ruler
Dedrick *m* people; ruler
Dee *f* black; dark
Deedee *f* beloved
Deems *m* judge; son

Deena *f* valley
Deepak *m* brilliant; candle; light
Deepan *m* lighting
Deependra *m* Lord/lord
Deepit *m* lighted
Degula *f* excellent; famous
Deidre *f* compassion; sorrow
Deirdre *f* complete; wanderer
Deka *f* pleases
Dekel *m* palm; tree
Del *m* gives
Dela *f* faithful; noble; woman
Delaine *m* descendant
Delainey *m* challenger; descendant
Delan *m* challenger; descendant
Delane *m* challenger
Delaney *f* challenger; descendant
Delaney *m* challenger; descendant
Delanie *f* challenger; descendant
Delano *m* alder; black; forest; grove; healthy; man; nut; trees
Delanos *m* alder; grove
Delbert *m* bright; brilliant; day; proud
Delcine *f* sweet
Delfina *f* delphinium; flower
Delfine *f* delphinium; flower
Delia *f* daughter; Delos; flower; heart; island; jewel; mighty; sea; star; visible; warm
Delicia *f* delightful; perfect
Delight *f* delight; pleasure
Delila *f* brooding; gentle
Delilah *f* brooding; gentle
Delisha *f* perfect
Della Delle *f* counselor
Della *f* elf; elves; great; jewel; kind; lady; noble; peaceful; rank; sea; wealth
Delle *f* elves
Delling *m* shining
Dellora *f* seashore
Delma *f* sea
Delmar *m* sea
Delmer *m* sea
Delmore *m* marsh

Delora *f* seashore; sorrows
Delores *f* sorrows
Deloris *f* sorrows
Delorita *f* sorrows
Delphina *f* calm; delphinium; flower; loving; serene; sister
Delphine *f* calm; delphinium; flower; loving; serene; sister
Delphinia *f* calm; loving; serene; sister
Delsey *m* dweller; island; ship
Delsin *m* he; truthful
Delta *f* fourth
Delu *f* forgetful; only
Delwin *m* friend; proud
Delwyn *m* friend; proud
DeMarco *m* martial; warlike
Demas *m* popular
Demetre *m* belonging; fertility; goddess
Demetria *f* fertile; goddess; Greek; land
Demetrio *m* belonging; fertility; goddess
Demetrius *m* belonging; fertility; goddess
Demi *f* half
Demitria *f* fertile; goddess; Greek; land
Demona *f* girl; sadness
Demos *m* people
Demothi *m* talks; walking
Dempsey *m* judge; wise
Dempster *m* judge; wise
Dempstor *m* judge; wise
Den *f* ancestors; asked
Dena *f* judged; valley; vindicated
Denby *m* Dane; loyal; settlement
Denice *f* Dionysus; God/god; Greek; wine
Denis *m* God/god
Denise *f* Dionysus; God/god; Greek; wine
Denisha *f* Dionysus; God/god; Greek; wine
Deniz *m* sea
Denley *m* dweller; meadow; valley
Denman *m* resident; valley
Dennis *m* God/god
Dennison *m* Dennis; son
Denton *m* farm; valley
Denver *m* dweller; green; valley

Denyse *f* Dionysus; God/god; Greek; wine
Denzel *m* Cornwall; place
Derby *m* deer; estate; free; man
Dercy *f* dark; girl; hair; princess
Derek *m* people; ruler
Dereka *f* people; ruler
Derian *m* man
Derica *f* people; ruler
Dericka *f* people; ruler
Derika *f* people; ruler
Derina *f* friend; good
Derinna *f* friend; good
Dermot *m* envious; free; man
Dermott *m* envious; free; man
Deror *m* flowing; freedom
Derora *f* bird; brook; flowing; freedom
Derori *m* flowing; freedom
Derrick *m* people; ruler
Derry *m* red
Derward *m* deer; guardian; warden
Derwin *m* animal; beloved; friend; lover
Derya *f* ocean
Desdamona *f* girl; sadness
Desdamonna *f* girl; sadness
Desdee *f* girl; sadness
Desdemona *f* girl; sadness
Deshad *m* country; nation
Deshal *m* country; nation
Deshan *m* country; nation
Deshane *m* God/god; gracious
Deshawn *m* God/god; gracious
Deshawne *m* God/god; gracious
Deshi *m* morally; upright
Desi *m* desired
Desirea *f* desired; hoped
Desireah *f* desired; hoped
Desiree *f* desired; hoped
Desito *m* desired
Desma *f* child; vow
Desmona *f* ill
Desmond *m* man; sophisticated; south
Desna *f* offering
Dessa *f* flat
Destiny *f* fate
Deston *m* destined; fate
Detta *f* watchtower
Deva *f* brave; divine; girl
Devadeva *m* all; Lord/lord; lords/Lord's

Devak *m* divine
Devaki *f* black; divine
Deval *m* divine; god-like
Devanee *f* divine; god-like
Devank *m* godly
Devanshi *f* divine
Devash *f* honey; sweet
Devasha *f* honey; sweet
Deven *m* god-like
Deverell *m* riverbank
Devi *f* goddess
Devika *f* goddess; little
Devin *m* poet
Devina *f* brave; girl
Devinna *f* brave; girl
Devlin *m* fierce; valor
Devmani *m* divine; jewel
Devona *f* brave; girl
Devonna *f* brave; girl
Devora *f* bee
Devraj *m* God's; ruler
Devrat *m* spiritual
Devsena *m* army; gods
Dewar *m* pilgrim
Dewayne *m* maker
Dewey *m* beloved
Dewi *f* goddess
DeWitt *m* blond; white
Dexter *m* dexterous
Dextra *f* dexterous; skillful
Dezba *f* war
Dhairya *m* patience
Dhanvanti *f* wealth
Dhanvi *f* money
Dharma *m* nature; religion
Dharti *f* earth
Dhatri *f* earth
Dhaval *m* fair
Dheeman *m* intelligent
Dheemant *m* intelligent; wise
Dheemanth *m* wise
Dheer *m* tolerant
Dheeraj *m* consolation; patience
Dhir *m* wise
Dhiraj *m* patience
Dhriti *f* patience
Dhruva *f* star
Dhumma *f* gentle; woman
Dhwani *f* melody; music
Dhyanesh *m* meditative
Dia *f* child
Diallo *m* bold
Diamanta *f* diamond
Diamond *m* bright; protector
Diana *f* divine; goddess
Dianna *f* divine; goddess
Diantha *f* divine; flower
Dianthe *f* divine; flower

Dianthia *f* divine; flower
Diarmit *m* envious
Dibbrun *m* eloquent; forthright
Dibby *f* fortune-teller
Dibri *m* eloquent; forthright
Dibrin *m* eloquent; forthright
Dibru *m* eloquent; forthright
Dichali *m* often
Dickson *m* Dick's; land; son
Didi *f* beloved
Diego *m* supplanter
Diella *f* girl; holy
Dielle *f* girl; holy
Dietrich *m* people; ruler
Digambar *m* unencumbered
Digant *m* horizon
Digvastra *m* clad; sky
Diksha *f* initiation
Dilan *f* faithful
Dilees *f* perfect
Dilen *f* faithful
Dilinn *f* faithful
Dilla *f* jackal; python
Dillan *f* faithful
Dillen *f* faithful
Dillon *m* faithful
Dillyn *f* faithful
Dilyn *f* faithful
Dilys *f* perfect
Dimitri *m* belonging; fertility; goddess
Dimphia *f* nurse
Dina *f* bold; divine; family; judged; people; prosperous; queen; voluptuous
Dinah *f* judged
Dinanath *m* protector
Dindayal *m* kind; poor
Dinesh *m* day; God/god; Lord/lord; sun
Dinh *m* crest; mountain; summit
Dinka *f* people
Dinna *f* arrived
Dinos *m* constant; firm
Dion *m* God/god
Dionne *f* divine; queen
Dionsio *m* God/god
Dionysus *m* God/god
Dior *f* golden
Dira *f* water
Dirk *m* people; ruler
Disa *f* active; double; sprite
Disha *f* direction

Dishi *f* direction
Dishita *f* focus
Dita *f* gift; rich
Diti *f* idea
Divija *f* born; heaven
Dixie *f* blessed; ten
Dixon *m* Dick's; land;
　Richard; son
Diza *f* joy
Doane *m* down; hill
Doba *f* war
Dobry *m* good
Docia *f* brave; child; father
Docie *f* good; repute
Docila *f* learn; willing
Docile *f* learn; willing
Docilla *f* learn; willing
Dodi *f* beloved
Dodie *f* beloved
Dody *f* beloved
Dohosan *m* bluff; small
Dola *f* baby
Dolan *m* black-haired;
　haired
Doli *f* doll
Dolores *f* sorrows
Domel *f* homelover
Domela *f* homelover
Domella *f* homelover
Domenica *f* belonging;
　born; Lord/lord
Domenico *m* belonging;
　born; day; Lord/lord;
　lords/Lord's; Sunday
Domina *f* lady
Dominga *f* belonging;
　born; Lord/lord
Domingo *m* belonging;
　born; day; Lord/lord;
　lords/Lord's; Sunday
Domini *f* belonging
Dominic *m* belonging;
　born; day; Lord/lord;
　lords/Lord's; Sunday
Dominica *f* belonging;
　born; Lord/lord
Dominick *m* belonging;
　born; day; Lord/lord;
　lords/Lord's; Sunday
Dominico *m* belonging;
　born; day; Lord/lord;
　lords/Lord's; Sunday
Dominika *f* belonging;
　Lord/lord
Dominique *f* belonging;
　born; Lord/lord
Dominique *m* belonging;
　born; day; Lord/lord;
　lords/Lord's; Sunday
Dona *f* deeply
Donah *f* deeply

Donahue *m* brown; war-
　rior
Donald *m* mighty; ruler;
　world
Donalda *f* ruler; world
Donata *f* donation; gift
Donato *m* gift
Donela *f* girl; little
Donell *f* girl; little
Donella *f* girl; little
Donely *m* brave; dark; man
Doni *f* ruler; world
Donia *f* ruler; world
Donica *f* morning; star
Donkor *m* humble
Donna *f* busy; girl; lady
Donnah *f* deeply
Donnan *m* brown-haired;
　haired; small
Donnel *m* brave; dark;
　man
Donnell *m* brave; dark;
　man
Donnelly *m* brave; dark;
　man
Donovan *m* dark; warrior
Dony *f* ruler; world
Dooley *m* dark; hero
Dooriya *f* deep
Dooya *f* deep
Dor *m* home
Dora *f* beloved; fountain;
　generous; gift; gifted;
　God/god; patient; wife;
　winged; wisdom
Doran *m* gift; strange;
　stranger
Dorcas *f* dark; eyes;
　gazelle; girl
Dorcas *m* forest; roe
Dorcea *f* dark; eyes; girl
Dorcia *f* dark; eyes; girl
Dorcus *m* forest; roe
Dore *f* golden
Doreen *f* bountiful; sullen
Dorein *m* gift; strange
Dorek *m* gift; God's
Doren *m* gift; strange
Dorena *f* bountiful
Dorene *f* bountiful; sullen
Doria *f* ocean
Dorian *m* Doria; man; sea
Dorice *f* generation; ocean
Dorin *f* beautiful; bounti-
　ful; gift
Dorin *m* gift; strange
Dorina *f* bountiful; friend;
　good
Dorinda *f* beautiful; boun-
　tiful; gift
Dorine *f* bountiful

Doris *f* ocean
Dorisa *f* sea
Dorise *f* ocean
Dorit *f* generation
Dorothea *f* gift; God/god
Dorothy *f* gift; God/god
Dorr *m* fountain; youth
Dorran *m* gift; strange
Dorren *m* gift; strange
Dorrin *m* gift; strange
Dorthea *f* gift; God/god
Dorthy *f* gift; God/god
Dorwin *m* animal; lover
Dory *m* golden; haired
Doshi *f* determined
Dosia *f* divinely; given;
　God/god
Dosya *f* gift; God/god
Dotan *m* law
Dothan *m* law
Doug *m* copper
Dougal *m* black; stranger
Douglas *m* black; dark;
　water
Douglass *m* black; dark;
　water
Dov *m* bear; quietly; speak
Dovev *m* quietly; speak
Dow *m* black-haired;
　haired
downward *f* flow
Doxia *f* brave; child; father
Doxie *f* good; repute
Doxy *f* good; repute
Doyle *m* dark; newcomer;
　stranger
Drake *m* dragon; sign
Dreda *f* friend; wise
Dreesa *f* daughter; sun
Dreesha *f* daughter; sun
Dreng *m* brave; man
Drew *m* manly; phantom;
　strength; vision; wise
Drida *f* friend; wise
Drisa *f* daughter; sun
Drisana *f* daughter; sun
Drishti *f* sight
Drishya *f* sight
Dristi *f* sight
Druce *m* man; son; wise
Drucie *f* strong
Druella *f* elfin; vision
Drummond *m* hilltop
Drury *m* darling
Drusa *f* strong
Drusie *f* strong
Drusilla *f* strong
Dryden *m* dry; valley
Du *m* elm; flattery; playful;
　tree
Duana *f* dark; little; song

Duane *m* dark; little
Duc *m* moral; virtuous
Duci *f* gift; rich; valuable
Dudas *m* trumpeter
Dudley *m* meadow; people's
Duena *f* chaperone
Duer *m* battle; valorous
Duff *m* dark; dark-haired; haired
Duffy *m* dark
Dugald *m* black; dark; water
Dugan *m* dark
Duka *f* all
Duke *m* bewitch; leader
Dukker *m* bewitch
Dulani *m* cutting
Dulcea *f* sweet
Dulciana *f* sweet
Dulcie *f* sweet
Dulcine *f* sweet
Dulcinea *f* sweet
Duma *f* gentle; woman
Dumah *f* gentle; woman
Dumaka *m* hand; help
Duman *m* mist; smoke
Dumichel *m* God/god
Duna *f* dark; little
Dunam *m* black; dark
Duncan *m* brown; chief; swarthy; warrior
Dunham *m* black; dark
Dunley *m* hill; meadow
Dunmore *m* fortress; great; hill
Dunn *m* dark
Dunstan *m* brown; fortress; stone
Dunston *m* farm; hill
Dunton *m* farm; hill
Duntson *m* farm; hill
Duque *m* duke
Dur *m* encircle
Durant *m* enduring
Durene *f* enduring
Durga *m* unreachable
Durja *m* invincible
Durriken *m* fortune-teller
Durril *m* gooseberry
Durst *m* heart; leader; strong-hearted
Durstin *m* heart; leader; strong-hearted
Durston *m* heart; leader; strong-hearted
Durward *m* gatekeeper; guard
Durwin *m* animal; beloved; friend; lover

Dusan *m* judge; Lord/lord; soul; spirit
Duscha *f* soul
Dustee *f* fighter
Dusti *f* fighter
Dustin *f* fighter
Dustin *m* destined; fate; heart; leader; strong-hearted
Dusty *f* fighter
Dustyn *f* fighter
Duy *m* moral
Dwana *f* dark; little; song
Dwayne *m* dark; little
Dwight *m* blond; white
Dyami *m* eagle
Dyan *f* divine; goddess
Dyana *f* divine; goddess
Dyane *f* divine; goddess
Dyani *f* deer
Dygal *m* born; daylight; son
Dygall *m* born; daylight; son
Dylan *m* sea; son; wave
Dylana *f* sea
Dylane *f* sea
Dylice *f* perfect
Dymphia *f* nurse
Dynah *f* divine; queen
Dyre *m* dear; precious
Dyumna *m* glorious

Eachan *m* horse; little
Eada *f* happy; prosperous
Eamon *m* prosperous; protector; wealthy
Earl *m* chief; nobleman
Earle *m* chief; nobleman
Earlene *f* noble; woman
Eartha *f* earth
Easter *f* baby; born; Easter
Eaton *m* estate; riverside
Eba *f* disagree; understanding
Ebarta *f* learning; woman
Ebba *f* flowing; giving; life-giving
Ebbie *f* darkness
Eben *m* help; rock; stone
Ebenezer *m* help; rock; stone
Eberhard *m* boar; brave; strong; wild
Eberta *f* learning; woman
Ebonee *f* dark; wood
Ebony *f* dark; wood
Echo *f* echo; sound
Econah *m* gift; Lord/lord
Eda *f* blessedness; fiery;

lovely; poetry; prosperity; rainwater; woman
Edan *m* fire
Edana *f* fiery; little
Edbert *m* brilliant; generous; prosperous; soul
Edda *f* fiery; poetry; rainwater; woman
Eddina *f* family; prosperous
Eddra *f* power; woman
Eddy *m* interesting
Ede *f* generation; prosperous
Edea *f* sorceress
Edel *f* fiery; woman
Edel *m* noble
Edeline *f* noble
Edelmar *m* famous; noble
Eden *f* delight; pleasure
Edena *f* rejuvenation
Edette *f* watchtower
Edgar *m* prosperous; spearman
Edgard *m* prosperous; spearman
Edgardo *m* prosperous; spearman
Edha *f* sacred
Edi *m* herb
Edia *f* God/god; Lord/lord
Ediah *f* God/god; Lord/lord
Edik *m* guardian; wealthy
Edina *f* family; friend; prosperous
Edison *m* Edward; son
Edita *f* gift; rich
Edith *f* gift; rich
Editha *f* gift; rich
Edithe *f* gift; rich
Ediva *f* gift; rich
Ediya *f* God/god; Lord/lord
Edlun *m* prosperous; village
Edlyn *f* little; noble
Edmanda *f* prosperous; protector
Edme *f* fortunate; protector
Edmea *f* fortunate; protector
Edmee *f* fortunate; protector
Edmond *m* prosperous; protector
Edmonda *f* prosperous; protector
Edmund *m* prosperous; protector

Edmunda *f* prosperous;
protector
Edmundo *m* prosperous;
protector
Edna *f* rejuvenation
Ednit *m* evolved
Edolf *m* prosperous; wolf
Edora *f* patient; wife
Edouard *m* guardian; pros-
perous
Edra *f* power; powerful;
prosperous; woman
Edrea *f* power; powerful;
prosperous; woman
Edrei *m* leader; powerful
Edric *m* prosperous; rich;
ruler
Edris *f* power; woman
Edroi *m* leader; powerful
Edsel *m* hall; house;
manor; prosperous
Edson *m* Edward; son
Eduard *m* guardian; pros-
perous
Eduardo *m* guardian; pros-
perous
Edva *f* diligent; joy; worker
Edvard *m* guardian; pros-
perous
Edveh *f* diligent; joy;
worker
Edwald *m* prosperous;
ruler
Edward *m* guardian; pros-
perous
Edwardine *f* guardian;
prosperous
Edwin *m* friend; prosper-
ous
Edwina *f* friend; prosper-
ous
Edya *f* God/god; Lord/
lord
Edyah *f* God/god; Lord/
lord
Edyth *f* gift; rich
Edythe *f* gift; rich
Effie *f* spoken; well
Efia *f* born
Efrain *m* abounding
Efram *m* abounding
Efuru *f* daughter; heaven
Ega *f* bird; palm
Egan *m* ardent; fiery
Egarton *m* hill; town
Egbert *m* bright; shining;
sword
Egberta *f* bright; shining;
sword
Egbertina *f* bright; shin-
ing; sword

Egbertine *f* bright; shin-
ing; sword
Egerton *m* hill; town
Egin *m* brilliant; friend;
quick
Eglantine *f* rose
Egwin *m* brilliant; friend;
quick
Ehimay *m* all; pervasive
Ehioze *m* jealous
Ehren *m* honorable
Ehud *m* lonesome; only;
son
Ehudd *m* son
Eiji *m* born; second-born;
son
Eila *f* earth
Eileen *f* bearer; light
Einar *m* leader; warrior
Eir *f* clemency; peace
Eirena *f* peace
Eirene *f* peace
Eithne *f* kernal
Ekaant *m* solitary
Ekanga *m* bodyguard
Ekani *m* one
Ekansh *m* whole
Ekaraj *m* emperor
Ekbal *m* dignity
Ekika *f* gift; valuable
Ekodar *m* brother
Ekon *m* strong
Ekram *m* honor
Ekua *f* born
Ela *f* blonde; God/god;
name; white
Elah *m* bitter; tree
Elaine *f* Lenka; light
Elamma *f* goddess; mother
Elan *m* friendly
Elane *f* light
Elanore *f* Lenka; light
Elata *f* elevated; lofty;
spirit
Elatia *f* elevated; lofty;
spirit
Elayne *f* light
Elbart *m* forthright; noble
Elbert *m* brilliant; forth-
right; illustrious; noble
Elberta *f* brilliant; noble
Elboa *f* fruitful
Elburt *m* forthright; noble
Elda *f* elder; fountain;
fresh; tree
Elden *m* elf; friend; old;
protector; valley; wise
Elder *m* dweller; elder;
tree
Eldin *m* friend; old; pro-
tector; wise

Eldon *m* hill; holy
Eldora *f* gifted; gilded; wis-
dom
Eldred *m* battle; counselor
Eldreda *f* friend; wise
Eldric *m* old; ruler; wise
Eldrid *m* battle; counselor
Eldrida *f* counselor;
friend; old; wise
Eldridge *m* king
Eldwen *m* adviser; wise
Eldwin *m* adviser; wise
Eleanor *f* light
Eleanore *f* light
Eleazar *m* God/god; help
Eleazaro *m* God/god; help
Electra *f* brilliant; star
Elek *m* defender; helper;
mankind
Elene *f* bearer; Lenka;
light
Eleni *f* Lenka; light
Elenora *f* light
Elenore *f* Lenka; light
Eleora *f* light; Lord/lord
Eleph *m* ox; strong
Elese *f* noble
Elewa *m* intelligent
Elfreda *f* counselor; elf;
good; peaceful; wise
Elfrida *f* counselor; elfin;
good; peaceful; wise
Elfrieda *f* counselor; elf;
good
Elga *f* consecrated; fighter;
holy; tiny
Eli *f* light
Eli *m* highest; Jehovah;
Lord/lord
Elia *m* God/god; Jehovah
Eliana *f* answered; Jeho-
vah; prayers
Eliane *f* answered; Jeho-
vah; prayers
Elianna *f* answered; Jeho-
vah; prayers
Elias *m* God/god; Jehovah
Eliath *m* Lord/lord
Eliathan *m* Lord/lord
Eliathas *m* Lord/lord
Elidad *m* beloved; God/
god; stranger
Elidi *f* gift; sun
Elihu *m* God/god; Lord/
lord
Elijah *m* God/god; Jeho-
vah
Elinore *f* light
Eliora *f* light; Lord/lord
Elisa *f* consecrated; God/
god

Elisabeth *f* consecrated; God/god
Elise *f* consecrated; God's; God/god; promise; truthful
Eliseo *m* God/god; Lord/lord; salvation
Elisha *f* truthful
Elisha *m* God/god; Lord/lord; salvation
Eliska *f* truthful
Elissa *f* consecrated; God/god
Elita *f* flower; honey; little; person; select; special
Eliza *f* consecrated; God/god
Elizabeth *f* consecrated; God/god
Elkan *m* belongs; God/god
Ella *f* beautiful; elf; fairy; maiden
Ellama *f* goddess; mother
Ellard *m* brave; nobly; warrior
Ellata *f* elevated; lofty; spirit
Ellen *f* Lenka; light
Ellerd *m* brave; nobly; warrior
Ellerey *m* elder; island; tree
Ellery *m* elder; island; tree
Ellette *f* Lenka; light
Ellga *f* fighter; tiny
Elli *f* Lenka; light
Ellice *f* God/god; Jehovah
Ellie *f* truthful
Elliot *m* God/god; Jehovah
Elliott *m* God/god; Jehovah
Ellis *m* God/god; Jehovah
Ellison *m* Ellis; son
Ellita *f* person; select; special
Ellon *m* invincible; mighty; oak
Ellora *f* seashore
Ellord *m* brave; nobly; warrior
Ellsworth *m* great
Ellwood *m* forest; old
Ellyn *f* Lenka; light
Elma *f* amiable; apple; elm; lovable; pleasant
Elman *m* elm; tree
Elmen *m* elm; tree
Elmer *m* famous; noble
Elmina *f* awe; fame; inspiring; tree

Elmira *f* clothing; exalted; famous; noble; truth
Elmo *m* friendly; helmet; lovable; protector
Elmon *m* elm; tree
Elmore *m* dweller; elm; moor; tree
Elodea *f* flower
Elodia *f* flower
Elodie *f* flower
Eloisa *f* famous; maid; warrior
Eloise *f* famous; maid; warrior
Elom *f* God/god
Elon *m* invincible; mighty; oak
Elrad *m* God/god; rules
Elrica *f* all; ruler
Elroy *m* king; royal
Elsa *f* given; God/god; maiden; noble; truthful
Elschen *f* truthful
Elsdon *m* hill; noble
Else *f* maiden; noble; truthful
Elsie *f* truthful
Elstan *m* little; small; stone
Elston *m* estate; little; noble; small; stone; town
Elsu *m* falcon; flying
Elsworth *m* estate; noble
Elton *m* dweller; estate; manor; old; town
Elu *m* full; grace
Elva *f* counselor; elf; elfin; good
Elvah *f* elfin
Elvera *f* blonde; white
Elvia *f* elfin; good
Elvin *m* elfin; friend
Elvina *f* elfin; elves; friend
Elvira *f* blonde; white
Elvire *f* blonde; white
Elvis *m* all; suitor; wise
Elvy *m* elfin; warrior
Elwell *m* old; spring
Elwin *m* elfin; friend
Elwina *f* elves; friend
Elwood *m* forest; old
Elyse *f* consecrated; God/god
Elysia *f* blissful; sweetly
Elza *f* truthful
Ema *f* beloved; universal
Emanuel *m* God/god
Emanuela *f* God/god
Emanuele *m* God/god
Emee *f* fortunate; protector
Emelda *f* flattering; industrious

Emelin *m* busy; father; son
Emelina *f* flattering; industrious; universal
Emeline *f* flattering; industrious; universal
Emelyne *f* universal
Emerald *f* jewel
Emeri *m* industrious; ruler
Emersen *m* Emory; son
Emerson *m* Emory; industrious; ruler; son
Emery *m* industrious; ruler
Emil *m* flattering; industrious; winning
Emilia *f* flattering; industrious
Emilie *f* flattering; industrious
Emilio *m* flattering; industrious; winning
Emily *f* flattering; industrious
Emina *f* lofty; noteworthy; prominent
Emlen *m* busy; father; son
Emlyn *f* flattering; industrious
Emlyn *m* busy; father; son; waterfall
Emlynne *f* flattering; industrious
Emma *f* universal
Emmaline *f* universal
Emmanuel *m* God/god
Emmet *m* industrious; strong
Emmett *m* industrious; strong
Emmott *m* industrious; strong
Emmuela *f* dedicated; God/god
Emory *m* industrious; ruler
Emuna *f* faithful
Ena *f* adorned; ardent; fiery; little
Enalda *f* omen; sign
Enam *m* gift; God/god
Encratia *f* maiden
Encratis *f* maiden
Ender *m* fountain; youth
Endor *m* fountain; youth
Endora *f* fountain
Eneas *m* praise; praised; worthy
Eng *m* place
Engedi *m* fame; fountain
Engelbert *m* angel; brilliant
Engelberta *f* angel; bright

Englebert *m* angel; brilliant
Engracia *f* attractive; graceful; maiden
Enid *f* fair; pure; purity; soul
Enlai *m* appreciates
Ennea *f* child; nine; ninth
Ennis *m* child; choice; ninth; one; only
Enoch *m* consecrated
Enola *f* alone
Enric *m* army; ruler
Enrica *f* estate; home; ruler
Enrico *m* home; ruler
Enrique *m* estate; home; property; ruler
Enriqueta *f* estate; home; ruler
Enya *f* kernal
Ephraim *m* abounding
Ephram *m* abounding
Eppie *f* spoken; well
Epua *f* born
Eradis *f* forthright
Eran *m* watchful
Eranthe *f* flower; spring
Erasatus *m* honored; loved; son
Erasme *m* lovable; love; worthy
Erasmo *m* lovable; love; worthy
Erasmus *m* kindly; lovable; love; worthy
Erastes *m* honored; loved; son
Erastus *m* beloved; honored; loved; son
Erda *f* child; earth; world
Erdah *f* child; earth
Erdda *f* child; earth
Erela *f* angel; messenger
Erena *f* peace
Eresenio *m* masculine; virile
Eric *m* powerful; ruler
Erica *f* flower; heather; powerful; regal; ruler
Erich *m* powerful; ruler
Erida *f* loved
Erik *m* powerful; ruler
Erika *f* flower; heather; powerful; regal; ruler
Erin *f* Erin; lass
Erina *f* Erin; lass
Erine *f* Erin; lass
Erinna *f* Erin; lass
Erl *m* chief; nobleman
Erland *m* eagle; land; noble; nobleman's

Erleena *f* elfin; girl
Erlene *f* noble; woman
Erlia *f* fruitful; spring; woman
Erlina *f* elfin; girl
Erlinda *f* lively
Erline *f* noble; woman
Erling *m* nobleman; son
Erlinna *f* elfin; girl
Erlond *m* eagle; noble
Erma *f* background; fine; high; noble; person
Ermina *f* background; fine; noble
Erminna *f* background; fine; noble
Erna *f* eagle; earnest
Ernald *m* city; foreign
Ernaldus *m* city; foreign
Ernaline *f* eagle
Ernest *m* earnest
Ernestine *f* earnest
Ernesto *m* earnest
Ernestus *m* earnest
Ernst *m* earnest
Errol *m* chief; nobleman; wandering
Erskine *m* cleft
Ertha *f* earth; world
Erwin *m* friend; sea
Erwina *f* friend; sea
Esau *m* hair; long
Esben *m* bear; holy
Esbern *m* bear; holy
Esburn *m* bear; holy
Escriba *m* scribe
Eshe *f* life
Esi *f* born
Eskil *m* protestor
Eskill *m* protestor
Esmael *m* God/god; hears
Esme *m* beloved
Esmee *f* beloved
Esmeralda *f* adorned; emerald; high; jewel
Esmerelda *f* high; jewel
Esmerolda *f* high; jewel
Esmond *m* gracious; protector
Esra *m* help; helper
Esraela *f* God/god; strength
Essien *m* born; sixth; son
Esta *f* east; star
Estas *m* Estes; house
Este *m* east
Esteban *m* crowned
Estefan *m* crowned
Estella *f* star
Estelle *f* star
Ester *f* star

Estes *m* east; Estes; house
Estevan *m* crowned
Esther *f* star
Estis *m* Estes; house
Estrella *f* star
Estrellita *f* star
Estus *m* honored; loved; son
Eta *f* ambitious; luminous
Etam *m* house; soldier's; son; warrior
Etana *f* strong
Etania *f* wealthy
Etash *m* luminous
Etenia *f* wealthy
Ethan *m* firmness; strength
Ethban *m* gracious; son
Ethben *m* gracious; son
Ethbin *m* gracious; son
Ethel *f* good; judge; people
Ethelind *f* good; judge; people
Ethelinda *f* good; judge; noble; people; serpent
Etienne *m* crowned
Etta *f* friend; little
Ettan *m* breath
Etu *m* sun
Euclea *f* glory
Eudice *f* praise
Eudo *m* child
Eudoca *f* brave; child; father
Eudocia *f* brave; child; father; good; repute
Eudora *f* generous; gift; splendid
Eudore *f* generous
Eudosia *f* brave; child; father; good; repute
Eudoxia *f* brave; child; father; good; repute
Eufemia *f* auspicious; good; repute; speech
Eugene *m* born; noble; well-born
Eugenia *f* born; noble; well
Eugenio *m* born; noble; well-born
Eula *f* fair; soft; speaking; speech; spoken; sweet; well; woman
Eulalia *f* fair; soft; speech; spoken; well; woman
Eulalie *f* fair; soft; speech; spoken; well; woman
Eunice *f* happy; victorious
Euphemia *f* auspicious;

fairest; famous; good; re-
pute; speech; spoken;
well
Euphemiah *f* fairest; fa-
mous
Euphemie *f* auspicious;
good; repute; speech
Eurydice *f* broad
Eustace *m* stable; tranquil
Eustacia *f* flowering; rich;
stable; tranquil
Eustacie *f* flowering; rich
Eustasius *m* stable; tran-
quil
Eustazio *m* stable; tranquil
Eva *f* bringer; giving;
good; life-giving; little;
news; nymph
Evadne *f* little; nymph;
singer; sweet
Evadnee *f* little; nymph
Evaleen *f* giving; life-giving
Evalina *f* giving; life-giving
Evan *m* born; God/god;
gracious; proud; warrior;
well-born; young
Evander *m* doer; well-doer
Evangelia *f* bringer; good;
news
Evangeline *f* bringer;
good; news
Evania *f* child; peace; tran-
quil
Evannia *f* child; peace;
tranquil
Evante *f* blossom; flower
Evanthe *f* blossom; flower
Eve *f* bringer; giving;
good; life-giving; news
Evelyn *f* giving; life-giving;
light
Everard *m* boar; brave;
strong
Evered *m* boar; brave;
strong
Everett *m* boar; brave;
strong
Everhart *m* boar; brave;
strong
Evers *m* boar; wild
Evetta *f* hunt
Evette *f* hunt
Evlyn *f* giving; life-giving
Ewald *m* bearer; good; law;
powerful
Ewan *m* born; warrior;
well-born; young
Ewen *m* born; warrior;
well-born; young
Ewert *m* ewe; herder
Ewing *m* friend; law

Ewold *m* bearer; good
Eyota *f* greatest
Ezar *m* treasure
Ezara *f* dear; treasure
Ezaria *f* dear; treasure
Ezarra *f* dear; treasure
Ezarras *f* dear; treasure
Eze *m* king
Ezechiel *m* God/god;
strength
Ezechiele *m* God/god;
strength
Ezekiel *m* God/god;
strength
Ezequiel *m* God/god;
strength
Ezra *m* help; helper
Ezraella *f* God/god;
strength
Ezrela *f* God/god;
strength

Faber *m* bean
Fabia *f* bean
Fabian *m* bean
Fabiana *f* bean
Fabiano *m* bean
Fabien *m* bean
Fabio *m* bean
Fabiola *f* good; woman
Fabiolas *f* good; woman
Fabria *f* girl
Fabriane *f* girl
Fabrianna *f* girl
Fabrianne *f* girl
Fabrienne *f* girl
Fabrin *m* hands
Fabrioni *m* blacksmith; lit-
tle
Fabron *m* blacksmith;
hands; little
Fabyola *f* good; woman
Fachan *m* enterprising;
skilled
Fachanan *m* enterprising;
skilled
Fadeel *m* generous
Fadey *m* father
Fadhila *f* outstanding
Fadil *m* generous
Fagan *m* little
Fagin *m* fiery; little
Fahdeel *m* generous
Faheem *m* intelligent;
learned
Fahim *m* intelligent;
learned
Faine *m* glad; joyful
Fairfax *m* haired; light
Fairleigh *m* bull; meadow

Faisal *m* good; judge
Faisel *m* good; judge
Faith *f* belief; fidelity;
God/god; loyalty
Faiza *f* victorious
Faizah *f* victorious
Faizal *m* good; judge
Fala *f* crow
Falda *f* folded; wings
Faline *f* catlike
Fanchan *f* independent;
woman
Fanchet *f* independent;
woman
Fanchette *f* independent;
woman
Fanchon *f* free; independ-
ent; woman
Fane *m* glad; joyful
Fanya *f* free
Fara *f* joyful; rejoicing
Farah *f* beautiful; pleasant
Faraji *m* consolation
Farand *f* beautiful; pleas-
ant
Fareed *m* unique
Farhani *m* happy
Farica *f* loving; peace;
peaceful; ruler
Farid *m* unique
Farida *f* unique
Farih *f* bright; confeder-
ate; light; perplexed;
playful; runs; white
Farika *f* loving; peace;
ruler
Fariq *m* general
Faris *m* knight
Farkas *m* wolf
Farlay *m* bull; meadow
Farlee *m* bull; meadow
Farley *m* bull; leader;
meadow; strong
Farman *m* sojourner
Farmann *m* sojourner
Farnall *m* fern; slope
Farnell *m* fern; slope
Farnham *m* fern; field
Farnley *m* fern; meadow
Faro *m* well
Farold *m* mighty; traveler
Farouk *m* discerning; truth
Farr *m* traveler
Farrah *f* beautiful; pleas-
ant
Farrand *m* gray; hair; iron
Farrant *m* gray; hair; iron
Farrel *m* valorous
Farrell *m* valorous
Farrica *f* loving; peace;
ruler

Farro *m* well
Farron *m* well
Faruq *m* discerning; truth
Fasta *m* sacrifices
Fasto *m* sacrifices
Fath *m* victory
Fatima *f* unknown
Fatimah *f* unknown
Faunia *f* deer; young
Faust *m* auspicious; lucky; opponent; strong
Fausta *f* lucky
Faustena *f* lucky
Faustina *f* lucky
Faustine *f* lucky
Faustus *m* opponent; strong
Favian *m* man; understanding
Favianus *m* man; understanding
Favient *m* man; understanding
Favin *m* man; understanding
Favor *f* approval; good; help
Fawn *f* deer; young
Fawna *f* deer; young
Fawnia *f* deer; young
Faxan *m* hair; renowned
Faxen *m* hair; renowned
Faxon *m* hair; renowned
Fay *f* belief; elf; fairy; fidelity; God/god; loyalty; raven
Fayette *f* fairy; little
Fayina *f* free
Fayme *f* lofty; renown
Fayola *f* honor; luck
Fayre *f* beautiful; pleasant
Faysal *m* good; judge
Faysul *m* good; judge
Fayzal *m* good; judge
Fayzel *m* good; judge
Fealty *f* allegiance; fidelity
Federica *f* peaceful; ruler
Fedor *m* gift; God/god
Feechi *f* God/god; worship
Felda *f* field
Felice *f* happiness; happy
Felicia *f* happiness; happy
Feliciana *f* happy
Felicidad *f* happy
Felicie *f* happy
Felicity *f* happiness; happy
Feliks *m* fortunate; lucky
Felipa *f* horses; lover
Felipe *m* horses; lover
Felise *f* happiness; happy

Felix *m* fortunate; lucky
Felton *m* estate; field; town
Femi *f* loved
Fenella *f* shouldered; white
Fenton *m* estate; farm; marsh
Fenyang *m* conqueror
Feodosia *f* given; God/god
Ferdinand *m* adventuring; daring; life; world
Ferdinanda *f* adventuring; world
Ferdinando *m* adventuring; daring; life; world
Ferdnando *m* adventuring; daring; life; world
Fergus *m* choice; man; strong
Feriga *f* loving; peace; ruler
Fern *f* delicate; feather; plant
Ferna *f* delicate; feather; plant
Fernald *m* alder; dweller; fern; slope; tree
Fernanda *f* adventuring; world
Fernandina *f* adventuring; world
Fernando *m* adventuring; daring; life; world
Fernas *f* delicate; feather; plant
Ferne *f* delicate; feather; plant
Ferran *f* adventurous
Ferran *m* baker
Ferrand *m* gray; hair; iron
Ferrant *m* gray; hair; iron
Ferrell *m* valorous
Ferris *m* rock
Festatus *m* gay
Festus *m* gay
Fhotima *f* friend; Lord/lord
Fia *f* ivory; lovely; wife
Fiala *f* violet
Fidel *m* faithful; sincere; true
Fidelas *f* faithful; woman
Fidele *m* faithful; sincere; true
Fidelia *f* faithful; woman
Fidelio *m* faithful; sincere; true
Fidelis *m* faithful; sincere; true
Fidelity *f* faithful; woman
Fidellia *f* faithful; woman

Fielding *m* dweller; field
Fifi *f* add; increase
Filbert *m* brilliant; radiant; soul
Filberte *m* brilliant
Filberto *m* brilliant
Filide *f* branch; green
Filippa *f* horses; lover
Filippo *m* horses; lover
Fillander *m* loves; man; mankind
Fillender *m* loves; man; mankind
Fillmore *m* famous
Filma *f* mist
Filmer *m* famous
Filmore *m* famous
Fina *f* bright; friend; girl; hair; Lord/lord; red
Finan *m* fair; little
Finbar *m* haired; white
Finbur *m* haired; white
Findlay *m* fair; little; valorous
Findley *m* fair; little; valorous
Finella *f* shouldered; white
Finlay *m* fair; little; valorous
Finley *m* fair; little; valorous
Finn *m* fair; haired; little
Finnin *m* fair; little
Fintan *m* fair; little
Finton *m* fair; little
Fiona *f* ivory
Fionan *m* fair; little
Fionna *f* ivory
Fionnula *f* shouldered; white
Fiora *f* flower
Fiorenza *f* blooming; flourishing; prosperous
Firmin *m* firm; strong
Fisk *m* fisherman
Fiske *m* fish; fisherman
Fisseha *f* happiness; joy
Fitch *m* ermine
Fitz *m* Gerald; Patrick; son
Fitzger *m* Gerald; son
Fitzgerald *m* Gerald; mighty; son; spear
Fitzhugh *m* intelligent; son; thoughtful
Fitzpatrick *m* Patrick; son
Flair *f* fragrant
Flammery *f* haired
Flann *f* flourishing
Flann *m* haired; red
Flanna *f* haired; red-haired

Flannery *f* red-haired
Flavia *f* haired; light; yellow
Flavian *m* haired; yellow
Flavio *m* blond
Flavius *m* golden; hair; yellow
Fleda *f* beautiful; clean
Fleta *f* beautiful; clean; fleet; swift
Fletcher *m* arrow; maker
Fleur *f* flower
Fleurette *f* flower
Flinn *m* haired; man; red; son
Flint *m* stream
Flita *f* beautiful; clean
Flo *f* arrow
Flo *m* arrow
Flora *f* flower
Florance *f* blooming; flourishing; prosperous
Flore *f* flower
Florence *f* blooming; flourishing; prosperous
Florencia *f* blooming; flourishing; prosperous
Floria *f* flower
Florida *f* blooming
Florinda *f* blooming; flourishing; prosperous
Florine *f* blooming; flourishing; prosperous
Floris *f* blooming; flourishing; prosperous
Flower *f* blossom
Floyd *m* gray; haired
Flynn *m* haired; man; red; son
Fola *f* honorable
Folk *m* people
Folke *m* people
Folki *m* people
Foluke *m* God's; hands
Fonda *f* affectionate; foundation; profound; tender; woman
Fontaine *m* fountain; water
Fontainne *f* fountain
Fontana *m* fountain; water
Fontayne *m* fountain; water
Fonya *m* immortal
Fonzi *m* battle; eager
Forbes *m* fields; man; owner; prosperity
Ford *m* cattle; crossing; resident; river; valley
Fordel *m* forgiving
Forest *m* dweller; forest; warden

Forester *m* forest; guardian
Forrest *m* dweller; forest
Forrester *m* forest; guardian
Fortuna *f* destiny; fate; lucky
Fortune *f* destiny; fate
Fortune *m* lucky
Fortunia *f* lucky
Fortunio *m* lucky
Fortunna *f* lucky
Foster *m* forest; guardian
Fotina *f* friend; Lord/lord
Fraine *m* foreigner; stranger
Francesca *f* France
Francesco *m* free; man
Franchot *m* free; man
Francis *m* free; man
Francisco *m* free; man
Francois *m* free; man
Frank *m* free; holder; land; man
Franklin *m* free; holder; land
Franklyn *m* free; holder; land
Frans *m* free; man
Franz *m* free; man
Fraser *m* curly; haired
Frasier *m* curly; haired
Frayne *m* alien; foreigner; stranger
Frazer *m* curly; haired
Frazier *m* curly; haired
Freda *f* holy; peaceful
Fredela *f* elf; peaceful
Fredella *f* elf; peaceful
Frederic *m* peaceful; ruler
Frederica *f* peaceful; ruler
Frederick *m* peaceful; ruler
Frederik *m* peaceful; ruler
Frederika *f* peaceful; ruler
Frederique *f* peaceful; ruler
Fredric *m* peaceful; ruler
Fredrich *m* peaceful; ruler
Fredrick *m* peaceful; ruler
Freeman *m* free; man
Fremont *m* free; noble; protection; protector
Freta *f* goddess; lady; love
Frewen *m* free; friend; noble
Frewin *m* free; friend; noble
Frey *m* Lord/lord
Freya *f* lady; noble

Freyah *f* goddess; lady; love
Freyne *m* foreigner; stranger
Frick *m* bold; man
Frida *f* peaceful
Fridolf *m* peaceful; wolf
Frieda *f* peaceful
Friedrich *m* peaceful; ruler
Fritzi *f* peaceful; ruler
Frodeen *f* intelligent; wise
Frodina *f* intelligent; wise
Frodine *f* intelligent; wise
Froma *f* girl; holy
Fromma *f* girl; holy
Fronde *f* branch
Fronia *f* teacher; wise
Fronnia *f* teacher; wise
Fronniah *f* teacher; wise
Fu *m* teacher
Fuji *f* wisteria
Fujita *f* field; rice; wisteria
Fujita *m* field; rice
Fukuda *m* field; fortune; good; rice
Fulbert *m* bright; shining; son
Fulki *f* spark
Fullan *f* blooming
Fuller *m* cloth
Fulmala *f* garland
Fulton *m* dweller; enclosure
Fulumirani *m* journey
Funsan *m* request
Furuta *m* field; old; rice
Fuyu *f* born
Fuyuko *f* born; child

Gaal *m* angry; son
Gabi *f* concealed
Gable *m* Gabriel; little
Gabriel *m* God/god; man
Gabriela *f* God/god; woman
Gabriella *f* God/god; woman
Gabrielle *f* God/god; woman
Gada *f* happy; lucky
Gadi *m* fortune
Gadiel *m* fortune
Gadmann *m* fortunate
Gadmon *m* fortunate
Gaea *f* earth
Gafna *f* vine
Gagan *m* heaven; sky
Gage *m* pledge
Gaia *f* earth

Gail *f* father; gay; joy; lively; sing; singer
Gaile *m* gay; lively
Gailen *m* healer; tranquil
Gainer *m* fair; head; son
Gainor *m* fair; head; son
Gaius *m* rejoicer
Gala *f* single; wealthy
Galatea *f* ivory; milky; white
Galatia *f* ivory
Gale *f* father; gay; joy; lively; sing; singer
Gale *m* gay; lively
Galen *m* bright; healer; little; tranquil
Gali *f* fountain; hill
Galiana *f* lofty
Galiena *f* lofty
Galina *f* light
Galitea *f* ivory
Gall *m* foreigner
Gallagher *m* eager; foreign; helper
Gallard *m* lively
Galt *m* ground; high
Galton *m* estate; owner
Galvan *m* bright; shining; white
Galven *m* bright; shining; white
Galvin *m* bright; shining; white
Galya *f* God/god; light; redeemed
Gamada *f* glad; pleased
Gamal *m* camel
Gamali *m* camel
Gamba *m* warrior
Gan *m* adventurous; near
Gana *f* garden
Ganak *m* astrologer
Ganesa *f* God/god; good; luck; wisdom
Ganesh *m* God/god; multitude
Ganice *f* garden
Ganit *f* garden
Gannon *m* fair; little
Garai *m* settled
Garda *f* garden; girl
Gardal *m* careful; guard
Gardel *m* careful; guard
Gardell *m* careful; guard
Gardenia *f* flower; fragrant; gardenia; white
Gardia *f* garden; girl
Gardiner *m* gardener
Gardner *m* gardener
Gareth *m* gentle
Garey *m* spear; spearman

Garfield *m* field; triangular
Gari *f* fair; maiden; spear; yellow
Gari *m* spear; spearman
Garibald *m* addition; welcome
Garibold *m* addition; welcome
Garima *f* warmth
Garjan *m* thunder
Garlan *m* crowned; great; honor
Garland *f* crown; flowers
Garland *m* crowned; great; honor
Garlanda *f* crowned; great; honor
Garlinda *f* crowned; great; honor
Garman *m* spearman
Garmond *m* protector; spear
Garmund *m* protector; spear
Garner *m* army; guard; guardian
Garnet *f* jewel; radiant; red
Garnet *m* compulsion; spear
Garnett *m* compulsion; spear
Garnette *f* jewel; radiant; red
Garnock *m* alder; dweller; river
Garrard *m* brave; firm; spear
Garret *m* brave; firm; spear
Garrett *m* brave; firm; spear
Garrick *m* ruler; spear
Garridan *m* hid
Garrison *m* Garret; son
Garritt *m* brave; firm; spear
Garron *m* Gary; son; spearman
Garroway *m* spear; warrior
Garry *m* spear; spearman
Garson *m* Gar; son
Garth *m* garden; gentle; yardkeeper
Garton *m* dweller; farmstead; triangular
Garv *m* pride
Garvan *m* little; rough
Garvey *m* honorable; little; peace; rough
Garvin *m* friend; spear
Garwin *m* friend; spear

Garwood *m* fir; forest
Gary *m* spear; spearman
Gaspar *m* master; treasure
Gasper *m* master; treasure
Gaston *m* Gascony
Gati *m* family
Gatian *m* family
Gatias *m* family
Gauri *f* fair; yellow
Gauthier *m* army; powerful; ruler; warrior
Gavan *m* field; hawk
Gaven *m* field; hawk
Gavin *m* field; hawk; white
Gavra *f* Lord/lord; rock
Gavrah *f* Lord/lord; rock
Gavriella *f* heroine; strong
Gavrielle *f* heroine; strong
Gavril *m* God's; hero
Gavrila *f* heroine; strong
Gay *f* bright; lively
Gayan *m* singing; sky
Gayle *f* gay; lively
Gayle *m* gay; lively
Gaylen *m* healer; tranquil
Gayler *m* lively
Gaylor *m* lively
Gaylord *m* lively
Gayner *m* fair; head; son
Gaynor *m* fair; head; son
Gazella *f* antelope; gazelle
Gazit *f* hewn; stone
Gazo *m* leader; powerful
Gazzo *m* leader; powerful
Geary *m* changeable
Gedraitis *m* calm
Geela *f* joy
Geet *m* song
Geeti *f* melody
Geier *m* vulture
Gelasia *f* inclined; laughter
Gelasias *m* bright; star
Gelasius *m* bright; star
Gelya *f* angel; messenger
Gemina *f* twin
Gemini *f* twin
Geminian *m* born
Geminine *f* twin
Geminius *m* born
Gemma *f* gem; precious; stone
Gen *f* source; spring
Gene *m* born; noble; wellborn
Geneen *f* God/god; gracious
Genesa *f* new
Genesia *f* new
Genet *f* Eden
Geneva *f* juniper; tree

Genevieve *f* phantom; wave; white
Genie *f* born; noble; well
Genisia *f* new
Genna *f* new
Gentilis *m* kind; soul
Geoffrey *m* divinely; peaceful
Georg *m* farmer; land; worker
George *m* farmer; land; worker
Georgene *f* farmer; watchful
Georgette *f* farmer; watchful
Georgia *f* farmer; watchful
Georgiana *f* farmer; watchful
Georgienne *f* farmer; watchful
Georgina *f* farmer; watchful
Georgine *f* farmer; watchful
Geraint *m* old
Gerald *m* mighty; spear
Geraldina *f* mighty; spear
Geraldine *f* mighty; spear
Geraldo *m* mighty; spear
Gerard *m* brave; spear; strong
Gerardo *m* brave; spear; strong
Geraud *m* brave; mighty; spear; strong
Gerault *m* mighty; spear
Gerbold *m* bold; spear
Gerda *f* enclosure; protected; protection
Gere *m* battle; comrade
Gereron *m* battle; comrade
Gerhard *m* mighty; spear
Gerhardine *f* mighty; spear
Gerik *m* prosperous; spearman
Gerita *f* bird; motherly
Gerius *m* steadfast
Gerlac *m* soldier
Germain *m* bold
Germaine *f* bold
Germaun *m* bold
Germin *m* bold
Gerold *m* mighty; spear
Gerrard *m* brave; spear; strong
Gersham *m* exile; stranger
Gershom *m* exile; stranger
Gershon *m* Gar; son

Gertruda *f* loved; spear
Gertrude *f* loved; spear
Gertrudis *f* loved; spear
Gervais *m* honorable
Gervase *m* honorable
Gery *m* changeable
Gesina *f* corn; rice
Gessica *f* wealthy
Geva *f* hill
Geyer *m* vulture
Ghalib *m* excellent; winner
Ghalyela *f* precious
Giacinta *f* flower; hyacinth
Giacomo *m* supplanter
Gialla *m* servant
Giamo *m* supplanter
Gianina *f* God/god; gracious
Gianna *f* God/god; gracious
Giannetta *f* God/god; gracious
Giannina *f* God/god; gracious
Gibbon *m* born; hill
Gibby *f* gap-toothed
Gibe *m* born; hill
Gibeon *m* born; hill
Gibor *m* strong
Gibrian *m* aristocrat; high; stern
Gibson *m* Gilbert; son
Gideon *m* destroyer; hewer
Gifferd *m* brave; gift
Gifford *m* brave; gift
Gigi *f* farmer; God/god; watchful; woman
Gil *m* bearded; downy; youthful
Gilad *m* camel
Gilada *f* eternal; joy
Giladah *f* eternal; joy
Giladi *m* camel
Gilane *f* downy; haired; youthful
Gilbert *m* brilliant; hostage; pledge
Gilberta *f* brilliant; hostage; pledge
Gilbertina *f* brilliant; hostage; pledge
Gilbertine *f* brilliant; hostage; pledge
Gilberto *m* brilliant; hostage; pledge
Gilboa *m* bubbly
Gilby *m* estate; hostage; pledge
Gilchrist *m* Christ; servant

Gilda *f* covered; gold
Gildas *m* heritage; wise
Gildus *m* heritage; wise
Gilead *m* camel; region; rocky
Giles *m* bearded; downy; youthful
Giletta *f* downy; haired; youthful
Gilford *m* ford
Gill *m* servant
Gillan *f* downy; haired; youthful
Gillead *m* region; rocky
Gilleod *m* region; rocky
Gilley *m* servant
Gilli *f* downy-haired; innocent
Gillian *f* downy; downy-haired; haired; innocent; youthful
Gilliana *f* downy; haired; youthful
Gillie *f* downy-haired; innocent
Gillie *m* song
Gilliette *f* downy; haired; youthful
Gilly *f* quiet; silent
Gilmer *m* famous; hostage
Gilmore *m* Mary; servant
Gilroy *m* haired; red; servant; youth
Gilus *m* heritage; wise
Gimbya *f* princess
Gina *f* maidenly; silvery
Ginata *f* maidenly
Ginger *f* flower; maidenly; spice
Ginia *f* maidenly
Gino *m* born; noble; well-born
Ginson *m* garden
Ginton *m* garden
Giordano *m* descending
Giorgia *f* farmer; watchful
Giorgio *m* farmer; land; worker
Giorsal *f* attractive; graceful
Giovanna *f* God/god; gracious
Giovanni *m* God/god; gracious
Giralda *f* mighty; spear
Giraldo *m* mighty; spear
Giraud *m* mighty; spear
Girilal *m* mountain; son
Girisa *f* Lord/lord; mountain

Girish *m* God/god; mountain
Girvan *m* little; rough
Girven *m* little; rough
Girvin *m* little; rough
Gisa *f* gift; hewn; stone
Gisela *f* hostage; pledge
Gisella *f* hostage; pledge
Giselle *f* hostage; pledge
Gita *f* good; pearl; song
Gitana *f* gypsy
Gitel *f* flatterer; innocent
Githa *f* warlike
Gitta *f* strength
Gitte *f* strength
Gittel *f* flatterer; innocent
Gittle *f* flatterer; innocent
Giuseppe *m* add
Givon *m* heights; hill
Gizi *f* hostage; pledge
Gladi *f* gladiolus
Gladwin *m* cheerful; friend; kind
Gladys *f* flower; gladiolus; lame; small; sword
Gleda *f* glad; gladden; glowing; happy; lame
Glen *m* dweller; glen; valley
Glenda *f* dweller; valley
Glenden *m* fortress; glen
Glendon *m* fortress; glen; shady; valley
Glenette *f* dweller; valley
Glenice *f* fair; holy
Glenise *f* fair; holy
Glenn *m* dweller; fortress; glen; valley
Glenna *f* dweller; valley
Glennette *f* dweller; valley
Glennice *f* fair; holy
Glennis *f* fair; holy
Glenwys *f* fair; holy
Glenys *f* fair; holy
Glinys *f* little; valley
Gloria *f* glorious; glory
Gloriana *f* glorious; glory
Gloriane *f* glorious; glory
Glyn *m* dweller; glen; valley
Glynas *f* little; valley
Glynis *f* dweller; fair; holy; little; valley
Glynn *m* dweller; glen; valley
Glynnis *f* fair; holy
Goar *m* fighter
Godana *m* child; male
Goddard *m* firm
Godderd *m* firm
Godfrey *m* divinely; peaceful

Godiva *f* gift; God/god
Godred *m* firm
Godric *m* God/god; ruling
Godrich *m* good; seafarer
Godwin *m* divine; friend
Goel *m* redeemer
Goer *m* fighter
Golda *f* flower; golden; haired
Goldie *f* golden
Golding *m* golden; son
Goldwin *m* friend; gold
Gomar *m* thorough
Gomer *m* thorough
Gonsalve *m* wolf
Gonzales *m* wolf
Gonzalo *m* wolf
Goodman *m* good; man
Goodrich *m* good; seafarer
Goodwin *m* divine; friend
Gopan *m* protection
Gorakh *m* cowherd
Goran *m* farmer; land; worker
Gordan *m* gore; hill; triangular
Gorden *m* gore; hill; triangular
Gordon *m* gore; hill; triangular
Gore *m* fighter
Gorman *m* blue; little
Gosheven *m* great
Gothar *m* flocks; God's
Gothard *m* flocks; God's
Gottfried *m* divinely; peaceful
Gouri *f* fair; yellow
Govind *m* cowherd
Gower *m* pure
Gowon *m* rainmaker
Gozal *m* bird
Gozy *f* skin
Grace *f* attractive; graceful
Grady *m* illustrious; noble
Graham *m* gray; home; land
Granger *m* farmer
Grania *f* female; romantic
Graniah *f* female; romantic
Grannia *f* female; romantic
Granniah *f* female; romantic
Grannias *f* female; romantic
Grant *m* great
Grantham *m* big; meadow
Grantland *m* big; meadow
Grantley *m* big; meadow

Granville *m* estate; great; town
Gratiana *f* girl
Gratianna *f* girl
Gray *m* judge's; son
Grayson *m* judge's; son
Grazia *f* attractive; graceful
Greeley *m* gray; meadow
Greer *f* watchful
Gregor *m* vigilant; watchful; watchman
Gregorio *m* vigilant
Gregory *m* vigilant; watchful; watchman
Gressa *f* grass
Greta *f* pearl
Gretal *f* pearl
Gretchen *f* pearl
Gretta *f* pearl
Grey *m* judge's; son
Greyson *m* judge's; son
Griffith *m* chief; fierce
Grigor *m* vigilant
Grimbal *m* bold; son
Grimbald *m* bold; son
Grimona *f* veneration; woman
Grimonia *f* veneration; woman
Griselda *f* battle; gray; heroine; maid; unconquerable
Grishilda *f* battle; gray; maid
Grishilde *f* battle; gray; maid
Grishm *m* heat
Griswold *m* forest; gray
Grover *m* grove; tree; trees
Grunella *f* brown
Guadalupe *f* black; river; stone
Guda *f* good
Guenna *f* browed; phantom; wave; white
Guenter *m* bold; warrior
Guenther *m* bold; warrior
Guibert *m* bright; hope
Guida *f* guide; maid; warrior
Guido *m* forest; guide
Guilbert *m* brilliant; hostage; pledge
Guillelmina *f* protector; resolute
Guillelmine *f* protector; resolute
Guillemette *f* protector; resolute
Guillermo *m* protector; resolute

Guin *m* blond; fair

Guinevere *f* phantom; wave; white

Gulal *m* colored; red

Gulika *f* pearl

Gunda *f* battle; maiden; warrior

Gunhilda *f* battle; maid; warrior

Gunnar *m* bold; warrior

Gunter *m* army; battle; bold; warrior

Guntero *m* bold; warrior

Gunther *m* army; battle; bold; warrior

Gur *m* cub; lion

Guri *m* cub; lion

Gurias *m* family; wandering

Gurice *f* animal; young

Guriel *m* God/god; lion

Gurion *m* lion

Gurit *f* animal; young

Gustaf *m* Goths; staff

Gustaff *m* Goths; staff

Gustav *m* Goths; staff

Gustava *f* Goths; staff

Gustave *m* Goths; staff

Gustavo *m* Goths; staff

Guthrie *m* windy

Guy *m* life; warrior

Guyapi *m* candid

Gwen *f* browed; haired; lady; moon; new; white

Gwenda *f* browed; white

Gwendaline *f* haired; lady; moon; new; white

Gwendoline *f* haired; lady; moon; new; white

Gwendolyn *f* browed; haired; lady; moon; new; white

Gwenore *f* phantom; wave; white

Gwyn *f* fair; haired; lady; moon; new; white

Gwyneth *f* blessed; haired; lady; moon; new; white

Gwynn *m* blond; fair

Gwynne *f* fair; white

Gyan *m* filled; knowledge

Gyasi *m* child

Gypsie *f* wanderer

Gypsy *f* wanderer

Gytha *f* warlike

Gytle *f* flatterer; innocent

Haadiya *m* guide

Haamid *m* grateful

Haas *m* hare

Habbai *f* festive; merry

Habib *m* beloved

Habibah *f* beloved

Habika *f* sweetheart

Hachman *m* learned; man

Hachmann *m* learned; man

Hachmin *m* learned; man

Hackett *m* hacker; little

Hackman *m* shopkeeper; woodcutter

Hadad *m* fertility; God/god

Haddad *m* fertility; God/god; smith

Hadden *m* moors

Haden *m* moors

Hadi *m* guide; leader

Hadiya *f* gift

Hadley *m* heath; meadow

Hadrian *m* dark

Hadwin *m* battle; dear; friend

Hadwyn *m* battle; dear; friend

Hafiz *m* guardian

Hagai *f* merry

Hagan *m* little; young

Hagar *f* flees

Hagen *m* little; young

Haggai *f* merry

Haggar *f* flees

Haggi *f* merry

Hagi *f* merry

Hagia *f* festive; joyful

Hagice *f* festive; joyful

Hagit *f* festive; joyful

Hagley *m* hedged; pasture

Hahnee *m* beggar

Hai *m* ocean

Haiba *f* charm

Haidar *m* lion

Haidee *f* honored; modest

Haig *m* dweller; enclosure; hedged

Haile *m* powerful; strength

Haily *f* hero

Haim *m* life

Haima *f* snow

Haimi *f* golden

Haines *m* cottage

Haji *m* born; pilgrimage

Hakan *m* fiery

Hakeem *m* wise

Hakeen *m* wise

Hakem *m* ruler

Hakesh *m* Lord/lord; sound

Hakim *m* doctor; wise

Hako *m* exalted; high

Hakon *m* exalted; high

Hakub *m* supplanter

Hal *m* army; ruler; stock

Haland *m* Henry's; land

Halbert *m* bright; brilliant; hero

Halda *f* battle; brave; reliable

Haldan *m* Dane; half

Haldana *f* Danish; half

Haldas *f* reliable

Halden *m* Dane; half

Haldi *f* reliable

Haldie *f* beloved

Haldis *f* reliable

Hale *m* army; hero; ruler; stock

Haleigh *f* hero

Haletta *f* queen; tiny

Halette *f* queen; tiny

Haley *f* clever; hero

Haley *m* ingenious; scientific

Halford *m* hall; manor

Halfrida *f* hall; heroine; home; peaceful

Hali *f* clever

Halian *m* belonging; Julius; youthful

Halie *f* clever; hero

Halil *m* friend

Halim *m* gentle; patient

Halima *f* gentle; kind

Halimeda *f* sea; thinking

Hall *m* house; master's

Halla *f* gift

Hallam *m* dweller

Halland *m* Henry's; land

Hallette *f* queen; tiny

Hallie *f* army; clever; ruler; sea; thinking

Halliwell *m* dweller; holy; spring

Hallvard *m* castle; king

Hally *f* army; hero; ruler

Halona *f* fortunate; pleasant; times

Halonna *f* pleasant; times

Halsey *m* Hal's; island

Halstead *m* house; manor

Halsted *m* house; manor

Halton *m* estate; hill; slope

Ham *m* black

Hama *f* shore

Hamako *f* child; shore

Hamal *m* lamb

Hamar *m* ingenuity

Hambleton *m* grassy hill; hill

Hamet *m* home; little

Hamford *m* black; ford

Hamid *m* God/god; praised

Hamida *f* gracious

Hamilton *m* estate; grassy hill; hill; home; lover's

Hamisi *m* born

Hamlet *m* home; little

Hamlin *m* army; home; little; lover; man; warrior

Hamlyn *m* home; little

Hammad *m* praised

Hammed *m* praised

Hammet *m* home; little

Hammond *m* home; protector

Hamon *m* faithful

Hamsa *f* swan

Hamza *m* powerful; strong

Han *m* fence; ocean

Hana *f* black; blossom; cloud; flower; graceful; happiness; sky

Hanae *f* blossom; flower

Hanako *f* blossom; flower

Hanan *m* God/god; gracious; mercy

Hanbal *m* pure

Haneef *m* believer; true

Hanford *m* ford; tall

Hania *f* place

Hanif *m* believer; true

Haniya *f* place

Haniyah *f* place

Hanley *m* high; meadow; pasture; warrior

Hanna *f* congratulations; forbidden; happiness; prevented

Hannah *f* graceful

Hannibal *m* Baal; grace

Hans *m* God/god; gracious

Hansa *f* swan

Hansan *m* Hans; son

Hansen *m* Hans; son

Hansin *m* soul; universal

Hansini *f* swan

Hanson *m* Hans; son

Hanzila *f* path

Hara *f* seizer

Hara *m* remover

Haralda *f* army; ruler

Harb *m* war

Harbin *m* glorious; little; warrior

Harcourt *m* court; fortified

Hardan *m* lively; town

Harday *m* hardy; stock

Harden *m* lively; town

Hardey *m* bold; daring

Harding *m* brave; son

Hardwin *m* brave; friend

Hardy *m* bold; daring; hardy; stock

Harel *m* God's; mountain

Harelda *f* battle; brave

Haresh *m* Lord/lord; Vishnu

Hargrave *m* grove; hare

Hargrove *m* grove; hare

Hari *m* tawny

Hariette *f* estate; home; ruler

Harilda *f* battle; brave

Harim *m* flatnosed

Harini *f* deer

Harish *m* Lord/lord; Vishnu

Harit *m* green

Harita *f* green

Harith *m* cultivator; plowman

Harithah *m* plowman

Harjeet *m* victorious

Harjit *m* victor

Harlan *m* army; land

Harley *m* hare; meadow; pasture; rabbit

Harlow *m* hill; rough

Harman *m* army; man; warrior

Harmon *m* army; man; unifying; warrior

Harmonia *f* concord; harmony

Harmony *f* concord; harmony

Haro *m* boar; first; son; wild

Harod *m* loud

Haroko *m* boar; first; son; wild

Haroku *m* boar; first; son; wild

Harold *m* army; ruler

Haroun *m* exalted; lofty

Harper *m* harp player; player

Harriet *f* estate; home; ruler

Harris *m* Harry; Henry; royal; son

Harrison *m* Harris; son

Harrod *m* loud

Harry *m* army; Harris; man; son

Harshad *m* delightful

Harshal *m* delightful

Harshil *m* delightful

Harsho *m* tricky

Harshul *m* deer; delightful

Hart *m* deer; hard

Hartman *m* austere; heart; man; strong

Hartmann *m* heart; man's

Hartwell *m* deer's; spring

Haru *f* born; spring

Haruko *f* born; child; spring; tranquil

Haruni *m* mountaineer

Harvey *m* army; warrior

Hasad *m* harvest

Hasan *m* laughter

Hasani *m* beautiful

Haseem *m* decisive

Hasen *m* laughing

Hasheem *m* destroyer

Hashi *f* bridge

Hashi *m* bridge

Hashim *m* destroyer

Hashum *m* rich

Hasika *f* laughter

Hasim *m* decisive; handsome; kind

Hasin *m* laughing

Hasina *f* good; strong

Haskel *m* understanding

Haskell *m* understanding

Hassan *m* handsome

Hassim *m* handsome; kind

Hassin *m* laughing

Hastin *m* elephant

Hastings *m* severe; son

Hateem *m* judge

Hatem *m* judge

Hatim *m* judge

Hau *m* desired

Havelock *m* contest; sea

Haven *m* safety

Haviva *f* beloved

Hawk *m* bird

Hawke *m* bird

Hawkeye *m* bird

Hawley *m* hedged; meadow

Haya *f* nimble; quick

Hayatt *f* life

Hayden *m* hedged; valley

Haydon *m* hedged; valley

Hayes *m* hunter; woods

Hayley *f* clever

Haylie *f* clever

Haymo *m* amiable; friend

Haynes *m* cottage

Hayu *f* born; spring

Hayward *m* enclosure; hedged; keeper

Haywood *m* forest; hedged

Hazel *f* hazelnut; tree

Hearn *m* horses; Lord/lord; owner

Hearne *m* horses; Lord/lord; owner

Heath *m* heath; wasteland
Heathcliff *m* cliff; heath
Heather *f* flower; heather; shrub
Hebbe *f* goddess; spring
Hebe *f* goddess; spring
Hebert *m* brilliance; man
Hector *m* fast; steadfast
Heda *f* fight; refuge; storm; strife
Hedda *f* strife
Heddi *f* strife
Heddy *f* strife
Hedeon *m* destroyer; hewer
Hedva *f* diligent; joy; worker
Hedvah *f* diligent; joy; worker
Hedve *f* diligent; joy; worker
Hedveh *f* diligent; joy; worker
Hedvig *f* fight; refuge; storm; strife
Hedvige *f* fight; refuge; storm; strife
Hedwig *f* fight; refuge; storm; strife
Hedy *f* fight; pleasant; refuge; storm; strife; sweet
Heidi *f* battle; maid
Heidy *f* battle; maid
Heinrich *m* estate; home; property; ruler
Helaku *m* day; sunny
Helbon *m* fruitful; valley
Helbona *f* fruitful
Helbonia *f* fruitful
Helbonna *f* fruitful
Helbonnah *f* fruitful
Helen *f* Lenka; light
Helena *f* Lenka; light
Helene *f* Lenka; light
Helga *f* holy; pious
Helice *f* spiral
Helki *f* touch
Helki *m* touch
Helma *f* protection; protector; resolute
Helmine *f* protector; resolute
Helmut *m* courage; helmet
Heloise *f* famous; maid; warrior
Helsa *f* given; God/god
Helse *f* given; God/god
Helsie *f* given; God/god
Hemakshi *f* eyes; good

Heman *m* steady
Hemkanta *f* girl; good
Hemlata *f* creeper; good
Henderson *m* Henry; royal
Hendrick *m* estate; home; property; ruler
Hendrik *m* home; ruler
Hendrika *f* estate; home; ruler
Henka *f* estate; home; ruler
Henleigh *m* clearing; high
Henley *m* clearing; high
Henri *m* estate; home; property; ruler
Henrietta *f* estate; home; ruler
Henriette *f* estate; home; ruler
Henrika *f* estate; home; ruler
Henry *m* estate; home; property; ruler
Hera *f* gods; lady; queen; ruling
Herbert *m* army; brilliant; glorious; warrior
Herma *f* child; earth
Herman *m* army; man; warrior
Hermina *f* child; earth
Hermine *f* earth; world
Herminia *f* earth; world
Hermione *f* earth; world
Hermosa *f* beautiful
Hernando *m* adventuring; daring; life; world
Herod *m* conqueror; heroic
Herra *f* gods; queen
Herrah *f* gods; queen
Herrick *m* army; ruler
Herrod *m* conqueror; heroic
Hersch *m* deer
Herschel *m* deer
Hersh *m* deer
Hershel *m* deer
Herta *f* earth; world
Hertha *f* earth; world
Heshum *m* rich
Hesper *f* evening; star
Hespera *f* evening; star
Hespira *f* evening; star
Hesta *f* goddess
Hester *f* star
Hesther *f* star
Hestia *f* goddess
Heti *f* beautiful; goddess; nymph; sea
Hetty *f* star

Hevel *m* breath
Hewett *m* Hugh; little
Hewitt *m* Hugh; little; smart
Hewlett *m* Hugh; little
Hewson *m* Hugh; little
Heywood *m* enclosed; forest; hedged; high; wood
Hiawatha *m* rivers
Hibernia *f* Ireland
Hibiscus *f* flower; plant
Hidalgo *m* Lord/lord; nobleman
Hideo *m* child; excellent; male
Hidie *f* battle; maid
Hien *m* good-natured; sweet
Hieu *m* admired; respected
Hignacio *m* fiery
Hija *f* daughter
Hilar *f* cheerful; friend; merry
Hilaria *f* cheerful
Hilary *f* cheerful; friend; merry
Hilda *f* battle; maid
Hilde *f* battle; maid
Hildebrand *m* sword; war
Hildegarde *f* battle; maid
Hildemar *f* battle; glorious
Hildie *f* battle; maid
Hildreth *f* battle; counselor
Hildy *f* battle; maid
Hilel *m* greatly; moon; new; praised
Hilier *m* battle; brave
Hillaria *f* friend; merry
Hillary *f* cheerful; friend; merry
Hillel *m* greatly; praised
Hillell *m* greatly; praised
Hilliard *m* battle; brave
Hilmar *m* famous; noble
Hiltan *m* hill; house
Hilten *m* hill; house
Hilton *m* hill; house
Himaadri *m* mountain; snow
Himesh *m* Lord/lord; snow
Himmat *m* courage
Hinda *f* deer
Hindi) *f* angular
Hinto *m* blue
Hinun *m* clouds; God/god; rain
Hira *f* chatty; palm; young
Hiram *m* noble

Hiramatsu *f* flat; pine
Hiramatsu *m* flat; pine
Hirata *f* field; flat; rice
Hirata *m* field; flat; rice
Hiroko *f* child; generous
Hiroshi *m* generous
Hirsch *m* deer
Hirza *f* delight
Hisa *f* long-lasting
Hisae *f* long-lasting
Hisako *f* long-lasting
Hisayo *f* long-lasting
Hisham *m* generosity
Hisoka *m* reserved; secretive
Hita *f* lovable
Hiti *f* hyena
Hiya *f* heart
Ho *m* congratulate; good; what
Hoa *f* flower; peace
Hoang *m* completed
Hoashis *m* God/god; loved
Hobart *m* brilliant; mind
Hoc *m* studious
Hod *m* splendid; vigorous
Hodia *m* Jehovah; splendor
Hodiah *m* Jehovah; splendor
Hodiya *m* Jehovah; splendor
Hoffman *m* farm; worker
Hogan *m* youth
Hokolesqua *m* cornstalk
Hoku *f* star
Hoku *m* star
Holbrook *m* brook; dweller; hollow
Holcomb *m* deep; valley
Holda *f* beloved; concealed
Holden *m* hollow; valley
Holen *f* holly tree; tree
Holic *m* barber
Hollah *f* girl
Holleb *m* dove
Holley *m* dove
Hollis *m* grove; tree
Holluh *m* dove
Holly *f* girl; holly tree; tree
Holman *m* island; river
Holmann *m* island; river
Holmen *m* island; river
Holmes *m* island; river
Holt *m* forest
Holuh *m* dove
Homer *m* pledge; security
Honda *m* base; field; rice
Hondo *m* warrior

Honey *f* sweet
Hong *f* pink
Hong *m* flank; red; side
Honon *m* bear
Honoria *f* honor; honorable
Honovi *m* strong
Hope *f* desire; hope
Horace *m* hours; keeper; light; sun
Horacia *f* hours
Horatia *f* hours
Horatio *m* hours; keeper; light; sun
Hortense *f* garden
Hortensia *f* garden
Horton *m* estate; gray
Horus *m* hawk
Hosana *f* Lord/lord; praise
Hoshi *f* star
Hoshi *m* star
Hosyi *m* conservative
Hototo *m* whistler
Houghton *m* dweller; estate; hillside
Houston *m* Hugh's; town
Howard *m* chief; guardian
Howe *m* eminent; high; hill
Howell *m* alert; eminent; little
Howi *m* turtledove
Howin *m* loyal
Howland *m* hills
Howlend *m* hills
Howlond *m* hills
Howlyn *m* hills
Hoyt *m* soul; spirit
Hridya *f* heart
Hu *m* tiger
Hua *f* flower
Huang *m* emperor; wealthy
Huang-Fu *m* future; wealthy
Hubert *m* brilliant; mind; spirit
Huberta *f* brilliant; mind
Huberto *m* brilliant; mind; spirit
Hudson *m* hooded; son
Huette *f* brilliance
Hugh *m* brilliant; intelligence; mind; spirit
Hugo *m* intelligence; spirit
Hui *f* intelligent; wise
Hui *m* intelligent; wise
Hulbard *m* brilliant; graceful
Hulbert *m* brilliant; graceful

Hulburt *m* brilliant; graceful
Hulda *f* beloved; concealed; gracious; prophetess; wise
Huldah *f* prophetess; wise
Huldie *f* gracious
Huma *f* bird; paradise
Humayd *m* praised
Humberto *m* famous; warrior
Hume *m* home; lover
Humita *f* corn
Humphrey *m* Hun; peaceful
Hunt *m* hunt
Hunter *m* hunter
Huntingdon *m* hill; hunter
Huntington *m* estate; hunting
Huntley *m* hunter; meadow
Hurd *m* hard; strong
Hurley *m* sea
Hurst *m* dweller; forest
Husain *m* beauty; little
Husam *m* sword
Huslu *m* bear; hair
Husni *m* good; handsome
Hussain *m* beauty; little
Hussein *m* beauty; little
Hutchens *m* Hugh; little; son
Hutchins *m* Hugh; little; son
Hutchinson *m* Hugh; little; son
Hutchison *m* Hugh; son
Hute *m* star
Hutton *m* estate; ridge
Huxford *m* ford; Hugh's
Huxley *m* Hugh's; meadow
Huy *m* glorious; radiant
Huyana *f* falling; rain
Huyu *m* born
Hwang *m* yellow
Hy *m* hope; wish
Hyacinth *f* flower; hyacinth
Hyam *m* life
Hyatt *m* gate; high

Ian *m* God/god; gracious
Iantha *f* colored; flower; violet
Ianthina *f* colored; flower; violet
Ibby *f* charcoal; kola
Ibrahim *m* father; multitude

Ichaa *m* desire
Ida *f* happy; industrious; prosperous
Idalia *f* happy; prosperous
Idalina *f* happy; prosperous
Idaline *f* happy; prosperous
Idden *m* man; prosperous
Iddo *m* loving
Idel *f* faithful; woman
Iden *m* man; prosperous
Idha *f* insight
Idhant *m* luminous
Idika *f* earth
Iditri *f* complimentary
Idola *f* lovely; vision
Idolah *f* lovely; vision
Idolla *f* lovely; vision
Idona *f* busy; girl
Idonah *f* busy; girl
Idonia *f* lover
Idonna *f* busy; girl
Iduna *f* lover
Ierne *f* Ireland
Igasho *m* wanderer
Iggi *m* lonesome; only
Ignace *m* fiery
Ignacia *f* ardent
Ignacio *m* fiery
Ignasio *m* fiery
Ignatia *f* ardent; fiery
Ignatius *m* fiery
Ignatz *m* fiery
Ignatzia *f* ardent
Ignaz *m* fiery
Ignazio *m* fiery
Igor *m* hero
Ihita *f* desire
Ijada *f* jade; stone
Ijaya *f* sacrifice
Ike *m* laughs
Ikov *m* supplanter
Iksha *f* sight
Ikshan *m* sight
Ikshita *f* visible
Ikshu *m* sugarcane
Iku *f* nourishing
Ila *f* island
Ileana *f* bearer; city; Lenka; light
Ilene *f* bearer; light
Ilesh *m* earth; Lord/lord
Ilia *f* city
Iliana *f* Lenka; light
Ilias *m* God/god; Jehovah
Ilisa *m* earth; king
Ilisha *f* truthful
Ilka *f* flattering; industrious
Ilom *m* enemies

Ilomerika *m* enemies
Ilona *f* beautiful; light
Ilsa *f* cheer; girl; maiden; noble
Ilse *f* maiden; noble; truthful
Ima *f* girl; lover; nature; now
Imako *f* now
Imala *f* disciplinarian
Imalda *f* wistful
Iman *f* believer
Iman *m* faith
Imani *f* trustworthy
Imelda *f* wistful
Imelida *f* wistful
Imena *f* dream
Immanuel *m* God/god
Imogene *f* image
Imperia *f* imperial
Ina *f* rendezvous; stutterer
Inas *m* capable
Ince *m* innocent
Inda *f* river
Indee *f* river
India *f* river
Indigo *f* blue; dark; India
Indira *f* splendid
Indra *f* splendid
Indria *f* splendid
Indrina *f* deep
Indu *f* moon
Indukala *f* moonlight
Indulala *f* moonlight
Induma *f* moon
Indumati *f* full; moon
Ines *f* pure
Inessa *f* pure
Inga *f* daughter
Ingar *m* army; son
Ingemar *m* famous; son
Inger *m* army; son
Inglebert *m* angel; brilliant
Ingmar *m* hero
Ingraham *m* Ing's; raven
Ingram *m* Ing's; raven
Ingrid *f* daughter
Ingvar *m* army; son
Inika *f* earth; small
Iniko *m* time
Innes *m* island; river
Inness *m* island; river
Innis *m* island; river
Inoa *f* chant; name
Inteus *m* shame
Inu *f* attractive
Ioakim *m* God/god; judge
Iola *f* cloud; color; dawn; violet
Iolanthe *f* flower; violet

Iole *f* cloud; color; dawn; violet
Iona *f* colored; stone; violet
Ione *f* colored; stone; violet
Ioseph *m* add
Iosif *m* add
Ipsita *f* desire
Iqbal *m* well
Ira *m* watchful
Iravan *m* earth; ocean
Irena *f* peace
Irene *f* peace
Ireta *f* angry
Iretta *f* angry
Irette *f* angry
Irina *f* peace
Iris *f* flower; iris; rainbow
Irisa *f* flower; iris; rainbow
Irma *f* high; person
Irra *f* castle; woman
Irvette *f* friend; sea
Irvin *m* friend; sea
Irvine *m* friend; sea
Irving *m* friend; sea
Irwin *m* friend; sea
Isa *f* consecrated; God/god; iron-willed
Isaac *m* laughs
Isabel *f* consecrated; God/god
Isabis *f* beautiful
Isadora *f* gift
Isaiah *m* Lord/lord; salvation
Isak *m* Lord/lord; salvation
Isamel *m* God/god; hears
Isas *m* meritorious
Isham *m* estate; iron
Ishana *f* desirable
Ishani *f* desirable
Ishat *m* superior
Ishi *f* stone
Ishie *f* stone
Ishiko *f* stone
Ishiyo *f* stone
Ishmael *m* God/god; hears; wanderer
Ishmul *m* wanderer
Isi *f* deer
Isi *m* deer
Isis *f* goddess; spirit
Isla *f* sweet
Islean *f* sweet
Isleana *f* sweet
Isleen *f* dream; sweet; vision
Isma *m* husband; loyal
Ismael *m* God/god; hears

Ismail *m* God/god; hears
Isman *m* husband; loyal
Ismeil *m* God/god; hears
Isoke *f* gift; satisfying
Isolda *f* girl; white
Isolde *f* girl; white
Israel *m* God/god
Issay *m* hairy
Istas *f* snow
Istu *m* sugar
Ita *f* enticing; thirst
Italia *f* Italy
Ithaman *m* man; sailor; sea
Ithnan *m* sailor; strong
Ituha *f* oak; strong
Iulia *f* downy; haired; youthful
Iva *f* promise; ripened; tree; yew-bow
Ivan *m* God/god; gracious
Ivana *f* gift; God's; gracious
Ivanah *f* gift; God's; gracious
Ivanna *f* gift; God's; gracious; tree; yew-bow
Ivar *m* army; bow; yew
Iven *m* bow; little; yew
Ives *m* bow; son; yew
Ivon *m* archer
Ivor *m* army; bow; yew
Ivria *f* Abraham's; land
Ivriah *f* Abraham's; land
Ivrit *f* Abraham's; land
Ivy *f* gift; God's; gracious; ivy; vine
Iwata *m* field; rice; rock
Iyla *f* moonlight
Iza *f* famous; maid; warrior
Izara *f* section; tree
Izusa *f* stone; white

Jaafar *m* river; small
Jaala *f* divine
Jaban *m* born; God/god
Jabari *m* brave
Jabilo *m* man; medicine
Jabin *m* born; God/god
Jabir *m* comforter
Jabon *m* born; God/god
Jacenta *f* beautiful; comely; flower; hyacinth
Jaci *f* moon
Jacinda *f* beautiful; comely; flower; hyacinth
Jacinta *f* beautiful; comely; flower; hyacinth
Jacintha *f* beautiful; comely; flower; hyacinth

Jacinthe *f* beautiful; comely; flower; hyacinth
Jacinto *m* hyacinth
Jackson *m* Jack; son
Jaclyn *f* supplanter
Jacob *m* supplanter
Jacoba *f* supplanter
Jacobah *f* supplanter
Jacobba *f* supplanter
Jacobina *f* supplanter
Jacqueline *f* supplanter
Jacquelyn *f* supplanter
Jacques *m* supplanter
Jacquetta *f* supplanter
Jacy *m* moon
Jacynth *f* beautiful; comely; flower; hyacinth
Jada *f* wise
Jadda *f* wise
Jadda *m* man; wisdom
Jaddan *m* man; wisdom
Jaddo *m* man; wisdom
Jade *f* jade; stone
Jaeger *m* huntsman
Jael *f* divine; goat; mountain
Jael *m* goat; mountain
Jaela *f* divine
Jafar *m* little; stream
Jaffa *f* beautiful; lovely
Jaffice *f* beautiful; lovely
Jafit *f* beautiful; lovely
Jagat *m* world
Jagdeo *m* God/god; world
Jagdish *m* king; world
Jagesh *m* Lord/lord; universe
Jagger *m* carter
Jagish *m* Lord/lord; universe
Jagrati *f* awakening
Jagrav *m* awakened
Jagruti *f* awareness
Jagvi *f* worldly
Jahan *m* world
Jahdai *m* directs; God/god; man
Jahdal *m* directs; God/god; man
Jahdiel *m* directs; God/god; man
Jahdol *m* directs; God/god; man
Jahi *m* dignified; dignity
Jahia *f* prominent
Jahsee *m* child
Jaichand *m* moon; victory
Jaidayal *m* kindness; victory
Jaideep *m* light; victory
Jaiman *m* victorious

Jaime *f* supplanter
Jaime *m* supplanter
Jair *m* enlightened; God/god; man
Jairia *f* enlightened; God/god
Jaival *m* life-giving
Jajdi *m* glorious
Jakarious *m* friend; peaceful
Jake *m* supplanter
Jakob *m* supplanter
Jakoba *f* supplanter
Jal *m* goes
Jala *f* bright; divine; glory; God/god; lion; polished; splendid
Jaldhar *m* clouds
Jalen *m* bright; healer; little; tranquil
Jalendu *m* moon; water
Jalesh *m* Lord/lord; water
Jalpa *f* discussion
Jalsa *f* celebration
Jamaine *m* German
Jamal *m* camel; elegance
Jameela *f* beautiful
James *m* supplanter
Jami *f* supplanter
Jamie *f* supplanter
Jamil *m* handsome
Jamila *f* beautiful
Jamilah *f* beautiful
Jamill *m* handsome
Jamillah *f* beautiful
Jamillia *f* beautiful
Jamin *m* righthanded
Jammal *m* camel
Jammin *m* righthanded
Jamnes *m* magician
Jamnis *m* magician
Jana *f* fruit; harvest
Janae *f* God/god; gracious
Janardan *m* helps; people
Janaya *f* fruit; harvest
Jane *f* God/god; gracious
Janesh *m* Lord/lord; men
Janet *f* God/god; gracious
Janette *f* God/god; gracious
Janice *f* God/god; gracious
Janina *f* God/god; gracious
Janis *m* God/god; gracious
Janisha *f* dispeller; ignorance
Janna *f* fruit; God/god; gracious; harvest
Janthina *f* colored; flower; violet

Janu *m* force; life; soul
Janulis *m* God/god; gracious
Janus *m* born
Janya *f* life
Japa *m* chanting
Japeth *m* fairest; son
Japheth *m* fairest; son
Jara *f* enlightened; God/god
Jardena *f* downward; Palestine; river
Jareb *m* contend; lively; son
Jared *m* descendant; inheritor
Jarek *m* born
Jari *f* bird; enlightened; God/god; motherly
Jari *m* control; man
Jariah *f* enlightened; God/god
Jarib *m* contend
Jarietta *f* earthen; water
Jarita *f* bird; earthen; motherly; water
Jarl *m* chief; nobleman
Jarlath *m* control; man
Jarlathus *m* control; man
Jarman *m* German
Jaron *m* cry; sing
Jaroslav *m* glory; spring
Jarred *m* descendant
Jarvey *m* honorable
Jarvia *f* keen; spear
Jarvis *m* keen; spear
Jaskaran *m* deeds; good
Jasmin *f* flower
Jasmina *f* flower
Jasmine *f* flower
Jasmit *f* famed
Jason *m* healer
Jasper *m* jasper; master; stone; treasure
Jasu *f* brainy
Jasweer *f* victorious
Jatan *m* nurturing
Jatasya *m* ocean
Javan *m* Greece
Javas *m* quick; swift
Javier *m* bright; house; new; owner
Javin *m* Greece; understand
Javon *m* Greece
Jawhar *m* essence; jewel
Jawole *f* clear; water
Jay *m* blue
Jaya *f* victory
Jayan *f* victory
Jayanti *f* victory

Jayavanti *f* victorious
Jaycee *m* moon
Jayin *m* conqueror
Jayita *f* victorious
Jayme *f* supplanter
Jayme *m* supplanter
Jaymi *f* supplanter
Jaymie *f* supplanter
Jayna *f* victory
Jayne *f* God/god; gracious; victorious
Jaysee *m* child
Jayson *m* healer
Jazeps *m* add
Jean *f* God/god; gracious
Jean *m* God/god; gracious
Jeanne *f* God/god; gracious
Jeannette *f* God/god; gracious
Jecoa *m* gift; God/god
Jecon *m* gift; Lord/lord
Jeconiah *m* gift; Lord/lord
Jed *m* beloved; hand; Lord/lord
Jedd *m* beloved; descendant; hand
Jediah *m* beloved; Lord/lord
Jedidiah *m* beloved; Lord/lord
Jedrek *m* manly; strong
Jedthus *m* Lord/lord; praise
Jeeval *m* full; life
Jeevan *m* life
Jeeven *m* give; light
Jeevika *f* water
Jeevitha *f* life
Jefferey *m* divinely; peaceful
Jefferson *m* Jeffrey; son
Jeffrey *m* divinely; peaceful
Jegar *m* love; witness
Jeggar *m* love; witness
Jegger *m* love; witness
Jehiah *m* Jehovah; life
Jehial *m* Jehovah; son
Jehias *m* Jehovah; life
Jehiel *m* Jehovah; son
Jehius *m* Jehovah; life
Jehosah *m* Jehovah; loyal; servant
Jehu *m* Lord/lord; praised
Jeks *m* supplanter
Jelani *m* mighty
Jelena *f* Lenka; light
Jelinek *m* deer
Jemena *f* dove
Jemima *f* dove
Jemina *f* dove

Jeminah *f* dove
Jemine *f* dove
Jena *f* bird; patience; small
Jendayi *f* give; thanks
Jenesia *f* new
Jenifer *f* phantom; wave; white
Jeniffer *f* phantom; wave; white
Jenna *f* bird; small
Jenni *f* phantom; wave; white
Jennie *f* phantom; wave, white
Jennifer *f* phantom; wave; white
Jennings *m* descendant; John
Jenny *f* phantom; wave; white
Jeno *f* heaven; heavenly; queen
Jens *m* God/god; gracious
Jeny *f* phantom; wave; white
Jephum *m* prepared
Jepum *m* prepared
Jerard *m* brave; spear; strong
Jereme *m* appointed; exalted; God/god; Jehovah
Jeremia *f* exalted; Lord/lord
Jeremiah *m* appointed; exalted; God/god; Jehovah
Jeremias *m* appointed; exalted; God/god; Jehovah
Jeremy *m* appointed; exalted; God/god; Jehovah
Jeri *f* exalted; Lord/lord
Jeritah *f* bird; motherly
Jermain *m* German
Jermaine *m* German
Jerman *m* German
Jermane *m* German
Jerome *m* holy
Jerred *m* inheritor
Jerri *f* mighty; spear
Jerrod *m* descendant; inheritor
Jerusha *f* married
Jervis *m* keen; spear
Jesh *m* man; upright
Jesher *m* man; upright
Jess *m* wealth
Jesse *f* wealthy
Jesse *m* wealth
Jessica *f* wealthy
Jessie *f* wealthy
Jessie *m* wealth
Jesu *m* God/god; salvation

Jesus *m* God/god; salvation

Jesuso *m* God/god; salvation

Jethro *m* preeminence

Jetta *f* encircled

Jette *f* encircled

Jeu *m* Lord/lord; praised

Jeuz *m* man; wisdom

Jeven *m* give; light

Jewel *f* gem; precious

Jezreel *m* God's

Jezus *m* God/god; salvation

Jhulier *m* precious

Ji *m* continuity

Jibben *m* life

Jigisha *f* superior

Jigna *f* curiosity; intellectual

Jignasa *f* academic; curiosity

Jignesh *m* curiosity

Jill *f* downy; downy-haired; haired; innocent; youthful

Jillian *f* downy-haired; innocent

Jilliana *f* downy-haired; innocent

Jillie *f* downy-haired; innocent

Jimoh *m* born

Jin *f* excellent; gentle; super-excellent

Jin *m* gold

Jina *f* name

Jing *m* pure

Jinx *f* charm

Jira *f* blood

Jiro *m* male; second; second-born

Jishnu *m* triumphant

Jitamitra *m* foes

Jivan *m* give; light

Jiven *m* give; light

Jivin *m* give; light

Jivvel *m* lives

Jiya *f* sweetheart

Jo Ella *f* Lord/lord; willing

Jo *m* add; God/god; increase

Joab *m* Lord/lord; praise

Joachim *m* God/god; judge

Joachima *f* pious

Joacima *f* pious

Joacimah *f* pious

Joakima *f* judge; Lord/lord

Joan *f* God/god; gracious

Joana *f* God/god; gracious

Joanne *f* God/god; gracious

Joappa *f* lovely; stranger

Joaquin *m* God/god; judge

Joash *m* God/god; loved

Joashus *m* God/god; loved

Joben *m* cleanliness

Jobi *f* afflicted

Jobie *f* afflicted

Jobina *f* afflicted

Joby *f* afflicted

Jocasta *f* lighthearted

Joceline *f* just

Jocelyn *f* just; merry; playful

Jocelyne *f* just

Jochbed *m* glory; God/god

Jochebed *m* glory; God/god

Jocosa *f* humorous

Jodi *f* praised

Jody *f* praised

Joed *m* goodness; lords/Lord's; witness

Joel *m* God/god; Lord/lord

Joella *f* Lord/lord; willing

Joelle *f* Lord/lord; willing

Joellen *f* Lord/lord; willing

Joette *f* add; increase

Johanan *m* gift; Jehovah

Johann *m* God/god; gracious

Johar *m* jewel

Johiah *m* Jehovah; life

John *m* God/god; gracious

Johnsten *m* John; son

Johnston *m* John; son

Johppa *f* lovely; stranger

Johppah *f* lovely; stranger

Joji *m* farmer; land; worker

Joktan *m* tiny

Jola *f* pretty; servant; tall

Jola *m* tall

Jolan *f* blossom; flower; violet

Jolanta *f* pretty; servant

Jolenta *f* pretty; servant

Jolie *f* pretty

Joline *f* increase

Jollanta *f* pretty; servant

Jollenta *f* pretty; servant

Jolon *m* dead; oaks; valley

Jomo *m* burning; spear

Jon *m* God/god; gracious

Jona *f* dove

Jonah *m* dove

Jonas *m* dove; God/god; gracious; peace

Jonathan *m* gift; Jehovah

Jonati *f* dove

Jone *m* God/god; gracious

Jones *m* John; son

Jonina *f* dove

Joosef *m* add

Jora *f* autumn; rain

Joran *f* autumn; rain

Jordan *f* Palestine; river

Jordan *m* Palestine; river

Jordana *f* Palestine; river

Jordane *f* Palestine; river

Jordanne *f* Palestine; river

Jordon *m* descending

Jordyn *f* Palestine; river

Jorge *m* farmer; land; worker

Jori *m* Palestine; river

Joriko *f* trustworthy

Jorn *m* farmer; land; worker

Jory *m* Palestine; river

Josceline *f* just

Joscelyne *f* just

José *m* add

Josecito *m* add

Josef *m* add

Josefina *f* add; increase

Joseito *m* add

Joselito *m* add

Josep *m* add

Joseph *m* add

Josephe *m* add

Josephina *f* add; increase

Josephine *f* add; increase

Joses *m* Lord/lord; loves

Josette *f* add; increase

Josha *m* satisfaction

Joshi *f* pious

Joshitha *f* pleased

Joshua *m* God/god; salvation

Josiah *m* healed; Lord/lord

Josip *m* add

Joska *m* add

Joszef *m* add

Jotham *m* God/god

Joub *m* Lord/lord; praise

Jov *m* God/god; judge

Jovan *m* God/god; gracious

Jovi *f* little; Lord/lord; servant

Jovia *f* little; Lord/lord; servant

Jovita *f* joyful; little; Lord/lord; servant

Jovitah *f* little; Lord/lord; servant

Jovitta *f* little; Lord/lord; servant
Joza *m* add
Joze *m* add
Jozef *m* add
Jozhe *m* add
Jozhef *m* add
Jozio *m* add
Jozka *m* add
Jozsi *m* add
Juan *m* God/god; gracious
Juana *f* God/god; gracious
Juanita *f* God/god; gracious
Juba *f* born
Judah *m* praise
Judas *m* praise
Judd *m* beloved; descendant; praised
Jude *m* law; praise; right
Judie *f* praised
Judith *f* praised
Judsen *m* Judd; son
Judson *m* Judd; son
Judus *m* beloved; descendant
Judy *f* praised
Jueta *f* friend
Juetta *f* friend
Jugal *m* couple
Jugnu *m* fire
Juji *f* heap; loved
Jula *f* downy; haired; youthful
Julcia *f* downy; haired; youthful
Jule *m* bearded; downy; youthful
Jules *m* bearded; downy; youthful
Julia *f* downy; haired; youthful
Julian *m* cheeked; downy; youthful
Juliana *f* downy; haired; youthful
Juliet *f* downy; haired; youthful
Julietta *f* downy; haired; youthful
Juliette *f* downy; haired; youthful
Julina *f* downy; haired; youthful
Juline *f* downy; haired; youthful
Julinka *f* downy; haired; youthful
Julio *m* bearded; downy; youthful

Juliska *f* downy; haired; youthful
Julissa *f* downy; haired; youthful
Julita *f* downy; haired; youthful
Julius *m* bearded; cheeked; downy; youthful
Juma *m* born
Jumah *m* born
Jun *f* obedient; truth
Jun *m* obedient; truth
Juna *f* heaven; heavenly; queen
June *f* born
Junella *f* born
Juni *f* heaven; heavenly; queen
Junius *m* forever; young
Junna *f* heaven; heavenly; queen
Junno *f* heaven; heavenly; queen
Juno *f* heaven; heavenly; queen
Juri *m* farmer; land; worker
Justin *m* just; upright
Justine *f* just
Justis *m* justice
Justus *m* justice
Juta *f* friend
Jutta *f* friend
Juzef *m* add
Juziu *m* add
Jwala *f* flame
Jynx *f* charm

Kaaliya *m* huge; serpent
Kaanan *m* forest
Kabibe *f* lady; little
Kabil *m* possessed
Kabir *m* honor
Kacey *f* guileless
Kachina *f* dancer; sacred
Kachine *f* dancer; sacred
Kacie *f* brave
Kadar *m* powerful
Kade *m* barrel
Kadee *f* battle; pure
Kadi *f* battle
Kadia *f* battle; pure
Kadie *f* battle; pure
Kadin *m* companion; friend
Kadir *m* green
Kaditula *m* sword
Kady *f* pure
Kafi *f* quiet

Kaga *m* chronicler; writer
Kagami *f* mirror
Kahaleel *m* friend; good
Kahlil *m* friend; good
Kai *f* forgiveness; sea
Kai *m* sea
Kaija *f* life
Kaiko *f* child; forgiveness
Kaila *f* crowned; laurel
Kaile *f* crown; victory
Kailey *f* beloved
Kain *m* tribute
Kaine *m* tribute
Kaiti *f* pure
Kaitlan *f* pure
Kaitleen *f* pure
Kaitlen *f* pure
Kaitlin *f* pure
Kaitlyn *f* pure
Kakala *f* flowers; fragrant; garland
Kakar *m* grass
Kaksi *f* perfume
Kala *f* art; black; laughs; princess; time
Kala *m* black; time
Kalama *f* flaming; Lenka
Kalan *m* moon
Kalanath *m* moon
Kalani *f* chieftain
Kalash *m* sacred
Kalb *m* dog
Kale *m* manly; strong
Kalea *f* brilliant; illustrious
Kaleb *m* bold; dog
Kaleela *f* girlfriend
Kaleena *f* sun
Kaleki *f* graceful; lovely
Kalena *f* pure
Kalere *f* small; woman
Kali *f* black; bud; destroyer; energy; goddess; maiden; rosebud; time
Kalica *f* rosebud
Kalie *f* rosebud
Kalifa *f* chaste; holy
Kalika *f* loud; rosebud
Kalil *m* friend; good
Kalila *f* beloved; girlfriend; loved; sweetheart
Kalilah *f* girlfriend
Kalin *m* mighty; warrior
Kalina *f* sun
Kalinda *f* sun
Kalindi *f* sun
Kaling *m* bird
Kaliq *m* creative
Kaliska *f* chasing; coyote; deer
Kalkin *m* God/god
Kalle *m* manly; strong

Kalli *f* lark
Kallol *m* joy
Kalman *m* manly; strong
Kalola *f* strong
Kaloosh *m* blessed; coming
Kalpana *f* imagination
Kalpesh *m* Lord/lord
Kalpita *f* imaginary
Kaluwa *f* forgotten
Kalvin *m* bald
Kalyan *m* welfare
Kalyani *f* fortunate
Kalyca *f* rosebud
Kama *f* love; nursling
Kama *m* loving
Kamadev *m* God/god; love
Kamal *m* lotus; man
Kamali *f* spirit
Kamali *m* spirit
Kamana *f* wish
Kamaria *f* moonlike
Kamea *f* one
Kameel *m* perfect
Kameka *f* blind
Kameko *f* child; tortoise
Kameo *f* one
Kami *f* Lord/lord
Kami *m* loving
Kamiko *f* Lord/lord
Kamil *m* perfect
Kamila *f* perfect
Kamilah *f* perfect
Kamili *f* perfection
Kamilla *f* perfect
Kamillah *f* perfect
Kammile *f* perfect
Kamna *f* wish
Kamran *m* success
Kamuzu *m* medicinal
Kamya *f* capable
Kana *f* atom
Kanan *f* jungle
Kanani *f* beauty
Kanasu *f* dream
Kanchan *f* gold
Kandace *f* glittering; glowing; white
Kande *f* born; daughter; first-born
Kandee *f* glittering; glowing; white
Kandi *f* glittering; glowing; white
Kandis *f* glittering; glowing; white
Kane *f* accomplished; bronze
Kane *m* tribute
Kang *m* bay; river
Kangee *m* raven; tin

Kangi *m* raven; tin
Kani *f* constancy; girl; sound
Kania *f* virgin
Kaniel *m* reed; stalk
Kanika *f* black; cloth; molecule
Kanjee *m* raven; tin
Kanko *m* thyself
Kanoa *f* freedom
Kantilal *m* lustrous
Kantimoy *m* lustrous
Kantu *m* happy
Kanya *f* virgin
Kapil *m* fair
Kapua *f* blossom
Kapuki *f* born; daughter; first-born
Kara *f* beloved; dear; friend; pure
Karan *m* instrument
Kardal *m* mustard
Kareem *m* generous
Kareema *f* generous
Kareen *m* exalted; noble
Karen *f* pure
Kari *f* little; strong; womanly
Karida *f* untouched
Karim *m* exalted; noble
Karima *f* generous
Karimah *f* generous
Karina *f* pure
Karisa *f* beloved; dear
Karise *f* beloved; dear
Karisha *f* beloved; dear
Karissa *f* beloved; dear
Karita *f* charity
Karl *m* farmer; manly; strong
Karla *f* little; strong; womanly
Karm *m* fate
Karma *f* action; destiny; fate
Karmel *f* farm; garden; vineyard
Karmel *m* farm
Karmen *f* crimson
Karmendra *m* duty
Karnam *m* famed
Karniela *f* horn
Karniella *f* horn
Karnis *f* horn
Karnit *f* horn
Karol *f* strong; womanly
Karolina *f* little; womanly
Karsten *m* blessed
Kartar *m* creation; Lord/lord
Karuna *f* merciful

Karuna *m* merciful
Karunesh *m* Lord/lord; mercy
Kaseem *m* divided; fertile
Kaseko *m* mock
Kasey *f* brave
Kashi *m* luminous
Kashif *m* connoisseur
Kasi *f* city; guileless; holy
Kasib *m* fertile
Kasim *m* divided
Kasimir *m* commands; peace
Kasmira *f* commands; peace
Kasper *m* master; treasure
Kass *m* blackbird
Kassandra *f* helper; men
Kassia *f* pure
Kassie *f* guileless
Kassy *f* guileless
Kassya *f* guileless
Kasturi *f* scented
Kata *f* worthy
Kateb *m* writer
Katelyn *f* pure
Katherine *f* pure
Katrina *f* pure
Katsu *f* child; victorious
Katura *f* better
Katy *f* pure
Katya *f* pure
Kauffman *m* merchant
Kaula *f* prophet
Kaulana *f* famous
Kausar *m* lake; paradise
Kaushal *m* clever
Kaushali *f* skillful
Kaustubh *m* immortal
Kautik *m* joy
Kavan *m* handsome
Kaveri *f* Kaveri; river; sacred
Kavi *m* poet
Kavika *f* poetess
Kavindra *f* mighty
Kaviraj *m* doctor
Kavita *f* poetry
Kavni *f* poem; small
Kawacatoose *m* lean; man; poor
Kawena *f* glowing
Kay *f* keeps
Kaya *f* elder; little; rush; sister; yew
Kaye *f* keeps
Kayin *m* celebrated
Kayla *f* keeps; pure
Kayle *f* crown; victory
Kayne *m* tribute

Kazuko *f* child; first; obedient
Kazuo *m* born; first
Kea *m* small
Keady *m* earth; man; red
Keahi *f* fire
Keahi *m* firm
Keala *f* fragrance
Kealan *m* little; slender
Kealy *m* handsome
Kean *m* ancient; bold; handsome; keen
Keandre *m* manly; strong
Keane *m* ancient; bold; handsome; keen
Keara *f* black; little
Keaton *m* hawks; place
Keb *m* Egyptian; God/god
Kedar *m* powerful
Keddie *m* earth; man; red
Keddy *m* earth; man; red
Kedem *m* ancient; east; old
Kedrick *m* battle
Keefe *m* barrel; gentle; handsome; lovable; maker; noble
Keegan *m* highly; little; spirited
Keelan *m* little; slender
Keeley *m* handsome
Keelin *f* fair; slender
Keely *f* beautiful
Keely *m* handsome
Keemaya *f* miracle
Keenan *m* ancient; little
Keene *m* ancient; bold; handsome; keen
Keerthi *f* eternal; flame
Kegan *m* highly; spirited
Kei *f* rapture
Keiki *f* child
Keiko *f* adored; child; joyous
Keir *m* bound; dark-skinned
Keira *f* black; little
Keisha *f* favorite
Keith *m* battle
Kekona *f* born; child
Kela *f* fountain; fresh
Kelan *m* little; slender
Kelby *m* farm
Kelcie *f* island; ship
Kelda *f* fountain; fresh; spring
Keldah *f* fountain; fresh
Kele *m* hawk
Kelemen *m* gentle; kind; merciful
Keli *f* warrior

Kelia *f* warrior
Kelii *m* chief
Kelila *f* crown; victory
Kelilah *f* crown; laurel; victory
Kelin *m* mighty; warrior
Kelisa *f* warrior
Kell *m* spring
Kella *f* fountain; fresh
Kellan *m* mighty; warrior
Kellda *f* fountain; fresh
Kelle *m* hawk; mighty; warrior
Kellen *f* warrior
Keller *m* companion; little
Kelley *f* warrior
Kelley *m* dweller; warrior; water
Kelli *f* warrior
Kellia *f* warrior
Kellie *f* warrior
Kellin *m* mighty; warrior
Kellina *f* warrior
Kelly *f* spring; warrior
Kelly *m* warrior
Kelsey *f* island; ship
Kelsey *m* ship; victory
Kelsy *f* island; ship
Kelsy *m* ship; victory
Kelula *f* crown; laurel; victory
Kelvan *m* narrow; river
Kelven *m* narrow; river
Kelvin *m* narrow; river
Kelwen *m* dweller; water
Kelwin *m* dweller; water
Kem *m* sun
Kemp *m* champion; warrior
Kenan *m* ancient; little
Kenay *m* brave; soldier
Kenaz *m* hunter
Kenda *f* child; cool; pure; water
Kendal *m* bright; clear; river; valley
Kendall *m* bright; clear; river; valley
Kendell *m* bright; clear; river; valley
Kendi *f* loved
Kendra *f* knowing; woman
Kendrah *f* knowing; woman
Kendrew *m* manly; strong
Kendrick *m* Henry; royal; ruler; son
Kendy *f* knowing; woman
Kenelm *m* brave; warrior
Kenisha *f* beautiful; life
Kenji *m* born; bright; second-born; son

Kenlay *m* king's/kings; meadow
Kenleigh *m* king's/kings; meadow
Kenley *m* king's/kings; meadow
Kenn *m* bright; clear; water
Kennard *m* bold; strong
Kennedy *m* head; helmeted
Kenneth *m* handsome; oath; royal
Kenrick *m* royal; ruler
Kensell *m* brave; royally
Kent *m* bright; white
Kenton *m* estate; farm; royal
Kenward *m* bold; guardian; royal
Kenway *m* bold; brave; royal; soldier; warrior
Kenweigh *m* brave; soldier
Kenyon *m* white
Kenzie *f* child; leader; wise
Kera *f* bells; sadness
Kerani *f* bells; sadness
Kerby *m* church; village
Kerel *m* man; young
Kerem *m* kind; noble
Kerey *m* bound
Keri *f* bells; sadness
Kerie *f* bells; sadness
Kermit *m* free; man
Kern *m* dark; little
Kerr *m* dark; spear
Kerry *m* captain; dark; ship; son
Kersen *m* cherry
Kersten *m* blessed
Kerwen *m* black; little
Kerwin *m* black; dark; little
Kerwon *m* dark
Kery *f* bells; sadness
Kesar *m* born; hair; leader; long
Kesava *f* fine; hair
Keshia *f* favorite
Kesia *f* favorite
Kesin *m* beggar; haired
Kesley *f* island; ship
Keslie *f* island; ship
Kesse *m* birth
Kessiah *f* favorite
Kessie *f* chubby
Ketura *f* incense
Ketzi *f* bark
Ketzia *f* bark
Keval *m* only
Kevan *m* gentle; lovable
Keven *m* gentle; lovable

Kevin m gentle; lovable
Kewal m only
Key m fiery; son
Kezi f bark
Kezia f bark
Khaim m life
Khairiya m charitable; good
Khalil m friend
Khang m hearty
Khatib m minister; religious
Khiem f humble
Khiem m humble
Khoury m priest
Khristina f Christian
Khushal m perfect
Khyati f fame
Kia f ancient; beginning; difficult
Kiah f beginning
Kian m ancient
Kiana f ancient
Kiandra f ancient
Kiandrea f ancient
Kianne f ancient
Kianni f ancient
Kibbe m bird; night
Kichi f fortunate
Kichiko f fortunate
Kichiyo f fortunate
Kiefer m barrel; maker
Kiele f blossom; fragrant; gardenia
Kiely f beautiful
Kienan m ancient; little
Kiera f black; little
Kieran f black; little
Kieran m dark; little
Kierra f black; little
Kieu f beautiful; graceful
Kijika m quietly
Kikilia f blind
Kiku f chrysanthemum
Kikuno f chrysanthemum; field
Kila f comely
Kilah f comely
Kilah m dog
Kilan m innocent
Kilby m farm; spring
Kile m fair; handsome
Kiley f beautiful
Kilian m innocent
Kill m dweller
Killian m little; warlike
Kim m chief; gold; ruler
Kimama f butterfly
Kimatra f seduce
Kimball m bold; chief; royal; warrior

Kimberly f fortress; meadow; royal
Kimble m bold; chief; royal; warrior
Kimi f peerless; sovereign
Kimie f peerless; sovereign
Kimiko f peerless; sovereign
Kimiyo f peerless; sovereign
Kin m golden
Kina f defender; helper
Kinaari f shore
Kincaid m battle; chief
Kineta f active
Kingdon m hill; king's/kings
Kingsley m king's/kings; meadow
Kingston m king's/kings
Kingswell m dweller; king's/kings; spring
Kini f God/god; gracious
Kini m king
Kinnard m high; hill
Kinnell m cliff; head
Kinsey m royal; victorious
Kinsley m king's/kings; meadow
Kinu f child; cloth
Kinuko f child; cloth
Kioko f child; happy
Kiona f brown; hills
Kipp m hill; pointed
Kira f sun
Kiraat m hunter
Kiral m king
Kiran m light; ray
Kirby m church; village
Kiri m mountain; summit
Kiril m lordly
Kirima f hill
Kirin m poet
Kiritan m crown
Kirk m church; dweller
Kirkley m church; meadow
Kirkwood m church; forest
Kiros m king
Kirsten f Christian
Kirsten m blessed
Kirstin f Christian
Kirsty f Christian
Kirt m blessed
Kirti f fame
Kirti m fame
Kirtin m celebrated
Kirwin m black; little
Kisa f kitty
Kishi f beach
Kishor m boy; young
Kiska f pure

Kismet f destiny
Kiss f small
Kiss m small
Kissa f born
Kissiah f favorite
Kistna f delightful
Kistnah f delightful
Kistur m Rider
Kita f kitten; north
Kito m jewel
Kiva m protect; supplant
Kivi m protect; supplant
Kiwa f border; born
Kiyoshi m quiet
Kizza m born; twins
Kizzy f cinnamon
Klarika f bright; brilliant; illustrious
Klarissa f bright; brilliant; illustrious
Klaus m army; people; victorious
Klein m little; short
Klementine f calm; merciful; mild
Kleon m famous
Klesa f pain
Kliment m gentle; kind; merciful
Kline m little; short
Knight m soldier
Knox m hills
Knut m knot
Knute m knot
Ko m yellow
Koa f princess
Koah f princess
Kodey f assistant; helper
Kodi f assistant; helper
Kodie f assistant; helper
Kody f assistant; helper
Kody m cushion
Koemi f small; smile
Koffi f born
Koi m panther
Koji m child; little; one
Kokila f singer
Koko f night; stork
Kokubas m supplanter
Kolala f womanly
Kolby m black; dark; settlement
Kolenya f cough
Kolika f ocean
Kolina f pure
Kolya m army; people; victorious
Komali f tender
Konane f bright; moonlight
Konane m bright; moonlight

Kong *m* hole
Konni *m* bold; counselor
Konrad *m* bold; counselor
Konstandinos *m* constant; firm
Konstantinos *m* constant; firm
Kontar *m* child; only
Korban *m* raven
Korben *m* raven
Korbin *m* raven
Kordell *m* little; maker; rope
Korigan *m* little; spear
Korin *f* maiden
Korina *f* sullen
Korrigan *m* little; spear
Korudon *m* crested; helmeted
Korwin *m* friend; raven's
Kosey *m* lion
Kosse *m* lion
Kostas *m* constant; firm
Kostis *m* constant; firm
Kostos *m* constant; firm
Kostya *f* constancy
Koto *f* harp
Kotoko *f* harp
Kovar *m* smith
Kovidh *m* wise
Kraanti *m* revolution
Kraig *m* crag; dweller
Kramer *m* shopkeeper
Kranti *f* revolution
Kripa *f* compassion
Kripal *m* compassionate
Kripasagar *m* mercy; ocean
Krisha *f* delightful
Krisha *m* delightful
Krishanu *m* fire
Krishna *f* delightful
Krishna *m* delightful
Krishnah *m* delightful
Krispin *m* curly; haired
Kriss *m* bearer; Christ
Krista *f* Christian
Kristan *f* Christian
Krister *m* anointed; believer; Christ
Kristian *m* anointed; believer; Christ
Kristin *f* Christian
Kristo *m* bearer; Christ
Kristopher *m* bearer
Kristophyer *m* Christ
Krisya *f* delightful
Kritanu *m* skilled
Kritiman *m* sculptor
Krolik *m* hare
Kruin *m* mountain; peak
Kruti *f* creation

Krysta *f* Christian
Krystal *f* clear
Kshantu *m* patient
Kshitij *m* horizon
Kudio *f* born
Kulani *f* sky
Kuma *m* bear
Kumar *m* boy; son; young
Kumi *f* braid
Kumiko *f* braid; child
Kumuda *f* lotus
Kumudesh *m* moon
Kumush *m* ancient
Kune *m* hare
Kuni *f* born; country
Kuniko *f* born; country
Kunjana *f* forest; girl
Kunshi *f* shining
Kuper *m* copper
Kurano *f* field
Kuri *f* chestnut
Kuroda *m* black; field; rice
Kurt *m* bold; counselor; courteous; well-bred
Kurtis *m* courteous; well-bred
Kuruk *m* bear
Kusa *f* grass; sacred
Kuzih *m* great
Kwabina *f* born
Kwaco *m* born
Kwaku *f* born
Kwaku *m* born
Kwam *m* born; God/god; gracious
Kwame *m* born
Kwamin *f* born
Kwamin *m* born
Kwan *m* shut
Kwanita *f* God/god; gracious
Kwashi *f* born
Kwasi *m* born; Sunday
Kwau *f* born
Kwesi *m* born; Sunday
Ky *f* abstain; sign; strange
Ky *m* abstain; sign; strange
Kyla *f* comely; crown; laurel; victory
Kylah *f* comely
Kyle *m* fair; handsome
Kyley *f* beautiful
Kylila *f* beloved
Kyna *f* intelligence; wisdom
Kyne *m* bold; royal
Kyoko *f* mirror
Kyra *f* God/god; Lord/lord
Kyrene *f* God/god; Lord/lord

La Reina *f* queen
La Roux *f* redhead
La Verne *f* alder; grove; tree
Laban *m* white
Labana *f* goddess; ivory
Labanna *f* goddess; ivory
Labannah *f* goddess; ivory
Labh *m* gain
Lacee *f* cheerful
Lacey *f* cheerful
Lach *m* dweller; invincible; water
Lachish *m* invincible
Lachlan *m* warlike; water
Lachus *m* invincible
Lacie *f* cheerful
Lacy *f* cheerful
Ladd *m* attendant; lad
Lado *m* born; boy; second-born; son
Ladonna *f* lady
Lael *f* devoted; Lord/lord
Lahar *m* wave
Lahela *f* ewe
Lail *f* devoted; Lord/lord
Laila *f* born; night
Laird *m* proprietor
Lais *f* adored
Lais *m* lion
Laise *f* adored
Laius *f* adored
Lajita *f* modest
Laka *f* attract; tame
Lakota *f* friend
Lakota *m* friend
Laksh *m* aim; target
Laksha *f* aim
Lakshan *m* aim
Lakshita *f* distinguished
Lakshya *m* target
Lakya *f* born
Lal *m* beloved
Lala *f* flower
Lalage *f* cheerful; speaker
Lalam *m* jewel
Lalasa *f* love
Lali *f* blushing
Lalita *f* charming; frank; pleasing
Lalitta *f* frank
Lalittah *f* frank
Lallage *f* cheerful; speaker
Lally *f* devoted; Lord/lord
Lamar *m* famous; land
Lambert *m* brilliant; land; light
Lamond *m* lawyer
Lamont *m* lawyer
Lana *f* air; beautiful;

bright; fair; harmonious;
light
Lance *m* adherent; atten-
dant; serves
Landa *f* crowned; great;
honor; honorable
Landbert *m* brilliant; land;
light
Landberto *m* brilliant;
land; light
Lander *m* grassy hill;
owner; plain
Landers *m* grassy hill;
green; owner; plain
Landis *m* native
Landon *m* dweller; hill;
long
Landor *m* grassy hill;
owner; plain
Landre *m* local; ruler
Landri *m* local; ruler
Landry *m* local; ruler
Lane *m* narrow; passage;
road
Lanette *f* lane; little
Lang *m* long; man; tall
Langdon *m* dweller; hill;
long
Langford *m* dweller; ford;
long
Langley *m* long; meadow
Langston *m* estate; man's;
tall; town
Langundo *m* peaceful
Langworth *m* enclosure;
long
Lani *f* chieftain; sky
Lani *m* sky
Lanna *f* beautiful; bright;
fair
Lantha *f* dark; flower
Lanzo *m* noble; ready
Lara *f* famous; shining
Laraine *f* gull; Lorraine
Laramie *m* love
Lareena *f* girl; sea
Lareina *f* queen
Larena *f* girl; queen; sea
Larentia *f* foster; mother
Laresa *f* happy
Larianna *f* girl; sea
Larimer *m* horses; lover
Larimor *m* horses; lover
Larina *f* girl; gull; sea
Larine *f* girl; gull; sea
Larisa *f* happy
Larissa *f* happy
Lark *f* lark; singer
Lars *m* crowned; laurel;
victory
Larson *m* Lars; son

LaSalle *m* hall
Lasca *f* weariness; weary
Lash *m* famous; warrior
Lashi *m* famous; warrior
Lasho *m* famous; warrior
Lassie *f* girl; little
Latacia *f* born
Latangi *f* girl; slim
Latasha *f* born
Latea *f* ivory
Lateefah *f* gentle
Lathan *m* boy; nearby
Lathrop *m* village
Lati *f* elevated; lofty; spirit
Latia *f* mother
Latif *m* gentle
Latika *f* creeper; small
Latimer *m* interpreter
Latin *f* bull
Latisha *f* gladness
Latona *f* mother
Latonia *f* mother
Latoniah *f* mother
Latoya *f* victorious
Latton *m* man
Lattonia *f* mother
Laughton *m* man
Laura *f* crown; laurel
Laurena *f* foster; mother
Laurene *f* crown; laurel
Laurentia *f* foster; mother
Laurenz *m* crowned; laurel
Lauretta *f* crown; laurel
Laurette *f* crown; laurel
Lavali *f* clove
Lavangi *f* angel
Lavani *f* grace
Laveda *f* purified
Lavella *f* cleansing
Lavelle *f* cleansing
Lavergne *f* alder; grove;
tree
Lavetta *f* purified
Lavette *f* purified
Lavi *m* lion
Lavina *f* purified
Lavinia *f* purified
Lawford *m* ford; hill
Lawler *m* half; speaker
Lawley *m* hill; meadow
Lawrence *m* crowned; lau-
rel
Lawry *m* crowned; laurel
Lawson *m* Lawrence; son
Lawton *m* man
Layak *m* capable
Layla *f* born; dark; night
Lazario *m* God/god; help
Lazaro *m* God/god; help
Lazarus *m* God/god; help
Lazauskas *m* willow

Le *f* pear; tree; weary
Le *m* pear; tree
Lea *f* bold; meadow; peo-
ple; weary
Leah *f* weary
Leal *m* faithful; loyal
Leala *f* faithful; loyal
Lealia *f* faithful; loyal
Lealie *f* faithful; loyal
Lealiki *f* shore; song
Leana *f* climbing; vine
Leander *m* lion; man
Leandre *m* lion; man
Leandro *m* lion; man
Leanna *f* answered; climb-
ing; Jehovah; prayers;
vine
Lear *m* joyful
Leatri *f* joyful; young
Leatrice *f* joyful; young
Leben *m* life
Lebna *f* fair; white
Lectra *f* brilliant; star
Leda *f* beautiful; birth;
city; clean; forgetfulness;
friend; girl; gladness; lit-
tle; lovely; patient; whole-
some; winged; young
Ledah *f* gladness; lovely
Ledda *f* lovely
Lee *f* child; meadow;
plum; plums; poetic;
weary
Lee *m* meadow; pasture;
plums; poetic
Leeba *f* heart
Leena *f* Lenka; light
Leesa *f* joy; joyful
Leeza *f* joy; joyful
Leggett *m* delegate
Leggitt *m* delegate
Legra *f* cheerful
Lehua *f* gods; sacred
Leib *m* lion
Leibel *m* lion
Leif *m* beloved
Leigh *m* meadow; pasture;
poetic
Leighland *m* meadow
Leighton *m* farm; meadow
Leila *f* beauty; born; dark;
night
Leilani *f* child; flower;
heavenly
Leilia *f* dark; night
Leith *m* river; wide
Leitha *f* forgetfulness
Leithia *f* forgetfulness
Lekh *m* document
Lekha *f* writing
Lekisha *f* life

Lel *m* takes
Lela *f* dark; night; noble
Leland *m* meadow
Lelith *f* wife
Lema *f* girl; peace
Lemmuela *f* dedicated; God/god
Lemuel *m* consecrated; God/god
Lemuela *f* dedicated; God/god
Lemuelah *f* dedicated; God/god
Len *m* flute
Lena *f* allures; mild; soft
Lencho *m* lion
Lenci *m* crowned; laurel
Lendar *m* parents
Leneta *f* mild; soft
Lenis *f* mild; soft
Lenita *f* mild; soft
Lenka *f* light
Lenmana *f* flute; maiden
Lenno *m* man
Lennon *m* cloak; little
Lennor *m* spring; summer
Lennox *m* elm; trees
Leno *m* man
Lenora *f* Lenka; light
Lenore *f* Lenka; light
Lenox *m* chief
Lensar *m* parents
Leo *m* lion
Leoda *f* people; woman
Leola *f* dear; lion; lioness
Leoma *f* bright; light
Leon *m* lion
Leona *f* lioness
Leonard *m* brave; lion
Leonarda *f* brave; lion
Leonardo *m* brave; lion
Leondra *f* lioness
Leonia *f* lioness
Leonice *f* lioness
Leonie *f* lioness
Leonora *f* Lenka; light
Leonteen *f* brave; lion
Leontina *f* brave; lion
Leontine *f* brave; lion
Leontyne *f* lion
Leopold *m* bold; people
Leopoldeen *f* bold; people
Leopoldine *f* bold; people
Leopoldo *m* bold; people
Leora Hindi) *f* light
Leora *f* light
Leorah *f* light
Leota *f* people; woman
Leotie *f* flower; prairie
Leron *m* song
Lerone *m* song

Leroy *m* king
Leska *f* defender; helper
Lesley *f* dweller; fortress; gray
Lesley *m* dweller; forest; gray
Leslie *f* dweller; fortress; gray
Leslie *m* dweller; forest; gray
Lester *m* camp; chosen
Lesya *f* defender; helper
Leta *f* beautiful; bring; clean; forgetfulness; gladness; lady
Letasha *f* born
Letha *f* forgetfulness; girl; trusted; truthful
Lethia *f* forgetfulness
Letice *f* gladness
Leticia *f* gladness; joyous
Letisha *f* gladness
Letitia *f* gladness
Letta *f* bird; graceful
Lev *m* lion
Levana *f* moon; rising; sun; white
Levania *f* moon; white
Leverett *m* rabbit; young
Leverton *m* farm; rush
Levi *m* joined
Levia *f* join; lioness
Levin *m* friend
Levina *f* flash; lightning
Leviya *f* lioness
Levona *f* moon; white
Levy *m* joined
Lewanna *f* beaming; moon; white
Lewis *m* famous; warrior
Lexine *f* defender; helper
Leya *f* law; loyalty
Li *f* blossom; plum; plums; tree
Li *m* black; plums
Liam *m* determined
Lian *f* graceful; willow
Liana *f* answered; climbing; Jehovah; prayers; vine
Liane *f* climbing; graceful; vine; willow
Liang *m* excellent; good
Lianna *f* climbing; vine
Lianne *f* answered; climbing; graceful; Jehovah; prayers; vine; willow
Liatrice *f* joyful; young
Liatris *f* joyful; young
Liayna *f* allures
Liba *f* fair; white

Libby *f* consecrated; God/god
Libna *f* fair; white
Libnah *f* fair; white
Libni *f* God/god
Licha *f* truthful
Lici *f* truthful
Lida *f* all; birth; city; gladness; loved
Lidah *f* all; gladness; loved
Lidda *f* all; loved
Liddie *f* all; loved
Lideah *f* birth
Lidi *f* happy
Lidia *f* cultured; happy; person; woman
Lidka *f* happy
Liem *m* honest
Lien *f* lotus
Liene *f* allures
Lien-Hua *f* flower; lotus
Liesel *f* consecrated; God/god
Liesl *f* consecrated; God/god
Liggett *m* delegate
Li-Hua *f* blossom; pear
Liko *m* Buddhist
Lila *f* brooding; capriciousness; dark; fate; flower; lilac; night
Lilac *f* flower; lilac
Lilah *f* brooding
Lilia *f* flower
Liliana *f* lily
Liliane *f* flower; lily
Liliha *f* disgust
Lilith *f* belonging; night; wife
Lilka *f* famous; maid; warrior
Lillian *f* flower; lily
Lilliana *f* flower; lily
Lillis *f* wife
Lillith *f* wife
Lily *f* beautiful; flower; lily
Lilybel *f* beautiful; lily
Lilybelle *f* beautiful; lily
Lilybet *f* God's; promise
Liman *m* man; plains
Limann *m* man; plains
Limber *f* joyful
Lin *f* beautiful; forest; jade
Lin *m* forest
Lina *f* allures; elfin; girl; high; tower
Lincoln *m* colony; pool
Linda *f* beautiful; pretty
Lindberg *m* hill; linden; tree

Lindell *m* dweller; linden; tree; valley
Lindley *m* linden; meadow
Lindly *m* linden; meadow
Lindo *m* gentle
Lindsay *f* island; tree
Lindsay *m* isle; linden; tree
Lindsey *f* island
Lindsey *m* isle; linden; tree
Lindy *m* linden; meadow
Linetta *f* comely; lass
Linette *f* comely; lass
Linford *m* ford; linden; tree
Linfred *m* gentle; peace
Ling *f* dainty; delicate; forest
Ling *m* forest
Linis *m* flaxen-haired; haired
Link *m* bank; ridge
Linley *m* field; flax
Linnea *f* lime tree; tree
Linnette *f* comely; lass
Linton *m* enclosure; flax
Linus *m* flaxen-haired; haired
Lio *m* lion
Liolya *f* Lenka; light
Liona *f* lioness
Lionel *m* lion; young
Liora *f* light
Liris *f* lyre; music
Lirit *f* lyrical; musical; poetic
Liron *f* song
Liron *m* song
Lirone *m* song
Lisbeth *f* consecrated; God/god
Liseta *f* consecrated; God/god
Lisette *f* consecrated; famous; God/god; maid; warrior
Lisha *f* darkness; midnight; mysterious
Lishe *f* darkness; midnight
Liska *m* fox
Lisle *m* city
Lissa *f* bee; honey
Lita *f* alone; beautiful; clean; frank; grove; little; olive; person; select; special; winged
Litha *f* girl; trusted; truthful
Lithea *f* girl; trusted; truthful
Litonya *f* dart
Litsa *f* angel; messenger

Litta *f* bird; graceful
Litton *m* estate; hillside; town
Liu *m* voice
Livana *f* moon; white
Livia *f* branch; lioness; olive; tree
Livingston *m* beloved
Liviya *f* lioness
Livona *f* incense; spice
Liwanu *m* bear; growling
Liza *f* consecrated; God/god
Lizabeth *f* consecrated; God/god
Lizanne *f* consecrated; God/god
Llewellyn *m* lightning; lionlike; ruler
Lloyd *m* gray; haired
Lochan *f* bright; eyes
Lochana *f* eye
Locke *m* dweller; enclosure; stronghold
Lockwood *m* deep; forest
Lodema *f* guide
Lodie *f* prosperous; woman
Lodmilla *f* all; loved
Loe *m* king
Loella *f* elf; famous
Logan *m* hollow; little
Lohendra *m* Lord/lord; three
Lohit *m* copper; Mars; red
Lois *f* famed; fighter
Lokanetra *m* eye
Lokelani *f* heavenly; rose
Lokenetra *m* world
Loknaath *m* Lord/lord; world
Lola *f* strong
Lolita *f* strong
Lolotea *f* gift; God's
Loma *f* peaceful
Loman *m* bare; delicate; little
Lomash *m* sage
Lomasi *f* flower; pretty
Lombard *m* beard; long
Lombardo *m* beard; long
Lombardy *m* beard; long
Lon *m* fierce; strong
Lona *f* lioness; lone; solitary
Lonato *m* flint
London *m* fortress; moon
Loni *f* lioness; lone; solitary
Lonna *f* lone; solitary

Lono *m* agriculture; God/god; peace
Lopa *f* learned
Lora *f* crown; laurel; lost; seashore
Lorain *f* Lorraine
Loraine *f* army; famous; Lorraine
Lorant *m* crowned; laurel; victory
Lorayna *f* Lorraine
Lorayne *f* Lorraine
Lorcan *m* crowned; laurel
Lorelei *f*
Lorelei *f* Rhine; river
Lorelle *f* little
Loren *f* crown; laurel; lost
Lorena *f* crown; laurel
Lorene *f* crown; laurel
Lorens *m* crowned; laurel
Lorenz *m* crowned; laurel
Lorenzo *m* crowned; laurel
Loretta *f* crown; laurel
Lorette *f* crown; laurel
Lori *f* flowers; goddess
Lorimer *m* horses; lover
Loring *m* famous; son; war
Loris *f* flowers; goddess
Lorita *f* crown; laurel
Lorn *m* crowned; laurel
Lorna *f* crown; laurel; lost
Lorne *m* crowned; laurel
Lorola *f* family; great
Lorolla *f* family; great
Lorollas *f* family; great
Lorraine *f* army; famous
Lorrane *f* Lorraine
Lot *m* veiled
Lota *f* cup
Lotario *m* famous; warrior
Lothar *m* famous; warrior
Lotus *f* flower; forgetfulness; lotus; tree
Lou *f* battle; graceful; maid
Louanna *f* battle; graceful; maid
Loudon *m* low; valley
Louella *f* elf; famous
Louis *m* famous; warrior
Louisa *f* famous; maid; warrior
Louise *f* famous; maid; warrior
Louisette *f* famous; maid; warrior
Lovell *m* beloved; little
Lovmilla *f* all; loved
Lowden *m* low; valley
Lowell *m* beloved; little

Luana *f* battle; graceful; maid
Luane *f* battle; graceful; maid
Luba *f* lover
Lubba *f* lover
Lubbi *f* lover
Luca *m* bringer; knowledge; light
Lucan *m* bringer; knowledge; light
Lucas *m* bringer; knowledge; light
Lucerna *f* circle; light
Lucerne *f* circle; light
Lucette *f* bringer; light
Lucia *f* bringer; light
Lucian *m* bringer; descendant; knowledge; light
Luciana *f* bringer; light
Luciano *m* descendant
Lucida *f* bringer; light
Lucie *f* bringer; light
Lucien *m* descendant
Lucienne *f* bringer; light
Lucile *f* bringer; light
Lucille *f* bringer; light
Lucita *f* light; Mary
Lucius *m* bringer; knowledge; light
Lucrecia *f* reward
Lucretia *f* reward
Lucy *f* bringer; light
Ludella *f* elf; famous
Ludlew *m* dweller; hill; low
Ludlow *m* dweller; hill; low
Ludly *m* dweller; hill; low
Ludmilla *f* all; loved
Ludvig *m* famous; warrior
Ludwig *m* famous; renowned; warrior
Luella *f* elf; famous
Luelle *f* elf; famous
Luigi *m* famous; warrior
Luis *m* famous; warrior
Luisa *f* famous; maid; warrior
Luister *m* listener
Luke *m* bringer; knowledge; light
Lulani *f* heaven; highest; point
Lulani *m* heaven; highest
Lulu *f* famous; influence; maid; rabbit; soothing; warrior
Luna *f* moonlight
Lundy *m* grove; island
Lunetta *f* little; moon
Lunn *m* fierce; strong
Lunna *f* moonlight

Lunt *m* grove
Luong *m* bamboo; large
Lupe *f* black; good; river; stone; wolf
Lupita *f* black; river; stone
Lurine *f* siren
Lusa *f* consecrated; God/god
Lutero *m* famous; warrior
Luthais *m* famous; warrior
Luther *m* famous; warrior
Lutherum *m* slumber
Luvena *f* beloved; little
Luwana *f* graceful
Luwanna *f* battle; maid
Luyu *m* head
Luz *f* light; Mary
Luz *m* light
Lydell *m* dell; open
Lydia *f* cultured; happy; person; woman
Lydie *f* cultured; happy; person; woman
Lyell *m* isle
Lyle *m* city; isle
Lyman *m* man; plains
Lymann *m* man; plains
Lynd *m* isle; linden; tree
Lynda *f* pretty
Lyndon *m* lime; wood
Lyndsey *f* island; tree
Lynette *f* comely; lass
Lynn *f* below; comely; lass; waterfall
Lynus *m* flaxen-haired; haired
Lyris *f* lyre; music
Lysandra *f* liberator; men

Maalik *m* experienced
Mab *f* baby; joy; joyous; mirth
Mac *m* son
MacAdam *m* Adam; son
MacDonald *m* mighty; son; world
MacDougal *m* dark; son; stranger
MacEgan *m* highly; spirited
Machas *m* God/god
Machi *f* ten
Machiko *f* child; fortunate
Machute *f* girl; valley
Machutte *f* girl; valley
MacKenzie *f* child; leader; wise
MacKinley *m* leader; learned; skilled
MacMurray *m* mariner; son

MacNair *m* heir; son
Macy *m* bearer
Madai *f* adorned; jewel
Madaih *f* jewel
Madalaine *f* elevated
Madalena *f* elevated
Madan *m* God/god; love
Maddock *m* beneficent; good
Maddox *m* benefactor's; son
Madea *f* sorceress
Madeline *f* elevated
Madella *f* elevated
Madelle *f* elevated
Madelline *f* elevated
Madelon *f* elevated
Madge *f* pearl
Madhur *m* melodious
Madi *f* adorned; devoted; jewel; Lord/lord
Madiah *f* adorned
Madin *m* delightful
Madina *f* beauty; land
Madison *m* God's; light; mighty; son; war
Madlen *f* elevated
Madoc *m* lucky
Madock *m* beneficent; good
Madora *f* child; middle; patient; ruling; wife
Madox *m* lucky
Madra *f* mother
Mae *f* great
Maeko *f* child; truthful
Maemi *f* smile; truthful
Maeve *f* joyous
Magaidi *m* fighter
Magan *m* engrossed
Magana *f* engrossed
Magara *f* sit
Magda *f* elevated; maiden; tower
Magdala *f* tower
Magdalen *f* elevated
Magdalena *f* elevated
Magdalene *f* elevated
Magee *m* fiery; son
Magen *f* coming; moon
Magena *f* coming; moon
Magid *m* glorious; illustrious
Magina *f* coming; moon
magistrate *m* foreman
Magna *f* large
Magnilda *f* battle; maiden; powerful
Magnolia *f* girl; magnolia; tree
Magnus *m* great

Maha *f* beautiful; eyes
Maha *m* gazelle
Mahala *f* melodious; song; tenderness; woman
Mahalah *f* tenderness
Mahalia *f* melodious; song; tenderness
Mahasvin *m* glorious
Mahesa *f* great; Lord/lord
Mahesh *m* great; Lord/lord
Mahi *m* world
Mahika *f* earth
Mahima *f* glorious
Mahin *m* earth
Mahina *f* moon
Mahir *m* expert; industrious
Mahira *f* energetic; quick
Mahit *m* honored
Mahla *f* melodious; song
Mahmoud *m* praised
Mahmud *m* praised
Mahogany *f* color; wood
Mai *f* blossom; brightness; coyote; May
Maia *f* great; mother; nurse
Maiah *f* mother; nurse
Maiara *f* wise
Maice *f* highest; star
Maida *f* battle; famous; glorious; maid; maiden; warrior; woman
Maidel *f* maiden
Maidie *f* maiden
Mailand *m* plains
Maili *f* breeze; gentle; summer
Maimun *m* lucky
Maire *f* bitter
Maise *f* highest; star
Maisha *f* life
Maisie *f* pearl
Maita *f* house; lady; mistress
Maitilde *f* battle; maiden; mighty
Maitland *m* plains
Maitreya *m* friendly
Maja *f* splendid
Majdi *m* illustrious
Majeed *m* glorious; illustrious
Majesta *f* majestic
Majid *m* glorious; illustrious
Majidah *f* splendid
Major *m* greater
Makadisa *f* always; selfish
Makana *f* gift; present

Makani *f* wind
Makenna *f* happiness
Makis *m* God/god
Makoto *m* honest; sincere
Makshi *f* honeybee
Maksim *m* excellence; greatest
Makya *m* eagle; hunter
Mala *f* string
Malachi *m* angel; Jehovah
Malaika *f* angel
Malak *f* angel
Malak *m* angel
Malaya *m* forest
Malca *f* active; industrious
Malcah *f* active; industrious
Malchus *m* angel; Jehovah
Malcolm *m* Columbia
Malena *f* gentle; mild
Mali *f* high; tower
Malia *f* bitter
Malik *m* little; man
Malika *f* queen
Malin *f* high; tower
Malin *m* little; mighty; war
Malina *f* gentle; high; mild; tower
Malinda *f* gentle; mild
Malinde *f* gentle; mild
Malita *f* flower; honey; little
Malka *f* queen
Malleta *f* flower; honey; little
Mallina *f* high; tower
Mallory *f* army; counselor
Maloney *m* devoted; Sunday
Malva *f* chief; colored; flower; lilac; polished; slender; soft; violet
Malvia *f* flower
Malvie *f* flower
Malvin *m* chief; polished
Malvina *f* chief; polished
Mamo *f* flower
Mamo *m* bird; yellow
Mamraj *m* affection; Lord/lord
Mana *f* power
Manaal *m* achievement
Manaba *f* coming; warlike
Manan *m* thinking
Manas *m* mind
Manav *m* man
Manchu *m* pure
Manco *m* king
Mandar *m* celestial; tree
Mandara *f* mandara; tree
Mandeep *m* light; mind

Mandek *m* army; man
Mandel *m* almond; designer
Mandell *m* designer
Mander *m* from
Mandisa *f* sweet
Manella *f* God/god
Manfred *m* hero; man; men; peace; peaceful
Mangal *m* planet
Mangena *f* melody; song
Mangina *f* melody; song
Manik *m* ruby
Manipi *m* walking; wonder
Manish *m* God/god; mind
Manit *m* highly; respected
Manjeet *m* conqueror; mind
Manjul *m* handsome
Manley *m* hero's; man's; meadow
Mannan *m* thought
Manning *m* coatmaker; good; hero; man; son
Mannuela *f* God/god
Manorath *m* desire
Mansa *m* king
Mansfield *m* field; river; small
Mansi *f* flower
Mansur *m* aided; divinely
Manton *m* estate; hero's
Manu *m* born; second-born; son
Manuel *m* God/god
Manuela *f* God/god
Manvel *m* grand; house
Manvell *m* grand; house
Manvil *m* grand; house
Manville *m* estate; great
Manya *f* bitter
Manzo *m* son; strong; ten; third
Mara *f* beauty; bitter; eternal; gentle; lamb
Maraam *m* aspiration
Marabel *f* beautiful; Mary
Marabelle *f* beautiful; Mary
Marala *f* sea; swan
Maralina *f* bitter
Maraline *f* bitter
Maralyn *f* bitter
Marana *m* dirt
Marar *m* dirt
Marc *m* Mars; warlike
Marcel *m* hammer; little
Marcela *f* belonging
Marcella *f* belonging; contestant; hammer; intelligent

Marcelle *f* belonging; contestant; hammer; intelligent
Marcellene *f* belonging
Marcellina *f* belonging
Marcelline *f* contestant; hammer; intelligent
Marcello *m* hammer; little
Marcellus *m* hammer; little
Marcelo *m* hammer; little
Marcie *f* belonging
Marcile *f* belonging
Marcille *f* belonging
Marco *m* warlike
Marcos *m* warlike
Marcus *m* Mars; warlike
Marcy *f* belonging
Mardav *m* softness
Marden *m* pool; valley
Mareechi *m* light; ray
Marela *f* Mary; tiny
Mareld *f* famous; maid; war
Marelda *f* famous; maid; war
Marella *f* bitter; Mary; tiny
Marelya *f* Mary; tiny
Maretta *f* bitter
Marette *f* bitter
Marga *f* pearl
Marganit *f* flower
Margaret *f* pearl
Margareta *f* pearl
Margarete *f* pearl
Margarita *f* pearl
Margaux *f* pearl
Marge *f* pearl
Margery *f* pearl
Margi *f* traveler
Margo *f* pearl
Margory *f* pearl
Margot *f* pearl
Mari *f* ball; bitter; flower; God/god; good; promise
Maria *f* bitter
Mariah *f* God/god; teacher
Marian *f* bitter; graceful
Mariana *f* bitter; graceful
Marianna *f* bitter; graceful
Marianne *f* bitter; graceful
Mariatu *f* pure
Maribelle *f* beautiful; Mary
Marid *m* rebellious
Marie *f* bitter; Mary; rose
Marietta *f* bitter
Marigold *f* flower
Marigolda *f* flower
Marigolde *f* flower
Mariko *f* ball; child; circle

Marilla *f* bitter
Marilyn *f* bitter
Marina *f* sea
Marini *f* fresh; healthy; pretty
Mario *m* bitter; martial
Marion *m* bitter
Maris *f* God/god; good; promise; sea; star
Marisa *f* sea
Marisha *f* sea
Marissa *f* sea; star
Marita *f* bitter; sea
Maritza *f* sea
Marius *m* bitter
Marje *f* pearl
Marjie *f* pearl
Marjorie *f* pearl
Marjory *f* pearl
Mark *m* warlike
Marla *f* bitter; Mary; tiny
Marland *m* lake; land
Marleen *f* elevated
Marlene *f* elevated
Marley *m* lake; meadow
Marlin *m* falcon; hawk; little
Marlisa *f* bitter
Marlon *m* falcon; hawk; little
Marlow *m* hill; water
Marmara *f* flashing; glittering
Marmion *m* small
Marni *f* rejoice
Marnie *f* rejoice
Marnin *m* creates; joy
Marny *f* rejoice
Maro *f* sea
Marola *f* sea
Marolda *f* famous; maid; war
Marques *m* marquis
Marquis *m* nobleman
Marras *f* sea; star
Marris *f* sea; star
Marrisa *f* sea
Marsden *m* dweller; marshy; valley
Marsdon *m* dweller; marshy; valley
Marsh *m* marshy
Marshall *m* horse; keeper; steward
Marston *m* farm; water
Mart *m* born; month
Marta *f* house; lady; martial; mistress; warlike
Martella *f* lady; mistress
Marten *m* warlike
Martha *f* lady; mistress

Marthena *f* lady; mistress
Martin *m* warlike
Martina *f* martial; warlike
Martine *f* martial; warlike
Martino *m* warlike
Martita *f* lady; mistress
Martiza *f* blessed
Marton *m* warlike
Marty *m* warlike
Maru *f* round
Marudeva *m* desert; Lord/lord
Marut *m* wind
Marvel *f* miracle; wonderful
Marvela *f* miracle; wonderful
Marvella *f* miracle; wonderful
Marvelle *f* miracle; wonderful
Marvin *m* famous; friend; sea
Marwood *m* forest; lake
Mary *f* bitter
Marya *f* brightly; pure; white
Maryam *f* bitter
Maryanne *f* bitter; graceful
Marybella *f* beautiful; Mary
Marybelle *f* beautiful; Mary
Maryl *f* fresh; new
Maryse *f* sea
Masa *f* honest
Masago *f* sand
Masara *f* emerald
Masato *m* justice
Masha *f* bitter
Masika *f* born; season
Maska *m* powerful
Maslin *m* little
Mason *m* stone; worker
Masud *m* fortunate
Matana *f* gift
Matelda *f* battle; maiden; mighty
Mateo *m* gift; Jehovah
Mathea *f* gift; God/god
Mather *m* army; powerful
Mathew *m* gift; Jehovah
Mathi *f* gift; prayed
Mathia *f* gift; God/god; prayed
Mathias *m* gift; Jehovah
Mathilda *f* battle; maiden; mighty
Mathilde *f* battle; maiden; mighty
Matilda *f* battle; maiden; mighty

Matilde *f* battle; maiden; mighty
Matland *m* plains
Mato *m* brave
Matrika *f* mother
Matrona *f* mother; motherly
Matronna *f* mother; motherly
Matsu *f* pine
Matsu *m* pine
Matsuda *f* field; pine; rice
Matsuda *m* field; pine; rice
Matsuhira *f* flat; pine
Matsuhira *m* flat; pine
Matsukawa *f* pine; river
Matsukawa *m* pine; river
Matsumoto *f* origin; pine
Matsumoto *m* origin; pine
Matsunaka *f* middle; pine
Matsunaka *m* middle; pine
Matsuo *f* little; pine
Matsuo *m* little; pine
Matsuoka *f* hill; pine
Matsuoka *m* hill; pine
Matsushima *f* island; pine
Matsushima *m* island; pine
Matsushita *f* below; pine
Matsushita *m* below; pine
Matsuyama *f* mountain; pine
Matsuyama *m* mountain; pine
Matta *f* gift; Lord/lord
Mattah *f* gift; Lord/lord
Mattea *f* gift; God/god
Matteo *m* gift; Jehovah
Matthaeus *m* gift; Jehovah
Matthea *f* gift; God/god
Matthew *m* gift; Jehovah
Matthia *f* gift; God/god; prayed
Mattias *m* gift; Jehovah
Mauli *m* dark-skinned
Maulik *m* precious
Maura *f* bitter
Mauralia *f* sympathizes; woman
Maureen *f* bitter; dark; little; Mary
Mauretta *f* dark; girl
Mauri *f* dark; girl
Maurice *m* dark
Mauricio *m* dark
Maurilia *f* sympathizes; woman
Maurilla *f* sympathizes; woman
Maurine *f* dark; little; Mary
Maurita *f* dark; girl

Maury *m* dark
Mausi *f* flower
Mauve *f* colored; lilac; violet
Mave *f* joyous
Maverick *m* independent
Mavis *f* joy; joyous; mirth; song; thrush
Maxama *f* girl; last
Maxantia *f* girl; great
Maxentia *f* girl; great
Maxia *f* girl; great
Maxim *m* excellence; greatest
Maxima *f* girl; last
Maximillian *m* excellence; greatest
Maximo *m* excellence; greatest
Maxine *f* greatest
Maxma *f* girl; last
Maxwell *m* near; spring
May *f* great
Maya *f* creative; God's; great; illusion; mother; nurse; power
Mayank *m* moon
Maybelle *f* beautiful; great
Mayce *f* highest; star
Mayda *f* maiden
Maydena *f* maiden
Mayer *m* farmer; greater
Mayfield *m* field; warrior
Mayhew *m* gift; Jehovah
Mayme *f* bitter
Maynard *m* brave; powerful; steady; strong
Mayon *m* black; God/god
Mayukh *m* brilliant; splendor
Mayur *m* peacock
Mayura *f* creative; God's; illusion; power
McKenzie *f* child; leader; wise
Mead *m* meadow
Meara *f* mirth
Meave *f* joy; merry; mirth
Meda *f* justice; Lord/lord; priestess; scholar; sea; thinking
Medarda *f* scholar
Medardas *f* scholar
Medea *f* child; middle; ruling; sorceress
Medeah *f* sorceress
Media *f* child; middle; ruling
Medor *f* patient; wife
Medora *f* child; middle; patient; ruling; wife

Medwin *m* friend; powerful
Meer *m* chief
Megan *f* great; mighty; strong
Megh *m* cloud
Meghan *f* great; mighty; strong
Meghnad *m* thunder
Meghraj *m* clouds; king
Mehal *f* cloud
Mehal *m* cloud
Mehala *f* melodious; song
Mehemet *m* praised
Meher *f* benevolence
Mehetabel *f* benefited; God/god
Mehika *f* dew
Mehira *f* energetic; quick
Mehitabel *f* benefited; God/god
Mehitabelle *f* benefited; God/god
Mehmet *m* praised
Mehtab *m* moon
Mehtar *m* prince
Meingolda *f* flower; golden
Meingoldas *f* flower; golden
Melanie *f* black; dark
Melantha *f* dark; flower
Melany *f* black; dark
Melar *m* prince
Melba *f* slender; soft
Melbourne *m* mill; stream
Melburn *m* mill; stream
Melcia *f* flattering; industrious
Melda *f* wistful
Meldon *m* hill; mill
Melena *f* gentle
Melentha *f* dark; flower
Meletius *m* saint
Meli *f* bitter
Melicent *f* bee; good; honey; worker
Melina *f* canary; colored; gentle; honey; mild; sweet; yellow
Melinda *f* gentle; mild
Melisande *f* industrious; true
Melisenda *f* industrious; true
Melissa *f* bee; honey
Melisse *f* bee; honey
Melita *f* bee; flower; honey; little
Melitta *f* flower; honey; little

Melka *f* black; dark
Mella *f* homelover; wistful
Mellicent *f* good; industrious; true; worker
Melodie *f* beautiful; music; song
Melody *f* beautiful; music; song
Melosa *f* gentle; sweet
Melva *f* chief; friend; polished; slender; soft; sweet; wine
Melvern *m* chief; great
Melville *m* estate; industrious
Melvin *m* chief; friend; polished; sword
Melvina *f* chief; friend; polished; sweet; wine
Melvine *f* chief; polished
Memtba *f* taste
Menachem *m* comforter
Menard *m* brave; powerful
Mendel *m* knowledge; wisdom
Mendeley *m* comforter
Menjuiwe *f* trustworthy
Menora *f* candelabrum
Menorah *f* candelabrum
Mera *f* girl; sadness
Merah *f* red-haired
Meraree *f* bitter; girl; sadness
Merari *f* bitter; girl; sadness
Meras *f* worthy
Merce *m* merchant
Mercedes *f* compassion
Merceer *m* merchant
Mercer *m* merchant
Mercia *f* kingdom
Mercy *f* compassion; merciful
Merdyce *f* famous; pleasant
Mered *m* revolt
Meredith *f* day; guardian; sea
Meredith *m* guardian; sea
Merial *f* bitter
Merick *m* dark-skinned
Meridith *f* day; guardian; sea
Merik *m* dark-skinned
Meris *f* worthy
Merisa *f* sea
Merissa *f* sea
Meriwa *f* Thorn
Merl *f* blackbird; thrush
Merle *f* blackbird; thrush
Merle *m* blackbird

Merlin *m* falcon; hawk
Merlina *f* blackbird; thrush
Merline *f* blackbird; thrush
Merna *f* gentle; polite
Merola *f* blackbird; thrush
Merras *f* worthy
Merrick *m* dark-skinned
Merrik *m* dark-skinned
Merrill *m* famous; little
Merripen *m* death; life
Merritt *m* famous; little
Merry *f* mirthful; pleasant
Merth *f* joy; pleasure
Mertice *f* famous; myrtle; pleasant
Mertle *f* myrtle
Merton *m* sea
Mervin *m* beautiful; famous; friend; sea
Merwin *m* beautiful; friend; sea
Merwyn *m* beautiful; famous; friend; sea
Meryem *f* bitter; rebellious
Meryl *f* blackbird; thrush
Mesha *f* ram
Messina *f* middle
Mestipen *m* fortune; luck
Meta *f* ambitious; goal
Metis *f* skill; wisdom
Mettah *f* ambitious
Metzger *m* butcher
Meyer *m* farmer; steward
Mia *f* God/god; mine
Miakoda *f* moon; power
Micah *f* God/god
Micah *m* God/god
Michael *m* God/god
Michaela *f* image
Michaele *f* God/god; image
Michaelina *f* God/god; image
Michail *m* God/god
Michak *m* God/god
Michalek *m* God/god
Michau *m* God/god
Micheil *m* God/god
Michel *m* God/god
Michella *f* God/god; image
Michelle *f* God/god; image
Michi *f* righteous
Michiko *f* righteous
Michio *m* man; strength; ten
Mickel *m* God/god
Midori *f* green

Mieko *f* child; prosperity
Mietek *m* God/god
Migina *f* moon
Mignon *f* dainty; darling; graceful
Mignonette *f* dainty; darling; graceful
Miguel *m* God/god
Mihail *m* God/god
Mihaio *m* God/god
Mihalje *m* God/god
Mihangel *m* God/god
Mihas *m* God/god
Mihir *m* sun
Mihkel *m* God/god
Mika *f* belonging; knowing; Lord/lord; stem
Mikael *m* God/god
Mikaela *f* God/god; image
Mikaila *f* god-like
Mikazuki *f* moon; night; third
Mikelis *m* God/god
Mikhail *m* God/god
Mikhalis *m* God/god
Mikhalka *m* God/god
Mikhos *m* God/god
Miki *f* God/god; image
Miki *m* tree
Mikie *f* stem
Mikiyo *f* stem
Mikka *f* days; three
Mikkel *m* God/god
Mikko *m* God/god
Mikul *m* comrade
Mikus *m* God/god
Mila *f* all; bracelet; loved; Milan; small
Milada *f* love
Milan *f* Milan
Milan *m* city
Milana *f* Milan
Miland *m* bee
Milanna *f* Milan
Milburn *m* mill; stream
Milburt *m* mill; stream
Milda *f* battle; famous; glorious; maid; maiden; warrior; woman
Mildred *f* counselor; mild
Mildrid *f* counselor; mild
Milena *f* black; dark
Miles *m* soldier; warrior
Milford *m* crossing; dweller; ford; mill
Milica *f* flattering; industrious
Milicent *f* industrious; true
Milla *f* bracelet; small
Millard *m* flattering; miller; strong; winning

Millburn *m* mill; stream
Millda *f* battle; maiden
Miller *m* miller
Millford *m* crossing; dweller; ford; mill
Milliani *f* caress; gentle
Millicent *f* bee; good; honey; industrious; true; worker
Millman *m* man; mill; miller
Milman *m* man; mill; miller
Milo *m* miller
Milore *m* prince
Milton *m* dweller; mill; town
Mimba *f* born
Mimi *f* bitter; dove
Min *f* quick; sensitive
Mina *f* background; child; dove; earth; fine; helmet; love; noble; noteworthy; protector
Minal *f* fruit
Minco *m* chief
Minda *f* knowledge; love; wisdom
Mindy *f* love
Mineko *f* child; mountain; peak
Minerva *f* force; thinking
Minetta *f* love
Minette *f* force; love; thinking
Ming *f* bright
Ming *m* bright
Mingan *m* gray; wolf
Minh *m* clear; luminous
Mini *f* twin
Miniya *f* expected
Minka *m* God/god
Minko *m* chief
Minna *f* background; fine; love; loving; noble; protector; resolute
Minnie *f* bitter
Minowa *f* moving
Minta *f* mint; plant
Mintha *f* mint; plant
Minya *f* older; sister
Mio *f* cord
Mique *f* counselor; wise
Mira *f* clothing; wonderful
Mirabel *f* beautiful
Mirabella *f* beautiful
Mirabelle *f* beautiful
Miranda *f* admirable
Mireil *f* God/god; spoke
Mirela *f* God/god; spoke
Mirella *f* God/god; spoke; wonderful

Mirelle *f* God/god; spoke; wonderful
Miri *f* mine
Miriam *f* bitter; pearl
Miriella *f* God/god; spoke
Mirilla *f* God/god; spoke; wonderful
Mirna *f* gentle; polite
Miron *m* basket
Mirth *f* joy; pleasure
Mirtle *f* myrtle
Miru *f* harmony; peace
Misao *f* loyal
Mischa *m* God/god
Misha *f* God/god; smile
Miska *m* God/god
Misko *m* God/god
Missim *m* sign
Mistie *f* mistress
Mistique *f* air; mystery
Misty *f* mistress
Misu *m* rippling; water
Mita *f* friend; industrious
Mitali *f* friendship
Mitali *m* friend
Mitchell *m* God/god
Mitena *f* coming; moon
Mitexi *f* moon; sacred
Mithil *m* kingdom
Mithun *m* union
Mitra *m* friend
Mitrajit *m* friendly
Mitul *m* friend
Mituna *f* roll
Mitzi *f* bitter
Miwa *f* farseeing
Miwako *f* farseeing
Miya *f* Shinto; temple
Miyo *f* beautiful; generation
Miyoko *f* child; generation
Miyuki *f* deep; snow
Moani *f* fragrance
Modak *m* pleasing
Modal *m* enjoyment
Modestia *f* modest
Modestine *f* modest
Modesty *f* modest
Moema *f* honey-sweet
Moh *m* love
Mohamad *m* praised
Mohamet *m* praised
Mohan *m* attractive; bewitching; delightful
Mohandas *m* attractive; charming; servant
Mohin *m* fascinating
Mohit *m* spellbound
Mohul *m* attractive
Moina *f* gentle; polite
Moir *f* great

Moira *f* bitter; dark; great; little; Mary; merit
Moksin *f* free
Molton *m* mule; stable
Mona *f* admonition; away; far; girl; lady; one; sadness; single; solitary; veneration; woman
Monal *f* bird
Monet *f* descendant; protector
Moneta *f* adviser
Monetta *f* adviser
Monica *f* admonition; counselor; wise
Monique *f* counselor; wise
Monish *m* Lord/lord; mind
Monisha *f* intellectual
Monroe *m* red
Montague *m* dweller; hill; pointed
Montana *m* mountainous; region
Monte *m* dweller; hill; pointed
Monteil *m* mountain
Montel *m* mountain
Montell *m* mountain
Montero *m* huntsman
Montgomery *m* castle; hill; wealthy
Monty *m* dweller; hill; pointed
Moore *m* dark; wasteland
Moorti *m* idol
Mora *f* blueberry; dark; little; Mary
Morathi *m* man; wise
Mordecai *m* counselor; wise
Moreen *f* dark; little; Mary
Morel *m* color; dark
Morela *f* apricot
Moreland *m* man; moors
Morella *f* apricot
Morena *f* bitter
Moreno *m* dark; little
Moretta *f* dark; darling; girl; little; lover
Morette *f* darling; little; lover
Morgan *m* dweller; sea; white
Morgana *f* sea; shore
Morgen *m* sea; white
Mori *f* chosen; forest; Lord/lord
Moria *f* chosen; dark; little; Lord/lord; Mary
Moriah *f* chosen; God/god; Lord/lord; teacher

Moriah *m* chosen; Jehovah; man
Moriann *f* long-haired
Morianne *f* long-haired
Moriko *f* child; forest
Morissa *f* sea
Morita *f* dark; field; forest; girl; rice
Morita *m* field; forest; rice
Moritz *m* dark
Moriyo *f* forest; generation
Morley *m* marsh; meadow; moor; wood
Morna *f* beloved; gentle; polite; tender
Morrell *m* color; dark
Morril *m* color; dark
Morrin *f* long-haired
Morris *m* dark
Morrison *m* Maurice; son
Morse *m* dark; son
Mortimer *m* still; water
Morton *m* estate; moor; town
Morven *m* mariner; sea
Morvin *m* sea
Mosa *f* fountain; girl
Moselle *f* saved; water
Mosera *f* bound
Moses *m* child; taken; water
Moshe *m* taken; water
Mosi *m* born; first-born
Mosira *f* bound
Mosora *f* bound
Moswen *m* color; light
Motega *m* arrow; new
Mouldon *m* mule; stable
Moulik *m* valuable
Moulton *m* mule; stable
Moya *f* bitter; great
Moyna *f* gentle; polite
Moyra *f* great
Moza *f* fountain; girl
Mozelle *f* saved; water
Mozza *f* fountain; girl
Mridul *m* delicate; tender
Mrigaj *m* moon; son
Mrigank *m* moon
Mrigendra *m* lion
Mrigesh *m* lion
Mrinal *m* lotus
Mudgal *m* saint
Mudil *m* moonshine
Mudit *m* pleased
Muhammad *m* praised
Muhammed *m* praised
Muir *m* moor; wasteland
Muireann *f* long-haired
Mukasa *m* administrator; chief; God's

Mukta *f* liberated; pearl
Muktananda *m* liberated
Mukti *f* liberation
Mukul *m* bud
Mukut *m* crown
Mu-Lan *f* blossom; magnolia
Muldon *m* mule; stable
Muliya *f* beat
Muna *f* Lord/lord; wish
Muna *m* desire
Munda *m* garden; wish
Mundan *m* garden
Muneera *f* illumination; light
Mungo *m* lovable
Muni *m* God/god; village
Munira *f* illumination; light
Munirah *f* illumination; light
Mura *f* village
Mura *m* village
Muraco *m* moon; white
Murad *m* wish
Muralee *m* flute
Murali *m* flute
Murdock *m* prosperous
Muriah *f* chosen; Lord/lord
Murial *f* bitter
Muriel *f* bitter
Murli *m* flute
Murphy *m* sea; warrior
Murray *m* mariner; sea; warrior
Musa *f* mouse
Musenda *m* nightmare
Musetta *f* mouse
Musette *f* mouse
Musidora *f* gift
Mustafa *m* chosen
Mu-Tan *f* blossom; tree
Mya *f* emerald
Myer *m* farmer
Myesha *f* life
Myeshia *f* life
Myisha *f* life; woman
Myles *m* soldier; warrior
Mylor *m* prince
Myra *f* abundance; wonderful
Myrilla *f* wonderful
Myrlene *f* blackbird; thrush
Myrna *f* beloved; gentle; polite; tender
Myron *m* fragrant
Myrtia *f* myrtle
Myrtice *f* myrtle
Myrtle *f* myrtle
Mystique *f* air; mystery

Naag *m* big; serpent
Naagarjun *m* ancient
Naagdhar *m* cobra
Naagendra *m* king; serpents
Naagesh *m* God/god; serpents
Naaghpati *m* serpents
Naagpal *m* savior; serpents
Naagpati *m* king
Naakesh *m* moon
Naam *f* agreeable
Naaman *f* agreeable
Naaman *m* agreeable
Naamana *f* agreeable
Naamann *m* agreeable
Naaraayan *m* man; refuge
Naarad *m* ancient; sage
Naarah *f* girl; heart
Naashom *f* enchantress
Naasir *m* defender
Nabal *f* comic; little
Nabala *f* comic; little
Nabalas *f* comic; little
Nabeela *f* born
Nabendu *m* moon; new
Nabhendu *m* moon; new
Nabiba *f* born
Nabil *m* noble
Nabila *f* born; noble
Nabilah *f* born
Nada Naddah *f* dewy
Nada *f* generous; hope
Nadab *m* ideas; liberal; man
Nadaba *f* democratic
Nadabas *f* democratic
Nadabb *m* ideas; liberal; man
Nadabus *m* ideas; liberal; man
Nadda *f* democratic; dewy; generous
Naddah *f* generous
Nadeen *m* ocean
Nadia *f* caller; hope
Nadine *f* charming; hope
Nadir *m* rare
Nadira *f* pinacle; precious; rare
Nadirah *f* precious; rare
Nadish *m* ocean
Naeem *m* benevolent
Nagid *m* ruler
Nagida *f* ruler; wealthy
Nagpal *m* savior; serpents
Nagy *m* husky; large
Nahama *f* comfort; God/god
Nahamas *f* comfort; God/god

Nahele *m* forest; grove; trees
Nahma *m* sturgeon
Nahshu *m* enchanter; great
Nahshun *m* enchanter; great
Nahshunn *m* enchanter; great
Nahson *m* enchanter; great
Nahtanha *f* corn; flower
Nahuel *m* jaguar
Nahum *m* comforter; compassionate
Naida *f* nymph; river; water
Naila *f* succeeds
Nailah *f* succeeds
Naima *f* graceful
Naira *f* big; eyes
Naisha *f* special
Naja *f* bright; eyes
Najah *f* bright; eyes
Najila *f* bright; eyes
Najilah *f* bright; eyes
Naka *f* middle
Naka *m* middle
Nakia *f* pure
Naksatraraja *m* king; star
Nakshatra *m* star
Nakti *f* night
Nalani *f* calm
Naldo *m* power
Nalor *m* maker
Nam *m* child; south
Naman *m* agreeable
Nami *f* child; wave
Namid *m* dancer; star
Namiko *f* child; wave
Namir *m* leopard
Namrah *f* tigress
Namrata *f* politeness
Nan *f* graceful
Nana *f* graceful; spring
Nanci *f* graceful
Nancy *f* graceful
Nandak *m* pleasing
Nandan *m* son
Nandin *m* destroyer
Nandor *m* fountain; youth
Nanetta *f* graceful; little
Nanette *f* graceful; little
Nani *f* beauty
Nanice *f* graceful
Nanji *m* safe
Nantan *m* spokesman
Naoma *f* pleasant
Naomi *f* pleasant
Napea *f* valley
Napier *m* city; new

Napoleon *m* dell; lion; woodland
Nara *f* daughter; girl; heart; moon; nearer; oak
Narah *f* girl; heart
Narain *m* God/god; Vishnu
Narcissus *m* loving; self-loving
Nard *m* chess; game
Narda *f* fragrant
Naren *m* manly
Naresh *m* king; Lord/lord
Naresha *f* king; Lord/lord
Nari *f* thunderpeal
Nariko *f* child; humble; thunderpeal
Narong *m* battle
Narra *f* daughter; moon
Narsi *m* poet; saint
Nartan *f* dance
Nartana *m* dance
Naruna *m* leader; men
Nasha *f* born; season
Nashom *f* enchantress
Nashoma *f* enchantress
Nashota *f* twin
Nasia *f* God/god; miracle
Nasr *m* vulture
Nasser *m* victorious
Nassor *m* victorious
Nastacia *f* resurrection
Nasya *f* God/god; miracle
Nata *f* creator; dancer; rope; speaker
Natal *m* born
Natala *f* birthday
Natalia *f* birthday
Natalie *f* birthday
Nataline *f* birthday
Natane *f* daughter
Natania *f* gift; God/god
Natanya *f* gift; God/god
Natasha *f* birthday; born
Nate *m* gift; given; God/god
Natene *f* Ben
Natesa *f* dance; Lord/lord
Natesh *m* king
Nathalia *f* birthday
Nathalie *f* birthday
Nathan *m* gift; given; God/god
Nathania *f* gift; given; God/god
Nathaniel *m* gift; God/god
Nathene *f* gift; given; God/god
Natonya *f* gift; God/god
Natraj *m* dancer; supreme
Natsu *f* born; summer

Nauka *m* boat
Nav *m* name
Nava *f* beautiful; pleasant
Navada *f* snowy
Navaj *m* born
Naval *m* wonder
Navashen *m* brings; hope
Naveen *m* new
Navice *f* beautiful; pleasant
Navin *m* new
Navit *f* beautiful; pleasant
Navrang *m* beautiful
Navratan *m* jewels
Navtej *m* light; new
Nawal *f* gift
Nawal *m* new; surprise
Nawat *m* hand
Nayan *m* eyes
Nayati *m* wrestler
Nayeli *f* love
Naylor *m* maker
Nazarius *m* aloof
Neal *m* champion
Neala *f* champion; princess
Nealah *f* princess
Neale *m* champion
Nealie *f* champion
Neall *m* champion
Nealson *m* champion; son
Neata *f* door
Nebula *f* cloud; mist
Neci *f* fiery
Neda *f* guardian; prosperous
Nediva *f* generous; noble
Nedra *f* guardian; prosperous
Nedrah *f* guardian; prosperous
Neel *m* blue
Neela *f* champion; cicada; dark; princess
Neelam *m* emerald
Neelambar *m* blue; sky
Neely *f* champion
Neema *f* born; prosperous; time
Neeooma *f* light; moon; new
Neerad *m* clouds
Neerav *m* quiet; silent
Nehal *m* handsome; rainy
Nehemiah *m* comfort; God/god
Nehru *m* canal
Neil *m* champion
Neila *f* champion; princess
Neisa *f* pure
Neisha *f* life; woman

Neka *f* goose; wild
Nela *f* rock; yellowish
Nelda *f* champion; cloud; elder; tree
Nelek *m* horn
Nelia *f* yellowish
Nelka *f* rock
Nell *f* elder; girl; little; tree
Nella *f* brown; colored; girl; little; plum; shouldered; white
Nellda *f* elder; tree
Nellwyn *f* bright; friend; light
Nelly *f* Lenka; light
Nels *m* champion
Nelson *m* champion; son
Nemo *m* glade; glen
Nemy *f* sweet
Nen *m* Nen; spirit
Nena *f* mighty; young
Nenah *f* girl
Nenet *f* goddess
Neom *f* light; moon; new
Neoma *f* light; moon; new
Neomah *f* light; moon; new
Nepa *f* backward
Neper *m* city; new
Nereen *f* nymph; sea
Neri *f* nymph; sea
Nerice *f* nymph; sea
Nerin *f* nymph; sea
Nerine *f* nymph; sea
Nerissa *f* nymph; sea
Nero *m* stern; strong
Neron *m* stern; strong
Nerone *m* stern; strong
Nessa *f* pure; resurrection
Nessi *f* pure
Nestor *m* departer; traveler; wisdom
Neta *f* door; plant; shrub
Netfa *f* free; woman
Netia *f* plant; shrub
Netis *f* friend; trusted
Neto *m* earnest
Netta *f* comely; door; lass; plant; shrub
Neva *f* extreme; snow; snowy
Nevada *f* snow; snowy; white
Nevan *m* holy; little; saint
Neveda *f* snowy
Nevil *m* estate; new
Nevile *m* estate; new
Neville *m* estate; new; town
Nevin *m* holy; little; nephew; saint; worshiper
Nevins *m* holy; little; saint

Nevlin *m* sailor
Newbold *m* building; new
Newcomb *m* stranger
Newland *m* land
Newlin *m* dweller; new; pool; spring
Newlyn *m* dweller; new; pool
Newman *m* newcomer
Newton *m* estate; new; town
Neysa *f* pure
Neza *f* pure
Nia *f* champion
Niabi *f* fawn
Nial *m* champion
Niall *m* champion
Nian *m* knows
Nibaal *m* arrows
Nibaw *m* stand
Nibodh *m* knowledge
Nicabar *m* away; steal
Nicanor *m* army; people; victorious
Nichele *f* army; people; victorious
Nichelle *f* army; people; victorious
Nichol *m* army; people; victorious
Nichola *f* army; people; victorious
Nicholas *m* army; people; victorious
Nick *m* belonging; born; day; Lord/lord; lords/ Lord's; Sunday
Nico *m* victory
Nicol *m* army; people; victorious
Nicola *f* army; people; victorious
Nicolas *m* army; people; victorious
Nicole *f* army; people; victorious
Nicolina *f* army; people; victorious
Nicoline *f* army; people; victorious
Nida *f* call
Nidhish *m* Lord/lord; treasure
Nidia *f* nest; refuge
Niela *f* Lord/lord
Niels *m* champion
Nien *m* year
Nigam *m* treasure
Nigan *m* ahead
Nigel *m* dark
Nihaar *m* fog

Nika *f* belonging; God/god; Lord/lord
Nikara *f* collection
Nike *f* victory
Niket *m* house
Niketan *m* house
Nikhil *m* entire
Niki *f* army; belonging; God/god; people; victorious
Nikka *f* belonging; God/god
Nikki *f* army; belonging; God/god; people; victorious
Nikki *m* army; people; victorious
Nikunja *m* enchanting
Nila *f* lady; river
Nilaya *f* home
Nilla *f* glorious; lady; river
Nils *m* champion
Nilson *m* champion; son
Nima *f* blessing; thread
Nimah *f* blessing
Nimat *f* blessing
Nimisha *f* momentary
Nina *f* fire; girl; mighty
Ninad *m* sound
Ninarika *f* misty
Ninetta *f* girl; mighty
Ninette *f* girl; mighty
Ninita *f* girl; little
Ninnetta *f* mighty
Ninnette *f* mighty
Nipa *f* stream
Nipha *f* snowflake
Nirad *m* given; water
Nirajit *m* illuminated
Niral *f* calm
Nirali *f* different
Niramay *m* blemish; without
Nirav *m* sound; without
Nirbhay *m* fearless
Nirbhik *m* fearless
Nirek *m* superior
Nirel *f* field; God's; light
Nirish *m* free
Nirmal *m* clear; pure
Nirmala *f* clean
Nirmay *m* pure
Nirmit *m* created
Nirmohi *m* unattached
Nirupam *m* comparison; without
Nirvan *m* blowing; liberation
Nirveli *f* child; water
Nisa *f* pure
Nisha *f* life; woman

Nishant *m* dawn
Nishar *m* cloth; warm
Nishat *m* tree
Nishchal *m* unmoveable
Nishesh *m* moon
Nishi *f* west
Nishil *m* night
Nishita *f* alert
Nishka *f* honest
Nishkarsh *m* result
Nishok *m* happy
Nishtha *f* determination
Nissa *f* brownie; elf; friendly; loved; test
Nissan *m* flight
Nisse *f* test
Nissim *m* miracle; unbounded
Nita *f* bear; confident; female; moral; pretty
Nitara *f* deeply
Niteesh *m* law; Lord/lord
Nithya *f* eternal
Niti *f* ethics
Nitika *f* angel; precious; stone
Nitin *m* master; path; right
Nitis *m* friend; good
Nitsa *f* Lenka; light
Nituna *f* daughter
Nitya *f* eternal
Nitza *f* bud
Nitzana *f* bud
Niva *f* renew
Niven *m* holy; little; nephew; saint; worshiper
Nivrutti *m* separation; world
Nix *f* haired; snowy; white
Nixie *f* little; sprite; water
Nixon *m* Nicholas; son
Niyati *f* destiny
Nizana *f* bud
Nizhoni *f* beautiful
Nnamdi *m* all; father; still
Noah *m* comfort; rest
Noami *f* pleasant
Nodab *m* Lord/lord; noble; son
Nodin *m* wind
Noel *f* birthday
Noel *m* born
Noelani *f* beautiful; heaven
Noelle *f* birthday
Noga *f* light; morning; shining
Nokomis *f* grandmother
Nola *f* bell; branch; famous; glorious; lady; olive; small; tree

Nolan *m* famous; noble
Nolana *f* bell; famous; small
Nolcha *f* sun
Noleta *f* lady
Noletta *f* lady
Nolita *f* grove; lady; olive
Nolitta *f* grove; olive
Noma *f* farming
Nona *f* child; ninth
Noni *f* gift; God/god
Nora *f* grace; honor; honorable; Lenka; light
Norah *f* honor; honorable; Lenka; light
Norbert *m* brightness; brilliant; hero; north
Norberta *f* brilliant; heroine
Nordica *f* north
Nori *f* doctrine; precept
Norie *f* doctrine; precept
Noriko *f* doctrine; precept
Norma *f* pattern; precept
Norman *m* northman
Norna *f* fate; goddess
Norris *m* north
Northrop *m* farm; north
Norton *m* estate; north; town
Norval *m* home; shepherd
Norvall *m* home; shepherd
Norvan *m* north
Norvel *m* estate; north
Norven *m* north
Norvil *m* estate; home; north; shepherd
Norville *m* estate; north
Norvin *m* friend; north
Norward *m* gate; guard
Norwell *m* north; spring
Norwin *m* friend; north
Norwood *m* forest; gate; guard; north
Norword *m* gate; guard
Norwyn *m* friend; north
Noton *m* wind
Noura *f* light
Nova *f* butterfly; new; person; young
Novah *f* new
Novella *f* birthday
Novia *f* new; person; young
Nowell *m* born
Noy *m* beauty
Nrip *m* king
Nripendra *m* king; king's/ kings
Nripesh *m* king; king's/ kings

Nuala *f* fair; shouldered
Nudahr *f* gold
Numa *f* pleasant; ripened
Numair *m* panther
Numidia *f* nomad
Nuna *f* land
Nuncia *f* good; news
Nunciata *f* good; news
Nuncio *m* messenger
Nunzio *m* messenger
Nuren *m* illumination; light
Nuri *f* fire; Lord/lord
Nuri *m* fire
Nuria *f* fire; Lord/lord
Nurice *f* flower; little; yellow
Nuriel *f* fire; Lord/lord
Nuriel *m* fire
Nuris *m* fire
Nurit *f* flower; little; yellow
Nurita *f* flower; little; yellow
Nusair *m* vulture
Nusi *f* graceful
Nuwa *f* goddess; mother
Nyagwa *m* ruler
Nyako *f* girl
Nydia *f* nest; refuge
Nye *m* dweller; island
Nyoko *f* child; gem
Nysa *f* pure
Nyssa *f* goal; point
Nyx *f* night

Oakes *m* oak; tree
Oakley *m* meadow; oak
Oba *f* ancient; goddess; river
Obadiah *m* God/god; man
Obala *f* hills
Oballa *f* hills
Obed *m* God/god; man
Obeded *m* God/god; man
Obel *f* pillar; pointed; rich
Obelia *f* pillar; pointed; rich
Obellia *f* pillar; pointed; rich
Obert *m* brilliant; wealthy
Obiel *f* pillar; pointed; rich
Obla *f* hills
Obola *f* hills
Ochi *m* laugh
Octavia *f* child
Octavie *f* child
Octavio *m* born; child
Octavius *m* born; child

Odab *m* Lord/lord; noble; son
Odeen *f* intelligent; wise
Odele *f* melody; song
Odelet *f* little; song
Odelette *f* little; melody; song
Odelia *f* little; wealthy
Odelinda *f* little; wealthy
Odell *f* melody; song
Odell *m* forested; hill; little; prosperous; wealthy
Odella *f* little; wealthy
Odera *f* plow
Odericus *m* good; man; son
Odessa *f* journey
Odetta *f* little; wealthy
Odette *f* little; wealthy
Odilia *f* little; wealthy
Odilo *m* refined; son
Odin *m* God/god; Odin
Odina *f* mountain
Odinan *m* born; child
Odine *f* intelligent; wise
Odion *m* first; twins
Odissan *m* born; son
Oditi *f* dawn
Odlo *m* refined; son
Odo *m* refined; son
Odolf *m* wealthy; wolf
Odon *m* prosperous; protector
Odongo *m* second; twins
Odoric *m* good; man; son
Odrick *m* good; man; son
Ofelia *f* help; serpent; useful
Ofilia *f* help; serpent
Ogano *m* deer; field; small
Ogden *m* oak; valley
Ogilvie *m* high; peak
Ogin *f* rose; wild
Oglesby *m* awe; inspiring
Ogun *m* God/god; war
Ogunkeye *m* earned; honor; Ogun
Ogunsanwo *m* gives; help; Ogun
Ogunsheye *m* honorably; Ogun
Ohanko *m* reckless
Ohara *f* bright; child; field; small
Ohara *m* field; small
Ohas *m* praise
Ohin *m* chief
Oira *f* great
Oisin *m* deer; little
Oja *f* vitality
Ojal *f* splendor

Ojas *m* luster
Ojayit *m* courageous
Oka *f* hill
Oka *m* hill
Okemos *m* chief; little
Oki *f* magic; middle; ocean; power
Okilani *f* heavens
Oko *m* God/god; Ogun
Okon *m* born; knight
Ola *f* ancestral; family; great; sea
Ola *m* man; noble
Olaf *m* ancestral
Olathe *f* beautiful
Olav *m* ancestral
Olcott *m* cottage; dweller; old
Olen *m* ancestor
Olena *f* Lenka; light
Olenta *f* pretty; servant
Olery *m* ruler
Oles *m* defender; helper; mankind
Olesia *f* defender; helper
Oleta *f* lady
Oletta *f* mystery; woman
Olette *f* mystery; woman
Olga *f* branch; consecrated; holy; olive; tree
Oliana *f* oleander
Olida *f* fragrant
Olin *m* ancestor
Olinda *f* fragrant
Olisa *f* God/god
Olive *f* branch; olive; tree
Oliver *m* affectionate; kind
Oliverio *m* affectionate; kind
Olivette *f* branch; olive; tree
Olivia *f* branch; holy; olive; tree
Olivier *m* affectionate; kind
Olnay *m* Olney; town
Olney *m* Olney; town
Olnton *m* Olney; town
Olorun *m* belonging; God/god; Olorun
Olufemi *m* God/god; loves
Olujimi *m* gave; God/god
Olukayode *m* brings; happiness; Lord/lord
Olushegun *m* God/god; victor
Olushola *m* blessed; God/god
Olva *f* holy
Olympia *f* gods; mountain
Olympias *f* gods; mountain

Olympium *f* gods; mountain
Oma *f* commander
Omar *m* loves; sea
Omari *m* God/god; highest
Omarr *m* God/god; highest; loves; sea
Omer *m* loves; sea
Omor *m* loves; sea
Omora *f* city; girl; laughing
Omusa *f* arrows
Ona *f* pattern; unity
Onan *m* prosperous
Onani *m* look
Onatah *f* corn; daughter; earth; spirit
Onawa *f* awake
Oni *f* born; child; desired; holy; prayed
Oni *m* cover; shelter; wanted
Onia *f* teacher; wise
Onida *f* desired
Ontina *f* brave; lion
Ontine *f* brave; lion
Onyx *f* gem
Oojam *m* enthusiasm
Oorjit *m* powerful
Opal *f* precious; stone
Opalina *f* precious; stone
Opaline *f* precious; stone
Opanas *m* immortal
Ophelia *f* serpent; useful
Ophelie *f* help; serpent; useful
Ophelila *f* help
Opportina *f* good; time
Opportuna *f* good; time
Oprah *f* fawn; freshness; runaway
Ora *f* gold; patient; seacoast; shore; wife
Orabel *f* beauty; gold; golden; seacoast; shore
Orabelle *f* beauty; gold; golden; seacoast; shore
Oralia *f* golden
Oralla *f* listener
Oram *m* enclosure; riverbank
Oran *m* pale
Orban *m* city
Ordando *m* famous
Ordella *f* elfin; spear
Ordway *m* fighter; spear
Orea *f* mountain
Orela *f* announcement; divine
Orelda *f* golden

Orelia *f* golden
Orella *f* announcement; divine; listener
Orelle *f* golden
Oren *m* pale
Orenda *f* magic; power
Oreste *m* man; mountain
Orestes *m* man; mountain; mountaineer
Orferd *m* cattle; valley
Orford *m* cattle; valley
Ori *f* corncake; field; weaver
Oria *f* girl; white
Orian *f* girl; white
Oriana *f* dawning; girl; golden; white
Orianna *f* girl; white
Oribel *f* beauty; golden
Oribella *f* beauty; golden
Oribelle *f* beauty; golden
Oriel *f* golden
Orielda *f* golden
Orielle *f* golden
Orin *m* pale
Orinda *f* light-skinned; pine; tree
Oringa *f* devout
Oringas *f* devout
Oringo *m* hunt
Orino *f* field; weaver
Oriola *f* golden
Oriole *f* golden
Orion *m* fire; giant; light; son
Orlan *m* land; pointed
Orland *m* land; pointed
Orlanda *f* famous; land
Orlando *m* famous; land
Orlann *f* golden
Orlanta *f* fame; great
Orlantha *f* fame; great
Orlena *f* golden
Orlenda *f* eagle; female
Orlene *f* golden
Orman *m* shipman; spearman
Ormond *m* armed; protector; spear
Orna *f* cedar; colored; olive; pale; tree
Ornas *f* colored; olive
Ornice *f* cedar; tree
Ornit *f* cedar; tree
Oro *m* golden
Orola *f* family; great
Orpah *f* fawn; freshness
Orpha *f* fawn; freshness
Orrick *m* ancient; dweller; oak; tree
Orrin *m* pale; river

Orsola *f* bear
Orson *m* bear; little; son
Orten *m* great; man; wealth
Ortensia *f* garden
Orton *m* great; man; wealth
Ortrude *f* maid; serpent
Orunjan *m* God/god; mid-day; sun
Orva *f* brave; friend; spear
Orvah *f* brave; friend
Orval *m* mighty; spear
Orvas *f* brave; friend
Orvil *m* Lord/lord; manor
Orville *m* estate; golden; Lord/lord; manor; town
Orvin *m* friend; spear
Orwin *m* divine; friend
Osa *f* god-like; God/god
Osana *f* mercy
Osanna *f* Lord/lord; mercy; praise
Osbert *m* brilliant; divinely
Osborn *m* bear; divine; warrior
Oscar *m* divine; spear; spearman
Osen *f* thousand
Osgood *m* divinely; gift; good; Lord/lord
Oshana *f* God/god; gracious
Oshanda *f* God/god; gracious
Oshawana *f* God/god; gracious
Osip *m* add
Osithe *f* Essex; saint
Osman *m* God/god; protected
Osmar *m* divinely; glorious
Osmen *m* God/god; protected
Osmo *m* God/god; protected
Osmond *m* divine; God/god; protected; protector
Osmund *m* divine; God/god; protected; protector
Osred *m* counselor; divine
Osric *m* divine; ruler
Osrick *m* divine; ruler
Osrock *m* divine; ruler
Ossa *f* God/god
Ossian *m* deer; little
Ossin *m* deer; little
Osten *f* east
Oswald *m* divinely; powerful
Oswell *m* divinely; powerful

Oswin *m* friend; God's
Osya *m* add
Osyth *f* Essex; saint
Otadan *m* plenty
Otha *f* little; wealthy
Othilia *f* little; wealthy
Othman *m* man; prosperous
Otina *f* friend; Lord/lord
Otis *m* wealthy
Ottah *m* thin
Ottavia *f* child
Otto *m* prosperous; wealthy
Ouray *m* arrow
Ova *f* born; sunshine overseer *m* foreman
Ovid *m* poet
Ovida *f* poetess
Owain *m* lamb; young
Owen *m* born; warrior; well-born; young
Owena *f* born; well
Oxford *m* ford
Oya *f* name
Oza *f* fountain; girl
Ozan *m* man; strength
Ozen *m* man; strength
Ozmo *m* God/god; protected
Ozora *f* Lord/lord; strength
Ozuru *m* large; stork

Pablo *m* little
Pace *m* man; peace
Pacian *m* man; peace
Pacien *m* man; peace
Pacifa *f* peaceful
Pacifica *f* peaceful
Pacificia *f* peaceful
Packston *m* afar; traveler
Packton *m* afar; traveler
Paco *m* pack
Padget *m* attendant; young
Padgett *m* attendant; young
Padma *f* lotus
Padraig *m* noble
Pagas *m* attendant; court; royal; servant; youthful
Page *f* child
Page *m* attendant; court; royal; servant; youthful
Paget *f* child
Pagett *f* child
Paige *f* child
Paka *f* cat; pussycat
Pakhi *m* bird
Paki *m* witness

Pakshi *m* bird
Pal *m* brother
Palani *m* free; man
Palash *m* tree
Palasha *f* sea
Palesa *f* flower
Palila *f* bird
Palin *m* protecting
Palla *f* distinguished; knowledge; maiden; wisdom; wise
Pallab *m* leaves; new
Palladin *m* fighter
Pallas *f* knowledge; maiden; wisdom; wise
Pallaton *m* fighter
Pallua *f* distinguished
Palma *f* palm
Palmer *m* bearing; crusader; palm; pilgrim
Palmira *f* palm
Palmyra *f* palm
Palnas *f* distinguished
Paloma *f* dove
Palua *f* distinguished
Pamela *f* all; honey
Pamelina *f* all; honey
Panas *m* immortal
Panav *m* prince
Pancho *m* free; man
Pandita *f* scholar
Pandita *m* scholar
Pandora *f* all; gifted
Pankti *f* sentence
Panna *f* emerald
Panna *m* emerald
Pannalal *m* emerald
Panphila *f* all; loving
Pansy *f* thought
Panthea *f* all; gods
Pantheas *f* all; gods
Panthia *f* all; gods
Panya *f* child; crowned; mouse; twin
Paolo *m* little
Papina *f* growing; oak; tree; vine
Parag *m* famous
Paramartha *m* highest; truth
Paramjeet *m* highest; success
Paranjay *m* Lord/lord; sea
Paras *m* touch
Parbarti *f* surrender
Pari *f* eagle; fairy
Pariket *m* against; desire
Parina *f* fairy
Parindra *m* lion
Parinita *f* complete
Parish *m* lives; parish

Paritosh *m* satisfaction
Parivita *f* free
Park *m* dweller; enclosed; land; park
Parke *m* dweller; enclosed; land; park
Parker *m* guardian; keeper; park
Parkin *m* little; Peter
Parlan *m* farmer
Parle *m* little; Peter
Parmaarth *m* highest; salvation; truth
Parmeet *m* wisdom
Parnal *m* leafy
Parnell *m* little; Peter
Parnella *f* little; rock
Parnik *m* creeper
Parrish *m* church; lives; parish
Parry *m* Harry; son
Parthena *f* sweet; virgin
Parthenia *f* maidenly; sweet; virgin
Parthinia *f* sweet; virgin
Parthiv *m* earth; prince
Parvat *m* mountain
Parvesh *m* celebration; Lord/lord
Pascal *m* born; child
Pascasia *f* Easter; season
Pascha *f* Easter; season
Paschasia *f* Easter; season
Pascia *f* Easter; season
Pasco *m* child
Pasha *f* sea
Pasha *m* net
Pashka Pelageya *f* sea
Pasia *f* Easter; season
Pat *m* fish
Patag *m* sun
Patakin *m* banner; holder
Patamon *m* raging
Pathik *m* traveler
Pathin *m* traveler
Patia *f* leaf
Patience *f* endurance
Paton *m* birth; noble
Patr *m* defender
Patrice *f* noble
Patrice *m* noble
Patricia *f* noble
Patrick *m* noble; Patrick; son
Patrin *m* leaf
Patrizia *f* noble
Patrizio *m* noble
Patsy *f* noble
Patti *f* noble
Pattie *f* noble
Pattin *m* leaf

Patton *m* combatant's; estate
Patty *f* noble
Patwin *m* man
Paul *m* little; small
Paula *f* little; rock
Paulette *f* little; rock
Paulina *f* little; rock
Pauline *f* little; rock
Paulita *f* little; rock
Paulo *m* place; rest
Pavak *m* fire
Pavan *m* wind
Pavel *m* small
Pavitra *m* pure
Pavla *f* little; rock
Paxon *m* afar; traveler
Paxton *m* afar; traveler
Pay *m* coming
Payas *m* water
Payat *m* coming
Payatt *m* coming
Payne *m* country
Payod *m* cloud
Payton *m* birth; dweller; estate; fighter; noble
Paz *f* peace
Paz *m* peace
Paza *f* golden
Pazi *f* bird; yellow
Pazia *f* golden
Pazice *f* golden
Pazit *f* golden
Peace *f* child; peaceful; tranquility
Pearl *f* pearl
Pearlina *f* pearl
Pearline *f* pearl
Pearson *m* Peter; son
Pedaiah *m* Lord/lord; protected
Pedaias *m* Lord/lord; protected
Pedro *m* rock; stone
Pedzi *f* finish
Pega *f* joined; together
Pegasus *m* attendant; court; royal; servant; youthful
Peggy *f* pearl
Pegma *f* joined; together
Pehlaj *m* born; first
Peirsen *m* Peter; son
Peke *f* glorious; shining
Pelaga *f* sorrow; woman
Pelagi *f* sorrow; woman
Pelagia *f* sea; sorrow; woman
Pelagias *f* sorrow; woman
Pelipa *f* horses; lover
Pelton *m* estate; pool

Pemba *f* existence; force; present
Pembroke *m* headland
Penda *f* admired; beloved
Penelope *f* weaver; worker
Penina *f* coral
Peninah *f* coral
Peninit *f* coral
Penley *m* enclosed; meadow; pasture
Penn *m* commander
Penny *f* weaver; worker
Penrod *m* commander; famous
Penrose *m* Penrose; town
Pentha *f* child; fifth
Penthea *f* child; fifth; mourner
Pentheam *f* child; fifth
Pentheas *f* child; fifth
Peony *f* giving; God/god; praise
Pepin *m* petitioner
Pepita *f* add; fruitful; increase
Percival *m* piercer; valley
Percy *m* piercer; valley
Perdita *f* lost
Perfecta *f* accomplished; perfect
Peri *f* dweller; mountain
Perkin *m* little; Peter
Perla *f* pearl
Pernella *f* little; rock
Pero *m* rock; stone
Perpetua *f* everlasting
Perri *f* pilgrim; strength; traveler
Perriann *f* pilgrim; strength; traveler
Perrie *f* pilgrim; strength; traveler
Perrin *f* pilgrim; strength; traveler
Perrin *m* little; Peter
Perrine *f* rock
Perry *f* pilgrim; strength; traveler
Perry *m* pear; pilgrim; stranger; traveler; tree
Persas *f* girl; peace
Persis *f* girl; peace
Peter *m* rock; stone
Petra *f* rock
Petronella *f* rock
Petronia *f* rock
Petronila *f* rock
Petula *f* seeker
Petulia *f* seeker
Peverel *m* piper; whistler
Peverell *m* piper; whistler

Peveril *m* piper; whistler
Peyton *m* birth; noble
Pezi *m* grass
Phalak *m* heaven
Pham *f* commit
Pham *m* commit
Phani *m* snake
Pheba *f* born
Phelan *m* little; wolf
Phelgen *m* man
Phelgon *m* man
Phemia *f* fairest; famous
Phenica *f* palm; tree
Phenice *f* palm; tree
Phia *f* ivory; lovely; nurse; wife
Phibba *f* born
Philan *m* loves; man; mankind
Philana *f* loving
Philander *m* loves; man; mankind
Philantha *f* flower; lover
Philbert *m* bright; brilliant; radiant; shining; son; soul
Philberta *f* brilliant
Philemon *m* beauty; great; man
Philender *m* loves; man; mankind
Philene *f* loving
Philida *f* loving
Philina *f* loving
Philip *m* horses; lover
Philipp *m* horses; lover
Philippa *f* horses; lover
Philippine *f* horses; lover
Phillada *f* loving; woman
Phillida *f* loving; woman
Phillip *m* horses; lover
Phillis *f* branch; green
Philo *m* friendly; loving
Philomela *f* lover; song
Philomena *f* lover; moon
Phineas *m* brass; mouth; oracle
Phiona *f* ivory
Phionna *f* ivory
Phira *f* beautiful; jewel
Phiroza *f* turquoise
Phoenix *f* eagle
Phonsa *f* aggressive Alphonsine; nature
Photina *f* friend; Lord/lord
Phyllis *f* branch; green
Pia *f* pious
Pias *m* fun
Pickford *m* ford; peak
Pierce *m* Peter; rock; son; stone

Pierette *f* rock
Piero *m* rock; stone
Pierpont *m* bridges; stone
Pierre *m* rock; stone
Pierrepont *m* bridges; stone
Pierrette *f* little
Pierro *m* flaming; hair
Pierson *m* Peter; son
Pieter *m* rock; stone
Pietro *m* rock; stone
Piki *m* cuckoo
Pilan *m* essence; supreme
Pilar *f* basin; fountain; pillar
Pilar *m* basin; fountain; pillar
Pili *m* born; second-born; son
Pilisi *f* branch; green
Pillan *m* essence; supreme
Pin *m* faithful; true
Pincas *m* oracle
Pinchas *m* oracle
Pinda *f* good
Ping *f* duckweed; peaceful
Pinga *f* dark
Pingal *m* reputed; sage
Piper *f* pipe
Pippa *f* horses; lover
Pippas *f* horses; lover
Pita *f* born; daughter; fourth
Pitney *m* island
Pival *m* tree
Piyali *m* tree
Piyush *m* milk
Placedo *m* calm; tranquil
Placia *f* calm
Placida *f* calm; gentle; peaceful
Placidia *f* calm
Placido *m* calm; tranquil
Placijo *m* calm; tranquil
Plasido *m* calm; tranquil
Plasio *m* calm; tranquil
Plato *m* broad; broad-shouldered; mankind; shouldered; teacher
Platon *m* broad-shouldered; shouldered
Platona *f* broad-shouldered; shouldered
Platt *m* flat; land
Platto *m* mankind; teacher
Platus *m* mankind; teacher
Pocahontas *f* playful
Pol *m* crown
Polard *m* man
Pollard *m* man
Pollerd *m* man

Pollock *m* little
Pollux *m* crown
Polly *f* little; rock
Pollyam *f* goddess
Polo *m* alligator
Poloma *f* bow
Pomeroy *m* apple
Pomona *f* apple; fertile;
    fruitful
Poni *f* born; child
Pontias *m* lover; sea; water
Pontius *m* lover; sea; water
Pontus *m* lover; sea; water
Poonish *m* Lord/lord;
    pious
Pooran *m* complete
Poorv *m* east
Poppy *f* flower; poppy
Porter *m* gatekeeper;
    porter
Portero *m* gatekeeper;
    messenger; royal
Portia *f* gateway; offering
Posala *f* burst
Pov *m* earth
Powa *m* rich
Prabal *m* mighty; strong
Prachur *m* abundant
Pradarsh *m* appearance;
    order
Pradeep *m* lamp
Pradhi *m* intelligent
Pradnesh *m* Lord/lord;
    wisdom
Pradosh *m* twilight
Pradvot *m* illuminate
Pradyun *m* radiant
Praful *m* blooming
Prafulla *m* cheerful; pleas-
    ant
Pragnya *f* scholar
Pragun *m* honest; straight
Prahalad *m* bliss
Prajeet *m* victorious
Prajin *m* kind
Prajit *m* kind
Prajval *m* brightness
Prajvala *m* flame
Prakalpa *f* project
Prakash *m* light
Praket *m* intelligence
Prakhar *m* shape; summit
Prakrit *m* handsome; na-
    ture
Pramad *m* delightful
Pramada *f* woman
Pramath *m* horse
Pramesh *m* accurate;
    knowledge; master
Pramit *m* consciousness
Pramod *m* delight; joyous

Pramsu *m* scholar
Prana *m* spirit
Pranati *f* prayer
Pranay *m* love
Pranesh *m* life; Lord/lord
Pranet *m* leader
Praney *m* obedient
Pranidhi *f* spy
Pranit *m* modest
Pranita *f* promoted
Pranjal *m* simple
Pranjivan *m* breath; life
Pransu *m* high; tall
Pransukh *m* joy; life
Pranya *m* friendship
Prapti *f* advantage
Prasanna *m* happy
Prasham *m* peace
Prashansa *m* praise
Prashant *m* calm
Prasheila *f* ancient; time
Prashray *m* love
Pratap *m* glory; vigor
Prateep *m* opposite
Pratichi *f* west
Pratik *m* symbol
Pratiti *f* faith
Pratosh *m* delight
Pratul *m* balanced; person
Pratyush *m* sun
Praval *m* fierce; strong
Pravar *m* excellent
Praveen *m* expert; skilled
Praveena *f* skilled
Praveer *m* excellent; king;
    warrior
Pravin *m* capable; expert;
    skilled; skillful
Pravir *m* brave
Pravit *m* hero
Preciosa *f* precious
Preetam *m* lover
Prem *m* affectionate; lov-
    able; love
Premal *m* full; love
Prentice *m* apprentice
Prescott *m* dwelling; priest's
Presley *m* dweller;
    meadow; priest's
Preston *m* dweller; priest's
Prianki *f* favorite
Price *m* ardent; son
Prima *f* child; first
Primavera *f* born; early;
    spring; springtime
Primo *m* born; child; fam-
    ily; first
Primrosa *f* first; flower; lit-
    tle; name
Primrose *f* first; flower; lit-
    tle; name

Prina *f* content
Prina *m* pleased
Prineet *m* content
Prior *m* head; monastery
Prisca *f* past; times
Priscilla *f* past; times
Prithu *m* broad
Prithvee *m* earth
Prithvi *m* earth
Prithviraj *m* earth; king
Pritish *m* Lord/lord; love
Priya *f* lovable; sweet-
    natured
Priyal *f* lovable; sweet-
    natured
Priyam *f* lovable; sweet-
    natured
Priyanka *f* lovable; sweet-
    natured
Priyata *f* lovable; sweet-
    natured
Priyesh *m* God/god; loved
Prochora *f* choir; leader
Procora *f* choir; leader
Procter *m* administrator
Procterl Pomo *m* leader
Proctor *m* administrator;
    leader
Prosper *m* always; blessed
Prospera *f* auspicious
Prospero *m* always; blessed
Prosperus *m* always;
    blessed
Prudence *f* forsight; intel-
    ligence
Prunella *f* colored; plum
Pryasha *f* lovable; sweet-
    natured
Pryati *f* lovable; sweet-
    natured
Pryor *m* head; monastery
Pua *f* blossoming; flower;
    tree
Pualani *f* flower; heavenly
Publias *m* man; people
Publius *m* man; people
Pukhraj *m* topaz
Pulak *m* ecstasy
Pulakesh *m* joyous
Pulcheria *f* beauty; girl
Pulchia *f* beauty; girl
Pulika *f* obedient
Puni *f* flower; heavenly
Punit *m* holy
Pura *f* pure
Puran *m* complete
Purumitra *m* city; friend
Purvis *m* food
Pusan *m* sage
Putnam *m* lives
Putul *f* doll

Pyrena *f* fiery; fruit; kernal
Pythia *f* diviner; prophet

Qianru *f* pretty; smile
Quaco *m* born
Quade *m* cross; son
Quaid *m* cross; son
Quami *m* born
Quanah *m* fragrant
Quanika *f* belonging;
 God/god
Quanikka *f* belonging;
 God/god
Quanique *f* belonging;
 God/god
Quanisha *f* life; woman
Quao *m* born
Quartana *f* born; fourth
Quartas *f* born; fourth
Quartis *f* born; fourth
Quartus *m* born; son
Quashee *m* born; Sunday
Queisha *f* favorite
Quenna *f* queen
Quennel *m* dweller; little;
 oak; tree
Quent *m* born; child;
 fighter
Quentessa *f* essence
Quentin *m* born; child;
 fighter
Quenton *m* born; child;
 fighter
Queri *f* loved
Querida *f* beloved; loved
Queridas *f* loved
Quesha *f* favorite
Questa *f* nightingale;
 searches; song
Queta *f* estate; home; ruler
Quiana *f* graceful
Quianna *f* graceful
Quico *m* estate; home;
 property; ruler
Quidel *m* burning
Quigley *m* distaff
Quilin *m* strong
Quillan *m* cub
Quimby *m* dweller; estate;
 woman
Quinby *m* dweller; estate;
 woman
Quincy *m* dweller; estate;
 fifth; son
Quinetta *f* born; fifth
Quinette *f* born; fifth
Quinlan *m* shaped; well
Quinley *m* strong
Quinn *m* intelligent;
 strong; wise

Quint *m* born; child;
 fighter
Quinta *f* essence
Quintessa *f* born; essence;
 fifth
Quintice *f* essence
Quintin *m* born; child;
 fighter
Quintina *f* born; fifth
Quinton *m* child; fifth
Quirita *f* citizen
Quirna *f* warlike
Quita *f* vital
Quiteria *f* vital
Quiteris *f* vital
Quito *m* born; child;
 fighter
Quon *m* bright

Raahi *m* traveler
Raajaa *m* king
Raakesh *m* Lord/lord;
 night
Raama *f* child
Rabbi *m* breeze
Rabi *f* breeze; harvest;
 spring
Rabi *m* breeze
Rabia *f* spring
Rabmet *m* compassionate;
 merciful
Rachaba *f* horse-woman;
 woman
Rachana *f* creation
Rachel *f* ewe
Rachele *f* ewe
Rachelle *f* ewe
Rachit *m* invention
Rachita *f* created
Rachna *f* creation
Rad burn *m* brook
Rad *m* counselor
Radbert *m* brilliant; coun-
 selor
Radborne *m* red; stream
Radbourne *m* brook; red
Radburn *m* red
Radcliff *m* cliff; dweller;
 red
Radella *f* counselor; elfin;
 elves
Radelle *f* counselor; elves
Radford *m* ford; red; valley
Radinka *f* active
Radley *m* field; meadow;
 pasture; red; valley
Radman *m* joy
Radmilla *f* people; worker
Radmund *m* counsel; pro-
 tector

Radnor *m* red
Radolf *m* counsel; swift;
 wolf
Radomil *m* lover; peace
Rae *f* deer; doe; ewe
Rafa *f* happy; prosperous
Rafael *m* God/god; healed
Rafaela *f* God/god
Rafaelle *m* God/god;
 healed
Rafaello *m* God/god;
 healed
Rafe *m* God/god; healed
Rafferty *m* prosperous;
 rich
Raffin *m* exalting
Rafi *m* exalting
Rafiki *m* friend
Rafiya *f* dignified
Ragnar *m* army; mighty
Ragnor *m* army; mighty
Rahas *m* delight
Rahel *f* ewe
Rahim *m* compassionate;
 merciful
Rahman *m* compassionate;
 merciful
Rai *f* next
Raidah *f* leader
Raiden *m* God/god; thun-
 der
Raiko *f* child; next
Raina *f* powerful
Rainah *f* powerful
Raine *f* creator
Rainelle *f* Lord/lord
Rainer *m* army; mighty;
 prudent; warrior
Rainger *m* forest; keeper
Raini *f* creator
Raini *m* Creator
Rainier *m* army; mighty
Rais *m* captain
Raisa *f* exalted; rose
Raissa *f* believer
Raizel *f* flower; rose
Raj *m* glorified; king's/
 kings
Raja *f* anticipated
Rajab *m* glorified
Rajan *m* king
Rajani *m* night
Rajas *m* arising; passion
Rajat *m* silver
Rajata *f* silver
Rajata *m* sovereignty
Rajdeep *m* best; king's/
 kings
Rajesh *m* king
Rajit *m* decorated
Rajkumar *m* prince

Rajnish *m* moon
Raju *m* prosperity
Rajul *f* brilliant
Rajul *m* brilliant
Rakel *f* ewe
Rakesh *m* Lord/lord;
night
Ralaigh *m* deer; meadow
Raleigh *m* deer; meadow
Ralfston *m* estate
Ralis *m* crowned; laurel
Ralleigh *m* deer; meadow
Ralph *m* counsel; protection; swift; wolf
Ralston *m* estate
Rama *f* child; exalted;
lofty; pleasing; restoration; thin
Ramadan *m* born; month;
Ramadan
Ramah *m* Lord/lord;
praise
Raman *m* pleasing
Rambert *m* brilliant;
mighty; prayed
Ramburt *m* prayed
Ramiah *m* Lord/lord;
praise
Ramila *f* fortune-teller
Ramirez *m* great; judge;
mighty; protector; wise
Ramiro *m* great; judge;
mighty; protector; wise
Ramla *f* future
Ramon *m* mighty; protector; wise
Ramona *f* mighty; protector; wise
Ramonda *f* mighty; protector; wise
Ramra *m* splendor
Ramsden *m* ram's; valley
Ramses *m* born; sun
Ramsey *m* island; ram's;
raven's
Rana *f* beautiful; eye-catching; queenly;
royal
Ranajay *m* victorious
Ranajit *m* victorious
Ranak *m* king
Ranana *f* fresh
Rance *m* all
Rancell *m* all
Randa *f* randa; sweet; tree
Randall *m* shield; wolf
Randell *m* shield; wolf
Randhir *m* brave
Randi *f* she-wolf
Randie *f* she-wolf
Randolf *m* shield; wolf

Randolph *m* protection;
shield; wolf
Randy *f* she-wolf
Rane *f* queen
Ranee *f* queenly; royal
Ranen *m* joyous; sing
Ranger *m* forest
Rani *f* bells; queen;
queenly; royal; sadness
Rania *f* queen
Ranita *f* confident; female;
joyful; song
Raniyah *f* beautiful; eye-catching
Ranjan *f* enjoyment
Ranjan *m* delighting
Ranjit *m* victor
Ranjiv *m* victorious
Rankin *m* little; shield
Ranon *m* joyous; sing
Ransell *m* all
Ransford *m* ford; raven's
Ransley *m* meadow;
raven's
Ransom *m* shield; son
Ranveer *m* battle; hero
Ranya *f* beautiful; eye-catching
Raoul *m* commander;
counsel; helpful; protection; swift; wolf
Raphael *m* God/god;
healed
Raphaela *f* God/god
Rapier *m* strong; sword
Raquel *f* ewe
Raseda *f* flower; tiny
Raseta *f* flower; tiny
Rasha *f* gazelle; young
Rashad *m* follows; path;
right; righteous
Rasheed *m* council; follows; good; guided; path;
right; rightly
Rashid *m* council; follows;
good; guided; path;
right; rightly
Rashida *f* righteous
Rashidi *m* thinker
Rashmi *m* sun
Rasia *f* rose
Rasik *m* feeling; full; passion
Rasmus *m* lovable; love;
worthy
Rasna *m* speech
Rasul *m* messenger
Ratan *m* precious; stone
Ratnakar *m* earth
Ratri *f* night
Raul *m* counsel; swift; wolf

Rave *m* sun
Ravi *m* conferring; sun
Raviv *m* sun
Rawdan *m* deer; hill
Rawden *m* deer; hill
Rawdin *m* deer; hill
Rawdon *m* deer; hill
Rawlins *m* counsel; little;
son; wolf
Rawnie *f* lady
Rawson *m* counsel; little;
son; wolf
Raybin *m* brook; deer;
fields; flower; roe
Raybourne *m* brook; deer;
fields; flower; roe
Rayburn *m* brook; deer;
fields; flower; roe
Rayen *f* flower
Raymond *m* mighty; protector; wise
Rayna *f* clean; powerful;
pure
Raynah *f* powerful
Raynard *m* brave; mighty
Raynata *f* powerful
Rayne *f* mighty
Rayner *m* army; mighty
Raynor *m* army; mighty
Rayzil *f* flower; rose
Razi *m* secret
Raziel *m* secret
Razil *f* flower; rose
Razilee *f* secret
Razili *f* secret
Raziya *f* agreeable
Rea *f* poppy; stream
Read *m* haired; red
Reagan *f* queen
Reagan *m* king; little
Reaganne *f* queen
Reagen *m* king; little
Reave *m* bailiff; steward
Reba *f* born; bound; fourth
Rebah *f* born; fourth
Rebba *f* born; fourth
Rebeca *f* bound
Rebecca *f* bound
Rebeka *f* bound
Rebekah *f* bound
Rechaba *f* horse-woman;
woman
Redford *m* ford; red
Redley *m* dweller;
meadow; red
Redman *m* counsel; horse-man; man
Redmond *m* adviser; counsel; protector
Redmund *m* counsel; protector

Redwald m counsel; mighty
Ree f riverbank; shore
Reece m ardent; swift
Reed m haired; red
Reena f dyed; embroi-
 dered
Reese m ardent
Reeta f shake
Reeva f riverbank; shore
Reeve m bailiff; steward
Regan f queen
Regan m king; little
Regen m king; little
Regin f queen
Regina f queen
Reginald m mighty; power-
 ful
Regis m regal
Reid m haired; red
Reiko f child; gratitude;
 next; pretty
Reilly m valiant; warlike
Reina f queen
Reinald m mighty; power-
 ful
Reine f queen
Reinhard m brave; mighty
Reinhold m mighty; pow-
 erful
Reinold m mighty; power-
 ful
Rema f girl; lover; nature
Remington m estate; fam-
 ily; raven
Remus m fair; white
Remy m oarsman
Ren f lily; lotus; water
Rena f despised; peace
Renaldo m mighty; power
Renard m brave; mighty
Renata f again; born;
 confident; female
Renate f again; born
Renato m mighty; power-
 ful
Renaud m brave; mighty;
 power; wise
Renault m mighty; power-
 ful
Rendor m policeman
Rene f again; born; peace
Rene m reborn
Renee f again; born
Renesh m Lord/lord; love
Reneta f confident; female
Renferd m maker; peace
Renfred m maker; mighty;
 peace; peaceful
Renia f queen
Renita f confident; female;
 resister

Reniti f confident; female
Rennold m lasting; power
Renny m little; mighty;
 powerful
Reno m deer
Renshaw m forest; raven
Renton m buck; deer; es-
 tate; roe
Renwick m nest
Reseda f flower; tiny
Reseta f flower; tiny
Resha f branch
Resham m silk
Resi f reaper
Reta f shake
Reth m king
Reuben m behold; son
Reva f Narmada; regain;
 river; riverbank; sacred;
 shore; strength
Revanth m horse; Rider
Rewa f swift
Rex m king
Rexana f grace; regal
Rexanna f grace; regal
Rexanne f grace; regal
Rexferd m castle; king
Rexford m castle; dweller;
 ford; king; king's/kings
Rey m king
Reyes m king
Reyna f queen
Reynard m brave; mighty
Reynold m lasting; mighty;
 power; powerful
Rez f copper
Rhea f stream
Rheta f orator; shake
Rhetta f shake
Rhiamon f witch
Rhiana f basil; sweet
Rhianon f witch
Rhlanna f basil; sweet;
 witch
Rhoda f rose
Rhodanthe f flower; rose
Rhodes m crucifix;
 dweller; roses
Rhodia f rose
Rhona f mighty; noisy;
 power
Rhonda f noisy
Rhonette f noisy
Ria f girl; Lord/lord;
 lover; mouth; nature;
 river
Riana f basil; sweet
Rianna f basil; sweet
Riannon f witch
Rianon f witch
Ribal m addition; welcome

Rica f all; famous;
 princess; ruler
Ricadonna f lady; ruling
Ricard m brave; powerful;
 ruler
Ricarda f powerful; ruler
Ricardo m brave; power-
 ful; ruler
Riccardo m brave; power-
 ful; ruler
Richard m brave; power-
 ful; ruler
Richart m powerful; ruler
Richerd m brave; powerful
Richma f leader; sign
Richmal f leader; sign
Richman m man; powerful
Richmond m powerful;
 protector
Rick m divine; ruler
Ricker m army; powerful
Rickert m brave; powerful;
 ruler
Rickward m guardian;
 powerful
Rickwood m guardian;
 powerful
Rico m home; ruler
Rida f favor; loved
Rida m favor
Riddock m field; smooth
Rider m horseman; knight
Ridge m ridge
Ridgeway m ridge; road
Ridglea m ridge
Ridglee m ridge
Ridgley m ridge
Ridhaa f good
Ridley m field; meadow;
 red
Rigby m ruler's; valley
Rigg m ridge
Rihana f basil; sweet
Riju m innocent
Rijul m innocent
Rika f all; ruler
Riki m peaceful; ruler
Rilda f armored; battle;
 girl; maid; war
Rilette f brook
Riley m valiant; warlike
Rilla f brook; stream
Rillette f stream
Rima f antelope; girl; lover;
 nature; poetry; white
Rimma f girl; lover; nature
Rimon m pomegranate
Rimona f pomegranate
Rin f park
Rina f dear; friend; girl;
 good; sea

Rinee *f* girl; little; purity
Riona *f* queen
Riordan *m* bard; poet; royal
Riorden *m* poet
Rip *m* full; grown; ripe
Ripleigh *m* valley
Ripley *m* valley
Ripp *m* full; grown; ripe
Ripu *m* enemy
Ripudaman *m* enemies
Risa *f* happy; laughter
Risha *f* flower; iris; rainbow
Rishab *m* superior
Rishabh *m* morality
Rishi *m* sage; saint
Rishima *f* moonbeam
Rishit *m* best
Risley *m* brushwood; meadow
Rissa *f* happy
Riston *m* brushwood; estate; town
Rita *f* bird; dark; generosity; girl; motherly
Ritesh *m* Lord/lord; truth
Rithik *m* stream
Rithwik *m* saint
Riti *m* motion
Ritsa *f* defender; helper
Ritter *m* knight
Ritvik *m* priest
Riva *f* riverbank; shore
Rnager *m* keeper
Roald *m* famous; ruler
Roarke *m* famous; ruler
Roba *f* brilliantly; famous
Robert *m* bright; fame; shining
Roberta *f* fame; shining
Roberto *m* bright; fame; shining
Robertson *m* bright; fame; shining
Robin *f* fame; little
Robin *m* bright; fame; shining
Robina *f* fame; shining
Robine *f* fame; shining
Robinetta *f* fame; little
Robinette *f* fame; little
Robinia *f* fame; shining
Rochak *m* tasty
Rochella *f* little; rock
Rochelle *f* little; rock
Rochester *m* fortress; rocky; sky
Rochette *f* little; rock
Rochus *m* soldier; valiant
Rock *m* rock; soldier; valiant

Rockley *m* meadow; rocky
Rockwell *m* rocky; spring
Rocky *m* rock; soldier; valiant
Roden *m* reed; valley
Roderica *f* famous; princess; ruler
Roderich *m* fame; famous; rich; ruler
Roderick *m* fame; famous; rich; ruler
Rodger *m* famous; spearman
Rodman *m* famous; hero; man; redhead
Rodmann *m* redhead
Rodmond *m* famous; protector
Rodmun *m* redhead
Rodmund *m* famous; protector
Rodmur *m* redhead
Rodney *m* famous; island
Rodolf *m* famous; wolf
Rodolfo *m* famous; wolf
Rodolph *m* famous; wolf
Rodrick *m* fame; famous; rich; ruler
Rodriego *m* fame; famous; rich; ruler
Rodrigo *m* fame; famous; rich; ruler
Rodwell *m* crucifix; dweller; spring
Rogan *m* haired; red
Roger *m* famous; spearman
Rogerio *m* famous; spearman
Rohak *m* rising
Rohan *m* ascending; sandalwood
Rohana *f* sandalwood
Rohin *f* rising
Rohin *m* path; upward
Rohit *m* red
Roi *m* king; son
Roice *m* king; son
Roid *m* clearing; forest
Rois *f* rose
Roland *m* famous; land
Rolanda *f* famous; land
Rolande *f* famous; land
Roldan *m* famous; land
Rolf *m* counsel; wolf
Rolfe *m* counsel; wolf
Rolfston *m* estate
Rolland *m* famous; land
Rollin *m* famous; land
Rollins *m* famous; land
Rolon *m* famous; wolf

Rolph *m* counsel; swift; wolf
Rolt *m* curving; famous; power; river
Roma *f* city; eternal
Romain *m* Rome
Romaine *f* city; eternal
Romalda *f* battle; famous; glorious; maid; warrior; woman
Roman *m* Rome
Rombert *m* prayed
Romelda *f* battle; famous; glorious; maid; warrior; woman
Romelle *f* city; eternal
Romeo *m* pilgrim; Rome
Romeon *m* pilgrim; Rome
Romila *f* city; eternal
Romilda *f* battle; city; eternal; famous; glorious; maid; warrior; woman
Romir *m* interesting
Romney *m* curving; river
Romola *f* Roman; woman
Romulus *m* citizen; Rome
Rona *f* joy; mighty; power
Ronak *m* brightness; radiance
Ronald *m* mighty; power; powerful
Ronalda *f* mighty; power
Ronan *m* little
Ronda *f* noisy
Ronel *m* God/god; song
Roni *f* joy
Roni *m* joy
Ronia *f* joy
Ronice *f* joy
Ronli *f* joy
Ronli *m* mine; song
Ronshan *m* illumination
Ronsher *m* battlefield; lion
Ronson *m* mighty; power; son
Rooney *m* red
Roper *m* maker; rope
Roque *m* soldier; valiant
Rory *m* king; red
Rosa *f* little; pretty; rose
Rosabel *f* beautiful; rose
Rosalba *f* lovely; rose; white
Rosaleen *f* little; pretty; rose
Rosalia *f* rose
Rosalie *f* little; pretty; rose
Rosalind *f* beautiful; little; pretty; rose
Rosalinda *f* beautiful; rose
Rosaline *f* beautiful; rose

Rosalynd *f* beautiful; rose
Rosamond *f* famous; protectress
Rosamund *f* famous; protectress
Rosamunda *f* famous; protectress
Rosamunde *f* famous; protectress
Rosanna *f* graceful; rose
Roscoe *m* deer; forest; roe
Rose *f* Mary; rose
Roselani *f* heavenly; rose
Roselba *f* lovely; rose; white
Roselind *f* little; pretty; rose
Roseline *f* beautiful; rose
Rosella *f* rose
Roselle *f* rose
Rosemari *f* Mary's; rose
Rosemarie *f* Mary's; rose
Rosemary *f* Mary; Mary's; rose
Rosen *m* ruler
Rosetta *f* rose
Rosette *f* rose
Rosh *m* chief
Roshan *m* dawn; light
Rosina *f* little; pretty; rose
Rosita *f* rose
Roslin *m* haired; little; red
Ross *m* peninsula
Roswald *m* horse; mighty
Roswell *m* horse; mighty
Roth *m* haired; red
Rothwell *m* red; spring
Rourke *m* famous; ruler
Rover *m* rambler; wanderer
Rowan *m* famous; haired; red
Rowe *m* haired; red; rest
Rowell *m* deer; roe; spring
Rowen *m* haired; red
Rowena *f* bosomed; famous; friend; haired; light; white
Rowland *m* famous; land
Rowley *m* dweller; meadow; rough
Roxana *f* dawning; new
Roxanne *f* dawning; new
Roxene *f* dawning; new
Roy *m* king; son
Royal *m* kingly; regal
Royale *f* regal
Royce *m* king; son
Royd *m* clearing; forest
Royden *m* flowered; valley
Rozamund *f* famous; protectress

Rozella *f* rose
Rozen *m* ruler
Rozene *f* flower; rose
Ruark *m* famous; ruler
Ruben *m* behold; son
Rubia *f* gem
Rubie *f* gem
Rubin *m* ruby
Rubina *f* gem
Ruby *f* gem
Ruchir *m* beautiful; radiant
Ruchira *f* tasty
Rudi *f* famous; wolf
Rudo *m* love
Rudolf *m* famous; wolf
Rudolph *m* famous; wolf
Rudyard *m* enclosure; red
Rue *f* grace
Ruella *f* elfin; lucky
Ruelle *f* elfin; lucky
Rufe *m* haired; red
Rufen *f* fragrance; pleasant
Rufena *f* bright; girl; hair; red
Ruff *m* haired; red
Ruffe *m* haired; red
Rufford *m* ford; rough
Rufina *f* bright; girl; hair; red
Ruford *m* ford; red
Rufus *m* haired; red
Rugby *m* estate
Ruhan *m* spiritual
Ruhi *f* soul
Ruhin *f* spiritual
Rujul *m* honest; simple
Rukm *m* gold
Rula *f* ruler
Rule *m* famous; wolf
Rumford *m* ford; wide
Runako *m* handsome
Rupak *m* sign
Rupang *m* beautiful
Rupert *m* bright; fame; shining
Rupesh *m* beauty; Lord/lord
Ruphina *f* bright; girl; hair; red
Rupin *m* beauty
Ruri *f* emerald
Rurik *m* fame; famous; king; red; rich; ruler
Rusalka *f* nymph; wood
Rush *m* haired; red
Rushabh *m* decoration
Rusham *m* peaceful
Rushford *m* ford; rush
Rushil *m* charming

Ruskin *m* haired; little; red
Russell *m* haired; red
Russom *m* boss; head
Rust *m* haired; red
Rustam *m* large; tall
Rusten *m* brushwood; home
Rustice *m* country
Rusticus *m* country
Rustin *m* brushwood; home
Ruston *m* brushwood; home
Rusty *m* haired; red
Rutajit *m* conqueror; truth
Rutesh *m* king
Rutger *m* famous; spearman
Ruth *f* beautiful; compassion
Rutherford *m* cattle; ford
Rutherfurd *m* cattle; ford
Rutland *m* land; root; stump
Rutledge *m* pool; red
Rutley *m* meadow; root; stump
Rutva *m* speech
Ryan *m* king; laughing; little
Rycroft *m* field; rye
Ryder *m* horseman; knight
Rye *m* riverbank
Ryker *m* Richard; son
Rylan *m* dweller
Ryland *m* dweller
Ryle *m* hill; rye
Ryley *m* valiant; warlike
Ryman *m* rye
Ryton *m* enclosure; rye

Saad *m* good; profit
Saada *f* helper
Saagar *m* ocean
Saanjh *m* evening
Saatvik *m* pious
Saba *f* eastern; morning; Saba; wind; woman
Sabah *f* rest
Sabal *m* strength
Sabaya *f* eastern; morning; wind
Sabba *f* rest
Sabel *f* black
Sabella *f* black; wise
Sabelle *f* black; wise
Saber *m* man; sword
Sabhya *m* civilized
Sabian *m* heaven
Sabina *f* lady

Sabine *f* lady
Sabir *m* man; sword
Sabira *f* patient
Sabirah *f* patience
Sabiya *f* eastern; morning; wind
Sabiyah *f* eastern; morning; wind
Sable *f* black
Sabra *f* cactus; patience; rest; thorny
Sabrang *f* rainbow
Sabrina *f* boundary; cactus; thorny
Sabu *m* boy; follower
Saburo *m* born; male; third-born
Sachetan *m* rational
Sachi *f* bliss; child; joy
Sachiko *f* bliss; child; joy
Sachio *m* fortunate; well-born
Sachit *m* joyful
Sachita *f* consciousness
Sachiv *m* friend
Sacnite *f* flower; white
Sada *f* chaste
Sadar *m* respectful
Sadavir *m* courageous
Sade *f* crown; honored
Sadella *f* princess
Sadira *f* lotus; tree
Sadirah *f* water
Sadiras *f* water
Sadiva *m* eternal
Sadoc *m* sacred
Sadonia *f* ensnare
Sadora *f* water
Sadzi *f* heart; sun
Safal *m* succeed
Safara *f* her; place
Saffar *m* coppersmith
Safford *m* ford; willow
Safina *f* Ark; Noah's
Safiya *f* pure
Sagar *m* ocean; sea
Sagara *f* ocean
Sage *f* healthy; knowing; whole; wise
Sage *m* healthy; knowing; whole; wise
Sahaj *m* easy
Sahale *m* above
Sahar *m* dawn; sun
Saharsh *m* joy
Sahas *m* brave
Sahasya *m* mighty
Sahat *m* strong
Sahen *m* falcon
Sahib *m* Lord/lord
Sahil *m* guide

Sahithi *f* literature
Sahitya *f* literature
Said *m* happy
Saida *f* happy
Sair *m* hermit
Saire *m* hermit
Sajal *m* moist
Sajan *m* beloved
Sajili *f* decorated
Sajiv *m* lively
Sajiva *m* full; life
Saju *m* traveling
Saka *f* slope
Saka *m* slope
Sakari *f* sweet
Sakash *m* illumination
Sakhi *f* friend
Saki *f* cape
Saki *m* cape; headland
Sakima *m* king
Saksham *m* able; capable
Sakshi *f* witness
Sakuna *f* bird
Sakura *f* blossom; cherry
Sala *f* sacred; tree
Salaam *m* peach
Salaman *m* peaceful
Salangi *f* good; shepherdess
Salangia *f* good; shepherdess
Salba *f* lovely; rose; white
Saleem *m* peace; peaceful; safe
Salena *f* moon
Salih *m* good; right
Salil *m* water
Salila *f* water
Salim *m* peace; peaceful; safe
Salina *f* salty
Salisbury *m* guard
Sally *f* peaceful; princess
Salmalin *m* taloned
Salokh *m* friendship
Salom *f* peaceful
Saloman *m* peaceful
Salome *f* peaceful
Salomon *m* peaceful
Salvador *m* savior
Salvatore *m* savior
Salvia *f* sage
Salvina *f* sage
Sam *m* hear
Sama *f* flower; lovely
Samaah *m* generosity
Samal *f* prayed
Samantha *f* flower; listener; lovely
Samanthia *f* flower; lovely
Samar *m* fruit; paradise

Samara *f* God/god
Samarpan *m* dedicating
Samata *f* equality
Samay *m* start
Sambha *m* shining
Sambit *m* consciousness
Sambodh *m* complete; knowledge
Sambuddha *m* wise
Sameep *m* close
Sameh *f* forgiver
Samen *m* happy
Samesh *m* equality; Lord/lord
Sami *f* exalted; listener; praised
Samik *m* peaceful
Samiksha *f* analysis
Samin *m* self-disciplined
Samina *f* happy
Samir *m* companion; entertaining; wind
Samita *f* collected
Samiya *f* incomparable
Sammad *m* joy
Samman *m* grocer
Sammon *m* grocer
Sampada *m* blessing
Sampson *m* man; son; splendid
Samskara *f* ethics
Samson *m* man; son; splendid
Samudra *m* sea
Samuel *m* God/god
Samuela *f* God/god; name
Samuele *m* God/god
Samuella *f* God/god; name
Samvar *m* content
Samyak *m* enough
Sana *f* word
Sana *m* word
Sanaatan *m* permanent
Sanborn *m* beach; brook; dweller; sandy
Sanborne *m* beach; brook; dweller; sandy
Sanburn *m* beach; brook; dweller; sandy
Sanchali *f* movement
Sanchay *m* collection
Sanchia *f* inviolable; sacred
Sanchit *m* collected
Sancho *m* companion; sanctified; sincere; truthful
Sancia *f* inviolable; sacred
Sander *m* defender; helper; helps; mankind; people

Sanders *m* Alexander;
  helps; people; son
Sanderson *m* Alexander;
  son
Sandesh *m* message
Sandiago *m* James
Sandiego *m* James
Sandon *m* hill; sandy
Sandor *m* helps; people
Sandra *f* defender; helper
Sandy *m* haired; sandy
Sanemi *f* perfect
Sanferd *m* crossing;
  dweller; ford; sandy
Sanfo *m* crossing; dweller;
  ford; sandy
Sanford *m* crossing;
  dweller; ford; sandy
Sanfourd *m* crossing;
  dweller; ford; sandy
Sanfred *m* counsel; peace-
  ful
Sangita *f* music
Sanhata *m* consciousness
Sani *m* old
Saniago *m* James
Sanika *f* flute
Saniya *f* moment
Sanjana *f* harmony
Sanjay *m* victorious
Sanjaya *f* triumphant
Sanjeev *m* giving; life
Sanji *m* admired; praised
Sanjiro *m* admired;
  praised
Sanjita *f* triumphant
Sanjiv *m* vital
Sanjog *m* coincidence
Sanjukta *f* union
Sankalp *m* determination;
  will
Sanket *m* signal
Sanoja *f* eternal
Sansen *m* brilliant; son
Sansita *f* praise
Sanskriti *f* culture
Sanson *m* brilliant; man;
  son; splendid
Sansone *m* man; son;
  splendid
Santan *m* tree
Santiago *m* James
Santo *m* holy; sacred;
  saintly
Santon *m* enclosure;
  sandy; town
Santosh *f* satisfaction
Santosh *m* happiness
Sanura *f* kitten
Sanurag *m* affectionate
Sanuye *f* cloud; red

Sanvali *f* dusky
Sapata *f* hug
Saphira *f* beautiful; blue;
  color; gem; jewel
Saphra *f* beautiful; jewel
Sapna *f* dream
Sapphera *f* beautiful; jewel
Sapphira *f* beautiful; blue;
  color; gem; jewel
Sapphire *f* beautiful; blue;
  color; gem; jewel
Saqui *f* favorite
Sara *f* princess
Sarad *m* autumn; born;
  survivors
Sarah *f* princess
Saral *m* simple
Sarana *m* injuring
Sarang *m* deer
Saranya *f* surrendered
Saras *m* moon
Sarasa *f* swan
Sarasi *m* lake
Sarasvat *m* learned
Sarat *m* sage
Saravana *m* clump
Sarayu *f* wind
Sarayu *m* wind
Saree *f* noble
Sarene *f* princess
Sarette *f* princess
Sargam *m* musical
Sargent *m* attendant;
  officer
Sari *f* noble; princess
Sarid *m* survivors
Sarik *f* sound
Saril *f* running; water
Sarilda *f* armored; battle;
  girl; maid; war
Sarin *m* helpful
Sarina *f* laughs; princess
Sarine *f* princess
Sarish *m* equal
Sarisha *f* charming
Sarit *m* river
Sarita *f* flowing
Sarjana *f* creative
Sarjena *f* creative
Sarna *m* deer
Sarngin *m* archer
Sarojin *m* lotuslike
Sarolta *f* laughs; little;
  princess; womanly
Sartaj *m* crown
Saruchi *f* wonderful
Sarvak *m* whole
Sarwar *m* promotion
Sasa *f* assistant
Sasha *f* defender; helper
Sashang *m* connected

Sashreek *m* prosperous
Sashwat *m* eternal
Sasmit *m* smiling
Sasmita *f* always; laughing
Sasta *m* rules
Satha *f* dishonest
Sathi *m* partner
Satinka *f* dancer; magic
Satish *m* hundreds; ruler
Satvik *m* victorious
Saubal *m* mighty
Saul *m* asked
Saumitr *m* friend; good
Saumya *m* handsome
Saunders *m* Alexander; de-
  fender; helper; mankind;
  son
Saunderson *m* Alexander;
  son
Saura *f* sun
Saurav *m* celestial; divine
Saval *m* born; farm; willow
Savan *m* moon
Savanna *f* barren; open;
  plain
Savannah *f* barren
Savil *m* born; farm; willow
Savill *m* born; farm; wil-
  low
Saville *m* born; estate;
  farm; willow
Savina *f* lady
Savir *m* leader
Sawa *f* Marsh; rock
Sawandi *m* founder
Sawyer *m* man; woods
Sawyor *m* man; woods
Saxen *m* Saxon; town
Saxon *m* Saxon; town
Sayen *f* lovely; sweet
Sayer *m* carpenter; cham-
  pion; people's
Sayers *m* carpenter
Sayo *f* born; night
Sayre *m* carpenter; cham-
  pion; hermit; people's
Scanlan *m* little
Scanlon *m* little
Scarlett *f* colored
Schaffer *m* shepherd
Schneider *m* tailor
Schreiner *m* cabinet;
  maker
Schultz *m* administrator;
  overseer
Schuman *m* maker; shoe
Schuster *m* repairman;
  shoe
Schuyler *m* hide; scholar;
  shield; teacher
Scott *m* Scotland

Shamir *m* flint-like
Shamita *f* peacemaker
Shamma *f* obedient; woman
Shamus *m* supplanter
Shana *f* God/god; gracious
Shanahan *m* sagacious; wise
Shanan *m* peaceful
Shanda *f* goddess; great
Shandar *m* proud
Shandeigh *f* rambunctious
Shandell *f* candle
Shandelle *f* candle
Shandler *m* candler; maker
Shandy *f* rambunctious
Shandy *m* boisterous; little
Shane *m* God/god; gracious
Shanel *f* canal; dweller
Shanell *f* canal; dweller
Shanelle *f* canal; dweller
Shani *f* marvelous; old; small; wise
Shanice *f* God/god; gracious
Shankh *m* shell
Shankhi *m* ocean
Shanley *m* hero; old
Shanna *f* God/god; gracious
Shannah *f* old; small; wise
Shannan *f* old; small; wise
Shannen *f* old; small; wise
Shannon *f* old; small; wise
Shannon *m* little; old; wise
Shanon *f* old; small; wise
Shanon *m* peaceful
Shansa *m* praise
Shanta *f* peaceful; rambunctious; serene; spiritual
Shantanu *m* whole
Shantel *f* place
Shanti *f* calm; peaceful
Shantidev *m* Lord/lord; peace
Shantimay *m* peaceful
Shantinath *m* Lord/lord; peace
Shanyu *m* benevolent
Shaphan *m* badger
Shappa *f* red; thunder
Shaquille *m* handsome
Shara *f* fertile; plain
Sharada *f* mature; ripe
Sharai *f* plain; princess
Sharan *m* shelter
Sharang *m* deer

Sharda *f* mature; ripe
Shardul *m* tiger
Shareefa *f* noble
Shari *f* honey-sweet; princess
Sharice *f* honey-sweet; princess
Sharie *f* honey-sweet; princess
Sharif *m* honest
Sharifa *f* noble
Sharifah *f* noble
Sharine *f* honey-sweet; princess
Sharissa *f* honey-sweet; princess
Sharlene *f* little; womanly
Sharma *f* bitter; princess
Sharmine *f* bitter; princess
Sharon *f* fertile; plain; princess
Sharvari *f* twilight
Shattesh *m* king
Shauna *f* old; small; wise
Shaunak *m* wise
Shaurav *m* bear
Shaurya *m* bravery
Shavon *f* God/god; gracious
Shavonne *f* God/god; gracious
Shaw *m* dweller; grove; tree; trees
Shawn *m* God/god; gracious
Shawna *f* God/god; gracious; old; small; wise
Shawni *f* old; small; wise
Shaya *f* asked
Shayana *f* learned; majestic
Shayfan *m* badger
Shayla *f* learned; majestic
Shaylee *f* learned; majestic
Shayleen *f* learned; majestic
Shaylene *f* learned; majestic
Shaylyn *f* learned; majestic
Shaymus *m* supplanter
Shea *f* asked; learned; majestic
Shea *m* courteous; ingenious; majestic; scientific
Sheala *f* learned; majestic
Sheba *f* daughter; Saba; vow; woman
Sheehan *m* beautiful; child; little; peaceful
Sheela *f* blind
Sheelah *f* blind

Sheena *f* God/god; good; gracious; virtue
Sheetal *f* cool
Sheffield *m* crooked; field
Sheila *f* blind
Sheilah *f* blind
Shekhar *m* peak; ultimate
Shela *f* asked; blind
Shelah *f* asked
Shelbie *f* grew; village
Shelby *f* grew; village
Shelby *m* farm; ledge
Sheldon *m* hill; ledge
Shelia *f* blind
Shelley *f* ledge; meadow
Shelley *m* dweller; hill; ledge; meadow
Shellie *f* grew; village
Shelly *f* grew; village
Shelton *m* farm; ledge; town
Shem *m* name
Shen *m* amulet; deeply; sacred; spiritual
Sheng *m* victory
Shep *m* meadow; sheep
Shepley *m* meadow; sheep
Sheply *m* meadow; sheep
Sherard *m* brave; soldier
Sherborne *m* brook; clear
Sherbourn *m* brook; clear
Sherbourne *m* brook; clear
Sheri *f* beloved
Sherice *f* honey-sweet; princess
Sheridan *m* man; wild
Sherie *f* honey-sweet; princess
Sherissa *f* honey-sweet; princess
Sherlock *m* fair; hair; haired; short; white
Sherlocke *m* fair; hair; haired; short; white
Sherman *m* cutter
Sherry *f* cherished
Sherwin *m* runner; swift
Sherwood *m* bright; forest
Sheryl *f* little; womanly
Shesh *m* cosmic; serpent
Shevi *m* return
Sheya *f* asked
Shiamak *m* flame; silver
Shika *f* deer
Shikhar *m* peak
Shikoba *f* feather
Shikoba *m* feather
Shila *f* rock
Shilang *m* virtuous
Shima *f* island

Shima *m* island
Shimatsu *m* island; pine
Shina *f* good; loyal; virtue
Shing *m* victorious
Shino *f* bamboo; slender
Shiona *f* God/god; gracious
Shipley *m* dweller; meadow; sheep
Shipton *m* dweller; estate; sheep
Shira *f* song
Shirah *f* song
Shiri *f* song
Shirlee *f* bright; meadow
Shirleen *f* bright; meadow
Shirlene *f* bright; meadow
Shirley *f* bright; meadow
Shiro *m* born; son
Shishul *m* baby
Shitiz *m* horizon
Shivadev *m* Lord/lord; prosperous
Shizu *f* clear; quiet
Shizue *f* clear; quiet
Shizuko *f* clear; quiet
Shizuyo *f* clear; quiet
shoda *m* field; level
Sholem *m* peace
Sholom *m* peace
Shoshana *f* rose
Shoushan *f* graceful; lily
Shreeman *m* person
Shrenik *m* organized
Shreyas *m* superior
Shringesh *m* Lord/lord; pearls
Shriyans *m* wealth
Shruthi *f* lyrics
Shubendra *m* Lord/lord; virtue
Shulamith *f* peace
Shuma *f* girl
Shumana *f* girl
Shura *f* defender; helper
Shushil *m* pleasant
Shvant *m* placid
Shwas *m* breath
Shyam *m* black; blue; dark
Shyamal *m* black; dark
Shymal *m* blue
Shysie *f* little; silent
Siamak *m* flame; silver
Siana *f* God/god; gracious
Sibelle *f* prophetess
Sibilla *f* prophetess
Sibille *f* prophetess
Siblee *m* brother
Sibley *m* brother
Sibyl *f* prophetess
Sida *f* lily; water

Sidak *m* wish
Siddell *m* sun; valley; village; wide
Siddon *m* fisherman
Siddra *f* star
Sidney *m* Denis
Sidon *m* fisherman
Sidonia *f* ensnare
Sidonie *f* ensnare
Sidonius *m* fisherman
Sidra *f* belonging; glittering; star
Sidras *f* star
Sidwel *m* sea; well
Sidwell *m* sea; well
Sidwohl *m* sea; well
Siegfrid *m* glorious; peace
Siegfried *m* glorious; peace; peaceful; victorious
Sierra *f* black; saw-toothed
Sigfreda *f* peaceful; victorious
Sigfrid *m* glorious; peace; peaceful; victorious
Sigismond *m* protector; victorious
Sigismund *m* protector; victorious
Sigmund *m* protector; victorious
Signa *f* signer
Signe *f* singer; victorious
Signi *f* singer; victorious
Signy *f* singer; victorious
Sigrid *f* beautiful; conqueror; counselor; victorious
Sigurd *m* guardian; victorious
Sigvard *m* glorious; peace; peaceful; victorious
Sigwald *m* government; ruler; victorious
Sihon *m* down
Sihonn *m* down
Sihu *f* bush; flower
Sihun *m* down
Sihunn *m* down
Sikander *m* victorious
Sikata *f* sand
Siko *f* crier
Sikta *f* wet
Sila *f* past; times
Silda *f* solitary
Siloa *m* forth
Siloam *m* forth
Siloum *m* forth
Silsby *m* farm; forest
Silva *f* white
Silvain *m* forest

Silvan *m* forest
Silvano *m* dweller; forest
Silvanus *m* dweller; forest
Silver *f* white
Silvester *m* forest
Silvestro *m* forest
Silvia *f* white
Sima *f* treasure; wealth; woman
Simah *f* treasure
Simbala *f* pond
Simen *m* alike; equal
Simeon *m* hearing; hears
Simon *m* hearing; hears
Simona *f* gladly; hearer; obedient
Simone *f* gladly; obedient
Simone *m* hearing; hears
Simonetta *f* gladly; obedient
Simonette *f* hearer
Simpson *m* Simon; son
Simrit *m* remembered
Simson *m* Simon; son
Sinclair *m* bright; Clair; clear
Sinead *f* God/god; gracious
Sinha *m* hero
Siobhan *f* admired; praised
Sion *m* exalted
Sipiana *f* Cyprus
Sirena *f* mermaid; singer; siren; sweetly
Sisi *f* born
Sisika *f* swallow; thrush
Sita *f* furrow; lady
Siva *f* God/god
Sivan *m* born
Sivia *f* doe
Skeat *m* swift
Skeet *m* swift
Skeeter *m* swift
Skelly *m* historian
Skelton *m* estate; ledge; town
Skerry *m* island; rocky
Skipp *m* owner; ship
Skipper *m* master; ship
Skipton *m* estate; sheep
Skylar *m* schoolmaster
Skyler *m* schoolmaster
Skylor *m* schoolmaster
Slade *m* child; dweller; valley
Slane *m* salty
Slaven *m* mountaineer
Slavin *m* mountaineer
Sleven *m* mountaineer
Slevin *m* mountaineer

Sloan *m* warrior
Sloane *m* warrior
Smaran *m* remembrance
Smedley *m* flat; meadow
Smirtiman *m* unforgettable
Smith *m* blacksmith; hammer; worker
Smrita *m* remembered
Snowden *m* hill
Snyder *m* tailor
Socrates *m* teacher
Sofia *f* wisdom
Sofian *m* devoted
Sohil *m* beautiful
Sol *m* sun
Sola *f* alone
Sola *m* hermit
Solana *f* sunshine
Solange *f* good; shepherdess
Solenne *f* sunshine
Solita *f* alonc
Solitta *f* alone
Soloma *f* peaceful
Solomon *m* peaceful
Solon *m* man; wisdom
Solvig *f* battle; maid; victorious
Soma *f* moon
Soma *m* king
Somerset *m* settlers; summer
Somerton *m* estate; summer
Somerville *m* estate; summer
Somhairle *m* sailor; summer
Somila *f* tranquil
Sona *f* wise
Sondra *f* defender; helper
Sonesu *f* wrong
Song *f* dwell
Song *m* dwell
Songan *m* strong
Sonia *f* wise
Sonja *f* sensible; wisdom
Sonny *m* little; son
Sonya *f* sensible; wisdom; wise
Soo *m* revive
Sophia *f* wisdom
Sophie *f* wisdom
Sophronia *f* sensible
Sora *f* songbird
Soran *m* stern; strict
Sorcha *f* bright; clear
Soren *m* stern; strict
Sorilda *f* armored; battle; girl; maid; war
Sorin *m* stern; strict
Sorka *f* bright; clear
Sorley *m* sailor; summer
Sorran *m* stern; strict
Sorrell *m* brown; hair; reddish
Sorren *m* stern; strict
Sorrin *m* stern; strict
Sosanna *f* graceful; lily
Sosthena *f* vigorous; woman
Sosthenna *f* vigorous; woman
Sosthina *f* vigorous; woman
Sothena *f* vigorous; woman
Southwell *m* south; spring
Sovann *m* golden
Sowa *m* owl
Spalding *m* meadow
Sparsh *m* touch
Spaulding *m* meadow
Speed *m* prosperity; success
Spencer *m* dispenser of provisions
Spengler *m* tinker
Spiro *m* breath; gods
Sprage *m* quick
Sprague *m* quick
Spring *f* springtime; year
Sproule *m* active
Sprowle *m* active
Squire *m* attendant; bearer; knight's; shield
Srijan *m* creation
Srikant *m* lover; wealth
Stacey *f* resurrection; stable; tranquil
Stacey *m* comrade; prosperous; stable
Stacie *f* stable; tranquil
Stacy *f* resurrection
Stacy *m* comrade; stable
Stafford *m* ford
Staford *m* ford
Stallone *m* stallion
Stamford *m* ford; stony
Stanbury *m* fortress; stone
Stancio *m* constant; firm
Stancliff *m* cliff; rocky
Standice *m* rocky; valley
Standish *m* rocky; valley
Stane *m* glorious; glory; stand
Stanfield *m* field; resident; rocky
Stanford *m* ford; rocky
Stanhope *m* hollow; rocky; stony
Stanislas *m* glorious; glory; stand
Stanislaus *m* glorious; glory; stand
Stanislav *m* glorious; glory; stand
Stanleigh *m* dweller; meadow; rocky
Stanley *m* dweller; meadow; rocky
Stanmore *m* lake; rocky
Stanton *m* estate; stony
Stanway *m* near; road; stony
Stanwick *m* dweller; rocky; village
Stanwin *m* friend; nature
Stanwood *m* dweller; forest; rocky; stony; woods
Star *f* star
Staunton *m* estate; stony
Stearn *m* austere
Stearne *m* austere
Stedman *m* farmer; farmstead; owner
Stedmann *m* farmer
Steele *m* resists
Stefan *m* crowned
Stefano *m* crowned
Stein *m* stone
Stella *f* star
Stelle *f* star
Stephan *m* crowned
Stephana *f* crowned
Stephania *f* crowned
Stephanie *f* crowned
Stephen *m* crowned
Stephenson *m* crowned
Sterling *m* house; yellow
Sterne *m* austere
Stevana *f* crowned
Steven *m* crowned
Stevena *f* crowned
Stevenson *m* crowned
Steward *m* bailiff; steward
Stewart *m* bailiff; steward
Stiggur *m* gate
Stila *f* quiet
Stilla *f* quiet
Stillas *f* quiet
Stillman *m* man; quiet
Stilwell *m* quiet; spring
Stine *f* earnest
Stinson *m* son; stone
Stockley *m* meadow; stump; tree
Stockton *m* estate; stump; town; tree
Stockwell *m* spring; stump; tree
Stoddard *m* horse; keeper

Stoffel *m* bearer; Christ
Stoke *m* village
Stonwin *m* friend; nature
Storm *f* storm
Strahan *m* poet; wise
Stratford *m* ford; river; street
Stroud *m* thicket
Struthers *m* stream
Stuart *m* bailiff; steward
Styles *m* dweller
Subali *m* strong
Subandhu *m* friend; good
Subhag *m* fortunate
Subhan *m* aware
Subhash *m* soft-spoken
Subhendu *m* moon
Subinay *m* humble
Suchendra *m* Lord/lord
Suchet *m* alert; attentive
Suchi *f* radiant
Suchir *m* eternal
Sudama *m* meek
Suday *m* gift
Sudha *f* juice; nectar
Sudhir *m* brave; resolute
Sudhit *m* kind
Sudi *m* luck
Sudip *m* bright
Sudir *m* bright
Suela *f* consolation
Suffield *m* field; south
Sugi *f* cedar
Suhaila *f* moonshine
Suhas *m* laughter
Suhruda *m* good-hearted
Suizuka *f* clear; quiet
Sujal *m* affectionate
Sujan *m* honest
Sujash *m* illustrious
Sujit *m* victory
Suka *m* wind
Suke *f* lily
Suki *f* beloved
Sukrit *m* wise
Sukumar *m* tender
Sula *f* bird; large; peace; sea; sun
Sulalit *m* graceful
Sulamith *f* peace
Sulek *m* sun
Suletu *f* fly
Sullivan *m* black-eyed; blue
Sully *m* meadow; south
Sultan *m* ruler
Sumant *m* friendly
Sumanyu *m* heaven
Sumay *m* wise
Sumed *m* wise
Sumedh *m* clever

Sumi *f* clear; refined
Sumiko *f* clear; refined
Sumner *m* church; officer
Sunar *m* happy
Sunki *f* overtake
Suran *m* pleasant; sound
Surata *f* blessed; joy
Suri *f* knife
Surush *m* shining
Surya *f* God/god; sun
Susan *f* graceful; lily
Susanna *f* graceful; lily
Susannah *f* graceful; lily
Susanne *f* graceful; lily
Susette *f* graceful; lily
Sushant *m* quiet
Sushim *m* moonstone
Susi *m* horseman
Suskov *m* gopher
Sussi *m* horseman
Sutapa *m* God/god; seeker
Sutara *m* holy; star
Sutcliff *m* cliff; south
Sutej *m* luster
Sutherland *m* land
Sutoya *m* river
Sutton *m* estate; south
Suval *m* placid
Suvan *m* sun
Suzanna *f* graceful; lily
Suzanne *f* graceful; lily
Suzu *f* bell
Sven *m* youth
Svend *m* youth
Svetlana *f* star
Swain *m* attendant; boy; herdsman; knight's
Swaine *m* boy
Swane *m* boy
Swanhilda *f* lady
Swapan *m* dream
Swapnesh *m* dreams; king
Swarit *m* heaven
Swayne *m* attendant; herdsman; knight's
Sweeney *m* hero; little
Swetlana *f* star
Sweyn *m* servant
Swithbart *m* landowner; respected
Swithbert *m* landowner; respected
Sybil *f* prophetess
Sybilla *f* prophetess
Sybille *f* prophetess
Sydney *m* Denis
Sylvan *m* forest
Sylvanus *m* dweller; forest
Sylvester *m* forest
Symington *m* dweller; estate

Syna *f* together
Syon *m* gentle

Taarank *m* serious
Tab *m* brilliant; people
Tabber *m* drummer
Taber *m* drummer
Tabia *f* talents
Tabib *m* doctor; physician
Tabina *f* follower
Tabita *f* graceful
Tabitha *f* gazelle; girl; graceful
Tabor *m* camp; misfortune
Taborri *f* carry
Tace *f* silent
Tacey *f* silent
Taci *f* washtub
Tacincala *f* deer
Tacita *f* silent
Tacy *f* silent
Tadan *m* plenty
Tadashi *m* faithful; servant
Tadd *m* father
Taddeo *m* courageous; heart; praiser
Tadeo *m* courageous; heart; praiser
Tadeta *f* runner
Tadewi *f* wind
Tadi *m* wind
Tadita *f* runner
Tagawa *f* field; rice; river
Tagawa *m* field; rice; river
Taggart *m* prelate; son
Taha *m* pure
Tahir *m* holy; pure
Tahya *f* precious
Tai *m* talented
Tailor *m* tailor
Taima *f* crash; thunder
Tainn *f* moon; new
Taipa *f* spread; wings
Taisha *f* God/god; loved
Tait *m* great; joy
Taite *m* cheerful; great; joy
Taizo *m* born; son; third-born
Taj *m* crowned
Taja *f* crown
Tajah *f* crown
Taji *m* crown
Taka *f* facon; honorable; tall
Taka *m* hawk
Takala *f* corn; tassel
Takara *f* precious; treasure
Takeo *m* bamboo; strong
Takeshi *m* bamboo; unbending

Taki *f* plunging; waterfall
Takis *m* rock; stone
Takoda *m* friend
Takoohi *f* queen
Takshak *m* cobra
Taksheel *m* character; strong
Takuhi *f* queen
Tal *m* dew; rain
Tala *f* runner; swift; wolf
Talajara *f* crown
Talanta *f* runner; swift
Talasi *f* corn; flower; tassel
Talbot *m* bloodhound; pillager
Talbott *m* bloodhound
Talfryn *m* high; hill
Talia *f* dew; gentle; heaven
Talib *m* seeker
Talie *f* maiden; pure
Talisa *f* life
Talish *m* earth; Lord/lord
Talisha *f* life
Talissa *f* life
Talitha *f* maiden
Tallbot *m* bloodhound
Tallbott *m* bloodhound
Tallulah *f* leaping; water
Talman *m* injure; oppress
Talmon *m* injure; oppress
Talor *m* dew; morning
Talula *f* leaping; water
Talvrin *m* high; hill
Talya *f* dew; gentle; heaven
Tam *m* born; child
Tama *f* astonishment; jewel; thunderbolt
Tamah *f* astonishment
Tamaki *f* bracelet
Taman *m* black; dark
Tamara *f* palm; tree
Tamas *m* darkness; twin
Tamasha *f* pageant
Tamaya *f* center
Tame *f* advantage; child
Tameko *f* advantage; child
Tami *f* people
Tamika *f* child; people
Tamike *f* people
Tamikee *f* child
Tamiko *f* child; people
Tamila *m* sun
Tamira *f* magic
Tamish *m* darkness; God/god
Tamiyo *f* child; people
Tammy *f* perfection; twin
Tamonash *m* destroyer
Tamus *m* Artemis; gift; goddess
Tan *m* fresh; new

Tanabe *f* field; rice
Tanabe *m* field; rice; side
Tanak *m* prize
Tanaka *f* field; middle; rice
Tanaka *m* field; middle; rice
Tanas *m* immortal
Tanav *m* flute
Tanay *m* son
Tanek *m* immortal
Tanesha *f* born
Tani *f* valley
Tani *m* valley
Tania *f* fairy; queen
Tanika *f* rope
Taniko *f* child; valley
Tanima *f* slenderness
Tanish *m* ambition
Tanisha *f* born
Taniya *f* sunshine
Tanjiro *m* precious; second; son
Tanner *m* leather; maker
Tanno *m* river; Tano
Tano *m* river; Tano
Tansey *f* immortality
Tansy *f* flower; tenacious
Tanton *m* estate; quiet; river; town
Tanveer *m* enlightened
Tanvir *m* strong
Tanya *f* fairy; queen
Tao *f* apple
Tara *f* crag; pinacle
Tarachand *m* star
Tarak *m* protector
Taral *m* liquid
Taran *f* crag; pinacle
Taran *m* heaven
Tarang *m* wave
Tarani *m* boat; sun
Tareek *m* door
Taresh *m* God/god; stars
Tarick *m* door
Tarik *m* door
Tarin *f* crag; pinacle
Tarina *f* crag; pinacle
Tariq *m* door
Tarit *m* lightning
Tarleton *m* estate; ruler's; thunder
Taro *m* born; first-born; male
Tarrant *m* thunder
Tarrsus *m* city
Tarsus *m* city
Tartan *m* chief; commander
Tarton *m* chief; commander

Tarttan *m* chief; commander
Taru *m* plant; small
Tarun *m* young; youthful
Tarusa *m* conqueror
Taryn *f* crag; pinacle
Tas *m* bird's; nest
Tasarla *f* evening; morning
Tasha *f* born
Tasida *f* rider
Tasida *m* Rider
Tassos *m* reaper
Tasya *f* resurrection
Tate *f* cheerful
Tate *m* cheerful; great; windy
Tatia *f* haired; silver
Tatiana *f* haired; silver
Tatianas *f* haired; silver
Tatianna *f* haired; silver
Tatsu *m* dragon
Tatum *f* cheerful
Tau *m* lion
Tauno *m* mighty; ruler; world
Taura *f* bull
Tautik *m* pearl
Tavas *m* inestimable
Tavi *m* good
Tavis *m* twin
Tavish *m* heaven; twin
Tavishi *f* courage
Tavor *m* misfortune
Tawia *f* born
Tawni *f* little
Tawnie *f* little
Tawno *m* small; tiny
Tawny *f* little
Tayen *f* moon; new
Tayib *m* delicate; good
Taylor *m* tailor
Tayma *f* queen
Taymus *m* Artemis; gift; goddess
Taysha *f* God/god; loved
Tazu *f* field; rice; stork
Teagan *f* beautiful; fair
Teage *m* man
Teague *m* man
Tearle *m* serious; severe; soul; stern
Tecla *f* divine; fame
Teddman *m* protector
Tedman *m* protector
Tedmann *m* protector
Tedmond *m* national; protector
Tedmund *m* protector
Tedora *f* gift; God/god
Tegan *f* beautiful; fair
Teillo *m* bright

Teilo *m* bright
Tejah *f* crown
Tejal *f* crown
Tejal *m* bright
Tekla *f* divine; fame
Telek *m* cutter; iron
Telem *m* cliff; ford
Telfor *m* cutter; hewer; iron
Telford *m* cutter; ford; hewer; iron
Telfore *m* ford; iron
Telfour *m* cutter; hewer; iron
Tellford *m* ford; iron
Telman *m* side
Tem *m* country
Tema *f* angels; custom; justice; order; sound
Teman *m* right
Temira *f* tall
Tempa *f* sanctuary
Tempest *f* storm; tempestuous
Templa *f* sanctuary
Templas *f* sanctuary
Templeton *m* religious; town
Templia *f* sanctuary
Teng *m* mound
Tenisha *f* born
Tennyson *m* Dennis; son
Tenskwatawa *m* door; open
Teodoro *m* gift; God/god
Teodosia *f* given; God/god
Tera *f* arrow; calm; farm; girl
Terena *f* earthly; pleasure
Terence *m* polished; smooth
Terencio *m* polished; smooth
Terentia *f* guardian
Teresa *f* reaper
Terese *f* reaper
Teresita *f* reaper
Tereza *f* reaper
Teria *f* child; third; vital
Terina *f* earthly; pleasure
Teritus *m* son; third
Terle *m* serious; severe; soul; stern
Terra *f* earth
Terrell *m* ruler; Thor; thunder
Terrena *f* earthly; pleasure
Terrene *f* earthly; pleasure
Terrill *m* ruler; thunder
Terris *m* son
Territus *m* son

Tertia *f* child; third
Tertias *f* child; third
Terza *f* farm; girl
Terzas *f* farm; girl
Tesfay *m* hope
Tesha *f* God/god; loved
Tesher *m* gift
Teshi *f* cheerful; laughter
Tesia *f* God/god; loved
Tessa *f* child; fourth
Tetsu *f* Iron
Teva *m* nature
Tevis *m* twin
Tevy *f* angel
Thaddea *f* courageous
Thaddeus *m* courageous; heart; praiser
Thai *m* many; multiple
Thaine *m* attendant; follower; warrior
Thais *f* giving; joy
Thakur *m* God/god; leader
Thalia *f* blooming
Thana *f* gratitude
Thane *m* attendant; follower; warrior
Thanos *m* bear
Thatcher *m* roof thatcher
Thayer *m* army; national
Thayne *m* attendant; follower; warrior
Thea *f* all; girl; God/god; goddess; gods; trusted; truthful; wholesome
Theano *f* divine; name
Thecia *f* divine; fame
Thecla *f* divinely; famous
Theda *f* divinely; gift; given; God/god
Thekla *f* divinely; famous
Thelma *f* nursling
Thema *f* custom; justice; order; queen
Themis *f* custom; justice; order
Thenna *f* vigorous; woman
Theobald *m* boldest; people
Theodora *f* gift; God/god
Theodore *m* gift; God/god
Theodoric *m* people; ruler
Theodorus *m* gift; God/god
Theodosia *f* divinely; given; God/god
Theola *f* God/god; speaker
Theon *m* godly

Theone *f* God's; godly; name
Theophania *f* appearance; God/god
Theophila *f* beloved; God/god
Theophilos *f* beloved; God/god
Theora *f* contemplater
Thera *f* untamed; wild
Theresa *f* reaper
Therese *f* reaper
Theron *m* hunter
Therron *m* hunter
Thesda *f* fountain
Thetes *f* beautiful; goddess; nymph; sea
Thetis *f* beautiful; determined; goddess; nymph; positive; sea
Thetisa *f* beautiful; goddess; nymph; sea
Thetos *f* beautiful; goddess; nymph; sea
Thia *f* all; gift; gods; prayed
Thien *f* expert; heaven; mind
Thien *m* expert; first; heaven; mind; narrow
Thieu *f* minority; short
Thieu *m* minority; short
Thilda *f* battle; maid
Thirza *f* delight; pleasantness
Thirzi *f* delight
Thirzia *f* delight
Thisbe *f* loss; lost; lover; romantic
Thisbee *f* loss; lost; lover; romantic
Thissa *f* delight
Tho *f* breathe; poem
Tho *m* breathe
Thomas *m* twin
Thomasa *f* twin
Thomasina *f* twin
Thomasine *f* twin
Thor *m* thunderous
Thora *f* city; girl; laughing; thunder
Thorald *m* ruler; Thor; thunder
Thorbert *m* brilliance; glorious; Thor; thunder
Thorberta *f* brilliance; Thor
Thorbjörn *m* bear; Thor's
Thorburn *m* bear; Thor's
Thordia *f* spirit; Thor
Thordis *f* spirit; Thor

Thorleif *m* beloved; Thor's
Thorley *m* meadow; Thor's
Thorlow *m* hill; mountain; Thor's
Thorma *f* city; girl; laughing
Thorman *m* protection; Thor's
Thormond *m* protection; Thor's
Thormora *f* city; girl; laughing
Thormund *m* protection; Thor's
Thorndike *m* dike; thorny
Thorndyke *m* dike; thorny
Thorne *m* dweller; tree
Thornley *m* meadow; thorny
Thornton *m* estate; thorny
Thorpe *m* village
Thorr *m* thunderous
Thorvald *m* ruler; Thor; thunder
Thu *m* autumn; born
Thurlow *m* hill; mountain; Thor's
Thurman *m* protection; Thor's
Thurmann *m* protection; Thor's
Thurmond *m* protection; Thor's
Thurstan *m* John; stone; Thor's
Thurston *m* John; stone; Thor's
Thyra *f* bearer
Tia *f* Aunt; child; third
Tiana *f* fairy; queen
Tiane *f* fairy; queen
Tianna *f* fairy; queen
Tianne *f* fairy; queen
Tiara *f* crowned
Tiaret *f* lioness
Tibelda *f* boldest; people
Tiberia *f* river
Tibold *m* boldest; people
Tica *f* city
Tichon *m* winegrower
Tichonn *m* winegrower
Ticon *m* winegrower
Tien *m* one
Tierell *m* serious; severe; soul; stern
Tiernan *m* Lord/lord; master
Tierney *m* lordly
Tiet *m* festival; season
Tifanie *f* God/god
Tiffanie *f* God/god

Tiffany *f* God/god
Tilda *f* battle; maid
Tilden *m* good; liberal; valley
Tilford *m* fertile; soil; tiller
Tillford *m* fertile; soil; tiller
Tillfourd *m* fertile; soil; tiller
Tillio *m* captive
Tillo *m* captive
Tilton *m* estate; good; liberal
Tima *f* born; final; last
Timin *m* fish; large; sea; serpent
Timon *m* honor; reward
Timora *f* tall
Timoteo *m* God/god
Timothea *f* God/god
Timotheus *m* God/god
Timothy *m* God/god
Timur *m* stately; tall
Tina *f* friend; Lord/lord; martial; warlike
Tinaret *f* friend
Tiponya *f* poke
Tirtha *f* ford
Tirumala *m* hills
Tirza *f* cypress; delight; desirable; tree
Tisa *f* born; ninth
Tisbe *f* loss; lost; lover; romantic
Tisbee *f* loss; lost; lover; romantic
Tish *f* gladness
Tisha *f* noble; strong-willed
Tita *f* honor
Titania *f* giant
Titir *m* bird
Tito *m* giants
Titus *m* giants
Tivon *m* lover; nature
Tivona *f* lover; nature
Tiwa *f* onions
Tobal *m* bearer; Christ
Tobbar *m* road
Tobia *m* good; Lord/lord
Tobias *m* good; Lord/lord
Tobit *f* good
Tobit *m* good
Toby *f* good; Lord/lord
Todd *m* fox
Todor *m* gift; God's
Toft *m* farm; small
Tohon *m* cougar
Toki *f* opportunity; time
Tokiwa *f* constant
Toland *m* country

Tolek *m* inestimable
Tolland *m* country
Tollman *m* collector
Tollmann *m* collector
Tolman *m* collector
Tolmann *m* collector
Tomas *m* twin
Tomasina *f* twin
Tomasine *f* twin
Tomaso *m* twin
Tomi *m* people; rich
Tomiko *f* child; happy
Tomkin *m* little
Tomlin *m* little
Tomo *f* intelligence; knowledge
Tona *f* rock
Tonda *m* inestimable
Tonek *m* inestimable
Tonese *m* inestimable
Toni *f* priceless
Tonia *f* beyond; mother
Tonie *f* priceless
Tonik *m* inestimable
Tonio *m* inestimable
Tonya *f* beyond
Topaz *f* gem
Tor *m* king
Tora *f* tiger
Torao *m* boy; tiger
Torbart *m* renowned; Thor
Torbert *m* renowned; Thor
Torey *m* knolls
Tori *f* bird
Torin *m* chief
Tormey *m* spirit; Thor; thunder
Tormoria *f* city; girl; laughing
Torpin *m* Finn; thunder
Torr *m* thunderous; tower
Torrance *m* knolls
Torray *m* tower
Torrey *m* knolls; tower
Torrlow *m* hill; mountain; Thor's
Torry *m* knolls
Toshan *m* satisfaction
Toshi *f* year
Toshi *m* boy; year
Toshio *m* boy; year
Tosia *f* priceless
Toski *f* squashbug
Tosya *m* inestimable
Totley *m* meadow; Thor's
Tova *f* good
Tova *m* good
Tovah *f* good
Tovah *m* good
Tovi *m* good

Towland *m* country
Townley *m* meadow; town
Townsend *m* end; town
Towrey *m* tower
Towroy *m* tower
Toy *f* tortoise
Toy *m* tortoise
Toya *f* victorious
Toya *m* water
Toyesh *m* Lord/lord; water
Toyo *f* plentiful
Toyo *m* plentiful
Tracay *m* brave; defender
Tracey *f* battles
Tracey *m* brave; defender
Traci *f* battles
Tracie *f* battles
Tracy *f* battles; bold; courageous
Tracy *m* battler; bold; brave; courageous; defender
Trahern *m* iron; leader; powerful; strength
Trahurn *m* leader; powerful
Trai *m* oyster; pearl
Tran *f* forehead
Tran *m* forehead
Trava *f* grass
Travers *m* crossroads
Traviata *f* astray
Travis *m* crossroads
Trayi *f* intellect
Tredway *m* mighty; warrior
Trela *f* evening; star
Trella *f* evening; star
Trellas *f* evening; star
Tremain *m* ruins
Tremayne *m* dweller; house; rock; ruins
Trent *m* rapid; stream; swift
Tresa *f* reaper
Treva *f* homelover
Trevah *f* homelover
Trevar *m* careful; traveler
Trevor *m* careful; discreet; prudent; traveler; wise
Trey *m* born; third-born
Triana *f* girl
Tridiva *m* heaven
Trigg *m* true
Trilbee *f* fluffy
Trilby *f* fluffy; sing
Trillbi *f* fluffy
Trilly *f* fluffy
Trina *f* girl; piercing; purity
Trinatte *f* girl; little; purity

Trinee *f* girl; purity
Trinetta *f* girl; little; purity
Trinette *f* girl; little; purity
Trinia *f* girl; purity
Tripp *m* traveler
Tripti *f* satisfaction
Trisha *f* thirst
Trishanku *m* ancient; king
Trista *f* melancholy; sadness; woman
Tristan *m* noisy
Tristas *f* sadness; woman
Tristis *f* sadness; woman
Tristram *m* bold; labor
Trixie *f* girl; happy
Trixy *f* girl; happy
Troy *m* curly; haired; people
Truda *f* maiden; spear; true; word
Trudy *f* loved; spear
True *m* faithful; loyal; true
Truesdale *m* beloved; farmstead
Truman *m* adherent; faithful
Trumble *m* bold; strong
Trusha *f* thirst
Tryphena *f* delicate
Tuan *m* goes; smoothly
Tudor *m* gift; Lord/lord
Tufan *m* storm
Tuhin *m* snow
Tuhinsurra *m* snow; white
Tuka *m* boy; young
Tulasi *f* sacred
Tullia *f* peaceful; quiet
Tullius *m* son
Tullus *m* son
Tullusus *m* son
Tully *m* devoted; God/god; mighty; peaceful; people; quiet; son; will
Tulsi *f* plant
Tunava *m* flute
Tungar *m* high; lofty
Tupper *m* raiser; ram
Turag *m* thought
Turanya *f* swift
Turner *m* lathe; worker
Turya *f* power; spiritual
Tusa *f* dog; prairie
Tushaar *m* frost
Tushar *m* winter
Tusya *m* inestimable
Tutto *m* all
Tuwa *f* earth
Tuxford *m* ford; national; spearman
Tuyen *m* angel
Twila *f* double; thread

Twyford *m* double; ford; river
Twyla *f* double; thread
Ty *m* city
Tybalt *m* boldest; people
Tychon *m* winegrower
Tychonn *m* winegrower
Tye *m* bound; Lord/lord
Tyee *m* chief
Tyler *m* maker; tile
Tyna *f* Christian; heavenly
Tynan *m* dark; gray; sovereign
Tyra *f* warrior
Tyrell *m* ruler; Thor; thunder
Tyrone *m* Lord/lord
Tyrus *m* city
Tyson *m* German; son
Tzigane *f* gypsy

Uba *m* father; Lord/lord
Ubald *m* brave
Ube *m* brave
Ubora *m* excellence
Uchit *m* correct
Uda *f* great; lady; wealth
Udale *m* tree; valley; yew
Udall *m* tree; valley; yew
Udant *m* correct; message
Uday *m* sunrise
Udbal *m* mighty
Udela *f* great; lady; wealth
Udele *f* great; lady; wealth
Udell *m* tree; valley; yew
Udella *f* great; lady; wealth
Udelle *f* great; lady; wealth
Udolf *m* prosperous; wolf
Udom *m* absolute
Udu *m* water
Udupati *m* Lord/lord; stars
Uduraj *m* Lord/lord; stars
Udyam *m* action
Udyan *m* garden
Uela *f* dedicated; God/god
Uella *f* God/god; name
Ujas *m* first; light
Ujjay *m* victorious
Ula *f* burdens; cat; dearest; estate; God's; jewel; laughing; Mary; owner; virgin; wealthy
Ulah *f* burdens; dearest; God's
Ulan *m* born; first-born; male; twin
Uland *m* land; noble
Ulani *f* cheerful

Vance *m* son
Vanda *f* braid; falling; kin-
dred
Vandan *m* adoration
Vanessa *f* butterflies
Vanhi *m* fire
Vani *f* child; peace; tran-
quil
Vania *f* butterflies; child;
peace; tranquil
Vanna *f* butterflies
Vanora *f* phantom; wave;
white
Vanthe *f* blossom; flower
Vanya *f* God/god; gracious
Varad *m* firm; God/god
Varana *m* holy; river
Varda *f* rose
Varden *m* green; hill
Vardia *f* rose
Vardice *f* rose
Vardina *f* rose
Vardis *f* rose
Vardon *m* green; hill
Vareck *m* stronghold
Varian *m* capricious;
clever; variable
Varick *m* stronghold
Varid *m* cloud
Varien *m* capricious; clever
Varina *f* stranger
Varindra *m* all; Lord/lord
Varion *m* capricious;
clever
Variya *m* excellent
Varney *m* alder; grove
Varsha *f* rain
Vartan *m* rose
Varun *m* God/god
Varunesh *m* Lord/lord;
water
Vasallo *m* vassal
Vasant *m* spring
Vashtee *f* fairest; woman
Vashti *f* fairest; woman
Vashtia *f* fairest; woman
Vasilek *m* protector
Vasilis *m* knightly;
magnificent
Vasin *m* Lord/lord; ruler
Vassily *m* protector
Vasta *f* healthy; large
Vastah *f* healthy; large
Vasti *f* fairest; woman
Vasuman *m* born; fire
Vasya *m* protector
Vasyuta *m* protector
Vatsa *m* son
Vatsal *m* affectionate
Vaughan *m* little
Vaughn *m* little; small

Vayya *m* friend
Vea *m* chief
Veda *f* knowledge
Vedetta *f* watchtower
Vedette *f* guardian; watch-
tower
Vedi *f* forest; spirit; wood
Vedis *f* forest; knowledge;
spirit; wood
Veedis *f* forest; spirit;
wood
Vega *f* falling
Vegenia *f* maidenly
Velda *f* governor; ruler;
wise
Velma *f* helmet; protector
Velvet *f* velvety
Vena *f* sweet; woman
Vencel *m* garland; wreath
Venda *f* filled
Venetia *f* blessed
Venice *f* palm; tree
Venita *f* beauty
Ventura *f* good; happiness;
luck
Venus *f* beauty
Vera *f* born; early; forth-
right; spring; true
Verada *f* forthright
Veradi *f* forthright
Veradia *f* forthright
Veradis *f* forthright
Verald *m* manly
Verbena *f* boughs; sacred
Verda *f* springlike
Vered *m* rose
Verena *f* defender; protec-
tor; springlike; true
Verene *f* true
Verge *m* acre; owner
Verina *f* true
Verine *f* true
Verla *f* true
Verna *f* springlike
Verne *m* springlike; youth-
ful
Verneta *f* springlike
Verney *m* alder; grove
Vernita *f* springlike
Vernon *m* springlike;
youthful
Veronica *f* harbinger; vic-
tory
Veronique *f* harbinger; vic-
tory
Verrall *m* true
Verrell *m* true
Verrill *m* manly; true
Veryl *m* manly
Vespera *f* evening; star
Vesta *f* dwells

Veta *f* alive; life
Vevila *f* harmonious; lady;
melodious
Vevina *f* sweet; woman
Vevine *f* sweet; woman
Vibhat *m* dawn
Vibhi *f* fearless
Vibhu *m* powerful
Vibhut *m* strong
Vick *m* village
Vickie *f* victory
Victoire *f* victory
Victor *m* conqueror
Victoria *f* victory
Victoriana *f* victory
Victorina *f* victory
Victorine *f* victory
Vida *f* beloved
Vidonia *f* branch; vine
Vidor *m* cheerful
Vidur *m* skillful
Vidvan *m* scholar
Vienna *f* Vienna
Vieva *f* alive
Vigilia *f* alert; awake
Vignette *f* little; vine
Vigor *m* vigor
Vihelmina *f* protector; res-
olute
Vijaya *f* electricity
Vijendra *m* victorious
Vijeta *m* victorious
Vijval *m* intelligent
Vika *f* victory
Vikas *m* development
Viki *f* victory
Vikram *m* valor
Vikrant *m* powerful
Viktoria *f* victory
Viktorie *f* victory
Viktorka *f* victory
Viljo *m* protector; reso-
lute
Villette *f* country; estate
Vilochan *m* eye
Vilok *m* see
Vilokan *m* gaze
Vimal *m* pure
Vimla *f* clean
Vina *f* bright; haired;
sweet; vine; vineyard;
woman
Vinamar *m* humble
Vinanti *f* request
Vinati *f* prayer
Vinay *m* modesty
Vinaya *f* humble
Vince *m* conquering
Vincent *m* conquering
Vincenta *f* victorious
Vincente *m* conquering

Vincentia *f* conquering; victorious
Vincenz *m* conquering
Vineet *m* unassuming
Vinesh *m* godly
Vinia *f* life; quiet
Vinil *m* blue
Vinita *f* beauty
Vinna *f* vine
Vinod *m* pleasing
Vinson *m* son
Viola *f* flower; violet
Violante *f* flower; violet
Viole *f* flower; violet
Violet *f* flower; violet
Violette *f* flower; violet
Vipin *m* forest; grove
Viplav *m* revolution
Vipreet *m* different
Vipul *m* extensive
Vir *m* brave
Viraaj *m* shine
Viraat *m* giant
Viraj *m* sun
Viral *m* rare
Viranath *m* brave; Lord/lord
Virat *m* supreme
Virata *m* bravery
Virendra *m* brave; Lord/lord
Viresh *m* brave; Lord/lord
Virge *m* bearer; staff
Virgil *m* bearer; staff
Virgilia *f* bearer; flourishing; staff
Virgilio *m* bearer; staff
Virginia *f* maidenly
Virida *f* green
Viridis *f* blooming; fresh; green
Virina *f* springlike
Virna *f* springlike
Virochan *m* sun
Virudh *m* opposition
Vishaal *m* broad
Vishal *m* huge
Vishalya *m* painless
Vishesh *m* special
Vishikh *m* arrow
Vishram *m* rest
Vishvam *m* universal
Vishvas *m* faith
Vishvatma *m* soul; universal
Vishvesh *m* Lord/lord; world
Vismay *m* surprise
Vismaya *f* amazing
Vita *f* alive; life; little; Lord/lord; servant

Vitia *f* life
Vito *m* alive; living
Vitola *m* peaceful
Vitoria *f* victory
Vitorio *m* conqueror
Vittesh *m* Lord/lord; wealth
Viva *f* alive; spring
Vivash *m* bright
Viveca *f* battle; fortress
Vivi *f* alive
Vivian *f* alive
Viviana *f* alive
Vivianna *f* alive
Vivica *f* battle; fortress
Vividha *f* strange
Vivien *f* alive
Vivienne *f* alive
Vivyan *f* alive
Vlad *m* all; famous; peaceful; royally; ruler
Vladamar *m* all; famous; peaceful; royally; ruler
Vladi *m* all; famous; peaceful; royally; ruler
Vladimar *m* all; famous; peaceful; royally; ruler
Vladimir *m* all; famous; peaceful; royally; ruler
Vladislav *m* glorious; glory; royal; ruler
Vlas *m* lisps
Vola *f* mystery; woman
Volante *f* flying
Voleta *f* mystery; woman
Voletta *f* mystery; woman
Volkov *m* wolf
Volkow *m* wolf
Volney *m* national; people's; popular; spirit
Vona *f* brave; girl
Voss *m* fox
Vovcenko *m* wolf
Vrishin *m* peacock
Vritika *f* thought
Vyan *m* air
Vyom *m* sky

Waban *m* wind
Wade *m* advancer; advancer's; castle; crossing; dweller; estate; river
Wadesworth *m* advancer's; castle; estate
Wadley *m* advancer's; meadow
Wadsworth *m* advancer's; castle; estate
Wagner *m* maker
Wainwright *m* maker

Waite *m* guard; watchman
Waitimu *m* born
Wakanda *f* inner; power
Wake *m* alert; watchful
Wakefield *m* dweller; field; wet
Wakeley *m* meadow; wet
Wakeman *m* watchman
Wakil *m* lawyer
Walcott *m* cottage; dweller; enclosed; walking
Wald *m* bearer; good
Walda *f* ruler
Waldemar *m* famous; ruler; strong
Walden *m* forest; mighty; ruler; valley
Waldo *m* mighty; usurper
Waldon *m* hill; wooded
Waldos *m* usurper
Waldron *m* raven; ruling
Walford *m* resident
Walfred *m* peaceful; ruler
Walker *m* cleaner; cloth
Wallace *m* man
Wallache *m* man
Waller *m* army; builder; ruler; walking
Walmond *m* mighty; protector; ruling
Walsh *m* man
Walston *m* corner; stone
Walter *m* army; powerful; ruler; warrior
Walther *m* army; powerful; ruler; warrior
Walton *m* city; fortified
Walworth *m* farm
Walwyn *m* friend
Waman *m* short
Wanda *f* lithe; shepherdess; slender; wanderer
Wandis *f* lithe; slender; wanderer
Waneta *f* charger
Wang *m* prince; yellow
Wangari *f* leopard
Wanita *f* God/god; gracious
Wannetta *f* little; pale
Wanonah *f* first-born
Wapasha *m* leaf; red
Wapeka *f* skillful
Wapi *m* lucky
Warburton *m* castle; enduring; town
Ward *m* guardian; watchman
Warda *f* guardian
Warde *m* guardian; watchman

Wardell *m* hill
Warden *m* guardian; watchman
Wardley *m* guardian; meadow
Ware *m* always; careful
Warfeld *m* resident
Warfield *m* resident
Warfold *m* resident
Warford *m* ford; walking
Warfourd *m* ford; walking
Waring *m* cautious; soul
Warmond *m* protector; true
Warner *m* army; defender; warrior
Warren *m* defender; man; true; watchman
Warrick *m* defender; family; fortress
Warrin *m* cautious; soul
Warring *m* cautious; soul
Warton *m* town; walking
Warwick *m* defender; family; fortress
Washburn *m* brook; dweller
Washi *m* eagle
Washington *m* estate; family; keen
Watkins *m* son
Watson *m* son
Wattan *m* black
Waverly *m* aspen; meadow; tree
Wayland *m* land; property
Wayna *f* young
Wayne *m* maker
Wayra *f* wild
Wazir *m* minister
Webb *m* weaver
Weber *m* weaver
Webley *m* meadow
Webster *m* weaver
Weddell *m* advancer's; dweller; hill
Welborne *m* brook; dweller; spring
Welby *m* farm; spring
Welcome *f* gladly; welcome
Welda *f* ruler
Weldon *m* hill; spring; well
Welford *m* crossing; ford; spring
Welk *m* wolf
Wellington *m* estate; wealthy
Wells *m* dweller; spring
Welton *m* dweller; estate; spring; town

Wemilat *m* all; given
Wemilo *m* all; speak
Wen *m* born; winter
Wenceslaus *m* garland; glory; wreath
Wenda *f* wanderer
Wendelin *f* wanderer
Wendelina *f* wanderer
Wendeline *f* wanderer
Wendell *m* wanderer
Wendolyn *f* wanderer
Wendy *f* wanderer
Wenoa *f* first-born
Wenona *f* born; daughter; first-born
Wenonah *f* first-born
Wentworth *m* estate; white
Wera *f* castle; woman
Werner *m* army; defender; warrior
Wes *m* cottage; dweller; west
Wescott *m* cottage; dweller; west
Wesh *m* forest; woods
Wesla *f* meadow; west
Wesley *m* meadow; west
Westbrook *m* brook; west
Westcott *m* cottage; west
Westleigh *m* meadow; west
Weston *m* estate; west
Wetherby *m* farm; sheep; wether
Wetherell *m* corner; sheep; wether
Wetherly *m* dweller; meadow; sheep; wether
Weylin *m* son; wolf
Wheatley *m* meadow; wheat
Wheaton *m* estate; town; wheat
Wheeler *m* maker
Whistler *m* piper; whistler
Whitby *m* farmstead; settlement; white
Whitelaw *m* hill; white
Whitfield *m* field; white
Whitford *m* ford; white
Whitley *f* white; wood
Whitley *m* meadow; white
Whitlock *m* stronghold; white
Whitman *m* haired; man; white
Whitmore *m* moor; white
Whitney *f* island; white
Whitney *m* haired; island; white
Whittaker *m* dweller; field; white

Wicent *m* conquering
Wichado *m* willing
Wickham *m* enclosure; meadow; village
Wickley *m* meadow; village
Wier *m* always; careful
Wilber *m* beloved
Wilbur *m* beloved; brilliant; firm; fortress; resolute
Wilda *f* untamed; wild
Wildee *f* wild
Wildon *m* hillside
Wilford *m* dweller; ford; willow
Wilfred *m* determined; peaceful; peacemaker; resolute
Wilhelm *m* protector; resolute
Wilhelma *f* protector; resolute
Wilhelmina *f* helmet; protector; resolute
Wilhelmine *f* protector
Wilhemine *f* resolute
Wilikinia *f* maidenly
Wilkes *m* protector; resolute
Will *m* determined; firm; resolute
Willa *f* continuation; protector; resolute; resolution; succession; true; word
Willabelle *f* protector; resolute
Willard *m* brave; resolute
Willette *f* protector; resolute
William *m* protector; resolute
Williamson *m* protector; resolute
Willis *m* protector; resolute; son
Willoughby *m* farm; willow
Willow *f* freedom; tree; willow
Willtrude *f* true; word
Wilma *f* helmet; protector; resolute
Wilmer *m* famous; resolute
Wilmette *f* protector; resolute
Wilmot *m* mind; resolute; spirit
Wilona *f* desired; wish
Wilonah *f* desired; wish
Wilson *m* protector; resolute; son

Wilton *m* farm; spring
Wilva *f* determined
Winchell *m* drawer; water
Winda *f* hunt
Windsor *m* bank; boundary; river
Winema *f* chief; woman
Winfield *m* field; friend's; grazing
Winfred *m* friend; peaceful
Wing *f* warm
Wing *m* glory; warm
Wingate *m* divine; protection
Wingi *m* willing
Winifred *f* friend; holy; peaceful; spiritual
Winn *m* brilliant; fair; friend; quick; white
Winna *f* friend; relaxed
Winola *f* friend; friendly; gracious; princess
Winona *f* born; daughter; first-born; generous
Winonah *f* born; daughter; first-born
Winslow *m* friend's; hill
Winston *m* estate; friend's; town
Winter *m* born
Winthrop *m* dweller; estate; friend's
Winton *m* estate; friend's
Winward *m* forest; friend; friend's; guardian
Wira *f* castle; woman
Wirt *m* master; worthy
Wisia *f* victory
Witt *m* man; wise
Witter *m* warrior; wise
Witton *m* estate; man's; wise
Wivina *f* life; quiet
Wivinah *f* life; quiet
Wivinia *f* life; quiet
Wolcott *m* cottage; dwells
Wolfe *m* wolf
Wolfgang *m* advancing; path; wolf
Wong *m* body; water; wide
Woodman *m* woodcutter
Woodrow *m* dweller; forest
Woodruff *m* bailiff; forest; warden
Woodward *m* forest; warden
Woolcott *m* cottage; dwells
Woolsey *m* victorious; wolf
Worcester *m* alder; army; camp; forest

Wordsworth *m* farm; guardian; wolf
Worth *m* farmstead
Worthington *m* riverside
Worton *m* dweller; enclosure
Wray *m* corner; property
Wright *m* carpenter
Wulff *m* wolf
Wuliton *m* well
Wunand *m* God/god; good
Wuyi *m* soaring; turkey; vulture
Wyanet *f* beautiful
Wyatt *m* little; warrior
Wyborn *m* bear; war
Wycliff *m* cliff; white
Wylie *m* beguiling; charming
Wyman *m* warrior
Wymer *m* battle; famous
Wyndham *m* enclosure; path; winding
Wynifred *f* holy
Wynn *m* battle; dear; fair; friend; white
Wynne *f* fair; white
Wyome *f* plain
Wystand *m* battle; stone
Wythe *m* dweller; tree; willow

Xandra *f* defender; helper
Xanthe *f* yellow
Xanthus *m* golden; haired
Xavier *m* house; new; owner; savior
Xaviera *f* house; new; owner
Xena *f* hospitable
Xene *f* hospitable
Xenia *f* hospitable
Xenos *m* guest; stranger
Xerxes *m* prince; royal; ruler
Ximena *f* heroine
Xochitl *f* flower
Xuxu *f* graceful; lily
Xylon *m* forest
Xylona *f* forest

Yachi *f* eight; thousand
Yachiko *f* eight; thousand
Yachiyo *f* eight; thousand
Yachne *f* gracious
Yaci *m* God/god
Yadim *m* God/god
Yadin *m* judge

Yadon *m* God/god; judge
Yagya *m* sacrifice
Yahto *m* bluebird
Yaj *m* sage
Yakecan *m* sky; song
Yakecen *m* sky; song
Yakez *m* heaven
Yakim *m* establish; God/god
Yakini *f* truth
Yale *m* corner; land; secluded; slope
Yama *f* mountain
Yama *m* mountain
Yamha *m* dove
Yamika *f* noble
Yamini *f* nocturnal
Yamir *m* moon
Yamka *f* budding; flower
Yamya *f* noble
Yana *m* bear
Yanaba *f* enemy
Yancy *m* Englishman
Yannis *m* God/god; gracious
Yarb *m* herb
Yardley *m* enclosed; meadow
Yarin *m* understand
Yarkona *f* green
Yarmilla *f* marketplace
Yaro *m* son
Yasar *m* wealth
Yaser *m* wealth
Yash *m* fame
Yashas *m* fame
Yashmit *m* famed
Yashodev *m* fame; Lord/lord
Yasir *m* wealth
Yasmeen *f* flower
Yasmine *f* flower
Yasser *m* wealth
Yasti *m* slim
Yasu *f* tranquil
Yates *m* dweller; gate
Yazid *m* add
Yedda *f* sing; singer
Yehudi *m* Lord/lord; praise
Yelena *f* Lenka; light
Yemina *f* hand; strength
Yemon *m* gate; guardian
Yen *m* calm; serene; swallow
Yens *m* God/god; gracious
Yeoman *m* retainer
Yepa *f* maiden; snow
Yerik *m* appointed; exalted; God/god; Jehovah
Yesima *f* hand; strength

Yeska *m* add
Yesya *m* add
Yeta *f* house; mistress
Yetah *f* house; mistress
Yetta *f* give; house; mistress
Yetti *f* house; mistress
Yeva *f* giving; life-giving
Ygnocio *m* fiery
Yin *f* silver
Yin *m* silver
Ynes *f* pure
Yobachi *f* God/god
Yochana *f* thought
Yohance *m* gift; God's
Yoi *f* born; evening
Yojit *m* planner
Yoki *f* bluebird
Yoko *f* positive
Yola *f* firefly
Yolanda *f* flower; modest; shy; violet
Yolande *f* flower; modest; shy; violet
Yolante *f* modest; shy; violet
Yolanthe *f* flower; violet
Yona *f* dove
Yonah *f* dove
Yonina *f* dove
Yonita *f* dove
Yori *f* trustworthy
York *m* boar; estate; tree; yew
Yoshi *f* good; respectful
Yoshi *m* quiet
Yoshie *f* good; respectful
Yoshiko *f* good; respectful
Yoshino *f* fertile; field; good
Yoshio *f* good; respectful
Yoshiyo *f* good; respectful
Yosif *m* add
Yousef *m* add
Yovela *f* rejoicing
Ysabel *f* consecrated; God/god
Yseulta *f* girl; white
Yseulte *f* girl; white
Ysmael *m* God/god; hears
Yu *f* jade
Yu *m* brightly; shining; universal
Yucel *m* sublime
Yuki *f* deep; lucky; snow
Yuki *m* boy; snow
Yukie *f* lucky
Yukiko *f* lucky
Yukio *m* boy; snow
Yukio *m* boy; snow
Yukiyo *f* lucky

Yukta *m* idea
Yukti *f* solution
Yul *m* beyond; horizon
Yula *f* downy; haired; youthful
Yule *m* born
Yulinka *f* downy; haired; youthful
Yulka *f* downy; haired; youthful
Yuma *m* chief; son
Yumi *f* arrow
Yumiko *f* arrow; child
Yunus *m* dove
Yuri *f* child; lily
Yuri *m* farmer; land; worker
Yuriko *f* child; lily
Yursa *f* bear; nymph; sky
Yusef *m* add
Yusif *m* add
Yusra *f* ease
Yusuf *m* add
Yuti *f* union
Yutu *m* claw
Yuval *m* brook
Yuvraj *m* prince
Yuzef *m* add
Yves *m* bow; son; yew
Yvette *f* archer; bow; yew-bow
Yvonne *f* archer; bow; yew-bow

Zacaria *m* Jehovah; remembered
Zacarias *m* Jehovah; remembered
Zacharias *m* Jehovah; remembered
Zachary *m* Jehovah; remembered
Zaci *m* fatherhood
Zada *f* lucky
Zadam *f* prosperous
Zadok *m* just; righteous
Zaelea *f* blossom; flower
Zahara *f* flower
Zaharita *f* princess
Zahid *m* ascetic; self-denying
Zahir *m* shining
Zahira *f* princess
Zahra *f* flower
Zahur *m* flower
Zaid *m* abundance; add; great
Zaida *f* prosperous
Zaidah *f* prosperous
Zaidee *f* princess

Zaila *f* female
Zaim *m* brigadier; general
Zaira *f* princess
Zajac *m* hare
Zajicka *m* hare
Zaki *m* intelligent
Zakoc *m* just; righteous
Zale *m* power; sea
Zalika *f* well-born
Zaltana *f* high; mountain
Zamir *m* song
Zana *f* alert; bud; merry; quick
Zandra *f* defender; helper
Zane *m* God/god; gracious
Zanna *f* God/god; gracious
Zara *f* brightness; coming; dawn; dear; east; princess; treasure
Zarah *f* princess
Zareb *m* enemies; protector
Zared *m* ambush
Zarek *m* king; Lord/lord; protect
Zarelda *f* armored; maid
Zaria *f* blessed; God/god; princess
Zarifa *f* graceful
Zarina *f* golden
Zarrah *f* coming; dawn
Zawadi *f* gift
Zayda *f* prosperous
Zayit *f* olive
Zbik *m* wildcat
Zea *f* grain
Zebadiah *m* gift; Lord/lord
Zebe *m* gift; Lord/lord
Zebedee *m* gift; Lord/lord
Zebulon *m* dwelling
Zedekiah *m* justice; Lord/lord
Zeeman *m* seaman
Zeeshan *m* strength
Zeheb *m* gold
Zeke *m* God/god; strength
Zeki *m* intelligent; quick-witted
Zel *f* bell; cymbal
Zela *f* blossom; flower; lacking
Zelda *f* heroine; unconquerable
Zelea *f* blossom; flower
Zelenka *f* green; little
Zelia *f* ardent; devoted
Zelimir *m* peace
Zelina *f* ardent; devoted

Zella *f* lacking
Zellah *f* lacking
Zelotes *m* zealous
Zenas *m* gift; living
Zenda *f* womanly
Zendah *f* womanly
Zenia *f* hospitable
Zeno *m* living
Zenon *m* living
Zenos *m* gift
Zephaniah *m* God/god; hidden
Zera *f* seeds
Zeralda *f* warrior
Zerdali *f* apricot; wild
Zerelda *f* armored; maid; warrior
Zerlinda *f* beautiful; dawn
Zesiro *m* elder; twin
Zeta *f* olive; Z
Zetana *f* olive
Zetta *f* olive
Zeus *m* father; gods; living; men
Zeva *f* sword
Zewek *m* living
Zhen *f* treasure
Zhiyuan *m* ambition
Ziana *f* bold
Ziegler *m* brick; maker; tile
Zigana *f* girl; gypsy

Zihna *f* spinning
Zikomo *m* thank
Zilla *f* shadow
Zillah *f* shade
Zima *f* wealth; woman
Zimmerman *m* carpenter
Zimmermann *m* carpenter
Zina *f* abundance; name; secret; spirit
Zinah *f* abundance
Zinan *m* born; second-born; son
Zinon *m* living
Zippora *f* beauty; bird
Zipporah *f* bird
Zita *f* enticing; seek
Zitah *f* enticing
Ziv *m* living
Ziven *m* all; vigorous
Zivon *m* all; vigorous
Zizi *f* consecrated; God/god
Zoa *f* daughter; life; little; ruler; woman
Zoara *f* little; woman
Zoarah *f* little; woman
Zoba *f* daughter; ruler
Zobe *f* daughter; ruler
Zody *f* beloved; desired
Zoe *f* daughter; life; ruler
Zofia *f* wisdom
Zoha *f* bright; child

Zohar *f* bright; child
Zohara *f* bright; child
Zoheret *f* shines
Zohra *f* blooming
Zoi *f* child; fortune
Zoie *f* life
Zoila *f* child; fortune
Zoilla *f* child; fortune
Zona *f* girdle
Zora *f* aurora; bargain; dawn; golden
Zorah *f* dawn; golden
Zorana *f* dawn; golden
Zori *f* dawn; golden
Zorie *f* dawn; golden
Zorina *f* dawn; golden
Zorra *f* bargain
Zory *f* dawn; golden
Zorya *m* star
Zosema *f* wealth; woman
Zosi *f* wealth; woman
Zosima *f* wealth; woman
Zula *f* ahead; brilliant
Zuleika *f* bright; fair
Zuni *f* Indian
Zuri *f* beautiful
Zuri *m* good-looking
Zuriel *m* God/god; rock; stone
Zuza *f* graceful; lily